Into the Black

Into the Black

JPL and the American Space Program,

1976–2004

Peter J. Westwick

Yale University Press　　New Haven & London

Set in Stempel Garamond and Syntax type by Duke & Company, Devon, Pennsylvania.
Printed in the United States of America by Sheridan Books, Ann Arbor, Michigan.

Library of Congress Cataloging-in-Publication Data
Westwick, Peter J.
   Into the black : JPL and the American space program, 1976–2004 / Peter J. Westwick.
      p. cm.
   Includes bibliographical references and index.
   ISBN-13: 978-0-300-11075-3 (cloth : alk. paper)
   ISBN-10: 0-300-11075-8
   1. Jet Propulsion Laboratory (U.S.)—History. 2. Astronautics—United States—History.
I. Title.
TL862.J48W47 2006
629.4072′079493—dc22

                              2006013349

A catalogue record for this book is available from the British Library.

The paper in this book meets the guidelines for permanence and durability of the Committee on Production Guidelines for Book Longevity of the Council on Library Resources.

10 9 8 7 6 5 4 3 2 1

For Dane and Caden, who look up at night and wonder

Contents

Part III. Beyond the Cold War: The Stone Years, 1991–2001

Preface

IN JANUARY 2004 THE JET PROPULSION LABORATORY (JPL) IN PASADENA, California, captured the public imagination by landing two rovers on Mars and sending another spacecraft through the tail of a comet. Four years earlier JPL attracted a different sort of attention when two spacecraft failed in their missions to Mars, one of them free-falling from 40 meters after its rockets shut off too early, the other augering into the planet owing to a failure to convert English into metric units. Twenty years before that the twin Voyager spacecraft began a triumphant tour of the outer planets by flying by Jupiter in 1979 and returning a remarkable collection of images and data.

This book is the second volume in the history of JPL, a sequel to *JPL and the American Space Program* by Clayton Koppes; it picks up the story from the end of Koppes's detailed account in 1976 and carries it to 2004. During this period JPL accomplished a string of engineering feats and scientific advances, from Voyager to the Mars rovers; but it also encountered periodic failures, questions about its national relevance, and doubts about its adaptation to new social realities. This book recounts these events and traces basic changes in priority at the lab itself, at NASA, and in American science and technology in general.

JPL is the premier builder of scientific spacecraft in the world, and it has incubated diverse technologies, from digital image processing to microelectronic sensors. But that is not the only source of its interest. With current annual budgets of well over a billion dollars and a staff of near 5,000, including about 800 PhDs, it represents a substantial national investment of money and brainpower. It also illustrates the relation of the individual to the organization, a central question of the twentieth century and with special significance for science and technology and their dependence on personal creativity. Complicating this relationship was JPL's status as a hybrid institution, a laboratory owned by the federal government but operated as part of a university; it thus required a delicate balancing act between technical independence and public accountability.

JPL's most important impact came in the realm of the intellect and imagination. Its spacecraft provided an abundance of new knowledge about the planets, Earth, and stars. It is fair to say that JPL spacecraft revolutionized our knowledge of the solar system, by transforming the planets and their moons from blurry dots of color in the night sky to entire worlds of astonishing diversity and complexity. JPL spacecraft also looked down on Earth for new perspectives on such phenomena as global warming, El Niño, and ancient civilizations; in doing so they changed the methodology of earth scientists, who came to accept electronic data from remote satellites as equivalent to that gathered on the ground or at sea. As for the stars, JPL built two of the most fruitful infrared telescopes as well as the camera that saved the Hubble telescope. More broadly, JPL's work provided perhaps the most promising way scientifically to address fundamental questions about man's place in the cosmos, including the possibility of life beyond Earth.

The planetary and earth sciences are attracting increasing attention from historians of science, and the history of JPL illuminates major research endeavors in these fields.[1] In addition, the period covered by this book, the last quarter of the twentieth century, offers rich historiographical ground that few historians of science and technology have tilled.[2] This book extends cold war history past the countercultural rebellion of the 1960s and the Vietnam War into the thaw of the 1970s and then to the renewed chill that started in the late 1970s and lasted into the 1980s. For the space program, this includes the post-Apollo drawdown and then the remilitarization of space that culminated in the Strategic Defense Initiative. And then there is that central event of the last half century, the end of the cold war. How did American science and technology and the American space program adapt to the loss of their primary driver? The absence of cold war competition helped doom big federal projects in other fields, such as the Superconducting Super Collider, and reoriented the U.S. space program, but many cold war scientific institutions survived its end, including JPL. How and why did the nation justify these continued investments? How sharp was the break from patterns of support of science and technology that had predominated for the previous forty years? Historians have just begun to address these questions; the history of JPL provides an important illustrative case.

This book covers in detail the twenty-five years from 1976 to 2001. The opening chapter summarizes the history of JPL up to 1976 and sets the context for the story that follows. The starting point in 1976 marks a transition to the post-Apollo space program, an apparent dwindling of national commitment to planetary exploration, and JPL's subsequent diversification into energy research. The narrative is divided into three main sections by two additional turning points: one in 1982, after a crisis in the planetary program renewed JPL's military connections; the other in 1991, when the dissolution of the Soviet Union ended the cold war and sparked a new approach to spaceflight known as faster-better-cheaper. The endpoint in 2001 covers the response to the Mars failures of 1999, and an epilogue includes the effects of the 9/11 attacks and brings the narrative up through several important missions in 2004, including the Mars rovers and the Cassini spacecraft's arrival at Saturn.

The periodization is based not only on social turning points, reflected in programmatic shifts, but also on changes in lab directors. Bruce Murray arrived in 1976, replacing longtime leader William Pickering, and resigned after the crisis in 1982; Lew Allen oversaw the recovery in the 1980s and retired in 1991; Ed Stone then tried to change JPL's culture in the 1990s, until his retirement in 2001 and the appointment of Charles Elachi. Each director imparted his personality to the lab, from the frenetic, freewheeling imagination of Murray, through the unruffled restraint of Allen, to the combination of cautious consensus-building and revolutionary cultural change of Stone. And their character determined their response to tests: Murray, combative in the face of budget cutbacks; Allen smoothly shifting emphasis to technology after the Challenger shuttle accident; Stone adapting to faster-better-cheaper to fend off more critical attacks. There is of course a danger to identifying an entire organization with an individual, to writing what is known as great-man history. But people matter, and scholars are giving increased attention to the role of individual authority and leadership in large organizations, including R&D labs.[3]

In each of the three main sections I devote particular chapters to planetary missions, to diversification into such fields as energy, defense, earth science, and astronomy, and to institutional issues, in particular JPL's evolving relationship with NASA and Caltech. Writing the history of a lab with diverse programs entails some jumping about either in time or topic, and in this book I adopt a thematic organization instead of a chronological one in order to sharpen the analysis.

Planetary spacecraft remained the main program in this period. I will not attempt a detailed history of each project, which would require exposition of diverse institutional, scientific, and engineering developments. For such narratives the reader may consult recent or forthcoming books on Voyager, Galileo, and the Deep Space Network, as well as several popular works and memoirs.[4] This book focuses on the history of JPL as an institution. As

William McNeill, a practitioner of "big history," has observed, historians must treat certain events as background noise in order to discern the most important patterns, much as people at JPL digitally process images to bring out particular features.[5]

The book's title echoes a Neil Young song that includes the line: "out of the blue and into the black." The words capture not only the trajectory of JPL's spacecraft, which hurtled beyond earth's atmosphere into deep space, but also the implications for JPL's work. As Young's song continued, "and once you're gone, you can never come back"—nor is anyone else going out to help you. To meet the challenge of launching irreparable, and highly expensive, machines, JPL helped develop the regime known as systems engineering, which reduced risk by imposing discipline on individual engineers and their relation to scientists and managers.[6]

The title has two other connotations that represent primary themes of this history. The first is the relation between the civil space program and the secret—or "black"—space programs of the military.[7] After starting as a military lab, JPL largely shed its defense ties by the early 1970s before re-mobilizing in the 1980s, when it committed up to one-fourth of its program to defense. JPL's renewed commitment to the military required negotiation of a different social context from comparable responses in the post–World War II and post-Sputnik periods. It also required an integration of civilian and military space programs, with lasting effects. Most notably, military space programs engendered the faster-better-cheaper approach that permeated the civil program in the 1990s, and JPL's adaptation to it drew on its military experience.

This book's concern with civil-military relations in space departs from the usual political-science focus on civilian political control over the military, and it also goes beyond the concept of technology transfer or spin-off, which focuses on the flow of military technologies to civilian applications.[8] The case of JPL illuminates the mutual interaction of civilian and military realms, including the two-way flow of people, institutions, and management techniques as well as technologies, at both the programmatic and the political level. What conduits ran between the two realms, and what obstacles existed to the flow of information? And how did these change over time? Did JPL's exposure to defense work overcome previous ignorance of classified programs? How did JPL's civilian programs contribute to the military? Answers to these questions emerge in this book.

The book's title suggests yet another, economic meaning: the sort of "in the black" desired by accountants on fiscal balance sheets. Since JPL is a nonprofit, government-funded entity producing such intangible returns as scientific knowledge and cosmic exploration, the term does not apply exactly to JPL. The substantial national investment in JPL, however, encourages some consideration of the returns, and people in Pasadena and Washington at times spoke of JPL as a sort of national resource. The economic metaphor suggests as well the effects of the end of the cold war and the search for new justifications for the civil space program in the 1990s, which settled on international economic competitiveness to replace the military and political competition of the space race. Space exploration, this argument ran, would keep the American economy operating in the black by creating new technologies and enticing younger generations into science and engineering careers.

JPL reflected this new rationale in its post–cold war emphasis on technology transfer, industrial partnering, and outreach, features that appeared in a broader trend toward commercialization of research and higher education; cold war concerns over military domination of science and technology gave way to worries about industrial influence.[9] An economic mindset appears also in the entrepreneurial attitudes of JPL staff: strategies of diversification, "marketing" efforts in new fields, references to "business models" for planetary spacecraft, and the application of corporate management techniques to planetary exploration. The economic metaphor finally suggests a basic long-term trend in the operation of JPL, from the independence of an academic research lab to the more regulated environment of an industrial contractor.

Acknowledgments

TWO PEOPLE DESERVE PARTICULAR THANKS FOR THIS BOOK. DANIEL J. KEVLES proposed the project at Caltech and provided valuable feedback throughout its execution. Winston Gin was the prime mover at JPL and provided much good guidance to JPL's people and programs, as well as comments on successive drafts. Dan's and Winston's wisdom and friendship helped sustain me from the first outline to the final revisions, a longer road than expected. This project was performed under the auspices of Caltech, with a grant from the discretionary funds made available to the JPL director by Caltech. I thank Ed Stone and Charles Elachi, who as JPL directors approved the funding and granted me free access to lab archives and staff. It is important to state that JPL exercised no editorial control over the work; I held a faculty appointment at Caltech and had complete academic freedom in the writing of this book.

Caltech was a great place to work. Diana Buchwald, Jed Buchwald, Bill Deverell, Moti Feingold, Robert Rosenstone, and Judy Goodstein and the Caltech archives welcomed me to the community, and Michelle Reinschmidt and Helga Galvan provided administrative and moral support. I have profited from discussions with many other historians of the space program, including Roger Launius, Glenn Bugos, Robert Smith, Bettyann Kevles, Douglas Mudgway, and Michael Meltzer. John Logsdon shared unpublished manuscripts, as did Steven Dick and James Strick. I thank in particular Erik Conway, the JPL historian, for conversations and thoughtful comments on the manuscript. Cathy Carson, Christophe Lécuyer, and Jochen Kirchhoff provided insights on management, and Zuoyue Wang, Jessica Wang, and Alexei

Kojevnikov shared Chinese food and good conversation. In Santa Barbara, Peter Neushul, Nick Rasmussen, and Patrick McCray gave helpful advice on many subjects and, most important, joined me for surf sessions.

This history rests on research at several archives, first of which is JPL's. This book would be far poorer without the consistent help of JPL archivist Michael Hooks and the archives staff: Everett Booth, Russell Castonguay, Averell Spicer, and especially Charles Miller. The late John Bluth, former director of the archives, not only put resources at my disposal, but also shared many insights. I also thank the NASA History Office, especially Jane Odom and Steven Garber as well as its directors, Roger Launius and now Steven Dick, and the space history group at the National Air and Space Museum for oral histories. For help with images, thanks to Gregory Hoppa; Susan LaVoie and Jerry Clark in JPL's Image Processing Lab; and especially David Deats of JPL's Photolab.

I talked to many former and current JPL staff, a few informally, most in formal oral histories: Lew Allen, Blaine Baggett, Phil Barnett, John Beckman, Walt Brown, James D. Burke, John Casani, Moustafa Chahine, Frank Colella, Clifford Cummings, James Cutts, Duane Dipprey, Larry Dumas, Tom Duxbury, Charles Elachi, Alexander Goetz, Richard Goldstein, William Green, Norm Haynes, Ross Jones, Charles Kohlhase, Krishna Koliwad, Carl Kukkonen, Richard Laeser, Arthur Lonne Lane, Pete Lyman, Bruce Murray, Don Rea, MacGregor Reid, Tony Spear, Rob Staehle, James Stephens, Ed Stone, Eugene Tattini, Jurrie van der Woude, Giulio Varsi, and Gary Ureda. Several shared documents from their files, and I thank in particular Walt Brown, Ross Jones, Bruce Murray, and Donna Shirley. Phil Barnett loaned a copy of his very useful dissertation. Susan Foster provided many inside stories as well as videotapes and documents, and Annette Ling provided invaluable administrative help. For those interviews that I tape-recorded, I intend (with permission of the interviewee) to deposit copies of the transcripts in the JPL archives.

Several former and current NASA staff provided their perspectives: Daniel Goldin, Ed Weiler, Wes Huntress, Kurt Lindstrom, Tom Sauret, and Brent Bennett. At Caltech, I profited from discussions with David Baltimore, Fred Culick, Rochus Vogt, Steven Koonin, John Ledyard, and David Schiminovich. Lawrence Gilbert and Rich Wolf in Caltech's office of technology transfer shared particular insights, and Melinda Bakarbessy and Fred Farina provided patent data. In the wider community of space science and aerospace, I thank Michael Griffin, Noel Hinners, Norman Ness, Trevor Sorensen, Steve Squyres, and Albert D. Wheelon. I would finally thank my editor at Yale

University Press, Jean Thomson Black, her assistant Laura Davulis, and copy editor Eliza Childs for shepherding the manuscript to publication.

My deepest thanks go to my wife Medeighnia, whose support and forbearance made this possible, and to our kids Dane and Caden, whose penetrating questions about space reminded me what this is all about.

Abbreviations

APL	Applied Physics Laboratory
ASAS	All Source Analysis System
C^3I	command, control, communications, and intelligence
CCD	charge-coupled device
CRAF	Comet Rendezvous and Asteroid Flyby
DARPA	Defense Advanced Research Projects Agency
DOD	Department of Defense
DOE	Department of Energy
DSN	Deep Space Network
ENSCE	Enemy Situation Correlation Element
ERDA	Energy Research and Development Administration
GALEX	Galaxy Evolution Explorer
IPAC	Infrared Processing and Analysis Center
IRAS	Infrared Astronomical Satellite
IUS	Inertial Upper Stage
JPL	Jet Propulsion Laboratory
LESS	Low-Cost Exploration of the Solar System
LODE	Large Optics Demonstration Experiment
MER	Mars Exploration Rover
MOU	memorandum of understanding
MSTI	Miniature Seeker Technology Integration
NACA	National Advisory Committee for Aeronautics
NASA	National Aeronautics and Space Administration
NEAR	Near-Earth Asteroid Rendezvous

NOAA	National Oceanic and Atmospheric Administration
NRO	National Reconnaissance Office
OAST	Office of Aeronautics and Space Technology
OMB	Office of Management and Budget
QWIP	quantum-well infrared photodetector
SAR	synthetic aperture radar
SDI	Strategic Defense Initiative
SETI	Search for Extraterrestrial Intelligence
SIR	Shuttle Imaging Radar
SSEC	Solar System Exploration Committee
TQM	Total Quality Management
VLSI	very large-scale integration
VOIR	Venus Orbital Imaging Radar
WF/PC	Wide Field/Planetary Camera

The Inheritance

THE JET PROPULSION LABORATORY (JPL) STARTED AS A GRADUATE-STUDENT rocket project at Caltech in the 1930s. At the time Caltech was already a center for science and engineering in the United States, a position it would occupy for the rest of the century. In 1930 Caltech lured Theodore von Kármán, a leading authority on aerodynamics, to become director of its Guggenheim Aeronautical Laboratory, or GALCIT. Von Kármán's lab at first studied airplane flight until a graduate student, Frank Malina, proposed thesis work on rockets. Malina banded together with two other rocket enthusiasts, John Parsons and Ed Forman; they fired their first rocket motor in fall 1936 at an isolated spot in the Arroyo Seco, a dry wash three miles above the Rose Bowl in Pasadena. The wisdom of using a remote site was confirmed when subsequent tests on campus misfired, one explosively. By spring of 1938 Malina and his group had a rocket that ran on the test stand for over a minute. The rocket work piqued military interest, and in January 1939 the National Academy of Sciences began funding GALCIT for work on rocket-assisted takeoff for airplanes. The following year the Army Air Corps took over, and the expanding program soon shifted for good to the Arroyo Seco site.[1]

Arsenal for the Army

The onset of World War II brought big budgets and secrecy to the rocketeers. It also led to the formal establishment of JPL. Following intelligence reports in 1943 of German rocket development, von Kármán, Malina, and Hsue-shen Tsien, a Chinese mathematician performing theoretical analyses for GALCIT, proposed a long-range program. The army responded with enthusiasm, although Caltech's trustees approved the contract only for the duration of the war. The arrangement nevertheless illustrated a basic watershed in the history of American science and technology: the wartime use of research contracts to enlist academic science in service for the federal government, particularly the military. In this case the army paid for new facilities and operating expenses, while Caltech contributed its administration, faculty, and graduates, as well as its name, to the enterprise. The army thus obtained access to expertise outside its ranks, lab staff got a technical challenge and the resources to pursue it, and both scientists and university administrators earned a patriotic sense of contributing to the war effort. The campus also received a fixed fee on top of the operating budget, a more concrete and compelling inducement that aided recovery from the Depression.[2]

The Jet Propulsion Laboratory officially opened on 1 July 1944, the new name shedding the speculative stigma of rockets. When von Kármán's increasing work for the air force took him to Washington later that year, Malina stepped in as director. JPL did not demobilize at the end of the war, although that required accommodations with campus. Caltech had agreed to only a wartime project, and many campus faculty wanted to return to peacetime research. Caltech barred classified research on campus and required military contracts to involve fundamental research instead of strictly applications. Malina and von Kármán suggested that Caltech set up its own rocket laboratory for unclassified, basic research on rockets for scientific use. Caltech's trustees instead decided to continue the existing arrangement, after the army assured them that JPL could focus on basic, unclassified research. Thus, like other large wartime labs, JPL survived through the postwar flux and was ready for service at the onset of the cold war.[3]

The decision to continue JPL as a cold war military lab had its costs. Domestic anticommunism perhaps encouraged Malina to resign as director in 1946, as he had moved in left-leaning circles in the 1930s and come under the suspicion of the FBI. It certainly cost the lab the later services of Tsien; when he sought to return to Maoist China, the federal government detained him in the United States and barred him from classified material and thus from JPL.[4] Military work had programmatic consequences as well. The army had pushed for a broad program on guided missiles, and the lab began to acquire expertise in electronics as well as in aerodynamics and propulsion. To highlight the shift, in 1954 William Pickering, an electrical engineer from Caltech, assumed the directorship of JPL, replacing Louis Dunn, Malina's successor.

Pickering's low-key geniality and informality belied the increasing organization of the lab. From the war through the late 1950s JPL designed and built a series of larger and longer-range missiles, designated by military rank: from the Private to Corporal and finally Sergeant. The work initially entailed much basic research in chemistry, physics, aerodynamics, and electronics; but the army wanted an operational weapon in the end, and the national emergency of the early 1950s—the Soviet atomic bomb, war in Korea, and development of tactical nuclear weapons—increased the urgency for a tactical missile. In 1950 the army asked JPL to weaponize the Corporal, primarily to carry nuclear warheads, and over the next several years JPL moved from research into development and then production functions, and even into training troops in use of the weapon.[5]

Corporal started JPL's transition from a small, unclassified, academic research outfit to a large, secret, development organization. The transition intensifed in 1954 when JPL undertook Sergeant, which would use solid instead of liquid propellants. An ad hoc, academic design process and loose organization had proved insufficient to handle the many problems on Corporal, including component failure, integration of components into subsystems and systems, oversight of contractors, and operation and training. The solution was managerial, not technological. The Sergeant managers—Robert Parks and his deputy, Jack James—included reliability, testing, and maintenance factors in the component design process, standardized the test and safety procedures, and, a crucial step, insisted on a progressive design freeze, with documented control of all changes. These procedures enabled JPL to develop Sergeant largely on schedule. From a longer view, they represent the initial steps toward the techniques of systems engineering.[6]

By 1953 JPL had more than 1,000 staff and a budget of $11 million. Despite the army's assurances, most of the work was secret: by 1958 almost two-thirds of lab publications were classified. The increasing secrecy, formality, and production nature of the work weakened links with campus, but Caltech administrators and trustees rebuffed suggestions to transfer the lab to another contractor or to the army itself.[7]

Onward and Upward with NASA

Von Kármán had initially intended to extend the missile series up through colonel, "the highest rank that works." But Pickering chafed under the pressure of developing weapons systems, and he and Caltech president Lee DuBridge determined not to go beyond Sergeant. The lab instead looked outward, and upward, for new opportunity. JPL rocketeers had always kept an eye on space as a destination for their hardware. In 1949 they reached it, with a version of the Corporal launched on top of a V-2 rocket to a height of 250 miles. In 1955 JPL renewed this collaboration with expropriated German rocket scientists at the Army Ballistic Missile Agency (ABMA), for whom JPL developed a radio-guidance system and reentry vehicle for an intermediate-range ballistic missile. This work led to a tracking system that could detect very faint radio signals thousands of kilometers away and to a proto-satellite vehicle.[8]

The federal government was meanwhile prosecuting the crash program for an intercontinental ballistic missile and beginning to appreciate the appeal of space for international prestige as well as military uses. The United States declared its intent to launch a satellite as part of the International Geophysical Year in 1957–58, but President Eisenhower insisted on a civilian, science-oriented precedent and thus sank a collaborative proposal from the army's labs at JPL and ABMA. Then, on 4 October 1957, the Soviets launched Sputnik. When the hurried American response failed dismally on the launch pad, JPL and the army got the green light to enter the space race. JPL's tracking system and reentry vehicle earned it the right to build the satellite, known as Explorer 1. The triumphant launch of Explorer on 31 January 1958 propelled JPL into the public eye and also into a leading role in the nation's space program.[9]

JPL followed with more Explorers and two Pioneers, the last of which aimed for the moon and signaled JPL's intent to push beyond earth orbit. Meanwhile, after much debate, Eisenhower and Congress in mid-1958 created the National Aeronautics and Space Administration (NASA). NASA coveted JPL's space expertise, and on 1 January 1959 the lab transferred to the new agency. JPL would thence have to negotiate its role amidst the often overlapping missions of other NASA centers. NASA assigned JPL responsibility for automated spacecraft for lunar and planetary exploration, which solidified the shift away from its titular interest in propulsion. In the heady days of the early space race, JPL planners laid out a series of flights to the moon, Venus, and Mars, culminating in a manned flight around Mars and back in 1965. They worried that this program lacked ambition. NASA instead accepted a more measured plan for three main flight series: first, reconnaissance flights to the moon known as Ranger; then Surveyor, to soft-land a spacecraft on the moon; and, concurrently, Mariner probes to Venus and Mars.[10] But even this scaled-back program would push JPL to the breaking point and beyond, and force the lab to forge a new regime.

The shift from rockets to spacecraft was not just a matter of mastering new technical fields. JPL engineers went from developing production-line weapon systems, with dozens or hundreds of test flights, to designing custom-built spacecraft that were too elaborate and expensive to test in flight. The Corporal and Sergeant programs in the 1950s had impelled the first steps toward systems engineering, but in the rush of the early space race JPL managers had dispensed with formal methods in favor of quick results, firing off spacecraft until project engineers learned how to make one fly.[11]

JPL learned the hard way that space missions might not resemble production-line missiles. From 1961 through 1962 the Ranger program suffered a series of mishaps. The launch vehicles failed for Rangers 1 and 2. Ranger 3 survived launch vehicle problems only to be bitten by a bug in JPL's flight software: a single reversed sign altered the trajectory, sending the craft in a direction opposite to that intended. Ranger 4 flew the correct path, but its communications failed and the spacecraft sailed silently, dumbly, into its perfect impact on the moon. After Ranger 5 missed the moon altogether NASA called a halt. It was not just the cost the nation could not tolerate, but also the embarrassment. The space race put a premium on quick results, but above all on results alone, and each failure undermined international perceptions of American prestige.

NASA's failure review board traced the problem to JPL's "shoot and hope" approach. JPL needed to test components and verify systems on the ground beforehand to ensure that spacecraft would work right the first time. To correct what NASA called "a loose anarchistic approach to project management," Pickering assigned new managers to Ranger, bringing in Bob Parks, the former Sergeant manager, as head of the lunar program and Harris "Bud" Schurmeier as Ranger project manager. Parks and Schurmeier applied the rigorous methods of systems engineering, including a formal design review and failure reporting system. The most important management technique involved design freezes and change control: at particular stages the project manager froze the design of a component, allowing modifications only with his written approval. The project manager thus kept individual engineers and scientists from pursuing indefinite improvements at the expense of the overall schedule, budget, and reliability. All of this relied on formal documentation to record, report, and enforce management decisions. JPL thus helped originate the discipline, in both senses of the word, of systems engineering.[12]

The crucible of Ranger also forged a new organizational structure. Through the 1950s Pickering had favored a functional organization, with staff divided among several technical divisions akin to disciplinary academic departments. Such a structure served well while JPL worked mainly on one large project at a time, but as the lab entered the space program and undertook a number of concurrent projects, it adopted a matrix organization. The matrix overlaid the technical divisions with a number of small, temporary project offices. Almost all the permanent staff resided in the technical divisions, which each project would draw on as necessary. The matrix thus allowed technical people to float from project to project while providing them a permanent home in the organization. In effect, the project offices controlled money and the technical divisions controlled people. The original matrix, however, was weak; the technical divisions kept most of their authority and left little to the project offices, which hired technical staff subject to the whim of the technical managers. After the failures Pickering gave project managers authority over all staff assigned to their project.[13]

Although Ranger may have been on the brink of success in its original mode, its subsequent results cemented the foundation of project management. The 1960s may have been the heyday of the technological fix—the tendency of American society to seek solutions to almost any problem through wonderful new technologies—but Ranger, though itself a technological tour de force, represented instead a managerial fix. Jack James was meanwhile already applying the formal approach to Mariner in parallel to Ranger, including failure reporting, design freezes, and change control. Although the launch vehicle failed on the first Mariner, doomed by the omission of a single hyphen in the guidance equations, Mariner 2 flew flawlessly to Venus in late 1962. After Mariner 3 failed, Mariner 4 in 1964 returned the first close-up pictures of Mars and showed up the Soviets after their five failures to reach the red planet. Subsequent Mariner flights—to Venus in 1967, Mars in 1969, to orbit Mars in 1971, and to Venus and Mercury in 1973—demonstrated JPL's mastery of high-reliability spacecraft and built up a cadre of experienced project managers.[14]

There was another, less publicized product of the early space missions, albeit a physically large one. JPL had won the Explorer mission in part thanks to its radio tracking work, and it began setting up a worldwide network of radio antennas, capable of communicating at any time with satellites in any orbital position around the earth. Such a network required three sites about 120 degrees apart in longitude. For the first and main site communications engineers, led by Eberhardt Rechtin, a Caltech PhD in electrical engineering, chose the Goldstone dry lake bed in the Mojave desert, about a hundred miles east of JPL. For the other nodes of what was called the Deep Space Network, JPL eventually settled on stations at Tidbinbilla in Australia and near Madrid in Spain, each of which by the early 1970s had antennas 26 meters and 64 meters in diameter.[15]

The massive antennas of the Deep Space Network enabled reception of signals transmitted by very low power spacecraft transmitters across hundreds of millions of kilometers. But large aperture alone was not enough. Hydrogen masers provided a precise frequency standard to ensure phase coherence of uplinked and downlinked signals, and cryogenic cooling of the ground receivers helped reduce signal noise. JPL engineers also developed complex codes to apply to the signals to screen out noise and transmission errors, as well as ones for data compression and pseudo-noise codes to prevent anyone—say, the Soviets—from eavesdropping or hijacking the spacecraft. Such techniques made JPL an important early center for telecommunications coding, and the techniques and the people themselves would help drive the emergence of the telecommunications industry, especially cellular phones, decades later.[16]

JPL's new regime in the 1960s had a breaking-in period. Ranger 6, the next flight in the series, seemed to go without a hitch right up to impact on the moon, but the live television pictures of the headlong descent to the lunar surface, supposed to be the highlight of the mission, never appeared. The blank monitors before the assembled dignitaries and media led to renewed grilling by NASA, joined now by Congress. The political castigation signified another important transition for the lab. As a sponsor, Army Ordnance had provided little oversight. The shift to NASA as sponsor brought account-ability to JPL, and the high visibility of the space race ensured that failures would receive political scrutiny. NASA also cultivated its own technical staff, as capable or more so than JPL engineers, at least in their own view; these NASA engineers tried to exercise their perceived prerogative as program managers, against JPL resistance.

Much political scrutiny centered on JPL's anomalous position within NASA: unlike the other NASA centers, JPL was owned and paid for by the government but operated by a contractor, in this case Caltech. Where the boundary lay between the public and the private depended on one's point of view. From the perspective of NASA and Congress, the govern-ment was paying for the work and thus had a right to say how it should be done. Caltech and JPL, however, replied that the point of contracting was to provide an independent environment free from the constraints of civil service bureaucracy; if NASA wanted to dictate how the lab was run, why not run it as a government lab in the first place? NASA did in 1962 consider this step, but it also appreciated the independence Caltech imparted and the cachet, and circumvention of civil service regulations, that aided recruitment of top-notch staff. Nevertheless, amid the Ranger failures, NASA tilted the balance from autonomy to accountability.[17]

The contract with Caltech added a third leg to the NASA-JPL relation-ship. What, wondered NASA, did Caltech contribute to JPL? JPL initially had relied on Caltech faculty as senior managers, and every director of the lab had come from the faculty; into the early 1950s, one-third of the professional staff were Caltech graduates. But joint appointments between lab and campus declined, as did the fraction of Caltech grads at the lab. Caltech was also supposed to provide administrative oversight, but the president and trust-ees of Caltech had little say in programmatic or operational matters at JPL. NASA, in particular, felt Caltech did little to earn its management fee, a sum awarded the institute on top of indirect costs. The fee was intended to cover Caltech's liability in case the contract was terminated and to compensate for intangible costs to the campus, such as the effect of JPL failures on Caltech's reputation. In practice, Caltech came to rely on the fee to boost the general campus budget. Caltech's main contribution to JPL may have been its name and image, although that could cut both ways as traditional campus elitism could make lab staff feel like second-class citizens. For its part, besides the fee, Caltech did not see many other benefits conferred by its association with JPL, although it would come to appreciate the public attention to spaceflight successes, and individual faculty were starting to capitalize on access to JPL spacecraft.[18]

JPL maintained relationships across another boundary, with industry. It was not by chance that JPL resided in southern California, the geographic epicenter of the aircraft and aerospace industry in the United States. Caltech's aeronautics programs had close ties from the 1920s to nearby aircraft firms, and its research and graduates helped fuel the prewar growth of the local aircraft industry.[19] JPL itself spun off Aerojet during the war, to mass-produce rockets to assist aircraft takeoffs; the firm would become a major defense contractor. The symbiosis continued in the cold war, and JPL's evolution resonated with the diversification of local industry from aircraft to aerospace. Several industry leaders would later serve as Caltech trustees, and as such they oversaw JPL policies and injected industrial perspectives. Meanwhile, cold war appropriations to the aerospace industry helped transform the Los Angeles basin from sunbelt orange groves and movie studios into a gunbelt metropolis.[20]

The common evolution and interests of JPL and industrial firms brought them into competition for programs as well as personnel. The political influence of the aerospace industry ensured that NASA would try to limit in-house research at its own labs and instead contract work to industry. JPL engineers, however, viewed the nascent space industry as incompetent to carry out advanced R&D and inefficient in production roles, especially in the fields of electronics and rocket propulsion.[21] The Surveyor project illuminated skirmishes along the public-private divide. Although JPL built most of the Ranger and Mariner spacecraft itself, for Surveyor NASA turned to an industrial contractor, Hughes Aircraft, under JPL supervision. Unlike Ranger, Surveyor was trying not to hit the moon head-on but to land a spacecraft gently on it, and technical optimism led to major cost overruns and schedule slips. JPL blamed a lack of experience at Hughes, but NASA and Congress also noted JPL's own disinterest. Lab staff had little personal incentive to look over the shoulders of Hughes engineers when they could be engineering Ranger or Mariner spacecraft themselves. In response to criticism, JPL stepped up its oversight, detailing 500 staff to ride herd on Hughes. The episode illustrated the political tightrope that JPL had to tread: NASA and Congress insisted on strict oversight of contractors but also demanded a role for private industry.[22]

Despite prickly relations with NASA, the space program proved a fertile environment for JPL. Lab staff mushroomed from about 2,500 in 1960 to 4,650 in the late 1960s before declining to around 4,000 in the early 1970s, with a professional staff of largely young, almost exclusively white males, reflecting the technical labor pool of the time.[23] The lab culture reflected the attitudes of bright young men who were willing to work hard—and play hard. The early missile test flights had required sites more remote than the Arroyo, and JPL rocketeers had trekked to the White Sands missile range in New Mexico, where all-night poker games on the train ride to the desert were followed by tequila-fueled runs to Juarez.[24] They found different diversions at the boomtown spaceport of Cape Canaveral in the 1960s, where a number of JPL engineers would go to prepare each spacecraft for launch. These road trips merged work and social lives and bound lab staff with a shared experience and values, including a formidable work ethic. Launches, and lab life in general, were not all play. Far from it—the bacchanalia blew off steam from hundred-hour work weeks around launches and planetary encounters, and sometimes not much less in normal business.

The work paid off in results—and in confidence, a can-do attitude that to outsiders smacked of arrogance. T. Keith Glennan, the first director of NASA, attributed the Ranger failures to JPL's "ambitious, cock-sure attitude," and even JPL admirers spoke of the lab's esprit as "almost offensive. It's like the Marines."[25] Although JPL people at times complained of the snobbery of Caltech faculty, some campus elitism may have rubbed off through association. The results, however, were real. The most tangible products were the spacecraft themselves. In order to keep antennas pointed at Earth for communication and solar panels at the sun for power, the Ranger and Mariner craft were stabilized in three dimensions, requiring complex guidance and control systems to keep proper attitude. Three-axis stabilization marked a major advance past the spin-stabilized Explorers and early Pioneers, which simply spun about their roll axis like a rifle bullet to maintain their trajectory.[26] It also perhaps encouraged imaging experiments, which required a stable platform, against experiments on particles and fields that benefited from spinning to sample all directions.

These spacecraft returned scientific data that revolutionized our knowledge of the solar system, starting with Explorer 1 and the discovery of charged particles trapped in Earth's magnetic field, now known as the Van Allen belts. Planetary missions replaced the fuzzy images from ground-based telescopes with up-close views across the electromagnetic spectrum. Mariner flights found a hothouse Venus, with surface temperatures of 900°F and pressures ninety times greater than on Earth.[27] Numerous craters detected by Mariner 10 on Mercury indicated a large number of planetesimals shooting through the inner solar system early in its history, a period dubbed the "Great Bombardment" that supported catastrophist theories of Earth's geological and biological history.[28] Perhaps the most surprising results came from Mars. Mariner 4 found no evidence for an earth-like atmosphere or water on its surface, no magnetism or radiation belts to betray an earth-like dynamic metal core, and signs that the polar ice caps were solid carbon dioxide, or dry ice. Later flights revised this Mars-as-moon picture by revealing geological features dwarfing any on Earth: volcanoes hundreds of kilometers across and almost twenty kilometers high, and a grand canyon thousands of kilometers long and five kilometers deep, called Valles Marineris in honor of its mechanical discoverer. Most surprising was evidence that Martian canyons had been carved by running water, probably from subterranean sources in a brief, ancient aqueous phase in the planet's history. The past presence of water rekindled speculation about life on Mars, with important consequences for the future of the planetary program.[29]

Ranger and Surveyor returned evidence that the moon had gone through a hot, molten phase and had not always been cold and hard, but they could not resolve competing theories about lunar origin: whether it was captured by Earth, fissioned from it, or had emerged at the same time as Earth as a sort of double planet.[30] The moon missions were primarily intended to prepare the way for Apollo, not to produce scientific data; plans for several experiments on Ranger were dropped to concentrate on television images to scout landing sites as well as spark public interest.[31]

The space program, that is, had two aims, science and exploration, which did not always converge. Rockets and spacecraft gave scientists direct access to space for the first time and thus promised—and delivered—remarkable advances. But space also beckoned humankind in general, with the fulfillment of primitive dreams of flight to the heavens.[32] The "new frontier" of space appealed in particular to the tradition of the frontier in American history, and NASA thus pursued in parallel both robotic probes and human spaceflight, despite the arguments of scientists that robots could do anything a human could do in space, and cheaper and more safely. The dual goals were not expressed just in terms of human versus robotic missions. JPL's planners also weighed tradeoffs between scientific goals and other priorities. In their first proposals for space projects, JPL mission designers ranked public relations second only to feasibility as a priority, ahead of scientific and technical objectives.[33] Mariner 2 landed Pickering on the cover of *Time* magazine and as grand marshal of the Rose Parade in 1963, indicating the public interest in the planetary program.[34]

Despite the popular interest in space, JPL was driven from its creation most fundamentally by the demands of national security, at first directly as an army lab, then as a leading element in America's space race against the Soviets. National security proved a potent and reliable source of support, fueling JPL's growth from a small rocketry project to a diverse R&D organization, but the association with national security could subordinate scientific goals to sociopolitical ends. It also exposed JPL to shifts in the cold war climate, which could threaten to dry up the political and social support for JPL's planetary missions.[35]

JPL circa 1976

The United States in the mid-1970s entered a new era. The Vietnam War, Watergate, and the energy crisis combined to erode the confidence of a postwar generation unaccustomed to hardship. Despite détente with the Soviet Union and rapprochement with China, the cold war continued, with a Soviet strategic arms buildup raising the nuclear stakes. American economic hegemony seemed to end, with an industrial challenge from Europe and Japan especially strong in high-tech fields. As the country tried to muster enthusiasm for its bicentennial year, the celebrations were tempered by a deepening sense of malaise.

American science and technology in this period meanwhile had come under criticism for their association with military weapons and environmental degradation. The 1960s counterculture challenged Enlightenment assumptions that knowledge equals progress, especially scientific knowledge; Pickering lamented in 1974 that "science and technology changed almost overnight from hero to antihero." Federal funding of basic research also came under question at a time of heightened concern about poverty, crime, pollution, and other pressing social problems. From presidents and program managers, the word went out to emphasize social applications of science and technology instead of knowledge for its own sake.[36]

The American space program reached its zenith amid the crescendo of counterculture criticism of science and technology. After Apollo won the space race, NASA's space budgets fell from a peak of more than $5 billion in the mid-1960s to less than $3 billion in the early 1970s, in current dollars; in constant dollars the decline was even more precipitous, with mid-1970s budgets at about one-third of the 1966 peak.[37] To provide a new focus for the space program and aerospace industry after Apollo, NASA and President Nixon decided to build the space shuttle, a reusable booster and orbiter that would, in theory, cut the cost from expendable launch vehicles; in practice, the shuttle development would cost far more and take longer than expected.[38]

Nixon's policy of détente with the Soviet Union also curtailed cold war competition as a driver for the space program, replacing it with cooperation; the centerpiece of this program, the Apollo-Soyuz rendezvous, flew in July 1975.[39]

The space shuttle program perpetuated the division between the human and robotic space programs. Within the robotic program itself, NASA managers encouraged competition to prod JPL's performance. Thus the Mariner 10 spacecraft beat out an alternative design proposed by the Goddard Space Flight Center; the Ames Research Center in Palo Alto, California, ran the Pioneer missions, which included two spin-stabilized spacecraft sent to Jupiter in 1973 and 1974, and an orbiter and probe to Venus in 1978; and NASA's Langley Research Center in Virginia developed the Viking mission in 1976, an ambitious plan for two identical orbiters and landers to visit Mars and soft-land a biological laboratory to test for life. JPL built the Viking orbiters, but not the more glamorous landers.[40]

NASA could encourage competition in prosperous times, but amid declining budgets these overlapping programs appeared as a luxury. A NASA study of "roles and missions," completed in 1976, retreated from the principle of competition and assigned JPL sole responsibility for planetary flight projects.[41] But the lab had no active planetary missions besides the Voyager mission to Jupiter and Saturn, approved in 1972 and slated for launch in 1977. The deepening sense of malaise at JPL belies portrayals of the 1970s as a "golden age" of planetary exploration—while the planetary program was indeed reaching its apogee, the impulse that had propelled it had burned out.[42]

By 1976 flight projects occupied about half of JPL staff, down from two-thirds in the mid-1960s. The rest of the staff had mostly worked on technology development and the Deep Space Network, but to pick up the slack in the 1970s JPL diversified. Diversification was an institutional strategy but also expressed technocratic ideals; in the afterglow of Apollo, systems engineering could appear as the source of American success.[43] The urge to apply science and technology to social problems reached through NASA to JPL, where Pickering proclaimed, "We must learn to satisfy the human condition with technological means." JPL engineers turned their techniques to problems in biomedicine, urban transportation, and police surveillance and communications. Social problems would prove difficult to solve with space technology and techniques, but the civil systems program did help keep JPL afloat.[44]

Having made the transition from army rocket arsenal to NASA spacecraft center, in 1976 JPL faced a shift from the buoyant Apollo-era program to an austerity plan of diversification. It also confronted a change in directors for the first time in more than twenty years. Pickering was turning sixty-five, the mandatory retirement age for Caltech administrators. The lab had quadrupled in size on his watch, and many JPL staff had known no other director. That, as Caltech president Harold Brown noted at the retirement ceremony, made "the institution the lengthened shadow of a man": the 3,000 guests that day wore buttons featuring Pickering's caricature and the words "Mr. JPL."[45] As America entered a new era of unease, Pickering's successor would inherit a large enterprise with a strong record, but one maturing into middle age with increasing insecurity.

PART I

Acclaim and Agitation

The Murray Years, 1976–1982

Planetary Exploration Triumphant

AS IT HAD DONE WHEN NAMING PICKERING AND HIS PREDECESSORS, CALTECH looked to its own ranks to fill the JPL director's chair in 1976. The search settled on Bruce Murray, a forty-three-year-old geology professor—a relatively young man, as Pickering had been when selected, but unlike Pickering, a scientist and not an engineer. JPL at Pickering's retirement numbered more than 4,000 people, with budgets of $250 million. The man chosen to lead it had managed a six-person team of geologists with a $200,000 budget.[1] Murray seems to have been selected not for his managerial skills, but rather for his imagination and dynamism. He also came as a champion of imaging experiments, both for scientific return and public appeal; for example, Murray used photos of Mars from Mariner 4 to wow the Senate Space Committee in 1965.[2] This knack for political salesmanship and public engagement, which Murray demonstrated in several books for a popular audience, would serve him well in his tenure as director.

Murray had earned his PhD in geology in 1955 at MIT. He had been in the ROTC as an undergraduate and had fulfilled his required two-year service as a lieutenant in the air force, studying the earth's gravitational field to help guide ballistic missiles. He later won a postdoctoral position at Caltech for planetary studies, starting with ground-based telescope observations and then joining the camera teams for the Mariner flights. By Mariners 9 and 10, Murray was head of the camera team, a full professor on campus, and recognized as a leading authority on Martian geology.

Whereas Pickering admitted to "an outlook that is too conservative—short-sighted of the possibilities," Murray counted himself a dreamer and visionary, and he would prove fond of cooking up blue-sky plans for deep space.[3] But he, too, betrayed a measure of conservatism. Unlike his good friend Carl

Sagan, who felt free to ponder Martian microbes and balloon animals floating through the atmospheres of Venus and Jupiter, Murray shied away from speculation. His main scientific contributions in the Mariner series helped puncture the possibility of life on Mars, leading Sagan to criticize Murray as living "on the side of pessimism." Murray's conservatism extended to his programmatic approach, where he favored cautious, incremental advances in missions instead of large leaps with complex, expensive spacecraft. He had thus opposed what he saw as overly ambitious plans for Mars exploration in the 1960s, dismissing a forerunner of the Viking mission as an "extravagant fantasy" and favoring the step-by-step approach of the Mariner series.[4]

Murray also exuded a whiff of the counterculture, even as he maintained his connections to military space programs through government advising and consulting for the Rand Corporation through the 1960s.[5] Murray viewed the 1970s as a period of unprecedented revolutionary change. In a talk in 1977 he declared that "materialism, in the sense of simply more and more, just does not make sense any longer"; instead, "quality will rule over quantity." Unlike many counterculture critics, Murray did not reject technoscience; on the contrary, technological advances were, in his view, driving the social revolution. He did, however, urge that technologists shed their elitist isolation and integrate with society, and he called as well for smaller, decentralized technological systems.[6] Murray's approach extended to his sartorial style, which consisted of shorts and sandals before he became director and tended toward casual shirts instead of conservative suits and ties afterwards.

Above all, Murray represented change—not just in the director's seat, but also as a personal philosophy, an attitude that perhaps won him the job from Caltech administrators seeking "a breath of fresh air" at JPL.[7] Murray's forthright, opinionated personality ensured a stiff breeze. Change could be good for an institution that had developed set ways of doing things and was seeking new directions in an uncertain environment. But change also threatened the stability offered by a highly organized institution. Like all large organizations, JPL faced the basic problem of balancing stability and change, of reducing risk without stifling innovation. JPL had been tilting toward the risk-reduction side for years. Murray would jump on the other side of the balance, rhetorically at least, but his underlying conservatism also led him to perpetuate certain traits of the lab, most importantly its approach to building spacecraft.

A Ticket for the Grand Tour?

Murray's public persona and his advocacy of imaging made him an ideal leader to trumpet JPL's most spectacular success, the Voyager tour of the outer planets. Planetary exploration had been limited to the inner solar system —the solid, smaller planets Mercury, Venus, and Mars. The gaseous giant planets of the outer solar system, much different from Earth, remained unexplored except from ground-based telescopes because of their distance. A direct flight to Neptune, for example, would take about thirty years even when powered by the huge Saturn V launch vehicle.

In the 1960s, however, JPL mission planners found an easier, elegant way to reach the outer planets in the technique known as gravity assist, which sought to use gravity from planets as a means to slingshot spacecraft to higher velocities. The effect of gravity on interplanetary trajectories was well known, but in 1961 Michael Minovitch, a graduate student at JPL for the summer, found that a close encounter with a planet could not only change the trajectory but also increase the velocity of a spacecraft, in a sort of celestial crack-the-whip, and that a spacecraft might thereby slingshot around the solar system indefinitely, using only enough rocket propulsion to reach the first planet.[8]

Gravity assist was useless without a spacecraft that could fly it. At the time of Minovitch's work, JPL was struggling to shoot a spacecraft into the moon; the lab first had to learn how to do that, then get one to another planet, before it could think about building spacecraft that could survive a trip to multiple planets. The gravity-assist concept itself was not proven until Mariner 10 in 1973, which swung by Venus on the way to Mercury. But its real payoff lay in the outer solar system. In 1965 Gary Flandro, a Caltech graduate student similarly at JPL for the summer, plotted detailed trajectories to Jupiter and Saturn. He found not only prime launch windows in the late 1970s, but also that Uranus and Neptune at that time would be on the same side of the sun as Jupiter and Saturn, a conjunction that Flandro calculated would occur once every 176 years. A spacecraft launched toward Jupiter in the late 1970s could thus conceivably hit all four giant outer planets, and if JPL started soon, it would have ten years to design a mission and build a spacecraft for this rare opportunity.[9]

A gravity-assisted trajectory past Jupiter promised to cut the flight time to Saturn from six years to three, to Uranus from sixteen years to six, and to Neptune from thirty years to eight. Better yet, it allowed a single spacecraft to cover the outer planets in one fell swoop. What Homer Joe Stewart of JPL called the "Grand Tour" produced a profusion of mission design studies, which soon concentrated in the Thermoelectric Outer Planet Spacecraft (TOPS) program. The overall mission called for identical twin spacecraft to launch for Jupiter, Saturn, and Pluto in 1977 and another pair for Jupiter, Uranus, and Neptune in 1979, with the four TOPS thus covering all the outer planets.[10]

Planetary scientists responded with enthusiasm to NASA's initial request for experiments in 1970, but ambitious experiment proposals, coupled with the engineering challenge of just getting a spacecraft to the outer solar system, doubled initial cost estimates toward the billion-dollar range. In December 1971 NASA administrator James Fletcher canceled the Grand Tour. The cancellation surprised fans of the Grand Tour at the Office of Management and Budget, who abandoned their usual hard fiscal line and offered funds for a scaled-back mission. JPL managers countered quickly with a mission to Jupiter and Saturn based on the Mariner spacecraft, with two identical craft to be launched in 1977; the early cost estimates of $250 million were about one-third those of the Grand Tour. The scaled-back plan addressed technical as well as fiscal doubts, since stopping at Saturn required the spacecraft to survive only four years instead of ten or twelve. Mariner Jupiter-Saturn '77, or MJS77, quickly won approval in 1972, just a few months after Fletcher killed the Grand Tour.[11]

The shift from the Grand Tour to MJS77 suggests a tendency by JPL to think big unless otherwise constrained. The tendency is understandable; without it the outer planets mission in particular, and space missions in general, would have been more timid endeavors, if they ever got off the ground at all. The Grand Tour concept in theory cut costs by precluding the need for individual probes for each outer planet, each of which would have had to run the political gauntlet in Washington. But the development of the Grand Tour nevertheless suggested a lack of restraint and, perhaps, of political acumen. Even before Grand Tour got the ax, Murray had advanced his incrementalist philosophy from an advisory role, suggesting that a less ambitious proposal based on the Mariner spacecraft might be technologically and politically more realistic.[12] In this case JPL was encouraged to return with just such a plan, but it would not always have a fall-back position.

Pork Chops and the X Factor

The theoretical existence of a gravity-assisted trajectory did not guarantee that a spacecraft could fly it in practice. JPL mission designers had to demonstrate that they could navigate the required ballistic trajectory to the outer planets with sufficient accuracy to hit the limited window at each planet that would sling the spacecraft in the right direction. Voyager aimed for 10-kilometer accuracy over distances of billions of kilometers, compared to an accuracy of 10,000–100,000 kilometers for the Mariners in the early 1960s and 100 kilometers for Viking at Mars.[13] They also had to choose where, exactly, the spacecraft should fly. Mission planners—notably Roger Bourke and then Charles Kohlhase—plotted possible launch dates and trajectories, seeking to fly close, but not too close, to Jupiter and Saturn and as many of their moons as possible. The daily rotation of the earth and the wheeling of all three planets about the sun and the moons about their planets, each at its own rate, made for a mind-boggling job. Computers helped. Terrestrial concerns did not. Mission designers tried to avoid planetary encounters taking place on Thanksgiving or Christmas, and they also sought to complete the Saturn encounter before the end of the 1981 fiscal year. Keeping such constraints in mind, Kohlhase and his crew generated 10,000 possible trajectories from plots of constant launch energy, called "pork-chop curves" from their distinctive shape. From these possibilities they selected a hundred or so trajectories that best satisfied mission objectives.[14]

The multiple goals of the mission further complicated calculations. The general scientific objectives had first been hammered out by a committee of planetary scientists in 1970.[15] Following their recommendations, for MJS77 NASA had selected ninety scientists for eleven different teams, each team working on a single experiment, such as imaging, radio science, or infrared spectroscopy. The objectives of the different groups did not always align. Imaging scientists, for example, wanted to view the sunlit side of a satellite whereas radio science and ultraviolet (UV) spectrometer experimenters preferred to fly behind it to see radio waves or sunlight pass through the atmosphere. Even within teams there could be a diversity of approaches, such as imaging team members preferring planetary rings to planets or satellites. And once everyone agreed on a trajectory, squabbles still arose over the sequence of experiments: one science team—for the imaging camera, say, or the ultraviolet spectrometer—could seek several hours of precious time during a close encounter for a single measurement they considered crucial, while the other teams clamored on behalf of their equally crucial experiments.[16]

Moderating such disputes required "a Solomon and a half," in the words of Arthur Lonne Lane, a member of the science integration team. Voyager scientists were dedicating several years to a project that returned most experimental data during the few days of encounters, and their results—and careers—depended on securing scarce observing time. "It never came to fisticuffs . . . but there were some pained and pointed discussions."[17] The pleasant role of referee fell to Edward Stone, a professor of physics at Caltech who served as the project scientist. Stone, a genial Midwesterner, had obtained a PhD in physics at Chicago in 1964; he had come to Caltech as a postdoc to study cosmic rays and earned a spot on the faculty. In 1972 Voyager project manager Harris ("Bud") Schurmeier asked him to be Voyager project scientist and Stone reluctantly agreed; he proved an adroit consensus-builder who had the scientific stature to enforce unilateral decisions when he could not negotiate a compromise.[18]

Although JPL planners made the most of it, MJS77 was a disappointing substitute for the Grand Tour. Since Ames was already sending Pioneer spacecraft to both Jupiter and Saturn, MJS alone would not break new ground, although it promised a much higher scientific return (and in particular a stable platform for imaging, unlike the spinning Pioneers). But MJS picked up most of its managers directly from the Grand Tour, from Schurmeier on down; they brought their initial plans with them but kept them under their hats, and as they designed the MJS mission they quietly ensured the possibility of extending it. The trajectory set included aim points to swing a spacecraft to Uranus; the radio system included an upgraded encoder to protect against failure but also to augment the capability to transmit from Uranus; and the sun sensor had amplifiers to boost its sensitivity to the level necessary at Uranus. Other features justified for reliability and redundancy on the nominal mission could also be reconfigured for use beyond Saturn.[19]

The notion of a conspiracy at JPL to end-run the approved mission and pull off the Grand Tour—the clever engineers subverting the timid bureaucrats—has some appeal, and it has acquired legendary status.[20] But Schurmeier's team also embraced versatility for the opposite reason. They assumed in the early design stages that a second, separate mission for Jupiter, Uranus, and Neptune would be approved for launch in 1979, using the same MJS spacecraft with different instruments bolted onto it. NASA declined to pursue the second round, probably for lack of launch vehicles, but the unfulfilled plans left the legacy of a spacecraft designed to go beyond Jupiter and Saturn.[21] The eventual Voyager spacecraft design, that is, displayed continuity with the go-for-broke Grand Tour approach, but it also reflected in part the incremental philosophy of spacecraft standardized to carry out a more cautious series of missions in the Mariner tradition.

By 1976 JPL engineers began to publicize the possibility of an extended mission, capitalizing on the existence of two spacecraft and a time interval between them. The two craft would fly slightly different trajectories, with arrivals at the planets separated by several months. The first to get there would take a riskier approach, flying near to Jupiter and past Saturn and its rings for a close flyby of Saturn's moon Titan; the second would approach Jupiter and its radiation fields at a safer distance, to back up any failure of the first spacecraft. The chosen distance would also, not coincidentally, allow it to hit the aim point necessary to swing past Saturn toward Uranus. The trajectory for Uranus, however, would compromise the science data from Titan. So if the first spacecraft failed, JPL engineers planned to retarget the second spacecraft as it approached Jupiter, to allow it to complete the objectives at Titan; but if the first spacecraft got the Titan data, the second could continue on the path to Uranus. The option became known as the X factor: the first spacecraft was the JST mission, after Jupiter-Saturn-Titan, and the second one JSX; the X would become either T or U, depending on the performance of the first spacecraft.[22]

As the launch dates approached, project managers began to push for a name change for the mission, to provide something catchier and, perhaps, to escape the mission constraints implied in the MJS name. After considering possibilities from Argus to Zeus, NASA staff and John Casani, who had succeeded Schurmeier as project manager, agreed on Voyager.[23] Names like Voyager, following earlier Explorers, Rangers, Mariners, Pioneers, and Viking, evoked the early emphasis on exploration in the planetary program.[24]

The abandoned name of Mariner indicates the expected inheritance from earlier spacecraft. JPL engineers would indeed capitalize on the Mariner experience, but Voyager was not a simple extension of that series. Although gravity assist cut many years off the flight time, the Voyager trajectory still required a couple of years just to reach Jupiter, at a time when the two-year duration of the Mariner trip to Mercury represented the limits of longevity. The whole Grand Tour would require a spacecraft to survive a dozen years, avoiding mechanical and electrical failures and withstanding micrometeorite and cosmic ray bombardment, all with no direct intervention from Earth.

The particular mission for Voyager presented new problems, especially the distance involved. To provide electrical power the Mariners used solar panels, but sunlight is 25 times less intense at Jupiter than at Earth, and 900 times less at Neptune. Colder temperatures exacerbated power problems, as mechanical and electrical components, computers, and propellants required heat to keep from freezing. Hence Voyager engineers turned to radioisotope thermoelectric generators, or RTGs, which generated electricity from the energy of radioactive decay. RTGs were smaller and lighter than solar panels, but since they gave off radiation they required isolation and shielding from spacecraft electronics, and their plutonium source also raised the issue of launch hazards.[25]

Long distance also complicated telemetry because radio signals, like sunlight intensity, fall off at the square of the distance. The spacecraft transmission power of 23 watts—about the power of a refrigerator light bulb—would give a signal at Earth of perhaps 1×10^{-18} watts, which would test the limits of the Deep Space Network, and the spacecraft itself needed an antenna three to four times the size of existing designs. Another advance was imposed by the science mission, especially the imaging experiments, which envisioned data rates of up to 115 kilobits per second; Mariners and Viking had maximum rates of 16 kilobits per second, from less distance. The high data rate required corresponding development both of telemetry systems and data storage devices and computers to process the data flow.[26]

The environment expected at Jupiter and Saturn forced other variations on the Mariner template. Schurmeier and his team had cut costs by not using electronic parts hardened to withstand high-radiation environments. Instead, they planned to use the Pioneer results to gauge how far away to fly from Jupiter to avoid its radiation fields. But Pioneer encountered a radiation environment at Jupiter a thousand times stronger than expected; the trajectory required to avoid lethal incidence of electrons on spacecraft circuits would greatly diminish Voyager's scientific returns. Schurmeier and Voyager engineers chose to save the science and brave the radiation by returning to radiation-hardened components, redesigning circuits to allow for radiation damage, and adding tantalum or titanium shielding.[27]

The spacecraft computer represented perhaps the most advanced and critical component and the most marked departure from Mariner. Two factors encouraged the departure, both stemming from the distances involved. First, radio signals would require much longer times to travel between the spacecraft and Earth—up to an hour and a half at Saturn. If the spacecraft developed a problem there, it would be three hours before it could receive a fix from engineers on Earth. So the spacecraft had to have a measure of autonomy, the ability to correct itself and compensate for failures. Second, the spacecraft would spend years in the cruise phase, just traveling across the void between planets, and the project had neither the money nor the people to look after it constantly. So the spacecraft was supposed to be able to take care of itself, operating for weeks at a time without any communication from the ground.

Advanced computers were intended to provide flexibility as well as autonomy. Given the relative lack of knowledge about Jupiter and Saturn, flight controllers wanted to be able to adapt to unexpected hazards or opportunities, which they could not do if the spacecraft was locked into a predetermined trajectory and sequence. In this regard computers distinguished American from Soviet planetary missions; the Soviets lacked onboard processing capability and hence tended to hard-wire the entire flight sequence on the ground before launch. That characteristic had cost them: when a Soviet spacecraft arrived at Mars in 1971 at the same time as both Mariner 9 and a huge dust storm, a reprogrammed Mariner 9 waited out the storm while a Soviet orbiter futilely exhausted its film and two landers plunged fatally into the maelstrom in a preset sequence.[28]

Integrating Voyager's subsystems tested the precepts of systems engineering. Managers first had to balance engineering tradeoffs, distributing mass and electrical power among the subsystems and science experiments. For instance, adding shielding to protect electronics against radiation added mass, forcing managers to cut mass elsewhere on the spacecraft to stay within margins or to recalculate the trajectory and fuel requirements (which in turn would affect the weight). They also had to trade science objectives against engineering options—such as the length of the boom isolating the magnetometer from spacecraft-generated electromagnetic fields—and science experiments with each other, as in deciding where to put the various instruments on the scan platform, a sort of turntable that allowed instruments to change position. Final responsibility for such decisions lay with the project manager, Schurmeier and, after 1976, Casani.[29] Schurmeier, who had a professional degree in aeronautical engineering from Caltech, had helped develop systems engineering as Ranger project manager, and he applied his experience to Voyager, not only integrating the diverse subsystems (such as power, propulsion, thermal, mechanical, computing, and control) but also ensuring reliability, through the now-familiar program of failure reporting and review boards to catch possible problems. The dozens of boxes filled with Voyager management reports in the JPL archives measure the rigor of the regime.[30]

The Skin of Their Teeth

Voyager's reliability program produced 3,500 problem/failure reports during spacecraft development, each requiring resolution. In the months and weeks preceding launch problems cropped up in various integrated circuits, resistors, and capacitors, forcing difficult decisions. If one capacitor failed, should they replace every such capacitor in the spacecraft? Was the tested part an outlier, or did it represent an inherent defect in the whole batch? Did the test failures threaten the mission, or could they go ahead and launch? As the launch approached, Thomas Gavin, the project assurance manager, was crossing his fingers: "I knew that, despite all our efforts, there was some unreliability in the spacecraft. And I'm thinking that I have a family to support; my oldest child is 14 years old. If this thing doesn't work, I don't want to have to meet a lot of important people who are going to be very angry with me. We launched."[31]

Voyager 2 blasted off on 20 August 1977, followed by Voyager 1 on 5 September, each on a combined Titan/Centaur launch vehicle. (The numbers on the spacecraft indicated the order of their arrival at the planets, not their launches: Voyager 2 launched first since its slower trajectory, to enable the grand tour, would get it to Jupiter second.) The problems began right away. And, of course, once the spacecraft was off the ground JPL flight controllers could not physically fix it; just to identify the problem meant deciphering the downlinked telemetry, and any solution would consist of new computer commands sent back by radio, either to forego the function of the afflicted component or find a substitute to perform it. Flight controllers had plenty of practice on such "work-arounds" from earlier missions, but Voyager would test their mettle.

Fixing failures, however, depended first of all on hearing from the spacecraft. The first inkling of trouble with Voyager 2 developed during the launch, when the launch vehicle went through a programmed roll maneuver. The roll rate was faster than anything JPL engineers had expected the spacecraft to do in deep space, and it overwhelmed the gyroscopes and thus disoriented the computer. Recalled Gavin, "As the reliability engineer, I'm thinking that the thing didn't last but a few seconds, and my career would likely do the same."[32] The gyros and computer recovered when the Centaur separated from the spacecraft, but then a more serious problem emerged. After separation the spacecraft deployed the boom holding the science instruments, but before it was fully extended the spacecraft ejected the spent solid-rocket motor that had provided a final boost. The combination of boom deployment and rocket ejection imparted angular momentum to the spacecraft. The computer sensed the tumble but attributed it to faulty firing of thrusters and switched to the backup thrusters. When the computer sensed that those, too, were not the source of the problem, it blamed itself and requested the central computer to switch to the backup attitude control computer. That step reinitialized the system, and the spacecraft thus set about reorienting itself from scratch by first finding the Sun. In the meantime the computer shut down the communication link with Earth.[33]

The whole process worked precisely as designed, since Voyager was supposed to fix itself in such an emergency in deep space. But JPL programmers had made the autonomy software too sensitive, so that it attributed an unexpected failure first to the thrusters and then to the computer itself. JPL flight controllers, still at the Cape, had to watch in idle panic for more than an hour as the spacecraft ran through its reorientation routines before it finally found its bearings. According to Raymond Heacock, the spacecraft systems manager, "The process had one or two steps left when it finally brought the spacecraft under control. If it had exhausted the opportunities, we could have lost the spacecraft."[34]

JPL engineers scrambled to correct the problems on Voyager 1 in the two weeks before its launch, installing springs and dampers to help the science boom deploy and adding software patches to the computer programs. That did not prevent an even closer call right off the bat. JPL engineers had learned from hard experience on Ranger and Mariner that success depended not only on their spacecraft but also on the launch vehicle. On Voyager 1 the first-stage Titan rocket did not burn all its fuel and thus left the spacecraft short of speed. The second-stage Centaur compensated by extending its burn, and thus got the spacecraft to the required velocity—with only 3.4

seconds of burn left in the Centaur's fuel tanks. Voyager 1, whose main mission would end at Titan, had a less demanding trajectory than Voyager 2 and a greater margin of fat in its pork-chop curve. If Voyager 2 had been riding on the faulty Titan it could not have made the grand tour. By the luck of the draw, the underperforming Titan went to the Voyager spacecraft that could still—by a three-second margin—fulfill its mission.[35]

The spacecraft were not yet out of the woods—indeed, they were heading in ever deeper. In November 1977 one of the two duplicate radio receivers on Voyager 2 began losing amplifier power, so flight controllers switched it to low-power mode. Both spacecraft suffered from shortages of hydrazine fuel, because exhaust plumes from the thrusters were impinging on the spacecraft and causing a larger than expected loss in thrust.[36] In February 1978 Voyager 1's scan platform stuck; the platform just as mysteriously freed itself, but flight engineers continued to test it gingerly into April. Preoccupied with the platform, mission controllers forgot to send a routine weekly command. The spacecraft computer interpreted the absence of a message as a failure in the primary radio receiver. When the computer switched to the backup receiver, however, flight controllers learned that a tracking-loop capacitor had shorted, so that the receiver could not adjust to the changing frequencies of signals produced by the Doppler shift. Programmers had anticipated a failure of the backup, and after twelve hours the computer switched back to the primary receiver, which promptly blew out completely. JPL lost all contact with the spacecraft. For seven frantic days, before the spacecraft was to switch automatically again to the backup receiver, engineers on the Deep Space Network devised computer tapes that varied the frequency of transmitted signals the precise amount necessary to mimic the Doppler shift expected at the spacecraft. The routine was extremely sensitive to spacecraft position and temperature—a change in the receiver's temperature of one-tenth of a degree centigrade would throw it off—but with time engineers on the ground reestablished communications with the spacecraft. Voyager 2 would hence have to get by with just the tone-deaf backup receiver.[37]

The problems with both spacecraft—especially, the failure by mission controllers to send the routine weekly command—suggested underlying failures of management. NASA, at least, viewed it that way. Casani, the Voyager project manager, in fall 1977 had also taken the reins of a new project, for the orbiter-probe mission to Jupiter that would be called Galileo. This new project consumed most of his time, and it was also siphoning key staff from Voyager. In addition, members of Voyager's mission operations team had planned to use the idle time of the cruise phase to develop sequences for the Jupiter encounter, but instead they found themselves dealing with the various emergencies. Planning for Jupiter fell behind schedule. In December 1977, the short-staffed mission control had to abort a complex maneuver when a software bug required a decision from a higher-level manager and none were present. The fiasco of April was the last straw.[38]

At NASA's request, JPL reorganized the Voyager project. Ray Heacock had succeeded Casani as project manager when the Galileo project had formally spun off in March 1978. Murray demoted Heacock and installed Bob Parks, whose project management experience went back to Sergeant, as Voyager project manager. Murray also brought in Peter Lyman, who had acquired a reputation as a mission operations guru on Viking, as another deputy under Parks. The management shuffle reflected the difference between building a spacecraft and flying it. In addition to the steady work that characterized spacecraft design, mission operations were punctuated by the chaos of emergencies and failures. Managing design required a different approach, perhaps even a different personality, from coping with the chaos of operations—Lyman compared it to running an army in peacetime versus wartime.[39]

That assumed that the project had committed people and resources to operations in the first place. Engineers tended to concentrate on how to build the spacecraft, and considerations of operations lost out to the preferences of designers in the development phase. Managers meanwhile often found it tempting to cover design cost overruns by raiding the operations budget. In addition, promotion into upper management tended to reward hardware designers, so top engineers could desert missions after launch for new design projects. Voyager exaggerated the problem. In the 1960s JPL built spacecraft in a couple years and flew them for at most a year or two, so the same people who designed the spacecraft could fly it with little cost to their careers. Voyager development took several years and operations would last decades, producing turnover from the project manager on down.[40]

JPL thence requested and got a budget increase to bolster Voyager operations, and Parks instated an informal division of labor, with Lyman pulling together an operations team and Heacock focusing on the hardware and software in the air. That software represented another of the main lessons drawn by JPL and NASA from the Voyager glitches, namely, the difficulty in testing and running complex software. Increasing on-board computing power and the desire for spacecraft autonomy encouraged JPL programmers to develop fault protection algorithms, which then displayed surprising sensitivity. Recalled Richard Laeser, then mission director, "We had some very clever programmers who put capabilities in the spacecraft, and the guys on the flight team couldn't understand why the spacecraft was doing what it was doing. . . . There are so many paths that you could follow through the automatics [steps] that the spacecraft sometimes appeared smarter than the people controlling it."[41] The role of software demonstrated the increasing centrality of computers and the difficulties scientists and engineers encountered in adapting to new practices—in this case, the need to bridge the gap between software designers and flight controllers.

The sensitivity of Voyager's software brought to mind HAL, the rebellious computer in "2001, A Space Odyssey," and Voyager team members similarly anthropomorphized their spacecraft. Voyager's computers "went crazy" and suffered from "vertigo"; they "displayed certain traits that seemed almost humanly perverse—and perhaps a little psychotic."[42] Although some managers, notably Heacock and Stone, declined to "animate the robot," as Murray put it, others developed "an emotional attachment to Voyager. It stopped being a spacecraft and became a personality, not just 1,800 pounds of nuts and bolts."[43]

Scientific Results at Jupiter and Saturn

Voyager's science teams were composed mostly of scientists from outside JPL, with a few exceptions. The engineering success of the Voyager project enabled these teams to return a treasure trove of data from Jupiter and Saturn, which would fundamentally alter our understanding of those two planets and the solar system as a whole. Scholarly analyses of the data filled thick volumes, and several books have summarized the findings for popular audiences.[44] Even a small sample of the results attests to Voyager's impact on planetary science.

Several surprises emerged from Voyager. Images of Jupiter's moon Io revealed a bewildering landscape of light and dark patches against a vivid orange background, provoking comparisons to a pepperoni pizza. More perplexing was the apparent absence of impact craters, which implied that some active geological process, such as volcanism or water erosion, had erased them. Confirmation of volcanism came not from scientists, but from a member of JPL's navigation team. Linda Morabito was studying an image of Io to find its position relative to two reference stars and thus to situate the spacecraft. She noticed a faint crescent extending some 300 kilometers above the edge of the planet, a plume from an active—very active—volcano (see figure 2.1).[45]

Io thus joined Earth as the only other body in the solar system to display active volcanoes. But if volcanism explained the lack of craters, it raised the question, why volcanoes? Where does the heat come from? Earth has a hot interior, which drives plate tectonics and forms plasmas; but Io occupies a much colder orbit, and any radioactive heat sources on the small moon should long ago have decayed. The heat engine was found instead in tidal forces from Jupiter's gravity and the other large moons, which combined to flex Io and

Figure 2.1. Voyager image of volcano erupting at the limb of Io. *Source:* JPL Photolab.

thus heat it. Another consequence of volcanoes was the massive amount of emitted material, which in Io's low-density atmosphere could reach escape velocity. The Io effluvium thus solved the mystery of the magnetosphere, the puzzling extent of which had forced radiation hardening of the spacecraft. The couple of tons of sulfur and oxygen emanating from Io every second flowed into a torus around Jupiter, which glowed in the ultraviolet; as the spinning torus expanded centrifugally it inflated the magnetosphere by a factor of two or three. Temperatures in the plasma torus ranged up to 100,000 degrees Kelvin and the magnetic flux tube linking Io and Jupiter carried an electric current of more than a million amps.[46]

Voyager also detected several new moons at both Jupiter and Saturn. And the known moons turned out to be much more idiosyncratic than previously thought. Since they appeared in ground-based photos as small smudges, planetary scientists tended to extrapolate from Earth's moon and hence expected to find geologically dead satellites, pockmarked by impact craters. Murray and planetary geologists had struggled to persuade Voyager planners that the satellites deserved close scrutiny.[47] The results justified the attention. Whereas scientists had anticipated craters on Io but found none, they expected none on Ganymede, whose ice surface was expected to absorb them, but found them in abundance; other regions on Ganymede exhibited a corduroy pattern indicating extensive ancient fault lines. Europa, another icy satellite, by contrast turned out smooth as a billiard ball, its icy crust obliterating craters but retaining a lacy pattern of dark cracks in the ice. Among Saturn's moons, the main attraction, Titan, was a relative disappointment visually because cameras could not penetrate its atmosphere. But infrared sensing and radio occultation revealed an unexpectedly dense atmosphere of nitrogen and some methane, above a cold surface of methane; atmospheric chemical reactions produced heavy hydrocarbons and carbon-nitrogen compounds, including hydrogen cyanide, a basic biological molecule.[48]

Except for Titan, most of Saturn's satellites were small and not dense; attention at Saturn instead focused on the famous ring system. As with Jupiter's moons, the rings displayed unanticipated complexity. The B ring exhibited dark radial lines in several places; how the spokes formed and how they survived the shear forces, arising from differential rotation rates at different radii, that should have dispersed them remained a puzzle (see figure 2.2). Other rings followed eccentric orbits and, most baffling of all, the F ring consisted of several intertwined or braided rings (see figure 2.3). Voyager also detected a faint ring around Jupiter, whose presence confounded the theory that tidal forces from Jupiter's huge moons—the same forces that powered Io's volcanoes—prevented rings from forming.[49]

The large planets themselves, though easier to study from Earth, also served up surprises. Initial views of Jupiter's weather emphasized its turbulence, but large-scale order soon emerged in alternating belts and zones of global wind patterns and convective action. Voyager's radio antennas meanwhile picked up whistlers from cloud-top Jovian lightning bolts. Saturn, almost featureless from terrestrial telescopes and so even less understood, displayed a large anticyclonic spot similar to Jupiter's Great Red Spot and alternating wind streams similar to Jupiter's at higher latitudes, but near the equator Saturn had a single, nearly supersonic jet stream—another puzzle, since Saturn received less solar energy than Jupiter and hence should have had slower winds. Attempts to integrate lateral wind patterns and vertical convection zones raised deeper questions about the source of energy driving the weather and whether it stemmed from processes in the deep interior of each planet or from the action of sunlight on the upper atmosphere alone.[50]

Voyager rewrote the textbooks—or, perhaps more accurately, drafted them from scratch, since knowledge of some of Jupiter's and Saturn's satellites and features was previously too scant to support detailed description.[51] In recognition of Voyager's scientific impact, *Science* and *Nature* magazines dedicated special issues to the encounters at Jupiter and Saturn, as did the more specialized *Journal of Geophysical Research*.[52] Above all, Voyager scientists turned the two planets and especially their moons from blurry smears on astronomer's plates to complex individual bodies, from the sulfurous calderas

Figure 2.2. Voyager image of Saturn's ring spokes. *Source:* JPL Photolab.

of Io to icy Europa, each undergoing dynamic processes—external bombardment to the point of cracking or splitting entirely, or flexing gravitationally, outgassing, and erupting. The twin Voyagers emphasized the solar system's diversity and thus helped to correct the geocentric perspective of planetary scientists, evident, for example, in the surprise at volcanic and tectonic activity in cold regions of the solar system.[53] And they were not done yet; as Voyager 1 swung up out of the ecliptic, Voyager 2 headed toward Uranus and Neptune, where more surprises awaited.

Public Relations and Instant Science

Although Voyager produced a profusion of scholarly publications, its scientific results were not first announced in academic journals, after months or

Figure 2.3. Voyager image of Saturn's braided F ring. *Source:* JPL Photolab.

years of data analysis. Instead, scientists publicized them in press conferences within days or less of getting the data. Science by press conference avoids peer review and thus violates the norms of the scientific community because half-baked analyses can slip through, as in the later, famous nondiscovery of cold fusion.[54] Voyager and other planetary encounters put a new twist on this approach in the very short time between data return and publication; hence the common term at JPL, "instant science." Planetary scientists put up some resistance to instant science. Murray had opposed quick release of photos from Mariner flights, seeking instead to hold them back for scholarly publications, and Caltech biochemist Norman Horowitz had complained on Viking that "having to work in a fishbowl like this is an experience that none of us is used to." Murray and Horowitz would see reason to resist: on Mariner 10 the press seized on reports of a moon around Mercury, which on closer examination turned out to be a distant star; initial ambiguity in Viking's data produced media accounts that flip-flopped daily on whether life existed on Mars.[55] But on Voyager, scientists would come to accept, and even relish, the new mode of publicity.

Planetary missions offered particular opportunities for instant science. As a matter of practicality, the media knew in advance the time of encounter and so could converge on JPL with pencils and cameras ready when results started arriving. But particle physicists, for example, also know in advance when they have beam time on accelerators, are often in a hurry to publish, and have proven willing to resort to press conferences—indeed, in August 1979 they were embarrassed by "the great 'gluon' fiasco," resulting from overstated press announcements of the discovery of a new elementary particle.[56] Yet particle physicists still do not turn around their results so quickly. What distinguished Voyager? For one, scientists' relative ignorance going in: as Stone put it, "one can, within a period of days, go from essentially no knowledge to quite a bit of knowledge, and in some cases even to understanding."[57] And some of that knowledge came in the form of images, a visual framework accessible to a nontechnical audience—for example, the volcanoes on Io, an unexpected discovery readily apparent from the pictures. Even if viewers did not comprehend the scientific importance of images, they could appreciate the aesthetic appeal of Jupiter's swirling cloud patterns or the abstract arrangement of Saturn's rings.

There was another factor fostering instant science, apparent for other planetary missions but especially evident on Voyager: the people involved were very good in public, starting with Stone, who as project scientist chaired most of the media sessions. Stone proved a master not only of presenting scientific results himself, but also in coordinating which results to present and who would present them.[58] The performance of Stone and his colleagues in the press conferences counteracted the popular image of the scientist as a reclusive nerd; on the contrary, Voyager scientists conveyed considerable aptitude and even enthusiasm for public appearances (see figures 2.4 and 2.5). Not all scientists had the knack, however, and journalists quickly learned the best sources for their sound bites. The imaging team in particular had media-friendly members and subject matter, while certain fields-and-particles experimenters suffered doubly, from the less visual subject matter (which could also require more lengthy data analysis) and from a charisma deficit; one dissatisfied reporter jokingly dubbed them "the morticians of space."[59]

Amid the phenomenon of daily press conferences, Stone tried to retain a measure of peer review. Before the press conference each morning during encounters, Stone convened the principal investigators to report on each experiment, but he forbade the presentation of this material to the press that day. Instead he called another meeting each afternoon of the entire science contingent, over a hundred scientists, to review incoming data in detail. This afternoon meeting concluded with decisions on what material to present at the next morning's press conference and which experiments needed more data. This compressed review process prevented major mistakes with instant science, although a few small ones—such as the assertion that Saturn's rings

Figure 2.4. Voyager imaging scientist Laurence Soderblom (at left, gesturing) meets the press during the Saturn encounter in August 1981. *Source:* JPL Photolab.

contained thousands of separate ringlets (later analysis determined that there were waves in the rings, but not discrete gaps)—snuck through.[60]

The media attention was not entirely unsolicited. JPL and NASA each had its own active public relations staff, whose job was not just to accommodate media queries but actively to generate public interest in the space program. NASA from its creation cultivated media relations, evident first in the Mercury program and then in Apollo. JPL's previous role as a classified rocket arsenal for the army had not encouraged publicity, but Pickering, who got a good look at the possibilities in the reaction to the first Explorer satellite, appreciated the importance of public relations for the lab's new mission. In 1957 he created a public information office, led after 1963 by Frank Colella, a salty, straightforward New Yorker. The Ranger series focused attention on JPL, initially unflattering; then Mariner and Viking built up interest outside of JPL and experience within the lab in handling the public attention.[61] JPL's embrace of public relations is a particular example of a more general phenomenon of the twentieth century, the deployment of professional public affairs specialists on behalf of science. The institutionalization of public relations in American science was led by industry—notably by Thomas Edison and General Electric—and then spread to scientific societies and finally universities, which by the 1970s were forming public information offices to publicize campus research.[62]

Figure 2.5. Voyager project manager Robert Parks, project scientist Ed Stone, and imaging team leader Brad Smith at a press conference. *Source:* JPL Photolab.

JPL joined the vanguard of this trend, and by the time of Voyager had a well-oiled public relations machine. One difference between Voyager and earlier flight projects: the relative status of television and print media.[63] In the 1960s JPL's public affairs was print dominated, but by the 1970s television had acquired a powerful role in American mass media. Because minute-long news stories on television relied on snappy visuals, the increasing attention to television reinforced the importance of imaging science.[64] It also promoted the development of graphical displays, including pioneering work on computer animation. JPL programmer James Blinn collaborated with Kohlhase to generate three-dimensional animations simulating Voyager's flight past Saturn, at each point calculating the relative appearance of planets and stars. The 3-D movies—in which the viewer rode along with Voyager as the spacecraft swooped over Saturn's rings and satellites—proved a hit with television news editors and viewers.[65]

Public relations had its costs. It diverted the attention of flight controllers and scientists to briefing the press in the midst of crucial encounters. It also required money. NASA had long demonstrated its commitment to public relations; when its public affairs staff presented NASA's science program manager with a budget for $600,000 for Viking, the manager "didn't flinch." Within JPL, most public affairs funding came out of general institutional funds, and in general the PR staff did not lack for resources. For special items, such as a spacecraft model or the Blinn-Kohlhase animations, the flight project itself would provide the funds, perhaps recognizing that PR was part of the mission.[66]

So much for the supply of science news from JPL. What about the demand for it? As American journalism grew increasingly specialized in the twentieth century, and as science acquired increasing relevance to economic and military strength, science writing had developed from a small niche to a recognized specialty after World War II. By the 1970s most major newspapers and newsmagazines supported science sections and writers, with coverage often dominated and defined by an "inner club" of reporters at leading papers. Many in this small group were first exposed to the science beat in assignments on the human space program in the 1960s, and subsequent polls of this cohort revealed a distinct preference for space and astronomy topics.[67]

Although professional science journalists in general shed the celebratory tone of earlier writers on science, the inner club's personal interest in space, combined with the sometimes symbiotic relationship between reporters and their sources, produced sympathetic, if not partisan, coverage of JPL. Amid the excitement of planetary encounters, seasoned journalists struggled to stay free of bias; younger reporters, one old hand observed, abandoned even the appearance of objectivity and led the cheerleading while wearing Voyager T-shirts. The same writer described Voyager encounters as "working festivals and reunions that were eagerly anticipated by the tribe that covered science. They would be to the space junkies what Grateful Dead concerts were to rock 'n' rollers."[68]

These journalists were not just satisfying their own curiosity; they were also fulfilling a perceived public demand for news about science in general and planetary exploration in particular. The late 1970s and early 1980s witnessed a resurgence of media interest in popular science, reversing a slump that had dated from the mid-1960s. Several new popular science magazines appeared, newspapers added weekly science supplements and columns, and science programs multiplied on television. The trend, perhaps spurred by such stories as Three Mile Island, Skylab, and gene splicing, added up to what *Newsweek* in 1979 called "the science boom."[69]

Popular culture provided several indicators of public interest. In the late 1970s Hollywood shifted its attention to outer space. The success especially of "Star Wars" in 1977 sparked a spate of space films, from "Close Encounters of the Third Kind" to "The Cat from Outer Space," in addition to the Star Wars sequels, and JPL managers suggested that NASA "consider ways of using this increased public interest to its advantage."[70] One space movie from this period capitalized on a built-in fan base. The "Star Trek" television series, set in the distant future and premiering in the mid-1960s, had inspired

Figure 2.6. Star Trek at JPL. Mariner 5 managers in mission control, October 1967: Ted Parker, Dave Shaw, and Dan Schneiderman (left to right). *Source:* JPL Photolab.

a devoted following after a decade on the air (see figure 2.6).[71] "Star Trek: The Motion Picture" (1979) would feature a mysterious, nearly sentient object known as V-GER, whose full name eventually revealed it as an interstellar relic from our time. The homage might have run the other way: several names considered for MJS77 ("Planet Trek," "Trekker") suggested a link to the television series.[72]

The Star Trek phenomenon represented just one segment of the science-fiction community, to which JPL was well connected. Many JPL staff, such as Casani and Kohlhase, had honed an early interest in space as sci-fi buffs.[73] Murray maintained an active correspondence with Arthur C. Clarke and had signed up Clarke and Ray Bradbury for a panel at Caltech in 1971 on "Mars and the Mind of Man," to coincide with the Mariner 9 encounter.[74] Sci-fi novelists for their part were a strong presence at JPL for planetary encounters, and at least one of them acknowledged, or rather advertised, the public relations function of "us Buck Rogers types."[75]

The clearest sign of public interest in space science came from the work of Murray's friend Carl Sagan. A planetary astronomer from Cornell, Sagan in the early 1970s began establishing a name as an enthusiastic popularizer of science, and especially planetary science, with a string of popular books and television appearances. In August 1977, as the Voyagers prepared for launch,

Sagan turned up on the cover of *Newsweek;* at the time he was preparing what would cement his celebrity, a thirteen-part series on astronomy for public television titled "Cosmos." The series, with Sagan as host, aired in 1980 and was an instant hit, eventually reaching not quite billions and billions, but about a half billion viewers worldwide; the book version stayed on best-seller lists for seventy weeks. The Cosmos series used Voyager images of Jupiter and several computer graphic sequences from Kohlhase and Blinn at JPL, and the visual dazzle—and Sagan's salesmanship—brought JPL's work to a wide audience.[76]

Sagan was on Voyager's imaging science team, but his most publicized contribution would be the Voyager records, phonographs carried on board each spacecraft with a message to any extraterrestrial civilizations. The idea of sending a message out with a spacecraft was not new: the Pioneer 10 and 11 spacecraft each bore a plaque with a likeness of male and female human forms and the location of Earth within the solar system.[77] The Pioneer plaques generated wide publicity, and in 1974 John Casani noted on a standard problem report for Voyager: "No plan for sending a message to our extra solar system neighbors." What to do? "Send a Message!"[78]

Casani took matters into his own hands when he became project manager. In December 1976, during Viking mission operations, he ran into Sagan and asked him to organize a message for Voyager, perhaps a modest extension of the Pioneer plaques. Sagan, typically, thought bigger. A long-playing record could include many more encoded pictures than a plaque and, even better, sounds and music. Sagan and several friends and colleagues hence set about collecting sample songs from various periods and cultures, arguing the merits of different genres (should we send out rock 'n' roll?) before settling on a playlist, including, yes, one Chuck Berry. Three-fourths of each record was music, ninety minutes' worth, with the remainder given to pictures and sounds of Earth and spoken greetings in fifty-five languages. The records—gold-plated copper in silver covers, with stylus and cartridge mounted nearby—added more than a kilogram of mass to each spacecraft, and Casani interrupted pleasant debates about music to enforce project deadlines on Sagan's group. He also provided some project funds to the effort. Some outside consultants perceived that the real audience for the Voyager records would not be extraterrestrials, who were unlikely ever to receive the records, but people on Earth, who should get the message that we are one people, sharing a planet. The records did spark much terrestrial interest and debate, although perhaps not at the desired depth; one late-night television skit featured aliens beaming back a message: "Send more Chuck Berry!"[79]

All of this public interest in space science, combined with a finely tuned PR operation, ensured a wide audience for Voyager. For the Jupiter encounter about 300 media representatives registered at JPL's news center; two years later, for Saturn, more than 1,000 showed up, the most ever for a robotic space event. (The Apollo 11 moon shot had attracted about 3,500 journalists.) The Saturn story and pictures landed on the front page of every major American newspaper the day after the closest encounter of Voyager 1, and most large metropolitan dailies carried the story on the front page for several days during the encounter; editorial pages then took up the celebration, and the following week Voyager garnered the cover of both *Time* and *Newsweek*. Live television broadcasts from JPL reached a potential audience of 100 million in the United States, and the interest extended abroad: the assembled media for Saturn included about 200 foreign news agencies, and 10 foreign countries sent television crews to JPL.[80]

The Legacy of Voyager

It is hard to overstate the acclaim earned by Voyager—within the science and aerospace communities, and from news editorials and public commentators—and its effects on the lab. Ed Stone, asked at a press conference what percentage of the science objectives had been met, thought for a moment and replied, "200 percent."[81] Thomas Mutch, associate administrator for space science at NASA, called Voyager "a truly revolutionary journey of exploration. . . . When the history books are written a hundred years from now, two hundred years from now, the historians are going to cite this particular period of exploration as a turning point in our cultural, our scientific, our intellectual development."[82] Press accolades for the Voyager 1 encounter at Saturn alone could fill a scrapbook. The *London Sunday Telegraph* and the *Wall Street Journal* looked back to the moon landing for comparison; the *New York Times* reached further, to Darwin's exploration of the Galapagos; and *Newsweek* furthest of all, to Columbus. *Time* enthused, "space exploration has already paid for itself many times over," and columnist George Will, no friend of federal activity, declared that "the dazzlingly precise flight of Voyager 1 is a smashingly successful government program."[83]

The evocations of exploration and Will's encomium suggest that the exploration ideal continued to take precedence over hard science in the public eye; just getting there sufficed. Voyager was first an engineering triumph, with the scientific bonanza a secondary payoff. JPL engineers, in a popular metaphor, hit a celestial home run, touching the four outer planets as they sent their spacecraft on a ride out of the solar system—even though they were not supposed to be swinging for the fences. The project came in on time, on budget (accounting for inflation), and then performed beyond the baseline requirements. Voyager boosted JPL's reputation, and its already formidable self-image, as the preeminent spacecraft builder, especially at a time when

NASA was struggling with massive cost overruns and delays in the shuttle program and also in the Large Space Telescope.[84] One JPL engineer summed it up: "Voyager was Camelot."[85]

Why did Voyager succeed? First, the particulars of the mission: because Voyager was the only large planetary flight project under development at JPL for much of this period, it could attract the best people, and the challenge of a 1-in-176-year opportunity also appealed to engineers. Voyager also benefited from redundancy, not just within each spacecraft but in the support of two spacecraft in the project—and the lab, in fact, built almost three whole spacecraft, counting the full-scale mock-up used for testing. Acquiring and assembling parts for three spacecraft turned up problems in components that might have slipped through if only one were built, and then when parts did fail in testing, engineers had spares at hand from the mock-up.[86]

Some general characteristics of JPL also enabled Voyager's success. Voyager's results rested, at the base, on the achievements of many talented and creative individuals, from Minovitch to Blinn, Schurmeier to Stone. The presence of these people was necessary but not sufficient; the lab had to get them to work together, compromising their professional and personal goals for the sake of the project, whether by agreeing to a different engineering or scientific approach or by giving up family or social life for eighty-hour work weeks. Motivation came from the mission itself, but also from management. Voyager represented above all the success of systems engineering: rigorous reviews and testing, detailed documentation, and communication across interfaces. JPL engineers by the late 1970s had about twenty years' experience designing high-reliability spacecraft. The size and complexity of Voyager honed that experience and tested it, and it proved sharp enough.

Voyager's triumphant tour, however, tended to obscure the early close calls that almost killed it. Both Voyager spacecraft survived by the skin of their teeth; but the rosy glow of congratulation after the encounters perhaps encouraged people—at JPL and NASA, but also politicians and the public— to forget that a very fine line separated success and failure. As the tribulations of the early space program receded in memory, the space community at large was becoming complacent. By 1968 the Space Science Board of the National Academy of Sciences already believed, "Now that technological advances have made failures infrequent, whether at launch or during the mission, . . . planetary exploration is no longer a primitive or risky act."[87] Subsequent successes only reinforced such attitudes. It was easier for people at JPL to forget that narrow margin because Voyager would be the only planetary project the lab launched for over a decade. JPL thus became accustomed to technical success, even as it endured a series of programmatic and political setbacks that threatened its foundations.

T H R E E

Planetary Exploration in Extremis

THE MEDIA INTEREST GENERATED BY VOYAGER AND THE SUPERLATIVES BESTOWED
upon it did not translate into political support. Even as the Voyager spacecraft
completed their triumphant encounter with Saturn, Murray and JPL were
waging a fierce campaign to save Voyager, the rest of the lab's flight projects,
and perhaps even the lab itself from extinction. The crisis in planetary exploration reached its peak in 1981, but it was germinating when Murray arrived
in 1976 and first blossomed the following summer, impelling lab managers
and Caltech trustees into the political arena.

National Priorities in Space and on Earth

In December 1980 NASA administrators and lab directors identified a para-
dox. "The apparently great public support that shows up at each new scientific achievement (e.g., the Voyager-Saturn encounter) does not seem to
translate into corresponding Congressional support." A year later, NASA's
deputy administrator, Hans Mark, informed a National Academy of Sciences
colloquium that the "Washington problem is that Americans don't *vote* on
[the] basis of the space program achievements."[1]

Several sources diluted public interest in deep-space missions and wa-
tered down political will: the slackening of the space race after the rush of
Apollo and the emergence of more pressing national priorities; continued
contention between the human and robotic programs, exacerbated especially
by the space shuttle; increasing competition within NASA's space science
program from space-based astronomy and earth sciences; and allocation of
priorities within the planetary program, which at times would array parts
of JPL against each other. At this time NASA also lacked the galvanizing

force provided by Soviet competition, at least until relations cooled later in the decade. The Soviets were emphasizing human orbital missions instead of planetary exploration, and the planetary missions they did pursue focused on Venus, abandoning Mars after 1973 and conceding the outer planets to the United States altogether; and both sides viewed Venus as an opportunity for cooperation rather than competition.[2]

The response to Viking provided early signs of dwindling interest. Planetary scientists complained of "the blasé attitude of the public toward the first transmissions of pictures," and the New York Times noted "the apathetic reaction of most Americans last week to the Viking miracle on Mars."[3] The publicity generated by Viking did not necessarily benefit the long-term planetary program. To drum up support, NASA had framed the mission as a search for life on Mars. By staking so much on the detection of life, the head of the biology team perceived, NASA managers set themselves up for "a bigger letdown than if they had taken a more neutral stand in the first place."[4] Despite the abundant data the mission returned, Viking's discovery that the Martian surface seemed downright hostile to life undermined one of NASA's key justifications for future missions.

In 1976 NASA commissioned a study of public interest. The study concluded, "The picture of NASA that is in focus is Big Budget, Big Spectaculars and, bottom line, a hundred pounds of moon rocks."[5] In a Roper poll in early 1977, 46 percent thought the federal government was spending too much on space exploration, 33 percent about right, and just 11 percent too little. Some Americans were not only uninterested but downright skeptical; a Gallup poll around the same time reported that 28 percent of Americans believed the space program was in fact an elaborate sham.[6]

NASA was not doing much to dispel the big-budget image. In 1972 President Nixon had approved the space shuttle program. To win approval, NASA had cut its cost estimates to $5 billion and inflated the projected number of launches to sixty per year. Both proved unrealistic. By the time the first shuttle flew in 1982, four years after the expected initial launch date, the program had doubled in cost and could deliver only about six flights in its first two years of operation. In the meantime, to ensure customers for the shuttle NASA had stopped buying expendable boosters, leaving planetary missions with no ride into space.[7]

The shuttle also affected JPL in terms of funding, where until late 1981 shuttle overruns came out of a zero-sum NASA budget. In 1978, for example, a House appropriations subcommittee created a $30-million contingency fund for the shuttle out of budgets for the Jupiter orbiter-probe, a solar mission at JPL, and the space telescope.[8] Proponents of human exploration could claim that big-budget programs provided coattails for cheaper robotic missions, and some planetary scientists came to accept "that one would not get *any* money . . . for space exploration without men in the loop." NASA tacitly supported this thesis by committing around 17 percent of its overall budget to space science each year through 1978, but that was a fixed percentage of the declining NASA budget, eroded further by inflation.[9]

Planetary flight projects meanwhile were facing increasing competition from astronomy and earth sciences. Planetary science had dominated the space science budget, receiving about a third of it in 1975, while earth sciences (including solar-terrestrial) and astronomy and astrophysics received between 10 and 15 percent each. By 1978 the planetary portion had declined to about 6 percent, a rapid switch from the largest to the smallest of the three programs. Astronomy meanwhile had started a slow climb that would take it to 30 percent of the space science program by the mid-1980s, completing the reversal of positions (see figure 3.1). The impetus for astronomy came from astronomers seeking a view of space not blocked or distorted by Earth's atmosphere; they agitated in particular for a large optical telescope in earth orbit, later renamed the Hubble Space Telescope, which by the early 1970s had reached the formal design stage.[10]

Similarly, but in the opposite direction, earth scientists were learning to appreciate the perspective offered from space. Meteorologists were among the first to capitalize on the potential of satellites, with the launch of the first Tiros weather satellite by NASA in 1960. Classified data from reconnaissance satellites and photos taken by astronauts stimulated geologists and geographers to seek a civilian remote-sensing satellite to monitor earth resources, culminating in the Landsat series launched first in 1972.[11] Relative to the planetary and astronomy programs, earth-science funding (including solar-terrestrial and ocean research) rose from about 14 to 23 percent from 1975 to 1980, making it in this period the dominant program of the three.[12]

NASA managers had primary responsibility for setting priorities among these fields, supplemented by an advisory apparatus centered on the Space Science Board of the National Academy of Sciences. In 1975 NASA commissioned a report titled "Outlook for Space" to orient the agency for the 1980 to 2000 time frame. The report proposed that "a major increase in emphasis and in resources should be directed toward Earth oriented space programs," and it also suggested more emphasis on cosmology and astrophysics.[13] NASA's associate administrator for space science, Noel Hinners, pronounced the belief that astronomy missions promised better scientific return for the investment, and staff in the Office of Management and Budget (OMB) shared the sense that space astronomy was the new "glamor" field in space science.[14] The Space Science Board reflected these priorities, consistently ranking the space telescope above the Jupiter mission; NASA managers then had to keep

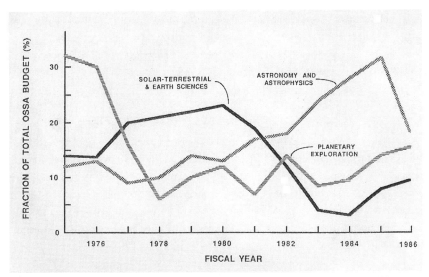

Figure 3.1. NASA's space science funding by program. OSSA stands for Office of Space Science and Applications. Before 1982 earth science was funded by a different NASA division, the Office of Space Technology and Applications; this graph includes those funds. *Source:* NASA Space and Earth Science Advisory Committee, "The crisis in space and earth science," November 1986 (JPL 198, 12/163).

astronomers and planetary scientists "from trying to shoot each other down to save their own project" in their lobbying for congressional approval.[15]

The decline of space as a national priority, the development of the space shuttle at the expense of robotic programs, and the emergence of disciplinary competition for flight projects had an accumulated effect on JPL: NASA's budget was contracting and with it the space science portion, and planetary projects within that were decreasing. The upshot: from 1974, the peak of Viking, to 1977, the planetary budget fell by a factor of almost three in current dollars and even more in constant dollars.[16] Five years passed between the start of Voyager in 1972 and approval of the Jupiter mission in 1977, and no more new starts for planetary projects at JPL were forthcoming through 1981.

Purple Pigeons and Gray Mice: Or, How to Fill a Bathtub

The decline of the planetary program manifested itself at JPL first in the projected rampdown from Viking and Voyager. The Viking workforce dropped off sharply from more than 400 staff in 1975 to almost zero by 1977; Voyager would undergo a similar decline starting in 1977. The lab expected to ramp back up for the Jupiter orbiter-probe and a possible lunar orbiter starting in 1978, but that left a deep two-year dip in the graph of staff levels. Even if the Jupiter or moon missions were approved for 1978, the lab would have to lay off staff; if neither project were approved that year, perhaps 500 JPL employees and a similar number of contractor staff at JPL would lose their jobs.[17]

The lack of new missions for 1977 and 1978 became known as the "bathtub," after the U-shaped bend in the workforce charts. The staffing shortfall had long-term implications. Experienced engineers were not easily replaced; despite the documentation of systems engineering, lab staff viewed their expertise as a form of tacit knowledge. Murray wrote to NASA's space science manager that "no amount of documentation or procedural manuals can enable inexperienced engineers to by-pass entirely the many subtle opportunities for potentially serious, even catastrophic mistakes. The knowledge and understanding now embodied in our staff was painfully acquired in the 1960s and has been maintained by the subsequent continuity of project activities."[18] The argument that JPL's expertise was a national resource meriting upkeep by the federal government would become a recurring theme.

JPL managers would seek to fill the bathtub in part with non-NASA work, especially in energy and then defense, but they also sought to keep planetary missions flowing. One of Murray's first acts as director in April 1976 was to assemble a team to come up with imaginative new missions. The group spent three months brainstorming and arrived at a list of seven candidates: Mars rovers; a Venus radar orbiter; a tour of Jupiter's inner moons with a landing on Ganymede; an orbiter to Saturn with a lander on Titan; a flyby of several asteroids; an unmanned station on the moon's south pole; and development of a "solar sail," which would use solar radiation pressure to propel a mission to Halley's comet.[19]

Murray dubbed the collective of missions the "purple pigeons." The name addressed perceptions of a lack of pizzazz at NASA, with the colorful pigeons replacing the "gray mice" generated by the current planning process.[20] Murray intended the pigeons to combine "first-rate science . . . with broad popular appeal"; the popular aspect, he noted, was required to generate and sustain political support for the several years from project approval to launch.[21] The purple pigeons coincided with the Viking encounter and aimed to capitalize on the media presence: when journalists asked what was next for the planetary program, Murray and the JPL public affairs people pushed the pigeons.[22] The colorful pigeons caught the media's eye, and NASA soon approved supplemental funds for the solar sail and Mars missions and added other pigeons to its long-range plans.[23] By the end of 1976 Murray concluded that "the outlook is more encouraging now than for some time."[24]

The lab meanwhile was awaiting formal approval of the Jupiter Orbiter-Probe (JOP) as a 1978 new start. With support from scientists, NASA, and OMB, approval seemed likely. But on 4 May 1977, the House appropriations subcommittee responsible for NASA's budget deleted all funds for the project. The chair of the committee, Rep. Edward Boland, had consistently pressed NASA to prioritize, and he now correctly judged the space telescope a higher priority for NASA and the Space Science Board. After the Senate appropriations subcommittee approved the Jupiter mission, and a House-Senate conference committee failed to resolve the impasse, the matter returned to the House for a special vote.[25]

In the week before the vote, Murray mobilized the lab to defeat Boland. The campaign recruited the California congressional delegation, the House and Senate science committees, planetary scientists, sympathetic media outlets, and the sci-fi community, including thousands of Star Trek fans convening for their annual convention.[26] On July 19 the House engaged in a dramatic floor debate over the Jupiter proposal. Boland and members of his committee stressed that they did not oppose NASA's mission or even the value of this specific project, but rather felt compelled to impose some discipline on NASA and space scientists. A succession of congressmen rose to defend the project and the overall deep-space program. Aside from scattered references to technological spin-offs and international prestige and cooperation, their justifications appealed mainly to the goal of space exploration, the importance of the science results and their relevance to terrestrial climate research, and the need to sustain the expertise at JPL. The time allotted for debate expired, and Boland called for a quorum. The final tally produced a sweeping victory for JPL: 280 supporting the Jupiter Orbiter-Probe to 131 opposed, with 22 abstentions.[27]

The possible loss of JPL's next major flight project was "a rude awakening" to lab staff.[28] The planetary program did appear to settle down after the flurry of activity to save the Jupiter mission, which was soon renamed Galileo.[29] But while Galileo sparked the recovery, its early development foreshadowed future trials. With no expendable rockets in NASA's inventory, Galileo was at the mercy of the shuttle schedule. JPL wanted to launch in January 1982 to take advantage of a gravity-assist trajectory past Mars to Jupiter. By 1979, however, it was apparent that the available shuttle at that time would be overweight and underpowered, and hence unable to lift the 30-ton Galileo spacecraft (a 2.5-ton spacecraft plus booster and support equipment). To meet the launch date, NASA asked JPL to split the spacecraft in two and launch the orbiter and probe separately. But that plan required the purchase of an additional transfer stage at $100 million, almost one-fourth the total project cost at that point. More important, a split launch required two shuttles—and

NASA would not have two by 1982. So Galileo was postponed until 1984, when a second shuttle would be available, with the delay inflating the cost increase to $225 million.[30] The saga of Galileo would not end there.

The delays and overruns in the shuttle program heralded an impending crisis. As the new decade dawned, *Science* magazine was reporting that planetary science was "on the brink again."[31] The newfound pessimism stemmed from a lack of new starts. Lab managers had planned for a lunar orbiter, Venus radar orbiter, Halley's comet rendezvous, and Mars sample return, but none of these won approval through 1981.[32] In 1978 NASA and JPL did win approval for the International Solar Polar Mission (ISPM), which would send two spacecraft, one American and one European, over opposite poles of the sun to map solar radiation out of the ecliptic plane for the first time.[33] But the ISPM spacecraft would be built by industrial contractors and would thus engage only a few dozen staff at JPL, and in 1980 it had its budget halved, forcing a two-year delay in the launch.[34]

Some of the crisis was self-inflicted. JPL mission planners presented congressional critics with fat targets, evident especially in Mars mission planning. Viking had revealed a Martian environment chemically hostile to life, suggesting that any life on Mars would have to be concentrated in remote oases or buried underground; hence scientists sought either rovers or penetrators.[35] JPL quickly drew up plans in early 1977 for two missions to Mars in the 1980s, an orbiter/rover to launch in 1984, and a sample return to launch in 1988. The first soon evolved into a proposal for a 400-kilogram rover capable of ranging 100 kilometers; the cost reached $1.4 billion—and NASA cost reviewers thought JPL had low-balled the figures to win approval.[36]

Even after the threat to Galileo in 1977, Mars planners had continued to disdain a lower-cost polar orbiter, on the theory that several smaller projects would be harder to sell than one big one. Although a few planetary scientists argued for an incrementalist approach, the majority soon abandoned plans for the billion-dollar rover in favor of a sample return that would cost twice as much; by contrast, the Jupiter proposal targeted by Boland was for $410 million. The rallying cry of "sample return or nothing," although based on a political calculation, again suggests a lack of political acumen among JPL managers and planetary scientists, who failed to recognize the prevailing political winds and instead indulged what one NASA manager called "delusions of grandeur."[37]

A tendency toward cost growth of JPL projects did not encourage political support. Galileo quickly ran into cost overruns, which also afflicted the Venus Orbital Imaging Radar (VOIR).[38] Initial studies of a Venus radar orbiter began at JPL in 1971 and received a boost from the purple pigeons. By 1979 the lab had developed a formal proposal for VOIR, for launch in 1984.

Its main instrument was a synthetic aperture radar, to penetrate the clouds of Venus and compare its hothouse environment to the frigid desert of Mars and Earth's more hospitable climate. NASA managers, however, expressed concern "about the high cost of this mission"—$400 million—and asked JPL to find ways to reduce it.[39] By 1981 cost estimates had far surpassed the levels that had alarmed NASA and now approached $700 million.[40]

VOIR also encountered competition from other JPL proposals. Although NASA's "roles and missions" review had removed Ames and Langley from the planetary program, that just displaced competition to within JPL, where champions of particular projects squared off. VOIR planners in particular jockeyed against a Halley mission.[41] Halley's orbital period of 76 years was due to return the comet to the inner solar system in the mid-1980s, and JPL in the mid-1970s began planning to take advantage of this once-in-a-lifetime chance. Halley met Murray's mandate that missions combine popular and scientific interest: its periodic and very visible appearance had attracted public attention throughout recorded history; and in the early 1970s space scientists had identified comets as a prime desideratum for inspection because they could provide clues to the initial constitution of the solar system.[42] Halley's retrograde and highly eccentric orbit and high velocity, however, put it out of reach of conventional chemical propulsion.[43] NASA and JPL managers then shot down a purple pigeon, the proposal to fly a solar sail to Halley, and an alternative proposal using solar-electric propulsion, also known as ion drive, saw its cost estimates balloon to $200 to $300 million. By 1979 JPL still had no Halley mission.[44]

The persistent effort to win a mission to Halley's comet would become the most visible victim of the planetary decline. Murray meanwhile tried to regenerate the excitement of the purple pigeons, by convening another study group in 1979 to study "far-out" ideas for deep-space missions twenty to forty years in the future.[45] Replicating the purple pigeons might have seemed a dubious exercise in retrospect: four years after the pigeons first flew, none of them had come to roost in approved flight projects. Beset by annual battles to save existing missions, NASA managers had little inclination to ponder the possibilities for forty years in the future. Any interest they might have had was definitely dispelled by a redoubled assault on the deep-space program.

Black September

The crisis in planetary exploration came to a head in 1981. If Murray spoke of low morale and soul-searching at JPL in October 1980, the effects of the presidential election the next month would not help. Ronald Reagan had campaigned on a platform of fiscal austerity, except for national security, and upon inauguration he immediately set about implementing it. In February 1981 Reagan's OMB not only cancelled VOIR, but it also required NASA to cancel either the space telescope, Galileo, or the solar-polar mission, even though each was years into development.[46] NASA elected to kill the solar-polar mission, an unprecedented cancellation of a well-established project that also involved international cooperation.[47]

The budget actions led Murray to paint a bleak picture to Congress: "Frankly, ... the U.S. deep space program is in deep jeopardy and even may face extinction."[48] Although spared the budget ax, Galileo now faced additional delays, again owing to the launch vehicle. The problem now concerned the so-called Inertial Upper Stage (IUS), a new solid-fuel rocket that would boost the spacecraft from the shuttle's orbit. In 1979, even as NASA decided on the split-launch configuration, problems with IUS performance required JPL to design new gravity-assist trajectories to reach Jupiter, and also spurred Representative Boland to press NASA to use the well-tested, liquid-fuel Centaur instead of the problematic IUS. The more powerful Centaur allowed a return to the original single-launch configuration of the Galileo orbiter and probe together, at the cost of a one-year delay in the launch, to 1985. JPL thus embraced the plan, and NASA committed to the Centaur in January 1981.[49] The decision, however, made Galileo dependent on a redesign of the Centaur, with its own technical and political hurdles; and the additional delay—eventually to 1986—would have important consequences. And Galileo engineers returned yet again to the drawing board to reintegrate the spacecraft and plot a new trajectory.

The Halley mission meanwhile was undergoing its own parallel odyssey. After the demise of the Halley plans of 1979, JPL the next year proposed a low-cost Halley Intercept Mission (HIM), with "low cost" soon defined as about $300 million. But comet scientists had earlier stated their distaste for a simple flyby, and NASA noted as well that the European Giotto mission to Halley would accomplish many of the same objectives.[50] Like the Grand Tour in 1971, the Halley intercept suffered from a lack of advocacy within NASA, the agency that is supposed to back space projects, despite indications of support from OMB, usually the enforcer of austerity. A Halley mission became Murray's personal hobbyhorse, and he made a determined push to procure it. Why did he perceive a Halley mission as so crucial? Since the 1960s JPL was accustomed to having two major flight projects in development, with one expanding while the predecessor ramped down. But after Viking and Voyager the lab had only one team, Galileo, at full strength.[51] VOIR could provide only a partial stopgap, since it would be built by industrial contractors; a Halley spacecraft promised to employ perhaps three times as many staff as VOIR.[52] Along with institutional considerations, Murray personally viewed

Halley as a unique chance to combine bold exploration with solid science and to make the first visit to an object of historical fascination.[53] But Murray's fixation with Halley would have its costs, both within JPL and without.

To replace HIM, JPL naturally suggested HER: Halley Earth Return, which would fly by Halley, unroll a long thin plastic tube "like a Chinese New Year party whistle" to sweep up cometary particles, then reel the tube back in and swing the spacecraft back toward Earth to return the sample.[54] The plan quickly earned approval from the Space Science Board, and it offered a different approach than the European or Soviet Halley missions. But after a month of negotiations between NASA and the White House, on 30 September 1981 NASA directed Murray to stop all work on Halley missions.[55]

The official end of JPL's hopes for Halley came as a jolt to Murray, who spoke bitterly of "Black September."[56] That was not all. First, budget cuts on the Centaur project again put Galileo at risk, until JPL designers came up with yet another gravity-assist trajectory to get to Jupiter on the IUS booster.[57] Then NASA floated a proposal to shut off the Voyager spacecraft, saving $222 million by foregoing the Uranus and Neptune encounters.[58] It finally became clear that not just single projects but the entire deep-space program was at stake. In summer 1981 the OMB cut $1.1 billion from NASA's budget request.[59] The new NASA administrator, James Beggs, insisted that such a shortfall would require dropping one of NASA's major programs, such as the shuttle, earth applications, or planetary exploration, and requested higher-level policy approval. But he did offer a suggestion. At his confirmation hearings in June, Beggs had called planetary exploration "a hallmark of the agency. It would be a disaster if we gave it up." He now pushed the planetary program on the table as a high-stakes wager in the budgetary standoff, naming it as the first item NASA would be willing to cut. He again cited the program's value, but he ranked it below astronomy in immediate potential: "the most important missions" in deep space had already been done, and the next phase of landers and sample returns could await the shuttle. He added, "Of course, elimination of the planetary exploration program will make the Jet Propulsion Laboratory in California surplus to our needs."[60]

The budget standoff continued through the fall, as dire rumors swirled concerning JPL's possible demise.[61] The lab got little support from Reagan's science advisor, George Keyworth. In an interview published 2 December, a week before the final budget review, Keyworth "recommended halting all new planetary space missions for at least the next decade," in favor of astronomy and shuttle-borne experiments. He soon backtracked, stating that he did not propose ending missions altogether, just doing them more cheaply.[62] Despite the public statements, Keyworth's testimony to the budget review board supported the decision to cancel Galileo and VOIR; "the cut in planetary exploration represents an example of good management."[63]

JPL likewise lacked support from key elements of NASA. In particular, Hans Mark, deputy to Beggs, proved an unreliable ally. Mark had long viewed the space shuttle as the focus of the space program, a necessary step toward the longer goal of a space station, and also held an ambivalent view of planetary exploration. In 1975 he had noted the substantial investment in the program, from which he believed "no *fundamental* or *unexpected* discovery" had emerged.[64] And the program itself, he observed two years later, was running out of steam: "we have reached a point in the planetary exploration where, for the missions planned between now and the early 1980's, we will have done just about everything we can given our current technology. In other words, we soon will have 'saturated' our capabilities."[65]

Mark brought these views with him to NASA. In August 1981 Mark and his aide Milton Silveira circulated a long-range plan for NASA. The document noted the space agency's role in scientific exploration, but it urged a focus on shuttle-borne experiments, especially for astronomy or cosmology, and a hiatus in planetary exploration until the construction of a space station as a base for spacecraft launch and sample return.[66] As for what to do with JPL, Mark had long-held opinions on that too, which reinforced his views on the expendability of planetary exploration: JPL would have to seek other sponsors, which to Mark meant the military. He was thus pursuing, in parallel, a campaign to enlist JPL's skills for the Department of Defense.

Into the Political Arena

Mark's statements on the planetary program undermined NASA's defense of JPL.[67] Beggs did not help with his negotiating ploy of August, which backfired in December when the OMB cited his assignment of a lower priority to the deep-space program in its arguments before the budget review board.[68] With a lack of advocacy at key levels, JPL undertook its own political campaign, one that would bring lobbying for programmatic goals to a new level of coordination and organization. But Murray first had to overcome an initial aversion to political activism, instilled not so much by principle as by practical considerations of JPL's relations with NASA. In 1976, for example, several JPL staff proposed Project Columbus, a long-term planetary program of one launch per year through 1992; the planners, however, bypassed NASA and took the proposal straight to OMB and Congress. Murray quickly reined them in and considered firing their leader, Lou Friedman, for insubordination.[69]

A few years later Murray would institutionalize political freelancing far beyond that undertaken by Friedman, as Murray himself would admit.[70] The congressional struggle over the cancellation of the Jupiter mission in summer 1977 provided the first test for Murray's misgivings. There remained perceptions of limits. NASA, at least, thought the lab had crossed a line. A legal affairs manager chastised Murray in May about direct contacts between JPL and Congress and reminded him that NASA policy required all congressional contacts with NASA personnel to go through his office. The lab's lawyers, however, pointed out that JPL was *not* a NASA field center; JPL staff were Caltech employees and as such were not bound by NASA's policy.[71] JPL's distinctive, dual status as a Caltech-run lab under NASA thus gave Murray and his managers leeway for lobbying. They also took refuge in semantics. What, exactly, constituted lobbying? The lab's NASA liaison was careful to refer instead to the "education" of Congress.[72]

Murray and his staff also attended to the sources and justifications for political support. JPL had started as an army lab, which gave it a strong political advocate, but its new mission in planetary spacecraft made its main political constituency the community of planetary scientists—a narrow group with little political clout, as interest groups go. In the late 1970s *Science* magazine estimated that the community numbered about "600 or so" scientists in the United States.[73] And it was competing with a formidable array of other interests, within NASA and without, for a share of the federal budget. Since JPL did most of its work in-house, the lab's projects elicited little political support from industry. To broaden the constituency, Murray and his friend Carl Sagan in late 1979 created the Planetary Society, together with Friedman. The society quickly built up a membership of 70,000 in its first year, a substantial base of enthusiasts to enlist in support of JPL's political initiatives.[74]

Why *should* the public get excited about very expensive missions that return data on distant planets to a small group of planetary scientists? Murray appealed to the ideal of exploration: "More than just science is involved, and it should be—for what it has cost. If there isn't a justification beyond what you might call narrow scientific objectives, then planetary is far overpriced in terms of what it has cost to accomplish. The reason it has been justified and continues to be is because it has broad cultural and social significance beyond the changing of the perceptions of individual scientists."[75] Similar attitudes permeated NASA. Program manager Dan Herman observed that "above a certain dollar level, science-for-science sake is not a salable commodity in the planetary program area"; missions had to include exploration.[76]

The decline of planetary prospects in 1980 quickened political activity at the lab, inspired by the rescue of Galileo in 1977. In its political campaign to defend the deep-space program, JPL had an important ally in the Caltech board of trustees. As part of Caltech, an elite institution with friends in high places, Murray and the lab sought to capitalize on connections to the inner circles of government. In 1976 Murray had created an advisory council for JPL, consisting of Caltech faculty, trustees, and eminent public citizens, to provide a source of high-level advice but also advocacy. An especially dedicated partisan was trustee Mary Scranton, wife of William Scranton, a one-time Republican candidate for president and then governor of Pennsylvania. Mary Scranton had extensive connections in Washington and she exercised them assiduously on behalf of JPL, advising Murray on congressional sentiment and urging him in October 1980 to find a back-door approach to the White House, perhaps with the aid of other trustees: "Bruce, you have a good fight and an important one, and it's time to use these big guns."[77]

With Reagan's election that November Murray brought in the artillery. At Reagan's private victory party on election night, Caltech trustee Earle Jorgensen delivered a JPL position paper on the Halley mission to Reagan aide Michael Deaver.[78] A week later trustee Stanley Rawn, Jr., sent the same Halley plea to Vice President-elect George Bush in a "Dear George" letter, followed by a letter in February 1981 to Chief of Staff James Baker III ("Jimmy," to Rawn).[79] On the day of inauguration, 20 January 1981, Murray sent a letter to Edwin Meese III pleading for the Halley mission and the future of space exploration in general.[80]

The responses to these missives were noncommittal.[81] As the Reagan administration settled in and the OMB budget targets began circulating in early 1981, Murray became a whirlwind, making several East Coast trips for meetings with dozens of congressional representatives and staffers, NASA and OMB officials, science writers and editorial boards, and key aerospace executives.[82] He also created an institutional framework within JPL for the campaign. In January 1981 he set up the Director's Interface Group (DIG) to devise "marketing strategies," produce campaign literature, and cultivate contacts in Washington, industry, and the media.[83] Murray also apparently hired a prominent local Republican, Robert Finch, who had access to the Reagan administration. Although Finch was not a professional lobbyist, his hiring tested and perhaps exceeded the limits imposed by the lab's relation with NASA.[84]

JPL's campaign found endorsements from across the political spectrum. In November 1980 Senators Strom Thurmond and Alan Cranston—a Deep South Republican and a left-coast Democrat—used the occasion of the Voyager encounter with Saturn to laud the deep-space program.[85] The budget cuts of spring 1981 raised editorial objections from both Edmund (Pat) Brown and George Will, and from the *New York Times* as well as the *Wall Street Journal*.[86] Perhaps the strangest bedfellows were California Governor Jerry Brown and Representative Newt Gingrich. As the highest expression of socially directed technical innovation, the early space program had received its main support from politicians on the left, especially for the ideal of exploration against a more limited focus on science. But in the late 1960s political liberals sought to direct federal spending toward social problems instead of technoscientific extravaganzas that seemed to benefit only a few scientists and aerospace corporations. Like others on the left, Brown had come to oppose large, centralized technologies as symptomatic of the ills of modern society, but inspired in part by his attendance at the Viking encounter, Brown embraced space with a typically visionary approach. He no doubt recognized a political constituency, at JPL and in the California aerospace industry, but he also acquired a keen personal interest. The *Los Angeles Times* commented on the conversion of "our new, spaced-out governor": "Gov. Brown is blasting into space. But to achieve lift-off he has had to jettison much of his old rhetorical baggage. He no longer speaks of an 'era of limits.' His new high is the 'era of possibilities.' Nor is small always beautiful. 'In space,' he exults, 'big is better.'"[87]

For his part, Gingrich, the young Republican firebrand from Georgia, proved an equally ardent space buff, founding the Congressional Space Caucus and suggesting $9 billion instead of $6.6 billion as an appropriate budget for NASA in 1983.[88] The support from Gingrich, Thurmond, Senator Barry Goldwater, and other conservatives stemmed from an ideological sea change concerning the space program. As political liberals drifted down to earth, conservatives were abandoning fiscal austerity and embracing the vision of space as new frontier first advanced by Kennedy: the space program could rekindle the old pioneer spirit, inspiring noble achievements and opening up a new realm for commerce. Liberal commentators for their part came to view the frontier myth as an emblem of imperial conquest, environmental damage, selective government subsidies, and corporate profiteering.[89] Hence public opinion polls in the early 1980s showed that conservatives were more likely than liberals to see space spending as inadequate.[90]

The support from political conservatives and liberal iconoclasts failed to stem the tide. Although the Reagan administration would come to extol the frontier image of space, its initial priority remained fiscal conservatism. In July 1981 Caltech president Marvin "Murph" Goldberger, prodded by Murray, created a new trustees subcommittee on JPL, chaired by Scranton, to mobilize more fully the potent influence of the trustees. The initial membership packed considerable political punch and included, among others, former Secretary of Defense Robert McNamara; Shirley Hufstedler, education secretary under Carter; Simon Ramo, a founder of the aerospace firm TRW and a longtime adviser to presidents; and Hollywood mogul and political insider Lew Wasserman.[91]

As the budget crisis deepened in fall 1981 Caltech and its trustees again waded into the fray on behalf of JPL. Their preferred approach remained the back door of the White House. At the suggestion of Arnold Beckman, a longtime trustee, Goldberger in October sent a letter to Reagan via Attorney General William French Smith. Goldberger defended the deep-space program on three main grounds: intellectual curiosity, international prestige, and technological spin-offs for industry and especially defense; two of the three justifications thus derived from the cold war. Beckman followed with a letter of his own to Meese, with a more practical political justification: the cuts threatened "rapid disintegration of a 5,000/person, $400 million Southern California enterprise. . . . There are obvious implications to the support of the President and to his Party should the Administration permit such a catastrophe to take place."[92] In addition to Scranton's persistent activity, and further interventions with Vice President Bush by Finch and Rawn, Goldberger made his own trip to Capitol Hill, where he pressed his case in particular with Senate Majority Leader Howard Baker. Baker wrote Reagan and followed up with repeated phone calls, stressing that he had no "parochial Tennessee interest" but rather a strong personal concern in the issue.[93]

Dénouement

The combination of Beckman's pressure on Meese and Goldberger's button-holing of Baker proved decisive. The White House budget review committee met on 15 December 1981 to resolve the fate of the planetary program. Keyworth suggested a compromise: preserving Galileo, and hence JPL, at a cost in fiscal 1983 of $90 million. The budget would include neither VOIR, effectively killing it, nor the Centaur upper stage, forcing yet another Galileo redesign, but the lab was safe for the immediate future.[94]

The crisis scarred JPL, however, both externally and internally. Murray approached the political battles with the enthusiasm of the true believer: "we must be zealots."[95] Indeed, although he decried the need to play the political game, Murray seemed to relish the stratagems and the chance to roll up his sleeves for a good fight. But Murray proved perhaps too zealous. His end-runs to Congress and the White House exasperated NASA.[96] He also moved away from his pragmatic, incrementalist approach toward a harder political line. In October 1980 he chastised comet scientists for insisting on a rendezvous instead of a flyby: "The coalition got itself into the position of saying 'All or Nothing,' and it got nothing."[97] But a few months later, as his worst fears materialized in early 1981, Murray rejected compromise, for instance, the possibility of sacrificing one mission to save another—say, forsaking Halley to preserve Galileo. "We must not permit the staff in OMB or Congress to trap us or other advocates in a no-win situation. There is no way to win by giving up one thing to get another, even if that were possible, which it normally is not. The only way to win is to protect Galileo, to get a successful reconsideration of some kind of U.S. Solar Polar mission in 1986, and to get the Halley in as an option. Anything else will mean losing. That is JPL's position." In short, Murray proclaimed to lab staff, "In the deep space area we do not bargain. . . . We have to go for the whole enchilada."[98]

Murray's tactics exposed Galileo and roused resentment at NASA and within JPL. In October 1980 Murray had warned planetary scientists to provide balanced advocacy: "We have to avoid overselling of a particular mission."[99] Some NASA managers now viewed him as doing just that on behalf of Halley and noted that "the actions taken by JPL management to 'sell' the Halley mission created, at times, the general impression that NASA and/or JPL were willing to forego the development of the Centaur and/or delay the Galileo project in the interest of committing to a Halley Intercept Mission." They added that a byproduct was morale problems on Galileo; John Casani, Galileo project manager, and others on Galileo questioned Murray's high-stakes wager with their work. Murray, for his part, viewed the Halley mission as the linchpin, "the key link in the trestle across the gorge," and he could not understand why his staff did not share his assessment. At a retreat held by the lab's executive council of senior managers, Murray asked how many thought cancellation of Halley and Venus missions would be a really serious problem. Only one person besides Murray thought it serious while fourteen others thought it not so bad.[100]

Murray was not the only planetary scientist to mobilize politically, but his especial activism stemmed from the failure of other lobbying efforts. In fall 1981 David Morrison, chair of the Division of Planetary Sciences of the American Astronomical Society, sent a circular letter to his colleagues: "The time has come to politicize the planetary science community."[101] But resistance to such appeals persisted among scientists, and both the division and the Space Science Board sought to preserve their objectivity by staying out of the political arena. The Planetary Society also proved an ineffectual means of influence. A society campaign organized in August 1981 to support the Halley mission generated 10,000 letters to the White House, which simply routed them all to NASA unopened.[102]

Why did the apparent public interest in space fail to translate into political support? The planetary program had attracted unprecedented interest from the Voyager encounters and Carl Sagan's "Cosmos" and received endorsements from a range of public and political commentators. But the general American public, the ultimate underwriters of the endeavor, did not share the commitment. NBC News polls in 1980 and 1981 found that most people still thought the United States was spending too much or just enough on the space program; only one-fifth thought support was inadequate. A clear majority also thought the space program should emphasize defense over science, a view that cut across political and demographic categories.[103] JPL itself was already starting to reflect such an orientation.

FOUR

External Relations and the Internal Environment

MURRAY'S POLITICAL ACTIVITY IN THE EARLY 1980S HIGHLIGHTED A CENTRAL characteristic of JPL: the triangular relationship among the lab, Caltech, and NASA. As the only NASA center operated by a contractor, JPL maintained a delicate balance between the independence offered by the Caltech association and the accountability demanded of government programs. The maturation of the aerospace industry added a fourth leg to the triangle and introduced basic questions about JPL's identity. All the while JPL itself was evolving in its internal organization and culture in response to changing contexts.

JPL and Caltech: Biting the Orange

Like the previous directors of JPL, Murray came to the job from Caltech, and he took office with the explicit intention of building up relations with campus.[1] Faculty animus dated back to the lab's early years under the army, when professors questioned Caltech's peacetime association with military work, and had continued through the 1960s, when the Ranger failures produced calls for divestment of JPL. In 1969 Caltech president Harold Brown had appointed a faculty committee to study Caltech's association with JPL; the resultant report recommended continuing the affiliation but encouraging greater interaction between campus and lab. No substantive change in the relationship ensued, however, and in 1975 Brown appointed another study committee, this one counting six members each from the faculty and the lab, with physics professor Rochus Vogt and Jack James from JPL sharing the chair.[2]

The committee began by canvassing faculty and lab staff. Many of the responses noted the poor state, if not nonexistence, of relations between

59

the two institutions. Each side naturally viewed the other as the cause of trouble, with JPL staff regarding faculty as "supercilious and snobbish" while professors complained of "arrogant," "hostile and insulting" lab managers. More substantive critiques attributed the gulf to a difference in cultures and objectives. The lab organized the efforts of many people toward a specific goal, with the requirements of risk-averse systems engineering and government accountability fostering bureaucratic formality, whereas the campus preserved the freedom of individual faculty to define their own approach to research and pedagogy.[3]

The committee issued its findings, bound in orange and hence known as the "orange report," in April 1976. The report laid out twenty forthright recommendations, from the practical to the programmatic. It suggested several concrete steps to foster interaction, including joint appointments for faculty and postdocs, work-study programs for Caltech students at JPL, clear policies to compensate collaborative work, and a greater role for faculty in mission planning. The committee also repudiated classified research as inimical to campus-lab collaboration in particular and to academic research in general, "except in times of national emergency."[4]

The most pointed critique concerned the nature of JPL's work. "At one time," the committee reported, "JPL was an undisputed leader in the fields in which it generally practiced." Now, however, the lab had fallen behind industry and other NASA centers in many areas; only in long-range telecommunications did JPL remain preeminent. Campus faculty, the report suggested, should not be expected to collaborate in second-rate work. The committee noted a few sources of the decline in JPL's engineering capability: increased contract monitoring, dwindling attention to research and advanced technology, and general conservatism. But it also suggested an underlying issue concerning the basic identity of JPL. Did the lab aspire to leadership in science, engineering, or management? Were JPL staff first and foremost scientists, engineers, or managers? The committee urged that JPL focus on engineering, not management. "To remain a necessary and valuable resource, JPL must regain the status of an innovator, not just a user, of high technology."[5]

At the same time, the committee recommended boosting the profile of science at JPL. The lab lacked first-rate scientists, according to the report. Scientists at JPL had no time for research, they lacked a role in mission planning, and personnel classifications provided no place for promotion. Goddard, by contrast, though not associated with a university, had still managed to develop a top-notch research reputation. The orange report advised JPL to recruit leading scientists and give them half their time for research, accommodate senior scientists in personnel classifications, and appoint a chief scientist. Thus strengthening science would also build a bridge from "the engineering character of JPL to the predominantly scientific character of the Campus."[6]

The orange report met with a cool reception at JPL. Some observers noted that it focused its criticism on JPL and presented largely the faculty's perspective: "Where were the six JPL members when all this happened?" R. W. Davies of JPL responded with a critique titled "Where to bite the orange?" in which he singled out several recommendations for censure. The condemnation of classified research aroused resentment among the many JPL staff members who had cut their teeth on military projects, and Davies noted that the strong wording would surely scare off possible military sponsors if NASA work evaporated. He pointed out that increased campus involvement in mission planning would provoke charges of insider trading from planetary scientists at other universities, who would think Caltech scientists unfairly capitalized on their JPL connections to win experiments on NASA missions.[7] As for the nature of JPL's work, Davies agreed that this was the central issue and that the committee's critique had merit: "All of us are concerned that our work has become less innovative." Davies concurred that the lab should return to its strengths in engineering instead of management. The issue, however, was not so much one of campus-lab relations but more an issue in public policy: NASA's insistence on contracting work to industry forced lab engineers into management roles.[8]

Both Murray and Brown immediately engaged the orange report's recommendations.[9] Turning proposals into policy, and policy into practice, proved more difficult. Plans to double the number of Caltech students employed at JPL foundered on a limit imposed by campus on the number of hours students could work.[10] The campus also shot down efforts in the following couple of years to grant course credit for work at JPL, as faculty committees refused to delegate academic responsibility to JPL staff, and joint faculty appointments raised questions about compensation and tenure.[11] Hence by October 1977, a year and a half after the orange report, only three people had joint appointments; by 1980 there were eleven, but many more JPL staff taught at other local colleges than at Caltech.[12]

Given these barriers to exchange in the teaching function of campus, the other prime function of research remained for possible collaboration. The Caltech President's Fund in the JPL budget provided short-term grants to university faculty for work with JPL, with the grants usually divided about equally between Caltech faculty and proposals from other universities; in 1980, for example, about $750,000 supported twenty grants, ten from Caltech.[13] Voyager was also providing a prime opportunity for Caltech researchers, with Vogt, Ed Stone, Andrew Ingersoll, and Eugene Shoemaker working on experiment teams; Stone's particularly prominent role highlighted the fruits of collaboration.

To encourage such research opportunities, the orange report had recommended raising the status of science at JPL. In October 1977 Murray created the position of chief scientist and filled it with Vogt in a joint appointment. (Vogt soon resigned to chair the physics division on campus and was replaced by Arden Albee, a Caltech planetary geologist.)[14] Later in 1978 Murray established the job categories of senior scientist and staff scientist, intended to be equivalent to full professor and associate professor rank at universities; the new positions replaced the title of "member of the technical staff" previously held by research scientists.[15] Fostering science at JPL, however, would involve more than new job categories and, indeed, would involve issues beyond the question of campus-lab interactions.

The orange report had noted one disincentive for Caltech to divest from JPL: the management fee that NASA awarded Caltech on the JPL contract. Since the 1960s the fee plus overhead had amounted to about 12 percent of the campus budget, and in the late 1970s the proportion started to rise.[16] The orange report supported the status quo; it did not recommend diverting the fee from campus to lab, as some JPL staff suggested, but it did urge enlightening the faculty to the fact that the JPL contract contributed as much to the campus budget as student tuition.[17]

Some JPL staff wondered what Caltech did to earn the fee. Caltech's trustees provided little oversight. In 1970 the trustees ended the practice of approving the lab program each year; as Donald Fowler, Caltech's lawyer, pointed out, NASA owned the facilities, set the budget and staff levels, and directed the program, "thus leaving virtually nothing to be 'authorized.'"[18] In terms of resources, the job of administering JPL seemed bigger than running the campus: in 1976 the JPL budget of $250 million was five times the size of the campus budget, and JPL's staff was about three times the size of Caltech's.[19] Caltech administrators nevertheless continued to view JPL as the tail to the campus dog, leaving most programmatic direction to the director and NASA and stepping in only for programs involving non-NASA diversification. Otherwise Caltech just concerned itself with broad policy issues at the lab, such as personnel. As these often involved legal questions, in practice Caltech's general counsel, Fowler, provided the main contact between Murray and the campus.

These issues were not unique to JPL and Caltech. Several universities besides Caltech, including the University of California, Chicago, MIT, Johns Hopkins, and Stanford, struggled to integrate large government-owned labs with research and teaching on campus. Although the University of California benefited from longer interactions with the national lab at Berkeley, it still wrestled occasionally with the blurry boundary between lab and campus; it also endured increasing questions in the 1960s about its association with nuclear weapons design at Livermore and Los Alamos. At Stanford, to take another example, physicists on campus maintained prickly relations with the Stanford Linear Accelerator Center, including squabbles over joint appointments, teaching privileges, and thesis supervision.[20] In preparation for the orange report, JPL staff had visited several similar university labs for comparison: the Applied Physics Lab at Johns Hopkins, Draper and Lincoln Labs at MIT, and Lawrence Livermore Lab under the University of California. They noted that staff at each lab expressed concern about their relation with the campus and that none seemed to have significantly higher interactions than did JPL with Caltech. They did perceive distance to be a general barrier to interaction: any lab farther than walking distance from campus found collaboration difficult—and JPL was a fifteen-minute drive from Caltech.[21]

The orange report impelled no great change in Caltech's relations with JPL. Neither the lab nor campus resolved the central issue, the conflicted identity of JPL and the decline of its engineering capability. As Davies had pointed out, the issue transcended the campus-lab nexus. And the underlying attitudes persisted, exacerbated in the early 1980s by Murray's political and programmatic activity, including the possibility of defense work, amid perceptions of lax campus oversight.[22] Hence Murray would judge, "The greatest single failure I know about as director of JPL was my inability to solve this problem" of campus-lab relations.[23]

The failure, however, was not due just to Murray and JPL. It takes two to tango. Caltech was distracted by its own struggles in the 1970s, when the post-Sputnik surge in science and engineering education receded and domestic economic woes eroded endowments.[24] Even in easy times many campus faculty focused on their own work and paid little mind to the distant lab. And however much attention Caltech and JPL could give to their interactions, the role of NASA presented the clever technicians on campus and lab with a three-body problem, whose solution proved far more difficult.

JPL and NASA

NASA employed two main instruments, in addition to the budget, to manipulate the actions of JPL and Caltech: the contract and a memorandum of understanding. The contract established the legal parameters of NASA's relationship with Caltech and so delineated the boundary between the public and the private—or, who really ran the lab. The basic difference in perspectives —Caltech defending its independence, NASA demanding responsiveness—

had produced contentious contract negotiations in the early 1960s, when the Ranger failures provoked NASA to question Caltech's oversight.[25] JPL's subsequent successes settled the relationship, however, and by the 1970s Caltech and NASA negotiated new contracts every three years with little acrimony. In 1978 Caltech proposed extending the contract to five years and carrying over the current contract with few modifications, and NASA agreed, indicating the acceptability of the current relationship to both parties.[26]

A few issues did remain between the two sides, often stemming from the basic ambiguity in JPL's role as both independent contractor and NASA lab. For example, NASA managers and Caltech's lawyers argued occasionally over the issuance of NASA Management Instructions. These thick documents provided official guidelines on how to run NASA's business, covering such subjects as publication, training, travel, safety, reporting, and procurement. Since JPL was not technically a NASA center it did not have to obey these instructions, although Caltech accepted some in the contract and JPL went along with others voluntarily. Thus the lab's refusal to accept the instruction limiting contacts with Congress gave it some leeway for lobbying during the Galileo debate in 1977. As this episode demonstrated, NASA managers nevertheless tried to enforce them at times, requiring Fowler to fend off the requests.[27]

NASA staff, especially at lower levels, also continued to grumble about the management fee paid to Caltech. In 1969 NASA had more than doubled the fee, from $1.6 million to $3.4 million, or from 0.75 percent to 1.6 percent of the baseline JPL budget; then in 1975 Caltech extracted another increase, to $4.2 million or almost 2 percent of the budget. Caltech justified the increases by appeals to inflation and "extraordinary effort and contributions"; NASA staff dismissed the latter and noted that neither the JPL budget nor NASA's had kept pace with inflation. Caltech, however, had the upper hand in negotiations; a local NASA manager observed that NASA was not even submitting the existing contract for full negotiation, let alone opening it up for outside bids.[28] NASA may have gotten wind of the suggestions among Caltech faculty that the institute divest itself of the lab; the prospect of finding a new contractor would have encouraged appeasement.

The stabilized contract negotiations benefited from JPL's relatively benign relationship with NASA management at the time. In particular, the on-site NASA Resident Office at JPL, created to exert local oversight, in practice proved friendly to JPL—for instance, by giving lab staff the opportunity to review and rebut annual performance evaluations.[29] JPL also enjoyed greater autonomy than the NASA centers in the human spaceflight program, which had more centralized management at headquarters; in the robotic program NASA worked with a relatively small staff at headquarters and delegated much technical authority to strong project managers at the labs.[30]

In addition to the contract, NASA relied on a joint memorandum of understanding, or MOU, to spell out the respective responsibilities of the agency, institute, and lab. Caltech and NASA had signed the first memorandum in 1968, at the insistence of NASA, apparently as a way to encourage certain activities not covered by the contract—in particular, campus-lab interactions and non-NASA work. NASA won some concessions, such as the right to approve senior staff appointments, and Caltech and the lab got two discretionary funds—the JPL Director's Discretionary Fund and the Caltech President's Fund—and the right to pursue non-NASA programs. Campus representatives viewed non-NASA work as "the most significant single result," since it led to the civil systems activity, and cited the MOU as a good reason to keep the JPL contract.[31]

The expansion of non-NASA work, especially in energy programs, spurred Caltech and NASA to negotiate a new MOU in 1978. Caltech and JPL took the position that lab staff were Caltech employees and as such should be allowed to accept contracts from any potential sponsor, without approval from NASA and at equal priority to NASA programs, except if NASA facilities were involved. But Fowler, again Caltech's lead negotiator, also recognized "an almost certain desire on the part of NASA to put a limiting percentage of some kind on work for non-NASA sponsors." Fowler insisted that "contrary to legend, no percentage limitation has ever been agreed upon, at least in writing," and he further urged that Caltech resist any such limitation.[32]

NASA, however, did not want to see its substantial investment in JPL diverted to other ends. NASA's negotiators indeed insisted on a limit and also sought the right to approve all such work. Caltech accepted the limit but wanted to keep it high, from 30 to perhaps 50 percent, and flatly rejected NASA oversight of non-NASA work. As a tradeoff, Caltech proposed that NASA accept institutional responsibility for JPL; in case of a major cancellation of non-NASA work, NASA would step in to sustain the lab.[33] After much haggling, NASA and Caltech settled on a compromise, dividing work for others into two categories. For category A work, NASA allowed JPL to perform another agency's work as if it were NASA's, with no limits. At the time the MOU defined category A to cover only JPL's programs for the Department of Energy. Category B included work for all other agencies, such as the Departments of Defense and Transportation; the lab could pursue such programs on a noninterference basis with NASA work and only if they occupied less than 10 percent of the total JPL workforce.[34]

As with the contract negotiations, the new memorandum of understanding hinged on the dual nature of JPL. Was it a Caltech lab, which happened to have most of its current work for NASA? Or was it a NASA lab, run for the time being by Caltech? From the perspective of Pasadena, history supported the former: JPL was a Caltech lab that found a sponsor in the army, then transferred to NASA—and perhaps could switch sponsors again in the future. From Washington, JPL appeared as a NASA-owned facility, which NASA had agreed to let Caltech run for the next five years—but not necessarily any longer.

The memoranda of 1968 and 1978 were not legally enforceable documents, but rather a general statement of intentions. Hence some NASA managers viewed the MOU as at best superfluous: NASA should handle any agreements formally, in the contract, or not at all. Caltech faculty meanwhile found the new MOU "full of good things," and Murray himself viewed the MOU as "more important" than the contract.[35] The MOU hence added to the relatively pacific environment conferred by the latest contract negotiations, at least in the view from Pasadena. And in the end, NASA-JPL relations came down to performance: if JPL did its job, NASA was happy. The acrimony amid the Ranger failures evaporated thanks to the overall success of Mariner, Viking, and above all Voyager. Even in 1981, while NASA's support of planetary exploration looked doubtful and while Murray was exasperating NASA with his end runs, the institutional relationship remained healthy, certainly in better shape than two decades earlier.[36] The old question remained, however, as Fowler had observed while negotiating the contract in 1978: "Is it 'NASA's Jet Propulsion Laboratory' or 'Caltech's Jet Propulsion Laboratory'?"[37]

JPL and the Aerospace Industry

Another persistent issue in the NASA-JPL-Caltech relationship concerned the part played by industry. As the aerospace industry matured and acquired capabilities previously monopolized by JPL, it added a fourth leg to the triangle. The issue was not new to NASA, whose predecessor agency NACA (National Advisory Committee for Aeronautics) had wrangled with aircraft companies over the performance of aeronautics R&D, or to government support of industrial research in general, which required defining a boundary between public and private sectors.[38]

Aviation, automobile, and chemical firms entered the space business in the 1950s but struggled at first to acquire the expertise in electronics, materials, and chemistry required by guided missiles and spacecraft, as well as an appreciation for state-of-the-art R&D instead of standardized mass production. Hence JPL engineer Clifford Cummings characterized the aircraft industry in 1958 as "hopelessly inefficient," with "little understanding of research and advanced development."[39] This "cockeyed image of ourselves" persisted through the 1960s, according to JPL engineer Brooks Morris, even as such firms as TRW and Hughes developed extensive satellite expertise, most of it through spacecraft for military reconnaissance and commercial communications.[40] For groups like the Hughes Space Division, which might have sales of several hundred million dollars a year, a NASA contract for $50 or $100 million spread out over several years provided a very small fraction of business. That did not keep them from competing for NASA contracts, or from complaining that NASA kept work in-house instead of contracting it to industry. And a decline in military space spending in the early 1970s, alongside NASA's cutbacks, left these companies scraping for business.[41]

The aerospace industry's attitude counted in Congress and the executive branch. With hundreds of thousands of jobs at stake, the aerospace industry was the most powerful interest group for the space program.[42] Constant questioning of in-house development at JPL and other NASA labs sensitized the agency's managers. Thus, for example, NASA administrator Fletcher in 1976 sought to shift more work to industry to preempt congressional criticism.[43] The policy extended to JPL flight projects, which followed two main modes of industrial contracting. In the first, known as subsystem mode, JPL contracted only for industrial production of selected components and otherwise kept in-house the design, assembly, and testing of hardware and its integration into the final spacecraft. In the second, system mode, JPL delegated the design, assembly, and testing of the entire spacecraft system to industry; the lab only planned the overall mission, oversaw the industrial program, and ran flight operations.[44]

JPL traditionally favored the subsystem mode, owing to its presumed technical superiority and perhaps to its legacy as an army lab; the army's arsenal model kept much design and development in-house even to the prototype stage.[45] But it did have experience, both good and bad, with both modes. The in-house Ranger series endured failures before meeting success, and the system-mode Surveyor similarly experienced both failure and success. Most of the successful Mariners were in subsystem mode, but the equally successful Mariner 10 was an industrial job.[46] The performance of two of the main flight projects in the late 1970s could have tilted the balance, although here too it was not clear-cut. JPL built Voyager in subsystem mode, within cost estimates, but succeeded only after early mishaps. Seasat, an earth-orbiting oceanographic satellite built by industry in system mode, came in over budget and failed three months after launch in 1978, but it still fulfilled much of its mission.

The question of subsystem versus system mode became known as the "make-or-buy" issue, which Bruce Murray early identified as "probably the most difficult single question JPL must resolve." In July 1977 he called a special retreat for senior staff to consider it. The assembled managers perceived several problems with the current subsystem mode. The ebb and flow of project assignments forced them to cope with peaks and valleys in staff levels, which in turn put pressure on facilities. Lab staff were then kept busy building hardware instead of spending their time on innovative design. And subsystem mode opened JPL to complaints from industry about competition. Against these, however, were the advantages of subsystem mode, in keeping technical experience and responsibility for budgets and schedules within JPL. Above all was the question of whether the lab could give up the old way and learn to do all its projects in system mode.[47]

Another factor favoring system mode was the political support industry could provide for planetary projects. NASA managers certainly recognized this benefit, and thus for instance had planned first Grand Tour and then Voyager for system mode and had used possible aerospace contractors, such as Boeing, to help sell the mission; Pickering had undercut this support by fighting for and winning Voyager as an in-house project in July 1972.[48] Five years later NASA and even some JPL staff suggested that the lab contract the Galileo spacecraft to industry, but the status quo prevailed and it would be built in-house.[49]

The political context highlighted the dilemma of the make-or-buy decision. Involving industry would shore up dwindling political support for deep-space missions, but at the same time it would decrease the amount of work performed at JPL at a time of institutional stress. In addition to cutting the amount of work, system mode would also change its character. Contracting to industry would turn engineers into managers, by requiring them to supervise industrial work instead of building things themselves. It thus revived the fundamental question about the identity of the lab: was it a technological or managerial organization? If JPL staff were engineers, they should be designing and building new technologies in-house; but if they were really managers, they could be overseeing technical projects at industrial contractors. If the lab was indeed a managerial institution, that would cancel the benefits of the Caltech connection because campus expertise was strictly technical.[50]

The lab would struggle with this identity crisis for the next twenty-five years. At the time Murray and his staff resolved that JPL remained a technological organization, but that it was in the lab's interest to contract as much work as possible, thus allowing its engineers to focus on advanced development. Contracted work should include those functions for which industry had the ability and which required "no special degree of innovation or advancement in state of the art," as well as those requiring a large workforce over short time frames. JPL would continue to do advanced concepts, and also those activities necessary to keep the expertise necessary to supervise work under contracts. This last justification became known as the "smart buyer" argument—lab staff had to know what they were getting from industry to avoid being fleeced—and resulted in a determination to have one major flight project under way in-house at all times.[51] The memorandum of understanding of 1978 codified the policy, which underpinned the battle to defend Galileo and win a new mission to succeed it.[52]

LESS Is More?

Part of the impetus for system contracting came from a concurrent push by NASA to cut costs. Planetary exploration was, and is, an expensive endeavor. Ballooning budgets, represented particularly by the billion-dollar Viking, compounded the problem of obtaining political support.[53] In response, NASA in 1973 had created a Low Cost Systems Office, and by 1976 a general plan had emerged to promote smaller, standardized missions instead of sophisticated, unique spacecraft. More modest mission goals would simplify both the technology and flight operations; and standardized spacecraft would rely on proven, off-the-shelf hardware instead of new technologies and so, in effect, would save money twice—first by not spending money on technology development, and second by not needing costly proof testing. The initiative thus removed one of the justifications for in-house development at JPL.[54]

JPL provided a particular target for cost-conscious NASA managers because of perceptions that it was "too high-priced and gold-plated in its approach." As Fred Felberg, JPL's assistant director for plans and programs, observed, "We have the image of producing 'Cadillac class' products; very good, luxurious, possibly cost effective, and costly. . . . Only in a few instances have we put out Model A type proposals." The image of "Jet Posh Lab" had wide play among NASA and industry managers, although some admitted privately that sometimes you get what you pay for: JPL did deliver quality. The extensive testing, redundancy, and design conservatism that fostered quality made JPL seem more costly in comparison to other NASA labs.[55] Part of JPL's expensive appearance stemmed also from its status as the sole contractor-operated lab among the NASA centers. The civil service centers had separate budgets for internal, institutional costs, including civil service labor, whereas JPL took labor costs out of the R&D program. As a result, JPL looked less productive for a given R&D budget than the other NASA centers.[56]

Factors external to JPL also drove up the cost of missions. Political calculations produced the belief that it was easier to sell one big mission than many small ones, and ensuring scientific support for missions tended to increase the number of experiments, which made for complex spacecraft. Resisting these factors required backbone in program and project managers. NASA managers found it too easy to accept the wish lists of planetary scientists, who said, in effect, as long as we are headed that way, maybe we should take a look at such-and-such. The agency's lab directors identified overly ambitious mission requirements as "by far the most important reason for high costs," and NASA and its labs then too often caved into investigators' requests to change those requirements midstream.[57] Finally, JPL and NASA managers recognized a basic tradeoff between cost and risk. The space program was paying for its own success: "During the early days of the Lunar Exploration Program, the public was conditioned to failure. Today the Agency [NASA] conditions the public for 100 percent success. . . . What image does the Agency want and is it willing to pay for it?"[58]

The low-cost initiative forged ahead against these obstacles. It supported development at JPL of standard spacecraft components such as computers, tape recorders, transponders, and solar cells.[59] Although Voyager later came to represent the epitome of the custom project, as a scaled-down proposal from the Grand Tour—at one-fourth the cost of Viking—it meshed with the low-cost effort, especially since it was initially intended to serve as a standardized template for subsequent missions to Uranus and Neptune. Voyager thus used funding from the Low Cost Systems Office to develop inertial reference units, hydrazine propulsion systems, and other standard components.[60] In 1980 JPL developed what it called the LESS program, for Low-Cost Exploration of the Solar System. LESS aimed for missions with short lead times, of two or three years, and costs of perhaps $100 to $200 million through now-familiar measures of focused mission goals and inherited technology.[61]

JPL had one low-cost model at hand in the Mariner 10 mission of 1973–74. JPL had developed the spacecraft in system mode, with a budget of under $100 million, about 30 percent less than other Mariners. The project came in under budget and on schedule, with only a few years between approval and launch, and returned the first photos from Venus and Mercury. It achieved this through a management approach based on strict mission guidelines and experiment selection, delegation of responsibility to experimenters within rigid budget ceilings, and a generous weight margin to trade off against costs. But NASA and JPL managers viewed these management lessons as mixed, owing to the many emergencies that cropped up after launch—at least forty-one failures or anomalies, several of them serious enough to threaten the mission. JPL mission controllers had saved it only by a series of ingenious but nail-biting work-arounds, and JPL and NASA managers wondered whether "shortcuts in the design, development, and test program" overly imperiled the mission.[62]

There were additional reasons for reluctance. As Robert Parks pointed out, reducing the requirements for missions at some point became pound-foolish: "if the scope of a mission is reduced to too low a level, it will not be cost effective since too high a percentage of the cost will be paid for just getting there (including the cost of the launch vehicle)." This applied especially to the outer planets. Parks also observed that new concepts could sometimes reduce costs as well as inflate them, but that NASA at some point had to pay to flight-test them; otherwise the low-cost initiative would stifle technology development and perhaps cost more in the long run.[63]

Lab engineers meanwhile were learning from experience that standardized hardware might not match the various environments throughout the solar system. Mariner 10, for example, had used leftover parts from earlier Mariners, but they then had to be modified to handle the thermal environment at Mercury.[64] The Seasat project of 1978, although an earth-orbiter, highlighted the hazards of standardization. The spacecraft failed after three months. A NASA failure review board traced the direct cause of failure to an electrical short in a slip ring, which connected the rotating solar arrays to the stationary satellite bus. The board located the indirect cause in the assumption that the Agena bus was standard equipment and hence did not need detailed testing, when in fact it was substantially modified for Seasat. The review warned, "the world of space flight is an unforgiving one and words like 'standard,' 'existing,' and 'similar to' can be traps for the unwary."[65] The lessons of Seasat, however, were lost on JPL and NASA, as would be evident twenty years later.

These factors stalled the low-cost drive. In 1980 Murray noted that budget pressures required JPL to "really put some muscle into a study and analysis of how to carrry out solar system exploration more cheaply. Those are old words and they've been said many times, but they haven't had enough conviction." He pinpointed two common sources of expense. One was the assumption that each mission required new technology — or, was an opportunity to develop new technology: "That requires self-discipline because we are technologists." The other was pressure from scientists to add to mission requirements — again, a difficult task, "because the reason we're here at JPL is that we *believe* in the science and the exploration." In both cases JPL staff were complicit in cost run-ups: "we have met the enemy and he has a familiar countenance."[66]

But Murray himself could have looked in the mirror. In the 1960s Murray had advocated incrementalism in planetary missions, and in early 1976 he argued for the Lunar Polar Orbiter as a model for low-cost missions. Just a few months earlier, however, as he prepared to take the helm of JPL, Murray seemed to believe "more ambitious space missions to be more cost-effective than less ambitious ones," at least in the perception of Felberg.[67] Viking and Voyager then may have provided the clinching evidence that bigger was better, at least in the deep-space program. In a talk to planetary scientists in 1980, Murray admitted that he had opposed Viking as "too big a leap," seeking instead a simpler investigation of Martian chemistry before searching for life. He continued, "I was right, in a narrow technical sense. . . . But I was dead wrong in a programmatic sense. Viking *was* the right thing to do. If that hadn't been done, if there hadn't been something on that scale to respond to the widespread *public* aspiration for the search for life, we would know far less about Mars now."[68] Two years later, NASA deputy administrator Hans Mark tried to persuade Murray that smaller, specialized missions were politically more palatable, pointing out that Voyager cost 2.35 times as much as the Pioneer 10–11 mission, and that Galileo would be close to four times as much, accounting for inflation and stretchouts. Murray replied that the volume and significance of the data returned by Voyager more than made up for the added investment, and that Voyager and Pioneer in fact cost about the same in average annual funding since Voyager took years longer to develop. Murray concluded, "it could be more cost effective . . . to launch 'Voyagers' once every N[times]2.35 years rather than 'Pioneers' once every N years."[69]

One NASA manager hence noted in 1981 that "JPL has not really accepted the fact that things must be done cheaper."[70] The agency thus blamed the budget crisis of 1981 in part on the lab's top management, which failed to develop "realistic plans to gain new business," including "low cost efforts . . . and less sophisticated, standardized missions."[71] It was not the last time NASA would push for cheaper, smaller planetary missions against the resistance, perceived and real, of JPL.

JPL's Internal Organization

JPL's organization in this period sought a balance between continuity and change, reliability and risk. Organizational inertia viewed from one perspective was a source of strength, producing the loyalty and esprit de corps that characterized JPL. But the appointment of Murray had revealed perceptions, at Caltech and JPL, that the lab had become hidebound. The sheer size of the lab contributed to inertia, as did aging staff, a lack of management turnover, and Pickering's long tenure of easygoing leadership.[72]

Murray took office with a mandate to shake things up.[73] On 30 July 1976 Murray announced a major reorganization, what became known as the "Thursday night massacre." The stated justification was to streamline the organization in order to eliminate overlapping functions, reduce overhead, and cut the number of people reporting directly to the director. But the organizational consolidation also offered a means to clear out deadwood at higher levels, since reducing the number of offices effectively demoted a number of senior managers. Murray acknowledged the effects on particular individuals but asserted that change was necessary for renewal and growth.[74]

The reorganization simplified organization charts, but it did not promote morale. It coincided with the prospect of 5 to 10 percent staff cuts owing to the bathtub problem in flight projects. Despite new termination policies to soften the blow, including help with outplacement, a regional union—the Engineers and Scientists of California—was encouraged to revive attempts to organize JPL employees, prompting active dissuasions from Murray and senior managers. Those remaining on the lab payroll meanwhile looked over their shoulders for the next round of layoffs.[75] A week after the massacre Murray sought "to put to rest the speculation, the uncertainty, the anxiety over what is going on" by declaring that "I don't have any more shoes to drop." But change appeared to apply to Murray's assurances. In his inaugural comments to lab staff four months earlier, before the bloodletting, Murray had stated: "Are s[w]eeping changes imminent? Do I have a list of jobs that I've already decided to destroy or replace or remove? The answer is no."[76]

Murray's standard managerial mode exaggerated the morale problem. He appeared to proceed from one crisis to another, with the lab always mobilized to meet current emergencies but also with better days just around the corner.[77] This state of perpetual crisis entailed a focus on the short term, which counteracted Murray's own embrace of strategic planning and also perhaps contributed to Murray's early burnout from the director's job. But despite the fire-drill atmosphere, Murray's activism encouraged initial perceptions that he was tightening up management.[78] One might extend the Camelot image from Voyager, modified by analogy to the Kennedy presidency: a dynamic, youthful leader with public relations savvy taking over from the genial, conservative grandfather figure, promising new ideas and promoting young up-and-comers, and combining idealism with cool political calculation.

Murray also battled bureaucracy. Coordinating the many interfaces in a planetary spacecraft required formal procedures and documentation, two prime indicators of bureaucracy. The trend in flight projects toward fewer, larger missions exacerbated these features, since larger teams, longer development, and more complex technology required ever-finer levels of coordination. From the freewheeling, small-team days of the 1950s, JPL had evolved into a big, hierarchical, formal bureaucracy.[79] The low-cost effort bucked the trend, but the Ranger experience had taught JPL engineers to appreciate the high costs of failure as a counter to material costs. Jack James, a progenitor of systems engineering, thus argued that bureaucracy was a strength as well as weakness: "every new organizational interface or operational requirement or report was imposed to fix a problem and prevent its recurr[e]nce."[80]

By the 1980s, however, a general perception emerged among lab staff that "things are harder to get done than they used to be." In their periodic meetings with lower-level staff, Murray and deputy director Charles Terhune received one consistent message: "Too much bureaucracy."[81] Some of the red tape came from Washington, in the "ever-growing requirements for reports, audits, etc.," but much of it derived from the lab itself.[82] Lab staff exhibited a common tendency to form study groups to approach a problem. For example, in response to an employee's complaint about the lack of information on open jobs at the lab, the requisite special committee assembled and generated an inch-think report.[83] And then there was the, yes, Paperwork Reduction Task Group of 1970, whose twelve subcommittees and three advisory subcommittees prompted the *New Yorker* to comment, "We can hardly wait for their written reports."[84]

Above all, noted John Heie, "bureaucracy is a means of maintaining *control* and minimizing *risk*." Conservatism ultimately flowed from the top down, and Heie declared that "management has to be willing to live with a certain mistake threshold." However, he continued, conservatism had become "a way of life and to change it, in my opinion, would be revolutionary."[85] Conservatism does not encourage revolutionary action. In 1981 Murray launched an attack on bureaucracy through several policy changes, including delegation of authority to lower levels.[86] These measures treated the symptoms of bureaucracy but did not address the underlying causes. The lab's attitudes toward risk and general conservatism had been forged twenty years earlier and continued to determine how JPL conducted its business.

The People of JPL

The laboratory, as Murray and his senior staff recognized, was at its base a collection of people. Who were they? The lab's disciplinary diversity confounds any identification of a typical employee. Hardware designers, software programmers, flight navigators, mission controllers, systems managers, quality control engineers, and research scientists all mingled in flight projects, not to mention the myriad smaller programs pursued at the lab. Several characteristics of JPL staff nevertheless may be discerned against this background.

JPL's reputation could attract the cream of technical talent. The relative lack of military connections may have provided an additional attraction for young scientists and engineers in the 1970s; a survey of lab staff in 1980 found that between 10 and 20 percent would not want an assignment to defense work.[87] But JPL's declining prospects limited its ability to recruit new staff, and instead the core of veteran lab staff remained intact, with the average age advancing steadily into the forties; by 1981 well over a quarter of scientists and engineers were over fifty years old.[88] The staff remained also largely white and male: in 1976 minorities filled 13 percent of full-time positions and women 16 percent. Asian ethnic groups made up the largest proportion of minorities, followed by Latinos and blacks.[89]

The JPL labor force in this respect followed the demographic of science and engineering disciplines nationwide, and it had almost twice the proportion of minorities as NASA as a whole.[90] The lab nevertheless resolved to improve minority and female representation. In 1971 Pickering had started an affirmative action program and in 1975 created an Advisory Committee for Minority Affairs, to report to the director on minority concerns. Murray continued both programs and established a similar Advisory Council on Women.[91] But while Murray and Terhune gave affirmative action their full support, the program depended as well on attitudes of lower-level staff, not all of whom necessarily shared the commitment.[92] And during a period of national debate over affirmative action, which saw the Supreme Court strike down minority quotas in the *Bakke* case of 1978, some JPL staff, including some minorities, repudiated the lab's program as a "degrading" quota system that undermined merit-based advancement.[93] It did, however, increase minority representation to 17 percent and female representation to 21 percent by 1980.[94]

The lab needed affirmative action in promotion as well as hiring. Murray noted that the improved statistics for minority and female employment did not show "the very serious problem . . . of upward mobility."[95] In 1977 minorities constituted 27 percent of clerical staff and 21 percent of technicians, but only 14 percent of professional staff and 9 percent of managers. The numbers were worse for women: 88 percent of clerical staff, 11 percent of technicians, 8 percent of professionals, 9 percent of managers.[96] The age demographic clogged the managerial ranks with senior people still years from retirement, affecting promotion not just of women and minorities but of younger staff in general.[97] By 1977, Caltech electrical engineer John Pierce was warning Murray that "very good people have left JPL."[98] Unlike industry, JPL offered no bonuses or stock plans and a constrained salary scale, and unlike academia, no lab staff enjoyed tenure. Competition for technical talent with industry in particular increased as the aerospace sector revived in the late 1970s.[99] Lack of individual recognition further handicapped employee relations. JPL's work and culture stressed collective instead of individual achievement. As flight projects manager Robert Parks put it, "The result of several modestly competent efforts all directed to the same goal can be much greater than the brilliant efforts of an equal number of extremely competent people if they are pulling in opposite directions."[100]

How did JPL get individuals to work toward collective goals? There were several possible motivations: the chance to advance national priorities, the romance of space exploration, technical and scientific challenges, and personal ambition. Selfish considerations proved stronger. A staff survey in 1980 asked what factors should influence selection of lab missions: lab employees rated national and social needs the least important and personal satisfaction and career goals the most important.[101] But the work itself enticed many lab staff. Lab managers identified two general categories of people at JPL: "One part includes those individuals who are *inspired* by the Space Exploration Program itself to make their careers at JPL. They tend to be associated with mission and system analysis and design functions. The other part includes the expert engineers who build their careers around challenging application of forefront technology. They tend to be more heavily in the subsystem and operations development functions." The attraction of the work helped compensate for lack of material rewards: mission designers, noted their manager, "do not believe that JPL is competitive in terms of salary and benefits. (They stay here because they like the work.)"[102]

Not all JPL staff were starry-eyed about space. Half the lab consisted of administrative or office staff, technical assistants, and other support staff, for whom the paycheck remained a prime motivation. Some of these nontechnical employees echoed public apathy toward the space program. In the midst of the Viking encounter, David Golidy, a twenty-eight-year-old janitor, took a cynical view: "At first, I thought it was great, but, more and more, I wonder. I mean, it's just a political game, another step in the great space race with the Russians. Like, look at the moon. What did we get? Nothing but rocks. And now, here we go again." Ron Goldbach, a twenty-two-year-old security guard, likewise failed to catch the excitement of Viking. "I've worked here maybe three months and, so far, the most interesting thing that's happened was a rat. . . . It was a big rat and it ran right across the auditorium and jumped into a secretary's wastebasket."[103]

In one respect JPL perhaps more closely followed industrial than academic employment patterns: lab staff did not have to possess a PhD to succeed. By the late 1970s about half of the 4,000 or so lab staff were scientific/engineering professionals; of those, about half had advanced degrees, including 350 doctorates—a substantial number in absolute terms, but less than 10 percent of total lab staff.[104] The relative scarcity of PhDs may have contributed to putdowns from Caltech faculty; but few on campus would have questioned the capabilities of, say, John Casani, who had just a bachelor's degree. JPL engineers believed that on-the-job training more than made up for a lack of advanced degree and that graduate schools did not necessarily teach the sort of specialized skills, such as spacecraft navigation or systems engineering, that planetary exploration demanded.[105]

Whether inspired by the mission or ambition, JPL technical staff did work hard toward the lab's goals, often at great personal sacrifice. Hundred-hour work weeks took their toll, and a saying in the space-science community held that "any sizeable project generates a divorce for everybody that's really involved."[106] Despite the cost to families and marriages, this commitment produced the esprit de corps that had long characterized JPL culture. By 1980, however, the lab had changed in subtle but important ways from two decades earlier. The lab was larger than ever, surpassing the earlier peak of the late 1960s with more than 4,600 staff.[107] With size came a change in culture, affected also by a lack of launches: in the late 1970s the lab launched only the Voyagers in 1977 and Seasat in 1978. As Jack James pointed out, the dwindling launch rate threatened "continuity in lore and know-how"; the result was "a decline in what was once the 'JPL spirit,'" which James traced to poor morale after layoffs, NASA harassment after Ranger, and poor recognition for individual contributions.[108]

James might have added: a shortage of social interactions. The lack of launches precluded the bonding experience provided by the combination of intense work and play off-site. James would have known: he himself was a cigar-smoking raconteur prized at parties for tales told in his Texas twang.[109] Lab staff complained about the lack of communication among various groups and of informal social interaction in general.[110] The lab newsletter exemplified the trend as the breezy, often bawdy accounts of fishing trips and "Canaveral Capers" in the 1950s gave way to dry administrative reports in the 1970s.[111] Perhaps it was just a matter of getting older: the energetic, twenty-something new graduates of the 1950s now had families and mortgages and lacked both the priorities and the stamina to work night and day and then go out for drinks. John Casani, a hail-fellow-well-met sort, did try to provide a social environment on Voyager, finding any excuse to throw a party and blow off steam. But the sheer size of the Voyager project, with its several hundred workers, let alone the thousands of lab staff in different programs, precluded the sort of camaraderie that earlier characterized the lab and instead contributed to the depersonalization of the large organization.

FIVE

Diversification

HOW DID JPL CONTINUE TO GROW DESPITE THE BUDGET CUTS IN THE PLANE-tary program? Instead of defending its main mission, JPL had a second option for institutional survival: find a new mission. If planetary spacecraft could not keep JPL in business, perhaps it was time to try different products and customers. After all, the lab had changed missions and sponsors before, with great success.

The lab found particular opportunities for diversification in three fields: astronomy, earth sciences, and energy. The first two appeared as competitors to planetary exploration within NASA's space science program. As astronomy and earth science acquired increasing support from NASA, JPL managers concluded: if you can't beat them, join them. Diversification into these fields required no change in sponsor and drew on space technology and systems engineering. Energy programs, however, brought a new sponsor, and although Murray and his managers argued that energy research would benefit from space technology and techniques, diversification in this direction represented a greater departure for the lab, with important long-term effects.

Energy

JPL had already started to diversify in the late 1960s with what was called the civil systems program. By 1976 civil systems had a budget of $21 million, about 10 percent of total lab funding, and employed more than 200 staff on work in energy, transportation, the environment, and biomedicine. Government agencies funded 90 percent of this, with the Energy Research and Development Administration (ERDA) the largest sponsor and solar energy the largest program, at about two-thirds of the effort.[1] In 1975 Murray decided that civil systems work had grown too diffuse, and he sought to focus on one field outside of unmanned space exploration where JPL could make clear practical contributions. He identified energy research as a prime candidate.[2]

Energy occupied a central place in the American consciousness in the mid-1970s. Cheap, plentiful oil had fueled the postwar American economy and suburban culture, and it is hard to recapture the sense of crisis, almost panic that gripped the United States when that supply was threatened. The oil embargo, imposed in 1973 by Arab nations as a consequence of their war with Israel, provided the immediate context for the crisis, but underlying issues of supply and demand had been causing shortages and blackouts since the late 1960s and would keep energy a national priority for years afterward. In April 1977 President Carter declared the energy challenge "the moral equivalent of war," and policymakers at the time warned darkly of "social upheaval and revolution" if factories, furnaces, or freeways shut down for lack of fuel.[3] Murray thus chose energy as a second main mission for JPL in addition to planetary exploration. To signal the lab's commitment, in one of his first acts as director Murray reassigned Bud Schurmeier from manager of the high-profile Voyager project to lead the energy work.[4]

JPL's response to the energy crisis derived from four main sources. The first was institutional—not only in the self-interested preservation of JPL amid space program cutbacks, but also in the sense of public service. Caltech and lab staff viewed the lab as "a national resource which should be put to its best and fullest possible use."[5] Murray embraced the concept of JPL as a "national laboratory," with "expertise in a wide variety of disciplines" available for application to national needs. The key criterion for a non-space mission was that it be "of national importance," and energy clearly qualified.[6] Murray advanced this view despite the presence of several other large, multidisciplinary labs, at Argonne, Brookhaven, Oak Ridge, and elsewhere, already designated as national labs and committed to the federal energy program.

Technical expertise provided the second source for the lab's response. JPL could argue that it contributed technological capabilities different from those of the national labs, especially in non-nuclear fields. Energy offered plentiful opportunities for the transfer of space techniques: lab engineers listed chemical catalysis and combustion, electrochemistry, heat transfer and thermodynamics, and systems analysis as among several skills they could apply to energy conversion technology.[7] In particular, solar energy research promised to capitalize on the lab's long experience with spacecraft solar power arrays, which had provided an important early demonstration of the use of photocells for electrical power.[8]

JPL, however, was not content with technological tasks. Murray at the outset stressed that the lab sought major projects in the energy field and that smaller jobs were just a means to that end. A special meeting of senior staff on energy in April 1977 revealed a strong desire to push beyond a "device-oriented approach" to the systems level—from "energy with a small e" to "energy with a large E."[9] The lab's skills, in other words, were as much managerial as technical, and the energy program should tap the well of systems management. This managerial perspective served as a third source for the lab's response.

A fourth source lay in the push for better Caltech-JPL relations. Campus strengths in chemical and nuclear engineering, geology, environmental science, plasma physics, and economics and public policy seemed readily applicable to energy research and promised to attract sponsors; according to Murray, ERDA director Robert Seamans had stated "quite clearly that JPL and the Campus together constitute a much more interesting resource for the country than either by itself."[10] Lab staff proposed that Caltech's budding program in social sciences could take the lead on short-term problems of economics, pricing, and distribution logistics; JPL engineers could meanwhile pursue long-term problems of alternative energy sources, with support from technical faculty on campus.[11] One such collaboration, for example, emerged on nuclear waste disposal, with JPL staff providing systems management and nuclear engineering and campus faculty studying environmental science and geology.[12]

There was yet another possible motivation for energy work at JPL: its political implications. Solar energy was not only a clean, renewable energy source; it also had the advantage of decentralization, with dispersed collectors instead of central generating stations and hence less need for long-line energy transmission and associated losses.[13] By thus breaking up electricity generating and distribution systems, solar power had social and political as well as technical benefits. As the authors of an article in *Science* in 1977 put it: "Solar energy is democratic. It falls on everyone and can be put to use by individuals and small groups of people."[14] As a potentially small-scale, decentralized system, solar power resonated in particular with the philosophy of economist E. F. Schumacher, whose best-selling book of 1973, titled *Small Is Beautiful*, popularized a combination of small-scale socioeconomic operation, environmentalism, and Buddhist philosophy. Schumacher argued against the need for centralized, capital-intensive systems and instead advocated what he called "intermediate technology," also known as "appropriate" or "alternative" technology, intended to reflect the resources and capabilities of local communities.[15]

Murray similarly called for small-scale technologies to enable economic and political decentralization, and he and his staff kept up with the trend, including discussions with Amory Lovins, a proponent of "soft energy paths" and supporter of Schumacher, and with Schumacher himself.[16] The resonance with Schumacher appeared not only in the push for solar power, in which JPL staff explicitly recognized the needs of small communities, but also in an approach to coal and geothermal sources that addressed regional problems and sponsors.[17] Some of the lab's more politically conservative engineers, however, resisted Murray's embrace of the appropriate-technology movement.[18]

These several factors combined to produce a rapid increase in energy work at JPL, which by early 1978 had an $80-million budget supporting 350 staff—about the size of a planetary project. Murray proclaimed that the lab was "well along toward the goal of a dual mission, in energy and space." The buildup contributed to the glut of work at JPL in the late 1970s, overflowing available facilities and forcing energy program staff into a leased site several miles away in Pasadena. As non-NASA work reached 18 percent of the lab program, most of it for the Department of Energy (DOE), Murray and the lab's executive council in December 1977 met to consider segregating it in either a new laboratory or a separate contract.[19] In 1975 Murray had proposed that Caltech provide start-up capital for a Pasadena Applications Laboratory, a new entity to exploit commercial opportunities from Caltech and JPL activities, in particular from the civil systems program. The venture, likely a for-profit corporation owned and run by Caltech, would recruit people and inventions from the campus and lab and provide a new source of income for the institute, as well as financial assets to give JPL some reserves. But Caltech failed to act on the proposal.[20]

The idea of a separate contract with another agency received more discussion. JPL since its inception had operated under a single prime contract, but the growth and diversity of civil systems projects spurred consideration of multiple contracts. The need to transfer funds through NASA was discouraging large projects for other agencies, and a separate contract would satisfy sponsors of the lab's commitment. A lab study group in 1976 found no great obstacle to multiple sponsors, if NASA and Caltech acquiesced, and a subsequent report viewed a separate contract as "probably inevitable" owing to the growth of energy work. But it also pointed out significant drawbacks, especially inconsistencies between the contracts and allocation of indirect costs and overhead, not to mention the fee, and a DOE contract would likely be less favorable than the current one with NASA.[21] As much as JPL and Caltech sparred with NASA, they did enjoy a historical relationship with the agency and its people. The lab's executive council decided against a separate contract or laboratory, and the issue was instead handled through the new memorandum of understanding with NASA of 1978, which included the special provision for energy work.[22]

Most of JPL's energy program concerned solar power, a subject receiving much attention at the time amid environmental concerns about fossil-fuel pollution and nuclear waste disposal. A congressional act on solar energy in 1974 tripled solar funding from 1975 to 1976, and in 1975 JPL started the Low-Cost Silicon Solar Array (LSSA) project, to develop photovoltaic cells with higher efficiency, longer lifetimes, and larger volumes.[23] In 1978 Congress created a ten-year, $1.5-billion national program for photovoltaics, and JPL won assignment as the Department of Energy's lead center for photovoltaic technology.[24] By 1980 the photovoltaic program provided over 150 work-years, supplemented by another 100 work-years on solar thermal power systems.[25] As of March 1980 the low-cost solar array was the largest lab program, in terms of outstanding cost commitments, ahead of Galileo and other space flight projects.[26]

Despite this buildup and the underlying justifications, energy work did not capture the allegiance of JPL. In a survey in 1980 lab scientists and engineers rated energy lower than space exploration in terms of individual and institutional importance.[27] Schurmeier, dissatisfied with the program, sought renewal in a sabbatical in 1981.[28] Aside from the low-cost solar array project, much of the work involved smaller projects in coal utilization, electric/hybrid vehicles, geothermal and biomass energy, and nuclear waste management, especially disposal in space.[29] One Caltech professor perceived "a conglomeration of minor activities . . . rather than a well-planned and coherent set of subtasks."[30] The scattershot programs reflected the general diffusion of interests in the national energy program, all of them lumped under the ill-defined Department of Energy.[31]

Energy work also drew on a limited portion of JPL's technical skills, primarily in chemical engineering, materials, and applied mechanics. It did not tap into expertise in electronics, communications, and information systems or into the high-reliability approach that characterized JPL's systems engineering, and it did not make much use of the special facilities at the lab, especially the elaborate spacecraft test chambers. And although it did not have the threat of embarrassing and expensive failures, neither did it provide the public appeal of launches and encounters. Finally, energy spurred disciplinary diversification into what one lab report called "the 'soft disciplines' of economics, policy analysis, social analysis, and law."[32]

The justification for energy work based on technological spin-offs proved as tenuous as institutional considerations. By the end of 1977 Murray recognized that "the thought that DOE work is a NASA spin-off is an outgrown thought."[33] Lab managers worried that the solar array project mostly involved evaluation and use of technology developed elsewhere—that is, the work was more management than engineering.[34] Caltech faculty and trustees similarly expressed concern over a lack of technical innovation and traced it to an emphasis, instilled by the Department of Energy, on short-term demonstrations instead of long-term research.[35]

The expected synergies with campus likewise failed to materialize. Faculty viewed the lab's energy work as inappropriate and undemanding, and the orange report of 1976 expressed the concern that diversified programs would not meet Caltech's standards. An anonymous faculty member observed that "out of desperation the Laboratory people will undertake any kind of work for survival and then do an embarrassing second-rate job. . . . Typically they will transfer a good space engineer onto a non-space job he knows nothing about."[36] For its part, Caltech's traditional base rested in technical fields, despite its increasing strength in the social sciences. Lab staff recognized that energy work involved "social, economic, and political considerations" and was "primarily program management rather than R&D," and hence it might not be "the right sort of thing for Caltech to be doing."[37] Energy programs also departed from campus strengths in dealing with products for the commercial market. As Murray noted, "energy work differs profoundly from space or DoD work because the government is not its own customer." JPL engineers and managers struggled to shift from space projects, which sought reliability at any price, to the cost-conscious mode of electrical utilities, which continually pressed for economic as well as technological feasibility.[38]

Energy work did, however, keep lab staff on tap through the uncertainties of the planetary program in this period, occupying as many as 400 full-time staff. In early 1980 JPL assumed that its energy R&D would continue to thrive for another decade, perhaps growing to 1,000 work-years.[39] But the oil crisis was already ebbing and the Reagan administration soon imposed precipitous cuts on the energy program, slashing in particular the solar-energy budget from $578 million in 1981 to $70 million in 1983. The budget cuts would effectively end JPL's major engagement with energy research, although not its legacies.[40]

Earth and Ocean Science

The lab had alternatives besides energy to fill the bathtub in planetary exploration. JPL staff listed earth and ocean science among the "utilitarian" activities pursued at the lab.[41] From 1975 to 1980 earth and ocean science enjoyed a larger proportion of NASA's space science budget than both planetary exploration and astronomy, thanks to consistent support from Congress; the subject resonated with the search for social benefits from the space program, since it embraced weather and climate, the environment, and resources such as food, forests, and minerals. JPL staff noted the emphasis on earth observations in NASA's "Outlook for Space" report of 1976 and, after considering whether to "get out of the space program as rapidly as possible" in favor of an earth-oriented program, resolved to develop earth observations in parallel to planetary exploration.[42]

The lab had a small but thriving earth and ocean program in place, which had tripled in size from 1973 to 1975 to a $10-million program. This work had focused at first on earth dynamics, drawing on the lab's experience in planetary geology, but in the mid-1970s the land-oriented work leveled off alongside a new and rapidly growing program in ocean dynamics.[43] Several factors spurred JPL into oceanography, a field seemingly distant from its expertise. At the time, even as humankind was venturing into space, much of the earth's oceans remained unexplored. In an expanded analog to the International Geophysical Year of 1957–58 that had helped to launch the space race, the 1970s were designated the International Decade of Ocean Exploration.[44] The oceans attracted popular interest as well: in the 1970s, just as Carl Sagan was popularizing planetary science, Jacques Cousteau was performing a similar role for ocean science. In May 1976 Cousteau visited JPL, where discussions likely included a proposed satellite program for biological data on oceans.[45]

Programmatic considerations also recommended oceanography. Meteorology, geology, and geography were already well covered by existing satellites, but oceanography had yet to capitalize on satellite remote sensing, and Goddard Space Flight Center, which otherwise dominated NASA's earth-orbiting satellite program, had a weaker claim for any projects. JPL beat out Goddard in competition for an ocean-sensing satellite, dubbed Seasat, proposed in the early 1970s. JPL's proposal appealed to the lab's experience in remote sensing and also to recent results from airplane-borne flights of a synthetic aperture radar by a JPL team, which suggested the radar's utility for ocean sensing.[46]

Seasat gave JPL an entry, or reentry, into earth-orbiting projects, and it subsequently anchored the lab's ocean science program. JPL thus won designation by NASA in 1976 as lead center for earth and ocean dynamics and as an alternate to Goddard for earth-orbiting science satellites, and it thence considered earth and especially ocean science as a third main focus for its R&D program, alongside planetary exploration and energy.[47] As a NASA program, earth science did not entail as great a change as did the energy program, but it still complicated JPL's external relations. Goddard and JPL squabbled over turf, and JPL adjusted to a new sponsor within NASA, the Office of Applications.[48] The boundary between science and application was not so neat as the organizational distinction. Seasat, for instance, was intended not as a research tool but instead as a technology demonstration en route to an operational system, which would provide oceanographic data for military and commercial as well as scientific users. These operational customers backed the inclusion of the synthetic aperture radar, for sea-surface texture, against oceanographers arguing for a microwave radiometer to provide surface temperatures. After scientists complained of being shut out of Seasat, NASA elected to appease each group and accept the cost of both instruments.[49]

Seasat data thus entailed interactions outside of NASA. Early support for the radar instrument came from the National Oceanic and Atmospheric Administration (NOAA), an agency created in 1970 under the Department of Commerce in response to the increasing interest in oceans as well as in weather; the new agency combined the Bureau of Commercial Fisheries, U.S. Weather Bureau, and Coast and Geodetic Survey.[50] Seasat reflected the different interest groups: it intended to provide wind and wave data for ship design and routing, storm warnings, and coastal and harbor protection; current and temperature patterns for shipping and fishing; and ice-field charts for shipping and weather forecasts.[51] Military and intelligence agencies meanwhile maintained their own interests in the project, though for less-advertised reasons.

Murray in April 1977 noted two differences on Seasat from planetary projects: first, the array of interests—"one does not have the narrowness, in a sense, of a scientific constituency consisting of a few tens of people selected by NASA"—and, second, "one does not have the discipline of a planetary launch window."[52] These factors promoted the proliferation of instruments and encouraged last-minute changes that vexed engineers and pushed up costs, forcing NASA to consider jettisoning the synthetic aperture radar, a prime motivation for the project.[53] The failure of the satellite three months into the mission did not improve NASA's disposition. The agency issued a scathing performance evaluation; the NASA program manager perceived that "outside JPL, there was little confidence in many areas that anything of value would come out of Seasat."[54]

Murray took a rosier view. Seasat was not a "mission failure," as NASA characterized it: the sensors worked, especially the synthetic aperture radar, and they were the crux of the mission. Seasat had succeeded in demonstrating that satellite-borne sensors could return important information on sea surface conditions from hundreds of miles away.[55] The voluminous data that gradually emerged from JPL's data processors vindicated Murray, and first NOAA and then, a year after launch, NASA stamped the project a success.[56] In June 1979 Seasat graced the cover of a special issue of *Science,* just a few weeks after the one for Voyager at Jupiter, and more specialized journals also dedicated their own issues to the subject.[57]

The technical success of Seasat failed to ensure continuity in JPL's oceans program. A planned follow-on to Seasat, called Seasat-B, foundered on the divide between development and operations. Since Seasat was intended to prove feasibility, how could more R&D on the operational mode be justified?[58] NASA instead backed the so-called National Oceanic Satellite System, or NOSS, a proposed collaboration with NOAA and the Defense Department to launch an operational system of two satellites on the space shuttle by 1984.[59] But the desire of the military to classify parts of the NOSS data clashed with the needs of scientific and commercial users—according to a NASA aide, NOSS was "the bastard baby of the closed and open worlds"—and the Defense Department pulled out of the agreement in 1981.[60] JPL thus failed to maintain momentum in its earth and ocean science program, which peaked with Seasat at 13 percent of the total lab program in 1977 and declined to 8 percent by 1981.[61] The Seasat and NOSS experience led Murray to scale back the expectations for oceanography, although JPL did begin plans in 1980 for another oceanographic satellite, called Topex.[62] The lab did maintain a fruitful program in geodynamics, and the synthetic aperture radar would continue to produce important contributions to archeology and anthropology as well as geology and oceanography.[63]

In addition to its conceptual influence, the JPL program reinforced a methodological shift away from traditional field approaches and toward quantitative physical approaches. Instead of geologists tramping through the landscape looking at rocks and oceanographers setting off in ships for weeks at sea, the practitioners of a new interdisciplinary field of earth science studied data disgorged from remote sensors, computers, and other instruments.[64] Physical techniques required different expertise than fieldwork. At JPL, for example, people like Walt Brown and Charles Elachi, with backgrounds in electrical engineering and electromagnetic theory, pushed the application of synthetic aperture radar to earth science, devising techniques to translate backscatter data into information on ocean wave heights. Their efforts at times met resistance. When Brown's team first detected ocean waves from their airborne radar in 1971, oceanographer Walter Monk at Scripps dismissed their claims as an artifact; other oceanographers argued that shorter capillary waves would scatter so much radar energy as to blur images of larger swells.[65] One JPL oceanographer perceived in 1977 that "the oceanographic community, although intrigued, is still skeptical about quantitative results and adequate precision of measurements from remote sensors."[66] The Seasat radar, however, produced images of long-wavelength swells, and the correlation of other Seasat data with surface measurements helped to overcome skepticism. NASA managers observed that in the late 1970s and early 1980s earth scientists became "convinced that studying the earth from space was part of science."[67] In 1988 *Time* magazine declared that "remote-sensing devices are revolutionizing the study of the seas."[68]

Astronomy

Astronomy provided a third target for diversification, owing to NASA's increasing support of it. JPL staff had recognized NASA's interest and pondered how to tap into it.[69] The first opportunity appeared in the Infrared Astronomy Satellite (IRAS), which NASA awarded to JPL in April 1976, apparently to draw on JPL's experience in systems engineering and perhaps also the proximity to Caltech astronomer Gerry Neugebauer, a longtime proponent of the project. JPL handled overall project management on IRAS, while Ball Brothers built the telescope itself under guidance from Ames; the Netherlands provided the satellite bus.[70] Then, in March 1977 NASA announced a competition to provide a key component for the Space Telescope, for what would be known as the Wide Field/Planetary Camera (WF/PC). A team led by Caltech astronomer James A. Westphal responded with a proposal based on charge-coupled devices (CCDs), which converted light falling on individual solid-state pixels into electrical signals. A prime advantage of CCDs over familiar television-tube devices was their response to red light, but with corresponding poor response in the ultraviolet. Westphal had the idea to coat the device with a fluorescent substance that would absorb ultraviolet and re-emit blue light, which the CCD could better detect.[71]

JPL engineers had recognized the potential of CCDs for planetary imaging soon after their invention in 1970, because of their small size and power requirements, and the lab quickly became the center for CCD expertise within NASA. Westphal's proposal drew on this capability, especially the effort to build CCDs for Galileo's camera. But Galileo's CCDs were imaging relatively bright planets and moons; for faint distant stars, by contrast, every photon was precious. The WF/PC also had its CCDs illuminated from the backside owing to its layout. To improve the response of the devices JPL engineers led by James Janasek had developed much thinner silicon layers, about 8 microns, which ensured that photoelectrons would reach the electronic gates, or collection points, and thus increased their low-noise response to about 30 times that of existing astronomical detectors. The JPL group had considered their own proposal for the Wide Field/Planetary Camera and then joined forces with Westphal and landed the part of prime contractor. The role would require a longer run than expected.[72]

Both IRAS and the WF/PC provided the sort of campus-lab interactions sought by the orange report, especially since astronomy had been a strength of Caltech since George Ellery Hale first founded the institute.[73] Although most of JPL's efforts aimed at space-based astronomy, it had a substantial asset that got it into ground-based observations: the Deep Space Network, or DSN. The network served the primary mission of deep-space exploration but was isolated from the rest of the lab, institutionally as well as geographically. DSN funding came in a separate account, which provided about one-fifth of the total JPL budget each year. Because the network had to continuously track spacecraft, the budget was much more constant than for spacecraft missions, which had to obtain approval for each new start. NASA managers appreciated the shelter this arrangement provided from congressional scrutiny, and they allowed DSN engineers to develop new technology for the network over time. The DSN thus fostered a different culture, a longer-range view instead of a succession of short-term projects, and produced what Murray would term an "Auslander kind of mentality" among the rest of the lab.[74]

By the mid-1970s the DSN consisted of three 64-meter antennas at Goldstone and in Australia and Spain, all now operating at higher X-band radio frequencies, along with the older 26-meter dishes.[75] These antennas not only tracked spacecraft and received data transmissions, but they also could serve as state-of-the-art scientific instruments themselves: for radio science, using the signals sent by spacecraft to reveal information about planetary atmospheres and the interplanetary environment; radar astronomy, using active transmission and reception of signals for planetary astronomy; and radio astronomy, with passive detection of radio signals emitted by distant stars and galaxies. In the late 1970s, however, the DSN faced a heavy workload tracking Viking, Pioneer, and Voyager spacecraft, and frustrated astronomers began complaining about lack of access to the antennas.[76]

Even as astronomers clamored for scarce observing time, Murray and DSN scientists were backing a new mission in the Search for Extraterrestrial Intelligence, or SETI. The possibility of detecting signals from extraterrestrial civilizations emerged in the late 1950s as astronomers began probing nonvisible portions of the spectrum, and received boosts in the 1960s from calculations of the theoretical existence of such civilizations. In the 1970s SETI proponents, including several JPL staff, turned their attention to observation instead of theory, and a series of workshops in 1975 and 1976 outlined observing programs. They aimed high, comparing SETI to the Apollo program and seeking to build up to a $1-billion-per-year program in the 1990s.[77]

NASA managers found the plans "not at all realistic" and agreed instead to a more modest program proposed jointly in 1976 by JPL and Ames.[78] Murray, whose friend Carl Sagan was one of the main SETI prophets, had attended a planning workshop, and SETI meshed with his search for projects to engage the public: "Communicating with other intelligent beings is one of the most exciting ventures I can envision." He thus created a SETI office at JPL, with plans to outfit the DSN antennas with new wideband receivers and a multichannel spectrum analyzer to sort the signals by frequency.[79] While JPL cast a broad net, searching most of the sky over the frequency range from 1.4 to 25 GHz, Ames would pursue a targeted survey, using other radio observatories to focus on nearby stars at frequencies around the "water hole" at 1420–1720 MHz, which was deemed a likely frequency for communication.[80]

Although Ames and JPL had to prod lower-level NASA managers for backing, SETI enjoyed support at the highest levels of NASA, and beyond. As a lay minister in the Church of Jesus Christ of Latter Day Saints, NASA administrator James Fletcher adhered to the Mormon doctrine that God created a plurality of worlds, populated with intelligent beings. In a speech to the National Academy of Engineering in 1975, Fletcher backed the idea of a search for extraterrestrial signals, based on the belief that the universe, even our own galaxy, "must be full of voices, calling from star to star in a myriad of tongues."[81] Congressmen were skeptical. After NASA submitted a SETI plan to Congress in February 1978, Senator William Proxmire awarded it his monthly Golden Fleece, intended to highlight wasteful government programs.[82] Congressional appropriations committees thence cut most of the SETI budget, and in 1982 a Proxmire amendment killed off the surviving remnants of the program, though not for good.[83]

Space Science at JPL

Earth science and astronomy experiments, such as synthetic aperture radar and the Wide Field/Planetary Camera, indicated a growing role at JPL in space science research. Although JPL built the spacecraft that carried science instruments into deep space, the instruments themselves usually came from researchers in other institutions, who then also analyzed the data that came back. Only one of the lab's several proposals for experiments on Voyager, the photopolarimeter, was selected by NASA. Although a number of JPL scientists would join the other Voyager experiment teams, they were far outnumbered by Goddard scientists.[84]

JPL now sought to build its science capability. NASA's "roles and missions" review of 1976 had given JPL an increased role in space science, and the same year the orange report encouraged an in-house science presence.[85] Outside experimenters could also support a science presence at the lab, to balance the predominant force of engineers and represent their interests on flight projects. Spacecraft engineers tended to view their main goal as just getting the spacecraft to its destination in working order; adding science experiments, with their demands on subsystems and trajectories, only added to the risk of failure. Scientists by contrast viewed spacecraft as the means to the end of returning data from new places.[86]

The tension between engineers and scientists went back to the earliest days of NASA, when scientists complained that JPL engineers viewed scientific instruments only as threats to project schedules and spacecraft survival.[87] Norman Ness at Goddard, head of the magnetometer on Voyager, referred to "that old problem that the engineering expertise of JPL is often so potent a force or tradition that it tends to dominate many aspects of a mission." On Voyager, for example, science representatives in the project office served at lower levels than the engineers; and Stone, despite his strengths, was handicapped by coming from campus and in only a part-time capacity. Hence Ness and another Voyager scientist, Herbert Bridge of MIT, lamented in 1977, before launch, that Voyager was becoming more an engineering mission than a scientific one.[88]

The main impetus for in-house science at JPL came from programmatic considerations. The growing programs in earth-orbiting spacecraft for astronomy and earth sciences and the prospect of shuttle-borne instruments spurred JPL's push to develop flight experiment capability.[89] But this effort first had to overcome obstacles within the lab. One was the JPL culture of reliability, which did not seem to encourage scientific creativity; Philip Abelson, editor of *Science*, pointed out to Murray that "people are unlikely to do imaginative science in a building where the value system favors highly dependable engineering."[90] JPL researchers complained that they were "shoved aside" by the lab's engineers in the development of flight experiments, that reliability and accounting practices handicapped them, and that the lab in general evinced no great commitment to their work.[91] As a result, noted one Caltech professor, "morale among these people is very low. They are all considering leaving, and . . . the group of good scientists that remains is now close to the edge of viability—a few more losses, and the flow will become a flood."[92]

Murray's own apparent ambivalence did little to stem the tide. When Goddard in 1976 proposed to increase its role in data analysis from flight projects, Murray disdained such a role for JPL: the flight projects themselves remained the top priority, and in-house research would conflict with their scientific users. Furthermore, "because of our relationship with the Caltech Campus there is little incentive to develop separate research organizations here."[93] Murray thus reversed the logic of the orange report, which had urged a research role to encourage collaboration with campus, and he would continue to view research as a service function, supporting the basic end of flight projects.[94]

JPL scientists also contended with academic colleagues. In 1976 NASA, at the urging of university scientists suspicious of the agency's in-house research, instituted a policy of peer review for all space science programs.[95] Murray and other NASA scientists protested that academic scientists enjoyed the advantages of tenure and graduate students; NASA centers, in other words, needed support equivalent to that provided by the teaching function of university faculty. NASA stuck to its position, and JPL scientists thereafter had to submit proposals at least every few years for peer review.[96] The process did not promote job security. The orange report had urged that JPL scientists should have half of their time for research, and Murray had approved such a policy. But scientists now had to find money for that half of their time, by winning grants through open competition; if a proposal did not pass muster, that scientist was out of a job.[97] The result was a constant pressure to win grants, cutting into the time spent on research, which then degraded a scientist's reputation over time and hurt grant prospects. And since many scientists spent the other half of their time managing—that is, coordinating and monitoring the work of others and planning future projects—it further blurred the distinction between scientist, engineer, and manager.[98]

Implications of Diversification

In 1975 JPL gave 83 percent of its effort, measured in work-years, to space exploration; by 1979 that proportion was below two-thirds, with the other third given to "utilitarian" programs, mostly energy (up from 5 to 16 percent) and earth-orbital projects (from 7 to 13 percent).[99] The lab program now embraced earth science and astronomy as well as planetary exploration in the space program; outside of space, JPL was pursuing diverse aspects of energy research as well as smaller programs in biomedicine, transportation, and other fields. By the early 1980s total lab staff numbered more than 4,600, even as flight projects staffing dropped from its peak of about 1,400 in the mid-1960s to below 800 by the early 1980s; the difference lay in the 850 work-years given to non-NASA programs by 1980. JPL was the exception among NASA labs; all of the others suffered decreases in this period, when NASA overall shrank by about 15 percent.[100]

Diversification, however, had its costs. Some JPL staff worried that the lab was "becoming too fragmented. . . . A jack of all trades and master of none." Murray admitted that "these utilitarian programs do not have a single unifying glue; they're different kinds of things. And if we move to all of those or to some mix of them . . . the Lab simply couldn't work as well. It would not be bound by the hidden threads that bind us together—the shared purpose of space exploration."[101] The dedication and sacrifice by individuals that enabled

JPL's performance rested in part on a commitment to the deep-space mission, which new fields did not necessarily command. Diversification threatened to turn JPL into a job shop, as Caltech professor John Pierce repeatedly warned Murray; the lab might have diverse sponsors but no clear purpose.[102]

Diversification also affected the composition of JPL staff: whereas new fields, such as energy, could keep engineers and technologists on tap, they did not sustain so well the other general category of lab staff, those in mission design and systems analysis who came to JPL because of their interest in space exploration.[103] The systems engineering regime and matrix organization had evolved to meet the needs of one or a few large flight projects, but the lab now faced a large number of smaller tasks that lacked the risk and reliability factors of space flight.[104] JPL also struggled to find enough experienced managers for proliferating tasks, not for the last time.[105]

Murray and his senior managers decided the benefits of diversification outweighed the costs. The subsequent crisis in planetary exploration of 1981 coincided with the deep cuts in the energy program and also with declining prospects in earth science. These factors combined by early 1982 to convince Murray and the lab's executive council that the second major period in the lab's history was ending: after the initial phase as an army rocket lab and then as the lead NASA lab for planetary exploration, JPL was beginning an "inevitable and rapid transition to JPL 3."[106] The evident success of the earlier move from rockets to robotic spacecraft could only have encouraged consideration of another such shift. The lab meanwhile had already begun to look for another major mission to sustain it, and it again found opportunities in the historical context—but ones that raised a new set of issues for Caltech and the lab.

SIX

Return to the Military

IN THE EARLY 1980S CONTEMPORARY COMMENTATORS PERCEIVED A "MILITARI-zation of space," a trend that began in the 1970s but reached its zenith during the Reagan administration.[1] Or, rather, remilitarization: a military presence in space was nothing new, and national security had been a primary driver of the American space program from the outset, from intercontinental missiles to satellite reconnaissance. But this period did witness a pronounced reorientation of the U.S. space program, evident in the relative funding from NASA and the military. In 1959 NASA supported one-third of the U.S. space program, with the Department of Defense (DOD) supporting almost all of the remainder. By the mid-1960s the proportion had reversed, thanks to Apollo. In the mid-1970s defense spending on space began to rise steadily, overtaking NASA in 1982, and by 1984 the ratio had reverted almost to that of 1959.[2] The trend reflected increasing recognition of the military importance of space, especially for reconnaissance satellites; it indicated as well a general cooling of cold war relations after the thaw of détente, and the American response to Soviet attainment of strategic parity and perceptions of Soviet technical achievements in space.

JPL could hardly avoid intersecting national security programs. The lab specialized in such things as survivable spacecraft, remote sensing, data telemetry, and image processing—all areas of keen interest to the military and intelligence communities. At the same time, the declining prospects in the planetary program motivated the lab to seek new programs that could sustain idled staff. JPL thus joined in the remilitarization of space. Not all of its defense work was in space, as it also pursued large projects for the army. As with the general mobilization, JPL's role in defense would start to increase in the late 1970s and peak in the 1980s. But its resumption of defense work came in a very different climate from its work under the army in the 1950s, and it would have to overcome antimilitary sentiment, particularly among campus faculty, spawned by the Vietnam War and the cold war arms race.

Dancing with the DOD

JPL originated as a military lab, and even after it shifted to NASA it never abandoned its original sponsor. In the early to mid-1970s JPL maintained a number of small defense projects, parallel to but not part of civil systems (although the civil systems work had at one time included a program called Space Technology Applications, whose benign name belied its purpose in designing weapons—such as nail-laced shells and target-marking rockets— for the Vietnam War).[3] But most of the work was unclassified, and defense programs constituted less than 1 percent of the total lab effort as of 1975.

The memorandum of understanding (MOU) of 1968 and the development of the civil systems program opened the possibility of expanding the defense work. In 1975, as lab managers began to look for "bathtub fillers" after Voyager, defense programs caught their eye. William Pickering sat on an advisory committee for the army, where he learned that the army was seeking technical help in several areas. He responded with interest, and H. H. Haglund and Phil Eckman, after a visit to the Pentagon, identified several areas where JPL could help. They perceived that the military would want a continuing commitment "rather than a short-time use of personnel to fill in a manpower deficit at the Laboratory," which would require a policy decision.[4] NASA presented no objections, and Caltech president Harold Brown welcomed "the idea of experimenting with a limited DOD activity." Brown, a former nuclear weapons designer with long experience managing defense programs, displayed the combination of institutional and patriotic motives behind defense work: it not only would provide sustenance for the lab, but would contribute to national needs.[5]

Some military programs, however, entailed secrecy and possible campus opposition. Lab staff recognized classification as "a particularly sensitive issue with some of the faculty," since it might restrict access to parts of JPL or prevent publication of lab research and hence restrict peer review.[6] Eckman and Haglund, after discussions on campus, feared that with the presence of defense work, "some faculty might feel that JPL should be severed from Caltech." Brown thought the problems "not insurmountable," but he certainly did not want to risk Caltech's relationship with the lab.[7]

The case of the Vista Laboratory, a highly classified surveillance program, highlighted qualms about the propriety of military programs. JPL's connections with Vista dated back to the 1950s.[8] The Vista Lab was located off the main JPL site, in Pasadena, and was sponsored by the National Security Agency and Central Intelligence Agency. Vista staff deciphered telemetry intercepted from Soviet launches in order to chart Soviet space capabilities and anticipate their plans; JPL staff in effect served as intelligence analysts for the spy agencies. JPL participation involved perhaps twenty people, including such key figures as Robert Parks, Jack James, Eb Rechtin, and Pickering himself, with younger staff rotating through Vista as consultants and, at times, as managers on leaves of absence.[9]

In the early 1970s Harold Brown grew squeamish about the association with Vista, which he perceived would not sit well with faculty on campus if word got out. At the time, recent revelations of the CIA's involvement in Watergate, domestic spying, and assassinations of foreign leaders had aroused public protests and congressional investigations, and defense labs on other college campuses had provoked protests, including a fatal bombing at the University of Wisconsin. JPL arranged to sever its institutional ties to Vista, and the sponsors chose Electro-Optical Systems, a Pasadena subsidiary of Xerox, to take over the Vista Lab. As Xerox assumed control, Murray stressed that he was reviewing JPL's role "with the intent of making sure that even the appearance of any institutional relationships with Vista and the intelligence community is eliminated."[10]

Although Caltech and JPL severed institutional ties to Vista, unofficial connections continued. JPL staff working on Vista had the option of joining Xerox or staying with JPL. Those who stayed could still serve as consultants, provided they did so as individuals and not as representatives of JPL. Xerox made wide use of consultants in its management of Vista, and JPL provided "the principal source" at the outset.[11] In October 1976, after the lab had officially divested, Murray was "both clarifying and strengthening the relationships between individuals at JPL and the VISTA organization."[12] Eckman served on Vista's advisory committee under Xerox, and Vista staff used JPL computers and other facilities for brief, occasional projects.[13] And the appearance of an official JPL role persisted with a Vista task called Dub/Galaxy, which seems to have involved a JPL contract. Although Murray "stated his strong personal support of the work," he worried that it "may be construed as an institutional commitment which would present him with serious problems with the Campus."[14]

The divestment from Vista indicates concern by JPL and Caltech administrators about the propriety of classified national security programs. The solution—official divestment and continued unofficial participation by consultants—allowed JPL to avoid campus concerns while still contributing to intelligence problems. JPL staff also thus maintained access to the black world of space reconnaissance. Coincidentally, the Vista program brought

Murray and JPL into contact with the head of the National Security Agency, an air force general named Lew Allen.

Military Spin-offs

Despite the divestment of Vista, defense work made gradual inroads at JPL in the late 1970s. Two programs exemplify how JPL flight projects overlapped military interests: Seasat and autonomous spacecraft. They also indicate how political disinterest in civil space missions changed attitudes toward defense programs, resulting in a mutual embrace between the lab and the military.

The military took a strong interest in Seasat from the outset. As JPL staff contemplated possible payloads they considered their customers and the relative clout they had with Congress and the Office of Management and Budget (OMB); the DOD ranked first, NOAA second, and the scientific community last. The DOD's primary interest in Seasat was in altimetry data for geodesy, necessary for the inertial guidance systems of ballistic missiles, but it also helped support an imaging radar and microwave radiometer. The inclusion of the radar raised the issue of classification. The synthetic aperture radar (SAR) had a long history of surveillance use; Seasat was just its first civilian flight. JPL staff by April 1974 had recognized "the problem of the position we should take if classified systems are flying."[15] The next year NASA terminated all contacts with foreigners regarding Seasat, an edict that cut several Canadians out of a collaboration on data processing; it also threatened to limit the data return since a Canadian ground station was needed to receive SAR data from the northwestern Atlantic.[16] In 1976 the Defense Department insisted on classifying the altimetry data, which would entail either encryption or a secure radio link, and it also demanded a secure link for the synthetic aperture radar. Gene Giberson, the project manager at JPL, thought there was "no quantitative reason to classify" the data, that it was a knee-jerk reaction by the military.[17] Giberson, Pickering, and then Murray lobbied Harold Brown, recently installed as secretary of defense, to prevent classification, while NASA's advisors pondered "where the borderline between the classified and the unclassified lies."[18] The issue finally went to President Carter, who overruled the military and allowed access to the Seasat data.[19]

The launch of the satellite in 1978 did not put the issue to rest. On the contrary, the military would wish it had clamped down harder. Incoming data from Seasat alarmed military analysts, first by detecting stealth aircraft, early prototypes of which were undergoing test flights off the coast. The change in polarization of radar pulses reflected off the ocean left a telltale shadow in the data, revealing the planes. Recalled Walt Brown of the radar team, "Well, when we showed them the stuff back in Washington, that's when they kind of all turned red and [said], 'What the hell is this?' . . . So they went back and looked through and found, yeah, a stealth airplane. Not so stealthy with that mode."[20]

Further analysis of SAR images also raised the possibility of submarine detection. The radar provided ocean-surface signatures, at high resolution, of subsurface phenomena including internal waves (see figure 6.1). The bow waves from submerged submarines could thus show up in radar images of the ocean surface.[21] The prospect of detecting submarines raised fundamental strategic problems for the United States, which depended on ballistic missile submarines as a crucial, invulnerable line of nuclear deterrence. Seasat's early demise fueled speculation about military connections. After NASA managers entertained the possibility of external causes of the failure, front-page headlines floated theories about killer satellites and ground-based laser beams—speculation encouraged by recent Soviet tests of anti-satellite weapons and reports of satellite-blinding incidents.[22] Recognition of the SAR's capabilities spurred conspiracy theories closer to home: once the American military learned about the possibility of submarine detection, one theory ran, it took the satellite out of operation rather than allow the release of unclassified results. Rumors of clandestine cover-ups persisted for years, despite the identification of Seasat's failure mode by the review board.[23]

Seasat managers at JPL had seen military interests as an intrusion and had fought them off, but as they pondered what to do with their team after Seasat they came to the opposite view. In early 1979 Murray wrote to the navy and air force proposing that JPL develop the SAR for military applications, under military sponsorship. The proposed program would be unclassified, but JPL would push to transfer the technology when it reached the classified development stage, and Murray allowed the possibility of classified work at JPL in the future.[24] The lack of classification, however, scared off the navy, and a similar proposal to the Defense Advanced Research Projects Agency (DARPA) made managers there "nervous" because all their space-borne sensing programs were classified.[25]

The lab's primary mission in interplanetary flight projects also piqued military interest—not in the direct results, but in the technologies involved. A JPL staff paper of March 1981 listed some military spin-offs from deep-space missions. Voyager and Galileo had to survive the harsh radiation environment of Jupiter and operate for extended periods without ground support; the staff paper noted the air force's concurrent interest in reliable, autonomous spacecraft working in high-radiation environments. The VOIR spacecraft would operate an SAR and associated high-capacity data system in orbit around a distant planet, with strong applications to earth-orbit surveillance. Then there was the Halley intercept mission:

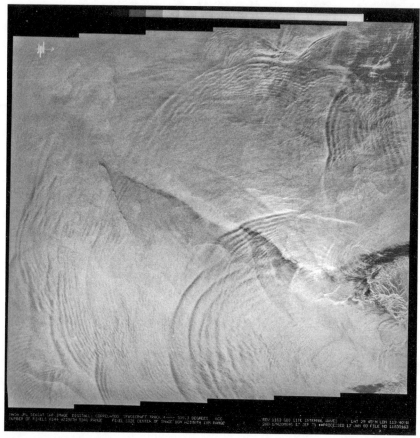

Figure 6.1. Seasat view of internal waves in the Gulf of California, 17 September 1978. These waves are associated with the twice monthly cycle of spring tides. *Source:* JPL Photolab.

the craft must find and track a fast moving, unpredictable target, Halley's comet, using on-board, autonomous closed-loop systems because there is not time for intervention from the ground (the relative speed of spacecraft and comet at encounter is nearly 60 km/sec or 130,000 mph). It must quickly maneuver and accurately point a high-precision camera system at the target. It must do this while surviving high-velocity impacts of cometary debris, maintaining autonomous on-board functions and attitude stability for high-quality imaging. These technologies have application to defense satellites which may be required to find and examine other satellites, and to protect themselves against hostile acts, such as a pellet weapon attack.[26]

The staff paper cited these spin-offs not as an argument for further defense work, but as justification for government support of deep-space missions. But as this support waned, JPL turned to the DOD to occupy the people and the technologies. The Air Force Space Division had embarked on a major upgrade in the survivability of surveillance and early-warning satellites, to reduce dependence on ground stations and the possibility of single-point failures as well as vulnerability to attack. According to Jack James, "Knowledgeable individuals in the space and defense community generally agree that the Voyager spacecraft now on their way to Saturn are an order of magnitude closer to meeting future Air Force survivability requirements than are the typical defense spacecraft now deployed."[27] In spring 1980 the Space Division's commander approached Murray and Goldberger to enlist JPL for what was called the Autonomous Spacecraft Project, conceived as the initial design phase of a seven-year, $90-million effort. The project planned to ramp up to 100 work-years by the mid-1980s; it hence fell within the 10 percent limit outlined in the NASA-Caltech MOU.[28] Murray noted that it would be the first new classified program at JPL since the 1960s: "Thus, we have crossed a threshold." But the project was small and a tight fit with the technologies of planetary missions, and so "the acceptance of this new classified task does not represent a bold new initiative with the DoD generally."[29]

The Autonomous Spacecraft Project, along with the proposals for synthetic aperture radar, indicates the inroads made by defense programs. By early 1979 JPL had thirty-five tasks under way for the Defense Department, all unclassified, totaling about $10 million in contracts — an order of magnitude increase from 1975.[30] Although a small fraction of the laboratory program, defense work had a broader impact. In 1978 Murray had identified information systems and energy conversion technology as the two main technological thrusts for JPL. In June 1981 the executive council held a special retreat on JPL's future and took autonomous systems as the primary technological focus. The following year Murray proclaimed that the lab had "the very strong unifying technological theme of autonomous systems," a shift no doubt influenced by the lab's new direction.[31]

Defense Research and Caltech

JPL's small but growing role in defense would greatly increase in the early 1980s, motivated by the moribund state of the planetary program and the redoubled military mobilization of the Reagan administration. Lab managers realized that acquiring additional defense work required more open-ended commitments to military sponsors and, in particular, two major policy changes: the acceptance of classified work and abolition of the 10 percent limit on work for outside sponsors.

After the shift from the army to NASA, JPL had jettisoned classified work: the proportion of classified lab publications dropped from 62 percent in 1958 to less than 1 percent in 1970. The orange report of 1976 had stressed that it should stay that way: "The faculty would not tolerate the conduct of classified research, civilian or military, on Campus, except in time of universally recognized national emergency. For this reason, no single issue could be more divisive and inimical to Campus-Laboratory relations than the performance of classified work at JPL."[32] The Seasat results and the Autonomous Spacecraft Project revived the issue in spring 1980.[33] The prospect of secrecy did not alarm lab managers. One report predicted little effect on the current open atmosphere, even with the assumption that classified work could involve up to 800 lab staff. More than half of JPL staff already had secret-level clearances: they had been routinely cleared through the late 1960s and these clearances did not lapse. That percentage was higher for technical staff, and it approached 90 percent for managers and supervisors; only clerical staff largely lacked clearances. The lab also already had restricted-access facilities, in order to protect fragile spacecraft, reduce safety hazards, and house old classified documents.[34]

Another aspect of classification, however, remained in the background. JPL's previous lack of classified work had made it attractive to a particular subset of aerospace engineers. Up until 1975 an admission of homosexuality was grounds for denial of clearance, and even afterwards the clearance process required a statement of sexual orientation. Checking the wrong box would set off a more thorough investigation, including questioning of colleagues and neighbors, so that acquiring a clearance in effect entailed coming out of the closet. Because of its relative lack of classified work compared to the aerospace industry, JPL had attracted a significant number of gay engineers, and these engineers had much to fear from an increase in secrecy.[35]

The Autonomous Spacecraft Project forced the issue of classification on Caltech. Goldberger recommended accepting classified work as long as it met an "important national need" and matched JPL capabilities, its general purpose was unclassified and could be made known to faculty, and it could be segregated to keep the rest of the lab accessible.[36] The faculty were not so sure and debated the issue at a special meeting on 11 June 1980. Astrophysicist Kip Thorne pronounced himself "unalterably opposed" to classified work, based on the fundamental principle of academic openness; Noel Corngold added, "I don't believe we should put our virginity on the line." Others responded with pragmatism instead of principle: the project would help both JPL and the air force and cause no great harm, so why not do it? It would keep secrecy safely distant at JPL and isolated from campus. And it seemed a better match to the technological skills of JPL staff than some of the other civil systems work: Robert Christy preferred that "JPL do first rate work for the DOD than second rate work for the DOE."[37]

The most troubling aspect for faculty was, as Murray put it, "the possibility that this could be the 'camel's nose under the tent.'"[38] As Goldberger had admitted: "It is hard to be only slightly involved with respect to defense work. Once the door is open, substantial pressures may be exerted to continue evolution over the long-term until the Laboratory might become a predominantly defense-oriented organization." He vowed to resist such pressures, but the faculty wondered whether the policy would "result in our going from 5% DOD work to 10%, 15%, and so on." The faculty did not vote on the proposal, but an informal show of hands produced no clear consensus for either side.[39]

Caltech's board of trustees approved the classified air force project later that summer. To cope with the camel's nose, Murray created a new office for defense programs to enhance their visibility. As a signal of the lab's commitment, he assigned Jack James, a primary architect of the systems engineering regime, to lead it. Schurmeier would also play a role as chair of a new subcommittee of the executive council to oversee all non-NASA programs.[40] In the fall of 1980 Goldberger created a faculty committee, chaired by Christy, to oversee classified work at JPL.[41] Caltech's approval did not assume a major influx of defense programs. On the contrary: the chair of the faculty reminded Murray that the faculty had authorized only the Autonomous Spacecraft Project, "reluctantly," as a small, short-term stopgap. Murray got the message and pledged to limit the Autonomous Spacecraft Project to 5 percent of JPL staff, and total defense work to 8 percent; he added that the Caltech-NASA MOU capped all non-NASA work at 10 percent.[42] But Murray had earlier hinted that if support for the planetary program disappeared, or if threats to national security increased, defense work could increase, to the point "of having JPL become primarily a DoD installation." If so, and if campus opposition toward defense work persisted, "there could be a genuine problem of whether JPL should continue as a Caltech laboratory."[43]

Events in 1981 tested Murray's predictions and realized faculty fears, bringing the military up to its neck inside the JPL tent. The crisis in planetary exploration coincided with the gutting of energy research; meanwhile the Reagan administration began a military buildup, including a strong space component. As an indicator of military influence on space policy, in July 1981 Reagan appointed Hans Mark as NASA's deputy administrator. Mark personified the integration of the military and civilian space programs through his directorship of Ames and his subsequent service as undersecretary and then secretary of the air force under President Carter. As undersecretary Mark by statute had directed the National Reconnaissance Office; then as secretary he initiated the creation of the Air Force Space Command. Mark's evident talents had almost brought him from Ames to JPL as a successor to Pickering. He had taken himself out of the running after visiting Pasadena; he strongly recommended that Caltech select the next director from its own senior faculty, in part because "only a man who is highly respected by the faculty at CalTech could persuade the institute to lift the restriction on classified work." And Caltech would need to remove the restriction soon. "The basic problem faced by the laboratory is that its purely NASA business will probably decline. This means that the laboratory must either be cut back or that it must find new business. . . . The major opportunities for new business lie in the Department of Defense."[44]

This opinion, expressed in 1974, guided Mark's approach to JPL when he rejoined NASA in 1981. In October, in the depths of Murray's despair over the planetary program, Mark sent a sympathetic handwritten note. He stressed his strong support of JPL as an institution, even if his policies at NASA indicated otherwise, and of Murray as its director. But he differed from Murray on "whether the popular support enjoyed by the planetary exploration program can be translated into the necessary long-term political support to assure a stable level of funding large enough to carry out what the planetary community thinks of as an adequate program. I have never believed that this could be achieved and I still do not believe that it can be done. . . . After having watched 'big science' closely in the United States for almost three decades, there is no doubt in my mind at all that national defense is the only truly *stable* source of large research and development funds." He thus endorsed Murray's pursuit of defense work for JPL.[45]

Mark had already taken steps to encourage JPL in the direction of defense. In July 1981 he and Murray began discussing ways to increase defense work, in particular the need to bypass the 10 percent limit on non-NASA, non-DOE work imposed by the Caltech-NASA MOU of 1978. Mark proposed raising the limit to 25 percent, with the restriction that the increase apply only to "DOD space program activities." Murray accepted the 25 percent limit but broadened the definition of "space program activities" to include any defense programs relevant to JPL's skills, even outside of space.[46]

Although NASA and Murray were amenable, the expansion required the approval of Goldberger, which again brought in the Caltech faculty and trustees. At a meeting in October 1981 the faculty noted with alarm Reagan's budget cuts for science and technology, especially those for NASA. The cuts revived faculty suggestions for Caltech "cutting loose from JPL" in order to reduce campus exposure to the vagaries of federal budgets. Goldberger reminded the faculty that the JPL overhead and fee provided 20 percent of the campus budget and thus stifled talk of cutting ties. But he also called a special faculty meeting for 20 October to discuss JPL's expansion of defense work.[47]

In preparation for the meeting Murray wrote a paper laying out the lab's predicament and offering three options: maintain the status quo, with limited defense work; take on defense work up to perhaps 30 percent of the lab program while remaining a NASA lab; or abandon NASA completely and become a DOD laboratory. Murray advocated the second option. "Continuation of present policies would result, at best, in JPL becoming a much less distinguished and important Laboratory, and at worst, in the actual demise of JPL." The third option "would certainly change the character of JPL itself as well as substantially diminish relations with the Campus." The second option, taking on a significant fraction of DOD work, would keep technical staff on tap while maintaining the lab's special status as a NASA center; it would satisfy the DOD's need for long-range commitments and NASA's desire to sustain flight project capabilities for the future. Classified work would increase but would still be only a fraction of the defense work, and hence a small part of the total lab program; JPL could remain an open laboratory with just a few restricted areas, and Caltech's current overview process for classified work would suffice. But, Murray added, "a fully DOD-sponsored JPL cannot be entirely excluded in the future, even by pursuing option 2," and that would face Caltech with either running a military lab or ending its association with JPL.[48]

The faculty meeting attracted close to 200 faculty members, who debated Murray's proposal for more than an hour. An informal straw vote came down about two to one in favor of Murray's preferred option, a substantial increase of defense work to 30 percent. The faculty suggested two conditions for the proposal. First, all projects should have unclassified titles: "The faculty ought to know, in general, what is going on at JPL." Second, the campus should wean itself over the next five or ten years from reliance on the JPL management fee.[49] The matter then proceeded to the trustees, who likewise engaged in a "vigorous discussion" before approving Murray's proposed option. The trustees noted that perhaps a third of the faculty strongly opposed an expansion of defense work but were consoled that "feelings were not so strong that . . . it would cause a major split between the Trustees and the faculty."[50]

Embracing the DOD

With campus approval of defense work, Murray could report to lab staff in December 1981 that "during the period since last April, and especially in the last several months, we have executed a modest but significant 'mid-course maneuver.'" The 30 percent limit allowed enough work to support key technical capabilities and convince the DOD of the lab's commitment, but it also ensured that NASA remained the dominant, responsible sponsor.[51] Murray admitted to the faculty that JPL was changing; defense work was no longer a short-term gap filler, pending a revival of planetary missions, but rather was a long-term presence within a permanently changed NASA program.[52]

The Reagan military buildup gave ample opportunity for new work, especially for space. The capabilities of reconnaissance satellites had increased dependence of intelligence and military communities on them and had also sparked an arms race in anti-satellite devices and directed-energy weapons, such as lasers, which also offered potential for ballistic missile defense.[53] Amid talk in defense circles of creating a fourth military service for space, the existing services competed to establish their roles. The air force had long viewed outer space as an extension of its domain, but the navy also staked a claim, since it relied on satellites for reconnaissance, ocean-condition sensing, and communication with its far-flung fleets.[54]

Jack James and his group pursued new customers with vigor. A gung ho marketer, James aimed to have 600 work-years committed to defense by 1983, more than a fourfold expansion from 1981.[55] The effort soon paid off in a long-term agreement signed with the Air Force Space Division in October 1981 projecting air force funding of $100–150 million per year for the next several years, supporting about 200 staff and encompassing the Autonomous Spacecraft Project and a major program called Talon Gold. An existing DARPA project managed by the air force, Talon Gold aimed to apply to ballistic missile defense the sort of expertise described for the Halley's comet mission, in a high-precision system for acquisition, tracking, and pointing of lasers or other kill mechanisms at targets traveling through space; JPL was to build a prototype system for test flights on the shuttle.[56]

JPL did not enter the military market without resistance. The aerospace industry did not welcome a new competitor. James, drumming up business at a navy symposium in October 1981, was buttonholed by representatives from TRW, Rockwell, and Westinghouse who were concerned that JPL would steal their business. James replied that "the problem is big enough for all of us."[57] The military itself also presented obstacles—in particular, mismatches between JPL's approach and the military's, or what JPL director Murray termed "substantial cultural differences" between their individual modes of R&D.[58] Many military managers had no notion of what JPL did or how it might help them, and even those who knew JPL could be frustrated in putting the lab to work. JPL's mode of performing projects differed from the military's: JPL received full responsibility for NASA projects and developed most of them in-house; the DOD contracted large projects with industry and vested responsibility for them in its own officers and civil servants. Lab staff thus either had to convince the DOD to assign it responsibility for large in-house projects or accept nonaccountable roles and smaller projects. Military sponsors also confronted JPL's bureaucracy. Defense contractors, for example, typically had thirty days to respond to requests for proposals, whereas JPL was accustomed to spending several months. James thus urged the lab to streamline the proposal review process, "to eliminate some of JPL's ponderous bureaucracy," but the old mode persisted, as JPL would learn ten years later.[59] The military also sensed that it had second priority to NASA flight projects in the allocation of staff.[60] Finally, JPL brought to defense work a reputation for accepting certain types of work and rejecting others, despite its newcomer status. The lab's selectivity, combined with its association with Caltech, conveyed "an image of arrogance and dilettantism" that turned off military officers, many of whom doubted the depth of JPL's commitment.[61]

Defense managers also faced a dilemma in marketing to the different services. Air force space programs meshed well with JPL's technological expertise and came at an acceptable classification level, but the air force was reluctant to give JPL an in-house, accountable project role. Navy programs likewise were a good technological fit, as in the synthetic aperture radar program, but they came at a higher classification level and also not in an accountable role. The army was the most interested and required mostly low or no classification; its traditional arsenal system also inclined it more toward the JPL mode of in-house work. The army had the added advantage of familiarity since senior officers and JPL staff remained from pre-NASA days under army sponsorship. But it lacked a significant role in space and offered a weaker technological fit with JPL's expertise.[62] JPL also sought a relationship with DARPA, which was getting more into demonstration projects as well as research; lab staff thought JPL could become "a principal laboratory for DARPA."[63]

JPL's first choice, the air force, failed to meet lab expectations. The Autonomous Spacecraft Project sputtered after a promising start, and Talon Gold offered only a low-level role, not project management. No other major missions had emerged to anchor a long-term program.[64] The relationship apparently foundered on the resistance of air force officers to JPL's desire to run projects itself, in-house. The air force already had the Aerospace Corporation, a dedicated outfit for technological support, although it did not build hardware. The air force also had a poor opinion of NASA thanks to the shuttle program; NASA had persuaded the military to sign on to the shuttle, but the military, particularly the air force, at the time was still waiting for the first launch and hence was regretting its support. One air force general warned JPL managers: "We have been burned in space. Be careful in identifying yourself too closely with NASA when selling to the AF."[65]

Defense marketers also failed to make inroads with the navy, whose officers, according to TRW executive Simon Ramo, formed a "closed club" and also did not want their contractors working for the air force or army.[66] JPL thus turned to the army. Instead of space research, JPL offered the army its expertise in information systems, which jibed with the current military emphasis on C³I, or command, control, communications, and intelligence—in particular, the application of computers to tactical as well as strategic problems and distribution of information to officers in the field.[67] In 1979 it had started on a project called MAFIS, for Mobile Automated Field Instrumentation System, intended to attach electronic transmitters and receivers to each soldier, vehicle, and weapon in training exercises, with information on the position and status of each unit available to commanders on graphic displays. In 1980 the army expanded the work, and JPL managers enthused that it "promises to be comparable in scope and challenge to a small flight project."[68] The next year the army added another project called SAWE, for Simulation of Area Weapons Effects, which would mimic the effects of artillery and mines in training exercises. The projects involved work in electronics, optics, information software, and systems engineering, and they gave project responsibility to the lab. And they were unclassified and hence more palatable for Caltech.[69]

By 1982 the army was providing about two-thirds of defense funding at JPL, centered around training and simulation systems and C³I, with space projects for the air force and navy providing the other third. By that time defense work engaged about 200 JPL staff, approaching 5 percent of the workforce and allowing Murray to conclude that JPL had "passed successfully last fall through the nadir point in JPL's future prospects."[70]

Implications of Defense Programs

The mobilization of JPL in the early 1980s was not instantaneous: lab managers first discussed a revival of defense work in the mid-1970s and ramped up their effort through the rest of the decade. JPL thus reflected continuity in the national mobilization, which likewise began in the Carter administration, driven by Soviet challenges for strategic parity and then their invasion of Afghanistan, before accelerating under Reagan.

The main obstacle to defense work lay not in the lab, nor in Caltech's administration or trustees, but in the Caltech faculty. To lab veterans, the new programs represented not a radical break but a reprise. Many people at

JPL remained from the days of army sponsorship, and Murray himself had worked for the air force. While perhaps 10 to 20 percent of lab staff did not themselves wish to work on military programs, only 5 percent at most opposed their presence in principle: "Most of our staff, and virtually all of our supervisors and managers, enthusiastically welcome DoD work."[71] Caltech, for its part, had a tradition of defense-oriented leaders, dating back to Robert Millikan; after Harold Brown left Caltech to become secretary of defense, the institute hired Goldberger, who had been a defense consultant since the 1950s and had helped to found the JASON group of scientific defense advisors. Caltech's trustees also provided a sympathetic forum: the subcommittee on JPL included Ramo; former Caltech president Lee Dubridge, another prominent defense advisor; and former Secretary of Defense Robert McNamara. But the support of defense work by senior administrators and managers at JPL and Caltech also suggested a generation gap, between older professors and lab staff who came of age during World War II and the early cold war, and a younger cohort that came out of the 1960s and the Vietnam War period with different attitudes toward the military. This younger group's simmering opposition to defense work would boil over in the future.

JPL managers viewed defense programs as a way to keep staff employed at the lab amid the decline in the planetary program. They thus reversed the standard cold war argument for scientists-on-tap, which sought basic research programs for government-funded labs in order to keep talented staff on hand for future defense work. At JPL, defense work would keep talented staff on tap at the lab for future diversion to civilian science missions. But defense programs at JPL had another important consequence: exposure to classified military research and development, and support for advanced technology.

S E V E N

Space Technology

JPL RESUMED DEFENSE WORK IN ORDER TO RETAIN ITS STAFF, WHICH DECLIN-
ing NASA budgets could no longer support. These people had produced a series of remarkable achievements in high-reliability spacecraft, which entailed
not only systems engineering but also the development of new technologies.
Examples of these technologies include hardware, such as charge-coupled
devices in place of vidicons, and software, such as the computer programs that
provided autonomy for Voyager. Two technologies in this period exemplify
the ingenuity and effort of JPL engineers: synthetic aperture radar and image
processing. Both relied on and helped drive advances in data processing and
thus demonstrate the increasing role of computers in opening up new fields
of scientific knowledge.

Synthetic Aperture Radar

After World War II astronomers turned the military technology of radar to
the study of the planets, using it as a way to determine their size, rotation,
orbits, and surface features. The space age offered a means to deliver radar
systems to the planets themselves, and NASA almost from its inception conceived of radar as a key component of planetary exploration.[1] In the 1970s
JPL developed a new type of radar for satellite remote sensing. Known as
synthetic aperture radar, this technology provided fresh views of Earth and
the planets.

As with a camera aperture, larger radar antennas provide higher image
resolution. Synthetic aperture radar (SAR) takes its name and operating principle from the simulation of a large antenna, or aperture, by combining observations from many points along the antenna's flight path. An SAR records

the amplitude and phase of radar echoes as a function of time, with each point on the planet's surface identified by a combination of time delay and Doppler shift. The SAR then integrates the data along the flight path to synthesize a large aperture (see figure 7.1). In effect, an SAR system substitutes software for hardware—that is, data processing for a physically large antenna.[2]

The smaller size of SARs was only one of several features that recommended them for use on satellites. Unlike real aperture radars, whose resolution is proportional to altitude, SAR resolution is independent of height and in fact varies directly with antenna size (a smaller antenna providing finer resolution). In practice, the altitude determines the antenna size required for signal transmission and acquisition, but SAR could still reduce satellite-borne radar resolution from tens of kilometers to tens of meters. Radars have the further advantage of collecting data at night and receiving pulses through clouds or through certain surface covers, such as sand or vegetation; the longer wavelengths than optical images also provide different information on the roughness and material properties of target surfaces.[3]

The ability to penetrate clouds had suggested, in particular, the use of radar on a mission to Venus, whose hazy atmosphere precluded optical observation of the surface. In 1960 JPL started a radar program with Venus in mind. A radar team under Walter E. Brown, Jr., first tested standard radars on rocket flights in conjunction with aircraft-borne radar in order to scale radar backscatter behavior with altitude. The radar team shifted to aircraft flights starting around 1970, and the detection of ocean waves by JPL's airborne SAR in 1971, as we know, led to the Seasat radar.[4] The successful tests of the SAR also earned it a central place in initial planning for the Venus Orbiting Imaging Radar mission.[5]

JPL's shift to synthetic aperture radar came at the recommendation of radar scientists at the University of Michigan. JPL did not originate SAR; the concept dated back to the end of World War II, when the military began sponsoring highly classified programs. By the 1960s commercial geological survey were using airborne SAR systems, and reconnaissance aircraft no doubt were as well.[6] JPL's contributions came not in inventing a new technology, but through innovative use of existing technology. The lab departed from current practice first by using longer wavelengths, around 23 centimeters instead of the military's 3-centimeter wavelengths. Unlike the military programs, which wanted the highest possible resolution (and hence smaller antennas and short wavelengths), JPL sought resolution sufficient for scientific purposes, balanced with other mission requirements. In particular, the dense atmosphere of Venus threatened to attenuate shorter wavelengths; at the same time, at longer wavelengths the little-understood Venusian magnetic field might affect signal polarization. So Brown's team settled on an intermediate

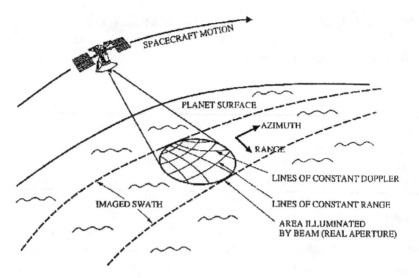

Figure 7.1. A synthetic aperture radar combines information on range and Doppler shift to improve resolution in the azimuth or along-track direction. *Source:* Magellan fact sheet, April 1989 (JPL 198, 3/26).

wavelength of 30 centimeters, later shortening it to 23 centimeters when they encountered interference from military aircraft radars.[7]

Seasat's radar resolution of 25 meters would not have excited military interests in advance, but the JPL program more than compensated in other ways. The longer wavelength proved crucial to detecting ocean waves and hence justifying Seasat: higher-resolution systems had been picking up short-wavelength capillary waves on the ocean surface that obscured long-wavelength swells, whereas the JPL radar just saw the swells. The opportunity to map direction and wavelength of wave patterns had piqued ocean-ographers' interest, and the longer wavelength also more easily mapped the internal waves that enabled submarine detection. As the first outfit to try putting an SAR on a satellite, JPL had also to adapt the system to the space environment, including vacuum, low temperatures, and especially vibration. Existing airborne SARs were generally mounted on elastic shock absorbers, but JPL's radar group instead built components rugged enough to handle the vibration of launch and spaceflight. Active radar systems also needed power that passive cameras did not; hence the need for the large solar arrays on Seasat, which would prove its undoing.[8]

Transferring radars from airplanes to satellites likewise entailed a shift from recording data onboard to transmitting it. That was no easy feat. Syn-thesizing a large aperture imposed formidable demands in data processing — not only in the integration of radar returns along the flight path, but also in accounting for phase shifts (as the distance changed to each point with the spacecraft motion), planet curvature and rotation, spacecraft attitude drift, atmospheric distortion, and a host of other variables. The SAR data from Seasat emerged at the rate of 111 megabits per second, requiring real-time transmission to Earth instead of onboard processing or recording. On the ground it took an entire day to process about five minutes' worth of data, covering about 200,000 square kilometers; lab staff predicted that at that rate it would take them seventy-five years to process all the images if Seasat worked for three years as planned.[9]

As it turned out there were only three months of data to worry about, though even that taxed JPL's capability. The lab had initially pursued an all-digital data system for the Seasat SAR, with an onboard processor and digital downlinks and recorders at the ground stations, but technical obstacles and escalating costs shelved the digital system in favor of an existing analog alternative.[10] The radar team thence had to reduce the data on the ground with an optical correlator, in which the radar signal patterns, recorded on film, formed a Fresnel lens; together with corrective optics in the correlator, the lens focused light to reproduce each radar image of the surface (a bit like the production of a hologram). The optical correlator proved a bottleneck in the Seasat data flow, greatly slowing the processing of SAR images and spurring subsequent attempts to develop digital SAR processors.[11]

The Seasat SAR signaled the increasing centrality of data processing to mission success. The flood of data threatened to swamp scientists. How to select particular bits of information from this incessant stream? How to convert downlinked telemetry to user-friendly data formats? To solve these problems NASA and JPL established the Seasat Data Utilization Project, which converted raw telemetry to scientific data, correlated this with location data, and developed algorithms to extract geophysical information, such as wind or wave patterns. One NASA manager called it "the least glamorous project ongoing at JPL" but at the same time recognized its crucial role in converting and distributing the data, and thus in changing perceptions of Seasat from failure to success.[12] Seasat thus demonstrated that space-based SAR could overcome the limited spatial and temporal coverage of airborne radars and provide synoptic, repetitive observations.[13] Even before Seasat, JPL managers recognized the programmatic potential for earth and ocean science as well as planetary exploration.[14] Venus mission planning continued to include an SAR, and JPL also parlayed the radar into a series of flights on the space shuttle, known as the Shuttle Imaging Radar (SIR). The first of these, SIR-A, flew on the second shuttle flight, in November 1981, and returned images of 10 million square kilometers, about 2 percent of Earth's surface.[15]

SIR-A confirmed the utility of SAR for both geology and oceanography and provided surprising uses in archeology and anthropology. Airborne SAR flights by JPL in 1977 and 1978 had revealed a system of canals buried under vegetation in Guatemalan rain forests; archeologists attributed the canals to ancient Mayan civilization and concluded that population pressure forced the Maya to develop intensive agriculture instead of primitive slash-and-burn farming.[16] SIR-A images of the deep Sahara Desert then revealed prehistoric river channels buried under two meters of sand; the very dry, fine-grained sand of the region proved transparent to radar. The images sent JPL radar scientist Charles Elachi and geologist Ronald Blom on an expedition to Egypt with other geologists and archeologists, where they verified that major rivers had traversed the area in the Tertiary period, carving valleys through a now-featureless landscape in which rain falls at thirty- to fifty-year intervals. The expedition confirmed as well that early human settlements had congregated near these river systems.[17]

A subsequent flight, SIR-B in 1984, was hampered by antenna and electrical problems and met only 40 percent of its goals, though it did prove the technique of stereo imaging and onboard digital processing.[18] The SIR series would continue in the 1990s, after an interruption by the Challenger disaster, and the similarly delayed Venus mission would fly with an SAR as Magellan in 1992. Synthetic aperture radar thus provided programmatic continuity through three decades. It had other implications as well. As with Voyager's flight computer, the complexity of the technology outran its developers. Tony Spear, the Seasat SAR manager, noted before launch that despite pre-flight testing, "we will fly Seasat-A SAR not completely understanding its performance." Spear added, "Some sensors now and some future sensors . . . are as complicated as whole, earlier spacecraft."[19]

Image Processing

SAR proved a particular harbinger in its reliance on data processing, which would become ever more crucial as digital components and data rates multiplied in spacecraft instruments. In 1976 Al Hibbs warned of a "data avalanche" facing JPL and the space program. "Modern electronics has placed at our disposal, quite suddenly and to the surprise of many, an enormously increased power of communication and computation." JPL engineers previously assumed that if the spacecraft and DSN worked properly, the mission would succeed, in that it would return scientific data. "This may no longer be true. The spacecraft can work perfectly, the data can be returned to earth and successfully processed and filed—and yet fall far below its potential usefulness because our information management techniques are inadequate."[20] Nuggets of important scientific information could be buried in the accumulated mountains of data. NASA's "Outlook for Space" study of 1976 had identified data management as a pressing need, and the next year Murray chose information systems as one of two main technological themes for JPL, alongside energy conversion.[21]

Hibbs identified image processing as a particular example of information systems and as a key asset of JPL. Image processing, Hibbs observed, involved much more than just cameras and was more properly viewed as an information system, encompassing selection of features for photographs, onboard processing, telemetry and data compression, and ground-based analysis.[22] The interpretation of images is not a straightforward task: pictures do not necessarily convey understanding by themselves; rather, researchers manipulate and analyze them to reveal particular sorts of information. From Galileo's sketches of the moon to photos of elementary-particle tracks in bubble chambers, the parsing of pictures has entailed decisions about which features to emphasize and which to ignore, and it has thus determined what people would see.[23]

As with the radar program, JPL's effort in image processing evolved in the 1960s. Processing data from space-borne camera experiments took two stages, one before launch, one after. All JPL spacecraft before the Galileo mission used cameras called vidicons to capture images. In a vidicon, light falls on a photoconductive surface, which builds up an electric charge proportional to the light received at each point. An electron beam then scans the charge-density pattern to record the image. In practice a vidicon required careful calibration on the ground: first, to correct for photometric distortion caused by uneven response in different portions of the photoconductor; second, to correct geometric distortion caused by warping of the electron beams, for instance, owing to external electric fields; and last, to remove residual images on the photoconductor.[24]

The second stage involved processing of images returned from the spacecraft. Images came to Earth in streams of telemetry, for the early missions as analog waves, later as digital bits. Processing required first extracting imagery data from the telemetry, relating it to cartographic coordinates, and, for analog signals, digitizing it. The digital data were then arrayed in a two-dimensional grid and translated to a gray-scale image, based on the intensity ascribed to each pixel. The first Ranger pictures proved too fuzzy to see craters, let alone finer features. Robert Nathan, a Caltech PhD who had worked with pattern recognition in crystallography, began cleaning them up. At first he focused on correcting distortions and removing signal noise, such as a particular frequency superimposed on an image by vibration of the camera. (Applying a Fourier transform from spatial to frequency variables revealed a bright spot for noise at particular frequencies; wiping out the spot and transforming back produced a clean image.) He then thought to use similar digital filters to enhance images in general: for instance, to average the contrast in local areas around each image point, subtract the averaged pattern, and then stretch the remainder, which had the cumulative effect of sharpening the overall picture. Nathan produced the first computer-enhanced images from Ranger 7 in 1964 and similarly enhanced the low-contrast, featureless images returned later that year by Mariner 4, and he proceeded to evolve ever more sophisticated techniques over the decade for Surveyor and Mariner flights (see figure 7.2).[25]

By the mid-1970s what was known as the Image Processing Laboratory at JPL had more than 50 staff and a library of software and image processing algorithms, all developed in-house. Since the reconnaissance community was just switching from satellite film drops to real-time digital telemetry, JPL had perhaps the most advanced digital image-processing capability in the country at the time. The software included routines for contrast enhancement, cartographic projection, constructing mosaics, motion compensation, foreshortening and topographic corrections, and full-color composition from black-and-white cameras and single-color filters.[26] The resultant high-resolution pictures enabled many of the image-driven scientific advances from robotic spacecraft—for example, composing the rich color pictures from Jupiter and Saturn on Voyager as well as revealing the fine detail in their atmospheres and satellites, including the volcanoes on Io and Saturn's rings.

The Image Processing Lab also provided a key resource for JPL's public relations program. Image processing removed unsightly distractions, such as reticles or blank patches, and created color photos, in some cases expressly to wow the public.[27] Public relations also encouraged the creation of motion pictures, especially the need for dynamic film clips instead of static images for television news. JPL staff first combined still photos from Ranger and Mariner to produce motion pictures; in 1987 Kevin Hussey, Bob Mortensen, and Jeff Hall projected topographic elevation data from Landsat to simulate the three-dimensional view from an aircraft swooping through the Los Angeles basin, in a video titled "LA, the Movie."[28] More elaborate simulated flights over Venus and Mars would be produced using data from Magellan and Mars Global Surveyor in the 1990s.

JPL did not necessarily invent digital image processing. It drew on earlier work in pattern recognition (such as Nathan's) as well as digital computing, and digital pictures themselves had been around since newspapers digitized photos for telegraph transmission in the 1920s.[29] What JPL engineers did was to realize the possibilities and by example spark subsequent applications far afield from space science. Several of these successive efforts acknowledged the inspiration provided by JPL, including a review article of 1977 in *Computer*

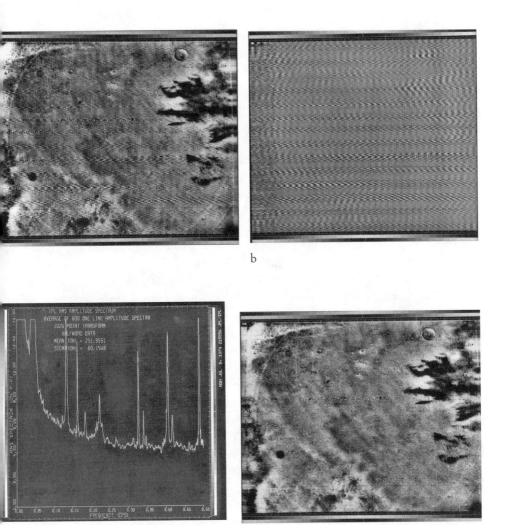

b

d

Figure 7.2. Image processing by Fourier transform. The first is the original image of the cratered surface of Mars, taken by Mariner 9. Second is the interference pattern superimposed from the coincident transmission of spectrometer data. Third is the Fourier transform showing the frequency peaks of the noise pattern. Fourth is the final image, with coherent noise suppressed. *Source:* JPL Image Processing Lab.

magazine that called the Ranger images "essentially the beginning of digital image processing technology."[30] Proliferating textbooks and special journal issues in the 1970s, including several standard texts and review articles by JPL engineers, helped to spread the techniques.[31]

JPL's image processing attracted the interest of industry. NASA in the 1970s made JPL software available through its licensing program, but the scarcity of specialized hardware and documentation initially limited the market until the emergence of higher-performance work stations and graphics accelerators starting in the 1980s.[32] A more direct approach was the recruiting of JPL staff by industry, including William Green, head of the Image Processing Lab in the late 1970s. JPL staff also formed their own spin-off companies, although criticism about capitalizing on government-funded work soon stifled these endeavors.[33] The availability of JPL software, people, and publications helped to catalyze a commercial software industry for image processing starting in the mid 1970s, and two decades later desktop packages, such as Photoshop, were deploying many of the techniques—contrast enhancement, image stretching, color corrections, and so on—developed at JPL.

The nearby movie business also drew on JPL's work. Although James Blinn was not a part of the Image Processing Lab, his computer animations for Voyager and the "Cosmos" series shared some of its methods, such as reconstructing viewing geometries and surface reflectance.[34] Blinn had been recruited to the lab by his mentor Ivan Sutherland, now at Caltech, and he was making a name as a guru of computer graphics. As Sutherland, himself no slouch, would say, "There are only a dozen great people in computer graphics, and Jim Blinn is six of them." Blinn's work attracted offers from movie studios, and he accepted one in 1980 from George Lucas to help establish a special-effects studio for the "Star Wars" sequels.[35] The image-processing group soon formed its own data visualization section, including the group that would produce "LA, the Movie"; among their tools was the sort of three-dimensional volume rendering used by Blinn and later embraced by movies and video games. Kevin Hussey would similarly leave this group for Disney in the mid-1990s.[36] By that time JPL had a separate Digital Image Animation Laboratory, funded mostly from outside NASA, with IMAX its largest sponsor.[37]

In November 1976 Caltech and JPL convened a conference on image processing to spread the work to a wider audience. Nearly 400 people attended—from academia, government agencies, and industry—to hear about its potential in such fields as geology, oceanography, astronomy, and biomedicine.[38] Researchers in these fields were beginning to realize the possibilities: Nathan had shifted entirely to biomedical research, in particular image processing for X-rays and microscopy, and in 1979 Green created an astronomy image-processing group alongside the existing planetary group.[39] Image processing found application even further afield—for fingerprint analysis in law enforcement, to interpret photos of the Loch Ness monster, and, most famously, to analyze the Shroud of Turin.[40]

The new digital techniques met some resistance. Although planetary geologists had some prior experience with ground-based astronomical photography, their field for the most part matured with digital imaging in the 1960s. To radiologists and astronomers, however, digital techniques meant a departure from accepted practice. As Green put it, "they knew and trusted their film." Radiologists resisted the digitizing of their X-rays through sampling since that meant an initial loss of information. Likewise, astronomers accustomed to peering at photographic plates adapted uneasily to scanning and scaling pixels on a graphics workstation.[41]

Image processing merged with synthetic aperture radar in yet another archeological find: the lost city of Ubar. A main city of the 'Ad people of antiquity, on the edge of the vast Rab' al-Khali desert of central Arabia (in today's Oman), Ubar flourished from about 300 BC to AD 300. The 'Ad people prospered from the harvest of frankincense from groves in the Dhofar Mountains; Ubar sat on the trading route north to Mesopotamia, Egypt, Israel, Greece, and Rome. The people of Ubar perhaps prospered too much. According to legend, the prophet Hud warned them about their decadent ways; when they failed to heed the warning, the city bore God's wrath and sank beneath the sands.[42]

In 1982 the documentary filmmaker Nicholas Clapp was investigating the legend of Ubar. Recalling press accounts of the radar-detected Mayan ruins, he contacted JPL and ended up talking to Blom, the geologist who had helped unearth the ancient Saharan riverbeds. Blom then brought in Elachi, who agreed to make Ubar a target of the SIR-B radar in 1984. The SIR-B glitches scuttled the plan, but Bob Crippen in the Image Processing Lab then ran images from Landsat 5 and the French SPOT satellite through a gamut of filters and wavelength shifts. The manipulated images eliminated modern tracks through the desert, leaving only a wide compressed track left by centuries of camel hoofprints. Blom and later Elachi joined Klapp and a team of archeologists on an expedition in Oman, where they traced the paths back to likely sites. Using a portable radar, they located a well shaft buried in sand in a sinkhole—the very pit, it turned out, that had swallowed the ancient city of Ubar sometime around AD 300–500 and had thus spawned the stories of its calamitous end.[43]

Technology and the Relation between
Civil and Military Space Programs

Despite these achievements, technology development in general at JPL was in decline in the late 1970s. The focus on big flight projects could stifle advanced technology both by demanding absolute reliability and by monopolizing resources—people and facilities—within the lab. Small technology projects offered little job security or upward mobility to technical staff and had low priority for computing time or machine shop orders.[44] Caltech engineering professor Fred Culick perceived more generally that technology development—what he called engineering research or applied science—fell between the cracks at JPL: "It is not 'engineering' if by that one means design and development of working hardware (other than experimental apparatus); and it is not 'science' if by that one means studies carried out primarily for their intrinsic value." Culick wondered whether the lab was neglecting such long-term technology research.[45]

The trend was wider than JPL. At a time when "technology utilization" was a priority, NASA concentrated on the application of existing technology instead of development of new technology—or, on short-term payoffs instead of long-term investments.[46] In 1982 Noel Hinners, director of Goddard, perceived "widespread agreement . . . that NASA has lost its technology zip." Hinners attributed NASA's conservatism to tight budgets that encouraged the use of reliable, proven technologies for space flight.[47] Technology development also lacked a clear home within NASA. The Office of Aeronautics and Space Technology (OAST) had nominal responsibility, but other offices often supported technological R&D within their missions, such as that provided for flight projects by the Office of Space Science. As a result each office could hope another one would pick up the funding for particular technologies. The arrangement also required an office to support flight testing of new technology. The Office of Space Science did not want to pay for technology research; OAST meanwhile wanted to spend its money on cutting-edge development, not flight-testing.[48] Finally, OAST gave half of its name, and much more support, to aeronautics, such as advanced helicopters and hypersonic aircraft. For example, aeronautics got two to three times the funding of space technology within the OAST budget in 1977 and 1978. And for space technology, the office emphasized the space shuttle, not planetary missions: the entire space technology budget in 1978 was dedicated to shuttle experiments.[49]

The neglect of technological R&D stemmed in part from the presence of the aerospace industry. Aerospace firms lobbied Congress and NASA to shift work from government labs to industry contracts; in propulsion, for instance, its eponymous specialty, JPL relinquished R&D to industry in the mid-1970s.[50] To take another example, JPL failed to win long-term support of the synthetic aperture radar program because of bickering over the role of industry.[51] Even unproven technologies, however, lacked support. In propulsion, for instance, NASA furled the solar sail and then unplugged the ion drive; the agency meanwhile rejected JPL's proposals in 1977 for nuclear-electric systems based on thermionics technology, leaving no alternatives to the standard chemically propelled rockets.[52] Even the most successful programs could struggle for support. Both SAR and image processing built on work from the 1960s; Murray complained in 1979 that the radar program lacked "adequate support for new innovative efforts," and the next year image-processing managers warned that an absence of long-term support threatened them with "obsolescence."[53]

But here was another motivation for defense work. JPL engineers and managers were not just pursuing defense programs for funding, but also for the technologies they supported. At the time lab staff shared a perception that the military represented the cutting edge of certain space technologies, especially in such critical areas as advanced sensors.[54] Some of the most advanced military technologies, however, were classified. The question thus arises whether people at JPL knew what was going on in so-called black or secret programs, which were developing technologies very similar to those used at JPL. Did the lab suffer from lack of contact with classified work? Was the government paying JPL engineers to reinvent wheels already developed by the military? There is substantial evidence that people at JPL and elsewhere perceived a disconnect between civil and military space programs in this period. The orange report of 1976 recognized "that in refraining from classified work, JPL will not have automatic access to or be able to work at the forefront of some new technologies which would benefit its primary missions."[55] Two years later Murray advised Caltech faculty that JPL paid a price for denying classified work: "In certain areas of satellite technology we are blind and it is possible that in the future our desire to avoid secret work may conflict with our equally valid desire to be the best in the business."[56]

Synthetic aperture radar was a prime example. In 1977 Murray wondered whether JPL was unwittingly duplicating secret military work on radar technology, including synthetic aperture radar. "We at JPL have little appreciation of similar or parallel technical developments which might be under way other than under NASA sponsorship. Hence, it is difficult for JPL to benefit effectively from or contribute to the total national space radar effort. More serious, I have little basis upon which to anticipate (and perhaps avoid) potential national security issues which conceivably could be encountered in an aggressive but 'blind' technology development and utilization program."[57] The following year Murray and NASA managers noted a concern that JPL could find itself "laundering" classified radar information.[58] Outsiders shared a sense of a disconnect. A visitor from TRW in 1978 asked if JPL engineers were giving "adequate consideration . . . to what has already been accomplished, or is planned for the near future, by the military in this area."[59] Four years later, another visitor from Hughes spoke of "a great gap" between open and black radar programs, and Harold Brown advised that JPL needed to be aware of similar work, "some highly classified," under the air force.[60]

Similarly, William Green confessed that JPL's image-processing staff could not tell whether they were lagging reconnaissance programs, which were then switching from analog to digital imaging: "that was always something we wondered about at JPL. Who was ahead? And we could never figure it out, because they wouldn't tell us."[61] Hence, in an early discussion of classified work with Caltech faculty, Murray submitted that the lab could not keep up with the technological state of the art in some fields without access to classified information, what he called "a secondary consideration" for undertaking defense work.[62]

The issue was not new. JPL in the late 1950s had unknowingly replicated the secret Agena missile program of the air force. After NASA cancelled the parallel JPL program, JPL engineers struggled to get crucial information on the Agena rocket past security barriers in order to build Ranger.[63] Twenty years later an electrical short in the slip ring on an Agena killed Seasat. A review board attributed the failure in part to the fact that "the heritage/pedigree of inherited military systems (i.e., launch vehicles, encrypting systems, etc.) cannot be as well known to NASA as is NASA's own hardware." Bruce Murray was more blunt: "What was supposed to be a flight qualified part was not. But because of the classification within Lockheed, the project manager from the Air Force side wasn't talking to the project manager from Seasat."[64]

The issue was also not limited to JPL, but rather affected the entire American space program. There is a common, perhaps apocryphal story about aerospace engineers having lunch in a company cafeteria: some of them, working on an unclassified civilian project, start talking about a particular problem they cannot fix, and their colleagues in secret military programs just sit there smirking.[65] More concretely, astronomers who worked on the Large Space Telescope complained that engineers from black programs handicapped the telescope by not sharing crucial information obtained building reconnaissance satellites. NASA manager Charles Pellerin claimed that the telescope's engineers suffered from "a fear of the black world mystique" and encountered statements like, "Well, we'd like to show you how this works, but you really don't have the clearances, and so you have to take my word for it."[66]

The space telescope, however, capitalized extensively on classified programs. NASA chose two of the main contractors, Lockheed and Perkin-Elmer, based on their work in reconnaissance satellites, which would now aim their cameras at the stars instead of Earth.[67] JPL likewise was not entirely cut off from the classified world. Some fields, such as chemical propulsion and lasers, kept in touch with military developments through classified literature and conferences.[68] Other programs benefited from indirect connections. Voyager, for example, capitalized on military space programs in two ways: first, in hardening electronics to survive the radiation environment at Jupiter, since American electronics manufacturers had experience designing components that could survive radiation from nuclear weapons; second, in its radioisotope power sources, which were available because the air force had wanted them for a classified communication satellite.[69]

A substantial traffic in people also crossed the classified border. The top-secret Vista Lab continued to employ a number of JPL staff as consultants, and a number of JPL staff came and went from defense contractors and agencies: for example, Bill Green came to the Image Processing Lab from an industry job analyzing reconnaissance images, and after a decade at JPL he returned to similar work in industry; several engineers, including James Burke, Clifford Cummings, and Philip Eckman, went from JPL to the CIA and back.[70] Murray himself had enjoyed, as he put it, "a window on the dark side of space" as a consultant for the Rand Corporation in the 1960s and as a member of defense advisory committees while he was director of JPL.[71] Murray helped bring into the planetary program Merton Davies from Rand, a pioneer in reconnaissance imaging who contributed his experience to missions from Mariner to Voyager.[72] At the NASA level, in addition to such people as Hans Mark, there were managers at lower levels like Dan Herman, who joined NASA's planetary program office in 1970 from Northrup, where he worked on SARs for the navy; at NASA Herman became a prime mover of the Venus radar mission.[73]

Whatever isolation from classified programs existed did not necessarily hurt the lab. JPL engineers generally preferred using technologies they had developed themselves, a common aversion to external R&D known as not-invented-here. So they may in fact have wanted to reinvent the wheel.[74] And when they did, their wheels worked: for example, the resolution of cameras on Mariner 10 in 1973 compared favorably with that of American spy satellites at the time.[75] And sometimes, as in the case of synthetic aperture radar, JPL engineers perhaps benefited from lack of contact, by pursuing a different approach, which then enabled important scientific results—and unexpected military payoffs. Furthermore, we may attribute some of the duplication and lack of communication not so much to secrecy but rather to mundane tendencies of rival bureaucracies. One might see similar disconnects among the various military services or between civilian agencies with overlapping missions.[76] Finally, any disconnects between the open and black worlds were bridged by JPL's entry into the classified community, as it joined the remilitarization of space. Subsequent support from and access to defense technology programs would indeed prove crucial for the future of JPL and planetary exploration.

But first the lab faced a transition to a new director following Murray's resignation in April 1982. The battles of 1981 took their toll. In April 1982, in his annual state of the lab address, Murray dropped a bombshell: he was retiring after six years as director. When appointed as a forty-four-year-old, he conceivably could have, like Pickering, provided twenty years of stability. But the trend for large government labs was for shorter-term directors; Harold Brown had called Pickering "the last of a breed of 20-year lab directors."[77] Murray maintained that he had taken the job assuming a five-to-ten-year term and was stepping down at a natural transition point. He was careful not to leave the impression that "'Murray has given up on the future of JPL and so he is bailing out'"; instead he claimed victory, having guided the lab through the crisis and hence ensuring security for a successor.[78] But Murray perhaps also recognized that he had burned too many bridges in the battle to save the lab. His energy and enthusiasm, attributes that helped win him the job, proved his undoing. By antagonizing NASA managers and some of his own staff with his missionary zeal, Murray diminished his effectiveness as director and hastened his departure.

PART II

Restoration

The Allen Years, 1982–1991

The Rise and Decline of Defense Programs

MURRAY'S SUCCESSOR AS DIRECTOR OF JPL WOULD NOT HAVE TO WORRY ABOUT ignorance of classified work. In July 1982 Caltech named Lew Allen as director, effective October 15 (deputy director Charles Terhune served as acting director from July to October). A native small-town Texan, Allen had graduated from West Point in 1946 and served in the Strategic Air Command. He then obtained a PhD in nuclear physics at Illinois in 1954, under a new air force program aiming to produce technically trained officers. Allen's career rewarded the investment. After stints working on nuclear weapons design and effects for the air force, in 1961 Allen joined the defense research and engineering office of the DOD, where he focused on space technology. His subsequent exposure to the reconnaissance satellite program led to his appointment in 1973 as deputy director of the CIA and soon thereafter as head of the National Security Agency. After four years Allen returned to the air force as a four-star general, and in 1978 he was named air force chief of staff, a position he held until his retirement in June 1982. The unprecedented appointment of a scientist and space expert as air force chief, instead of the traditional commander of combat pilots, indicates the military's reorientation toward space in this period.[1]

Allen's retirement from the air force coincided with Murray's from JPL, and his long acquaintance with Harold Brown and Murph Goldberger through defense work brought him to the attention of Caltech. Allen's appointment signaled a shift in style from Murray's leadership. The mercurial Murray often seemed to manage by the seat of his pants, and he did not shy away from rocking the boat. Allen, by contrast, brought a methodical managerial approach and a taciturn, buttoned-down personality—a "steady hand" to Murray's perpetual crisis mode and embrace of change. Like Murray,

Allen was very much attuned to the political context, as his experience in Washington attested, but he preferred quiet negotiations to public campaigns and political lobbying. Indeed, his neglect of public appearances would cost JPL. Allen similarly shunned the visionary approach, although he too could demonstrate enthusiasm for far-out projects and for space science itself; his evident interest in science and technology would win over lab staff and Caltech faculty. Finally, Allen was not so straitlaced as his image suggested: an occasional twinkle in his eye betrayed an understated sense of humor, and he liked to skydive and fly hot-air balloons in his spare time.[2]

Above all, whereas Murray generated enthusiasm and imagination, Allen commanded respect. Within higher circles in the military and aerospace communities, Allen enjoyed a reputation for probity and keen intelligence, and Caltech was quick to capitalize on his availability.[3] When he was first named, however, Allen's military background was his most conspicuous trait. Caltech president Goldberger and Allen were sensitive to perceptions that the institute selected him as a former general whose connections could bring in defense work. Allen stressed that his main interest would be planetary exploration, not defense, and he and Goldberger agreed that he would use the title "Dr." instead of "General." To those who asked, as did several local and national publications, why a military man was chosen to lead the civilian space science lab, Bruce Murray replied that, on the contrary, military experience would help the director judge what the lab should and should not do: "Allen will be a very good buttress against the people who might want to push JPL further into DOD work than it should go."[4]

Allen did bring deep experience with military space missions and technology, which would prove useful for JPL's growing participation in military programs. But the importance of the military as a stopgap sponsor decreased, owing to NASA's revitalization of the planetary program early in his tenure. Allen thus presided over a remarkable turnaround, from the pessimism of Black September 1981 to optimism by early 1983, and his main problem became not generating business, but finding people and facilities to handle all the work. The military, however, would continue to provide important support for advanced technology research at JPL, with long-term consequences for the planetary program.

Star Wars

When Allen came on board JPL had already undertaken two major projects for the air force: Autonomous Spacecraft and Talon Gold, for acquisition, tracking, and pointing. In late 1982 they combined for about one-third of defense work, but the different institutional approaches and "cultural problems," as Allen called them and which Murray had identified, continued to hinder relations with the air force.[5] Projects like Talon Gold, which related to missile defense, soon received a tremendous boost. Ballistic missile defense attracted increasing attention in the late 1970s, and then in March 1983 President Reagan called for a crash program, what would be named the Strategic Defense Initiative (SDI), more popularly known as Star Wars.[6]

In February 1984 DARPA, the primary sponsor of Talon Gold, decided that for SDI projects the NASA mode of "one of a kind" missions was more appropriate than the air force's aim of operational weapons systems. DARPA thus asked JPL to take an expanded role not only in Talon Gold but in the two associated aspects of the "Triad" laser project: Alpha, for a high-power, ground-based laser, and LODE (Large Optics Demonstration Experiment), for an advanced electro-optical system in orbit with a four-meter mirror. Although JPL had maintained small research programs on lasers since the 1960s, it declined to take over Alpha because it involved "devices used for destructive purposes" and the design of actual weapons systems. The optics part, LODE, was more tempting because of its relevance to astronomy. Although the lab declined that specific job in the end, it did undertake a similar project for the SDI program office two years later. Called the Space Relay Experiment, this project involved an orbital mirror and optics system to relay a laser beam from one ground station to another.[7]

The acquisition-tracking-pointing work under Talon Gold meanwhile led to a new project, also under the SDI office, in early 1985, which would soon be dubbed Pathfinder (not to be confused with the later Mars Pathfinder, a civilian planetary mission).[8] The SDI Pathfinder experiment, a complex array of instruments to fly on the space shuttle, aimed to observe the booster plumes of ascending missiles in infrared, visible, and ultraviolet wavelengths and then to continue tracking the missile with strict pointing stability at high slew rates. In particular, JPL was pushing ultraviolet observations, based on its experience with CCDs, against the military's preference at the time for infrared detectors, which required complex cryogenics.[9] Pathfinder initially involved a $100-million effort; the detectors would come from contractors, but JPL would build the precision pointer in-house, since it related to work underway on the Mariner Mark II planetary spacecraft. The experiment was slated for a shuttle flight in late 1987, but the Challenger shuttle explosion in January 1986 delayed plans and the Pathfinder apparently never flew. It did, however, occupy up to 70 staff for about two years, and the acquisition-tracking-pointing work in general had sustained similar levels since 1981. JPL did fly an ultraviolet detector on SDI's later Delta experiments, although its engineers never overcame the military's attachment to infrared detection.[10]

JPL's work suggests a corrective to popular perceptions of Star Wars, which commonly focus on exotic beam weapons, such as nuclear-pumped X-ray lasers. Most of the initiative focused on less dramatic technologies, especially sensors and mechanisms for automatic acquisition and tracking, instead of the destruction phase. As James Fletcher, chair of the SDI Defensive Technologies committee, testified in Congress in March 1984: "The popular press has emphasized the exotic nature of certain technologies included in our study. . . . I feel compelled to set the record straight on this illusion. Our recommended program does not concentrate on so-called 'Star Wars' weapons. The directed energy area, which I suppose has elicited the most attention, is less than a fourth of the program. The largest portion of the recommended effort is to develop effective surveillance, acquisition, tracking, and assessment sensor systems."[11] The SDI budget would consistently stress sensors over directed-energy research in ensuing years.[12]

The popular attention to beam weapons, combined with the public advocacy of Edward Teller and his protégé Lowell Wood, has resulted in a focus on Livermore as the main SDI laboratory, which neglects the much broader permeation of American scientific institutions by Star Wars research. JPL not only worked on the key technologies but also helped define the parameters of SDI itself, by participating in the SDI Pilot Architecture Study from 1984 to 1985. Jack James, Ronald Boain, and Clifford Cummings of JPL worked on the study, and Schurmeier served on its executive review panel.[13]

Star Wars, however, also rekindled debate over the propriety of defense work. For some engineers and scientists at JPL, the absence of defense work had been a prime attraction of employment—the chance, as one put it, "to go home and tell their kids what they do for a living."[14] The increasing military presence had already begun undermining this attraction; in May 1982 Allan Klumpp and 40 other lab staff denounced the "creeping militarism" of JPL in a letter to the *Los Angeles Times*.[15] Star Wars spurred broader considerations. In 1985 lab employee Paul Weissman, in a letter to Allen, criticized several consequences of defense work, including moral and political implications. Star Wars projects seemed to go beyond research into development of weapons systems. The cost and difficulty of the SDI concept and its strategic implications furthermore suggested that JPL refuse to work on it: "Are we not treading on . . . dangerous ground in pursuing SDI, a program that has been heatedly debated around the nation as unworkable, unaffordable, and destabilizing to the nuclear arms race?"[16]

Caltech faculty likewise raised wider objections to SDI research. A group of professors and students organized a "Committee against Space Weapons" that sought to circulate protest petitions and organize critical forums on campus and at the lab. The initial round of protests in the summer of 1984 forced JPL to take a stand on political activity. Since JPL was not a civil service lab, NASA allowed political activity by lab staff.[17] But since JPL was government property, Allen decided that lab facilities could not be used "for the advocacy of any particular political or social issue or cause," as he put it to one of the organizers, ruling out petitions or any sort of gathering.[18] Although some JPL staff spoke out against defense work and Star Wars, the protests seemed to gain more traction on campus. A petition drive in 1985 netted 500 signatures on campus, including those of 6 Nobel laureates. The previous summer, after Goldberger allowed the group to organize as long as they disavowed official association with Caltech, senior lab managers Schurmeier and Robert Parks criticized the politicization of campus. Parks wrote Goldberger, "Our impression [at JPL] is you are leaning over backwards to be as lenient as possible and we would tend to be slightly less lenient."[19]

The proposals to expand Talon Gold in early 1984 renewed campus attention to JPL programs. A series of faculty meetings debated not just the effects of classified defense work, but also whether Caltech should consider moral and political objections.[20] At a meeting on 6 June, professor Barclay Kamb, identifying a "moral issue," declared, *the United States is making a grave error in entering into star wars*" and asked "whether the Institute should support the nation in error through work at JPL." Goldberger sought to leave aside such concerns, despite his personal opposition to SDI on technical and strategic grounds: "Private disagreement of any part of the Caltech community with the President's aspirations for the SDI . . . is not a proper basis for Caltech to make a decision as to whether to undertake the proposed work."[21]

Goldberger continued to suggest that politicians defined national policy, which citizens then followed; the role of Caltech lay not in "a dramatic gesture" of disobedience, but rather in public education to induce changes in policy. Faculty, however, persisted in criticizing SDI as "'morally repugnant' research" and insisting that "political concerns are relevant"; "a policy of ruling out political considerations amounts to putting 'our heads in the sand.'"[22] In response to the campus protests, Schurmeier and James drew up guidelines for defense programs. In addition to existing requirements for unclassified descriptions of each project to allow campus oversight, the guidelines declared that "JPL will not pursue work on weapons systems," to placate apparent campus concerns that the lab would be building operational hardware for combat. The guidelines acknowledged, however, that much of the work would "have relevance to eventual weapon development," which begged the question of where to draw the line.[23] The adaptive optics of the LODE experiment seem to have involved too much of the business end of a laser weapon, which helped persuade JPL and Caltech to decline the work. The pointing device in Talon Gold, by contrast, appeared acceptable to Goldberger as a "component," as opposed to a weapon system, and as an experimental device "3 to 5 orders of magnitude away from any conceivable weapons capability."[24]

A system of Caltech committees helped oversee the defense work. The faculty committee on classified research, set up in 1980 and chaired by Robert Christy, reviewed new defense proposals with Schurmeier from JPL.[25] Far from isolating the lab from campus, classified work thus appeared to increase campus involvement, as faculty were now poking their noses into the early definition and negotiation of JPL proposals. But the oversight committee seems not to have taken an activist stance. Although several members had appropriate clearances, Christy did not have one himself and the committee work was unclassified.[26] Amid the Talon Gold debate in 1984 the committee did set up a cleared subgroup that could receive classified briefings. Goldberger also created a broader advisory committee on JPL in January 1985, chaired by engineering professor Fred Culick and charged with considering the overall policies and direction of the lab, including the presence of both secret and unclassified defense work.[27] The trustees meanwhile set up their own cleared subcommittee to review classified work.[28]

In addition to persistent moral and political concerns about Star Wars, the practical effects of secrecy raised hackles on campus. Culick's committee, reporting to the faculty in late 1985, accepted the need for some classified work but announced, "We are nervous." Even work undertaken within the guidelines "may slowly erode the Laboratory's special relationship with the campus." Although less than 5 percent of lab work-years went to classified work, Culick observed that a much higher percentage of staff dealt with classification because of part-time involvement. He added that "many JPL employees were uncomfortable with the Lab's classified activities but there seemed to be no alternative to taking on work for DOD."[29]

As Goldberger pointed out, however, the only classified aspects of Talon Gold were the launch dates, pointing accuracy, and slew rate, so that faculty could gain a good general idea of the work.[30] Furthermore, the military was not the only source of secrecy: Goldberger viewed proprietary research for industry alongside classified military research as "moral equivalents" and banned both from campus.[31] The issue of technology transfer, a hot topic at the time owing to declining American economic competitiveness, could also limit publication of unclassified work; NASA, for example, reviewed JPL papers submitted to unclassified conferences on photo-optics and space-borne imaging radar for industrial as well as military relevance.[32] In this context, and amid the general mobilization, JPL and Caltech accepted the presence of SDI programs despite the principled protests and the practical hassles.

The Arroyo Center

Campus faculty opposed Star Wars programs on moral or political grounds; but as a technological project, SDI meshed with JPL's disciplinary orientation, even if some scientists and engineers thought the mission technologically impossible. Different sorts of opposition arose against another defense initiative in the early 1980s, a think tank called the Arroyo Center. The Arroyo Center aimed to draw heavily on the humanities and social sciences and hence represented a disciplinary departure from the JPL program. Its proposed formation sparked heated debate on campus over JPL's mission and its relation to campus and also tapped internal tensions at Caltech between faculty and administration, and between technical and nontechnical disciplines.

The Arroyo Center episode emerged from the army's plans for a think tank. The air force had Rand and the navy had the Center for Naval Analysis at the University of Rochester, both of which pursued studies of technical programs, tactical and strategic doctrine, and policy and hence engaged such disciplines as economics, political science, history, and psychology in addition to technical fields.[33] In 1978 the army, then recovering from Vietnam and contemplating recent Soviet technological advances, started identifying candidates for its own think tank, and in May 1982 it approached JPL about "what might be described as a Rand Corporation for the Army." The proposal drew on the existing relationship between the army and JPL and allowed the army to avoid the creation of a new, separate lab, a step Congress would likely disapprove. JPL set up a study group, which noted possible concerns about campus participation, classification, and academic credibility but also touted the potential relationship with the army.[34] Goldberger approved, and in September the Caltech board of trustees authorized JPL to contract for an Army Analysis Program for three years, not to exceed $15 million per year, and the army provided $2 million for 1983 under a block grant to NASA. The justification stressed the development of a top-level relationship with the army that would generate even more business.[35]

The proposal envisioned a center with about 150 staff. At the time JPL had less than 10 percent of its work for the DOD, and so the army program would not push against the 30 percent limit. Although Goldberger backed the plan, he approached it "with some caution" and brought the issue before the faculty board that October. Goldberger recognized that the program "would be significantly different from the past efforts of the lab." Work in operations research, game theory, and decision analysis might require new hires. The army aimed to capitalize on Caltech for some of this work and involve faculty in the research projects, and it also hoped to send some of its officers to Caltech under an educational program. The issue of classification reappeared, although Goldberger assumed much of the work would be un-classified. Finally, "will this new entity simply respond to tasks set it by the Army, or will it have an opportunity for independent research?" In other words, what would the project do, who decided that, where would it be located, and what would be its relation to campus?[36]

The faculty expressed reservations. Military think tanks had acquired sinister connotations in the 1960s for their involvement with nuclear strat-egy and the Vietnam War; one faculty member "shuddered at references to Rand." Others worried about JPL's expansion into policy analysis, especially when even its technological competence appeared to be slipping, and some questioned the association with the army instead of the navy or air force, whose technologies seemed closer to JPL's experience. Finally, faculty feared that they faced a fait accompli since the project was already months into the definition phase. Goldberger assured them that the proposal was still open for discussion. He had formed a special committee in September under Picker-ing, which included two faculty members as well as several outside defense advisors, to provide a forum for the various issues (although Goldberger, to placate concerns, doubled the faculty representation to four members).[37]

The Pickering committee, however, would only encourage perceptions of a done deal. Its report to the faculty in December 1982, one professor noted, "does not appear to be a discussion of *whether* to go ahead with this project, but rather of *what* it will look like." The committee recommended that the program start small and grow slowly, with an initial staff of 25 to 40 professionals; that it have 25 percent of its budget for discretionary studies not requiring army approval; and that it have the right to reject any research topics. It also recommended the appointment of an all-faculty committee to consider the program.[38]

Faculty disagreement simmered behind the scenes. When Pickering cir-culated a separate memo extolling the program, the other faculty members castigated him for presenting his own views as those of the committee as a whole.[39] One of those members, Fred Culick, had earlier written to Pickering of "ill-founded expectations" and "a serious mismatch" between the army's goals and the character of JPL and, especially, campus: "there is practically no professional commitment by Caltech faculty in their work *on campus* to the subjects involved." Culick thus questioned Caltech's sponsorship of the center through JPL. More broadly, he concluded that the shift to defense work was leading JPL away from campus interests.[40]

The faculty committee appointed by Goldberger, however, was directed to keep the faculty at large informed about the evolution of the program—not ask whether it should exist at all—and to insure that it met JPL and Caltech standards. Its chairman, William Bridges, admitted to the faculty board that it did not "examine the ultimate rationale for the program." That did not placate the professors. Kip Thorne pointed out that the army think tank departed from the original motive for DOD work of keeping JPL staff on tap; "Now . . . we are hiring people from the outside to do work which is not within the existing expertise of JPL." Marshall Cohen added that Murray had originally proposed a small and narrow defense program for a short time frame, whereas the new program looked broad and long-lasting. The members of the faculty committee replied that the program provided a source of insight into the army's problems, which would then help the lab compete for army technology work. As for size and duration, no sponsor would agree to only a short-term relationship, and 150 people would be less than the 270 lab staff currently engaged in defense work and only a small fraction of total lab staff.[41]

Faculty reservations and committee studies did little to divert the center's growing momentum. Bud Schurmeier took the initial lead in organizing it and Martin Goldsmith then served as program manager, and in March 1983 Allen appointed a search committee for a permanent director.[42] At that time the project had 20 staff, most of whom came from JPL; the project thus fulfilled the purpose of keeping lab staff on tap.[43] The existing contingent of economists and systems analysts at the lab, many of them engaged either in defense or the dwindling energy program, provided enough people to get the center off the ground, if not enough for all of the eventual staff.[44] But JPL employees did not flock to the program, and the staffing challenge perhaps encouraged lab leaders to embrace a slow buildup against the initial desires of the army for "getting the show going."[45]

The staff of the center concentrated in four broad areas: military technology, which made use of engineering expertise; force utilization, such as war-gaming and simulation, which required operations analysis and game theory; support systems, including logistics, training, and recruiting, which employed economists and business administrators; and national security, which entailed studies of the political, economic, and geographic environment. The effort was entirely analytical, with no lab research.[46] The lab chose for the first director Richard Montgomery, a Caltech PhD who worked for R&D Associates, across town in Marina Del Rey, and also chaired the Army Science Board. Montgomery started work in October 1983. In May the program had acquired the name of the Arroyo Center, which referred to the nearby Arroyo Seco and was otherwise acceptably ambiguous.[47]

The gathering momentum revived faculty fears of a fait accompli. After the Bridges oversight committee reported on the project in November 1983, the steering committee of the faculty board raised several objections: Caltech should not, "in the absence of a recognizable national emergency," take responsibility for a lab "substantially directed toward classified research." Furthermore, "The name of the California Institute of Technology should be associated with the highest levels of scholarship particularly in science and technology and should not directly serve as a hallmark for other endeavors," a veiled reference to the social sciences.[48]

At the subsequent faculty meeting in December, Goldberger acknowledged that "there were and are negative aspects to the relationship to which I was insufficiently sensitive" and apologized for "inadequate" consultation of the faculty. The underlying issues, which the faculty chose not to air in a formal meeting, tapped not only long-standing disdain for JPL on campus but also interdepartmental politics, especially between the scientific and engineering disciplines and the social sciences, and friction between the faculty and Caltech administration.[49]

The location of the Arroyo Center presented the main issue.[50] The faculty assumed that the center would sit on the lab site; the lab, however, had no room for it and sought to lease a permanent site "within walking distance of campus."[51] Physical proximity would help satisfy the army's desire for faculty participation. But campus faculty speculated that the Arroyo Center's location, as well as its name, were intended to distance it from JPL and instead link it to Caltech.[52] Faculty feared the "closeness of a classified operation to Campus" and, what was more important, "contamination of [the] Athenaeum," the exclusive faculty club, by center staff.[53] The faculty thus abandoned their earlier preference, expressed in the debate over classified work in 1980, for the physical segregation of secret research from JPL. They wanted to keep the lab clean, but not if it meant soiling the campus.

Also at issue was the program. The Arroyo Center seemed to violate the guideline that defense work should draw on the lab's technical strengths. Because the emphasis on social science and the humanities departed from the existing expertise of JPL, the army sought connections with campus, but Caltech likewise had traditionally emphasized science and engineering. Humanities had been present since the formation of the campus, and in the late 1960s Caltech had begun to strengthen the social sciences, adding a number of eminent faculty, much of whose research, especially in economics and social sciences, displayed a quantitative bent that resonated with systems analysis. Nevertheless, the perception persisted among the faculty that "using humanities is not using Caltech," and some scientists and engineers on campus still wished they could get rid of their colleagues in social sciences.[54] They thus did not welcome the possible presence of a new group of nonscientists. Not only might the Arroyo Center pollute the faculty club, but with the worst sort of people: "social scientists don't get to [the] Athenaeum."[55]

Several other issues complicated the debate: classification; procedures for campus oversight; faculty and student participation; how to hire top-quality staff in the rapid buildup; and relation to the rest of the JPL program.[56] Finally, behind all of these issues lurked residual mistrust between campus and the lab, evident in such statements as "Some faculty just don't like JPL" and in constant faculty invocations of Caltech's high standards, which suggested that JPL research did not always live up to them.[57]

In short, JPL wanted the Arroyo Center close to campus since there was no room at the lab and since the army wanted faculty involvement; the faculty feared the proximity of classified work and shoddy social scientists and resented the perceived misrepresentations of Goldberger. The debate devolved into a standoff between Goldberger and the faculty. Professors complained that Goldberger "just hasn't leveled with faculty," especially about the location, and felt they were being railroaded. Goldberger, meanwhile, dug in his heels and did "not want to give in to Faculty" by backing out of the project.[58]

In January 1984 JPL and Caltech administrators tried to stem the rising tide of opposition. Pressed by Goldberger, JPL retreated on the location issue, even though it had already entered negotiations on a lease. The Arroyo Center would move to the main lab site, though this would displace NASA programs, to NASA's displeasure.[59] But Allen thought also of the interests of the army and raised the possibility of renouncing the center altogether: rather than string along the sponsor, he urged a quick decision to allow the army to move on if Caltech could not commit. The JPL managers involved with the center responded that the military would view Caltech "as less than dependable in its commitments" and predicted a "'ripple effect' on JPL programs for the Army." The army had negotiated its agreement with Caltech and the lab "*in good faith*" and invested nearly two years in the program. Montgomery warned that "the debate within Caltech surrounding the Arroyo Center is widely known in the defense community."[60] Montgomery also wondered why JPL was letting campus faculty "dictate JPL internal administrative decisions, such as the site of leased office space."[61]

Matters came to a head at a well-attended faculty meeting on 30 January 1984. The issue was dividing the faculty among itself and from the administration and was receiving prominent play in the local press.[62] Goldberger and Rochus Vogt, now the Caltech provost, presented two options to the faculty: divestment, which they discouraged, or the current course.[63] The lab's efforts to defuse the location issue did not appease the assembled professors. After an hour and a half of intense debate, an "overwhelming" majority rebuked the administration and voted to divest "at the earliest possible time."[64] Although the faculty at Caltech did not have the formal power of colleagues at some other universities, in practice they wielded informal influence over the president thanks in part to their scientific stature, and no administrator could hope to govern the campus without faculty support. The faculty vote, though officially nonbinding, sealed the fate of the project, especially after Richard Feynman, a legendary figure on campus, stood up and said that Caltech should get rid of the Arroyo Center at once.[65]

In September 1984 the army, which had sought to avoid creating a new laboratory from the outset, decided to transfer the center to Rand. The Arroyo Center closed at JPL in January 1985 and remains at Rand today.[66] The center collapsed at JPL because of competing conceptions from three parties—lab, contractor, and sponsor. Lab managers perceived it, like the rest of defense work, as a way to keep lab staff on tap while contributing to national security. But hardware-oriented JPL engineers were not the sort of analysts the army wanted, and the center required instead some new hires. The on-tap justification for defense work applied only indirectly, as a sort of market survey of army programs. The army, for its part, perceived the Arroyo Center as an analysis organization drawing on the social sciences and humanities at Caltech, and hence encouraged physical proximity to campus. The close military association, however, perturbed Caltech faculty, who also stressed their traditional technical focus and lack of respect for the social sciences. The fate of the Arroyo Center demonstrated the distance, physically and programmatically, between the laboratory and the campus.

Back to the Army

The army did not hold a grudge. Although Star Wars programs attracted much attention and constituted substantial portions of JPL's defense work, the main military sponsor in the 1980s was the army. JPL returned to its original sponsor not for rockets, but now for battlefield simulation and command, control, communications, and intelligence (C^3I), derived from its experience in information systems and systems engineering. The lab under Murray had already undertaken the MAFIS (Mobile Automated Field Instrumentation System) and SAWE (Simulation of Area Weapons Effects) projects, which integrated electronic sensors and computers with the army's training exercises. In July 1982 the army began discussing a new project, called the All Source Analysis System (ASAS), to extend electronics and computers into the actual battlefield to cut through the fog of war. The system comprised computer workstations mounted in trucks or trailers, which would combine data from satellites and airplanes as well as the field and then display it in a quickly useful form; it would thus channel the flood of information while at the same time allowing field commanders to focus on particular areas of a battle or pull up certain intelligence sources in real time. The army soon chose to collaborate with a similar project under the air force, called the Enemy Situation Correlation Element (ENSCE), and together the services chose JPL to manage ASAS/ENSCE.[67]

JPL managers perceived several benefits: "This effort will utilize some of the most advanced and sophisticated sensor and computer systems in current Army and Air Force inventory. It will provide significant challenges in the areas of communications, data handling/processing, graphic displays, command and control. . . . Furthermore, it provides JPL the opportunity to manage a major project in the mode it has performed on NASA space missions."[68] It also provided substantial support. Conceived as a "crash project," it quickly built up to engage 180 staff by March 1985, close to 40 percent of all defense work.[69] But ASAS had associated costs in headaches. It came with a high classification level of SCI (Sensitive Compartmented Information).[70] Although it drew on skills in information management, such as the integration of spacecraft telemetry into ground data systems, Allen acknowledged that "we have little background" in the particular systems involved.[71] The army then could not decide what it wanted, changing the specifications as new technology became available. The constant redefinitions of the job frustrated JPL managers trying to freeze the design in order to build a baseline system for production.[72]

The military meanwhile worried about JPL's commitment. General James Ambrose early expressed concern that the army "be treated as [a] first-rate customer, not as buffer."[73] The memorandum of understanding by the army and JPL of 1982 placed a limit of 300 work-years on army work, reflecting concerns that NASA would view army programs as not so relevant but also thus irritating the army.[74] ASAS had occasional trouble obtaining staff, apparently because of fears that defense work was a career dead-end. Defense manager Philip Eckman recalled a sense of "unease" about ASAS, owing to the view that it "wasn't mainstream JPL." Managers complained that critical personnel were leaving the project for "more important" assignments, and replacements had to wait to obtain high-level clearances. To forestall desertions, Allen declared the project a high priority, equivalent to that of major NASA flight projects.[75]

The military benefited in the long run. JPL adapted to changing plans and eventually produced a system, first tested in field exercises in 1985, refined into a final product by 1989, and then deployed in the Gulf War.[76] Duane Dipprey, who succeeded Jack James as defense program manager, visited army headquarters in West Germany regarding some other work but found the commanding general preoccupied by ASAS. The general viewed it as his most effective weapon to balance the overwhelming Soviet forces: "That's all he wanted to talk about, that he was absolutely ecstatic about it."[77] JPL thus played a little-recognized role in the transformation of combat, from the field commander wielding binoculars and radios while perusing unscrolled maps, to the arcade of graphic displays and real-time satellite data links that have come to constitute the electronic battlefield.[78]

High Tide

The ASAS/ENSCE project remained by far the largest single defense program at the lab through the 1980s and helped make the army the main military sponsor; less than 30 percent of military work concerned space in 1985, although that would increase thanks to Pathfinder and SDI.[79] Defense work in general was limited to 30 percent of the total program in terms of work-years, but amid the Arroyo Center flap Goldberger revised that to 20 percent, with all non-NASA work—including energy—capped at 25 percent. Defense work bumped against the lower ceiling only in 1987, when it rose to 21 percent after the Challenger disaster. But because of a greater amount of subcontracting, defense programs provided a much larger fraction in terms of dollars instead of work-years: 35 percent of JPL's budget in 1987, or $355 million, came from defense, close to the 40 percent ($390 million) provided by NASA for space science.[80]

Military work continued to intersect diverse fields. The air force helped fund the SIR-B imaging radar experiment in 1984, and along with the navy it supported SIR-B analyses to test the possibility of cruise-missile detection; DARPA then supported later work on the synthetic aperture radar, which led to airborne tests of submarine detection off of Scotland in 1989 and 1991.[81] The air force also helped fund data processing from the IRAS telescope, to "acquire improved IR signatures of selected orbiting objects and full sky background."[82]

A substantial program through the middle of the decade concerned war-gaming and simulation, which combined techniques from operations research and game theory with the electronic computer to evaluate combat strategies and tactics. The fiscal, environmental, and political costs of field exercises, especially in foreign countries, encouraged the military in the 1980s to boost support of simulation, and JPL's skills in computer networking, visualization, and image processing attracted military sponsors.[83] By 1985 war-gaming had become the second largest defense program at JPL, occupying about 40 staff, many of them software programmers. When Allen proposed scaling back the work the following year, General Fred Mahaffey, head of U.S. Readiness Command, replied that "no others in the simulation field have matched your level of success. . . . JPL has a unique array of expertise . . . ranging from simulation skills to worldwide networking of computers and communications." Mahaffey appealed to Allen that "your simulation expertise has become, in a very real sense, a national asset." The lab agreed to continue until industrial contractors caught up to its capabilities; meanwhile it signed an agreement with the Readiness Command for a long-term effort of about 60 work-years per year.[84]

Allen's attempt to scale back the war-gaming stemmed from a glut of work. The variety of programs led to early criticism within JPL that defense marketers had "sought work on too broad a front."[85] By mid-1983 defense programs had more than 350 work-years, and James was proposing "a realistic scenario" of defense work peaking at 750 staff in 1985, then holding steady at around 600, and certainly "no less than 500." But as the planetary program recovered, managers reached a consensus to cut defense instead of NASA programs.[86] By 1985 the defense program had its staff allocation cut below 500 and was fending off further cuts to 400 staff.[87]

By seeming to run back to NASA when the planetary program revived, JPL might have confirmed earlier military doubts about the depth of its commitment to defense. The staff shortage led the lab to decline or delay military programs, including several SDI missions.[88] The loss of the space shuttle Challenger in 1986 and the associated hiatus in planetary launches, however, revived defense programs. By 1987 the total lab budget had doubled from 1983, to more than $850 million, with much of the increase courtesy of the military; and total lab staff had climbed past 5,000, with about 1,000 work-years going to defense.[89]

Defense work gradually declined through the end of the decade, especially as ASAS started ramping down with nothing of comparable size to replace it. NASA business increasingly pressed the limits of staff and facilities, and then the end of the cold war squeezed military programs in the early 1990s—not so much through budget cuts, since military R&D budgets in fact held steady, but rather through competition from military labs and aerospace firms seeking new business. By 1992 defense work had dropped to about 7 percent of the program, with 234 work-years.[90] But defense work did not disappear altogether, and its legacy would prove crucial to the subsequent evolution of JPL.

Effects of DOD work

The primary motivation for defense work was to keep experienced staff on tap for future planetary programs. How well did it serve this purpose? In February 1983, of the 270 people working in defense, 260 had been at the lab previously. As Goldberger concluded, "defense work, therefore, in general has gone a long way to keep people at JPL."[91] Would these people have otherwise left the lab? Did defense work attract only the second-string engineers, people whose absence would not have hurt the planetary program? One can identify several individuals in defense projects who would return to leading roles in planetary exploration: the Pathfinder experiment had David Evans and Glenn Cunningham as managers and Wesley Huntress as project scientist; Anthony Spear was a lead manager on ASAS and other army programs.[92] In the 1990s Evans and then Cunningham would serve as project manager for Mars Observer, and Cunningham later ran Mars Global Surveyor; Spear would manage Magellan and the other Pathfinder, the Mars mission of 1997; and Huntress directed NASA's space science office. It is doubtful that any of these people would have left JPL without defense assignments, but amid the dearth of deep-space missions, defense projects provided an opportunity for up-and-coming staff to get management experience.

Defense work at times diverted staff from the main mission. At the top levels, Bud Schurmeier and Jack James devoted their extensive experience to defense, not to planetary exploration. At lower ranks, ASAS borrowed programmers from Galileo's flight-software development, the autonomous satellite project appropriated Voyager engineers, and SDI experiments tapped Galileo and Cassini project staff. One engineer complained to Allen that "key personnel are being siphoned off to the military projects at the expense of planetary programs" and that "the military projects are hurting the scientific programs they were meant to protect."[93] Although Galileo manager John Casani tolerated the temporary loan of engineers to the SDI Pathfinder experiment, others, such as W. E. Giberson, head of the flight projects office, objected to such assignments.[94]

Defense programs brought back secrecy to JPL, with high-level clearances for staff, restrictions on publication, and the associated apparatus of secure facilities and document handling. Military research also exposed divisions within the lab as some staff refused to work on defense programs while others resented the political activity of SDI protesters.[95] More prominent were the fissures between lab and campus. Professorial pronouncements on the immorality of SDI research could rouse resentment at JPL. Faculty meanwhile feared that lab managers were pursuing programs of dubious military, technological, or political value, and which, in the case of the Arroyo Center, threatened to contaminate the campus itself with a military presence.[96]

The campus criticism suggests a changed environment for American science in the later cold war, when academic scientists did not readily accept associations with military research. Unlike the early cold war, when questions about military sponsorship were soon swamped by the consensus of anticommunism, in the 1980s students and faculty at many leading campuses protested the renewed military mobilization.[97] On the other hand, the Caltech

confined to NASA support, JPL could work directly with the military and thus integrate civil and military space technology.

The lab's defense program fostered technology from the outset. By 1985 small defense technology tasks were supporting about 140 engineers, not counting those engaged in such larger projects as ASAS and Talon Gold; this work included remote sensing, propulsion and power, materials, autonomous systems and robotics, and artificial intelligence and software. In 1988 Allen stated that about half of all advanced technology development at JPL was funded by the military.[5] Much of this effort picked up the slack from NASA programs. In late 1985, for example, JPL undertook work on CCDs for an earth-orbiting reconnaissance spacecraft as the CCD work for Galileo and the space telescope wound down.[6] Similarly, the military supported work on alternatives to chemical propulsion, including nuclear-electric and solar-electric propulsion.[7]

Two technologies in particular highlight the importance of military support: microelectronics and supercomputing. JPL, abetted by Caltech research, had unique resources to offer in both of these front-line fields that attracted military sponsors, and both returned benefits to JPL's main mission in planetary exploration, demonstrating the increasing symbiosis between civil and military space in this period.

Microelectronics

In the 1970s JPL began converting its computer designs from hard-wired logic boards to integrated circuits, which had logic elements etched onto a semiconductor chip. The conversion capitalized on advances in the microelectronics industry; in particular, the greatly increased number of elements on a single chip enabled by metal-oxide semiconductors and the flexibility afforded by programmable microprocessors. By the end of the decade circuits with so-called large-scale integration (LSI) contained up to 100,000 elements per chip, and very large-scale integration (VLSI), or 1 million elements, was within reach.[8] The processing power offered by integrated circuits persuaded JPL engineers to incorporate them in spacecraft computers, payload instruments (such as synthetic aperture radar), and the Deep Space Network.[9]

Military interests supported JPL's microelectronics push. DARPA, for example, provided half the initial funding of a VLSI design center at JPL, which was up and running by 1982.[10] Before that, however, the lab had laid the foundation for a microelectronics program through its energy work. The contributions of energy research to space technology are not immediately apparent, since it was at times perceived as technically deficient, but it provided both people and facilities for microelectronics. In 1979 Bud Schurmeier hired

Terry Cole to act as the JPL's chief technologist, especially for the energy program. Cole, a chemist and chemical engineer with a joint appointment on campus, had previously worked for Ford in thermal-to-electric conversion. Although not technically involved in microelectronics, he perceived its importance and initially led the program.[11]

At lower levels, despite appeals to space spin-offs, energy research had proved to require different expertise and led to a number of new hires, bringing skills and techniques that then connected to other programs. In particular, photovoltaic research benefited not so much spacecraft solar arrays as spacecraft electronics. Photovoltaic cells use semiconductors to convert sunlight into electrical current; JPL's job was to improve the efficiency of this process for silicon solar arrays, which entailed detailed understanding of silicon's properties and its interaction with radiation. This sort of knowledge was of prime interest to JPL engineers designing spacecraft computers and sensors. The abrupt termination of energy work in the early 1980s cast adrift all these solid-state physicists and electrical engineers, many of whom found refuge in the microelectronics program. As important were the facilities. The solar-cell effort acquired an assortment of tools to produce doped silicon materials, lay them down in ultrathin layers, and deposit electrical contacts. Many of these devices—chemical vapor deposition, sputtering, molecular-beam epitaxy—were equally useful in the fabrication of semiconductor microelectronics.[12]

The microelectronics program thus aimed to combine the semiconductor fabrication expertise from the energy program with the circuit design work for VLSI, radiation-hardening, and other space electronics. The Departments of Energy and Defense provided much of the foundation, but NASA was not entirely absent from the effort; on the contrary, it was happy to redeem the investments of other agencies. In July 1983 NASA's manager for space science, Burton Edelson, sat in on a meeting of the Caltech trustees' subcommittee on JPL. Edelson noted the lab's work in VLSI and also in microwave circuits and suggested that JPL could become a national center for microelectronics.[13] At the time semiconductor firms, in addition to the usual industrial focus on short-term payoffs, shied away from the small product lines for high-reliability, radiation-hardened devices, and defense-related federal R&D for sensors tended to neglect the X-ray, extreme infrared, and submillimeter wavelengths of interest to NASA.[14]

Edelson's suggestion fired the enthusiasm of the trustees and of Allen, and by early 1984 JPL had assembled what was known as the Advanced Microelectronics Program.[15] Microelectronics drew together existing research in a unified program, including the people and facilities left over from energy work, and capitalized more generally on the lab's long experience in electrical engineering, going back to its work on radio and guidance in the 1950s.

In response to the orange report of 1976, Caltech professor John Pierce had extolled JPL's expertise, especially in signal processing and control and in electronic systems, complementing Caltech's strength in integrated circuits, and urged campus-lab collaboration. Pierce added, "The best people there [at JPL] are as good as or better than the best Caltech EE faculty."[16] The microelectronics program explicitly sought to realize the potential for campus-lab collaboration.[17] The initial VLSI effort, for example, drew heavily on the "silicon foundry" approach developed by Carver Mead at Caltech, which decoupled circuit design from fabrication. JPL engineers began pilgrimages to campus to learn the technique and then installed Caltech-licensed design software on the lab's VAX computer.[18] Similarly, high-content, content-addressable computer memories capitalized on neural network research by Caltech's John Hopfield; solid-state lasers for optical communication, on work by Amron Yariv.[19]

Microelectronics also received impetus from within JPL, starting at the top. Allen seized on microelectronics as the central theme for his technology movement; years later, Allen's reverence for microelectronics would be a running joke in a skit at his retirement ceremony.[20] Microelectronics acquired an enthusiastic promoter in 1984 when JPL hired Carl Kukkonen to take over the program from Terry Cole, who was more a researcher than a manager. Like Cole, Kukkonen came to JPL from Ford, where he had worked on engine design and hydrogen fuels. Kukkonen had little direct experience with microelectronics, but as a PhD in theoretical physics from Cornell he had intellectual credibility to back up his considerable entrepreneurial talent, which he would exercise with great energy on behalf of microelectronics at JPL.[21]

Kukkonen was not content to collect existing work into one program; instead he set about expanding the current effort and adding substantial new lines.[22] In 1985 he convinced NASA to approve a new building, the Microdevices Laboratory, to bring the existing facilities and people under one roof together with new clean rooms and requisite vibration, temperature, and humidity controls.[23] But NASA would provide only the building; to outfit it Kukkonen undertook a marketing campaign targeting the military. He found a prime sponsor in SDI, which was still ramping up and which perceived a way to capitalize on Caltech's reputation and capabilities through JPL. As electronics manager Krishna Koliwad recalled, "SDI came and said, 'we'll pay for equipment, what do you want.' So it was like taking kids to the candy store. We had a long list of stuff—man, we got the best e-beam lithography, and you name it."[24]

In July 1985, even before the Microdevices Lab was approved, the Department of Defense had been funding half of the Advanced Microelectronics

Program. A year later the Caltech trustees perceived that SDI support introduced programs "which are significantly different in character," which put further plans "on hold until the issues of character and support are resolved."[25] At the time Edelson had proposed to double the size of the program within a few years, with eventual funding levels of $30–40 million coming equally from NASA and Caltech.[26] Instead the lab resolved the issue in favor of the military. In January 1987 NASA and Caltech signed an agreement establishing a formal Center for Space Microelectronics Technology at JPL, with the Microdevices Lab (then under construction) as its principal facility.[27] NASA provided one-third of the center's initial budget of $22 million. Almost all of the rest came from national security agencies, and the directors of DARPA and the SDI technology office sat on the center's board of governors, along with NASA and Caltech representatives.[28] Caltech accepted the military funding but insisted that "all work in the Center is explicitly required to be unclassified."[29]

The center had about 170 staff at its inception and soon grew to about 250 staff. The program continued to concentrate on the four areas of solid-state device research, custom circuit design, photonics and optoelectronics, and computer architecture, all capitalizing on the resources of the Microdevices Lab. The electron-beam lithography device served as a centerpiece, like "the altar in a temple," as deputy manager James Cutts called it. E-beam lithography could deposit semiconductor layers at exceedingly fine scales, on the order of 20 angstroms, with no defects; hence, for example, it was essential for producing high-density memory chips based on neural networks, which promised a thousandfold increase in information storage and retrieval.[30]

E-beam lithography also enabled JPL to push into submillimeter astronomy. The lab had programmatic reasons to pursue a field where spacecraft provided a unique opportunity; because the atmosphere blocks most submillimeter radiation, space-based detectors make that portion of the spectrum accessible to astronomers. Microelectronics provided technological entry since existing detectors could not separate signals from background thermal noise. Caltech professor Tom Phillips had proposed using thin Josephson junctions, consisting of a superconductor-insulator-superconductor sandwich, for a detector; incident radiation created electron pairs that tunneled through the insulating barrier to produce a signal. Using niobium instead of lead compounds, JPL engineer Satish Khanna and Caltech professor David Rutledge developed new versions of these junctions that were more sensitive to submillimeter radiation and did not need as complex cryogenics to screen thermal noise; the sensitivity depended on the thickness of the layers and hence on the ultrafine deposition provided by e-beam lithography.[31]

A few more examples will indicate the scope and output of the program.

The Microdevices Lab also acquired a scanning tunneling microscope, a recent invention that could resolve material at nanometer scale. William Kaiser, another Ford recruit, devised a technique—called ballistic electron emission microscopy—to use the microscope to study subsurface interfaces in semiconductors, in addition to surface properties, which promised to help design ever-smaller devices.[32] Kaiser then thought to use the principle of electron tunneling not as a microscope but as a displacement sensor: electron tunneling across a very narrow vacuum gap between two electrodes varies greatly with the size of the gap, with the tunneling current jumping an order of magnitude if the electrodes move 1 angstrom (10 nanometers) closer together. The idea promised to reduce greatly the size of accelerometers, seismometers, and other displacement sensors and at the same time increase their sensitivity by a factor of 10,000. Similar quantum effects underpinned the quantum-well infrared photodetector (QWIP), an existing device in which electrons tunnel out of potential wells in a semiconductor to produce the output signal. JPL engineers adapted QWIPs for space science, taking advantage of the opportunity to tailor the shape of the quantum wells in order to tune the detector to certain wavelengths. The same approach appeared in tunable diode lasers, useful as spectrometers for detecting chemical molecules based on absorption of particular wavelengths.[33]

At the time these research results remained a good distance from realization in flight hardware. But their evident potential indicated the value of the Microdevices Lab, at least to the eyes of the sponsors. The center's visiting scientific committee found the program "competitive with . . . top ranked industrial and academic institutions," and an SDI manager pronounced it "first class."[34]

Hypercube

Another prime component of the microelectronics program, and another fruit of campus-lab collaboration, was the effort in computer architecture, which centered on concurrent or parallel processing. The idea of parallel processing had been around for decades, but it received renewed impetus starting in the late 1970s as supercomputers grew in performance and expense, and as VLSI enabled small, cheaper chips. Many small processors working in parallel offered potentially comparable performance to a single very fast processor taking programming instructions sequentially; such parallel processing, however, required sophisticated operating software to separate the instructions, direct them through particular processors, and recombine the results. In 1982 Caltech professors Charles Seitz and Geoffrey Fox started building a series of concurrent computers called "cosmic cubes," using standard Intel 8086/8087 chips and working up from a 4-node device to 64 nodes. Instead of connecting each node only to its immediate neighbors, they linked each processor in the 64-node model to 6 others; the 64 corners of a 6-dimensional cube inspired a new name, the hypercube. Seitz and Fox's design would greatly influence the subsequent embrace of parallel processing by the supercomputing industry. The hypercube had 1/10th the computing power of a Cray-1 sequential supercomputer but at $80,000 had 1/100th the cost.[35]

Such performance caught the eye of JPL engineers, who were contemplating the demands of real-time data processing for synthetic aperture radar and other sensors. The hypercube was also particularly proficient at fast Fourier transforms, a staple of image processing.[36] In 1982 JPL began supporting the campus work and its own effort using discretionary funds. Two years later the JPL group had built a 32-node machine called the Mark II hypercube, following the Mark I on campus, and had plans under way for a 128-mode Mark III and, beyond that, a 1024-node, ten-dimensional device.[37]

NASA funded none of this. DARPA and then the Department of Energy sponsored the Caltech program, and JPL relied on discretionary funds and then military sponsors. In 1985 Allen noted that "all of the JPL's outside funding support for the hypercube, other than that which we get from campus, comes from the Defense community."[38] The air force's Electronic Systems Division became the main sponsor, but after 1985 the hypercube focused on immediate applications concerning Star Wars, especially the simulation of complex scenarios for missile interception.[39]

The SDI work raised the issue of classification. In December 1988 the Department of Defense tightened secrecy around SDI, a directive which classified some of the hypercube SDI simulations. Air force general Gordon Fornell called the work "invaluable . . . a significant component of the SDI research program," and asked JPL to undertake classified runs on the large 128-node Mark III.[40] JPL and Caltech had built that device on campus, however, where Caltech banned classified work, so SDI had to settle for the 32-node Mark II at JPL. Kukkonen told the air force manager that "JPL is willing to do at JPL whatever classified work is necessary."[41] But the Center for Space Microelectronics Technology, which included the hypercube, was also supposed to be unclassified, so JPL built another small hypercube in a classified facility.[42]

Caltech and JPL assumed that they would let industry take over the production of mature hypercube designs. By 1984 Seitz was transferring the initial cosmic cube to Intel, and Fox negotiated with IBM for subsequent Caltech designs; JPL meanwhile signed an agreement with Ametek in 1985 to help build the Mark III, while Ametek developed its own commercial 256-node device.[43] As the lab waited for commercial versions of the hypercube it met increasing demand at JPL and Caltech with a series of Crays, which used standard sequential supercomputing. In the early 1990s Cray itself, whose approach the original hypercube had challenged, adopted so-called massively parallel processing into its T3D design, under a license from Caltech, and JPL wound up with a T3D of its own. The hypercube thus resulted in a long-term supercomputing program at both JPL and Caltech.[44]

Microspacecraft

Microelectronics intersected another effort at JPL, in microspacecraft, which likewise built on a military foundation. The microspacecraft program sought to use SDI technologies to produce shoebox-sized spacecraft that would revolutionize planetary exploration. The revolution did not occur. Against such examples as image processing or microsensors there are instances where JPL failed to realize the potential of new technologies. The history of microspacecraft at JPL illustrates that miniaturization entailed more than just technological advances.

The idea of microspacecraft first emerged at JPL in 1979. Veteran manager James D. Burke started doodling designs for tiny spacecraft components, and Robert L. Staehle, a young mission designer, proposed "miniature spacecraft" later that year. An ensuing study produced in 1981 a proposal for a 20- to 30-kilogram spacecraft, 66 centimeters wide, launched on a small Scout rocket to probe the solar corona with radio waves. The main technological novelty lay in the electronics, which drew on the Caltech-JPL work on VLSI.[45] The concept was subsequently taken up by Ross Jones, another young engineer like Staehle who saw microspacecraft as a way to pursue space exploration without billion-dollar budgets or teams of several hundred people; the movement thus merged young enthusiasts with old hands who perhaps saw a return in some respects to the first Explorer satellites, which had been limited to 10-kilogram scale by available rockets. For such people, as for Burke, the microspacecraft study provided "an unrestrained outlet for their creativity and was fun."[46] It also perhaps resonated with the democratization of technology, exemplified at the time by the emerging personal computer.

The movement was not confined to JPL. At the time a group of space engineers had formed the Amateur Radio Satellite Corporation (Amsat) and were building small, cheap satellites in their spare time, cobbling together donated or surplus components and launching on the new French Ariane rocket.[47] The military provided a more influential model. Plans to orbit electromagnetic railguns in space for strategic defense suggested a way to launch many microspacecraft without the expense of rockets. Jones then began borrowing SDI concepts for spacecraft technology, such as kilogram-sized projectiles built by SDI contractor General Dynamics, which Jones visited in 1986. These kinetic-kill vehicles included many common spacecraft subsystems, including propulsion, power, guidance and control, and remote sensing.[48]

Despite their appeal, microspacecraft failed for several years to generate interest at JPL. Although they faced the problem of aperture—bigger solar arrays provided more power, bigger antennas sent more data, and bigger instruments collected more photons—the constraints were more programmatic than technological. A half-meter spacecraft had plenty of aperture for most missions, and the cost of microspacecraft compensated for their size by offering a way to take data from many points at once.[49] Microspacecraft could carry only one or a few instruments, however, and they thus entailed a fundamental programmatic adjustment: instead of a comprehensive mission once every several years, where a single complex spacecraft provided a variety of data from its destination, the planetary program would comprise dozens of microspacecraft, each with limited objectives. The concept thus confronted JPL's internal organization, which was set up to prosecute one or major projects at a time; the customary practice of space scientists, who assumed that each mission would accommodate a full complement of proposals; and NASA's planning process, which aimed at just one or two new starts every budget cycle.

At first microspacecraft foundered on resistance within JPL. After several proposals for discretionary funds were rejected, Jones lost faith. But in 1988 Carl Kukkonen got wind of his ideas and brought them under the umbrella of the microelectronics program.[50] With Kukkonen, microspacecraft acquired not just a high-level advocate but also one with some resources. The Microdevices Lab had concentrated on sensors and not the components of the spacecraft itself. At the time university and industrial researchers were beginning to use photolithography techniques to make not just electronic circuits, but also mechanical devices—what was called Micro Electromechanical Systems, or MEMS, although it was also becoming known as nanotechnology from the nanometer scale of the devices.[51] The Microdevices Lab had the apparatus to apply MEMS techniques to spacecraft components, such as gyroscopes and reaction wheels, or rocket nozzles and combustion chambers.[52]

The growing interest at JPL drew not only on SDI technologies but also on a military trend toward "lightsats" or "cheapsats." In 1987 DARPA started an Advanced Satellite Technology Program to shrink earth-orbiting spacecraft an order of magnitude, from thousands to hundreds of kilograms or less; by distributing many lightsats in orbit the military hoped to reduce vulnerability to Soviet anti-satellite attacks. The lightsat trend also embraced a multiplication of launch vehicles after the Challenger explosion in 1986.

The space shuttle did not encourage economy in spacecraft weight, since it launched a big satellite about as easily as a little one. The loss of the Challenger reopened the use of expendable launch vehicles, including existing small rockets such as the Scout and new vehicles such as the Pegasus.[53]

Kukkonen's first contribution to microspacecraft was to sponsor a workshop at JPL in July 1988. Like Bruce Murray's brainstorming sessions, the workshop convened noted blue-sky thinkers such as sci-fi author Robert Forward and physicist Freeman Dyson, who had recently proposed a scheme to release a flock of microspacecraft, dubbed "astrochickens," that would spread out through the solar system, consuming interplanetary ice and hydrocarbons for fuel and reporting back to Earth.[54] On a more practical plane, the workshop, sponsored by NASA and SDI, included several people from the SDI office and its contractors.[55] Lew Allen's opening remarks made clear the military impetus. He first noted planetary science's current reliance on large, expensive spacecraft launched every several years and predicted a proliferation of small, simpler spacecraft, which could attain higher speeds and hence distances, cover many locations, and attain reliability through sheer numbers. Allen cited the technology base in microelectronics and miniaturization of other components and added, "Here, I'd like to point out that the DOD has been interested in advanced micro technology for many years. I am especially pleased to note that SDIO technology and personnel are well represented here today."[56]

The end of the cold war accelerated the application of SDI technology to civil space missions in the early 1990s. In particular, kinetic-kill vehicles, such as the Brilliant Pebbles scheme from the Lawrence Livermore Laboratory and the Lightweight Exo-Atmospheric Projectile of Boeing and Hughes, provided an array of miniature components. In 1990 Jones visited Boeing, Hughes, and other SDI contractors, where he learned about propulsion systems weighing a few kilograms and inertial guidance systems of a few hundred grams; he also heard about a star tracker from Livermore, about the size of a cigarette pack and weighing 300 grams. Jones and other mission designers began proposing microspacecraft for near-earth asteroid flybys, lunar rovers, and a Mars rover/sample return.[57] At a conference in Pasadena, meanwhile, Rob Staehle had met a Livermore scientist, who had pulled out of his pocket a mock-up of the new star tracker. At the time Staehle was planning a mission to Pluto and was contemplating, among other things, the 10-kilogram star tracker standard at JPL. A subsequent visit to Livermore convinced him to redefine the Pluto mission as a 35-kilogram microspacecraft, with a total payload of 7 kilograms and a power supply of 6 watts.[58]

Microspacecraft, however, remained only a prospect for JPL, as the technology continued to confront programmatic obstacles within JPL, NASA, and the scientific community—in particular, what microspacecraft advocates viewed as "the stranglehold of the big planetary mission."[59] The subsequent history of microspacecraft, the Pluto project, and JPL in general would demonstrate the difficulty in adapting to new modes of space exploration.

Consequences

JPL's efforts in microelectronics, concurrent computing, and microspacecraft highlight the critical role of the military, specifically DARPA and SDI, in developing advanced space technology. The military supported hundreds of engineers and outfitted state-of-the-art laboratories at JPL, producing an array of new devices and techniques, and technologies developed elsewhere for the military inspired new programs at JPL. Star Wars provided a crucial stimulus by turning technological concepts into hardware. As Ross Jones put it, SDI "actually did it; they didn't just make colored viewgraphs the way we do here, they had real money and they went out and *built* miniature propulsion tanks and miniature engines. . . . I took some pictures of that stuff to my section manager and said, look, this is why I'm talking about microspacecraft. He said, shit, I didn't know that you could actually do it."[60]

Some of this work was connected tenuously at best to national security missions. For example, although the military considered the uses of submillimeter sensors in orbit, the opacity of the atmosphere at most wavelengths limited their utility, and JPL engineers, whose interest stemmed from astronomy, employed mostly hand-waving arguments to justify SDI support. Scanning tunneling microscopy seemed similarly distant from military missions. SDI managers, however, could advertise JPL's research accomplishments, such as the extension of sensing into new regimes, and they appreciated more generally the association with Caltech. JPL's contribution in this respect was more as a showcase for SDI's support of long-range, cutting-edge research than for any specific devices that resulted; it conferred cachet and credibility that SDI program managers could use to bolster their own political position.[61]

The growth of the microelectronics and hypercube programs complicated the mid-decade efforts to cut back on defense work. In 1985 Jack James at first declined to take on additional hypercube work, noting that he had already committed available staff to the ASAS and SDI Pathfinder projects. Instead Allen approved an increase in defense staff to accommodate microelectronics and hypercube, which he deemed "important for the intellectual growth of JPL."[62] Two years later Allen was hoping "that JPL does not become so heavily tasked by NASA that it will be unable to assume invigorating technological tasks supported by the Department of Defense."[63]

JPL's success in defense programs encouraged Allen to look to the military as a general basis for civil space policy. With the human program in limbo following Challenger and science missions unevenly supported, Allen suggested broadening NASA's mission to include "support to national security through technology."[64] He did not propose simple spin-offs from civilian programs but rather a two-way interaction: "Sometimes that technology will be directed to a NASA mission and, incidentially [sic], useful to Defense but there will certainly be times when the situation is reversed."[65] Microspacecraft offered one way to link NASA and the Defense Department since military missions suffered from the same constituency-building that afflicted planetary exploration, with accumulating requirements and instruments producing ever-bigger satellites. JPL's efforts toward small, more frequent spacecraft could support both NASA and the military.[66]

The integration of civil and military space programs was already apparent at JPL, as SDI projects applied JPL expertise to military purposes while other JPL engineers borrowed SDI products for civilian missions. That is, it was not just a case of JPL working for the military; rather, JPL engineers used military funding and technologies to advance their own interests in planetary exploration. Whatever disconnect existed between civil and military space, or between open and classified programs, was thus bridged in the 1980s. Lew Allen personified the interaction in his background and in his continued service on several high-level advisory committees for national security. Some of these connections provided a useful conduit to military programs: for example, Allen sat on a visiting committee for Livermore and tipped off JPL engineers about Livermore's advances in computers and microsensors.[67] At lower levels, JPL staff managed to keep up with much military space technology. Engineers in JPL's defense programs stayed informed through their contacts with SDI and DARPA program managers and labs, and engineers outside these programs could plug into this network through their own initiative. Most of the work for the SDI Innovative Science and Technology program, which was a prime sponsor of microdevices R&D, was unclassified and accessible. Ross Jones had little trouble visiting SDI contractors or learning about Livermore's results, and Rob Staehle similarly encountered Livermore technology and then visited there.[68]

Any limits to communication between civil and military programs could come more from informal obstacles than from official secrecy. Competition for business provided a particular barrier. When JPL shopped its synthetic aperture radar to military managers, it found them happy to ask a lot of questions but unwilling to divulge their own efforts.[69] Then at the end of the cold war, military-oriented labs sought new markets for their technology in the civil space program. Since JPL represented a potential competitor, Livermore engineers at times held their cards close to their vest; Jones recalled them as being "less than forthcoming." JPL managers meanwhile "were pretty circumspect when it came to Livermore," as Duane Dipprey put it.[70] When the two labs did cooperate, JPL engineers encountered a different mindset. For example, Livermore in 1990 began pushing Brilliant Pebbles systems for NASA earth-orbiting missions, and several JPL managers visited Livermore for a classified briefing. The two groups reached no agreement, however: the Livermore people enthused about a slew of small satellites seeking unexpected phenomena, while the JPL team talked in terms of one or two big platforms in polar orbit to provide precise refinements of existing scientific models.[71] The application of military techniques to civil space missions would have to overcome similar philosophical divides in the future.

Thriving defense technology programs finally spurred NASA into action. In 1988 NASA announced a Civil Space Technology Initiative (CSTI), the name alone suggesting a need for a civilian effort to match the military's.[72] The initiative and its successors, however, in practice focused on human missions, and it then was gutted by congressional budget cuts in 1989 and 1990.[73] The military thus continued to support most of the key technologies at JPL; in 1990 lab managers perceived NASA's attitude toward electronics to be, "Let DOD do it."[74]

In its pursuit of space technology, JPL had a crucial advantage over other NASA centers as a contractor lab. Its status fostered technology development in two ways. First, JPL could diversify to new sponsors, who supported technologies neglected by NASA. Thus the Department of Energy laid a foundation for microelectronics, upon which the Department of Defense built a thriving program; the resulting devices—submillimeter and infrared detectors, accelerometers and siesmometers—proved useful for space science. Second, JPL capitalized on its association with Caltech, with research programs deriving from faculty advances in VLSI, neural networks, and concurrent computing. As a result, by the end of the 1980s JPL had developed capabilities that existed nowhere else in NASA, and at few places in the nation as a whole, which gave it a technological leg up as the lab entered the new decade.

Space and Earth Science

MICROELECTRONICS PLAYED A ROLE IN THE DEVELOPMENT OF THE WIDE FIELD/ Planetary Camera (WF/PC) for the Hubble telescope, a major JPL effort in the 1980s. Along with several other large science instruments, and the primary work of the Microdevices Lab in experimental sensors, the camera highlighted the increasing diffusion of JPL beyond its focus on the systems engineering of spacecraft. Instead of just building the spacecraft to carry instruments for science teams, JPL increasingly sought to build the instruments themselves. The trend continued the diversification of the lab into space-based astronomy and earth and ocean science and was strengthened by its ties to Caltech, for infrared astronomy as well as the Hubble camera. But it also raised broader questions about JPL's relation to a primary constituency, the community of space scientists, and hence about its mission.

Astronomy

In the late 1970s JPL had joined with James Westphal at Caltech to build the Wide Field/Planetary Camera. The collaboration produced the sort of friction that had appeared between spacecraft engineers and science teams on Voyager, but in this case the engineers and scientists were teamed up to build a science instrument across the campus-lab divide. JPL in effect served as subcontractor to Westphal, the WF/PC principal investigator, who maintained technical and fiscal control. He thereby forced a role reversal on JPL engineers, who were more accustomed to managing subcontractors, not being overseen themselves, and hence chafed at Westphal's dictates.[1]

Then in June 1984 thermal-vacuum tests at JPL revealed a curious phenomenon that threatened to cripple the telescope. The CCDs were displaying ghost images, where traces of previous exposures showed up in succeeding images. The effect became known as quantum efficiency hysteresis and appeared to be generic to CCDs. A simple fix involved shining bright ultraviolet light on the CCDs, essentially burning out the residual images; but there was no room in the telescope to put a floodlamp, and pointing the telescope at the sun, another source of ultraviolet light, was anathema to the telescope's designers. After months of intense debate, Dave Swenson of JPL found a spare half-inch amid the telescope components to fit a light-pipe, which would reflect enough light from the side of the telescope to reset the CCDs, and that solution was adopted.[2]

JPL's work on the WF/PC did not end there. The Challenger disaster delayed the Hubble's deployment from 1986 until April 1990. Then the first images after launch displayed spherical aberration, indicating the telescope's primary mirror was distorted. The $2-billion telescope was apparently worthless. Lew Allen, who had had extensive experience with advanced optics in his military career, chaired the NASA review committee that traced the aberration to a faulty measuring device at Perkin-Elmer, the mirror's builder. A corrective for the Hubble's myopia, however, existed in the space shuttle's ability to service satellites in orbit. The importance of the WF/PC to the telescope's mission, and the possibility that it might fail or that quantum efficiency hysteresis might degrade its performance, had spurred NASA to approve a backup version. JPL had thus built a clone of the WF/PC as an insurance policy, with the added benefit of keeping the team intact until launch after work on the first camera ended.[3]

The team and the backup were thus on hand to address the spherical aberration. Art Vaughan at JPL had designed the camera's optics so that a set of secondary mirrors relayed the primary image to the CCDs, and his optics group now redesigned the relay mirrors to correct the distortion from the primary. In 1993 space-walking astronauts inserted the backup camera along with corrective lenses for the other instruments, which restored most of the performance of the telescope, albeit at great additional cost—about three times the initial estimate for the clone of $27 million, and much more than the first WF/PC price of $68 million. That was a small price to pay, however, to recover the Hubble; according to NASA manager Ed Weiler, JPL's camera enabled the ensuing slew of scientific results and "brought us from being a national disgrace to a great American comeback."[4]

Because of the Hubble's delayed launch, JPL's main contributions to astronomy in this period came from the Infrared Astronomy Satellite (IRAS). Technical gremlins continued to plague IRAS into 1982, in particular the infrared detector array at the telescope's focal plane. When JPL engineers cooled the telescope to 2 degrees Kelvin for ground tests they discovered whole banks of failed detectors and noisy, cross-talking, or just plain dead electronics. Rather than warm up the telescope and expose it to thermal stress, they decided to keep it cold and fix the problems from the outside, even as the launch date slipped several more months.[5] Another late problem emerged when a capacitor failed in the gyroscope electronics. The failure was generic to the part, and a review board noted that "hundreds of suspect capacitors are functioning in the spacecraft and the telescope electronics boxes." Changing all the capacitors would delay launch several months, and further testing turned up no other failures. Engineers speculated that moisture caused the failure, which would not be a problem in the vacuum of space. The review board voted to roll the dice and launch.[6]

The spacecraft launched in January 1983 and survived in orbit for 300 days before it ran out of helium coolant. As with Seasat, and unlike Voyager, IRAS did not produce instant science; instead results trickled in after painstaking data analysis. But even as the telescope expired it was generating increasing excitement among astronomers. Gerald Neugebauer and colleagues hailed IRAS for providing "what might be termed their first view of the infrared sky on a clear, dark night," finally free from the atmospheric absorption and thermal distortion of ground-based telescopes. The telescope detected a vast halo of cool solid material around several nearby stars, including Vega and Beta Pictoris; such proto-planetary systems suggested that extrasolar planets might be much more common than expected. Infrared data also provided a new window into the process of star formation. More discoveries awaited beyond the Milky Way, including tens of thousands of previously unseen galaxies and smaller infrared sources. The data suggested that many galaxies, unlike their component stars, emit the bulk of their energy in the infrared rather than visible wavelengths owing to interstellar dust, and that the dust included wispy clouds spread through much of the sky, a sort of "infrared cirrus." The dust clouds, together with IRAS data on the density and distribution of galactic clusters, sparked a reappraisal of current theories of dark matter and Big Bang cosmology (see figure 10.1).[7]

All told, IRAS surveyed more than 96 percent of the sky and produced a vast database of infrared sources to occupy astronomers for the next decade and more—more than 250,000 sources, compared to the 1,000 previously catalogued, prompting NASA managers to applaud "one of the most successful space science missions ever conducted."[8] The success vindicated JPL after the troubled early history of the project and provided a welcome infusion of scientific results during the long hiatus in planetary data between Voyager's encounters at Saturn in 1981 and Uranus in 1986; together with the Voyager encounters, IRAS burnished JPL's reputation and self-image.

Unlike the Hubble camera, JPL's work on IRAS entailed traditional systems

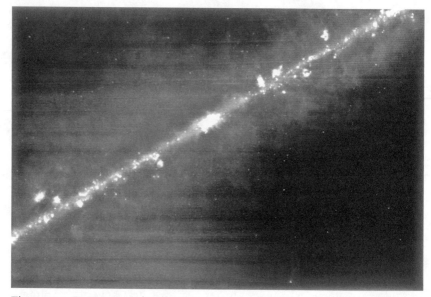

Figure 10.1. IRAS image of Milky Way; the bright bulge in the middle is the center of the galaxy. *Source:* JPL Photolab.

engineering, not instrument development. But IRAS did involve JPL in the data analysis and thus left a lasting legacy at Caltech. JPL and NASA had already recognized the need for formal systems to handle the increasing flood of data returned from remote sensing satellites, and the Seasat Data Utilization Project had demonstrated the potential payoffs. IRAS expanded on this experience, the difference in this case being the particular interest of Caltech faculty in the data, including astronomers Neugebauer and Thomas Soifer. To enhance Caltech's role, while maintaining that of JPL, Caltech administrator David Morrisroe worked out a deal for an IRAS data center, wherein Caltech would provide a new facility on campus, NASA supplied the operating budget, and JPL managed it.[9]

The Infrared Processing and Analysis Center (IPAC) opened at Caltech in 1986, with almost 60 staff transferred from JPL. The center was intended to serve the astronomy community at large, distributing and archiving the data and with one-fourth of the budget supporting visiting scientists, but its name indicated that the center's Caltech staff also did some science themselves.[10] A similarly blurry line between service and research had appeared in the Space Telescope Science Institute, established at Johns Hopkins University in 1981 for the Hubble Space Telescope. NASA and other astronomers were trying to curb the ambitions of the institute's managers, who sought to analyze as well as process data.[11] IPAC and Caltech appear to have escaped the resentment roused by the Hubble's institute, in part because they did not have the responsibility of doling out observing time on the telescope; IRAS had already shut down and the data was on the ground and available.

But that raised another issue: what would happen to these institutes and their staffs when the data was processed and archived? IPAC answered by providing the data center for ensuing missions in infrared astronomy, and it thus helped secure one of those missions for JPL. Since the early 1970s NASA had planned to follow IRAS with a larger infrared telescope, one to join the Hubble and two other planned "Great Observatories" for gamma- and X-ray wavelengths. As Ames at the time was designing IRAS it also undertook the early studies for the follow-on, which would be called the Space Infrared Telescope Facility, or SIRTF.[12]

After years of budget delays, the success of IRAS finally pushed SIRTF to the front burner in the late 1980s. JPL at first went along with the NASA policy of giving Ames first crack at the project, but after NASA decided to give it instead to a lab "with recent experience in managing large-scale projects," JPL entered into a vigorous competition with Goddard and Marshall and emerged the victor at the end of 1989. As Norm Haynes, who would later temporarily manage the project, recalled, "JPL lusted after SIRTF—JPL and Caltech, I might point out, because there are a lot of infrared scientists and astronomers on campus."[13] The interest of Caltech astronomers and the presence of the IPAC data center, in combination with JPL's experience on IRAS, proved decisive, although the subsequent history of SIRTF would test the lab's fortitude.

JPL focused on infrared astronomy, but the Microdevices Lab fostered a push into submillimeter astronomy. Several JPL scientists also undertook research into relativistic gravitation, the results of which helped encourage NASA managers to consider a major effort in gravitational-wave astronomy.[14] The research resonated with a general interest in gravity waves around that time, and JPL engineers would contribute to a major ground-based collaboration between Caltech and MIT, the Laser Interferometer Gravitational Wave Observatory funded by the National Science Foundation. But individual lab staff would continue their own lines, spurred also by JPL's practical interest in relativity: spacecraft navigation and telemetry required extremely precise knowledge of the transmit times of electromagnetic signals, including the effects of massive bodies and the behavior of clocks as well as possible variance of the speed of light.

Finally, JPL also continued work on SETI, whose backers managed to restore limited congressional funding in 1983. After five years of preliminary work on the instruments, in 1988 JPL and Ames won approval from NASA for a formal SETI project, a ten-year, $100-million effort that started in 1990.[15]

But unlike Bruce Murray, Lew Allen was not a big fan of SETI: "I'm frankly not impressed with the reasoning that says there are billions of galaxies with billions of stars, and in each, uncountable numbers of planets. . . . We're doing SETI, but it has a small chance of observing anything when one works out the statistics involved. One can question whether SETI is a scientific endeavor or an exercise of imagination and faith." Instead Allen backed a "soundly based scientific exploration of other solar systems," taking as an example work by Richard Terrile of JPL and Brad Smith of the University of Arizona that seemed to confirm the detection of protoplanetary systems by IRAS.[16] Based on the IRAS image of Beta Pictoris, Allen directed a substantial portion of his discretionary funds, about a half million dollars a year, toward further study of extrasolar planets.[17]

The IRAS results also inspired Allen to push for missions beyond the solar system as a potential new realm for JPL and NASA and one that would spark public as well as scientific interest. He hence allocated additional discretionary funds to plan a Thousand Astronomical Unit (TAU) mission, which would send a spacecraft with a telescope out to interstellar space, using nuclear-electric propulsion to enable the fifty-year flight. The main scientific justification was to achieve a far longer baseline for positional astronomy than parallax available from the earth's orbit around the sun; but Allen, demonstrating Murray-like enthusiasm, seems to have been taken as much by the exploration aspect, and he touted the idea in a number of public speeches in the mid-1980s. The plan did not lead to a flight project, but it did help get people at JPL and NASA thinking about more far-out possibilities. It also signaled a wider redirection of the search for extraterrestrial life in the 1990s.[18]

Earth Observations

JPL also continued its pursuit of earth and ocean science from the 1970s. Although JPL failed to obtain approval for a Seasat follow-on with synthetic aperture radar, it did win responsibility for the Ocean Topography Experiment, or Topex, an earth-orbiting satellite for precise altimetry of ocean surfaces. In December 1979 NASA asked JPL to study the concept, and after years of delay, including combination with a similar French mission called Poseidon, Topex/Poseidon launched in August 1992.[19]

More earth-observing work came through individual instruments instead of entire satellites. For example, NASA initially planned for Topex to include a scatterometer, an active radar to measure sea-surface winds, and JPL won the project after a vigorous competition with Goddard.[20] The NASA Scatterometer (NSCAT) finally flew in 1996 on Japan's Advanced

Earth Orbiting Satellite and was followed by similar successive instruments.[21] The scatterometry settlement thus produced a long-term program for JPL and, coming on the heels of Seasat, sealed its role in physical oceanography. It also implied a rough division of labor between the competing labs, with JPL pursuing observational systems and Goddard developing global modeling from the resultant data.[22]

JPL earth scientists flew instruments on the space shuttle and airplanes as well as satellites. In 1985 JPL scientist Taylor Wang flew as an astronaut on a shuttle flight, in order to run his own experiment on the physics of liquid drops in microgravity as well as the Atmospheric Trace Molecule Spectroscopy experiment (ATMOS), an infrared interferometric spectrometer that could detect trace molecules in the stratosphere at concentrations of a few parts per trillion.[23] The following year JPL's lead investigator on ATMOS, Crofton Farmer, would use a similar airborne interferometer to measure the abundance of trace gases in the Antarctic atmosphere. The experiment provided important evidence regarding the ozone hole, the growing gap in the earth's atmospheric shield against ultraviolet radiation that was then attracting increasing environmental concern; the paper from Farmer's group appeared just as representatives from thirty-five countries were meeting in Montreal to address the issue. The marked presence of halogen compounds in Farmer's data suggested that human activity caused the hole, not meteorological variations, since laboratory experiments had demonstrated that halogenated hydrocarbons (produced by aerosols and refrigerators) deplete ozone. JPL then provided further detailed maps of ozone depletion with the Microwave Limb Sounder, an instrument launched in 1991 aboard Goddard's Upper Atmosphere Research Satellite.[24]

The embrace of earth observations at JPL, and at NASA in general, reflected political support of programs with clear social relevance. The trend was evident in 1982, after the crisis in the planetary program, when a reporter asked NASA chief James Beggs, "Does NASA still have a mission to explore outer space, the planets, comets, etc., or has it become a Department of Agriculture?"[25] Although the Reagan administration would push for commercialization of land remote sensing and weather satellites, NASA continued to tap the popularity of earth-observing programs.[26] As a companion to deep-space exploration, NASA's space science office created a "Mission to Planet Earth," which had an increasing presence in the space science program at the end of the 1980s. A prime component of the mission was the Earth Observing System, or EOS, a planned series of large platforms, similar to a small space station but in polar orbit, to carry a host of earth-observing instruments. NASA managers and other administration officials noted strong congressional interest in EOS and pushed ahead despite criticism of the big-platform approach. NASA saw its ambitious early plans gradually whittled down, but in the meantime the prospect of big platforms full of science instruments encouraged JPL's pursuit of the earth-science market.[27]

JPL and Scientists

When Lew Allen arrived at JPL in 1982 he noted "the increasingly important role of flight experiments" and set about updating JPL's statement of objectives. Pickering had defined three main goals in 1963: flight projects; the Deep Space Network; and supporting research and development. Allen now added two more: scientific study of space and the earth, and defense and other selected national priorities such as energy.[28] In 1984 Allen supplied another indicator of the trend by appointing atmospheric scientist Moustafa Chahine as chief scientist, to replace Caltech planetary geologist Arden Albee. Then in 1987 Allen elevated the technical division for earth and space science, led by Charles Elachi, to a new program office for space science and instruments. Elachi's entrepreneurship had parlayed the synthetic aperture radar and other instruments into a thriving flow of new business; he observed the following year that "over the last several years, the instrument activity at JPL has expanded significantly and will continue to grow," with the prospect of soon doubling from its current level of $100 million per year.[29]

Elachi's program ranged from the WF/PC for astronomy to spectrometers for planetary missions to the radar, scatterometer, and other instruments for earth observations, with particular emphasis on earth science.[30] In 1988 JPL's executive council noted that a number of the lab's planetary scientists had moved into earth science, helping to make it three times larger than the planetary research effort. The council cited stronger NASA and public support for earth science than for planetary missions and also the important results obtained. As for competition with other centers, "we should carefully avoid the appearance of an overt campaign to displace others in this field." Ames, however, seemed to be doing "very little science," while Goddard's strengths lay in global modeling, not observational techniques. The managers concluded that JPL should aspire to a lead role in earth science as well as planetary, with an additional major role in astrophysics and space physics: "A major mission for JPL is emerging in this field. . . . Historically we're planetary exploration, but today we're space science and exploration."[31]

Elachi observed that the increasing complexity of science instruments provided a technical and managerial challenge now comparable to that of entire spacecraft.[32] Experiments such as SIR-C, WF/PC, and NSCAT each cost well over $100 million and involved dozens of people in their design, and the instruments themselves could weigh hundreds of kilograms and encompass diverse power, thermal, mechanical, and electrical subsystems. The scale, cost, and complexity of individual instruments thus approached the neighborhood of small flight projects, which seemed to justify the application of JPL's systems engineering experience. But flight experiments also brought potential pitfalls. Albert Wheelon, an eminent aerospace executive brought in by Allen to survey JPL's programs in 1988, hoped that "the opportunity to build more sophisticated instruments will not become a substitute for building and launching American spacecraft to explore the solar system." Other labs could do instruments, but JPL at the time enjoyed a monopoly on deep-space missions, and Allen recognized "that we should take care not to become just an instrument lab."[33]

The pursuit of flight experiments threatened not only to distract JPL from its role as spacecraft builder, but also to undermine its relationship with its own constituents. For more than two decades JPL had provided the platforms for instruments from outside researchers, many of them university scientists who in effect hitched rides on JPL vehicles into deep space. NASA selected the experiments for each process in a competition, with entries usually coming from universities, institutes, and other NASA centers; hence the principal investigators on Voyager came from places such as Caltech, the University of Arizona, MIT, Stanford, and Goddard. As JPL stepped up its pursuit of flight experiments, on planetary as well as earth-orbiting spacecraft, scientists elsewhere resented the new competition and complained that JPL scientists had the advantage of inside information: they could talk to spacecraft engineers and tailor their proposals to the spacecraft technology. JPL scientists responded that NASA had agreed to support a cadre of researchers at the lab and could not now deny them the opportunity to compete; without that opportunity they would surely desert JPL.[34] The increasingly complex instruments might also benefit from JPL's systems management, although university groups were also acquiring experience with scaled-up projects.

The lab failed to resolve the issue, which only added to the long-standing tension between JPL spacecraft engineers and outside scientists. A NASA committee studying science at NASA centers in 1988 stressed that labs such as JPL should not try to compete with university scientists, but rather should focus on those large programs beyond the capabilities of university groups.[35] Planetary geologist Albee had earlier expressed concern about JPL's increasing work in flight instruments, specifically the possibility that it would compete for experiments on Mars Observer and Cassini. After much discussion, the lab's executive council agreed that "JPL should consciously restrict its participation in the scientific payloads" for these missions "to what is a reasonable share for JPL." "Reasonable" was defined as the visible and infrared mapping spectrometer and the imaging camera plus two smaller instruments on each spacecraft.[36] Whereas JPL built no instruments for Voyager and only one for Galileo, the Cassini orbiter wound up with three, or one-fourth the total complement of twelve: the mapping spectrometer, a radar mapper, and a radio science instrument.[37] The lab, however, did not adopt any long-term policy regarding its pursuit of instruments and instead settled on a sort of laissez-faire: lab staff were free to enter proposals for any spacecraft, recognizing that NASA managers would consider institutional factors—just as they did for geographical distribution, and hence political interest—in the apportionment of flight experiments. If the aerospace industry provided a fourth leg on the Caltech-NASA-JPL triangle, the space science community perhaps constituted a fifth. The additional legs, however, did not necessarily enhance stability.

JPL under Allen

BRUCE MURRAY HAD RESIGNED AS DIRECTOR OF JPL BECAUSE HE PERCEIVED A turning point in the history of the lab, from the Mariner-Voyager era of planetary exploration to a combination NASA and military lab no longer sustained by planetary projects.[1] This transition would entail changes in JPL's internal management, starting at the top, and also in the lab's relations with Caltech and NASA and with an increasingly mature aerospace industry. Murray, however, underestimated the prospects for the planetary program, and the subsequent revival of the primary mission on top of new programs made growth a key issue in the 1980s.

JPL's Internal Evolution

When Lew Allen arrived at JPL in October 1982 he did not perceive any great mandate for change and undertook no sweeping reorganization. That itself represented a change from Murray's tenure, as did Allen's pragmatic management style, which departed from Murray's more visionary initiatives. In 1987 Allen wrote, with regard to NASA's long-term goal of sending humans to Mars, "we tend to set goals that are inadequately realistic. The visionary approach may be inspiring but unfortunately it causes nearer term objectives to suffer." Finally, Allen was accustomed to overseeing much larger organizations than JPL and thus tended to delegate more responsibility than Murray had. The net result was a more measured environment inside JPL, although it lacked some of the drama of the Murray years.[2]

Murray's strategic planning and political activism had responded to the demands of the context. Allen was fortunate to preside over a recovery of the planetary program, which combined with diversified programs in defense, earth science, and astronomy to more than double the lab budget in a span of five years, eventually passing $1 billion by the end of the decade, and to drive staff levels toward 6,000, well above the 4,000 or so of the late 1970s. Far from seeking to generate new business, the problem became performing work already committed. Allen declared in 1986 that "the JPL workforce is too large" and pledged to reduce staff through attrition.[3] But lower-level managers had little incentive for restraint, and associate director Clarence Gates perceived that "everybody wants to grow except the Director's Office."[4] Exceptions to Allen's no-growth policy became a running joke, as managers appealed to Allen's enthusiasm for technology and new missions while assuring him that growth was only temporary.[5]

Growth began to shift demographics toward younger staff, especially as veterans from the initial buildup of the 1950s began retiring. Charles Terhune stepped down as deputy director in December 1983; Harris "Bud" Schurmeier and Jack James retired from their defense and civil systems positions at the end of 1985; and in 1987 the lab lost deputy director Robert Parks and associate director Fred Felberg. James, Parks, and Schurmeier were the main originators of systems engineering at JPL, and their departure alone represented a loss of a century of hard-won experience. Although successors like John Casani were in place, the turnover began to open up the managerial ranks to promotion and heralded a more thorough changing of the guard as the rest of that generation approached retirement.

JPL's demographics also reflected the brain drain from Asia and the Middle East. Among the more prominent emigrés were Moustafa Chahine, named chief scientist in 1984, and Charles Elachi, head of the space science division. JPL, with the rest of the space program and American science and technology in general, capitalized on the modernization efforts of developing countries, which often stressed science and technology education, and on their persistent lack of research opportunities at the highest levels. For example, Chahine and Elachi—born fifteen miles apart in Lebanon—won scholarships from the Lebanese government to pursue higher education abroad, with no strings attached. Their respective paths through American and European universities eventually converged at JPL.[6]

Another major change came to the work environment in this period in the influx of personal computers, networking, and electronic mail. The personal computer met initial resistance at JPL, where information-systems managers viewed the mainframe network as sufficient and denied requests to buy computers for individuals, but it would eventually bring powerful capabilities to the individual desktops of scientists and engineers.[7] As JPL staff adapted to the boon of personal computers, they also confronted that bane of late twentieth-century office life: the cubicle. DSN engineers first moved from private offices to "open landscaping," also called the "Action Office," in 1976, and the lab newsletter played up how roomy and functional cubicles could be.[8] Lab staff were not buying it. In 1984 the technical divisions as a whole were made to switch to cubicles and nearly rose up in revolt. Engineers complained about the lack of space and privacy, the noise from telephones and chit-chat, and secondhand smoke from cigarettes (as the lab still permitted smoking indoors); one compared the new layout to an "assembly line," another to the notorious "Bull Pens" of big aircraft firms, and both predicted that cubicles would alienate key staff.[9]

JPL and Caltech

Allen's appointment marked a break from the convention of hiring the JPL director from Caltech, and may have thus represented a decision by the Caltech trustees and administration to increase JPL's independence from campus.[10] Allen nevertheless succeeded in improving JPL-Caltech relations, perhaps because he tried that much harder to reach out to campus. Allen's military background was initially a worry for some faculty, but he defused concerns in personal engagements with professors and through his straightforward presentations at faculty meetings. As a result, even amid protests against defense programs the faculty were usually deferential toward Allen.[11]

Allen also enjoyed higher rank on campus, even if the title was only symbolic. Murray had strongly urged upon his retirement that the JPL director also be a vice president at Caltech, to provide a formal connection to the trustees and also to counter what Murray perceived as the growing influence of the Caltech provost—nominally concerned with campus teaching and research—over JPL. As a vice president, the JPL director would be organizationally separate from campus, but the Caltech administration, at least, seemed to view the appointment as a token. When faculty asked, "Vice President for what?" president Goldberger replied, "Vice President of nothing."[12]

Murray had sought greater independence from Caltech faculty because of their resistance to defense work, but the subsequent reception of the Arroyo Center and Star Wars suggest that campus influence persisted and even increased. Rochus Vogt, the provost after 1983, however, had worked at JPL and strongly supported it, a change from the lukewarm attitude of the previous provost, John D. Roberts.[13] Although Vogt stepped down as provost in 1987, followed shortly by president Goldberger, Caltech's new president, Thomas Everhart, was an electrical engineer who took particular interest in JPL's work.[14]

Increasing evidence of fruitful collaboration had meanwhile dispelled any lingering tensions. The lab had long worked with campus geologists on planetary missions and more recently with astronomers on the Hubble camera and IRAS, but it now began engaging faculty in diverse fields, including general relativity and gravity-wave research and especially through technology programs. The microelectronics and supercomputing initiatives derived from campus collaborations, as we know, and campus faculty in turn gained access to expensive facilities, such as the e-beam lithography and hypercube. Although campus teaching appointments for JPL staff remained sparse, by 1986 there were thirty-six collaborative research projects under way between JPL and Caltech groups, many of them supported by the military; defense work thus increased campus collaboration as well as oversight.[15] Caltech's agreement to help finance a new Central Engineering Building was just one concrete manifestation, literally, of increasing campus-lab ties, as was the Infrared Processing and Analysis Center, for which Caltech provided all the construction funds directly.

There was another threat to the campus-lab balance in JPL's growth. Both campus and lab administrators recognized that growth and diversification diluted Caltech overview and further distinguished the lab from the focused academic environment.[16] Caltech, however, did little to restrain growth, in part because of the compensating windfall in overhead. From 1982 to 1987 the combined overhead and fee rose from about $10 million to $17 million (about $11 million of which was the fee).[17] In early 1982, amid the crisis in the planetary program, president Goldberger had proposed to wean Caltech from the fee "with all deliberate speed," but by 1986 it still supplied 11 percent of the campus budget, about the same fraction as in 1976. Hence, while faculty continued occasionally to question campus dependence on the fee, Caltech administrators preferred instead to perpetuate the arrangement: "The emphasis today is on maintaining the good relationship with NASA to see that the fee continues."[18] In this respect Caltech could view its financing of the Central Engineering Building and construction of the Infrared Processing and Analysis Center as investments whose dividends appeared annually in the JPL fee; or, from NASA's perspective, overhead payments to Caltech produced a return in the institute's contributions.[19]

JPL and the Local Community

The Infrared Processing and Analysis Center (IPAC) also highlighted JPL and Caltech's increasing sensitivity to community relations. Caltech planned to build the center beyond the existing campus boundary, along a street extending into a residential neighborhood. Campus administrators neglected to consult local residents about the proposal, however, and were surprised by vehement protests at a public hearing. Neighbors feared an intrusive building with attendant noise, traffic, and parking, and above all they worried that the center would deflate property values. They demanded that Caltech "put the building somewhere else—anywhere else." Caltech agreed to improve a neighboring park and minimize the architectural impact in a low-slung, one-story design nestled in trees, which together with support from local press and politicians overcame the opposition.[20]

As a result of the IPAC affair, Allen resolved to improve community relations.[21] But the episode demonstrated the substantial influence with local media and city government that JPL and Caltech already enjoyed, by virtue of their size and prestige. With more than 4,000 staff, JPL by the mid-1970s was the largest employer in Pasadena.[22] This statistic relied on the fact that JPL staff were Caltech employees. JPL itself was not located in Pasadena; it lay outside the city limits on land annexed by the town of La Cañada-Flintridge when it incorporated in 1976. After much squabbling between rival city boosters, including a declaration by the Pasadena city manager that "to see it end up in some other corporate limits would be like losing the Rose Bowl," JPL retained Pasadena as its official location when the U.S. Postal Service left the decision up to the lab. Pasadena thus won continued association with JPL in media bylines, and La Cañada-Flintridge residents were still stewing about it twenty years later.[23]

Pasadena city managers soon had cause to regret JPL's proximity owing to the emergence of a more pressing issue. Increasing public sensitivity in the United States to environmental pollution resulted, among other things, in the Safe Drinking Water Act of 1976 and testing of water supplies. In 1980 state health authorities began testing water wells in Pasadena and found a number of them contaminated with toxic carcinogens, including four wells in the Arroyo Seco east of JPL. The lab had developed formal control of hazardous waste in the early 1960s; before that, in the 1940s and 1950s, JPL had used cesspools, dumping pits, and an incinerator to dispose of wastes at the east end of the lab.[24]

Pasadena officials assumed the contamination came from JPL's early liquid-rocket research. The lab initially denied blame, noting that the contaminants —trichloroethylene, carbon tetrachloride, and tetrachlorethylene—were common industrial solvents and that thirty other wells throughout the San Gabriel Valley had also turned up excessive traces. JPL nevertheless agreed in 1985 to fund jointly with Pasadena an engineering study, in the spirit of a "good neighbor" and without admitting liability. An outside consultant subsequently concluded that JPL was the "most probable source" and recommended construction of a water treatment plant.[25] NASA agreed to pay for the plant, built in 1990 at a cost of $1.3 million, and JPL planned to commit about $1 million a year for several ensuing years to cleaning up the contamination. In 1992 JPL was named a "Superfund" site, one of more than 1,000 polluted places identified by the federal government for environmental remediation.[26]

Environmental liability would be a major issue in contract negotiations the following year: Caltech feared exposing its endowment to lawsuits, and NASA found itself paying for damage likely incurred under the previous army contract.[27] This was not just splitting hairs: JPL was shortly slapped with a lawsuit alleging that pollution caused the death of one local woman and Hodgkin's disease in two others; thirty-one other local residents petitioned to join the case. A groundwater study by the federal Health and Human Services Department in 1998 found no current threat and judged past hazards "unlikely," but JPL would continue to grapple with lawsuits into the new century.[28]

JPL's response to the groundwater problem is instructive. Despite the lawsuits and bad publicity, JPL avoided the much more active environmental controversies that plagued some other government labs. Like other facets of society in the cold war, research labs had raced to beat the Soviets, at a time of more cavalier attitudes toward waste disposal and the environment, and then faced the consequences decades later. Brookhaven National Lab, to take one example, encountered an uproar after revelations in the 1990s that a plume of groundwater near a nuclear reactor contained tritium. Hundreds of community activists packed public hearings and vented their anger. Brookhaven scientists could not understand the fuss over what they saw as a negligible hazard, but local residents resented what they viewed as evasions and patronizing reassurances based on statistical risk analysis. Brookhaven learned a hard lesson in community relations: the lab director was effectively pressured out of his job, and the contractor, which had run Brookhaven for fifty years, saw its contract summarily terminated by the Department of Energy in 1997.[29]

The JPL case differed in that it dealt with common industrial chemicals, whereas that of Brookhaven and other national labs involved radioactivity, with its popular associations of danger and secrecy.[30] Another prime difference from such labs as Brookhaven was that JPL had a finely tuned public relations organization and decades of experience operating in the media glare, including highly exposed failures. At JPL, managers early emphasized to staff that any public comments "will not underestimate the important nature of the problem. For example, we will not cite statistics in an effort to demonstrate that chances of getting cancer from Pasadena drinking water are low."[31] Another internal memo stressed that JPL and NASA should "maintain a positive, cooperative attitude in dealing with the city. The contribution of a substantial part of the construction cost of a treatment plant is preferable to the consequences of sensational adverse press coverage of the situation."[32] Its public relations experience helped JPL largely avoid the antagonistic community reaction that could characterize environmental cleanup elsewhere.

JPL and NASA

Allen's style also helped rebuild bridges to NASA that had been burned by Murray's political end-runs in the crisis of 1981. Unlike Murray, who seemed to relish his charges into the political fray, Allen tried to operate outside the down-and-dirty of Washington power politics, although he was certainly aware of political factors. In 1987 Caltech trustee Mary Scranton, a prime political resource for Murray, prompted Allen about NASA's political situation; Allen replied, "I'm always uneasy about suggesting action in the political arena because I don't understand that arena and since I don't have the answers."[33] That typical self-deprecation may have belittled Allen's considerable experience in Washington, but it did indicate a preference for political detachment that reinforced his reputation for integrity.

At times, however, Allen's aloofness cost JPL. In March 1989 Senator Barbara Mikulski, chair of the appropriations subcommittee that determined NASA's budget, visited JPL along with her staff. Mikulski's district in Maryland included NASA's Goddard Space Flight Center, as well as the Applied Physics Lab at Johns Hopkins that built spacecraft for the military. She already had a reason to favor her constituents over JPL, but the handling of her visit would give her another one. Rather than roll out the red carpet, Allen chose to spend little time with the senator and instead had her meet informally with managers of individual projects. The approach backfired; Mikulski was miffed at the lack of attention from Allen, and her staff came away highly critical of the casual briefings. When word got back to JPL, Allen tried to repair the damage with an apologetic letter, but the impression remained of an arrogant laboratory with little concern for costs.[34]

Relations with NASA itself, however, were mostly smooth. Contract negotiations in 1982 raised no apparent disputes, and another negotiation five years later likewise came out favorably from Caltech's point of view, including an increase in the annual fee of $1.6 million per year, which exceeded Caltech's negotiating target.[35] The contract relationship seemed so strong that NASA discussed extending it to its other centers. A study report of 1986 cited the advantages of decentralized flexible management, less detailed oversight, and easier recruitment of staff outside of civil service regulations. As for the disadvantages, JPL had shown that conflicts of interest, diluted commitment to NASA, and contract squabbles could be "successfully managed." The main drawbacks would be the cost in time and money to make the change, which in the end deterred NASA from converting, but the discussion indicated the prevailing appreciation of the JPL contract. A top-level review of the U.S. space program in 1990, known as the Augustine Committee after its chair Norman Augustine, similarly advised that if civil service regulations continued to stifle recruitment, NASA should switch other centers to the contract mode, "using as a model the Jet Propulsion Laboratory."[36]

A few troublesome issues lurked in relations with NASA. One was discretionary funds. In 1983 a panel reviewing federal labs for the White House Science Council, known as the Packard Panel after its chairman David Packard, recommended that labs have up to 10 percent of their budget at the discretion of the lab director.[37] Even after NASA increased the director's discretionary fund to $3 million in 1986, that still left less than 1 percent of the budget as discretionary.[38] Albert D. Wheelon, a Packard panelist, Caltech trustee, and longtime head of the Hughes space division, observed during a visit in 1988 that most aerospace companies usually devoted several percent of their budgets to discretionary R&D, as did such government labs as Los Alamos and Livermore; he suggested a reasonable figure for JPL of $30 to 50 million a year.[39]

The lack of discretion exaggerated NASA's neglect of advanced technology. Several microelectronics projects and the hypercube, for example, relied initially on discretionary seed money. JPL suffered doubly in comparison with the other NASA centers, which had salaries covered separately from R&D and hence had more flexibility; JPL's discretionary funds were eaten up by salaries and could support perhaps 15 full-time researchers. With NASA unwilling to provide extra discretionary funds, the alternative was to find them internally. But when Allen proposed adding discretionary R&D to indirect costs, project managers protested that it would essentially raid their budgets to fund advanced research. Allen would instead continue to seek increased discretion from NASA, to no avail.[40]

Another sticking point was patent policy. JPL could not own patents itself, and according to NASA regulations and contract provisions the space agency owned the rights to JPL inventions since it paid for the work. NASA did allow Caltech to petition for a waiver of this rule for certain inventions, in which case Caltech could file for the patent, license it, and keep the royalties. The institute in effect retained a sort of right of first refusal for promising inventions. NASA, however, sought to restrict these petitions to cases where Caltech could ensure commercial exploitation, and the cost of filing for patents meanwhile deterred Caltech from often exercising this option. Nevertheless, JPL by the mid-1980s consistently accounted for half or more of Caltech's patent filings: for instance, forty-nine of the eighty-one applications for 1988 were from JPL.[41] JPL's work for outside sponsors tested this arrangement, in particular the consideration of work for industry. NASA continued to insist that the sponsor, in this case the industrial firm, got the rights to patents. Donald Fowler, Caltech's lawyer, asserted that Caltech had the opposite policy for industrial sponsors, namely, that Caltech retained patent rights and just granted a license, usually nonexclusive, to the sponsor.[42] The issue revived the fundamental question: was JPL a NASA lab or a Caltech lab? Whose policies should apply? In the case of industrial sponsors, as with defense work, JPL's work outside of NASA tilted the balance toward Caltech.

JPL and Industry

The patent issue reflected increasing attention to the relation between government-funded research and the private sector. Public concern about American industrial competitiveness, especially with the thriving economies of Japan and Western Europe, had spurred new policies to help transfer technologies from government labs to industry. The Bayh-Dole act of 1980 encouraged contractors to patent the results of federally funded research and thus supported NASA's policy of letting Caltech patent JPL inventions, and the Federal Technology Transfer Act of 1986 promoted Cooperative Research and Development Agreements, or CRADAs, between government labs and industrial firms; similar joint projects with industry had sparked the discussion over patent policy.[43]

The commercialization of space made it a site of economic as well as military competition. In 1982 NASA's Robert Allnut announced the dawn of a new "commercial era" in space: the booming market in communications satellites was spilling over into launch vehicles, and new markets were emerging in remote sensing and space manufacturing. The Reagan administration meanwhile made privatization a cornerstone of national space policy.[44] NASA, JPL, and the lab's other sponsors thus sought to encourage technology transfer from such programs as microelectronics, but first they debated how and when to transfer—for instance, by sending people along with their ideas to industry for development, or by releasing technologies after they reached the prototype production stage. The hypercube program provided just one prominent example of a technology incorporated into commercial products through a series of licensing agreements.[45]

Technology transfer, of course, did not extend to international competitors, at least in theory. Spacecraft systems and components were defined as export-controlled technology. NASA's concerns over technology exports affected international cooperation on space projects, an objective otherwise encouraged. In 1982 Hitachi approached JPL about helping develop synthetic aperture radar systems for Japan. Burton Edelson, the space science manager at NASA, strongly urged Allen to terminate the discussions because of the economic as well as military potential of the radar: "I would hate to see NASA embarrassed by charges that we had created a first-class capability and then encouraged it to compete with U.S. industry." Allen agreed to stop the talks with Hitachi, but he noted that NASA itself "has indicated clearly that it desires *more* participation by foreign groups in space science projects" and furthermore that the military had sought a greater role for Japan in mutual defense. He added, "It is unrealistic to presume that foreign governments do not have technological advances in mind when they agree to be major participants in space projects."[46] Fears of international technology transfer similarly reduced Caltech-JPL collaboration, which NASA likewise sought to encourage. The agency refused to let JPL hire Caltech students who were foreign nationals, which in fields like electrical engineering excluded up to half the students. JPL and Caltech fought these restrictions, and others on publication of technology research, with little success. Allen, however, would win some relief by chairing a National Academy of Sciences panel on export controls in 1987, whose recommendations for relaxed controls influenced congressional revision of the Export Policy Act.[47]

JPL's internal growth also affected relations with industry by reviving the old make-or-buy question. The need to keep staff levels stable while accepting more programs encouraged managers to subcontract work instead of performing it in-house. The commercialization of space reinforced this tendency. Against both of these trends ran the sense that JPL was an engineering organization, and that the shift to managing contracts would erode the technical capabilities of the lab.[48]

Amid these developments, Allen in 1988 asked his friend Albert Wheelon to spend a few days at JPL assessing its capabilities. Wheelon, surprisingly enough for an industry leader, did not dispute JPL's desire for in-house work. His philosophy at Hughes was never to leave mission-critical components to contractors; if you had to have something done right, build it yourself. And when JPL did farm out work, Wheelon advised, it should pick the right contractors. For some components, such as spacecraft transponders, JPL seemed to settle for second-best. And why go to industry in the first place? Transponders were critical; a silent spacecraft is worthless. Industrial contractors catered to the military and communications markets for earth-orbiting satellites, whose transponders had much shorter ranges and wider bandwidths than planetary spacecraft. Despite Wheelon's advice, JPL continued to rely on the same supplier, perhaps because of an unspoken preference for a pliable contractor, one whose engineers would more easily accept technical oversight without questioning decisions handed down from the lab.[49]

Recovery of Flight Projects

THE LAB'S GROWTH IN THE 1980S STEMMED FROM THE RECOVERY OF ITS MAIN mission in planetary exploration. The recovery, however, rested on plans for a new low-cost approach that did not translate easily into practice, and then the explosion of the space shuttle Challenger threw the entire space program into turmoil. The deep-space program did benefit from the examination of U.S. space policy that followed Challenger, as well as from increasing international competition—and collaboration. But cost overruns in spacecraft development and also technical problems after launches revived questions about JPL's approach at the end of the decade.

Low-Cost Missions Redux: To the Planets, Cheaply?

The immediate source for the recovery was a report by NASA's Solar System Exploration Committee (SSEC), an ad hoc panel of prominent space scientists convened by NASA in late 1980 to develop a long-range planetary program through 2000 within a limited budget. By summer 1981 the committee was converging on a consensus for smaller, cheaper, and more frequent missions. Its formal report of April 1983 proposed three classes of missions: a Planetary Observer class, under $150 million, for simple orbiters for the inner planets; a more ambitious Mariner class, for $300–500 million, for more complicated missions to outer planets, comets, or asteroids; and the billion-dollar Viking class, which was unacceptable in the existing environment. The Observers would derive from commercial, earth-orbiting satellites, while the middle-class missions would build around a standard, modular "Mariner Mark II" spacecraft proposed by JPL—another attempt to capitalize on the Mariner brand name. The report also urged that NASA establish a long-term planetary program, with fixed funding of perhaps $300 million each year, to support a series of missions, instead of having to seek separate approval for every new project. A stable program, like the Explorer series for astronomy satellites, would avoid the feast-or-famine pattern of the previous decade and also remove the incentive for scientists to pile objectives onto each spacecraft, as they would now be assured of ensuing missions. Standardized spacecraft in a long-term program might thus avoid two main drivers behind high costs: technology development and proliferating science objectives.[1]

The SSEC in another respect represented a shift toward emphasizing science rather than exploration. Instead of making the public the constituency, as Murray had tried to do, the SSEC report made the scientific community the constituency, albeit with scaled-back ambitions.[2] The SSEC plan had little to engage the public: there were no rovers, Mars sample returns, or new propulsion systems, and only the comet-asteroid mission promised to visit a new place. Rather than try to generate interest, the committee assumed a lack of political support, owing to decreasing Soviet competition and increasing contention within NASA for funds, and chose to live with it.

The Observer class seemed to embrace the logic of LESS, JPL's earlier proposal for cheaper, frequent, focused missions with high inheritance. But some SSEC members questioned JPL's ability to work in the new mode. In late 1982 James Arnold of UC San Diego expressed to Lew Allen the sentiment that JPL was giving only "lip service" to the Observer concept; JPL engineers were instead focused on Mariner Mark IIs, which threatened to grow in size and price. Arnold warned that "I (and most members of the SSEC) doubt that JPL could manage a small mission successfully," and that "smaller and leaner" labs such as at Ames, industry, or universities might make a better claim for such projects. Allen allowed to Arnold that "some people [at JPL] may have been prisoners of past successes" but that he was encouraging "fresh ideas on how to undertake smaller projects."[3]

Allen did recognize the SSEC plan as a good influence after the crisis of 1981. By February 1983 the planetary program seemed to have stabilized, and by that July Allen perceived "more work opportunities than we can do."[4] The SSEC report had listed four missions in order of priority: a Venus radar mapper; a Mars orbiter; a comet rendezvous and asteroid flyby, known by the acronym CRAF; and a Titan probe and radar mapper soon called Cassini.[5] NASA had already approved the Venus mission, to launch in 1988, after John Gerpheide of JPL presented a plan to cut the costs of the cancelled VOIR mission by more than half, from $700 million to $300 million. The proposed Venus Radar Mapper would still carry a synthetic aperture radar, but it left out the radar's high-resolution mode as well as all atmospheric experiments. Digital processing of the images allowed an elliptical instead of circular orbit, with software correcting for elevation and viewing angle. An elliptical orbit in turn eliminated the need for aerobraking and thus simplified operations as well as propellant requirements. Instead of separate antennas for radar and communications, engineers used just a single leftover antenna from Voyager and rotated the entire spacecraft for each function. Other spare parts for the mission, renamed Magellan in 1985, included a spacecraft bus and propulsion system from Voyager and computers and tape recorders from Galileo.[6] The Venus mission's creative recycling justified crow-barring it into the SSEC plan, although it was not considered part of the Observer series since it did not use a standard, earth-orbiting satellite. The first Observer, the Mars orbiter, was shortly approved to begin development in 1985, with a cost of about $200 million, and to launch in 1990. In addition to the standard satellite bus, development of a standard inventory of instruments and a multimission operations system would cut costs for the Observers.[7]

By the end of 1985 the planetary program seemed back on track. Voyager was due to arrive at Uranus in early 1986, followed by the launch of Galileo; the Venus and Mars missions were under way, and CRAF was supposed to follow as a new start in 1986. JPL had also rejoined the International Solar Polar Mission, now renamed Ulysses, and would provide navigation, tracking, and mission control for the European spacecraft.[8] The new projects increased the planetary program 71 percent from 1982 to 1986—and that did not include CRAF. Together with the arrival of Halley's comet and the launch of the Hubble telescope in August, the burgeoning slate encouraged NASA to declare 1986 the "year of space science."[9] JPL entered that year with renewed optimism, which events would soon dispel.

Challenger

JPL staff watched in shock with the rest of the nation as the space shuttle Challenger exploded after launch on 28 January 1986. Although their thoughts turned to the seven crew members killed in the accident, they also recognized the implications for their own work. The space shuttle fleet would be grounded and with it all JPL spacecraft, owing to NASA's abandonment of alternative launch vehicles, and NASA's resources and attention would go to analyzing the cause of the failure and returning the shuttle to service.[10]

The significance of launch delays grew as confident plans for recovery gave way to grim reality. At first JPL staff shared NASA's assumptions, as of March 1986, for one year of downtime for the shuttle and a launch rate of twenty-four per year by 1990. Instead the delay stretched out to two and a half years: flights resumed in September 1988, and the shuttle fleet never came close to the expected launch rate.[11] The result was a twelve-year gap in launches from Voyager in 1977 to Galileo and Magellan in 1989, with Voyager's infrequent encounters providing the sole sustenance for planetary exploration. Furthermore, in June 1986 NASA decided to cancel the Centaur upper stage as a booster for space shuttle payloads, owing to the danger of carrying a highly energetic, liquid-fuelled rocket in the shuttle bay. The decision put in doubt the Galileo, Ulysses, and the Mariner Mark II missions, all of which had depended on the powerful Centaur to provide velocities beyond those of the solid-fuel options. Engineers on the three projects began casting about for alternative means to fly their desired trajectories.[12]

The combination of delays and redesigns demolished morale at JPL. After the Centaur cancellation, Allen lamented that "the decade of the '80s turned out to be a dry hole. . . . Things have gone very sour indeed," and one anonymous administrator declared, "I've never been so depressed in my life."[13] The post-Challenger doldrums at JPL spurred the shift to earth sciences and instruments and also briefly revived the marketing of defense programs. Challenger also provoked much examination of the basis for American space policy. Motivated by the sense, as Allen privately put it, that "NASA, as a space agency, is at risk of becoming largely irrelevant," a succession of high-level committees considered the future of the space program.[14] First up in May 1986 was a White House panel chaired by former NASA chief Thomas Paine, followed the next year by a NASA panel under physicist and astronaut Sally Ride. Both the Paine and Ride reports envisioned human exploration of Mars as the next great goal, a plan that received official endorsement in July 1989 when President George H. W. Bush announced, on the twentieth anniversary of Apollo 11 and with lofty rhetoric, that the United States would return to the moon and then send humans on to Mars.[15]

The combination of a lunar outpost and human Mars mission, eventually called the Space Exploration Initiative, sought to revive the space program with ambitious goals. The enterprise was soon overtaken by world events—namely, the unraveling of the Soviet Union. In the meantime, it renewed the debate over robots versus humans in space. The initiative rated science as a lower priority than human spaceflight; the emphasis on the moon and Mars left little room for planetary exploration, and robotic spacecraft served mainly as advance scouts for human missions. The initial name applied to it in 1989, the Human Exploration Initiative, belied the emphasis, although "Human" was soon replaced by "Space." Even before then, Caltech trustees worried along with JPL that "the entire SSEC program for the exploration of the outer planets has been abandoned in these initiatives."[16] In response, first the National Research Council's Space Science Board in 1988 and then another ad hoc White House panel of 1990, this one under Norman Augustine, urged that NASA scale back human flight and instead emphasize space science.[17]

Scientists and JPL staff focused their concerns on the space station, which was included in most of the new plans as a stepping stone to the moon and Mars. As the shuttle had a decade before, the space station was threatening to siphon money from space science, as well as to monopolize shuttle launches. Furthermore, its orbit was of little use for Earth observations or for launching planetary or astronomy spacecraft, although it might help with sample return missions.[18] JPL's history with the shuttle reinforced its traditional aversion to human spaceflight programs and produced widespread opposition to the station at the lab. As Robert Staehle remarked, "It was almost a litmus test for a JPL person that they hated the manned space program."[19]

Not everyone at JPL passed the test. Staehle himself liked human missions, and a few others in the early 1980s worried that JPL's disdain would cause it to miss NASA's next gravy train.[20] But JPL's distaste for the space station started at the top. Allen preferred "incremental, enabling steps" and "less grandiose" programs and viewed the Space Exploration Initiative as "perhaps noble, but likely futile."[21] He considered the space station itself a boondoggle, and in non-NASA forums—for instance, before the Caltech faculty—stated that "JPL is not needed for, and not all that interested in, the space station."[22] Shortly after this declaration in 1986, NASA asked JPL to take on the job of systems engineering for the space station. Allen swallowed his objections and agreed, appointing Richard Laeser to lead a new office in Reston, Virginia. Laeser and others soon realized, as Norm Haynes put it, that "to do the system engineering on the space station is going to take all of JPL," and the lab gradually withdrew.[23]

A prime driver for the ambitious space initiatives of the late 1980s was the sense, expressed by the Ride report in 1987, that the United States had lost "leadership" in space.[24] The Challenger accident came amid renewed competition from the Soviets, magnified by the subsequent hiatus in American launches. The Soviet missions Venera 15 and 16 had already beaten JPL by orbiting synthetic aperture radars around Venus in 1983, and two Vega spacecraft had deployed landers and balloons at Venus in 1985 before flying past Halley's comet in 1986. By 1985 Lew Allen noted "rising concern about the Soviet space program, which appears to be doing the American program two years before the Americans." The following year a *National Geographic* cover story asked, "Are the Soviets ahead in space?"[25] The competition increased and shifted to Mars. In 1987 the Soviets startled American planners by laying out an ambitious series of Mars missions: redundant spacecraft, Phobos 1 and 2, for launch in 1988 to orbit Mars and skim over its moon Phobos; two orbiting craft in 1992 to deploy penetrators; rover/penetrator missions in 1994; and a sample return in 1996.[26] Although both Phobos missions ultimately failed, they sparked media jokes about the "red planet" and darker warnings about a "space gap" amid the presidential election of 1988.[27]

Competition was not confined to the Soviet Union. The commercial challenge from Western Europe and Japan was expressed also in their maturing space programs, exemplified by their separate pursuit of Halley missions. NASA managers and advisors, including the Paine committee of 1986, stressed that Europe and Japan, as well as China and perhaps India, were joining the space race.[28] Competition, however, also coexisted with cooperation. This is clear not only for Europe—for example, the Netherlands provided the satellite bus for IRAS and West Germany a propulsion system for Galileo, while JPL participated in Ulysses—but also for the Soviets. As with earlier periods of the cold war, the internationalist ideals of science spurred collaboration to offset national competition.[29] Although the chill in Soviet-American relations in the late 1970s curtailed collaborations in space from earlier in the decade, by 1984 some thawing was evident. That year President Reagan proposed space collaboration as a way to improve ties. Although Allen would at times cite Soviet competition to help justify JPL missions, he also began urging cooperation to senators and NASA managers, in part to allow American scientists to capitalize on the active European and Soviet programs.[30]

The delays in American launches following Challenger encouraged such considerations, and the emerging Soviet policy of glasnost provided impetus from the other direction. In September 1986 Allen and a team of American scientists visited Moscow to discuss specific possibilities, which led to a joint agreement on cooperation in planetary exploration "for peaceful purposes," signed in April 1987. The agreement, however, had modest goals: exchanges of data, coordination of planned missions, joint workshops, along with continued support by the Deep Space Network of Soviet missions.[31] The cold war continued, and the relevance of planetary spacecraft to national security hampered more substantial collaboration, such as joint missions. When the two countries agreed at the Moscow summit in May 1988 to extend "space glasnost" by flying science experiments on each other's spacecraft, the plan foundered on military fears of technology transfer.[32]

Hence, although JPL scientists would participate in planning and data analysis on Phobos and subsequent missions, collaboration with the Soviet Union was otherwise limited.[33] An ambitious plan by Carl Sagan and Bruce Murray, put forth even before Challenger and then taken up widely, called for joint human missions under the banner of "To Mars . . . Together."[34] The initiative fizzled with the subsequent collapse of Soviet Union, which removed incentives to collaboration, both idealistic and practical, along with the barriers. But collaboration with Europe meanwhile increased and Japan joined the mix, with JPL, for example, building CCD cameras for a Japanese space telescope.[35] Together with the prospects of Soviet cooperation, these international initiatives increased the complexity of JPL's external environment and balanced the competitive aspects of space exploration.

The SSEC Plan in Action

International competition spurred the Solar System Exploration Committee to reconvene in the summer of 1986. Committee members cited ambitious European, Japanese, and especially Soviet programs, which they had not anticipated five years earlier, as reason to rethink their plan, together with the consequences of Challenger and a new regime at NASA.[36] A year later the committee issued only slightly revised recommendations: the existing Mariner Mark II program, and a new Mars program to start with the Observer and proceed to rovers and sample return. It thus added an element of exploration to the earlier plan's emphasis on science.[37]

Beyond specific plans, however, the committee raised a general alarm about the planetary program, one which echoed in the space science community at large. As NASA figured out how to rebuild the shuttle program, and as new studies stressed the space station and human missions, space scientists feared getting lost in the shuffle. Another NASA panel, the Space and Earth Science Advisory Committee, summarized prevailing sentiment in November 1986 in a report titled "The Crisis in Space and Earth Science."[38] A month earlier Lew Allen had warned Burt Edelson, NASA's manager for space science, about "the already strained relationship between NASA and the planetary science community," and a year later Edelson's successor, Lennard Fisk, was still bemoaning the "bleak picture" for planetary missions.[39]

Why the gloom after the rebound in planetary budgets from the early 1980s? For one, NASA began diverting money from planetary exploration in 1987 and 1988. As a cost-cutting measure the agency postponed launching Mars Observer from 1990 until 1992. NASA blamed the delay on a projected shortage of launch capacity when the shuttle returned to flight, but scientists argued that an expendable booster could be used and that NASA's real reason was money: $40 million saved in 1997 and $50 million in 1998, although the delay would inflate the final cost of the project. As for CRAF, JPL had initially sought to start it in 1986, but NASA deferred it first to 1987 and then to 1988, with Cassini assumed to follow as a new start in 1991. The deferrals impelled planetary scientists to warn that NASA was playing off parts of the community against each other, by threatening to take money from CRAF to restore the earlier launch of Mars Observer.[40]

The planetary community also clashed over general approaches to projects, and this division was perhaps a deeper source for the sense of crisis. The crucial development, according to the Space and Earth Science Advisory Committee, was not the Challenger accident or Soviet competition but rather "the trend toward big science." Planetary spacecraft consisted now of "facility-class missions," not a small spacecraft with a single experiment but a complex flying laboratory with a multitude of instruments. The trend extended to astronomy and its Great Observatories, such as the Hubble telescope, and in fact was manifest in other fields ranging from particle physics to plasma physics. The committee thus did not see it as cause for alarm, but rather as a natural development that NASA's plans should accommodate: "the days of simple science in space are largely over."[41]

This view contradicted the SSEC's stress on smaller, focused missions. But the SSEC plan had also made the scientific community the constituency, which encouraged mission planners to seek a broad base among scientists in order to win support for new missions and hence multiplied science goals. This tendency was reinforced by the advisory committees, such as the Space Science Board of the National Academy of Sciences, that defined scientific goals for each mission, at times with little consideration for cost. In 1988 Caltech's Jerry Wasserburg blasted such panels for recommending "Christmas-tree missions adorned in excess with experiments of lesser significance, yielding a final product of excessive cost and high risk. . . . Neither the Space Science Board nor any other advisory body may act as if had just inherited a candy store and is passing out sweets to all the kids in the neighborhood."[42] The backlash against big science in space contributed to the appeal of microspacecraft; another manifestation of this movement would receive official sanction from NASA in the 1990s.

The science community also divided along the old line of science versus exploration. Murray, for example, viewed the SSEC plan as a political misstep; the public, in addition to scientists, for Murray remained the constituency. For this reason Murray, together with Carl Sagan, backed human missions to Mars as a way to invigorate the whole civil space program and so raised the ire of planetary scientists, who thought that Murray and Sagan's Planetary Society was supposed to be working for them.[43] Leaders of the Planetary Society and the SSEC recognized perceptions of "conflict" and "resentment" between the two groups; an example was the society's focus on Mars, which led to criticism that it was "soft on CRAF."[44] The Planetary Society at the time was also considering whether to try sponsoring its own space missions, to demonstrate an alternative to big, science-driven NASA projects. One such proposal for a Mars spacecraft stressed that "science should be given a low priority on this mission, if it is given any direct participation at all. . . . Imaging, imaging, and more imaging is the name of the game. . . . The aim here is to obtain images that are shameless crowd-pleasers and show Mars from a human perspective. If that's not good science, well then tough."[45]

These internal divisions indeed contributed to the demise of the SSEC plan—or, rather, they were symptoms of the ills that continued to plague the planetary program. Of the plan's two main legs, the Observer line was the first to give way. There were four main assumptions behind the plan: cheap and frequent shuttle launches; consistent long-term funding; standardized instruments; and a modified earth-orbital spacecraft. None worked in practice. The shuttle was unlikely to provide the first requirement even before the Challenger accident. The second, for a line item in the annual NASA budget for the Planetary Observer program, was rejected by the Office of Management and Budget in 1984 at the same time the individual Mars project was approved.[46] The refusal of federal budgeteers to yield long-term budgetary discretion in turn affected the selection of instruments. These were supposed to be treated as a single payload, in effect making the instruments fit the spacecraft instead of designing the spacecraft around the instruments.[47] For Mars Observer, however, a science working group allowed instruments to be integrated individually instead of bundled together, which a JPL manager warned would yield "control over the experimenters' appetites."[48] Sure enough, science teams proposed an array of fruitful experiments, and by 1986 NASA managers had accepted a complement of instruments that exceeded the design payload. To make matters worse, several of these instruments were not well understood, as the Observer concept assumed, but rather were highly developmental and hence were found to need more money, mass, and electrical power than expected.[49] The fourth and final assumption, of a modified earth-orbiting satellite, would prove equally unworkable, as the modifications required for deep space erased the expected inheritance.

Enhancements helped drive the budget from initial estimates of $293 million to more than $500 million by October 1987. The cost growth came from instrument and subsequent spacecraft modifications and from the decision after Challenger to delay the launch two years.[50] These factors do not absolve JPL itself. A sense persisted that the lab was "neither interested in the project nor willing to take on the job of bringing it to fruition." That was the judgment in 1988 of Michael Malin, head of the camera team. Unlike James Arnold, who had earlier questioned JPL's commitment to the low-cost Observer concept, Malin criticized JPL's "unwillingness . . . to recognize the importance of Mars Observer beyond the limited scope originally viewed for the mission."[51] Malin's camera typified the ambitious proposals helping to drive up costs, but he may have had a point about JPL's apparent indifference. The lab had consistently underspent allocated funds, up to about one-third of the planned budget by April 1987, suggesting a tepid commitment to the work.[52]

Another factor driving cost growth was NASA's and JPL's willingness to back-load the budget, accepting larger long-term costs in order to present lower short-term budgets. The launch slip to 1992 was a prime example. NASA blamed the delay on a lack of shuttle launches but refused congressional and contractor offers to help finance an expendable launch vehicle for 1990 (and the 1992 launch ended up using such a rocket anyway); the agency instead appeared set on saving $70 million in the next two years in exchange for higher final costs of $125 million. Those estimates soon inflated further, as JPL, NASA, and scientists took advantage of the delay to upgrade the spacecraft and instruments, with congressional support. The project manager at JPL declared in May 1987 that the launch slip "created something of a new situation and some of the limitations of the past may no longer apply." JPL managers increased reliability by purchasing a backup spacecraft and adopting a more thorough testing regimen. They also allowed the scientific teams to enhance instrument reliability and performance, in part to exploit increased mass and power margins, which in turn required redesign of the spacecraft. Although NASA sought to cut costs the following year by cutting or scaling back certain experiments, many enhancements crept back in ensuing years to push budgets ever higher.[53] By the time it launched in late 1992, Mars Observer had taken eight years from start to launch and $959 million, including the launch vehicle, a far cry from the $150-million Observers contemplated by the SSEC plan of 1983.

There was plenty of blame to go around for Observer's expansion, starting with the old problem of the shuttle as launch vehicle and the refusal of a consistent long-term program. The science community then unsurprisingly sought to maximize the scientific return; NASA managers indulged the scientists and in general tolerated long-term cost growth for short-term savings. The contractor, RCA (later bought by General Electric), was accused of lowballing its initial bid; JPL managers then complained that the company resisted JPL oversight and, with a fixed-price contract, "kept sticking it to us with the slow reveal," gradually divulging a series of overruns.[54]

But responsibility for project management ultimately resided at JPL, and the history of Observer suggested the lab could not keep the lid on costs. NASA managers thought the lab responded slowly to budget overruns and then resisted plans to cut costs.[55] JPL staff recognized at least the perception of complicity. In 1989 flight projects director John Casani commissioned a study of the project by Caltech economists. The resultant report ascribed some of the cost growth to JPL itself; it also concluded that within six months of approval the project had departed from the Observer concept.[56] Subsequent actions abandoned it altogether. Instead of a series of standardized spacecraft, the Mars mission was the first and last in the Observer line. As a programmatic initiative, Observer had failed long before it reached the launch pad. And its troubles were not over yet.

The collapse of the SSEC plan was also apparent in its other main component, Mariner Mark II. As with Observer, Mariner Mark II assumed that NASA would reward discipline on the part of JPL and planetary scientists with consistent funding. By 1985 Allen was pointing out to NASA that delays in the approval of CRAF, the comet-asteroid mission, threatened the arrangement.[57] Competition among disciplines also continued to undermine stable annual support. As Galileo had contended with the Hubble telescope, CRAF lost out to a large X-ray telescope called AXAF and the Topex oceanographic satellite.[58] The deferrals meant missed launch opportunities and hence new trajectories, propulsion requirements, and mass margins for instruments. The delay from a 1987 start, for instance, meant the target comet Wild 2 was out of range, so plans shifted to comet Tempel 2, which required a 1992 launch; additional delays then made the comet Kopff the target.[59]

Delays in CRAF also pushed back the Cassini mission to Saturn, which was next in the queue for Mariner Mark II. Then NASA suggested combining the two missions, to capitalize on commonality in the Mariner Mark II design.[60] The two spacecraft would still launch separately, but their design and development would overlap. The revamped CRAF/Cassini proposal won congressional approval as a new start for 1990, with CRAF due to launch in 1995 and Cassini the following year. Less than a year into the project, however, NASA found itself eliminating major instruments from CRAF in order to meet congressional cost caps, forcing still more redesigns, and even these steps seemed unlikely to solve funding problems—as subsequent events would confirm.[61]

By the end of the 1980s the SSEC plan for a stable planetary program had expired. A combination of external factors killed it: the Challenger accident, NASA's focus on human spaceflight, competition from astronomy and earth science, and the lack of a long-term political commitment. But tendencies within the program also contributed, including disagreement among planetary scientists over the goals and approach of the program, overambitious instrument payloads pushed by scientists doubtful of future missions, and acquiescence by JPL and NASA managers in the inflation of mission objectives, costs, and schedules. The expected benefits of the plan—especially cost savings from inheritance in spacecraft and instruments—failed to materialize. By 1990 the planetary program was back to where it was at the start of the decade, struggling to win approval for scarce, big missions and to fend off delays and overruns for the projects under development.

Voyager Redux, Galileo, and Magellan

IN SPITE OF THE FAILURE OF THE SSEC PLAN—THE BLOATED MARS OBSERVER, the deferral of Mariner Mark II—the decade of the 1980s closed on a generally upbeat note. The optimism of 1985, dashed by Challenger, returned. Mars Observer and CRAF/Cassini, although expanding beyond austerity, were still under way. Voyager meanwhile continued to sustain the lab with encounters with Uranus in 1986 and Neptune in 1989, and together with Galileo and Magellan it combined to restore confidence at JPL.

Voyager

Amid the drought in planetary launches, the main sustenance for planetary scientists in this period came from Voyager 2's encounters at Uranus and Neptune, which extended Voyager's triumphal tour of the outer solar system. But the encounters did not simply entail sitting back and waiting for the spacecraft to get there. On the contrary, getting there, and getting data back, required much new work. One problem had cropped up just as Voyager 2 left Saturn. The scan platform—the turntable that held the camera and several other science instruments—started sticking, probably because the drive actuators had lost lubrication over the several years of flight. Careful testing freed the platform, but project manager Richard Laeser (who succeeded Esker Davis and, before him, Ray Heacock) elected to limit any platform motions to low speed, and the threat remained that it might stick again during a crucial phase of an encounter.[1]

Much of the work for Uranus and Neptune involved not correcting malfunctions, but rather adapting the spacecraft for the more distant environment. Engineering on Voyager was not a case of build-it-and-launch-it;

instead it became a continuous process through the lifetime of the spacecraft. In effect, JPL engineers redesigned the spacecraft while it was flying. They had to address several issues associated with the fact that the spacecraft at Uranus was twice as old and twice as far away as at Saturn. One concern was the shrinking supply of hydrazine propellant, which required careful management of trajectory and attitude-control maneuvers. Another was the power supply from the radioisotopic generators, which by 1986 had decayed from 470 watts to about 400 watts. At the same time, the spacecraft needed more power at its greater distance to run heaters and transmit data. With 400 watts, the spacecraft could not run all the subsystems at once—for instance, moving the scan platform to take a picture while recording data on tape and beaming radio signals through a planet's atmosphere. Engineers choreographed "a careful ballet" of power use, turning instruments, heaters, and other components on and off to avoid overloading the power system.[2]

Another dwindling resource was light, which decreases with the square of the distance from the sun. Since the orbit of Uranus is twice as distant as that of Saturn, Voyager's camera would have one-fourth the light to work with. Quadrupling exposure times threatened to smear pictures, from both spacecraft jitter and its high velocity (almost 15 kilometers per second) relative to the planets and their moons. For jitter, JPL engineers beamed up new software to produce much finer control of thrusters and to correct for angular momentum imparted by the tape recorder. For high-speed smear, they resorted to "panning" the camera, much as a photographer in a moving car might swing a camera to keep nearby objects from blurring. The scan platform, however, had a step actuator whose jerks, however small, would also blur pictures. So engineers elected to turn the whole spacecraft, by substituting software to bluff the attitude-control system into thinking it was drifting to the degree needed to pan the camera. This solution entailed some risk since it meddled with the crucial attitude-control software and also interrupted radio communication by swinging the antenna away from Earth. It also affected the thermal exposure of the spacecraft, which in turn required recalculating frequency shifts to get signals to the crippled backup receiver. Project managers judged that the potential science return justified the risk—and, again, they were rewarded by the return of sharper images.[3]

Radio signal strength similarly decreases with the square of the distance. Voyager radiated its signals into space at 23 watts and it took close to three hours from Uranus, and more than four hours from Neptune, for them to reach Earth while traveling at the speed of light. Detecting the signals depended on the Deep Space Network; the Voyager encounters would thus highlight the central, underappreciated role of the DSN in enabling space exploration—not just JPL projects but all American and, indeed, worldwide space missions.[4]

Telecommunication to Uranus and Neptune required upgrades in hardware and software. For Uranus, engineers merged the signals from the single 64-meter and two 34-meter antennas in Australia and then arrayed them with the 64-meter dish at the Parkes observatory for radioastronomy. For Neptune, JPL won approval to enlarge the DSN's three 64-meter antennas to 70 meters, and then to combine them with the Very Large Array of 25-meter antennas in New Mexico and a 70-meter radiotelescope in Japan, along with the Parkes dish (see figure 13.1). Together these various antennas managed to collect enough bits to support a data rate of up to 30 kilobits per second.[5]

That still fell below the data rate at Jupiter and Saturn. A single Voyager image required more than 5,000 kilobits, and the Uranus encounter would return almost 6,000 images, not to mention other scientific and engineering data. JPL engineers turned to software to enhance data transmission. For images, new software programs commanded Voyager to transmit only the change in brightness from pixel to pixel instead of the absolute brightness for each pixel, halving the necessary bits per pixel. Engineers also changed the coding scheme for error detection. Error detection codes added a pattern of binary numbers to the downlinked data, to enable the detection of flipped bits (for instance, a 0 garbled into a 1 by background noise). The Jupiter and Saturn encounters used Golay encoding, where the number of code bits equaled the number of data bits, doubling the transmission load. For Uranus and Neptune, the Voyager team switched to Reed-Solomon coding, which used only one code bit for every seven data bits and hence provided a much more efficient data rate. The redesign was aided by the fact that Voyager's original designers had included the hardware needed for Reed-Solomon encoding as a backup to the Golay scheme, but also with an eye to the Uranus-Neptune mission.[6]

The Deep Space Network proved crucial not only to communication, but also to navigation. The standard way to locate a spacecraft used radiometric data, combining the round-trip signal time, the angle between the beam and a reference radio source in the sky, and the Doppler shift to determine spacecraft position and velocity. The Voyager encounters combined radiometry with a newer optical approach, which used the spacecraft's cameras to situate it relative to the planets and their satellites. The combination located Voyager to within 23 kilometers at Uranus, more than 3 billion kilometers distant.[7]

The demand for precise navigation stemmed from science and the geometry of the encounter. Unlike the other planets in the solar system, Uranus and its satellite system orbited around an axis parallel to the ecliptic (with the planet's south pole pointing toward the sun), presenting a vertical bull's-

Figure 13.1. Seventy-meter antenna at the Deep Space Network station at Canberra. *Source:* JPL Photolab.

eye to Voyager. The penalty for poor aim was deducted from the dwindling supply of hydrazine propellant: missing the aim point at Uranus by 225 kilometers took 1 kilogram of fuel to correct the trajectory to Neptune. The perpendicular target also concentrated the Uranus encounter into six hours on 24 January 1986, as the spacecraft zipped past.[8]

As before, engineers plotted the trajectory to maximize the science return from both planets. The results rivaled those from Jupiter and Saturn. At Uranus, flight planners had selected the moon Miranda for the closest flyby, and it did not disappoint. Images of Miranda proved almost as surprising as the ones of Io at Jupiter, revealing a cratered landscape scarred by extensive regions of sharp ridges and valleys, at some places in angular networks, with canyons 15 kilometers deep and sheer cliff faces several kilometers high (see figure 13.2). Scientists struggled to explain this evidently young terrain and pondered whether Miranda had been blasted apart by another large body and then re-accreted, or if it had geological activity unexpected at this distance from the sun, perhaps driven by tidal forces. The larger moons Titania and Ariel also displayed fault systems and canyons characteristic of recent internal activity.[9]

Images of Uranus itself showed only a dull blue-green ball, but fields and particles experiments yielded further surprises, in particular, a remarkably nonuniform magnetic field. The data indicated that the planet's magnetic poles were inclined 60 degrees from the poles of rotation, and further that the magnetic axis did not run through the center of the planet but rather was offset a third of the radius. The odd magnetic configuration suggested dynamic internal fluid flows powering the magnetic field that differed greatly from other planets.[10]

A similarly skewed magnetic field appeared three years later at Neptune, tilted 47 degrees from the rotation axis and offset half the radius. The off-kilter fields at both planets suggested that the perpendicular rotation axis for Uranus might not be the cause of its magnetic anomaly, and scientists struggled to find an explanation for the fields. Neptune also displayed striking weather patterns, including near-supersonic winds and extensive cloud formations of hydrogen sulfide, ammonia, or methane ice crystals, including one persistent storm about the diameter of Earth, dubbed the Great Dark Spot. At the cold distance of Neptune's orbit such weather seemed to derive energy from internal heat sources. Neptune's moon Triton meanwhile displayed few impact craters amid a varied landscape of ridges and valleys and icy plains. The scarcity of craters suggested recent geological activity, a theory apparently confirmed by the appearance of plumes of material 8 kilometers high extending from geyser-like vents on the surface (see figure 13.3). As with Io's volcanoes at Jupiter, scientists located the engine of Triton's unexpected geological activity in tidal forces from its orbit around Neptune.[11]

The science results from these encounters fed a stream of scientific papers and special journal issues.[12] More broadly, Voyager 2 continued the earlier trend from Jupiter and Saturn in revealing the diversity and dynamic character of the solar system. The large gaseous planets themselves displayed meteorological activity unexpected in the colder reaches of the solar system and odd electromagnetic fields, from Jupiter's extended magnetosphere to the skewed fields of Uranus and Neptune. The dozens of moons of these planets

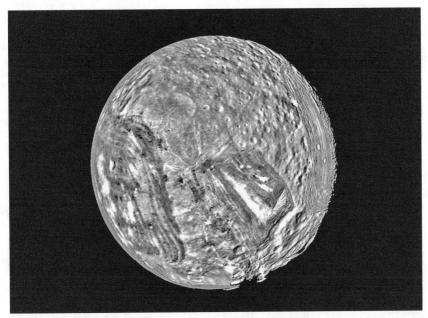

Figure 13.2. Voyager 2 image of Uranus's moon Miranda. *Source:* JPL Photolab.

exhibited a surprising range of geological features, including tectonics and volcanism similarly unexpected in the outer solar system. Andrew Ingersoll, a planetary scientist at Caltech, found that Voyager taught him "a certain humility. All the great knowledge we have of the Earth does not generalize very well. Uranus doesn't even generalize to Neptune."[13]

Voyager 2, however, also perpetuated the view that the science results were really secondary to the engineering achievement. At Uranus, for example, commentators marveled that Voyager arrived within one minute of the time calculated five years earlier when it departed Saturn. It then skimmed past Miranda at 72,000 kilometers per hour, rotating the entire spacecraft for camera exposures, and beamed back pictures of 500-meter resolution from an altitude of 29,000 kilometers. It repeated this feat at Neptune. Hence the conclusion of Burton Edelson, head of space science at NASA, on Voyager: "The big accomplishment there is an *engineering* accomplishment. It isn't a scientific accomplishment."[14]

Voyager 2, finally, continued as an object of media attention and acclaim, albeit in different circumstances. Five years had passed since the Saturn encounter, and the popular interest sparked by space movies and "Cosmos" seemed to subside by the mid-1980s. JPL also now had Lew Allen as director, a man whose personal reticence perhaps affected his attitudes toward public

Figure 13.3. Voyager 2 image of Neptune's moon Triton, with surface mostly of nitrogen ice. Dark smudges in the top half are evidence of dust deposits from geyser-like plumes. *Source:* JPL Photolab.

relations, at least when compared with the media attentiveness of Murray; in 1987 Allen demoted the public affairs manager from the lab's executive council.[15] By that time the Voyager team had long experience, but that could not prepare them for yet another consequence of the Challenger accident. Closest approach to Uranus occurred on 24 January. Four days later, scientists and reporters at JPL were preparing for a final celebratory press conference when the presumably routine shuttle launch playing on background television monitors turned into images of disaster. The assembled media decamped en masse for Cape Canaveral, depriving the Voyager team its final triumphal turn in the spotlight for Uranus.[16] Some JPL staff could not help expressing bitterness, especially with the space shuttle again as nemesis. As project manager Laeser recalled: "We knew we were going to have the cover of *Time* magazine and probably *Newsweek*, too. We were all charged up. . . . It was fascinating to see: the press just evacuated the press room. Everybody was down at the Cape or in Houston. We went through and had our encounter with practically no news coverage. It was a downer, quite honestly, because we had been building up to be national heroes."[17]

In addition to Challenger's immediate impact on the Uranus encounter, some historians have blamed it for a general shift toward a more critical media stance regarding NASA.[18] But if the Hubble telescope and other publicized failures represented and accelerated this trend, press accounts of Voyager's Neptune encounter gave little evidence of it; once again, front-page headlines and magazine cover stories gushed over Voyager.[19] On the contrary, NASA's evident failings could heighten media appreciation of Voyager's successes. The juxtaposition of triumph and tragedy in 1986 was not lost on Voyager engineers or on public commentators. The *New York Times*, for example, used the Neptune encounter to editorialize against the human spaceflight program. In the aftermath of Challenger, and at a time when NASA was pursuing the multibillion-dollar space station as a prelude to even more expensive human flights to Mars, robotic exploration seemed to offer a way to explore the solar system at less cost and less risk of human life.[20]

Galileo

By 1982 the Galileo mission for a Jupiter orbiter and probe had survived repeated threats of cancellation and delays owing to launch vehicles. The original launch date of 1982 had slipped to May 1986, and a series of redesigns—from single launch to separated and back, from the solid-fuel Inertial Upper Stage booster to the liquid-fuel Centaur—had doubled the cost of the mission, from $410 million to $874 million.[21]

The basic design of the spacecraft itself had already posed formidable engineering challenges. Planetary scientists in the early 1970s sought to follow the Voyager flyby with a more detailed visit to the Jovian system. Plans soon crystallized into competing orbiter-probe proposals from Ames, then building the Pioneer spacecraft for Jupiter flybys, and JPL, home of Voyager. The proposals reflected the design philosophy of each lab and also the old split in the scientific community between particles-and-fields experiments, for atmospheric science, and remote sensing instruments, for geology. The particles-and-fields camp preferred the spin-stabilized Pioneer design from Ames, which gave instruments a 360-degree survey of the environment. The remote sensing camp preferred the three-axis stabilized Mariner spacecraft from JPL, which gave a platform for imaging.[22]

Ames had the initial advantage. James Van Allen, discoverer of the eponymous radiation belts and a senior figure in the field, led the particles-and-fields side. This group perhaps resented JPL's dominance of planetary missions and its historic emphasis on three-axis stabilization for imaging; as John Casani put it, atmospheric scientists had "been in the kitchen trying to get into the banquet hall for years and years." Spinning advocates had the Pioneer design to promote. Based on the same principle as the rifle bullet, spin stabilization provided a simple way to guide a spacecraft to its target. It did not require the complicated sun and star sensors, gyroscopes, and thruster system of the Mariner spacecraft, with their associated mass, cost, and risk.[23]

NASA picked Ames in early 1975 to design the orbiter-probe as a Pioneer. At the time, however, the agency was also conducting its "roles and missions" review, which sought to reduce duplication, and so it awarded JPL primary responsibility for planetary missions. Several months after the Ames assignment, NASA transferred the spacecraft to JPL. The decision failed to settle the scientific squabble. Casani recalled imaging scientists clamoring after the initial selection of Ames, "you cannot send a major spacecraft to Jupiter without cameras." Then, after the switch to JPL, "the fields and particles guys are saying, 'over my dead body, this is our mission, we were the ones that put this together, you're going to come in and stabilize the damn thing and take half the value away.'" Van Allen suggested a compromise. What about a spacecraft that combined the two designs? Half of it could spin and carry the particles-and-fields instruments and probe; the other half could stand still and carry the cameras. NASA duly approved JPL to pursue what was called a spun/despun design.[24] The compromise reflected the common tendency to involve as many experiments and institutions as possible in a mission's definition in order to broaden the scientific constituency and help win approval.[25]

The idea seemed simple. Putting it into practice was not. The combination had a precedent in earth-orbiting communications satellites that had an antenna with a fixed orientation while the rest of the satellite spun above it. A less reassuring precedent was Seasat, which used a slip ring that allowed solar panels to track the sun while the spacecraft platform remained stationary—and that slip ring was the cause of Seasat's early demise. But it was one thing to despin a small, light antenna on top of a spinning spacecraft of a couple hundred kilograms. It was another matter to manage the momentum of two massive segments, each in the neighborhood of a thousand kilograms, with the despun part requiring very stable and precise pointing for the camera. The spin-bearing assembly connecting the two sat close to the center of the spacecraft, requiring engineers to route many subsystems—mechanical, electrical, thermal—through it. The propellant tanks, for example, were on the spinning section but the motor was on despun side, so that propellant lines ran through the annular center of the slip rings.[26]

The spun-despun design added considerable complexity as well as mass, as did the suite of instruments, larger and more complex than on Voyager, which in turn complicated the telecommunications, flight computer, and attitude control. Lew Allen judged Galileo "an order of magnitude or so more complex than Voyager."[27] The magnitude of the task became apparent, however, only after congressional approval. The people who wrote JPL's proposal were not the ones who would build the spacecraft. It was hard to get experienced engineers interested during the study phase, which meant not only that cost estimates could be far off the mark, but also that the proposal writers would not be responsible for their estimate and the engineers who built the spacecraft would feel no attachment to the estimate.[28] Casani assembled a team of spacecraft engineers off of Voyager, who soon "realized that it wasn't going to be anything like the slam dunk that had been represented in the study activities."[29]

This dawning recognition of difficulty spurred Galileo review boards as well as Murray, the old imaging advocate, to suggest dumping the dual-spin design and going back to a three-axis spacecraft. But by that time the engineers had figured out how to make the design work, and they could see no easier way to satisfy the particles-and-fields scientists.[30] The dual-spin design remained, along with revised cost estimates. As on Mars Observer, JPL engineers and scientists together acted to drive up the scope of a mission. In this case, JPL chose to satisfy the two main groups of planetary scientists, remote sensing and particles-and-fields, and the scientists helped win the new mission. But also as with Mars Observer, it was not just a case of indulging scientists; JPL's internal dynamics were in part to blame, in this case its process of cost estimation.

The dual-spin design not only increased the scope of the work; it also broke the chain of inheritance with the Mariner series. Voyager had as its template the Mariner platform and was supposed to provide a standardized model for subsequent missions in the incremental Mariner approach. At the time NASA and JPL were backing a program for high-inheritance spacecraft as a way to keep costs and risk down, but with Galileo they broke the mold technically and programmatically. To Bruce Murray, Galileo represented a departure from JPL's product line, and more basically it reoriented the planetary program from incremental missions to a more ambitious, customized approach.[31] Another major difference from previous missions was that Galileo did not have the luxury of redundant spacecraft—it was hard enough just to get one spacecraft approved—and so JPL had all its eggs in one basket. For the Mariner spacecraft to Mars, Viking, and Voyager the lab had built two spacecraft for each mission, so that if one failed—as occurred on some of the Mariners—a backup was ready to go. JPL's very success undermined this trend, and going two-for-two on both Viking and Voyager made it harder to sell the need for redundancy. Without the fallback position of a second spacecraft, however, Galileo required more work in the development phase, to engineer in reliability.[32]

John Casani steered Galileo through these shoals as project manager from the outset. Casani had started at JPL as a young electrical engineer in 1956 and mastered the art of systems engineering on Ranger and Mariner flights. He displayed a talent for making and enforcing difficult decisions while maintaining morale with a jovial personal style; Casani could lash engineers in a scathing design review and then head out with them to knock back a beer. His management of Voyager had confirmed his approach, but it would take all of Casani's irrepressible humor and persistence to sustain the Galileo team through trials that Van Allen compared to the Perils of Pauline.[33]

Challenger further tested the fortitude of Casani and his crew. At the time of the accident the Galileo spacecraft was at Cape Canaveral, in preparation for the next launch in May. Instead the spacecraft returned to its crate for a degrading retreat back to Pasadena, and the team set about redesigning the mission yet again. In particular, the return to the less energetic IUS booster required a new trajectory. The earlier, temporary plans for a 1985 launch on an IUS had compensated with a so-called Delta-VEGA trajectory, for Delta-V (or velocity change) Earth Gravity Assist, which sent the spacecraft in a long arc around the sun and then past Earth for a gravity boost to Jupiter. Roger Diehl and Lou D'Amario now transformed that trajectory into Venus-Earth-Earth gravity assist, or VEEGA: Galileo would launch toward Venus, swing back past Earth and then curve around for a second, very close flyby of Earth to kick it out finally to Jupiter.[34]

The VEEGA trajectory would get Galileo to Jupiter, albeit not until late 1995. But it also sent the spacecraft, against intuition, into the inner solar system as a way to get to Jupiter. That meant still another redesign of the spacecraft as it now had to handle the heat near Venus in addition to the cold of Jupiter. Engineers added sunshades and thermal blankets and reoriented the spacecraft to fly with the antenna facing the sun for more thermal protection—which in turn required additional low-gain antennas and sun sensors. In particular, the new route would expose the 5-meter, high-gain antenna to too much heat. Engineers had designed the antenna to deploy like an umbrella, to make sure it fit in the shuttle; they now planned to keep the antenna folded up until the outward leg beyond Earth. The longer flight time would also reduce the electric power supply at Jupiter, owing to decay of the radioisotope generators. Finally, engineers had to replace many aging parts: conductive tapes losing adhesion, electrical cables losing flexibility, corroding metal parts, and fractured O-rings. A NASA manager observed that the entire process required "the tear-down, modification, and retest plans of what was a flight ready spacecraft."[35]

One could argue, however, that Galileo benefited from the delays. The novel dual-spin design, perpetual mission replanning, and the need to withstand prolonged radiation exposure at Jupiter had put an extra burden on the design team to meet the launch dates, as did the diversion of much of the team early in the design phase to bail out Voyager in its post-launch distress. The 1982 launch would have been especially hard to meet, and if the shuttle had been ready, the spacecraft would have had a dicey trip. Testing revealed that electronic memories in the avionics were vulnerable to single-event upset, where a cosmic ray flips bits; the effect would have constantly reset the computer and put the spacecraft into safe mode, making for an emergency-filled flight. The delay to 1986 allowed engineers to replace the several thousand susceptible devices, and also to discover and correct contamination in the slip ring that would have intermittently cut off the electrical power supply.[36] Advantages accrued to the instruments as well as the spacecraft. The camera, for example, used the new charge-coupled devices, or CCDs, which strained Galileo's schedules. JPL's instrument engineers wondered in 1983 whether Galileo had lucked out with the launch delay, and whether flight projects in general should pursue technology on a deadline. "*The fundamental question,*" as they called it: "Did the [Galileo] project make the right decision when they opted for the 'new technology'?"[37]

Even the delay to 1989 proved beneficial. Norm Haynes, head of the systems division at the time, recalled: "We found out after we'd gone to Florida [in 1986] that we had huge problems in the spacecraft. We had problems with the computer memories, we had problems with the propulsion system. So we had three years to bring it back to JPL and work some of those problems out." And, as with Mars Observer, Galileo engineers saw the delay as an opportunity: they were creative people looking for technical problems to solve, they knew that certain parts of the spacecraft contained lingering weaknesses, and they now had time to reduce the risk. The scarcity of new planetary projects no doubt encouraged their desire to find meaningful work on Galileo.[38]

Another obstacle remained before launch. Like Voyager, Galileo used radioisotope generators, which converted heat from radioactive decay of plutonium-238 into electricity. Flying the toxic, highly radioactive isotope on spacecraft required White House approval. Challenger undercut assumptions about the safety of shuttle launches and ensured that such approval would no longer be routine. In February 1986 the *Nation* magazine noted that if Galileo had ridden on Challenger the explosion might have dispersed plutonium across the Florida coast. The subsequent Chernobyl reactor explosion in the Soviet Union intensified fears of radioactivity, and as the launch date approached in 1989 activist groups launched a widespread protest, including marches at the Cape and threats of a sit-in on the launch pad itself.[39] The protests attracted much media attention, caught NASA up in nuclear politics, and forced JPL engineers into murky statistical assessments of possible health risks not only at launch but also during the two flybys of Earth, especially the second close one. They insisted that no feasible alternatives existed—solar power was too weak at Jupiter's distance and electrochemical batteries would be too heavy—and that the units provided sufficient containment. Galileo's launch finally proceeded, amid heightened security, after the White House approved it and a last-minute lawsuit and appeals by protesters failed.[40]

Galileo launched from the shuttle on 18 October 1989 as the biggest planetary spacecraft ever built by the United States. The orbiter weighed almost 2,700 kilograms plus the 335-kilogram probe—about 1,000 kilograms more than Voyager at launch—and stood 9 meters tall (see figure 13.4).[41] The spacecraft cost $900 million, with another $500 million budgeted for mission operations and data analysis—an increase of almost $1 billion from original estimates, which the congressional General Accounting Office ascribed to the delays and redesigns caused by launch vehicles.[42] JPL engineers could finally celebrate, several years later than planned, and scientists could begin looking toward the encounter at Jupiter in 1995. Some of them by that time would have devoted almost two decades of their careers to the mission. The launch delays had taken a toll on the spacecraft as well, although the engineers and scientists did not know it yet. Galileo had more trials to endure.

Magellan

Galileo followed Magellan, launched five months earlier, on its trajectory toward Venus. The Venus radar mapper had negotiated its own troubles. NASA stressed that it viewed Magellan as a test of JPL's commitment to low-cost missions.[43] The lab did not pass the test with flying colors. Magellan's cost by the time of launch had increased from $300 million to about $550 million, which returned it to the budget neighborhood of the abandoned VOIR.[44] A General Accounting Office audit blamed about half the increase on Challenger's consequences and the other half on enhancements and over-runs.[45] As with Galileo, however, delays that inflated costs also provided relief to technology programs that might not have met the original deadline—in particular, the crucial synthetic aperture radar.[46]

Magellan launched on 4 May 1989, the first planetary spacecraft to set off from the shuttle. The spacecraft's namesake had not survived his major voyage in the sixteenth century, and the spacecraft threatened to follow suit.[47] It reached Venus on 10 August 1990, and on 17 August began transmitting data from the first test runs of the radar. In the middle of the second round of transmission, it turned to perform a routine star calibration, which oriented the spacecraft gyroscopes against the position of certain stars. But when the Deep Space Network began listening for the transmission to resume, it

Figure 13.4. Galileo spacecraft in the 25-foot space simulator chamber at JPL.
Source: JPL Photolab.

heard nothing. Such a loss-of-signal could have meant that the spacecraft was healthy and just pointing in the wrong direction, or that it was tumbling out of control or otherwise failing catastrophically.[48]

Engineers soon traced the problem to a loss of the spacecraft's "heartbeat," a memory address in the attitude control computer that switched back and forth more than once a second as a way for the main computer to monitor the health of the system. The heartbeat loss caused the main computer to enter safe mode: it swung the solar panels toward the sun to keep the batteries charged and began running through programmed options for recovery. One of these steps required another star calibration, at which point another failure occurred. The star sensor apparently locked on a floating, reflective particle that had flaked off the insulation, and as a result the disoriented spacecraft kept the antenna pointed away from Earth. Although the emergency had roused the project team in the middle of the night, project manager Tony Spear decided to let the spacecraft heal itself. After eighteen hours in safe mode it was supposed to start "coning," or scanning the sky with its medium-gain antenna in search of Earth, but after about twelve hours a third surprise occurred, this one because of a forgotten fix buried in the computer instructions that interrupted safe mode and began coning immediately. The Deep Space Network soon picked up a faint signal—fifteen hours after first losing it—and replied with instructions for the spacecraft to stay in contact.[49]

Three days later, on 21 August, as engineers tried to figure out what had gone wrong, Magellan's signal began fading and then disappeared again. Mission control gave the spacecraft four hours to cone and reacquire Earth. Meanwhile, the reassembled project team raced to diagnose the new loss-of-signal. Two factors contributed to the sense of urgency. First, if the spacecraft had not pointed the solar panels at the sun, it would be six to ten hours before the batteries drained and the spacecraft expired. Second, models at contractor Martin Marietta showed that the spacecraft might have started rolling back and forth instead of coning, and if so it was either wasting all its propellant or, worse, swinging ever harder until it entered a final, fatal spin. After the four-hour period ended with no signal, mission controllers decided to zap Magellan with all 350 kilowatts from the 70-meter dishes of the Deep Space Network, in hopes of punching through a command to the misaligned spacecraft antennas. After several such blasts, and seventeen hours of silence from Magellan, the network detected a reply. Exhausted engineers in mission control cheered, or wept; recalled one manager, "It was unbelievable. There were tears to be honest with you, because we had no expectation of ever seeing that thing again."[50]

Even as Magellan resumed radar mapping, people at JPL and Martin

Marietta did not understand what caused the loss-of-signals. Similar losses continued occasionally to plague the mission every few months, but programmers had beamed corrective software to help the spacecraft recover from such incidents, calming heartbeats in Pasadena if not on the spacecraft. Martin Marietta engineers eventually traced the problem to a damaged chip in the backup memory of the attitude control computer; the underlying cause, however, lay in a software shortcut that sent the computer into a loop when certain instructions happened to coincide within the same interval of two-millionth of a second (the low probability of coincidence explained the infrequency of the events). But other problems had meanwhile cropped up, including the failure of one of the tape recorders necessary to store the voluminous radar data before transmission. Then, in January 1992, the primary radio transponder failed, and a sort of whistle in the backup transponder limited transmission to less than half the design rate. Magellan survived all these failures because it had backup systems, demonstrating the virtues of redundant engineering.[51]

By the time of the transponder failure, Magellan had already mapped 95 percent of the Venusian surface. The synthetic aperture radar revealed the detailed geology for previously unseen regions of Venus; at a resolution of up to 150 meters, the Magellan images improved on those from the Soviet Veneras by an order of magnitude, and the Veneras had only covered part of the northern hemisphere, not the entire planet. The images revealed unexpected features—for example, dark splotches surrounding a number of craters, which scientists attributed to "ground slaps" or shock waves generated by asteroids when they hit the thick Venusian atmosphere. More generally, the images forced scientists to reconcile evidence of strong volcanism with crater counts that suggested the Venusian surface was about 500 million years old. Two theories competed to explain why the craters survived amid lava flows. One theory proposed that a period of volcanic activity several hundred million years ago had resurfaced all of Venus, after which volcanic activity declined as the planet cooled. Against this quasi-catastrophist position, another theory advanced the more steady-state view that different surface regions displayed a range of ages, and that a constant level of volcanism had just kept pace with cratering rates.[52]

To help answer such questions, Magellan scientists sought to shed light on the planet's internal structure through precise measurements of the gravity field (deduced from minute changes in spacecraft motion). Magellan's elliptical orbit limited the accuracy of these measurements, so engineers planned to circularize the orbit through a new technique called aerobraking, which used a planet's atmosphere instead of rockets to slow down a spacecraft. The aerobraking maneuver started in May 1993 and took about two months, during which time the spacecraft dipped into the atmosphere 730 times, lowering its apoapsis (or highest altitude) from 8,500 kilometers to 540 kilometers at very little cost in propellant. The test pleased the engineers, who added it to their repertoire for future missions, as well as scientists measuring gravity. The data gave evidence of a thick lithosphere or crust, which signified a cooling planet and thus tilted the scientific consensus toward the catastrophist theory. The thickness of the Venusian lithosphere, up to twice that of Earth's, suggested that Venus was much less like Earth than had been expected and perhaps more like Mars.[53]

Magellan meanwhile continued to accumulate failed components, including now a declining power supply and degraded solar panels. More important, it had exhausted the willingness of federal budgeteers to fund further operations. As with other large federally funded facilities, such as telescopes or accelerators, NASA managers had to weigh the marginal cost and return of existing projects against the desire for newer but more expensive ones. Mission controllers planned a final experiment for October 1994, when they sent the spacecraft on a fiery, fatal descent into the Venusian atmosphere in order to test atmospheric properties and spacecraft aerodynamics.[54]

Happy Days Are Here Again?

In spite of the general internal stability of JPL under Lew Allen, the roller-coaster ride in the planetary program continued. The crisis of 1981 gave way to optimism after the SSEC report; Challenger then cast all in doubt until hopes renewed at the end of decade. The return to space after a long hiatus, together with Voyager's final encounter, ended the decade on a high note. JPL still lacked a stable, long-term program, however, which it would again try to address in the 1990s. And the problems encountered by Galileo and Magellan in flight and Observer and CRAF/Cassini on the ground might have tempered optimism with a reminder of the pitfalls in planetary exploration.

Another consequence of the interlude in launches also lurked, unacknowledged. Constant delays and redesigns got the lab into bad habits. On Galileo, Magellan, Mars Observer, and CRAF/Cassini, stretchouts became the status quo, and JPL managers and engineers lost the cost and schedule discipline they had learned in the 1960s.[55] Launch slips turned into opportunities to improve the mission, as on Mars Observer and Galileo, and perhaps appeared to ensure a continued source of work for both individual engineers and the institution in general. The Challenger accident, in particular, encouraged laxity, but so did NASA's tendency to defer projects in exchange for short-term savings, a tactic accepted by Congress.

One other key trend of the 1980s, diversification, had meanwhile damped institutional fluctuations by diluting the dominance of planetary exploration at JPL. Flight projects were still the main mission, but in terms of budgets they had declined to only 37 percent of the lab program by 1991: about 25 percent went to non-NASA work, 20 percent to space science and instruments, and about 15 percent to the Deep Space Network.[56] As defense work dwindled, however, flight projects would acquire renewed focus, albeit in a new approach that derived substantially from military programs—even as the main impetus for those programs disappeared.

PART III

Beyond the Cold War

The Stone Years, 1991–2001

FOURTEEN

Faster, Better, Cheaper

LEW ALLEN STEPPED DOWN AS JPL DIRECTOR AT THE END OF 1990, AFTER reaching age sixty-five. To replace him, Caltech turned to Ed Stone, like Pickering and Murray a Caltech professor already familiar with the lab. While project scientist on Voyager, Stone had remained on the campus faculty, honing his administrative skills as chair of the physics, math, and astronomy division and then as head of the California Association for Research in Astronomy, the partnership, including Caltech, to build the ground-based Keck telescopes. Stone continued his research in space science, including his service on Voyager, through his tenure as JPL director. A wiry, bespectacled man with considerable enthusiasm for space science, Stone had seemingly boundless energy, but his tenure as JPL director would test his ability to juggle a number of different tasks.[1]

Several of Stone's personal traits recommended him for the job. He had demonstrated on Voyager the ability to cajole consensus on priorities, a skill required in a period of declining budgets after the end of the cold war. His substantial scientific reputation bolstered NASA's relations with the science community, and he had also displayed a talent for public relations, another valuable trait as public outreach would acquire increasing importance for the civil space program. Like Allen, Stone had a reputation for integrity and a methodical approach to problem-solving. But although Stone sought to avoid mistakes through careful analysis, at the same time he, like Bruce Murray, believed himself forced by the environment to undertake revolutionary change. The nature of the change compounded the contradiction of the conservative revolutionary: a new mode of deep-space exploration emphasized risk-taking, against Stone's innate caution. At times Stone's desire for consensus led to perceptions of overaccommodation, for instance, by appeasing NASA demands instead of holding out for the interests of JPL. But a restrained, logical approach would prove helpful in dealing with a new NASA administrator, Daniel Goldin, whose scattershot, often overbearing management style scarred other parts of NASA. In this respect, too, Stone's attributes perhaps proved appropriate to the time.[2]

As Stone made the rounds in Washington in 1990 before starting as director, he picked up signals that he faced a more difficult job than he had anticipated. Events were overtaking the prevailing optimistic outlook, such as that expressed by the Augustine Committee, which assumed the NASA budget would grow at 10 percent a year through the 1990s. Lew Allen had warned earlier that year that he did not trust "the projected large NASA budget" and that "if it doesn't come to fruition, we will be subjected to a painful downsizing later on."[3] Stone soon realized that he would have to administer the pain.

The End of the Cold War

Another characteristic of Stone was his strong view that the end of the cold war marked a fundamental turning point for the nation as a whole and for JPL in particular.[4] The demise of the Soviet Union removed the force that had served as the primary driver of the U.S. space program since its inception. In addition to continuing debates over NASA's mission—human versus robotic exploration, earth versus space science—the agency now faced a deeper, though related debate about its basic justification. Why should the nation devote billions of dollars each year, and the energy of many thousands of people, to exploring outer space?

Wesley Huntress, NASA's associate administrator for space science, declared in 1993 that exploration itself was insufficient. "Historical analogs show that serious, sustained exploration has only secured government funding for commercial, military, or religious reasons." Military competition with the Soviets had underpinned the space program in the cold war, but no longer. International collaboration offered one alternative (and one NASA would invoke for the space station), but Huntress judged this "not a compelling reason." Instead, Huntress declared that "Americans are more pragmatic than intellectual; they want real return for their tax dollars," and he hence settled on a primary justification of "near-and far-term economic vitality." The space program supported the aerospace industry, increasingly important in the international market for commercial uses of space, and would produce longer-term payoffs in technological spin-offs.[5]

Huntress's views jibed with new public surveys commissioned by NASA, which found that 75 percent of Americans had no interest in space, a proportion that had remained more or less constant through the 1980s. Of the 25 percent interested in space, an even smaller fraction considered themselves both interested and knowledgeable—and most of those did not want more money spent on it.[6] Most Americans, that is, were concerned with jobs and the economy, not space. In seeking to tap that 75 percent of uninterested Americans, NASA followed the lead of the new Clinton administration, whose campaign strategy in 1992 had declared, "It's the economy, stupid," and whose policies now stressed economic competitiveness, especially in high technology.

The end of the cold war had a more quantifiable effect on NASA budgets. The twilight struggle left a legacy of large deficits in the federal budget, which led Congress and the Clinton administration to make deficit reduction a top priority and put strict caps on discretionary spending, including NASA. The space agency got no help from the peace dividend, at least not in its budget. NASA and its congressional supporters tried to get defense cutbacks applied toward civil space, to no avail.[7] As military space budgets plummeted from their Star Wars highs, civil space budgets fell with them. Excluding aeronautics, NASA's space budget peaked in fiscal 1992 at $13.2 billion (in current dollars), then declined to $12.5 billion in 1995; factoring in inflation made the cut even more substantial. Military space had peaked in 1989 at $17.9 billion (in current dollars), then declined to $13.1 billion in 1994 and $10.6 billion the following year. In 1995, spending on the civil space program again surpassed the military space program for the first time since 1981—but only because military funding fell faster than NASA's.[8]

As NASA began absorbing budget cuts, JPL managers began to rein in and reverse the growth from the 1980s. Although the lab's budget in constant dollars peaked in 1988, the workforce had continued to grow; by 1992 JPL staff numbered more than 6,000 Caltech employees and 1,700 on-site contractors. Stone began drawing up plans to reduce the total workforce by 1,000 over the next five years.[9] And that was not the worst-case scenario. Stone and his staff, along with Caltech's administration and trustees, worried about the possible closure of the entire lab, a prospect not contemplated since the dark days of 1981. As Caltech president Thomas Everhart noted in 1992, at a trustees meeting on JPL, "this is a time of triage—[the] only question is what is going to die."[10]

The Programmatic Response

As with the early 1980s, when the crisis in the planetary program had produced the plan for low-cost Observer and Mariner Mark II missions, the budget cuts of the early 1990s provoked alarm in the planetary science community and a programmatic response to cut costs.[11] The new plan, which would become known as "faster-better-cheaper," derived from the same impulses that drove earlier schemes: namely, that infrequent, complex, and costly missions were hard to sell politically, delayed the return of scientific data, and increased the consequences of failure. Faster-better-cheaper stemmed more immediately from the ferment around microspacecraft in the late 1980s, which had spurred talk of launching flocks of satellites one-tenth the size of existing spacecraft.

The Challenger disaster had meanwhile highlighted the concentrated risk of big missions, whose expensive design and testing would come to naught if the launch vehicle failed. Challenger also revived the production of expendable rockets, and because these were considered less reliable than the shuttle, returning to rockets discouraged concentrated risk. At the same time, expendable launch vehicles could realize economies in launch costs; smaller rockets could launch smaller spacecraft cheaply—a Delta II launch cost maybe one-tenth that of a Titan IV—whereas shuttle launches had sunk costs no matter the spacecraft size. Thus another cumulative effect of Challenger was to encourage smaller missions.[12]

In the late 1980s Geoffrey Briggs, the head of planetary exploration in NASA's space science office, had arranged yet another study on low-cost missions, called the Discovery working group, which continued in 1990 under Huntress, Briggs's successor. A research scientist in astrochemistry, Huntress had come to NASA in 1988 from JPL, where he had suffered through the lack of data owing to the lack of launches in the 1980s. He arrived at NASA in time to watch Mars Observer double in cost. Huntress thus welcomed the idea of more frequent, cheaper missions, and Lennard Fisk, head of the space science office at the time, likewise began turning toward a new approach. In summer 1991 Huntress and Fisk organized a conference of 60 NASA managers and space scientists at Woods Hole, Massachusetts, an analogue to the earlier Solar System Exploration Committee. After considerable debate, the conferees agreed to shift the program away from "flagship" missions and toward smaller, more frequent flights.[13]

The Woods Hole meeting continued the debate over big science from the 1980s and the emerging backlash against ever-bigger projects. The issue affected astronomy and earth science as well as planetary science. In earth science, NASA had backed the large platforms of EOS, the Earth Observing System; in astronomy, the agency had sponsored one major observatory for each of the main portions of the electromagnetic spectrum (visible, infrared, X-ray, and gamma-ray). Like a big planetary spacecraft, such as Galileo, these missions spread their high cost over many years and promised a wide range of science data. But astronomy also had the Explorer class of smaller, specialized satellites, and earth science a similar line of Earth Probes, which had produced much important, albeit focused research. NASA in the 1980s had backed the evolution from small to big; but the debacle with the Hubble telescope's mirror in 1990 provided the immediate context for the Woods Hole meeting. Together with a glitch recently discovered in Galileo's high-gain antenna, the Hubble experience suggested the risk of putting many science eggs in single baskets. Although big missions remained in the picture after Woods Hole, NASA assigned a higher priority to a new Discovery series of small, focused planetary missions, to provide the counterpart to the Explorer and Earth Probe lines.[14]

NASA found an ally in the Office of Management and Budget. Like Congress, OMB managers guarded against delegating fiscal authority for a long-term program, as opposed to short-term projects, to an agency. But the current mode of big projects resembled a program, in that each mission effectively required many years of funding commitment, and by March 1992 OMB had announced its interest in smaller missions.[15] The next month the office of space science presented the Discovery program to Congress. It called for missions costing less than $150 million and taking three years from approval to launch, to be achieved through focused scientific goals, the use of "mature instrument and spacecraft technology," and "the acceptance of a modest increase in the level of risk." The anticipated benefits included better responsiveness to changing science goals, a broader program, more missions for scientists to work on, and more timely data return, which in turn would fit better with timelines for graduate students and hence train new planetary scientists.[16] The downside for scientists would be a basic change in approach: instead of comprehensive data about a few places, they would get limited data sets but from more places.

The formal presentation of the Discovery program coincided with the arrival of Dan Goldin as NASA administrator. Although regarded as an outsider to NASA, Goldin was a longtime space enthusiast who had started his career at NASA's Lewis center before moving to industry, where he rose to lead TRW's space and technology division. Upon his return to NASA he vowed to restore the agency to what he called the "Wonder Years" of the 1960s, and as a symbolic step toward that end he brought back NASA's old "meatball" logo, which the agency had replaced in the 1970s.[17] Goldin differed from preceding NASA administrators in his particular interest in deep-space exploration. That was a two-edged sword: it ensured attention to JPL from the top of NASA, but it also exposed the lab to Goldin's impetuous management style, which earned him a reputation for browbeating subordinates and critics into submission.[18]

It would take more than changing the logo and declaring that "the magic is back" to restore the space program to its former glory.[19] Goldin's rhetorical exhortations could not overcome the budgetary climate, which was much different from the early days of the agency. Goldin could, however, force changes on NASA from his position at the top. While at TRW he had proposed a low-cost series of earth-orbiting satellites, which NASA had denied amid plans for the big platforms of the Earth Observing System. Goldin remembered the rejection, and when he came to NASA he set out to eliminate what he saw as NASA's big-project mentality. Huntress and Fisk were ahead of the game; when Goldin arrived asking how they were going to reorient planetary missions, they could hand him the Discovery plan and add that they had already submitted it to Congress.[20]

The low-cost approach thus did not originate with Goldin, nor did the catchphrase "faster, better, cheaper," which had been in circulation at least since 1990.[21] But Goldin embraced it and pushed it hard. Within weeks of his instatement he was at JPL announcing a new era, and he would famously designate Cassini as the last "battlestar galactica," a reference to the popular television program featuring huge spaceships bristling with gear.[22] Goldin's evident commitment soon won what earlier low-cost efforts had not: line-item status for the Discovery program starting in fiscal 1994.[23] That meant the program could expect consistent funding each year of $85 million, which NASA managers had discretion to dispense to particular projects; they thus did not need to sell each individual project to Congress. Assurance of a steady stream of projects in turn would decrease the pressure to load each spacecraft with an expensive suite of instruments, since scientists now knew the current mission would not be the last one in a while.

The Discovery program started with two missions, Mars Pathfinder and NEAR (Near-Earth Asteroid Rendezvous). In 1982 JPL had proposed NEAR as a low-cost Pioneer-class mission, to start in 1991 and launch in 1994.[24] Shelved by the subsequent disarray in the 1980s, NASA dusted off NEAR for the Discovery program. But JPL's studies in the early 1990s came in way out of the expected cost range, and Huntress and Fisk instead awarded NEAR to the Applied Physics Laboratory at Johns Hopkins University, which had offered a competing proposal with a much lower budget. The loss of NEAR jolted JPL, whose managers had confidently come to assume their claim to every planetary mission over the past twenty years.[25]

As consolation JPL won Pathfinder. In the heady days of the late 1980s, amid talk of human missions to Mars, JPL and NASA had revived the post-Viking plans for a Mars rover/sample return mission. The Woods Hole meeting in 1991 led to a redirection of the Mars program, toward a network of small landers for meteorology and seismology known as MESUR (for Mars Environmental Survey). Both Ames and JPL had sought the demonstration mission for a single lander, which NASA awarded to JPL in late 1991.[26] At JPL, meanwhile, Tony Spear, the former Magellan manager, had taken over JPL's low-cost proposals after NASA's frustration with the NEAR submission. In February 1992 Huntress telephoned Spear to say that JPL could do the Mars mission under one condition: it would be a Discovery project with a fixed price of $150 million. NASA called the Discovery version MESUR-Pathfinder, although it was soon known more simply as Mars Pathfinder, the name indicating NASA's expectation that it would show the way to do cheaper missions.[27] The agency also restored one element of the Mars rover/sample return, albeit much scaled back in ambition. The Mars rover plans had contemplated a burly design of several hundred kilograms; for Pathfinder JPL would build a microrover of about 10 kilograms using an additional $25 million in NASA technology money.[28]

JPL managers, however, were not sure they wanted the job. Landing on Mars presented difficult challenges, more than the lunar or asteroid orbiters previously studied for Discovery. Much of the cost of the Viking mission of 1976 had come from those challenges, yet in constant dollars, Pathfinder's budget was one-twentieth that of Viking (although Viking also had much greater science scope and two landers).[29] Norm Haynes, an assistant lab director, recalled, "We had no clue how to do a project for $150 million."[30] When Spear presented Pathfinder to lab managers, "They'd say, 'you're going to ruin the lab, Tony. You're crazy.'" But Stone backed Spear and JPL accepted the challenge.[31]

By the time Goldin arrived at NASA to spread the gospel of faster-better-cheaper, JPL had already won Pathfinder but lost NEAR, and JPL managers had begun holding workshops on "low-cost spacecraft: the wave of the future."[32] NASA and JPL managers identified several techniques—some familiar from earlier low-cost efforts, others new—to build spacecraft faster and cheaper: accept limited science objectives, with only a few instruments on a spacecraft; specify a strict cost and accept a flexible definition of mission success, instead of vice versa; modify the mission to available hardware instead of designing hardware to suit the mission; buy parts in quantity, commercially when possible; and avoid excessive testing.[33] They anticipated feedback effects: for example, Discovery missions would have short cruise phases, for earlier data return but also to cut operations costs. Shorter cruise phases encouraged engineers and managers to stay with the project for its whole lifetime, and that in turn reduced the need for documentation, since projects need not worry that in ten years an engineer new to the team would need to look up the design of some component.[34] Finally, NASA proposed to delegate authority to a small, centralized program office, which would substitute informal communication among individuals for the formal documentation of systems management; in other words, to replace paperwork with teamwork. Faster-better-cheaper thus entailed a retreat from the principles of systems management.[35]

All of these techniques aimed at efficiencies in cost and schedule. But as JPL engineer Jeff Leising asked, "most of us understand what 'faster' means, and most of us understand what 'cheaper' means, but what does 'better' mean?"[36] Better would seem to mean more reliable, but faster-better-cheaper accepted *more* risk than the traditional approach. Better instead seemed to aim for more data return, both in frequency and volume, to be accomplished by flying many more missions. The Discovery program contemplated launching one or a few spacecraft each year, but Goldin was soon talking about launching one a month within a decade.[37] Faster-better-cheaper aimed to build a lot of spacecraft and launch them often, accepting some failures along the way. In other words, the end of the cold war spurred the United States to embrace the philosophy of the Soviet space program.[38]

The Discovery program remained far from Goldin's goal. Discovery's line-item funding of $85 million per year could cover maybe one mission every couple of years. This greatly improved on the existing rate, but not enough to reduce risk. It also did not sustain standardization. The initial Discovery plan of April 1992 shared a key drawback with earlier low-cost efforts from the 1970s and early 1980s in its reliance on standardized spacecraft and components. Spacecraft would carry "mature instruments" and would "require little or no new technological developments."[39] Since much cost went into design and testing, low-cost advocates had long claimed that standardized components would save time and money. But this assumed economies of scale that did not exist in the civil space industry. Aerospace firms would only support standardized lines if a sufficient market existed, and NASA and Congress would not commit to the number of missions necessary to sustain such a market, thus dooming earlier low-cost efforts to failure.[40]

Although faster-better-cheaper resembled the Soviet style of build-and-launch, Goldin soon seized on the defining characteristic of the American approach: high technology. Rather than rely on familiar components, Goldin instead declared that faster-better-cheaper should push new technologies. This was perhaps his main contribution to the faster-better-cheaper philosophy and one that meshed with the Clinton administration's emphasis on high-tech industry. Goldin envisaged a resonance effect: short development cycles meant technology would still be new; accepting risk encouraged use of new technology; and more use of system contracts with industry would promote technology transfer.[41] But the old dilemma remained: engineers did not want to risk a spacecraft failure by flying unproven technology, and without flight-testing new technology remained unproven. NASA now addressed the dilemma by agreeing to pay for flight testing of new technologies in what was called the New Millennium program, started in 1995.

Another feature of Discovery was that instead of institutions, such as JPL, proposing missions, the principal scientific investigators did. The principal investigators, not NASA, then decided whom to have manage and build the spacecraft. So a project could have a principal investigator from JPL, but not have JPL as project manager; or it could have a principal investigator from outside JPL but a project manager at JPL; or no JPL involvement at all.[42] In practice, many Discovery proposals kept the instruments, data analysis, and perhaps mission operations under the principal investigator but turned to other labs, including JPL, for systems engineering and oversight of the spacecraft.[43]

NASA's initial announcement of the Discovery program met an enthusiastic response, with 89 scientists submitting proposals, 18 from JPL.[44] The failure in August 1993 of Mars Observer, the poster child for cost overruns, added impetus to the program. In February 1995 NASA announced the results of the second round of Discovery selection, which came out like the first: JPL lost out to the Lunar Prospector mission from Lockheed (with project management by Ames); as consolation JPL later that year won the Stardust mission, with Donald Brownlee from the University of Washington as principal investigator and a plan to fly through the tail of a comet and snatch a sample of cometary debris for return to Earth.[45]

The Military Roots of Faster-Better-Cheaper

Why did faster-better-cheaper take root where earlier, similar efforts had withered? What was different in the 1990s? Several factors contributed: budget cuts, availability of smaller launch vehicles after the Challenger accident, and problems with big missions like the Hubble telescope, Galileo, and Mars Observer.[46] Individual personalities played a role as well, especially that of Goldin, who often has been viewed as the main driver of faster-better-cheaper, although the concept predated his arrival at NASA.[47] But another crucial factor was the availability of military space resources. The end of the cold war flushed military technologies, techniques, laboratories, and managers into the civilian space program, where they provided the basis for the new approach. NASA could not have implemented faster-better-cheaper without the capabilities developed by the military—in particular, the Strategic Defense Initiative. SDI projects provided models of the informal, team-based approach, and then testbeds for JPL to learn it; SDI project managers personally implemented it within JPL and NASA; SDI technologies provided miniaturized components to underpin the new mode; and SDI labs provided the competitive spur to force JPL to adapt. But military modes would prove difficult to graft onto civilian institutions and missions, a lesson JPL would learn the hard way in 1999.

Goldin himself embodied the military contribution, and his background at TRW, where he led the firm's extensive SDI programs, contributed to his hiring at NASA. In the early 1990s staff of the National Space Council—created by President George H. W. Bush to bring together the heads of various space-related agencies, especially the SDI office and NASA—agitated to redirect NASA toward SDI methods, including faster-better-cheaper. The criticism eventually forced out NASA head Richard Truly; after first considering Lt. Gen. James Abrahamson, former director of the SDI office, the council selected Goldin as the one to bring the SDI approach to NASA.[48]

The existence of the space council itself indicated the increasing integration of the civil and military space programs. This integration, however, did not just occur at high policy levels. Examination of JPL's experience with faster-better-cheaper shows the strong, if little recognized, influence of military space programs at the level of particular laboratories, projects, and technologies. One prime difference for the Discovery program from earlier low-cost efforts was its embrace of competition. In 1976 NASA had imposed a division of labor, to avoid expensive duplication, and assigned JPL as the lead center for planetary projects. Although limited competition remained, JPL had no real challenge to its dominance of deep-space exploration. The 1990s still had tight budgets, but now NASA viewed competition not as wasteful duplication, but rather as a spur to efficiency.

Furthermore, the competition now included non-NASA labs, especially in the military. Military space budgets were declining even faster than NASA's and encouraged defense-oriented labs to seek civil projects. Several of these labs had capabilities to match their motivation. The Naval Research Lab, for instance, had a long history in space flight dating back to the 1940s; Lawrence Livermore National Lab could likewise point to decades of relevant experience in its work on nuclear rockets, space-based weapons, and, more recently, Star Wars—some of which had helped spark JPL's work on microspacecraft.[49] Livermore presented a particular challenge, both in its geographical proximity and its typical ambition. At the time Edward Teller, Livermore's éminence grise, was pushing SDI techniques for NASA missions, and a group of Livermore scientists had recently proposed a radical alternative to NASA's Space Exploration Initiative, one that would use inflatable instead of rigid space structures, cost ten times less, and take one-third the time.[50]

JPL's main competitor would be the Applied Physics Lab (APL), which also had a long history in space science and had managed several Explorer missions and built flight instruments for JPL spacecraft, including Galileo.

It did not hurt that APL, like NASA's Goddard center, sat in the Maryland district of Senator Barbara Mikulski, a member of the Senate appropriations subcommittee that oversaw NASA's budget. More important was APL's experience on an SDI experiment called Vector Sum or Delta 180, a boost-phase intercept demonstration launched in May 1986. APL built the experiment in fourteen months from approval to launch, at a cost of $150 million, and in doing so provided an important early example of the streamlined management approach known later as faster-better-cheaper.[51]

The end of the cold war drove these management models, as well as their parent laboratories, from defense into civil space. The military had demonstrated how to do a faster-better-cheaper project before the term itself gained currency. Wes Huntress, for example, gained his first exposure to small, quick, innovative missions as the project scientist on the SDI Pathfinder experiment at JPL. This experience highlighted for Huntress the excesses of JPL's systems engineering, where the insistence on requirements, documentation, and reviews clashed with the tight schedule and budget and frustrated SDI managers.[52] In this respect NASA's later appropriation of the Pathfinder name for MESUR was suggestive: the Mars mission intended to show the way for the low-cost approach—and borrowed, apparently unintentionally, the name from an SDI mission that had already marked the trail ten years earlier.

SDI continued as a source of models in the 1990s. In April 1993 Huntress convened a workshop on the Discovery program and brought in several SDI managers to share their experience with quick, cheaper missions.[53] Huntress's nod to SDI, and perhaps even his push for the Discovery program itself, may have served to preempt competition from another NASA office that was itself a by-product of SDI. The Augustine panel of 1990 noted that it had been "asked to consider whether some altogether new form of management structure should be established to pursue portions of the nation's civil space program, as has been recommended by various observers. Such a model might include an altogether separate agency patterned after, say, the Strategic Defense Initiative of the Department of Defense, which would be established to pursue major new initiatives such as the Mars exploration program." The committee thought such a sweeping step unnecessary, but it did recommend that NASA create a new office to handle robotic and human exploration of the moon and Mars. In late 1991 NASA duly created the Office of Exploration, known as Code X (the space science office being Code S) and hired Michael Griffin, previously head of the SDI technology program (and even earlier at JPL), to lead it.[54] The new office tangled the lines of responsibility for robotic programs and seemed to intrude on the domain of Huntress and Code S. Griffin viewed low-cost robotic missions to the moon as the starting point for his program and poached lunar scout missions proposed for Code S. MESUR remained with Code S, but if Code X proved its ability at the low-cost approach, it threatened to take over the Mars program as well. Hence Huntress had added incentive to get low-cost missions underway in his program.[55]

The inroads by SDI led JPL's executive council to ponder the possibility of "NASA losing control of civil space."[56] The threats extended from NASA program offices to specific projects. One development viewed at JPL as a possible "encroachment upon NASA's charter" was a plan for the SDI organization to pursue its own mission to the moon and an asteroid.[57] The plan stemmed from conversations among SDI managers in 1989 about how to "demonstrate to the civilian community the great strides made by the Department of Defense and SDIO in lower-cost advanced space technology."[58] After more formal discussions SDI approved the mission, called Clementine, in 1992 and assigned the Naval Research Lab to build it and Livermore to provide the sensors. Clementine had the stated goal of technology demonstration, with science experiments at the moon and the near-earth asteroid Geographos secondary. In particular, Clementine aimed to demonstrate that infrared and ultraviolet sensors from the Brilliant Pebbles system could acquire and track a cold target in space—the asteroid—and withstand cosmic radiation. Some observers doubted this rationale and suspected the military was peeking its nose into NASA's tent. Physicist Richard Garwin, a prominent defense adviser and SDI critic, noted that "sending a Brilliant Pebble to the moon is an extremely costly way to study its radiation sensitivity."[59]

In its size, schedule, cost, technology, and management, Clementine represented the new approach. The spacecraft weighed 235 kilograms, plus about 200 kilograms of propellant, and it took less than two years to design and launch. It cost $80 million, or one-tenth the cost of Mars Observer, which failed just a few months before Clementine's launch. To achieve these efficiencies the Clementine team eschewed the decision hierarchies, design freezes, and documentation of traditional systems engineering and instead delegated responsibility to a small project team. The team operated informally and with little paperwork, making decisions on the fly and up to the last minute; instead of several layers of management it had two: the project manager and everyone else. Although the spacecraft tested a few new, miniature sensors, for the rest of the components it sought to use prequalified commercial parts. As a final symbol of austerity, the project set up its mission operations in a refurbished garage dubbed the Bat Cave.[60]

Clementine launched in January 1994 and soon returned a trove of images from the moon, including evidence of frozen water in a shadowed crater at the moon's south pole.[61] As it headed for the asteroid, however, a software error left a thruster open; the spacecraft spun out of control, and Clementine was lost and gone forever. The failure might have moderated Clementine's appeal as a model, along with several other characteristics. For one thing, it failed despite a relatively easy mission: the short trip to the moon and asteroid meant much less need for long-term reliability or autonomy and much simpler thermal, power, communications, navigation, and launch requirements.[62] The lack of documentation made it hard to track requirements and design changes.[63] Project managers also acknowledged the short time frame was too ambitious; the schedule perhaps contributed to the failure by leaving insufficient time to test software and by overstressing the operations team, whose success seemed "to have been as much triumph of human dedication and motivation as of deliberate organization." That at least was the conclusion of a "lessons learned" study of Clementine by the Space Studies Board of the National Research Council. The same report observed that Clementine's costs were deceptive, since they did not include technology development (borne by earlier SDI programs) or science (covered by NASA's space science office).[64]

The general reaction to Clementine, however, overlooked these caveats and the failure and instead celebrated it as a "model for NASA." The Space Studies Board's review declared Clementine "an archetype of the 'smaller, faster, cheaper' approach," and Wes Huntress similarly cited its influence.[65] JPL staff sat in on review meetings on the lessons of Clementine, and a delegation from JPL, led by Stone, visited the Bat Cave for enlightenment.[66] At NASA, Michael Griffin brought his personal experience on Clementine from SDI to Code X, along with other Clementine managers.[67] Thus Clementine's manager, Col. Pedro Rustan, could claim in 1994 that "the changes that are going on at the Jet Propulsion Laboratory and NASA headquarters on the future of space exploration could not be taking place without Clementine."[68]

Rustan's comment neglected the fact that JPL had already done a faster-better-cheaper mission, called Miniature Seeker Technology Integration (MSTI, pronounced "misty"), run by the same SDI office that sponsored Clementine. One might instead view MSTI, together with the earlier Delta 180, as a forerunner of Clementine. Even if MSTI's influence was confined to JPL, its effect there was substantial, providing a lab-level counterpart to Clementine's impact on NASA. In 1991 Stone had noted the growing interest in small missions but added, "JPL does not now have the expertise and reputation to do them."[69] The lab faced a dilemma: how could it acquire the expertise necessary to win small missions without getting the chance to try one? The solution: go to the source. Here JPL's previous experience with SDI proved useful. In 1991 the SDI office was planning a series of satellites to track missile launches, explicitly conceived within the faster-better-cheaper approach. An initial MSTI mission would demonstrate the concept and technologies. In August 1991 JPL won the right to develop MSTI, no doubt because of its previous experience with acquisition-tracking-pointing systems for the air force and SDI in the 1980s, including the similar SDI Pathfinder experiment.[70]

JPL could thus claim familiarity with the technical requirements, as well as with the spacecraft design, a three-axis stabilized, earth-orbiting satellite with a swiveling scan platform for the sensors. But if the technical outline was familiar, the details were not. JPL had nine months to design, build, and deliver the spacecraft, from August 1991 to April 1992. The spacecraft would launch that fall on a Scout rocket, which kept the spacecraft weight to 155 kilograms, and it cost $15 million (not including the launch vehicle or operations, which together were capped at $5 million). To meet this cost and schedule, project manager E. Kane Casani—younger brother of John— adopted a "hardware-driven design," as opposed to the old "requirements-driven design." Instead of defining the requirements and then designing hardware to meet them, Casani's team looked at available hardware and then defined the requirements to suit. This required what Casani called a "cultural adjustment" by JPL engineers, who were accustomed always to seek optimum performance. For example, engineers found a small leak in the propellant system and had to restrain themselves from fixing it, as the supply would still be sufficient to meet the four-day design lifetime of the spacecraft. MSTI also used a spare Magellan battery, although it had four times the necessary capacity, and had separate optics for the infrared and visual sensors, since coupling the optics complicated the design and testing. In the end Casani estimated what a requirements-driven approach would have cost and arrived at a figure of $100 million, versus $15 million for the new hardware-driven method.[71]

MSTI thus provided a crucial proving ground for JPL's conversion to faster-better-cheaper. Ed Stone in particular offered numerous testimonials to its importance, "as an opportunity to show that we are capable of doing such a small, quick mission."[72] MSTI launched on 21 November 1992 and met its objectives—and then some, surviving at least into March 1993 and returning more than 120,000 images, far exceeding its design specifications.[73] The lab could now claim experience in the new mode, just as Congress was approving the Discovery program. Stone appointed Casani to lead a new program to speed JPL's adaptation to faster-better-cheaper for planetary flight projects.[74]

Kane Casani was not the only one to capitalize on experience in military missions. The SDI Pathfinder experiment, in addition to Wes Huntress as project scientist, had David Evans as project manager and Glenn Cunningham as systems engineer. Evans, who had previously worked on the autonomous spacecraft project for the air force and then led the lab's entire defense space effort, went on to manage Mars Observer and in 1992 became deputy assistant lab director for flight projects. Cunningham succeeded Evans on Mars Observer, oversaw its replacement Mars Global Surveyor, and then ran the whole Mars program at JPL. Evans and Cunningham both had much experience with planetary missions and both struggled to keep Mars Observer under control, but their background also suggests that defense programs helped sustain a source of experienced managers at a time when scarce planetary projects were producing few of them. And perhaps exposed them to particular approaches: such projects as SDI Pathfinder and JPL's ultraviolet detector for the Delta series had compressed schedules, tighter budgets, and higher risk. Defense manager Jack James had argued in 1985 that SDI Pathfinder would counteract JPL's increasing conservatism and added, "The Defense and Civil Programs rather than the NASA Programs is the appropriate place to take such risks and to grow our people."[75] A couple years later Lew Allen, in a meeting with Caltech's trustees, had backed smaller spacecraft missions as a way to groom young project managers, and the ensuing discussion noted in particular the contributions of defense work in this regard.[76] It thus might not be a coincidence that the two lead managers on the first Discovery mission, Mars Pathfinder, also had experience in defense work in the 1980s: project manager Tony Spear and rover manager Donna Shirley. Spear's work on ASAS differed in important respects from flight projects, especially concerning risk, but he would also say of that experience, "I was learning how to do faster, better, cheaper on that, by the way. It was a short, fast thing, pulling people together."[77]

JPL's earlier diversification into defense work aided faster-better-cheaper in another way, through advanced technology. Much of the new technology considered for faster-better-cheaper derived from military programs. Goldin's main technological inspiration on his visits to JPL came from the Microdevices Lab, whose SDI funding was bearing fruit in new, miniature instruments and spacecraft components.[78] For example, the first two missions under New Millennium—called Deep Space 1 and 2—included a new CCD camera and tiny tunable diode lasers for detecting water on Mars.[79] In particular, the microspacecraft movement finally gained some momentum. Faster-better-cheaper did not necessarily mean smaller—sometimes it was cheaper to use bigger, readily available components—but smaller did provide some economy, especially in the launch vehicle. By 1991 JPL engineer Chris Salvo had a proposal to send a 25-kilogram, 60-centimeter-tall spacecraft with a single imaging camera to a near-earth asteroid, and had prepared studies of similarly sized lunar scouts and microrovers for NASA's new Office of

Exploration. Ross Jones was soon planning what he called second-generation microspacecraft, which would further shrink spacecraft to the 5-kilogram range. Mock-ups of the second generation attracted the attention of Goldin, whose New Millennium program shared many of the same goals, and the initiative also won converts at JPL—including Spear, who hailed microspacecraft as "one of the most important developments for the lab's future."[80]

Rob Staehle meanwhile had caught Goldin's eye with his microspacecraft plans for Pluto. As of 1992 NASA, at the recommendation of scientific advisory groups, was planning a Pluto flyby as a Mariner Mark II mission, with a suite of fourteen instruments and spacecraft subsystems derived from Cassini.[81] Such a mission required a heavy launch vehicle and a fourteen-year flight time, both of which multiplied the already high cost. Instead Staehle had proposed a 35-kilogram microspacecraft based on SDI technologies, with just a CCD camera and a radio for instruments. In May 1992 he noticed that Goldin would be visiting Los Angeles to return an Oscar award statue that had flown on the space shuttle. Staehle showed up at the ceremony and button-holed Goldin to pitch him the Pluto plan, and Goldin quickly approved what was called the Pluto Express (now revised to a 100-kilogram spacecraft to reach Pluto in seven years).[82]

By 1993 the microspacecraft plans included first- and second-generation concepts and the Pluto Express.[83] Three years later microspacecraft remained on viewgraphs, not blueprints. The persistent failure to realize the potential of microspacecraft had several causes. A debate over the use of radioisotope power sources diverted the Pluto project for several years; more generally, Staehle's plan, and his circumvention of scientific review, had roused the resentment of space scientists set on a comprehensive, Cassini-class mission.[84] Above all, microspacecraft advocates began to recognize the technological obstacles, and the distance from lab bench to launch pad. A wide gap separated technology people, who tended toward optimistic projections, from spacecraft engineers, who were responsible for delivering a particular component on a strict schedule. Microspacecraft in the end fell victim to short-term views, both of JPL engineers focused on delivering hardware for existing spacecraft, and of NASA managers indisposed to divert money from current missions toward technologies whose return lay many years in the future.[85]

JPL's Adaptation

The fizzling microspacecraft movement resembled the lukewarm initiation of faster-better-cheaper at JPL. In spite of the resources to aid conversion and the potential consequences of not doing so, many JPL staff resisted.

At the institutional level, JPL managers viewed faster-better-cheaper as an insufficient business model to sustain the lab, an attitude that went beyond the number of employees. A big project, such as Cassini, directly supported maybe 500 work-years, about 10 percent of total lab staff.[86] But many people worked part time on it, and over the lifetime of a long project many more people would do so, providing a shared experience. Big missions created an identity—or, as Stone put it, "a sense of a community for the laboratory."[87] Their fiscal influence was even greater; at its peak Cassini provided close to 20 percent of the lab budget. Big projects could thus provide infrastructure. They funded new technologies, such as spacecraft transponders or computers, and until the start of the New Millennium program in 1995 no such support existed in the cost-capped Discovery program.[88] Flight projects also paid for such items as test facilities and workstations that were then available to other projects. The influence of flight projects extended to the lab's basic rules and procedures: each project at its start issued a complete set of documents defining how the project would be run, and these applied de facto to the other lab programs.[89]

The lab's executive council thus wondered in 1994: "How can small projects survive at JPL without a Cassini 'cash cow'? . . . Without a big project how can we train our engineers, develop needed new technologies and attract the best talent?"[90] For his part, Stone labeled faster-better-cheaper a "cultural change . . . from the project driving the laboratory, to the laboratory somehow providing an infrastructure for the projects. You can see it's a different attitude. The projects really were the center because they had the money."[91] Deputy director Larry Dumas likened the lab to a large carnivore, accustomed to feeding on the occasional large kill, that now had to get by on a diet of nuts and berries.[92]

Adaptation to faster-better-cheaper extended to engineering practice. The shift to informal, nonhierarchical teams and little documentation abandoned the precepts of systems engineering that had underpinned JPL for thirty years. As Kane Casani learned on MSTI, JPL engineers had grown accustomed to design for performance, not cost. Some managers argued that JPL should not even try to change: in March 1992 Kirk Dawson, head of all the lab's technical divisions, defended large, in-house flight projects as the basis for JPL's reputation and expertise. "JPL will not prosper doing a series of small things with off-the-shelf technology (MSTI). Others can do [that] as well or better than JPL."[93]

The perception thus persisted that JPL really did not want to do things quickly or cheaply.[94] Despite Stone's push for change from the top down, and the presence of such converts as Spear and Kane Casani, much of the lab remained skeptical of the new approach, or at best agnostic; engineers wanted proof to justify the faith of advocates. Many JPL staff doubted that the first Discovery mission—Pathfinder—would succeed. The presence of Cassini complicated conversion: JPL could not just drop the old mode for the new because it still had to build Cassini, whose high cost, and associated high stakes, focused attention on it instead of smaller missions.[95] And JPL's plans beyond Cassini continued to hedge: the long-range program still contemplated occasional big expensive missions.[96] When Donna Shirley, head of the Pathfinder rover team, sought out MSTI manager Kane Casani for advice on faster-better-cheaper, Casani told her, "You want people who have been here more than twenty-five years or who have been here less than five years and nobody in between." The newcomers would not be corrupted from working on big missions like Galileo or Cassini, and old-timers would still remember the early missions from the 1960s, which had built spacecraft fast and less expensively.[97]

Goldin sensed resistance at JPL, but his style raised hackles there. On a visit in September 1994, Goldin gave a long, animated speech to lab staff on the global and domestic context and the absolute necessity of adaptation. The good news, Goldin announced, was that the survival of JPL was no longer in question, whereas "if you asked how JPL was doing a year and a half ago—right after the Mars Observer failure—I would have said the chances of survival at JPL were 50/50." The bad news: "JPL will never look the way it did. . . . You will not have a $3 billion Cassini. You must erase that from your minds." Resistance to change, Goldin perceived, had caused "an underlying fear and anger that permeates things, causing the Lab to be somewhat dysfunctional." In a memorable stunt, Goldin took a tall stack of documents from the Mars Global Surveyor project, a replacement for Mars Observer, as evidence that JPL stuck to the old bureaucratic ways: "The Mars Global Surveyor was supposed to be faster, better, cheaper. [*Drops stack of operations manuals on table.*] Gravity works."[98] JPL employees judged the paper drop a "grandstand act" and observed that Goldin's "very negative" tone would do little to help the morale problem he had criticized. They noted further contradictions in his philosophy. Goldin asked JPL to take risks, but he also announced that the lab could not fail. He had elsewhere warned that if Cassini failed—even if the launch vehicle failed—JPL would be "gone," and that "JPL must deliver on Mars Surveyor, and JPL must deliver on Mars Pathfinder—or at least one of them."[99]

JPL's resistance to another element of faster-better-cheaper, competition, was exacerbated by perceived claims from the Applied Physics Lab that it not only did things as well as JPL, but better.[100] JPL's defensive reaction to the small upstart belied the implications of competition. The lab had previously enjoyed a monopoly because it could claim that no one else could build robotic spacecraft of the same complexity and reliability. But NASA's embrace of competition suggested that other labs had caught up, and it hence punctured the substantial pride that JPL had nourished over three decades of space exploration.

JPL had sound reasons for resisting competition, however, in particular the issue of infrastructure: competition could discourage JPL from long-term investments in technology and facilities by raising doubt about future missions. JPL managers observed that Clementine and NEAR had artificially low costs because defense programs had paid for the technology and infrastructure. To NASA managers, however, this was precisely the attraction: the need to save money overcame the natural resistance of one government agency to give work to another agency's lab instead of one of its own.[101] But competition cut two ways. JPL had earlier competed eagerly with Goddard for earth-science missions, and JPL's diversification into earth science, as well as astronomy and space-science instruments, had already eased the adaptation to faster-better-cheaper by providing projects of similar size and cost. As Ed Stone pointed out to lab staff in 1994: "Look at what JPL actually does now—mostly small, mostly in-house projects. . . . So for most JPL employees the future of smaller flight projects is already here."[102]

JPL managers did recognize institutional advantages to faster-better-cheaper as well as the benefits to the planetary exploration program. As deputy director Larry Dumas put it: "When you have these massive projects going through the various phases—preliminary design, detailed design, integration and test, and so forth—the effect on the Lab was like a snake swallowing a pig. You could see this big thing moving through the system, and wherever it was at that moment was overloaded. Absolutely overloaded on capacities for test facilities, or overloaded on capacities for the design or whatever it was—and then it would go on to the next phase, and suddenly you wouldn't have any work for those areas."[103] Stone also tried to turn around the argument that the easy missions had been done and that rather than simple flybys scientists needed to go back for detailed—and costly—missions with landers, sample returns, and outer-planet orbiters. Stone argued that this new era, as he called it, on the contrary allowed smaller missions, since scientists could now zero in on local, specific phenomena identified by earlier comprehensive flights.[104]

Such considerations, and the constant encouragement of Stone, enabled faster-better-cheaper to make gradual inroads at JPL. Increasing evidence of the new mode's advantages helped persuade skeptics. By early 1996 JPL had one Discovery mission nearing launch in Pathfinder and another starting in Stardust, and the New Millennium program included a flight test in 1998 of electric propulsion called Deep Space 1. The Pluto Express remained on the drawing board, along with another Discovery proposal called Genesis to return samples of the solar wind.[105] The apparent success of faster-better-cheaper led NASA to apply it to the entire Mars program, which was becoming a focus of planetary exploration. The Mars Global Surveyor cost $131 million and would launch in 1996, and to follow Pathfinder NASA planned to send a pair of low-cost missions to Mars at the end of 1998, which JPL would likewise oversee.[106] Faster-better-cheaper had thus led to plans to launch five spacecraft in the next three years, with more in the works. But resistance remained, and JPL still had to show that its attempts in the new mode, starting with Pathfinder, would not meet with disaster.

Conclusion

The obstacles to faster-better-cheaper were not only within JPL. The new mode required NASA to provide technology funding, Congress to commit to a budget line-item for Discovery, scientists to accept specific data from many places instead of comprehensive data on a few places, and the American public to tolerate more risk of failure. To align these interests, and win over the skeptics, JPL first had to demonstrate results.

You can't teach an old dog new tricks. JPL, the former military lab, in its thirty-five years under NASA had developed strong ways of doing things, and many people there viewed faster-better-cheaper skeptically, whatever its advantages to the planetary program. But JPL had learned new tricks before, in its diversification into earth science, astronomy, and defense, and some of those tricks related strongly to faster-better-cheaper.

The idea of smaller, cheaper, faster missions had appeared before, in the 1970s and 1980s. Faster-better-cheaper differed in several respects, including its accommodation of advanced technology and embrace of competition. But the main difference from earlier low-cost models was that faster-better-cheaper was implemented. Why did it make it where earlier efforts failed? The usual answer is that the force of Dan Goldin overcame resistance. That is part of the story, but not all of it. A crucial, additional component was the role of military models and technologies, especially from Star Wars. The end of the cold war not only drove down NASA budgets but also flushed military labs and technologies into the civil space program.

The Strategic Defense Initiative provided managers who had exposure to faster-better-cheaper. It provided management models, especially that of flat, informal teams, for faster-better-cheaper missions. It provided specific projects, including Delta 180, MSTI, and Clementine, to demonstrate the new approach. It provided new technologies: microspacecraft components out of SDI programs, and miniaturized instruments and components out of the SDI-supported Microdevices Lab at JPL. And, in case all these proved insufficient, it provided incentive for adaptation, in the emergence of SDI-supported labs as alternatives to JPL. Star Wars was not the only source of faster-better-cheaper, but the new approach would not have happened without it.

That is not to say that the military took over the civil space program. NASA would not have welcomed the idea of forfeiting its missions to another agency, and not everyone there was convinced of the military approach. Alan Ladwig, a policy adviser to Goldin, pooh-poohed the Clementine mode, declaring that the United States should not "have to settle for space missions conducted out of former garages and things."[107] The Clementine team claimed that NASA rejected their subsequent proposals for Discovery missions so as not to "contaminate" the civilian program.[108] Proposals to fly a Clementine 2 to Mars as a replacement for the failed Mars Observer likewise failed to win approval.[109] The military did, however, maintain a strong role in Discovery: the Applied Physics Lab would compete for and win missions after NEAR, and the Lunar Prospector went to Lockheed's missiles and space division in Sunnyvale, California, whose expertise derived from extensive military and reconnaissance contracts.

Military models did not transplant easily onto civilian missions. The "lessons learned" review of Clementine by the Space Studies Board noted "the quite different 'cultures' operating within DOD and NASA." The reviewers highlighted several differences: "The greater resources available overall to DOD versus NASA; The underlying sense of urgency surrounding military projects contrasted with the more leisurely pace of civil programs; Less involvement by Congress, and reduced micromanagement on the part of DOD leadership . . . ; A narrower, more focused task-force-like management style that differs greatly from the broad, participatory approach more familiar to members of the scientific community associated with NASA's missions."[110] The last two, in particular, suggest that military programs such as Clementine benefited from a relative lack of political accountability, enhanced for some projects by classification. JPL's formal systems engineering may have started under military programs in the 1950s, but it had evolved amid intense political scrutiny of flight failures in the early space race. This basic political difference underpinned institutional, programmatic, and managerial resistance to faster-better-cheaper. It remained to be seen whether the new approach, and the military methods it represented, would stand up to sustained public and political scrutiny.

Reengineering JPL

THE NEW MODE OF FASTER-BETTER-CHEAPER IN THE 1990S REQUIRED JPL TO increase productivity. Amid layoffs and problems with cost control, lab managers turned to industrial management philosophies for solutions. In particular, they embraced in succession two management theories then sweeping corporate America: Total Quality Management, which stressed customer satisfaction and employee empowerment, and reengineering, which extended the approach by organizing not around particular tasks but around general processes. These management philosophies reflected a general shift in corporate organization in the last quarter of the twentieth century, away from the classic hierarchical structure of the vertically integrated firm to a flexible, nonhierarchical structure that responds to mobility and flux. They also suggested a reaction against technoscientific rationalism in their holistic lingo of enabling, nurturing, and partnering, and a departure from the lab's autocratic regime of systems engineering. But techniques for managing manufacturing processes proved difficult to transfer to an R&D environment, and despite a quantitative side that emphasized measurable "metrics," the holistic vocabulary encountered resistance among hard-headed technical staff at JPL. Lab staff nevertheless expended considerable effort on the management philosophies, indicating the amount of adaptation they felt the new context required.

The Rise of Corporatism

Total Quality Management, or TQM, originated in Japan in the 1950s, aided by the efforts of two American popularizers, W. Edwards Deming and Joseph Juran. The Japanese approach centered on "quality circles," which brought together small, workshop-based groups of employees with managers to give shop-floor workers a sense of participation in the company and at the same time to impart managerial goals to workers. TQM reflected emerging critiques of the dehumanizing tendencies of bureaucracy and of so-called scientific management, which stressed strict supervision and standardized tasks; the push for a consensual approach appeared also in the Management by Objectives theory of Peter Drucker and the movement for sensitivity training for corporate managers.[1]

These corporatist theories sought to foster a sense of community within an organization, through a participatory, democratic mode of management based on cooperation instead of conflict between workers and management. Giving workers a voice in formulating company goals would motivate them to work to reach them, thus increasing productivity and making everyone happy. Practice did not always follow theory, and the corporatist theories instead often offered a benign way for management to pacify labor, but the hopeful possibilities convinced increasing numbers of companies to adopt the theories. The new management philosophies found wider popularity in the late 1970s, amid international challenges to American manufacturing and the perceived decline of quality of American products and corporate performance. The challenge in particular of "Japan Inc." spurred major industrial firms to emulate their rivals and "Japanize" the American corporation. The main lesson, according to a *Time* magazine cover story of 1981: "Individuality at some point has to give ground to group needs. . . . Teamwork, however it is organized, is still the prerequisite for a prosperous society."[2]

These philosophies penetrated the realm of space science and technology. The aerospace industry was an early convert to the total quality movement, and NASA, which likewise felt the challenge of Japan and Europe in commercial space ventures, was among the first federal agencies to embrace it.[3] In 1982 the NASA administrator made Management by Objectives official policy, and NASA soon appointed a special manager to oversee quality and productivity in the space program. The NASA policy included quality circles, communication among managers and workers, and employee participation and in general sought to encourage "cooperation, informal discussions . . . decentralization . . . flexibility and creativity."[4]

High-level support did not ensure the conversion of NASA labs. As an observer from the aerospace industry noted: "NASA Center personnel are not productivity-oriented. They ignore or make fun of it. Get them on the bandwagon."[5] The people at JPL declined to climb aboard. Since JPL was a contractor lab, both Caltech and lab administrators felt free to reject NASA management initiatives not covered by the contract.[6] Senior JPL staff viewed productivity meetings and seminars as an onerous obligation and a waste of time and tried to get out of them or foist attendance off on subordinates.[7] Lew Allen also objected on principle. He wrote to NASA's productivity campaign manager, "There are fundamental differences between the goals, the roles, and, indeed, the very agendas of industrial companies and NASA R&D Centers."[8] Allen's objection identified a fundamental question: did management theories developed for the manufacturing industry apply also to science and technology? NASA and JPL never resolved this issue.

Total Quality at JPL

Attitudes toward the management theories at JPL changed in the early 1990s. The shift stemmed from the changing external context and also from the change in leadership at JPL. When Stone took over as director in January 1991 he had no knowledge of TQM.[9] Richard Laeser, the former Voyager manager, was working at the time as a special assistant in Stone's office. Laeser had long viewed JPL engineers as deficient in management skills; he had taken a three-month course at the Harvard Business School early in his career and continued to take a theoretical interest in the subject. Around the time he joined Stone's staff Laeser encountered TQM, embraced it, and began preaching its virtues to Stone. Stone himself had heard about it through briefings from aerospace industry leaders, and in April 1991, after only a few months on the job, he declared his support of TQM and appointed Laeser to a special top-level post to apply it throughout the lab.[10]

Why the emerging appeal of TQM at JPL? First, it seemed to address the demands of faster-better-cheaper. The shift in the new mode to informal teamwork and away from the formal hierarchies of systems engineering resonated with TQM, and the smaller projects of faster-better-cheaper further encouraged a team-based approach. Faster-better-cheaper also required JPL to reorganize to build many standardized spacecraft instead of a single custom spacecraft at a time, what one might characterize as a shift from a guild system to a production-line model. TQM presented a way to cut costs and schedules without sacrificing quality. Japanese manufacturing industry, in Laeser's eyes, had proved the merits of "designing the quality in at the beginning rather than checking it in at the end. Checking it in was the way JPL worked." For spacecraft, emphasizing design instead of expensive, time-consuming testing and reviews might help JPL adapt to faster-better-cheaper.[11]

TQM also emphasized customer service. JPL staff tended not to think in terms of customers for their products, at least in the eyes of NASA, whose managers saw themselves as the prime customer. A sampling of NASA managers in late 1991 returned views that JPL was "fat, complacent, arrogant, with little regard for cost," and Wes Huntress complained that JPL engineers tended to tell NASA what the agency should do, instead of responding to the agency's own plans.[12] Stone thus presented TQM as a new commitment to do "what the *customer* wants, not what we want," and hence to get back in NASA's good graces.[13]

Another incentive for TQM came from the arrival at NASA of Goldin, who had championed it during his time at TRW. The agency had itself adopted TQM only a couple months after JPL in 1991.[14] In his inaugural speech, Goldin declared himself a "true believer" and soon thereafter identified TQM as one of two "central tenets" of NASA alongside faster-better-cheaper.[15] Goldin's faith resonated with that of the incoming Clinton administration, which launched its ballyhooed "Reinventing Government" initiative with TQM as a centerpiece and with appeals as well to the doctrine of "better, faster, cheaper."[16] But while NASA urged TQM on all of its centers, some of them only tested the total quality waters, putting up a few posters and holding a few workshops; JPL, led by Stone, dove into the deep end.[17]

TQM also addressed some issues within the lab, especially the familiar but increasing complaint about red tape and the need to send decisions to senior managers for approval. Something as simple as, say, a request to buy a personal computer could acquire several signatures on its way up the hierarchy.[18] A central goal for the lab's executive council was to reduce the reliance on senior managers, whose power produced "the frustration that exists on the part of many in the lower levels of the organization." "TQM will force the empowerment of lower level people"; upper- and mid-level managers "need to prepare themselves to relinquish authority and control."[19]

Above all, Stone had embraced the need for revolutionary change and was casting about for ways to effect it. As Larry Dumas put it, Stone was "looking for a horse to ride," and he jumped on TQM. The management initiative intended to address the need, as Stone declared, "to develop a new modus operandi, one that requires fewer people to get the job done. Fewer people means that the organization as a whole will need to be more productive. This obviously requires a cultural change. . . . TQM is critical to bringing about cultural changes."[20] Among possible management approaches, TQM in particular meshed with Stone's personal preference for consensus instead of confrontation. He and several of his staff became enthusiastic students of management, subscribing to *Business Week* and circulating articles from *Fortune* and the *Harvard Business Review.*[21]

Installing TQM ended up taking two years, but by the end of 1993 almost every employee had gone through "total quality" training, consisting of three days of workshops.[22] These workshops were funded not through special accounts but instead came out of the budgets for flight and research projects—against the objections of technical and NASA managers, who tended to say, "Hey, that's soft stuff. We don't want to spend our program money on soft stuff."[23] The total quality approach rested on the five "pillars of quality" (see figure 15.1). Although the vocabulary of TQM included talk of "holistic" views, "care-about" meetings with customers, and laboratory "values," it also applied a market-based attitude, evident in an emphasis on customer satisfaction, to an R&D laboratory.[24] The central pillar of quality, "measurement," also betrayed a quantitative side to TQM. As the standard refrain ran, "If you can't measure it, you can't manage it."[25] Hence TQM stressed the use of metrics, and lab managers tried to quantify the care-abouts by having the customers—that is, NASA program managers—rate JPL's performance.[26] Senior managers also engaged in quantitative exercises, for instance, rating the dialogue and output of senior staff meetings.[27]

The TQM lingo could not hide less rosy connotations of the new environment. JPL implemented the new approach amid projected staff cuts of 30 percent from 1992 through the end of the decade. TQM might thus seem an underhanded attempt to pacify employees. That is how labor unions in general had viewed it, as another ploy by management to boost productivity without real compensation to workers, providing just a phony sense of participation instead of money and benefits.[28] At JPL, however, TQM did not appear to be a direct response to labor problems. Stone had already settled on TQM before the downsizing problems fully emerged, in an apparently earnest effort to control costs and cut bureaucracy.[29] JPL staff were employees of Caltech and continued to present little threat of unionization, and as an R&D organization JPL did not face the same labor pressures as manufacturing industry.

From Quality to Processes

If TQM was intended as a labor appeasement tool, it failed. Despite the apparent lack of a connection, the coincidence between downsizing and TQM seemed more than that to some staff, who wondered whether "you are only doing this so you can lay me off."[30] The new management approach was not a pacifier but an irritant to many JPL engineers and scientists, who viewed the workshops and paperwork as a hassle and the underlying philosophy as suspect, and middle management appeared reluctant to empower subordinates. In a lab-wide employee survey in 1993 less than half of the respondents viewed their immediate supervisor as committed to the initiative. A similar survey two years later likewise showed lukewarm support from middle management, and more than half of the lab staff doubted even the executive council's commitment.[31]

As with faster-better-cheaper, TQM undermined basic precepts of sys-

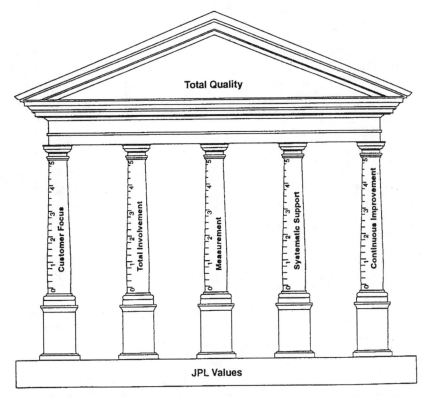

Figure 15.1. The five pillars of quality in Total Quality Management. *Source:* JPL 165, 2/18.

tems engineering that had supported JPL for thirty years. Project managers were often hard-driving autocrats; as Voyager manager Norm Haynes put it, they "were culled out to be sort of rugged individualists."[32] The otherwise good-natured John Casani, the epitome of the breed, was also known as the "Ayatollah Casani." At one point a consultant gave a personality test to senior managers; at one end of the scale were the counselor types, such as the professorial Stone, and at the other were what Casani called the "leg breakers," including himself.[33] Deputy director Pete Lyman, who himself was said to "manage by embarrassment," appreciated some aspects of TQM but viewed Laeser's initiative as a token effort. As Laeser recalled: "Pete didn't expect that the outcome of this was going to be—to put it quite bluntly—a clear statement that we didn't want to manage the way Pete Lyman managed anymore. . . . Command-and-control was out. That was really the bottom line. Teams were in." Lyman soon retired and Stone replaced him with Larry Dumas, who proved sympathetic to the new approach.[34]

By 1995 the perception prevailed among JPL staff "that little progress has been made since TQM."[35] Larry Dumas recalled the whole initiative as "god-awful painful," a sentiment seconded by Laeser: "It was a tooth-pulling exercise, because the executive council were all people who had grown into the position that they had [by] doing things a certain way. And now they were being asked to lead the laboratory in doing things a different way. And there was major resistance—*major* resistance. And that's the story for the next decade."[36]

One of the hang-ups for TQM had been its use of flow charts to diagram processes. A Laeser memo of 1993 reported: "The JPL culture does not typically think of work as a process with a flow that can be diagramed. Thus, even with TQM pressure to flowchart, deep-rooted culture drives [JPL staff] to resist it."[37] Despite this sentiment, Stone and Laeser turned to a new philosophy that made flowcharts and processes a fundamental principle. Laeser had recently come across the theory of "process-based management," the centerpiece of a movement in the 1990s that Michael Hammer and other management-consulting gurus called "reengineering the corporation."[38] He came away a convert and became, in his own words, "a disciple of Mike Hammer." Laeser brought the gospel to Stone, who agreed to reengineer JPL.[39]

Reengineering shared several attributes with TQM and could be seen as one more step of "continuous improvement." Dumas recalled the executive council's sense that "we've gotten about all we're going to get out of TQM—let's focus on reengineering as a possible mechanism for taking us to the next level."[40] Employees, however, viewed reengineering as "the fad de jour," according to a staff report: "many fail to see any common thread between TQM and reengineering and some believe that reengineering is a replacement for failed TQM."[41] One similarity lay in the need to address faster-better-cheaper. The many missions anticipated in the new mode would require many managers, and this in turn would entail standard processes to guide them—especially since many of the managers would lack experience. With faster-better-cheaper, instead of a single project propagating documents that defined the way the rest of the lab worked, the lab would define the way the projects would work; that is, the lab would standardize projects instead of projects setting standards for the lab.[42] Also like TQM, reengineering aimed to involve lower levels of the lab. In late 1995, after four years of TQM, lower-level technical staff still complained of a "disconnect" with senior management.[43] According to Laeser, the new policy involved removing "process and rule-making responsibility from a chosen and senior few, who are distant from the real work, and placing it with many who are close to that work," that is, "*at the lowest practical organizational level of the Laboratory.*"[44]

Finally, reengineering likewise aimed to reduce the bureaucracy, in particular by streamlining rules. By the 1990s JPL had accumulated more than fifty years' worth of rules, which in general were retained, not retired. The result was fourteen thick volumes of administrative guidelines. There were reasons for all this red tape: the proliferation of written rules at JPL was driven by the need for absolute reliability and government accountability. The lab now sought to simplify these rules and also to move them from the administrative manuals to searchable online databases, in which an employee could quickly learn, say, how to request a new office computer or hire a lab technician.[45]

A more fundamental aspect of reengineering, and one that differentiated it from TQM, was its organizational structure, or, rather, its attitude toward structure itself. TQM had left JPL's matrix organization intact, but the lab now used reengineering as a reason to switch from an organization based on function to one based on process, with process defined vaguely as "an organized group of related activities that together create an outcome of value."[46] Managers identified five general processes at JPL, each of which comprised a number of subprocesses and then sublevels, and at each level a particular process had a "process owner" to oversee it. By delegating responsibility down these tiers of processes, the lab hoped to empower lower-level staff. To highlight the organization around dynamic processes instead of static functions, reengineering replaced the standard, hierarchical organization chart with a profusion of flowcharts. Flowcharts, of course, were not new to JPL, since systems engineering also relied on them. But reengineering raised flowcharting to an art form and to a new level of abstraction (in addition to new status as a verb). Instead of specific functions or milestones on a schedule, these new flowcharts traced the generalized transformation of information and resources as the inputs and outputs of each process (see figure 15.2).

All of this added up to what one consultant described as a "paradigm shift."[47] Reengineering, according to a typical Hammer presentation, provided "a holistic perspective on work," one in which "intuition is as good as knowledge"; it switched from the belief that "controlling knowledge is power" to "sharing knowledge is power."[48] Laeser at the time called it "a major shift in perspective: from the vertical, hierarchical structure of the Industrial Age to the responsive, workflow-based organization of the Information Age."[49] These techniques thus brought to JPL the transition from the rigid, vertically integrated modern corporation to the flexibility, mobility, and flux of the postmodern firm.[50]

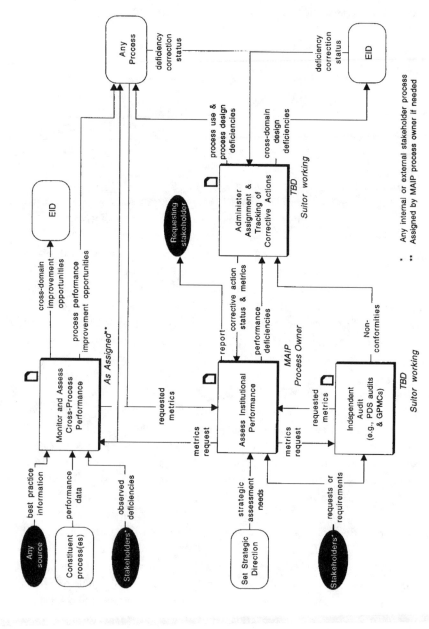

Figure 15.2. Monitor and Assess Institutional Performance process flowchart. *Source:* JPL 163, 1/1.

Consequences

What was the effect of reengineering on the work of JPL? It did get the massive rulebooks online, in searchable databases.[51] According to measurable metrics, it improved the length of time to process purchase orders and financial reports, although data for other performance categories was ambiguous.[52] Stone cited the restructuring of Voyager mission operations, which switched from functional to process-based teams and cut staff in half. The restructuring achieved this efficiency by making each individual do a broader range of work; Stone replied that "jobs are more demanding, but also more interesting."[53]

Beyond concrete payoffs, the management techniques in general conveyed the need for new ways of thinking. Dumas, once again: "We had to shake up the Laboratory; we had to shake it loose from the tried and true ways of doing business."[54] In particular, TQM and then reengineering spurred JPL staff to think in terms of customers and products, not only with respect to the main customer, NASA, but also within the lab. JPL engineers and administrators alike began to recognize, in Stone's words, "that when you do your own job you're actually doing it for somebody else. You're not doing it for yourself. You're doing it for somebody else, somebody else who needs something."[55]

Like TQM, however, reengineering management had its drawbacks. A devotion to the concept of a customer could have ill effects, in reducing the lab's independence and flexibility; believing the customer is always right could lead JPL to accept unreasonable demands. In one TQM talk, for example, Stone noted that satisfying the customer meant that JPL had to "make a deal and stick to it."[56] JPL and NASA together would learn the price of such an attitude. The management improvements had more immediate costs in money, time, and effort. As with TQM, implementation of process-based management went on for years: it started in 1995 and required frequent meetings and memos into 1999.[57] The material costs included consultants, seminars, workshops, and training manuals, all of which came out of budgets for flight projects, research, and technology, and all at a time of fiscal belt-tightening—and some of the consultants did not come cheap. Then there was the time and effort. Countless memos, viewgraphs, meeting minutes, and iterated revisions of flowcharts indicate the work involved. If reengineering aimed to reduce paperwork, it failed in the short term. Stone and the executive council devoted considerable attention to these management issues over a span of several years, attention necessarily diverted from the technical program, and the steady stream of seminars likewise distracted lower-level employees from their jobs building hardware and software.[58]

The management initiatives also occupied several senior staff full time.

When Stone took up process-based management, he and deputy director Dumas assigned it top priority. As Dumas put it: "We had to decide whether we really were going to put the first team in and assign a whole bunch of people full time to this, or were we going to try to work it with whomever we could find part time and cobble it together. And we decided to take the plunge." They pulled several key managers from their programmatic positions and assigned them to lead reengineering teams, and thus left, as Dumas acknowledged, some pretty big holes to fill. One gaping void was left by John Casani, JPL's preeminent project manager and now chief engineer, whom Stone reassigned first to revise the rulebooks and then to lead an industrial-standards certification drive.[59]

Reengineering also obeyed the law of unintended consequences. In 1998 Laeser wrote a memo entitled "Something's not right." In seeking to delegate authority to the process owners at the lowest possible level, the policy had produced a vast number of processes, which complicated instead of simplifying the bureaucracy. And the process owners at these levels in Laeser's view could lack the experience and inclination to take responsibility; they often had "insufficient big-hat viewpoint and expertise" and were "too often delegators, not leaders." The diffusion of authority alarmed the legal department; one Caltech lawyer perceived "purposeful mistakes by overly empowered process owners who are more than willing to spend Caltech's money or put the lab at risk." In a subsequent attempt "to rise above [the] fragmentation chaos and documentation quagmire," the lab consolidated processes, which then drove authority back up to senior managers.[60]

Reengineering only intensified the resistance that had earlier greeted Total Quality Management. Two years of effort, one lab leader observed in 1997, had failed to produce "real process improvement and payoffs from [the] current reengineering."[61] By that time, Dumas recalled, "we had really built up the antibodies to new initiatives to the point where anything—if you said the 'p' word, then everybody ran for the exits."[62] JPL engineers and scientists wrestled with the "abstraction" of processes and their lack of connection to the daily work of lab, as the feedback loops on flowcharts attained comical complexity (see figure 15.3).[63] Managers recorded "frequent complaints from inside," including, "rewards of process ownership [are] not worth the pain" and "this process stuff is too complicated, too esoteric and too much work."[64] In private, lab staff used more pungent language.

As important, reengineering did not replace the old functional organization but only overlaid it with the process regime. Each "process owner" now had an additional responsibility on top of his or her functional job, with no increase in compensation, but it was not clear whether or how process owners should exercise line authority.[65] The "tiers" of process owners perpetuated

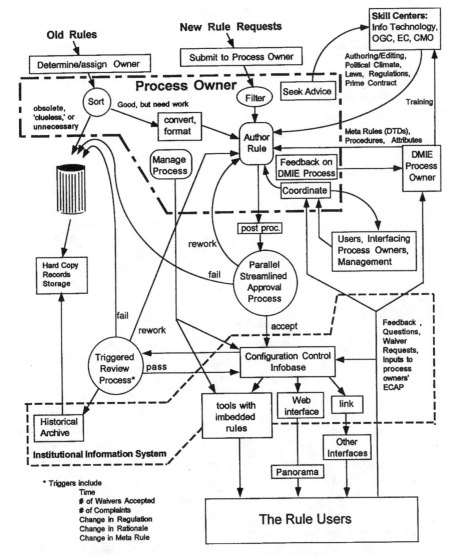

Figure 15.3. Define and Maintain the Institutional Environment process flowchart.
Source: JPL 163, 2/13.

vertical hierarchy, despite claims to the contrary. Reengineering, in effect, doubled the bureaucracy. Hence the judgment of Wes Huntress that the new regime acted to "constipate" JPL, clogging it up with new layers of people needed to approve any decision.[66]

More generally, reengineering, like TQM before it, sought to bring a countercultural sensibility to JPL's technical environment, with talk of "enabling," "nurturing," and "holistic" programs based on intuition instead of knowledge. One management consultant deployed techniques from Werner Erhard's est movement in workshops at JPL on "conversation management" and as a discussion facilitator for the executive council—the sort of management psychology viewed twenty years earlier as the white-collar equivalent to pot, flower power, and rock and roll.[67] The new management theories did appeal to scientific rationalism with their quantitative metrics, as well as with the term "reengineering" itself, and some scientists and engineers—starting with Laeser and Stone—found them persuasive. But other technical staff viewed the philosophies with suspicion, if not derision, as a bit too touchy-feely—as "the new rage in the enlightened age, the more liberal enlightened age, of how you interact."[68]

The management theories also met opposition on deeper, philosophical grounds. Although JPL's work required much coordination and teamwork, the lab viewed itself as fundamentally a collection of very talented individuals, and corporatist management theories challenged this individualistic, meritocratic ethos. As chief scientist Moustafa Chahine put it: "We have a bunch of mavericks here at JPL. . . . This new culture said 'no, there will be no mavericks at JPL. Each one will follow a set of rules.' Ninety-nine percent of the time, yes, but then what will save you is that one percent when you've got the maverick." At its extremes, reengineering held that with the proper rules in place, any individual could follow them. Pathfinder manager Tony Spear recalled: "He [Stone] thought if he could write it down on paper, anybody could do it. And I kept arguing, baloney!"[69] At a presentation attended by Chahine, Hammer claimed that "with the process-based management, you can get a person here at JPL, he doesn't have to be as educated as Ed Stone, you can get a gardener and make him the director of JPL, and with those rules he would be able to." Chahine's response: "No way. There's no way. And he should have been challenged at that time, because none of the people sitting there believed what he said. . . . But I didn't forget it, and many people did not forget it."[70]

At the same time, these management theories injected a commercial mindset to a university-run research laboratory. Management theories developed for manufacturing industry proved difficult to apply to R&D, not to mention government sponsorship. True, JPL was in the business of building things, namely, robotic spacecraft, and at the time was adapting to the production-line mode of faster-better-cheaper, and aerospace firms such as TRW had embraced TQM. Furthermore, these corporatist management theories had developed in response to the emergence of so-called knowledge workers, that increasing fraction of the workforce with an education, who sought challenging, skilled work instead of routine tasks. But the laboratory was not a factory; it remained an R&D organization, pursuing much scientific research as well as highly advanced technology. Lab managers did circulate a *Harvard Business Review* article arguing that TQM applied to development as well as manufacturing, and Stone sought to sidestep the line of argument previously raised by Lew Allen: "While some might question TQM's applicability to JPL's research and one-of-a-kind development environment, I've concluded that the potential benefits justify inauguration of a lab-wide TQM program. The basic tenets of TQM are intuitively correct—principles such as focusing on customer satisfaction, continuously improving processes, eliminating rework, and involving employees each step of the way."[71] But Michael Hammer seemed to view JPL as a test case, and Stone would note that "nobody in our situation had even done this, so there was no model we could just plug into and say, this is the way to do it."[72]

The assumption that scientific research and advanced technology are like any other product for market, and that a laboratory might be run like a business with customers and products, perhaps reflects a capitalist bent, a typically American approach. In particular, the appeal to corporate industry for management models suggests characteristics of the post–cold war context, when the search for new justifications for the civil space program settled on economic competitiveness. The commercialization of the civil space program thus might mean more than increasing reliance on industrial contractors, though there was that too. Rather, commercialization extended even to the mode of operation of academic and government labs under NASA, as well as to the underlying justification of their mission. JPL's embrace of corporate management models in the 1990s represented this broader trend.

SIXTEEN

The Tilting Triangle and Commercialization

AS TOTAL QUALITY MANAGEMENT AND REENGINEERING RESPONDED TO FASTER-better-cheaper, so were they linked to two other features of the 1990s: downsizing and regulatory pressure. These four threads — faster-better-cheaper, reengineering, downsizing, and accountability — intertwined and reinforced each other throughout the 1990s.[1] Post–cold war fiscal constraints, for example, drove faster-better-cheaper and downsizing, both of which in turn tied into the new management initiatives. Reengineering responded to NASA's interest in how JPL conducted its business, but at the same time its attempts to trim bureaucracy ran up against increasing demands for accountability. And downsizing produced an environment of fear and mistrust at lower levels of JPL, which affected reception of the management theories as well as faster-better-cheaper. The aerospace industry spooled another thread into this fabric, with persistent criticism of JPL's preference for building spacecraft itself instead of contracting their development to industry.

Stone's response as lab director to regulatory pressure and downsizing, as well as his embrace of management theories, reflected his personal distaste for confrontation and also his tendency to look inside the lab for solutions. Although he directed much attention toward the external environment, he did not try to change it as Murray had; instead Stone sought to understand the environment and adapt the lab to it. Stone accommodated increasing government audits amid calls from some quarters for pushing back, and he accepted budget and staff cuts rather than seeking new sponsors to pick up programmatic slack. In the post–cold war context there were no clear alternative sponsors, and the political environment, combined with Goldin's management of NASA, did not encourage resistance.

Downsizing

Behind the post–cold war budget-cutting lay a sense that the nation needed to reduce the federal infrastructure, including that for science and technology, which had grown to meet the needs of the cold war and which a number of politicians now viewed as excessive. By October 1992 Caltech's trustees were urging JPL to preempt political pressure by starting to shrink its staff.[2] The lab soon adopted an "employee displacement strategy," also known as "right-sizing" or, more bluntly, downsizing, with plans to cut 1,000 staff by 1998.[3] A second, deeper round of downsizing began two years later, in early 1995, when JPL completed a so-called Zero-Base Review demanded by NASA. The review required that JPL assemble its program from scratch instead of planning the budget for each year based on the previous year's work; it aimed at cuts of 22 percent on top of those already absorbed, reducing the JPL staff to 5,000 by the year 2000. Although JPL's downsizing seemed drastic, it was at the low end of cuts imposed on other NASA centers, which ranged from 20 to 35 percent; JPL's cutbacks were also not as drastic as those suffered in the aerospace industry. As Stone pointed out, the cuts would return JPL to its size in the mid 1980s, which itself was much bigger than the 1960s level of 4,000 staff.[4]

The net result of the downsizing was a loss of more than 1,400 employees from 1992 to 1998. Factoring in cuts in on-site contractors produced a decrease from more than 7,600 work-years in 1992 to 5,344 by 1999, or 30 percent of total staff.[5] The lab accomplished much of this through attrition, including a generous early retirement package, but the lab also laid off almost 900 people.[6] The layoffs occupied much management attention, especially the desire, not entirely successful, to avoid lawsuits for wrongful termination.[7] Downsizing had another effect on lab demographics. The net cutbacks, as Stone observed, were "not the whole story" since normal turnover continued. By 1998 more than 3,000 people had left JPL, so that almost one-third of staff were new hires.[8] The lab capitalized on downsizing as a way to bring in new, fresher faces amid renewed perceptions that the lab was littered with "dead-wood"—that is, older staff marking time until retirement, the demographic legacy of the buildup of the 1960s.[9] The early retirement program, however, inadvertently cleared out some strong timber, including several members of the executive council.[10]

The large turnover also presented an opportunity for affirmative action. The representation of ethnic minorities increased from 17 percent in 1984 to 25 percent in 1994, and the fraction of minority scientists and engineers increased over the same period from 14 to 22 percent. Lab staff, however, continued to see little diversity in the ranks of upper management; and Hispanics and especially Asian-Americans constituted most of the minorities (8 and 11 percent, respectively), in particular among scientists and engineers (14 percent Asian), so that whites, Asians, and Hispanics held better views of JPL's diversity than did African-Americans.[11]

Another prominent trend was the increasing presence of women. The proportion of female staff increased from 23 percent in 1984 to 27 percent in 1994. Most of them were concentrated in administrative positions, but the fraction of women among scientists and engineers also increased from 9 percent in 1984 to 15 percent in 1994. The lab in the 1990s was also promoting women at greater rates than men, and female faces began appearing on project review boards, mission study groups, and also in senior management—most in administrative positions, but also some who had worked up through technical management, such as Donna Shirley, promoted from the Pathfinder rover to lead the Mars program, and Barbara Wilson, who in 1998 became head of the microelectronics program and later the lab-wide chief technologist.[12] The trend culminated in the Deep Space 2 mission to Mars in 1999, which had women in the three top jobs: Sarah Gavit as project manager, Sue Smrekar as project scientist, and Kari Lewis as chief mission engineer, a trifecta that won headlines in *Working Woman* magazine as well as the *New York Times*.[13]

The inroads made by women at JPL mirrored their gains in the broader scientific/engineering labor pool and also represented the fruit of Bruce Murray's initiatives, years earlier, to make JPL more friendly to female careers.[14] The percentages suggest that JPL provided a better environment for women than NASA as a whole.[15] Although the space agency could point to achievements of individual women, such as female astronauts, it lagged the civilian labor force in hiring women for scientific and engineering fields. Goldin mocked NASA's "pale, male, and stale" culture and vowed to change it.[16] He perceived a political as well as a moral imperative for diversity in the increasing representation of women and minorities in Congress.[17]

The growing presence of women may have changed JPL's culture and practices. On the Pathfinder rover, for example, Shirley abandoned a hierarchical organization for a more collaborative, nurturing approach that she modeled on a biological cell. On the other hand, this management style may have derived more from such corporate philosophies as Total Quality Management than from feminine values. Shirley was a self-described Oklahoma tomboy who could steamroller critics and trade raunchy jokes as well as any old-school male manager, which might have helped her thrive in the JPL environment.[18] Other women claimed that their gender had little effect on their management approach. Gavit, the Deep Space 2 manager, stated that "the fact that we're women hasn't made a difference here." More important, she declared, was youthfulness.[19] The demographic bulge from the 1960s had moved through the system and was being replenished now by new hires; for the first time in decades, the largest cohort was in the thirty-to-thirty-nine-year age group in 1994.[20] The multitude of missions under faster-better-cheaper gave young engineers, as well as women and minorities, more chances at management experience.

Besides demographics, downsizing had a less salutary effect on morale. To take advantage of attrition, the lab spread out the process over several years instead of making a single large cut, but this approach kept staff looking over their shoulders for the next round of pink slips.[21] Stone and the executive council did not help morale by freezing wages for one year in 1995. The zero-raise policy unleashed protests from hundreds of angry staff, some of whom noted that with inflation it amounted to a pay cut, at a time when the lab was asking for more productivity from staff. The freeze was intended to signal NASA and Congress that JPL was committed to cost control, but it eroded morale and trust in management, especially since the decision first trickled out by e-mail, leading some staff to think it was a joke.[22]

The personnel policies propagated a sense of malaise. In 1993 the lab commissioned a survey of the entire staff. The responses shocked the executive council.[23] Only half the staff were satisfied with JPL's present state, most thought it had changed for the worse in the last year, and only 20 percent thought senior management was doing a good job. These figures included the views of senior management, who had a much more positive view of lab than lower-level staff; in general, older staff had a much more positive outlook than younger staff. The complaints about management conveyed a general sense that JPL managers were technically proficient but were poor as "people managers."[24]

A repeat of the survey in 1995 only strengthened these impressions. Downsizing had led, unsurprisingly, to greater fears about job security. Perceptions that the lab had changed for the worse increased 15 percent, and only 15 percent of staff thought the place was well managed. Above all, 35 percent pronounced themselves satisfied with JPL's present state, and more people viewed it as "just a place to work."[25] Two years later these perceptions persisted; one manager forwarding criticism to the executive council noted that "what is shared here does not fully reflect the intensity and feeling, much of it fear, frustration, dismay, and anger, that seems to exist throughout the Laboratory."[26]

One potential solution surfaced in a management meeting in late 1995: "Why aren't we pursuing other customers? . . . Why aren't we going outside the government to get work?" But few alternative customers existed outside NASA. The Departments of Energy and Defense were cutting their budgets and infrastructure, as were other agencies, and labs like APL and Livermore were themselves looking to NASA for business. The cold war had provided a compelling reason to keep scientists and engineers on tap at federal facilities in case of an immediate national emergency, but in the 1990s that justification disappeared.

An Affliction of Auditors

The issue of activism versus acquiescence also appeared in JPL's institutional relations with NASA and the federal government. The end of the cold war had another effect on the political environment, a corollary of fiscal compression. Although federal research labs had certainly suffered political scrutiny during the cold war, the contest with the Soviets also encouraged an emphasis on results instead of regulatory compliance. Thus JPL's one major experience of congressional investigation came after the Ranger failures. In the 1990s regulatory tolerance ceased, and the federal government began pressing for accountability from all of its research labs.[27] Meanwhile NASA's performance—the Challenger accident, Hubble telescope fiasco, and then the failure of Mars Observer in 1993—suggested an agency in disarray; congressional staff viewed NASA as "a trove for waste, fraud, and abuse."[28] The resulting pressure realigned relations among NASA and JPL and Caltech.

The first signs of a changed environment emerged in 1992, when the congressional General Accounting Office (GAO), at the request of a Senate subcommittee on oversight of government management chaired by Sen. Carl Levin, prepared a report criticizing control of federal labs. The review focused on labs under the Departments of Energy and Defense and did not include JPL. Levin's committee, however, was looking for ways to influence the negotiation of lab contracts, and it so happened that JPL's contract with NASA was coming up for renewal in 1993. As deputy director Larry Dumas put it, "JPL sort of drifted into their gunsights." The committee dispatched a team of GAO auditors, who spent several months at JPL "turning over rocks and looking at things. . . . And they found some things that they did not like."[29]

The auditors raised red flags about travel costs, tuition reimbursement for JPL employees at Caltech, and slack control of government property—in particular, the fact that JPL employees had taken much out-of-date computer equipment home with them. Levin threatened to hold public hearings and interrogate Ed Stone—again according to Dumas—about "why we were loaning JPL employees computers to take home so their kids could play computer games." Dumas and several Caltech administrators flew back to Washington to plead their case to Levin's staff and admit the need for changes, including an end to the computer policy. In the end Levin spared Stone a public grilling. But his threat and the GAO study had their effects, first by tightening the screws on JPL during its contract negotiations, and second by unleashing the auditors.[30]

The negotiations of 1993 involved a new team in NASA's on-site office. The longtime resident officer, Fred Bowen, had grown too collegial with JPL managers, in NASA's view. In 1993 the agency appointed Kurt Lindstrom as the NASA management officer and Tom Sauret as his deputy, with a mandate to impose discipline.[31] They started with the contract. Instead of opening up a few key issues for discussion, they sought to rewrite the whole document, even language formerly accepted as boilerplate. In particular, NASA wanted to tighten adherence to government regulations for procurement, health, safety, and security. The management fee provided another sticking point. The size of the fee irritated Congress and its auditors, and basing the fee on JPL's budget seemed a counterincentive to cost control; the annual performance review furthermore had no real consequences. NASA in the early 1960s had sought to switch to a performance-based fee, but Caltech had fended it off. The agency now revived the idea, to encourage JPL to do what NASA wanted—and reward it if it did.[32]

The contract negotiations dragged on from June to December 1993; the Mars Observer failure in August provided the backdrop. The process involved tedious wrangling and strong disagreements over fundamental points, including who really ran JPL: Caltech or NASA. NASA managers, for example, felt that Caltech wanted a free hand to run the lab but did not want fiscal or legal responsibility, such as for lawsuits over wrongful termination or environmental damage.[33] They argued that it was in JPL's and Caltech's interest to adhere to federal regulations—for example, by avoiding costly fines for health or safety violations—and that keeping out of regulatory trouble would in the long run decrease the administrative burden.[34] In the end Caltech accepted a performance-based fee: each year NASA managers would evaluate JPL's performance in the categories of the technical program, administration, and outreach and calculate the fee from the overall grade. The contract also imposed more federal regulations, such as those for procurement.[35] In general the contract tilted the balance from autonomy toward accountability and from Caltech toward NASA.

In addition to influencing the contract, the GAO study portended a flood of federal audits. The number of audits increased from 71 in 1989, to 138 in 1992, and to 152 in 1993. Several of these were internal Caltech reviews, but most were from NASA, the GAO, and the Defense Contract Audit Agency.[36] From 1992 to 1994 the number of on-site auditors doubled, so that there were almost 40 investigators residing at JPL and probing its business. Their activity occupied 12 JPL staff full time with much additional attention from JPL managers.[37] Recalled Dumas: "For a while, there was almost a feeding frenzy of audits at the Laboratory. . . . We were very much in a reactive role. We were sort of reeling, with more audits coming in over the transom every day. We had at one point nearly 100 individual audits and reviews under way at the same time."[38]

All these audits had an effect in increasing bureaucracy. They thus counteracted the attempts of faster-better-cheaper and new management initiatives to cut back on paperwork and red tape. In a talk at JPL in 1994, Goldin had mocked flight operations guidebooks and "the famous JPL procurement forms manual" and asked: "Do you want to spend your remaining days in the space program dealing with garbage like this? . . . This is not what we are about. We are about leaving Earth. We are not about paper."[39] At the same time, federal auditors—and the new contract with NASA—were asking for more records, not fewer.

The auditors struggled in particular to untangle JPL's finances. NASA managers argued that JPL needed an experienced, top-level *business* manager—as distinct from the technical managers who populated the lab. In particular, JPL seemed to need a chief financial officer. Wes Huntress of NASA declared in 1992 that "an institution of $1.3 billion with no CFO is hard to believe!"[40] Caltech's trustees, many of them industrial executives who wondered at JPL's academic approach to business operations, likewise pushed for a CFO, especially after accounting problems forced the lab to borrow money from Caltech to pay vendors and meet payroll. After much prodding from the trustees and a failed experiment with a controller, Stone appointed a chief financial officer in 1999.[41]

Regulatory pressure also contributed to unrest within the lab, expressed in murmuring about "pushing back" or what one JPL manager called "the 'wimp' issue."[42] Protests began simmering when the lab forced staff to return computers from their homes, heated further with new NASA rules on travel, and boiled over in 1995 in general complaints that NASA was imposing rules not accepted in the contract. The whole point of running JPL through a Caltech contract, after all, was to avoid the civil service bureaucracy. One manager noted, "people don't know why we just accept the impositions"; another cited a "perception that [the] Lab just salutes Goldin and doesn't push back."[43] Recalled Dumas: "From the employees' point of view, we heard a lot of 'why didn't you push back? Why do we have all of these new controls, and silly Work Authorization Memos (WAMs), and punching time clocks, and rules about not being able to take computers off-site, and a lot of bureaucratic obstacles to getting work done?'" Dumas went on: "The funny thing about that is that the IG [NASA inspector general] tells us that they just hate to work with us because they think we're so difficult and so uncooperative. And so you have this disconnect where the employees think we're just rolling over at every turn. And the IG thinks 'these people are just impossible.'"[44]

Some of the internal discontent implied a lack of backbone in Stone. His consensus-driven approach seemed ill-suited to strong action. Goldin felt compelled to defend Stone in a speech at JPL: "Your leader is not wimping out." The pressure for oversight, Goldin observed, ultimately derived from the American public. Wimping out, Goldin declared, would mean Stone "telling the General Accounting Office or the Inspector General they can't come in here"; instead JPL should stand up and "welcome them with open arms."[45] For his part, Stone viewed the audits as a temporary feature of the political environment: "My feeling was, we just had to get through it. Get out the other side, right? And if you push back, all you do is delay it." By letting the auditors in, he reasoned, the lab would get rid of them sooner and then could get back to its real work building spacecraft.[46]

Stone could soon see signs justifying his approach. By 1995 GAO auditors and Congress seemed satisfied by the new contract and by JPL's response to their investigations, and a meeting of the lab's executive council in 1997 suggested a sense that the crisis had passed.[47] Relations with NASA remained rocky, however, apparently exacerbated by personality conflicts. In 1996 NASA appointed a special committee to study NASA-JPL relations. The committee's ensuing report identified a basic breakdown in trust and spurred NASA to address the situation. NASA's resident management team meanwhile was completing its four-year term: Lindstrom, although a genial man, had seen his mandate as cleaning up the mess from his more lenient predecessor; his replacement, Robert Parker, arrived with the opposite mission of restoring frayed ties.[48]

At Caltech, in 1997 David Baltimore succeeded Thomas Everhart as president. Everhart, in NASA's view, had refused to accept the new, post–cold war political environment. Baltimore seemed more sympathetic to NASA's situation and got along better personally with Goldin.[49] Caltech also recognized that the performance-based contract could, in fact, increase the management fee. In 1994, the first year of the new fee, JPL's good grades for programmatic results and outreach outweighed a poor grade for institutional management, resulting in an overall mark of 88 percent (about a B+) and a fee of $16.5 million out of a possible $18 million. That represented a 25 percent increase over the previous year's fee of $13.1 million, and the fee would hover around the higher level for the next several years.[50]

The combination of increasing business focus, easing of audit pressures, and improved personal relations helped defuse the issue of accountability.

And no matter how contentious the relationship got, NASA did not seriously consider the possibility of allowing other institutions besides Caltech to bid for the JPL contract.[51] The agency also apparently never considered renouncing the contract arrangement altogether and trying to run JPL itself. On the contrary, at a time when the outcome of the cold war suggested the triumph of the private sector, contracting offered a way to satisfy new demands for privatization. It also offered practical advantages. NASA's Augustine Committee of 1990 had touted contracting as a way to avoid civil service regulations in recruitment. In 1995 a panel studying NASA's labs similarly recommended wider use of the contract model, based on the benefits from university affiliation and also the oversight provided by Caltech's eminent trustees.[52]

But attempts to extend contract operation to other NASA centers—for instance, to an extensive astrobiology program at Ames—ran into familiar obstacles, especially transfers of civil service employees.[53] And while Dan Goldin gave energetic endorsement to the JPL model, at the same time his management style reduced the benefits of independence. More broadly, the post–cold war push for accountability counteracted the coincident embrace of privatization. Despite the advantages of contract operation, increasing demands for accountability—and JPL's acceptance of them—compromised the independence of the lab. The smoother relationship that eventually resulted between the lab and the government did not remove the ultimate source of tension, as JPL and Caltech would learn in future contract negotiations.

The Triangle Tilts

The NASA-JPL-Caltech triangle had tilted toward Caltech in the 1980s, thanks to increasing campus ties and work for outside sponsors in the military. In the 1990s the triangle tilted back toward NASA, so that the old question of whether it was Caltech's JPL or NASA's was answered now for NASA. Caltech remained in the equation, and regulatory pressure reached it as well. Auditors threatened to make Caltech pay for certain unacceptable costs at JPL, and at one point these disallowances approached $10 million; hence the trustees' push for a chief financial officer and Caltech's own internal audits of JPL's business.[54]

The regulatory environment also affected campus-lab collaboration. The need for NASA approval limited the number of Caltech graduate students at JPL, and rules about reimbursement restricted faculty involvement. In the other direction, contract issues about subsidizing a university reduced the number of JPL staff teaching on campus from thirty to ten. Caltech's general counsel feared federal auditors probing the blurry boundary between campus and lab on such collaborative projects as the Infrared Processing and Analysis

Center (IPAC).[55] Above all, Caltech administrators and trustees denounced the "uncooperative 'gotcha' attitude" of NASA business managers and resolved that if NASA did not retreat from the current adversarial approach, "Caltech will need to think very hard about *any* future contract renewal."[56]

The trustees expressed this frustration to Goldin in a private meeting in 1996, which helped spark the move to improve relations. Goldin appreciated not only Caltech's scientific and technical contributions to JPL and NASA, but also the political ones. After Bruce Murray's end-runs, the lab and campus had soft-pedaled any political activity, but in a breakfast meeting at Caltech, Goldin now asked the trustees to get involved.[57] The trustees continued to offer a potent roster of political influence, and at their Washington meeting each year they pressed JPL's case with a number of congressional representatives. NASA managers welcomed the trustees' "heightened profile on Capitol Hill"—as long, of course, as they advocated NASA's program and not their own.[58]

From their end, Caltech administrators and trustees appreciated their affiliation with NASA. The campus continued to depend on the JPL fee and overhead for a substantial chunk of its operating budget—$28 million or 15 percent in 1995, an average of $100,000 per professor, an amount to give pause to even the most vocal campus critics of JPL.[59] Additional funds flowed to campus in the form of research contracts: about $25 million in 1998, one-third of that to IPAC. A number of professors worked on JPL missions—not only planetary, but also astronomy, where the campus investment in IPAC paid off in a leading role in the larger follow-on infrared telescope.[60]

But the sheer size of JPL programs revived fears that the affiliation would change the character of Caltech. As Baltimore observed, "JPL has much more to offer than the Campus and its student body can absorb." The size of the infrared astronomy program—$40 million and 180 staff—surprised him. "We can carry one of these and be small, but if we do one more of these we will loose [sic] our smallness."[61] People at JPL, meanwhile, still did not always appreciate the value added by its association with Caltech. In the employee survey of 1993, 60 percent of JPL staff felt a strong affiliation with NASA and only 26 percent with Caltech.[62] When the trustees stepped up their political activity, some lab staff thought it was about time the lab benefited from its relation to Caltech.[63] Baltimore recognized that "campus must care about the health of JPL, not just treat it as a cash cow."[64]

The Commercialization of JPL

The lab's tilt away from Caltech and toward NASA indicated in part its integration into the federal government, but even more it represented a shift from its original academic background to an industrial environment. The affliction of audits in the 1990s forced the lab to comply with procurement regulations and other rules developed for industrial contractors. JPL was indeed a contractor, but it was not the same thing as an aerospace company. Federal auditors nevertheless squeezed JPL's square peg into a round industry hole and thus squeezed its independence and distorted its technical focus.[65] The embrace of reengineering and the hiring of a chief financial officer represented JPL's efforts to adhere to industrial standards and techniques. More generally, faster-better-cheaper brought more of an industrial mind-set, where cost became the driving factor for deep-space missions instead of success-at-any-price.[66]

Several others factors also helped to commercialize JPL. The post–cold war environment that encouraged the celebration of the private sector also sparked an entrepreneurial spirit, which impelled efforts to apply JPL technologies to civilian products. The usual route ran through patents, which Caltech would license to industry for a fee or royalties. The number of licenses rose more or less steadily starting in the early 1990s, especially for software, which increased from about 10 in 1992 to 180 by 1996.[67] A few years earlier the lab had also started programs for "technology affiliates" and other cooperative agreements with industry, under which JPL helped firms, usually small companies, develop new technologies. The lab had thirty corporations as technology affiliates by 1992, sixty by 1994, most of them not from the aerospace industry but seeking help in such fields as software, robotics, microdevices, or remote sensing.[68] Licensing activity greatly increased after the institute created an office of technology transfer in 1995; by the late 1990s Caltech was reaping more than a million dollars in annual revenue from JPL products, most from software licenses.[69]

Another approach emerged amid the entrepreneurial buzz of the late 1990s: instead of transferring specific technologies, JPL started spinning off people and their ideas in small start-up companies. Since small start-ups lacked capital for license fees, Caltech began a "grubstake" grant program for start-ups, with an equity stake retained by the institute. By 1998 JPL had generated six start-up companies. But the firms cost the lab in loss of people. In 1998, for example, Carl Kukkonen, the architect of JPL's microelectronics program, left to start a company called ViaSpace, and he sought to bring some key people with him. Caltech agreed but asked that he keep his recruiting within reasonable bounds; Kukkonen agreed, but it was a voluntary gesture.[70]

The microelectronics program provided a prime example of spin-off. In the early 1990s a JPL team led by Eric Fossum developed a solid-state image sensor called the active pixel sensor, which connected an electronic amplifier to every pixel in an image and used the CMOS (complementary metal-oxide semiconductor) process to put the entire camera on a chip. A CMOS image sensor thus used much less power than a CCD camera and could also be much smaller. In 1995 Fossum and his wife, Sabrina Kemeny, left JPL to form Photobit Corporation, with a license from Caltech for the CMOS sensor; they soon led an industry that ranged from an ingestible "camera in a pill" for medical diagnosis to the cameras used in mobile phones. The sale of the company several years later made Fossum and Kemeny millionaires, and Caltech netted its own tidy profit.[71]

Photobit exemplified the new justifications for the space program: high technology as a source for economic growth. But it also suggested some resistance to the commercial spirit at JPL. Lab managers initially resisted such spin-offs, and not only for fear of losing staff and the distraction from the main job of building spacecraft. They worried that NASA auditors, despite the Bayh-Dole act promoting technology transfer, would charge that individuals were profiting from government-funded research. It took the intervention of the Caltech president and trustees to overcome JPL's discouragement of Photobit, and although the lab would later come to celebrate Photobit's success, concern about the private-public divide continued to dampen its embrace of entrepreneurialism. At the same time, many of the technology licenses derived from the Microdevices Lab and thus represented another legacy of defense work, but as military investment receded in the 1990s it threatened to dry up the flow of commercial technologies.[72]

JPL also continued to intersect the aerospace industry in spacecraft development. Agitation by the aerospace industry for JPL to contract out spacecraft work instead of performing it in-house increased in this period. Maturing aerospace firms continued to challenge JPL's technical superiority, and after the end of the cold war they also looked to make up for their declining military business with NASA contracts.[73] Furthermore, if privatizing was the mantra of the 1990s, industry could argue that contract operation was only a half-step away from the government; why not go all the way to the private sector?

These factors helped revive the make-or-buy question—that is, should JPL build spacecraft itself or buy them from industry. The usual arguments for in-house work, including doubts about industry's technical competence and the need to be a "smart buyer," had resulted in the assumption that JPL should have one big in-house project at all times. The Cassini project followed Galileo as a mostly in-house project, as was Pathfinder. It did not help that Mars Observer, a system-mode contract, failed in 1993. Although Magellan, likewise a system contract, succeeded, JPL had pulled much of its radar system in-house after the radar contractor ran into technical problems.[74]

In 1993 Stone hired an outside consulting firm to study the "make versus buy" issue. The firm's report concluded that "by almost all measures, JPL should be expanding its reliance on outside suppliers of technology." Industry had multiple suppliers, who would benefit from technology transfer, and infrequent deep-space missions taxed JPL's ability to maintain in-house expertise. If the lab did not make the shift on its own, NASA and Congress would no doubt impose it from above. The report acknowledged that the "shift from the end-to-end builder of spacecraft to the manager of missions" would make JPL "a very different place in five years," not least by redefining it as a source of "management effectiveness rather than internal technical expertise."[75]

The issue involved the basic identity of JPL: was it management or engineering? Lab staff stuck to their technical identity. When Ed Stone asked John Casani in 1995 to consider what JPL would look like with no in-house development—what disciplines to renounce, what jobs to cut—Casani considered the likely reception of the exercise and called it a "suicide mission."[76] Faster-better-cheaper and downsizing, however, were providing additional impetus. Discovery missions removed the possibility of one big project sustaining staff and provided more of an opening for industrial participation, and downsizing encouraged shifting the burden of maintaining staff to industry.[77] The lab had meanwhile developed a new approach to address problems of contracting. In the late 1980s the executive council raised the possibility of an "associate contractor," a single firm with something like a five-year, renewable contract for a series of projects. A longer-term commitment would overcome JPL's lack of trust, allow the contractor to invest in staff and facilities, avoid detailed negotiations for every project, allow informal relations to replace formal contacts, and in general promote continuity.[78] In the eyes of both JPL and industry the problem was "cultural," not legal or contractual: JPL needed to get over its pride and accept industry as an equal collaborator.[79]

In the 1990s this concept evolved into the approach known as "partnering." Lab staff did note several pitfalls. The lack of competition for contracts would invite complacency in the partner and lead other potential contractors to drop out of the business, eliminating potential sources of new ideas.[80] The end result might be a monopoly, surely not the sort of thing JPL or the federal government wanted. JPL nevertheless in 1997 entered a ten-year partnership in its Mars program with Lockheed Martin Astronautics in Denver. The company had built the Viking landers and the Magellan spacecraft; when it won the contract to build an orbiter and lander to launch to Mars in 1998, JPL agreed to buy subsequent spacecraft for launches in 2001, 2003, and 2005, assuming the company performed well and NASA funded the program. Even the losing bidders in industry reportedly agreed that a single competition for a ten-year, $500-million program was better than one every two years for $100 million; they just disagreed with JPL's choice of contractor.[81] The partnership included JPL's maintaining long-term staff in Denver, Lockheed's participating in Mars program planning and contributing technology developed with its own discretionary funds, and both sides aligning their organizations.[82] The upshot was the further integration of JPL and industry.

Conclusion

Instead of a triangle tilting toward NASA, then, the 1990s suggested a quadrilateral with JPL and Caltech on one end and NASA and industry at the other, with more influence accruing to the NASA and industry side. In a different light, the trend of the 1990s increased the connections between JPL and NASA and JPL and industry, with the same effect of reducing the lab's autonomy. As Stone announced in 1997, JPL was "changing from an era of independence to one of interdependence."[83]

The combination of downsizing and regulatory pressure in the early to mid 1990s produced a climate of uncertainty and mistrust of senior management and exacerbated the grumbling about reengineering and the doubts about faster-better-cheaper.[84] The results from its technical program, especially in deep-space exploration, promised either to push the lab further into gloom or to restore its optimism and vitality.

A Break in the Storm

THE DEEP-SPACE PROGRAM IN THE 1990S AT FIRST DID NOT DO MUCH TO EASE THE uncertain climate at JPL. The failure of the main antenna on Galileo in 1991, the complete loss of Mars Observer in 1993, and resistance to faster-better-cheaper produced a climate of doubt. The tide began turning mid-decade with the ultimate success of Galileo at Jupiter; then in July 1997 the Mars Pathfinder beamed back pictures of the Martian surface. As the lab's first faster-better-cheaper mission, Pathfinder seemed to confirm that JPL had adapted to the new mode and that technical creativity could thrive even when money was lacking. The Mars Global Surveyor followed with a steady stream of scientific data from Mars orbit, including images suggesting recent surface water flows.

Meanwhile, the discovery in 1996 of a meteorite on Earth with possible traces of Martian microbes sparked a new program, called Origins, that laid out transcendent goals for the post–cold war space program—namely, the origins and fate of the cosmos and of life itself. The new program, together with faster-better-cheaper, provided a flurry of new projects, in astronomy as well as planetary science, and lab managers began to realize that the new programs would provide more eggs for the lab's basket. The big-mission mode, however, persisted in the Cassini mission to Saturn and induced schizophrenia in JPL engineers trying to pursue faster-better-cheaper while still doing a flagship mission.

Gathering Clouds

JPL's technical trials began in 1991 with Galileo. The project's tortuous history of budget cuts and redesigns gave way to relief at its launch in 1989, but unexpected legacies lurked in the hardware. The delay after Challenger had allowed much fine-tuning, but it also forced the spacecraft to sit for another three years, and the redesigned trajectory required the high-gain antenna to remain stowed for two years of flight. The spacecraft first swung by Venus for a gravity assist and then returned to the neighborhood of Earth for two more gravity-assist passes; at this point, away from the heat at Venus, the high-gain antenna was supposed to unfurl like an umbrella. Pins holding eighteen graphite-epoxy ribs in the stowed position were designed to release and a small motor would drive the ribs outward, stretching a metallic mesh into a parabolic dish. But on the day of deployment, two of the umbrella's ribs stuck, producing an asymmetric—and useless—antenna.[1]

JPL engineers soon identified a probable cause in a lack of dry lubricant on the pins. In this respect the Challenger disaster again had a role: the spacecraft's two extra cross-country trips may have jostled the lubricant away from the pin contacts, and the longer, post-Challenger trajectory did not help. Another possible factor was the lack of a spare antenna, which limited preflight testing on the single available antenna so as not to wear it out. But the phenomenon was difficult to simulate; it required a long time in zero pressure so that the lubricant molecules could migrate, and even after the failure JPL engineers could not reproduce it on the ground.[2] At the time, the Galileo team focused its energy not on finding fault, but on fixing the problem. The high-gain antenna was to provide a data rate of 134 kilobytes per second, transmitting one image per minute alongside other data. The backup low-gain antenna had a rate of 10 bits per second, or about a picture a month, not including data from the other ten instruments. The loss of the big antenna would thus greatly limit the science return, which had aimed for some 50,000 images over two years.[3]

JPL engineers tried several ways to unstick the pins: turning the antenna into and then out of sunlight, hoping that thermal expansion and contraction would free it; rotating the spacecraft even faster to jog the antenna with centrifugal force; and finally "hammering" it with the antenna's drive motors. None of them worked. By 1993 Galileo managers accepted the stuck antenna and set about salvaging the mission. When the problem was first recognized, a team of engineers from the Deep Space Network had started working on ways to boost communication with only the low-gain antenna. The success of the mission now depended on their efforts.

Just as Galileo engineers were giving up on the high-gain antenna, the Mars Observer was nearing its destination. As with Galileo, project engineers had hoped Observer's launch in September 1992 would put an end to its travails—in this case, the technical problems, delays, and ballooning costs that killed the Observer concept itself. Their hopes were soon dashed. As the

258 • The Stone Years, 1991–2001

spacecraft approached Mars on 21 August 1993 it pressurized its propellant tanks, to prepare for firing its engines a few days later in order to enter Mars orbit. To protect the radio transmitter tubes from jolts during the pressurization sequence, JPL engineers had programmed them to switch off and then back on after the fourteen-minute process was complete. The appointed time came and went with no signal. As the spacecraft stayed silent JPL engineers again hoped that the loss-of-signal came from a software glitch, and they scrambled to find a fix. But as days and weeks passed they came to accept that they had lost the spacecraft.[4]

The failure of the billion-dollar Mars Observer followed closely on the problems with Galileo's antenna and the Hubble telescope, and the Challenger disaster before them. JPL and NASA became a laughingstock. Late-night television host David Letterman listed his "Top Ten Reasons for Losing Mars Observer," which ran from "Mars probe? What Mars probe?" to number one, "Space monkeys."[5] Letterman's gag suggested a persistent feature of JPL's environment: UFO believers and conspiracy theorists. The failure revived tabloid talk of the Great Galactic Ghoul (see figure 17.1), a mythical monster near Mars that ate Soviet and American spacecraft without discrimination and whose presence sprang from a joking comment by John Casani to a reporter back in 1964.[6] The *Weekly World News* revealed that a 750-mile-long space fish had swallowed Mars Observer as an hors d'oeuvre, while darker conspiracy theories held that NASA killed the mission after initial photos revealed a sculpted face on Mars, remnant of an extraterrestrial civilization.[7]

NASA and JPL review boards found more plausible explanations. Their postmortem was hampered by the lack of telemetry itself, which in turn stemmed from cost-cutting: rather than conduct a $375,000 shock test of the radio transmitter, project managers decided to switch it off during pressurization. But keeping the transmitter on would probably not have saved the spacecraft. The most likely failure scenario concerned leaky valves in the propulsion system: during the eleven-month trip to Mars a couple of spoonfuls of nitrogen tetroxide, the oxidizer for the hydrazine fuel, seeped through the valves into tubes where it mixed with hydrazine during the pressurization process. The resultant combustion melted the titanium tube like butter; when propellant then sprayed out of the tube it spun the spacecraft out of control, or, worse, the combustion reached the fuel tank and blew the spacecraft to smithereens.[8]

The original flight plans had called for pressurization of the tanks only five days after launch, which would have kept the oxidizer from leaking during the trip to Mars. Seven months before launch, however, a JPL engineer recalled that early pressurization had caused problems on Viking: leaky pressure regulators had caused potentially catastrophic pressure buildup in

Figure 17.1. The Great Galactic Ghoul. The original painting by G. W. Burton hangs in the JPL archives. *Source:* JPL Photolab.

the Viking fuel tanks. Rather than delay Observer's launch to install new pressure valves, project manager Glenn Cunningham decided to delay pressurization until arrival at Mars. As he put it after the failure: "We may have been damned either way. Sweeping the system clean on Day Five would work, but then we'd be facing the risk of a slow regulator leak overpressurizing the tank in those same 11 months." The NASA review did cite overpressurization as another possible cause of failure, albeit from a regulator that stuck open during pressurization and burst the tank. Other possible failure modes included a backfiring pyrotechnic device that punctured the fuel tank or a massive electrical short.[9]

The review boards traced these technical failures to several management assumptions. First was the fixed-price contract with the spacecraft supplier, which kept JPL engineers at "arm's length" from the contractor; the head of NASA's review board speculated that they might have dealt with the pressurization decision earlier had they had a better understanding of the spacecraft.[10] The fixed-price contract in turn assumed only minor modifications were required to a commercial earth-orbiting spacecraft. Fifteen years earlier Seasat had shown the pitfalls of standardization, but JPL forgot these lessons and now even extended standardization from Earth to Mars. A Mars mission, NASA's board observed, required not only design and testing of much different components—such as shock-testing the radio transmitter amplifiers or redesigning the propulsion system—but also the "discipline and documentation" required for a complex, custom spacecraft instead of a production-line model.[11] Observer finally suggested the virtues of redundancy. Unlike previous Mars missions under Mariner and Viking as well as Voyager, Observer had no backup spacecraft, despite calls from scientists and some NASA managers for a spare.[12] As with Galileo, JPL and NASA decided that the risks of planetary missions had dipped below the costs of insurance.

Mars Observer shook JPL out of complacency. JPL had not lost a spacecraft since 1971, when the launch vehicle for Mariner 8 failed, and JPL engineers from Voyager to Magellan had always managed to bail out a spacecraft in trouble. As Stone pointed out to the Observer team, "that record of success has made the sending of complex machines hundreds of millions of kilometers across the solar system seem easier, and less risky, than it is."[13] For planetary missions from Mariner 1 through Magellan, JPL had a batting average of .800, losing three spacecraft out of fifteen launches. Mars Observer made it four.

JPL's problems extended from spacecraft in flight to those in development. In 1990 JPL had started work on the combined CRAF/Cassini project. CRAF was the comet rendezvous/asteroid flyby, the first of the Mariner Mark II missions; Cassini planned an extensive orbital tour of Saturn and its satellites, including a probe dropped into Titan, doing for Saturn what Galileo would do for Jupiter. Congress had approved CRAF/Cassini with a $1.6-billion cost cap, but early cost increases on CRAF led NASA to cut the CRAF half of the mission in January 1992, to the chagrin of comet scientists already peeved at missing Halley's comet. CRAF had in fact been first in line for the Mariner Mark II missions, with Cassini second, but JPL and science advisory groups had long viewed Cassini as a higher priority.[14]

The demise of CRAF also doomed the Mariner Mark II concept, as NASA directed JPL to plan for a unique Cassini craft instead of a multimission model.[15] Even after CRAF's cancellation, Cassini was to cost $1.7 billion, not counting the launch vehicle and operations costs. That price was twice the cost of Voyager. Cassini had a longer, more complicated mission (Voyager, after all, was explicitly designed only to get to Saturn) and carried a larger complement of instruments, plus the Titan probe.[16] But Stone admitted that although science had contributed to high costs, "in-house dynamics led to making it bigger and bigger."[17] In particular, when faced with a choice between performance versus cost, JPL engineers—abetted by scientists and NASA managers—seemed to favor performance.

Conceived in a time of growth, Cassini now faced constricting NASA budgets. Deficit hawks in Congress in the early 1990s froze discretionary spending, including NASA's budget.[18] Within the zero-sum NASA budget, space science now contended with the space station. An early congressional vote on the station in 1991 rekindled the old issue of human exploration versus scientific research, which subsequent congressional debates would revisit through the decade. Once again, science lost. And, like Galileo, Cassini contended with astronomy (a major orbiting X-ray observatory, later called Chandra) and earth science (the ambitious Earth Observing System platforms).[19]

These budget pressures put Cassini on the chopping block in 1992, amid Goldin's fulminations against battlestar galacticas, and Stone worried about the threat, by extension, to JPL itself.[20] To save Cassini, project engineers shaved about $250 million and 200 kilograms off the spacecraft and greatly reduced annual funding by slipping the launch date two years, to 1997.[21] The main savings in cost and weight came through eliminating two booms that stuck out from the spacecraft, one holding a scan platform with the camera and the other with particles-and-fields instruments on a turntable; instead engineers bolted these instruments onto the spacecraft itself. The fiscal savings thus came at the expense of science, since the several instruments could no longer point and gather data independently. To take a picture, for instance, the whole spacecraft would have to rotate to aim the camera, so an individual instrument could spend much of the mission pointing in the wrong direction. The restructuring also greatly complicated operations, with the whole spacecraft turning this way and that and mission planners figuring out what sequence of positions would maximize the science return. Finally, the new plan entailed more risk, with the chance that the spacecraft might start rolling and not stop.[22] To criticisms that the new plan made for a more difficult mission, John Casani, one of its primary architects, replied: "Yeah, of course it does. But it means you have a mission to run."[23]

The complicated flight sequences, together with Cassini's cost, raised a broader issue with NASA, that of development versus operations. Outer-planet missions could soak up hundreds of millions of dollars over the several years they spent flying, on top of their billion-dollar development costs. High operations costs stemmed in part from the old problem that engineers focused on design and neglected planning for operations, and also from the large size of Galileo and Cassini, which required long, looping gravity-assist trajectories to reach their targets.[24] Goldin noted that spending on operations had more than doubled since 1986; the mounting costs provided an additional spur to faster-better-cheaper.[25]

Part of NASA's criticism, however, derived from a disconnect: NASA viewed operations simply as mission control; JPL took a more active view of operations that shaded into development, with software for trajectories and science sequences, for example, coded during the cruise phase—the sort of in-flight design that characterized Voyager.[26] In part to recognize the integration of development and operations, in 1994 JPL reorganized, combining mission planning, development, and operations in a single office. The reorganization elevated Cassini and the Mars missions to separate offices, and as a result abolished the vaunted flight projects office, for decades the home of planetary mission expertise. It also shuffled the flight projects director, John Casani, to a new position as chief engineer—a move that to some observers seemed like a kick upstairs for the epitome of old-school project management, amid the push for faster-better-cheaper.[27]

Even as JPL ramped up for the flagship Cassini, it began to learn the new mode of faster-better-cheaper on Mars Pathfinder. The early travails on this project added to the atmosphere of adversity in the early 1990s. The mission aimed to land on another body, something JPL had not tried since the 1960s. Furthermore, the Viking landers, run by NASA's Langley center, were dropped off by orbiters; Pathfinder had to combine the cruise vehicle with the lander, and then tack on surface operations with a robotic rover, something never before tried on another planet.[28] Overseeing this "three-in-one spacecraft" fell to project manager Tony Spear, a shaggy, mustached figure, whose reputation as a maverick had won him the Pathfinder job but whose casual demeanor belied his long experience in project management, most recently with Magellan.[29]

Many people inside and outside JPL assumed that Pathfinder would fail. Landing looked like the hardest part, especially after Spear decided to use a new landing system. Instead of retro-rockets firing to slow its final descent, the spacecraft would plummet to the Martian surface and cushion the shock with big, inflatable airbags. The airbag approach pleased NASA managers, who consistently pushed for novelty within faster-better-cheaper, as well as JPL engineers seeking a new challenge, but the lab had zero experience with airbags. Doubts increased after early tests in 1993 ended with shredded, useless bags. Said Spear: "Every time we showed a film, a simulation of airbags, the people in the audience would giggle. 'No way in hell is this going to work, Spear.'"[30]

A similar technical debate consumed the rover project. Spear did not welcome the added challenge of the rover; the initial mission had just called for a lander, and he viewed the rover as a drain on resources that could imperil the mission. Even after Spear acceded to NASA's rover plans, a clash continued between boundary-pushing technologists on the rover team and conservative spacecraft engineers.[31] The technologists had been working for years on autonomous rovers, which used artificial-intelligence software to avoid obstacles (the round-trip radio time from Mars to Earth of about 30 minutes ruled out real-time remote control). Spear, however, feared a free-ranging rover would lose radio contact with the lander and perish; instead he insisted on a tethered rover, to provide a secure radio link as well as electrical power. But the tether, too, had complications, not least of which was a possible tangle, and Spear eventually abandoned it after a successful test of the autonomous rover in spring 1993. Until then, the rover debate added doubt to Pathfinder, complicated by friction between Spear and rover manager Donna Shirley, two strong and forthright personalities.[32]

The technical obstacles produced cost and schedule pressures, and NASA budget managers watched for any excuse to cancel Pathfinder.[33] JPL staff meanwhile viewed it as something of a tar baby, and the project team was isolated within the lab.[34] That was in part by design: Pathfinder had adopted a "skunk works" organization, modeled on the legendary Lockheed group that had produced the U-2 and SR-71 spy planes and stealth aircraft. A skunk works features a small staff freed from bureaucratic constraints and conventional thinking, committed full time to a project, with minimal documentation but thorough testing and reviews, and it thus seemed to meet the demands of faster-better-cheaper.[35] The lab brought in Lockheed managers to learn how it worked, and Spear had Pathfinder staff report straight to him instead of through their managers in the technical divisions. The arrangement only reinforced Pathfinder's isolation, and as the project's problems mounted, Spear said, "our skunk works started to stink."[36]

Pathfinder's early travails merged with the questionable survival of Cassini, the failure of Mars Observer, and Galileo's antenna woes to foster uncertainty in JPL's flight projects in the early 1990s. Together with doubts about faster-better-cheaper, the turmoil of reengineering, and NASA's managerial meddling, JPL's future seemed to darken the deeper it entered the post–cold war environment.

A Fresh Breeze

The programmatic clouds around JPL started to lift in the middle of the decade. Pathfinder would provide the final puff to dispel them, but the initial break began with Galileo. Even as they continued to try opening the jammed main antenna, JPL engineers sought other ways to salvage the mission. The Deep Space Network provided the key. In early 1993 Leslie Deutsch, a mathematician in the DSN, led a study of how to boost the data return through the low-gain antenna. Once again, software would compensate for the limitations of hardware: as they had done for the later Voyager encounters, engineers developed algorithms for data compression, especially of images, and for telemetry encoding that would maximize the amount of useful data in a given packet of downlinked bits.[37]

The fix required replacing the software in the main computer's operating system, what one study paper called "a complete brain transplant over a four-hundred-million-mile radio link." The age of the components—1970s-vintage processors and an archaic software code—complicated the procedure, as did another relic of the 1970s, a reel-to-reel tape recorder included on the spacecraft to store data from the atmospheric probe. The recorder became the crucial link: it would store data from all the instruments during close flybys of Jupiter and its moons, and the low-gain antenna would transmit the compressed data during slack periods.[38] The risky transplant took place over six weeks in early 1995, at the end of which the spacecraft had its new brain. The procedure allowed Galileo to meet 70 percent of its original science goals; the low-gain antenna could transmit about 200 images a month—far from the 2,000 a month originally planned, but much better than the 1 per month possible without the fix. The bailout proved once again the central importance of the Deep Space Network to JPL's mission.[39]

Then, in October 1995, when the spacecraft acquired the first images during final approach, the tape recorder stuck in rewind mode. Since the recorder was now the crucial lifeline, project engineers feared a disaster, especially after ground tests of an identical recorder resulted in the tape ripping from the reel. Project engineers finally stopped the tape, and a fretful week later they gingerly tested it in play mode. It worked, but fears that it would stick again—or that the constant rewinding had worn that section of the tape to a precarious thread—led project manager William O'Neil to run the recorder only in low-speed mode in order to preserve the highest priority, returning data from the probe. Among other things, that meant skipping pictures of Europa and Io during close flybys on the probe's arrival day, to the disappointment of scientists.[40]

The probe had released from the orbiter in July 1995 and the two arrived in tandem at Jupiter on 7 December 1995. Although the encounter attracted flocks of media to JPL, Galileo seems not to have had the same public impact as Voyager. For one, it was a return visit after the Voyager flyby, so it lacked the excitement of seeing new worlds, and as an extended orbiting mission it lacked the concentrated drama of a flyby. Galileo was also something of a forgotten stepchild between Voyager and Cassini—a relic of the 1970s, strung out by Challenger, dogged by the antenna failure, and now the antithesis of faster-better-cheaper. That at least was the complaint of O'Neil, who earlier in 1995 had declared: "Galileo is not considered good and important. The signals are that Galileo is *the example* of how *not* to do things."[41]

The mission made up for any neglect with its science results. As the first spacecraft to orbit an outer planet, Galileo provided data from a variety of angles. Over the next five years it would make about thirty orbits of Jupiter, allowing multiple passes of the major moons Callisto, Europa, Ganymede, and Io and detailed study of the magnetosphere. On arrival in December 1995 the orbiter relayed data from the probe's descent into the Jovian atmosphere; the probe survived an initial deceleration of 228 g's before deploying its parachute, and it then returned data for almost an hour of descent before the increasingly dense atmosphere attenuated its signal deep below the clouds. The probe provided detailed profiles for chemical composition, temperature, wind and weather, lightning, and the magnetosphere; a particular surprise was the lack of water, which suggested that the probe had hit a "hot spot" on Jupiter, akin to a desert on Earth, and that Jupiter's weather was even more dynamic than had been thought. All of the data greatly refined models of planetary formation and structure for the outer solar system. In particular, the data revealed close coupling among the various phenomena and hence suggested the value of the comprehensive, simultaneous data sets provided by big, expensive missions.[42]

Galileo also provided close looks at the four major moons, including volcanic Io, but perhaps the most important result concerned Io's colder cousins. Voyager images of Europa from a distance of more than 100,000 kilometers had revealed curving cracks in its ice surface, linked in long chains extending hundreds of kilometers. Galileo imaged the cracks from only 200 kilometers away, with a resolution of 200 meters (see figure 17.2). The images inspired an explanation from Randy Tufts, Gregory Hoppa, and other geologists at the University of Arizona: Europa's elliptical orbit and diurnal rotation resulted in varying gravitational force from Jupiter, so that each arc formed over a single cycle of 85 hours, propagating at a speed of 3 kilometers per hour; for the next cycle slightly different gravitational forces produced a new arc. More important, the cracks themselves came from tidal swings of up to dozens of meters in a vast ocean of liquid water under the ice; the model of crack formation required a very deep ocean—perhaps a hundred kilometers deep, which would give Europa more water than Earth—and a thin ice crust, as little as 15 kilometers thick. Galileo's magnetometer backed up the theory with evidence of a global, electrically conducting layer, such as salt water, under the ice; and the lack of impact craters around the cracks implied that they formed recently and that the ocean still exists. Another surprise was magnetic data suggesting similar conducting layers, and hence subsurface saltwater oceans, on Ganymede and Callisto. The theory of extensive and perhaps accessible liquid oceans had profound implications: water is seen as a key ingredient for life, and Jupiter's icy moons, and Europa in particular, thus became a prime target in the search for extraterrestrial life.[43]

The results rewarded Galileo scientists for eighteen years of forbearance, beginning with the project's approval in 1977 and including the ten-year delay from the originally planned arrival of 1985. After its initial problems

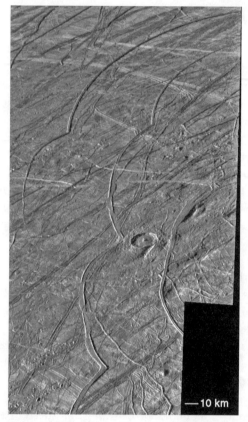

Figure 17.2. Cycloidal features on the northern hemisphere of Europa, taken by Galileo. The crater at center is about 10 kilometers across. *Source:* PIRL University of Arizona/JPL/NASA.

the spacecraft survived well beyond its planned twenty-two-month orbital mission, despite absorbing four times its specified radiation dose.[44] Galileo was still orbiting in 2000 when Cassini flew by Jupiter, enabling simultaneous measurements from different positions of the solar wind and magnetic fields.[45] Its end came in September 2003, fourteen years after launch, as its propellant dwindled. NASA decided to sacrifice the spacecraft by vaporizing it in Jupiter's atmosphere rather than risk the possibility of contaminating Europa with spacecraft-borne terrestrial microbes. Project manager O'Neil noted the irony that "Galileo gets a death sentence from NASA for its greatest discovery: the prospect of life on Europa."[46]

Pathfinder

As Galileo arrived at Jupiter the Pathfinder project entered its prelaunch homestretch with a firmer seat in the saddle. The spacecraft and rover teams came together in the skunk works and developed a remarkable camaraderie, and Spear's willingness to delegate responsibility and elide bureaucratic boundaries fostered a sense of teamwork. One longtime JPL manager who worked with Pathfinder summed up the common sentiment: "It was the most fun project I ever worked on, far and away. . . . The whole spirit on that project was just a bunch of entrepreneurs figuring out, hey, what do we do next?"[47] The youth of the team promoted this spirit. Pathfinder's younger engineers reflected JPL's changing demographics and also perhaps the fact that more experienced engineers were working on Cassini or doubted Pathfinder's odds.[48] Youth brought computer savvy: veteran engineers knew spacecraft computers, but fresh college graduates in the early 1990s were the first generation to grow up with personal computers and such tools as financial databases. More important, youth brought energy and enthusiasm, and as the launch date approached they geared up to work around the clock.[49]

Although later media accounts would emphasize the youngsters on Pathfinder, Spear provided crucial, experienced guidance, abetted by other veterans—most notably Bill Layman, chief engineer on the rover, who helped bridge the difference between technologists and spacecraft engineers.[50] Spear's management style appeared new in its embrace of teamwork and the skunk works, and novel components, such as the airbags, required a more empirical approach than traditional systems engineering. But in other respects Spear represented the old ways. He had authority to run the project with a strong hand, including enforcing discipline on the science team, and he insisted on a strict regime of intensive testing and reviews. The frequent reviews irritated project engineers, but they also caught a number of potential failures, right up to the preparations for launch in late 1996.[51]

The regimen did not prevent the usual crisis after launch. The in-flight failure of a sun sensor threatened the mission, especially after the spacecraft refused to accept a software patch beamed from Earth. Finally a telecommunications engineer, Gordon Wood, found a gap in the antenna's reception produced every five seconds by the spacecraft's rotation, which blocked crucial bits of the patch; compensating for the gap got the patch through.[52] The main drama, however, occurred on arrival at Mars. The sequence for entry, descent, and landing called for the spacecraft, protected by a heat shield, to hit the Martian atmosphere at 28,000 kilometers per hour; atmospheric drag would slow the spacecraft to a fraction of that before a parachute slowed it further, retro-rockets fired as a final brake, and then airbags cushioned the final 12-meter drop to the surface. After deflating the airbags, the tetrahedral lander would unfold its hinged sides, revealing the rover, which would then drive off onto the Martian surface, relying on its own solar power supply and artificial intelligence.[53]

Everything worked. The navigators hit their target, the parachute and airbags deployed as designed, and the lander bounced across the surface and rolled to a stop. The first signals of success and images of a rocky landing site released euphoria from vindicated engineers at JPL. After an anxious interlude clearing airbags from a ramp, the Sojourner rover rolled off the lander and left the first tire tracks on another planet (see figure 17.3). The date of the landing—4 July 1997—provided a patriotic flourish, and the end of the mission three months later, when the lander's batteries ran down as expected, leaving the forlorn rover to circle it helplessly, provided a poignant denouement.[54]

JPL and NASA were surprised not only by Pathfinder's success but also by the intense public interest it generated. The mission landed on the cover of *Time* and *Newsweek,* and the little 10-kilogram rover, the size of a small dog, captured the public's affection.[55] New media helped expand the audience. Cable television had multiplied the number of news outlets, with round-the-clock channels like CNN capitalizing on Pathfinder's unfolding drama. Another venue emerged in the Internet. The World Wide Web had grown exponentially from a handful of sites in 1991 to 300 million sites by the end of 1997, with the number of users increasing apace.[56] The potential of the medium dawned on Pathfinder managers after they set up a Web site in 1994 and received 2,000 visits in the first week.[57] That was just a teaser. After the landing JPL's Web sites began registering 80 million hits a day, and in the next three months recorded 670 million hits, leading the *New York Times* to declare Pathfinder a "defining moment in Web use" and "the start of a new interactive era in the mass consumption of news."[58]

The popularity of Pathfinder provided another entrepreneurial outlet. The CRAF mission, scheduled to fly by the asteroid Hamburga, had earlier inspired JPL staff to explore an advertising agreement with McDonalds.[59] These plans were, alas, unrealized, but for Pathfinder the lab licensed the Mattell corporation to build a Hot Wheels JPL Sojourner Mars Rover Action Pack. The five-dollar toy sold so well, reported the *Los Angeles Times,* "that even JPL's Mars Program manager had to buy a set off a scalper." The lab's technology transfer office convened a meeting with toy industry executives to develop new licensing agreements, and several future Mars missions would have toy tie-ins.[60]

Not all of the public interest was spontaneous. Ed Stone, the veteran of Voyager, as JPL director had further sharpened JPL's already well-honed public relations effort. Public relations—now called "outreach"—received

Figure 17.3. First tracks on Mars. Sojourner rover, imaged from Pathfinder lander. *Source:* JPL Photolab.

another boost from the new post–cold war justifications for the space program and for federal support of science and technology more generally. Instead of cold war military security, the Clinton administration stressed economic strength and viewed science and engineering education as key to the supply of technical labor and ideas for high-tech industry. The space program seemed an especially fruitful way to inspire children to careers in science and engineering; hence NASA and JPL redoubled their efforts on outreach in the 1990s, with particular attention to school-age children, and reaped the rewards on Pathfinder.[61]

Even more so than Galileo, Pathfinder restored luster lost by Mars Observer and, for NASA more generally, by the Hubble fiasco and Challenger.[62] Why did Pathfinder succeed in the face of doubt? Although Spear retreated from the public relations spotlight, he deserved much credit for merging the new team approach with the rigor of old-fashioned systems engineering.[63] NASA science managers for their part let Spear run the project without imposing additional demands, and within JPL Stone backed up his independence.[64] In the end, though, Pathfinder succeeded simply because people worked very hard. Pathfinder provided a model for faster-better-cheaper missions: gather a bunch of bright youngsters and turn them loose, with graybeards like Spear to watch over them, and through heroic effort they would get the job done.[65] Pathfinder achieved higher productivity (and hence lower cost) by overworking people, which raised the issue of how long the lab could sustain such an effort. One technical manager noted the "high stress and much overtime" on the project and asked, "how do we deal with this type of activity long term?"[66] Spear recalled, "We talked about that at great length after Pathfinder and said, we can't do that from one project to the next."[67] The lesson, however, would be forgotten.

Pathfinder did not exactly fit the Discovery program mold. For one, instead of giving a scientific investigator overall responsibility, Pathfinder had an experienced systems engineer in charge. Second, it was more a technology than a science mission; it was planned as a demonstration for the MESUR network of landers, but when NASA cancelled MESUR after the Mars Observer failure, Pathfinder remained.[68] The lander and rover carried cameras, and the rover a spectrometer to analyze the chemistry of Martian rocks, but in terms of the old tradeoff, Pathfinder was more exploration than science. That explained its public appeal, but the main scientific results from Mars in this period would come from another mission.

Mars Global Surveyor

Weeks after the Mars Observer failure, a group at JPL had begun studying ways to fulfill the mission. The process pitted scientists seeking full recovery of Observer's goals, for which they had waited ten years, against NASA's push for faster-better-cheaper. By early 1994 plans had settled on a new Mars Surveyor program to recapture Observer's science in a series of smaller missions, starting with an orbiter called Mars Global Surveyor in 1996, which would carry five of the seven Observer instruments, followed by launches in 1998 and 2001.[69]

To save mass, the Global Surveyor would mostly use aerobraking instead of propellant to enter orbit at Mars, but a major threat to this plan emerged after launch. When the solar panels deployed, one of the joints buckled, leaving one solar panel flapping like a broken wing. Relying on atmospheric resistance to slow the spacecraft would stress the crippled wing—and perhaps break it off. Project manager Glenn Cunningham decided to ease the spacecraft into circular orbit by stretching aerobraking over an extra year, to early 1999.[70] Delaying the primary mission proved a blessing in disguise. The extended elliptical orbit at its low point dipped below the ionosphere, allowing better maps of the gravitational and magnetic fields. It thus enabled the spacecraft magnetometer to detect remnant magnetism, or localized magnetic fields frozen in the planet's crust. Mars had previously shown no evidence of a magnetic field, but the remnant fields suggested that in the past Mars had a strong global field, in turn suggesting a more dynamic thermal and geologic history. And since a magnetic field would help protect the surface from high-energy cosmic rays, as Earth's does, the possibility of ancient magnetism on Mars had important implications for the search for life.[71]

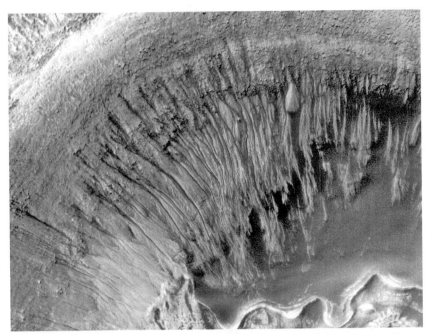

Figure 17.4. Evidence for recent liquid water on Mars: channels in a crater wall, imaged by Mars Global Surveyor. *Source:* JPL Photolab.

Similar implications emerged from images from the spacecraft camera, which could pick out objects 1.4 meters across. Pictures of cliff walls taken in early 2000 revealed widespread gullies, apparently cut by melting subsurface ice (see figure 17.4); other pictures of a curving canyon suggested channels carved by water. The lack of dust or other features across the gullies hinted that they may have formed recently, and that liquid water might currently exist just below the surface. As with Europa, the compelling evidence for liquid water on Mars raised hopes of finding signs of life.[72] Mars Global Surveyor also returned extensive data on Martian weather, topography and geodesy, volcanism, and the polar caps, all of which combined to change greatly our knowledge of the planet. Within a few years the results would make the cover of *Science* six times, and the volume and precision of the data set promised to occupy scientists for years to come.[73]

Cassini

The Cassini mission likewise gave grounds for optimism: the spacecraft sailed through development with few hitches once its survival was assured. Larry Dumas thought that "we finally got flagship development right on Cassini

. . . just when these missions went out of style."[74] Styles, however, can return, and this one would.

Cassini also provided one more example of the increasingly commercial mindset of JPL, one that extended into the practice of systems engineering. The number of instrument teams complicated the usual negotiations for mass, money, and power supplies. John Casani, the initial project manager, brought in John Ledyard, a Caltech economist, for advice on the allocation of resources among the teams. Instead of the standard, centralized allocation of reserves by the project manager, Ledyard recommended a decentralized marketplace: Casani would give all the reserves to the instrument teams at the outset and then set up an online bazaar. As Casani described it, "If you need more money, you say, 'I've got 3 kilograms, what am I bid for it?' You can sell some of your mass margin, or you can sell some of your power margin, or you can sell some of your money margin. Or you can say, 'I need money this year, if you give me a hundred [thousand] this year I'll give you a hundred twenty-five [thousand] next year.'" The scientists at first viewed this approach with suspicion, but eventually came to appreciate that decisions were in their hands instead of dictated from above. As for Casani, he loved it. He no longer had scientists constantly begging him for reserves, and, more important, with the market approach the collection of instruments came in within cost and mass limits—a first, in Casani's extensive experience.[75]

Cassini launched on 15 October 1997, but only after enduring widespread protests and a lawsuit, similar to those raised against Galileo, about the hazards of the plutonium isotopes it carried for electrical power.[76] The school-bus-sized spacecraft faced a seven-year journey to Saturn, but its terrestrial trials had ended.

A Multitude of Missions

The launch of Cassini was supposed to mark the final transition to faster-better-cheaper. The new mode was starting to multiply missions at JPL, and the shift to long-term programs instead of discrete projects allowed lab staff to focus on carrying out missions instead of constantly strategizing to win new starts.[77] The new programs also encouraged imaginative plans for harpooning comets, submarines on Europa, and airplanes for Mars. But JPL still faced the fact that Discovery missions, while cheaper, were not so cheap as to realize Goldin's dream of launching many each year—to "blacken the sky with spacecraft."[78] Discovery and Surveyor missions hence did not compensate for the Cassini workload: flight project staffing dropped about 300 work-years with the completion of Cassini, vindicating both those at JPL who viewed faster-better-cheaper as a poor business model and those at NASA who viewed JPL as overstaffed for the post–cold war program.[79]

Science instruments picked up some of the slack. In 1998 flight instruments passed flight projects as the largest effort, with more than 500 work-years.[80] Many of these instruments were for earth sciences; the large-platform concept for the Earth Observing System gave way to a series of smaller satellites, for which JPL built a variety of scatterometers, radiometers, and atmospheric sounders, the largest of which could occupy up to 100 engineers.[81] In 1992 the lab also launched the Topex/Poseidon satellite, whose altimeters could determine sea-surface heights to within a few centimeters; it tracked the El Niño events of 1994–95 and 1997–98, where warm-water masses in the Pacific Ocean showed up as sea-surface bulges, heralding severe weather patterns. The synthetic aperture radar program continued with SIR-C, which flew twice on the space shuttle in 1994, and the Shuttle Radar Topography Mission in 2000, which used two antennas, one at the end of a 60-meter mast, to perform radar interferometry; running the 12 terabytes of data through image-processing software produced high-resolution, digital elevation maps of all landmasses between plus and minus 60 degrees latitude.[82]

Perhaps the best example of JPL's new approach to spacecraft came from infrared astronomy. The Space Infrared Telescope Facility (SIRTF, later called the Spitzer Space Telescope) was a major observatory, comparable to the Hubble telescope, planned in the 1980s to follow the success of IRAS. Initial designs placed it in low earth orbit for launch and servicing by the shuttle. But that orbit entailed a large cryogenic cooler of liquid helium, to shield the infrared sensors from heat reflected from the earth, and articulated antennas and solar arrays to account for changing geometries. Project manager Larry Simmons switched to another plan based on a solar orbit, where the telescope would trail Earth at a great distance in its orbit around the sun. A high orbit away from Earth required fewer cryogenics and had easier viewing geometries, but it took away the possibility of shuttle servicing, which limited the telescope's lifetime to its few years' supply of coolant and also raised the stakes of failure.[83] Most important, it cut the telescope's mass from 5,700 kilograms to 900 kilograms and its cost from $2 billion to $450 million. The scaled-back SIRTF hence won approval in 1997, and Stone and NASA managers from Goldin on down viewed it as an exemplar of the faster-better-cheaper approach: use imaginative solutions to cut costs, and accept more risk with the possibility of flying more missions.[84]

Transcendence

JPL's program in the mid-1990s received a final boost from an unexpected direction. In August 1996 scientists at the Johnson Space Center published an article in *Science* declaring that a meteorite from Mars, discovered in Antarctica, contained evidence of organic molecules and fossils of microscopic organisms. The evidence was inconclusive and controversial, although it was reinforced by discoveries on Earth of life existing in surprisingly harsh environments: scientists found so-called extremophiles thriving around deep-ocean geothermal vents, in acidic hot springs and frozen Antarctic rocks, and in rocks several kilometers underground. In the meantime the Mars rock, announced at a White House press conference, set off a public frenzy about life on Mars. The White House convened a "space summit" later that year to plan the American response, which coalesced around a program already in the works, called Origins.[85]

The Origins program addressed basic questions: How did the universe evolve? What is the origin of life? Is there life beyond Earth?[86] JPL served as the lead center for Origins and had two clear roles in it: first, planetary exploration of Mars, Europa, and other possible homes for life; and second, astronomical searches for planets outside our solar system, which might likewise harbor life. This second aspect stemmed from JPL's work on extrasolar planets sparked by IRAS in the 1980s. In addition to infrared and submillimeter astronomy, which were suited to detect dim planets around other stars, in the early 1990s JPL pursued another avenue in optical interferometry, which hoped to combine light from two telescopes in order to cancel out the starlight and leave any planets in view.[87]

The Origins program thus merged the Mars rock and extremophiles with several other recent discoveries, including Europa's ocean, Hubble images of possible proto-planetary systems in stellar nebulae, and strong evidence for extrasolar planets.[88] It also addressed the criticism circa 1980 that planetary science had become pedestrian and that astronomy was the best route to fundamental questions. Instead, Origins enabled JPL to tie together its work in infrared astronomy, interferometry, and planetary exploration in a single theme—and one that addressed the most fundamental questions of all. This transcendent rationale held particular appeal in the post–cold war context as a justification for the space program to replace cold war competition and as an alternative to the more mundane invocations of economic competitiveness then prevalent. Hence Goldin included ethicists, religious leaders, and historians in Origins planning, and a *Science* editorial declared that Origins would transcend science itself, "to engage the larger philosophical and religious communities in an ambitious attempt to understand who we are, whence we came, and how we fit into the cosmic theme of things as wise, ethical human beings."[89]

JPL also tried to expand into the astrobiology segment of Origins. JPL had maintained a small exobiology program since the 1960s, as well as the Search for Extraterrestrial Intelligence—once again cancelled by Congress, amid mockery of "the great Martian chase," soon after observations finally started on the Deep Space Network in 1992. After the discoveries of the mid-1990s, a reoriented and broadly defined astrobiology began searching for signs of organisms and habitable environments. Astrobiology resonated with the general vitality of the biological sciences in the 1990s; Goldin worried that "the biological revolution has passed the space program by" and got NASA on the bandwagon. It also engaged the personal interest of Caltech president David Baltimore, whose wife Alice Huang, also a microbiologist, served on a NASA astrobiology panel. As Baltimore put it: "The raison d'être for the lab is increasingly the discovery of life elsewhere. And with that focus, it's a biology lab. Maybe a funny way to do biology." JPL thus expanded its own efforts in parallel with NASA, although NASA assigned the lead role in astrobiology to Ames.[90]

The Mars rock and a comet impact on Jupiter abetted a revival of popular fascination with space similar to that of the 1970s. The movie industry reflected this interest with several blockbusters, including "Deep Impact" and "Armageddon," both about meteor impacts on Earth, "Mission to Mars" and "Red Planet," about mysterious life forms on Mars, and several new installments slated for the Star Wars saga. JPL's executive council in 1999 noted the surprising interest in "space movies and the merging of entertainment and realities." The merging included a new mission, approved that year, which planned to fire a 500-kilogram projectile into the comet P/Tempel-1 and observe the resultant crater. JPL's project manager had to insist that the mission's name, Deep Impact, was in fact selected prior to the movie.[91]

The new public interest, nourished by Galileo, Pathfinder, and Mars Global Surveyor, signaled a recovery after the lows of the early 1990s. The space summit and Origins promised to boost JPL's budget by 20 percent. By early 1998 Stone could declare: "JPL's future has never been stronger. . . . Today the laboratory's challenge is not one of survival, but of delivering."[92] The programmatic recovery coincided with stabilization in JPL's administrative environment, especially its relations with NASA, and also with the long-desired funding for advanced technology. Together these developments had JPL flying high as it approached the end of the decade. Then came a crash.

Annus Miserabilis

JPL's HIGH HOPES CAME CRASHING BACK DOWN IN 1999 WITH A SERIES OF embarrassing failures, most notably of two spacecraft at Mars. The debacles and ensuing public scrutiny produced much soul-searching at all levels over the future of JPL, called into question the concept of faster-better-cheaper, and plunged the lab into its deepest crisis since the Ranger failures of the early 1960s.

The Failures

In his state of the lab address in March 1999, Ed Stone celebrated the launches of six space missions in the previous six months: Deep Space 1, testing an ion-drive propulsion system; Mars Climate Orbiter, Mars Polar Lander, and the Deep Space 2 surface penetrator experiment, all headed to Mars; Stardust for a comet sample return; and the Widefield Infrared Explorer astronomy satellite, to study evolution of distant galaxies.[1] Four of them would fail.

First came the Widefield Infrared Explorer, which began leaking cryogenic coolant soon after launch that March, ending the mission. Then the Great Galactic Ghoul reared its ugly head. Amid JPL's multiplying missions, Mars had remained the centerpiece, with two Surveyor missions launched in 1998: the Climate Orbiter and Polar Lander. Climate Orbiter would be a sort of Martian weather satellite, and the lander would provide for detailed, long-duration measurements at the south pole. The two missions together cost $193 million, a little more than Pathfinder's price tag of $175 million (but less in constant dollars), and they would take three years to design and launch. In effect, JPL was providing two missions for the price of one, and in the same amount of time—and the 1998 missions would carry much more science. The hard bargain resulted from NASA's desire for frequent launches under faster-better-cheaper but with insufficient funds to achieve them.

It was difficult enough trying to build two missions for the price of one, especially when the one was the cut-rate Pathfinder. But JPL also contended with continued attempts by NASA to tweak the mission. Part of this stemmed from a desire for international cooperation, which led NASA to add two Russian instruments to the Mars missions. It derived also from the old problem of human versus robotic exploration. With Mars again a focus of the space program, the idea of a manned mission to Mars returned to the front burner, and the human spaceflight program began jockeying for control of precursor missions, including the possibility of additional experiments on the Mars orbiter and lander.[2]

With project managers fending off NASA requests and struggling to get adequate staff within the limited budget, some worries surfaced at JPL. In March 1997 the executive council wondered whether the lab had recognized the increased risk that came with faster-better-cheaper. The leader of an internal study on risk management noted, "Some missions may be headed toward a cliff on this." Mars program manager Norm Haynes recalled, "We kept asking ourselves, 'can we do this, can we do this?'" But the overall assessment of managers at JPL and Lockheed Martin, the spacecraft contractor, was that the two spacecraft were in good shape heading to launch.[3]

The Mars Climate Orbiter arrived first at Mars on 23 September 1999. After it fired its main engine to slow its approach, the spacecraft passed behind the planet as it entered orbit, blocking its radio signal. But when engineers expected to recover the signal when it came back into view, they heard nothing—and continued to hear nothing even as they worked through troubleshooting sequences. Within a few days they recognized failure because a clear cause had emerged. The spacecraft had small thrusters to steer it. The software calibrating the thrusters was written by a young engineer at Lockheed Martin who had been on the job a short time. The software calibrated the thruster force in English units of pounds rather than the specified metric units of newtons, so that each time the thrusters fired the trajectory changes were off by a factor of 4.5. As a result, the Climate Orbiter came in toward Mars too low, at an altitude of 57 kilometers instead of 226 kilometers, and plunged into the planet.[4]

The failure was vastly embarrassing, both publicly—how could they just botch the units!—and within the space community. JPL had long prided itself on its navigation expertise, perhaps more so than its spacecraft hardware. Spacecraft, after all, had suffered many component failures, but navigators had always provided pinpoint precision, for instance in getting Galileo and Voyager to their far more distant targets with vanishingly small errors.

So how could they not notice accumulating errors in the Climate Orbiter trajectory?[5]

There were several opportunities to catch the error. Ground tests should have revealed it, but Lockheed Martin misclassified the software as not mission-critical, so it did not undergo the usual scrutiny.[6] JPL's navigators caught other errors in the software before launch, but rather than document them with a problem-failure report, they sent an e-mail to Lockheed Martin—the type of informal communication encouraged by faster-better-cheaper, but one that escaped the tracking system of systems management.[7] More galling was the fact that navigators did not correct the error after launch, when the trajectory showed an error of the same magnitude every time the thrusters fired, without the scatter one would expect from random errors. Engineers at Lockheed and at JPL did notice the discrepancies before arrival at Mars, but JPL's navigation team elected not to raise a red flag or call in peer review. The team was understaffed and dealing with turnover in management, but that did not excuse their neglect. The error did not just slip through the cracks; rather, it was identified but swept under the rug.[8]

As for the units issue, the Mars spacecraft might have seemed a casualty of the continuing American reluctance to convert to the metric system. But JPL had long used metric units for science and engineering, including interplanetary navigation. In 1992 NASA's space science office committed to the metric system, with the conversion to be complete by 1997, and JPL began converting the entire lab to metric.[9] JPL engineers' familiarity with metric units may have prevented them from considering the possibility of such a basic mix-up.

The Climate Orbiter failure raised the stakes for the Polar Lander. Stone declared to lab staff that the lander was now "the most important issue facing JPL."[10] That did not bode well. Managers had left Climate Orbiter's navigation team understaffed because it was supposed to be the easy one: landing a spacecraft is much harder than orbiting.[11] Furthermore, the lander would use not the airbag method proved by Pathfinder but rather retro-rockets, because Lockheed Martin had experience with them from Viking and future Mars missions would need the pinpoint location provided by rockets instead of the haphazard bouncing of airbags. Above all, the lander design had been finalized in 1995, well before Pathfinder showed that airbags indeed worked. The design thus resulted from the desire to launch to Mars at every opportunity, every twenty-six months, which meant that JPL could not apply lessons from one mission to the next one, but only to the next one in the queue after that, several years down the road.[12]

In response to the orbiter failure, for the lander JPL brought in additional experienced managers, beefed up the navigation team, and expanded peer review, especially for navigation and the landing sequence.[13] It still did not work. On 3 December 1999 the spacecraft started its descent to the surface, slowed first by a parachute and then by the retro-rockets. Mission control expected to lose radio contact with the lander during the descent; problems with geometry and antenna gain made communication difficult, and to save money designers decided to do without it. Pathfinder had similarly skipped telemetry, although a review board at the time had worried "that if the lander fails we won't know why." Pathfinder's success rendered the issue irrelevant, until Mars Polar Lander. After several minutes of blackout, JPL flight controllers expected to reacquire a signal. As on the Climate Orbiter, the moment passed with no contact. The moment turned into minutes, hours, days. JPL had lost another spacecraft at Mars.[14]

Engineers eventually found the likely cause in ground tests. After the rockets fired to slow the spacecraft's descent, sensors and software on the lander legs would detect touchdown and shut off the engine. But when the legs deployed during descent they shook a little, and the sensors, detecting the vibration, could shut down the engines too early. The spacecraft designers recognized this possibility and programmed the sensors to wait until the legs deployed, at over 1,000 meters altitude, but an error in the code allowed the sensors to signal landing at a height of 40 meters, thus shutting off the rockets and leaving the spacecraft to plummet to the surface. Project engineers should have caught this error, too, in testing. In a ground test of leg deployment the sensors had not worked at all. Engineers found a wiring mix-up, fixed it, and repeated the test—but only the touchdown part. The sensors detected touchdown and the test engineers declared success. They did not repeat the entire deployment sequence and hence missed the early shutdown signal.[15]

The thousand-odd journalists who had gathered at JPL for the landing quickly changed their story lines from redemption to redoubled ineptitude. Compounding the embarrassment was the simultaneous loss of the Deep Space 2 mission, which had piggybacked on the lander and then separated during the descent. That mission consisted of twin penetrators, each the size of a basketball, designed to fall unimpeded and drive small water-detection probes one meter into the ground from the force of impact. The probes likely plowed into the ground about the same time as the Polar Lander, but with much greater violence; like the lander they were never heard from again. Postmortems found no evident cause, but a review board declared unequivocally that "the microprobes were not adequately tested and were not ready for launch."[16]

A final screwup arrived in March 2000. Goddard had sent the High Energy Solar Spectroscopic Imager (HESSI), a spacecraft designed to study solar flares, to JPL for vibration tests. JPL engineers set the test level ten times too high, inflicting substantial damage to the $40-million spacecraft.[17] The HESSI incident came ten days after a critical report on the Mars failures by an independent review board and completed a miserable year at JPL.

The Young Report

After the failures Dan Goldin did not chew anyone out; he had viewed risk as a corollary of faster-better-cheaper and took the blame before the press and Congress for pushing JPL too hard.[18] But he also convened a review board called the Mars Program Independent Assessment Team—usually known as the Young panel after its chairman, Thomas Young, a retired Lockheed Martin executive and former director of Goddard and NASA's planetary program. Goldin viewed the review as a way to get JPL's attention, and the report came out purposefully blunt. Even before the second failure Stone warned Caltech's trustees that "this will not be pretty."[19] He was right.

The Young report looked beyond immediate, engineering causes to indict JPL and NASA management. Tangled lines of communication led JPL to hear NASA requests as nonnegotiable mandates, while NASA managers, for their part, seemed not to want to hear bad news from JPL. In the other direction, managers at JPL and Lockheed Martin developed a close working relationship. Maybe too close, since it led first to JPL managers accepting less oversight of the firm and also to what the Young report characterized as an "insular relationship."[20] Although the Young report did not question the use of a contractor in system mode, the Mars failures did demonstrate the risk in trusting mission-critical work to contractors, who might not—and in the case of the orbiter software did not—treat it as mission-critical.[21]

The most obvious cause for the failure was corner-cutting under faster-better-cheaper—that is, too little time and money to do the job right. This applied to all three institutions—NASA, JPL, and Lockheed Martin—and also involved deeper issues. The poor state of the aerospace business, combined with JPL's decision to select a long-term partner, no doubt encouraged Lockheed's lowball bid—what the Young panel called an "aggressive pricing strategy"—on the Mars '98 contract.[22] JPL's subsequent refusal to seek more money from NASA similarly may have derived from fear of competition; NASA could have interpreted such a request as proof that JPL could not do faster-better-cheaper, at a time when the Applied Physics Lab was returning unspent funds on its Near-Earth Asteroid Rendezvous mission.[23]

The main shortfall may have been as much time as money. Noel Hinners from Lockheed Martin cited schedule pressures as the main cause of shortcuts, and Norm Haynes recalled of the lander, "Part of the problem we missed the software bug was because the guys were in such a hurry in test.... A little more time and we'd have had a much better chance of catching that bug." Planetary space missions are almost unique in their need to launch during a particular window, and missing the window can be akin to failure. This especially affected the Mars program, where the next launch opportunity was twenty-six months away and where the Mars rock discovery had accelerated the timetable for a sample return mission. The Young report stressed that NASA and JPL should prefer to miss a launch window rather than launch an ill-prepared mission: "if not ready—do not launch."[24]

The Mars failures showed that heroic effort alone would not get the job done. And here the youth of the team perhaps worked against them. Unlike Spear and Cunningham, the experienced project managers on Pathfinder and Mars Global Surveyor, John McNamee had no project management experience prior to his appointment as head of the Mars missions. JPL, however, faced a dilemma: the profusion of spacecraft and big instrument projects in the late 1990s coincided with the retirement of several stalwarts of project management, including Spear, Cunningham, and Casani. Young managers no longer had the luxury of working their way up from subsystems through spacecraft system engineer to project manager; instead the lab thrust them straight to the top of projects. The skunk works approach meanwhile isolated the youngsters from the experienced managers in the technical divisions.[25]

The Young report cited the lack of experience and the need to mentor new project managers. The report itself did not say more, but others did. Arthur Lonne Lane, a veteran of many JPL projects, had warned Pathfinder people of the value of experience, speaking of the "scars and knifewounds" left by "hardware disasters.... I don't think until you've actually bled on the floor and been sliced up that you really understand the magnitude of certain decision pathways."[26] In the celebration after Pathfinder some of the young Pathfinder team, who had experienced nothing but success, perhaps got cocky. According to Bruce Murray, an advisor to the Young panel, "the Pathfinder people . . . went out and said, 'look, we showed these guys we can do it cheaper than the regular old line way of doing it.'" Pete Lyman, now retired from JPL and a Young panelist, similarly said: "They were all young ones. And they thought—and I don't blame them for thinking this—'man, this is easy, I can do this.' But they'd never been where they'd had their fingers burned before." Whether out of cockiness or complacency, they failed to appreciate how close even successful missions skated to disaster and hence ignored or explained away warning signs instead of pursuing them to ground. As Murray put it, "You come close, you can get seared in your soul."[27]

Others, however, thought the Young report overstated the lack of experience. Norm Haynes was confident before the launches in part because the project had review boards with many decades of project management, including Casani, Cunningham, and Spear. There were still plenty of senior people who had been around JPL for decades, and the many missions in earth science and astronomy, supplemented earlier by defense projects, had furthermore provided a number of management opportunities—enough so that JPL now had more experienced project managers on its staff than it had twenty or thirty years earlier. More important, according to Haynes, were the immediate effects of turnover on the Mars project, when the retirements of Cunningham and a navigation section manager roiled the mission midflight.[28]

Management Initiatives, Military Modes, and the Mars Missions

The Young report did not cite two other features of the context: the embrace of such management philosophies as reengineering and the military roots of faster-better-cheaper. Although neither was a direct cause of the Mars failures, both contributed to the environment around the failures and to JPL's response.

The management initiatives had not only diverted time and effort from the task at hand; they also introduced a focus on the customer. The new belief in customer service increased responsiveness to NASA and moderated the lab's reputed arrogance, but a belief that the customer is always right could reduce the lab's independence and lead it to accept unreasonable demands. In 1992, soon after the adoption of Total Quality Management, Stone had defined a new strategic goal that would become a refrain: "Make a deal and stick to it."[29] JPL stuck to its deal on the Mars missions and paid the price: the lab agreed to the initial cost cap and then refused to ask NASA for more money. Appeasement in part stemmed from the presence of Goldin, whose management style encouraged submission. After the earlier Mars Observer failure Goldin had come to JPL and declared: "If there was something wrong, you should have called it out and said we shouldn't have done it. If we at headquarters or anyone else forces a contract down your throat that's stupid, just say no." But a corollary, he continued, was that having agreed to a project, "The new rule is that you've got to do what you say you are going to do." JPL took the rule to heart and after accepting the initial budget on the Mars mission, refused to challenge the customer.[30]

Reengineering may also have diluted JPL's culture of peer review. Spacecraft design reviews, a key component of systems engineering, put engineers and their designs on trial before a critical review board, whose job was to probe—ruthlessly—for possible design flaws. The unfettered airing of opinions, which perhaps derived from the lab's association with Caltech, extended to everyday encounters. Larry Dumas cited the sense that "a person cannot stand up and start talking at JPL without it turning into a design review. We've got this analytical, critical approach, that's very tough on people . . . and sometimes it's not very polite, but I think that's an important part."[31] But reengineering stressed consensus instead of criticism and included the hiring of a management consultant for workshops on "conversation management"—and, as Casani recalled, "one of the things he admonished everybody against is to stop finding fault."[32]

Appeasing NASA on the budget and stressing consensus may not have caused the failures at Mars, but they did not help. As interesting is JPL's reaction to the failures. Amid the postmortems, grumblings over process-based management increased, some in an explicitly ideological framework. As one admittedly conservative JPL manager put it: "Under Stone, the lab moved—philosophically—to the left. We've moved to where individuals weren't responsible."[33] Unlike the Ranger failures, where the two senior project managers were dismissed, no one at JPL was fired or reprimanded after the debacles at Mars. On the contrary, Stone took great pains to stress to lab staff that "the loss of the Climate Orbiter is not about human failure. It is about the failure of our processes—our checks and balances. . . . Humans make mistakes and our processes must assure that we recognize and correct those mistakes. What we are not going to do—nor should you—is to fix the blame."[34] Meanwhile, Goldin's apologies for pushing too hard could be interpreted as absolving individuals at JPL; instead it was NASA's fault. These refusals to pin blame were commendable and warranted; neither McNamee nor the young Lockheed engineer, for example, deserved to bear the full weight of the orbiter failure. But blaming undefined processes dodged accountability. The same JPL manager concluded: "So all of this stuff was just the way the country was going, where there's no individual responsibility—the government or somebody else is responsible for everything."[35]

As for the military origins of faster-better-cheaper, we have seen that the new approach germinated in the relative shelter of military programs. The Mars failures gave faster-better-cheaper the full blast of civilian treatment. Military programs, of course, did not escape public scrutiny: Congress took regular delight in exposing overruns in military programs, such as the navy's mythical $435 hammers.[36] But as the Clementine review board noted, military projects in general benefited from less congressional involvement, agency oversight, and scientific participation than NASA missions, and this view did not account for classification.[37] The differences dated back to the start of the space race: the Discoverer program—the public name for the classified Corona spy satellites—had twelve failures before finally succeeding in

August 1960 but received little political scrutiny; five failures on Ranger were enough to call down criticism and NASA review boards, and a subsequent sixth failure produced a congressional investigation.[38]

Hence Goldin, in the same speech at JPL in 1994, noted that right after the loss of contact with Observer, "within eight hours, we lost a weather satellite. Then the Defense Department launched a classified spacecraft for a billion and a half that went into the drink. Do you know what the first headline was? 'NASA loses another satellite.'" He was a bit off on the timing of the military satellite but right about the overall impression from the headlines: Observer occupied the front page and editorials for several days, while the military failure faded quickly from sight. A spy satellite lost in 1998 and then the Mars failures in 1999 received similarly disparate public scrutiny.[39] The American public seemed consistently willing to accept missions that entailed risk, to machines as well as to human lives, for the sake of national security but not for space science or exploration. As a product of military programs, faster-better-cheaper entailed risk, but when the reality of risk appeared, JPL and NASA—and the American public—turned out not to have the stomach for it.

The Response

The Mars failures and other mishaps punctured the self-image of JPL. Lab staff had a habit of touting the lab's superlative expertise—how it attracted the smartest people and turned them loose on far-out projects. This confidence had characterized JPL since its first forays into space, but it now confronted its common fallibility. The lab fell into a funk. The malaise tapped into preexisting complaints about increasing bureaucracy and downsizing, especially at lower levels of the lab, and cast Pathfinder and Origins as only a temporary respite.[40] Former NASA manager Wes Huntress, on a visit to JPL two years afterward, called the failures the institutional equivalent of Vietnam and added, "There's a pall over this place."[41] The Ranger failures of almost forty years earlier provided a closer equivalent. The pointed criticisms of the Young report encouraged congressional critics to "sharpen up their knives," according to one news headline.[42] Unlike Ranger, however, when NASA had used congressional investigations to gain leverage over JPL, Goldin's reaction shielded the lab from congressional hearings. But on the Ranger failures Congress had acted to rein in a more independent laboratory. Thanks to NASA's growing leverage, the problem now was not JPL's lack of submission but rather too much of it.[43]

That did not stop scrutiny in public forums or pressure from NASA itself. The Young report, however, conditioned NASA's response, and the agency and the panel did not align. The result was another tug-of-war over faster-better-cheaper, this one conducted not in open debate but through the actions taken after the failures. Although the dispute did not exactly fall along generational lines, some of the older guard shared a sense that younger engineers had too easily abandoned the tried-and-true, if costly, precepts of systems engineering. The experienced membership of the Young panel ensured that it was weighted toward the old school. Although the panel stated its approval of the faster-better-cheaper concept, it also declared that the space program had proven the techniques of systems engineering over several decades, and that these techniques should apply to smaller missions.[44] Pete Lyman declared: "There were a lot of issues dealing with faster-better-cheaper, and mind-sets about 'golly, the old way had too much documentation, had too much this, too much that.' And they threw some of the babies out with the bathwater."[45] JPL responded to the report with increased reviews and management oversight, problem reporting, quality control, and integration with line management (that is, abandoning the skunk works)—in short, with a return to the conservative techniques of systems engineering.[46]

Faster-better-cheaper advocates viewed the reaction with dismay. They argued that JPL and NASA had tested the limits of faster-better-cheaper and now, having found them, just needed to back off a little. Haynes observed, "It's not like we threw this thing together and nothing worked." He thought the Mars missions, even at the two-for-one price, had ended up perhaps only 20 percent short of time and money.[47] Instead JPL now seemed on the verge of throwing faster-better-cheaper itself out with the bathwater. In July 2001 Stardust project manager Tom Duxbury criticized an "overreaction. . . . Faster-better-cheaper is out of vogue." For proof, he pointed to the resurrection of the flight projects organization, the bastion of systems engineering abolished by Stone in 1994.[48] Wes Huntress, who in 1998 had resigned as NASA space science manager, feared the failures "just brought the old school right back. Instead of backing off and figuring out 'what did we do wrong, let's fix that,' instead they went all the way back to the old way of doing business."[49]

The effects soon appeared in the next Mars missions in the queue. Plans for the 2001 launch opportunity had called for another orbiter and lander, with a total cost under $282 million and an option to carry a spare Pathfinder rover on the lander. At the time of the Young report the spacecraft were a year from launch and were already in system tests at Lockheed Martin, and NASA had spent perhaps three-fourths of the budget. But their design derived largely from the failed spacecraft—for instance, the new lander inherited 70 percent of its flight software from the earlier design (and the cause of the 1999 failure was, in fact, found in testing of the new one). NASA balked—in the view of Haynes, "they didn't want to have anything to do with anything that came out of that project that had two failures."[50] The agency pulled the spacecraft back for a major redesign, into what eventually became the Mars Exploration Rover mission, or MER, for twin rovers to launch in 2003. The budget ballooned to an eventual total of $800 million, siphoning funds from other potential missions, including ones to Pluto and Europa.[51] As Haynes put it in early 2003, "What's been going on the last year or two is, that giant sucking sound you heard was the sound of the MER projects sucking up all the available money from NASA and JPL."[52]

Conclusion

In May 2000, as JPL began addressing the Young report, Stone announced he would retire at the end of the year when he turned sixty-five.[53] Age, not events, dictated his retirement; he was not paying the price for the failures. On the contrary: Stone began the process of recovery even as he prepared to leave the lab, much as recovery from the crisis of 1981 began before Bruce Murray left. Yet deputy director Dumas admitted that the Stone regime toward the end had accumulated a number of unpopular decisions—downsizing, salary freezes, the management initiatives—that diminished its effectiveness.[54] In this respect, too, Stone resembled Murray, albeit again with the central difference that Murray's baggage stemmed from external activism and Stone's from internal decisions.

The Mars failures and the reaction marked a turning point in JPL's history. They forced the lab to reconsider its commitment to faster-better-cheaper, which it had engaged for almost a decade. In the longer view, the series of smashups marred an otherwise long record of success stretching back thirty years, and unlike the loss of Mars Observer, the lab could not dismiss them as a one-time aberration. The soul-searching in the aftermath demonstrated the depth of the impact, comparable only to the Ranger failures in the history of JPL. The adversity of Ranger had forged a new organization and discipline in the 1960s; it remained to be seen whether JPL would similarly emerge stronger in the new century.

N I N E T E E N

Epilogue, 2001–2004

CALTECH PRESIDENT DAVID BALTIMORE TAPPED CHARLES ELACHI TO SUC-
ceed Stone in 2001. It was far from a slam-dunk choice. Members of the
search committee thought JPL needed someone from outside the lab to respond to the Mars failures—"a breath of fresh air," as Baltimore put it—and
Elachi was about as much of an insider as one could be, having spent his
entire career at JPL after graduate school at Caltech.[1] But he also had several
attributes that recommended him. He had demonstrated his technical skills
in the 1970s on synthetic aperture radar and proved himself an energetic en-
trepreneur in parlaying that work into the Shuttle Imaging Radar. Whereas
Stone retained traces of the college teacher, Elachi was more of a salesman.
As one JPL veteran put it, "When Elachi makes a presentation, it's a pitch;
when Stone makes a presentation, it's a lecture."[2] The growth in flight instruments for earth and space sciences owed much to Elachi's leadership, and
by 1995 lower levels viewed him as "a preeminent 'marketeer'" and one of
the "saviors of the lab."[3]

Elachi did not lack ambition, but he tempered it with good-natured enthusiasm and an ever-present grin.[4] Like Bruce Murray, he tried to have a
long-term vision, but he also stayed hands-on with current projects, delving
into technological details in a way that Ed Stone, who focused more on management and the external environment, had not.[5] Elachi differed from Stone
as well as from Murray in another respect: he felt no need to change JPL's
culture. This may have, in part, reflected the questioning of faster-better-
cheaper after the Mars failures and the renewed appreciation for traditional
modes of systems engineering. But it was also an indication of Elachi's personal preference for slow evolution; if Stone was a cautious revolutionary,
one might say Elachi was a daring conservative. Elachi would say: "A lot

of people talk that we need to change the culture. My attitude is, I love our culture. . . . I get very leery when people say, 'we are going to change the culture.' Culture doesn't change easily, and I'm not sure it's a good idea to change the culture."[6] A corollary of this was his attitude toward JPL's embrace of corporate management philosophies, to which he had not exactly hidden his earlier opposition. In his first address as director he announced diplomatically that the lab would reconsider its commitment to them.[7]

Elachi inherited an organization of just over 5,000 employees and a $1.2 billion annual budget.[8] Although Elachi, unlike Stone and Murray, had not been a Caltech professor, he still carried credibility on campus through his Caltech PhD and his many years of teaching the physics of remote sensing there. The campus response to the Mars failures had been remarkably restrained: in a sign of improved faculty appreciation for JPL since the 1970s, professors issued no calls for divestment or claims that JPL had sullied Caltech's reputation.[9] The Young report did not fault Caltech for the failures, but it did recommend that the institute provide more technical oversight. Baltimore duly created a visiting committee of Caltech faculty, outside scientists, and industry leaders with a mandate to get deeper into technical issues than the Caltech trustees, whose advice tended to focus on institutional and strategic issues. The new visiting committee included, not accidentally, several members of the Young panel.[10]

The visiting committee also provided Elachi some leverage against NASA, a way to push back in case NASA, as it had for the Mars missions, made unreasonable demands.[11] JPL's relation with NASA was further tempered by Goldin's resignation in 2002; his replacement, Sean O'Keefe, had a budget and policy background (albeit also with a stint in the Pentagon) and suggested the possibility of stability after ten tumultuous years. Goldin, however, had appreciated the concept of contract operation and the presence of Caltech. In negotiations over a new contract for JPL in 2003, NASA raised the possibility of allowing other institutions to compete for the contract, apparently the first serious consideration of taking JPL from Caltech, at least since the 1960s. The notion perhaps stemmed from similar suggestions for other federal labs, including Los Alamos; whatever the motivation, it signaled NASA's intent to continue tightening accountability, reflected in the new contract by more regulations. The general effect was to tilt the JPL-Caltech-NASA triangle further toward NASA.[12]

Elachi did extract a significant concession from NASA in support for advanced technology. Despite Goldin's desire to push new technology under faster-better-cheaper, the programs set up to do so—known as New Millennium and X2000—had soon reverted to short-term problems instead of long-term development. Then in 1998 Congress demanded that NASA contract more technology development to industry. The result: by 2001 JPL's advanced technology funding was almost half what it had been in 1996, in constant dollars, and much of it went to short-term needs.[13] The cutbacks compounded the shortfall stemming from JPL's withdrawal from military programs—the Microdevices Lab, for example, now depended mostly on NASA funding—and discretionary funds could not compensate, since they amounted to a few million dollars each year, less than 1 percent of the budget.[14] Other federal and industrial labs enjoyed so-called institutional R&D of several percent each year, or tens of millions of dollars. Elachi managed to overcome objections within JPL to carving such funds out of indirect costs, as Lew Allen had tried and failed to do, and NASA readily agreed since it would not cost extra money. JPL hence had up to 3 percent, or $35 million, in institutional R&D.[15]

Elachi had been on the job a few months when terrorists attacked the United States on 11 September 2001. The lab shut down for two days and security thereafter tightened. Security had increased in previous years, owing to investigations of other federal labs—most notably Los Alamos, with the Wen Ho Lee case and later security breaches—and restrictions on international technology transfer, especially International Traffic in Arms Regulations (ITAR).[16] The terrorist attacks further cut off access to the lab, particularly for foreign nationals. JPL had a substantial presence of people of Middle Eastern ethnicity, starting with Elachi, who himself encountered pointed questions about his allegiance. But Elachi and other well-established figures met little outright discrimination. The effect fell instead on visitors, postdocs, and students, including those from Caltech, as new restrictions on foreign nationals in federal programs cast a chill across all of American science and technology.[17]

Another effect of 9/11 was to remobilize the lab for national security. JPL's technologies for remote sensing and in-situ detection of trace chemical and biological elements clearly related to the war on terrorism. The renewed interest in national defense differed from the earlier remobilization of the late 1970s, which had been driven from the top down, from decisions taken by Murray and senior NASA leaders, and by institutional considerations of JPL's survival. The post-9/11 response, rather, reflected a spontaneous reaction across a spectrum of individual lab workers, who immediately began proposing ways their work could contribute to national security. It also differed in its scale: instead of undertaking a number of large defense projects, JPL contributed through a number of small research programs, so that the fraction of the effort given to defense work did not rise above 5 percent.[18]

Another substantial event occurred in 2003: the disintegration of the space shuttle Columbia as it returned to Earth on 1 February. The accident provided further indictment of faster-better-cheaper, which for the human spaceflight program had meant schedule pressures and cuts in operations budgets—the sort of corner-cutting that doomed JPL's Mars missions. The accident also revived the debate over human versus robotic exploration and led to a basic reconsideration of the policy that for thirty years had focused the space program on the shuttle and space station. Finally, an accident review board expressed pointed criticisms of NASA's culture, especially an insulated management style that stifled dissenting technical views in bureaucratic procedures.[19] JPL had already had its equivalent of Columbia in the Mars failures, and the Young report had expressed similar concerns about "circling the wagons" with regard to risk and a refusal to tell NASA bad news. Another criticism of the Columbia review board applied equally to JPL: the plague of PowerPoint presentations, which provided a mesmerizing appearance of competence while obscuring technical detail.[20]

Columbia raised the stakes for JPL's next missions, which were already high after the Mars failures in 1999. Signs of a rebound had appeared in 2001, on Valentine's Day, when JPL navigators helped the APL-designed Near-Earth Asteroid Rendezvous maneuver into a landing on the asteroid Eros. The tricky landing, greatly complicated by the irregular gravitational field of the odd-shaped body, began to restore the reputation of JPL's navigators. Then Deep Space 1 flew by the comet Borrelly in September, capturing images of the comet nucleus and tail from 2,000 kilometers' distance and proving the ion drive technology in the process.[21] Meanwhile Mars Global Surveyor continued to return data, joined in early 2002 by Mars Odyssey, the one spacecraft launched during the 2001 opportunity. Odyssey's successful encounter would begin the rebound of the Mars program. Its gamma ray spectrometer had been part of Mars Observer's instrument suite; finally arrived at the red planet, it detected substantial deposits of ice less than a meter below the surface and thus helped explain what might have happened to any ancient bodies of surface water.[22]

The true test of recovery, however, was the Mars Exploration Rovers (MER). A failure of MER might mean the end of the Mars program, and perhaps of JPL.[23] MER served as a sort of test bed for the Young panel's recommendations, and the panel followed up to make sure JPL adhered to them.[24] The response encouraged perceptions of a retreat from faster-better-cheaper, evident not only in the budget but in the size and complexity of the spacecraft. At 174 kilograms each, the new rovers, about the size of a golf cart, weighed seventeen times as much as Sojourner, and each carried a color camera, an infrared instrument, two spectrometers, a microscope, and a tool for grinding rocks.[25] Instead of a small team in a skunk works, the large MER team—perhaps two or three times the size of Pathfinder's—was integrated into the technical divisions in big-project mode.[26] MER also represented a return to redundancy after the single-spacecraft approach of the 1980s and 1990s.

But MER did not represent a complete rejection of faster-better-cheaper. Post-Pathfinder plans, before the failures, had called for much larger rovers for the Mars 2001 mission, which were just carried over to MER. Although NASA did throw some money at MER, it was still perhaps one-fifth the cost of Viking in constant dollars. And unlike, say, Mars Observer, it was not strung out for years under scientific and engineering refinements; MER took three years from design to launch. Engineers and managers had long said of faster-better-cheaper: pick two.[27] NASA did so, implicitly, for MER: it was faster and better—but not cheaper. In other words, MER sought a happy medium between the bloated mode of Mars Observer and Goldin's dream of faster-better-cheaper. NASA manager Ed Weiler and JPL deputy director Larry Dumas both thought the Young report forced JPL to implement faster-better-cheaper right.[28] This middle way required merging the two approaches of faster-better-cheaper and traditional systems engineering—a not entirely smooth merger, as Pathfinder and Cassini alumni clashed within MER.[29]

The Mars rovers—one named Spirit, the other Opportunity—planned to land in January 2004. As if to highlight the difficulty, two other spacecraft failed at Mars in the preceding month: a Japanese orbiter sailed helplessly past the planet, and the European Beagle 2 lander disappeared without a peep.[30] If JPL and NASA needed more pressure, President George W. Bush was planning a major new initiative to send humans to the moon and Mars. Intead of announcing it a month earlier, as expected, Bush and NASA were quietly waiting to see if the first Mars rover landed successfully. People at JPL evidently did not know it, but if the Mars rovers failed it might scuttle the nation's big plans for Mars.[31]

The science team picked the landing sites to maximize chances of finding signs of water at acceptable risk. Spirit would land in Gusev crater, which appeared to have held a lake in the distant past; Opportunity, on Meridiani Planum, a flat plain with concentrations of hematite, a mineral often formed in liquid water. The sites needed a sizable landing zone, since MER returned to the airbag system after the failure of the retro-rocket system on Mars Polar Lander. Pathfinder had proven the airbag concept, but MER would test it greatly by requiring the bags to cushion 540 kilograms instead of the 360 kilograms of Pathfinder.[32]

Spirit arrived at Mars first, on 3 January 2004. As on Pathfinder, MER engineers endured "six minutes from hell" as the spacecraft slowed from 5.4 kilometers per second to zero in its entry, descent, and landing sequence. The spacecraft plunged into the Martian atmosphere, shed its heat shield and deployed its parachute and then airbag, fired small rockets to brake further and stop swinging, and then cut its tether to free-fall 15 meters to the ground. Flight controllers this time followed radio telemetry all the way to the ground but lost the signal for several minutes while the lander bounced and rolled inside the airbag. When the Deep Space Network finally locked onto a strong signal, the mission control room erupted in cheers. To top it off, Spirit had landed right side up, on an almost perfectly flat surface, which allowed it to start sending back images just three hours after landing. The images set off another round of celebration, and at the post-landing press conference a jubilant Sean O'Keefe toasted the team with champagne and the words, "We're back." He meant it literally, back on Mars, but also figuratively: after the disasters of Columbia and Mars in 1999, JPL and NASA were redeemed.[33]

Spirit's landing also sparked public interest to levels reminiscent of Pathfinder, perhaps evident more on the Internet than in media coverage. In the first four days after Spirit landed NASA Web sites logged 1.2 billion hits, and they received 4 billion by 24 January, the day that the second rover, Opportunity, was due to arrive.[34] Just a few days earlier Spirit had fallen silent, and when it finally made contact again flight controllers found its computer rebooting repeatedly. Project manager Pete Theisinger judged it a "critical" threat to Spirit's survival, and JPL seemed on the verge of losing half the mission before the other half even got there. The combination of the Spirit drama and the bandwagon effect heightened interest in Opportunity, and a host of media and VIPs descended on JPL.[35] Opportunity rewarded them with another flawless landing, within 24 kilometers of the aimpoint after a trip of 200 million kilometers, the inaccuracy due to uncertainty in the atmospheric density of Mars. Mission control again burst into cheers and a few tears, punctuated by waving brooms to signify a clean sweep. By that time engineers had stabilized Spirit and had a tentative diagnosis of its problems, and within a couple weeks JPL had two healthy rovers exploring Mars.[36]

The MER mission demonstrated the increasing gender and ethnic diversity of JPL, evident in project scientist Joy Crisp and in Spirit's mission manager Jennifer Trosper, who had been a flight controller on Pathfinder at the age of twenty-seven (see figure 19.1). MER also demonstrated the value of the Caltech connection: half of the ten top managers on MER were Caltech graduates.[37] They included project manager Pete Theisinger, another stocky, mustached figure, who had worked on projects from Mariner in the late 1960s to Mars Global Surveyor before taking over the rovers, and who like Spear on Pathfinder provided a gray-haired, experienced presence among the youngsters.[38] Theisiniger had a pessimistic appreciation of risk, evident in his warnings even amid the post-landing celebrations, and his engineering conservatism paid off. The other key ingredient, once again, was sheer hard work. The three-year development period made for sixty-hour weeks from the beginning, and as the launch dates approached MER engineers worked themselves beyond exhaustion. Success erased fatigue, but the effort required again raised the question, asked after Pathfinder, whether JPL could expect such commitment on every mission.[39]

Despite the euphoria over the landings, MER's mission was incomplete without science. That came soon enough. After several weeks of roving the science team had enough data to announce that Mars had once had extensive, shallow, standing bodies of salty water (see figure 19.2). The chemical and geological evidence provided ground truth for the earlier hints of water from orbital images and greatly increased hopes of finding life on Mars. Even as Spirit and Opportunity continued to rove kilometers across the Martian landscape, spurring John Updike to poetic speculation about them one day meeting, the MER mission could go down as a triumph.[40]

MER stole the spotlight from Stardust, which on 2 January passed 300 kilometers from comet Wild-2, snapping the highest resolution images yet obtained of a comet core and, more important, catching samples of comet dust for return to Earth. Another sample return from space occurred in September 2004, although not exactly as planned. A helicopter over a Utah desert was supposed to snag a capsule from Genesis with samples of the solar wind, but the parachute failed to deploy and the capsule instead crashed into the desert floor at about 350 kilometers per hour and cracked open. The crash landing, later traced to a switch installed backwards, threatened to contaminate the precious samples, although scientists managed to salvage some intact. Genesis and Stardust thus provided the first sample returns from space since Apollo. The Genesis crash suggested that JPL's adaptation to faster-better-cheaper continued to struggle, but Stardust's subsequent successful landing in January 2006 provided some vindication, as well as important clues to comet formation.[41]

At the other end of the scale sat Cassini, which entered orbit at Saturn on 30 June 2004. Cassini's arrival may have lacked the compressed drama of the Mars landings, but it had far higher stakes—four times the cost and much more time in development and in transit, and thus much harder to replace. From a weltering array of possible orbits, with science observations, viewing geometries, and telecommunications factored in with the orbital mechanics of Saturn and its satellites, flight planners had settled on seventy-four orbits of Saturn, including forty-four Titan flybys. Cassini promised to provide many more and closer looks than Voyager: its camera had five times the resolution of Voyager's, and Cassini carried a JPL-designed synthetic aperture radar to peer through Titan's opaque atmosphere. At the end of 2004 the Huygens

Figure 19.1. Times change. On the left, space flight operations in 1962, just before Ranger 5. Note the desktop hand calculators. On the right, space flight operations in 2004, after landing of Spirit rover on Mars. Left to right: Joel Krajewski, Jennifer Trosper, Chris Lewicki, Jason Willis. *Source:* JPL Photolab.

probe, built by Europe, dove through Titan's atmosphere. Together with the radar images, it provided evidence of methane rainfall and rivers of methane flowing around icy ridges on the surface. The following year Cassini's camera yielded striking images of geysers emanating from the south pole of Enceladus, another of Saturn's moons. The icy plumes were apparently expelled through surface vents by an internal heat source, and the presence of water and heat made Enceladus another promising target in the search for life on other planets.[42]

NASA had intended Cassini to be the final battlestar galactica, "the last of a class of 'flagship' missions."[43] But Galileo had likewise been planned, in 1983, as "the last of the elaborate old-style planetary expeditions."[44] Plans now emerged that made Cassini and Galileo look positively puny. The Prometheus program aimed to develop a new nuclear-electric propulsion system using an onboard nuclear reactor; early designs envisioned a spacecraft perhaps 30 meters long, several times the height and mass of Galileo. To direct this endeavor JPL brought out of retirement John Casani, avatar of old-school systems engineering.[45] The increasing scale reflected an admission by JPL and NASA that they could not do some missions, such as outer

planets or Mars rovers, smaller or cheaper; but that meant a range of approaches persisted.[46]

JPL's program in earth science continued, but its consistent growth starting in the 1980s was leveling off and focusing on two main lines. Earth scientists were extending the synthetic aperture radar program into differential interferometry: high-resolution radar topography taken at different times (say, different orbital passes) could detect earth movement of a few centimeters, revealing earthquakes—or, even better, predicting them from a telltale bulge in a fault. In ocean science JPL hoped through remote sensing to track changes in the ocean and the coupling between the ocean and the atmosphere.[47]

As earth science leveled off, astronomy looked to grow. In April 2003 JPL launched the Galaxy Evolution Explorer (GALEX), a collaboration with Caltech astronomer Christopher Martin that would study very early star formation. GALEX marked a new foray into ultraviolet astronomy, but the program otherwise had concentrated in two main lines: infrared astronomy and interferometry for extrasolar planet detection. For the first, the Spitzer telescope, the infrared equivalent of the Hubble, launched on 25 August 2003. At infrared wavelengths the Spitzer could see through interstellar dust, track the possible formation of planetary systems in cool gas clouds, and see stars at a great distance—and hence a very early stage in the universe—whose light had red-shifted to longer wavelengths.[48] For optical interferometry, JPL was planning an orbiting version of two linked telescopes

Figure 19.2. Evidence of past liquid water on Mars: ball-bearing-sized "blueberries" of hematite, which usually forms in water, scattered around a drill mark from the Opportunity rover. *Source:* JPL Photolab.

called the Space Interferometry Mission, whose precision in locating stars would allow it to detect wobbles in a star's position caused by planets. JPL's two main astronomy lines, infrared and interferometry, thus intersected in the extrasolar planet search, since dim planets would also show up at longer wavelengths. Together with the search for life on other bodies of our solar system, the prospect of finding earth-like planets around other stars offered JPL a chance at a transcendent discovery.

A possible major new direction, equally transcendent, was emerging in astrophysics and cosmology. As theory in high-energy physics far outstripped the energies available from particle accelerators, physicists early in the new century looked to space as the next source of experimental advance. JPL had several programs to build on, including tests with spacecraft radio signals of general relativity and gravity waves, and another planned orbiting interferometer called LISA (for Laser Interferometer Space Antenna), which would fly three spacecraft in extremely precise formation to detect gravity waves free from Earth's environmental noise. In addition to gravity waves, JPL helped research on cosmic background radiation, the electromagnetic vestige of the big bang: Caltech physicist Andrew Lange had flown a submillimeter bolometer from the Microdevices Lab on a balloon-borne experiment and found evidence of small irregularities that suggested the universe has flat geometry—that is, that its mass counteracts its expansion just enough to prevent the universe from one day collapsing. That experiment, the journal *Nature* announced, opened "a new era of precision cosmology," which JPL hoped to lead.[49] The Caltech connection greatly helped here, too, by giving JPL access to campus astronomers and physicists like Lange. Just as JPL allowed Caltech to do big science while staying small, Elachi noted that Caltech allowed JPL "to be involved in a small way in new areas which could become big things" without the need to hire cosmologists of its own.[50]

Astrophysics offered possible institutional as well as intellectual stimulation, but JPL and Caltech were not the only institutions contemplating this avenue: physicists and astronomers at Berkeley and Stanford, for example, had the same idea. At the federal level, NASA would have to define its responsibility against the traditional roles of the National Science Foundation in physics and astronomy and the Department of Energy in high-energy physics. For JPL itself, if it did pursue this line, it could mean a major reorientation, comparable perhaps to the shift from rockets to planetary spacecraft at the end of the 1950s. Although cosmology had some technological connections to current work, as in detectors, it would introduce JPL to a much different scientific constituency. Planetary missions promised to remain the lab's identity in the short term, but a major push into astrophysics and cosmology would bring large changes.[51]

By the middle of 2004 JPL looked stronger than ever, after the success of Spitzer and GALEX, Stardust, MER, and Cassini. As a symbol of JPL's resiliency, the Voyager spacecraft, launched in 1977, had kept flying through the ups and downs of the 1990s. By 2004 Voyager 1 was about 14 billion kilometers from Earth, with Voyager 2 almost as distant, and both still were transmitting data to the Deep Space Network. At that range the two spacecraft were approaching the outer limits of the sun's influence, and they would soon pass into interstellar space and begin the trip to other stars.[52]

Conclusion

FROM 1976 TO 2001 JPL CONSUMED ABOUT $30 BILLION (IN CONSTANT 1999 dollars) and consistently employed several thousand people, a fair fraction of them science and engineering PhDs. What did the government and the American people get for this investment? To people at JPL, the images from their spacecraft provided sufficient, if not spectacular, returns. When asked the question "why spend all that money?" Jurrie van der Woude borrowed a riff from Louis Armstrong: If you have to ask, I couldn't tell you.[1] But to elicit taxpayer money from the federal government, JPL would have to be more specific.

Investments and Returns

For much of its history JPL traded in the currency of the cold war, first as an army rocket arsenal, then under NASA in the space race for international prestige. But the cold war itself proved insufficient to sustain JPL's mission. The shortfall of the mid-1970s, amid détente, first impelled JPL managers to seek another major sponsor, and even in the early 1980s, after the renewed chill in U.S.-Soviet relations, the Reagan administration considered abandoning the planetary program altogether. Tied by the cold war to federal support, JPL suffered the vagaries of the political climate—that is, JPL managers could not just invoke the cold war or national security; they still had to generate political support for particular initiatives. Not for nothing did Congress define NASA's budget as "discretionary."[2]

That meant JPL had to find a constituency, whether in the planetary science community, the aerospace industry, or the interested public. But the several hundred or so planetary scientists produced barely a blip on political radar screens, planetary spacecraft added only a pittance to the bottom line of big aerospace corporations, and opinion polls revealed the American public's consistent lack of interest. With no single clear constituency, allocation of resources to space exploration required negotiation among a tangle of stakeholders. Planetary science itself contained subcommunities for comets, inner or outer planets, and so on, and disciplinary divides between geologists and space physicists; NASA's space science program then unified these groups against astronomers and earth scientists; the space science program contended with human exploration within NASA and with other sciences (such as high-energy physics or molecular biology) within the federal government. All of these scientific and political decisions played out in the usual congressional maneuvers, including calculations involving the equally fractious aerospace industry. For example, comet scientists in the late 1970s debated the merits of different Halley missions, then squared off against Galileo and a Venus orbiter as well as two astronomy telescopes, while enduring shuttle overruns that ate into the space science budget and the general decline of NASA's budget against military space programs.

A particular, persistent issue throughout this period was the relation between robotic and human exploration. Despite the scientific return and public interest in robotic missions, NASA's top priority remained human exploration, through the shuttle and then the space station. Many problems in the robotic program, even ones seemingly unrelated to human spaceflight, could be traced back to the space shuttle, including Galileo's tortured history of delays. The failure to provide cheap launches encouraged more ambitious planetary missions; managers reasoned that with large sunk costs for each launch, they should maximize scientific return, in the sort of reasoning that produced Mars Observer. Perceived public demand for a human presence in space justified NASA's priorities, although some commentators, including Bruce Murray, charged that NASA viewed the aerospace industry as its real constituency and therefore sought the biggest projects as jobs programs.[3] NASA managers replied that space science received a fixed portion of NASA's budget, so that big human projects in fact boosted science funding. A rising tide did lift all boats—until the tide fell, as it did in the mid-1970s and again in the 1990s, and NASA found itself committed to costly human programs that drained money from robotic missions.[4] Not all the problems of the planetary program stemmed from the shuttle, but it did have extensive impact, even far downstream of the original commitment to it in the early 1970s. The Columbia accident of 2003 and subsequent turmoil are only the latest manifestation, but they also signaled a reconsideration of thirty years of policy. The resultant plan to send humans to the moon and then Mars, however, revived the threat to robotic exploration and suggested that the issue remained relevant.

Another consequence of federal support was to subject the planetary program to the short-term focus of the American political system. Even programs declared a high national priority, such as Apollo, could not escape persistent political scrutiny. A NASA manager conveyed the general mind-set to a JPL engineer: "Long-range planning? Ha! Are you kidding? Long-range planning is 'what do we do this afternoon?'"[5] Hence attempts to establish a long-term, low-cost exploration program, instead of proposing projects individually, foundered when Congress refused to yield discretion to NASA, which in turn concentrated risk in overloaded, infrequent missions. Technology programs with payoffs ten years or more down the road, such as microelectronics, microspacecraft, or new propulsion systems, likewise languished.

The national investment in JPL was substantial. But so were its accomplishments, which were not just the product of public relations machines or the prolific pens of popularizers like Carl Sagan. JPL launched spacecraft into the black of space, where they had to endure many years of temperature extremes, high radiation doses, and vacuum, with no hope of repairs save those possible over a tenuous radio link. Complex calculations of celestial mechanics delivered these spacecraft with pinpoint accuracy to their destination, where they commenced a ballet of imaging and other observations constrained by lighting angles, viewing geometries, and scientific interests, and the giant antennas of the Deep Space Network retrieved signals broadcast across billions of kilometers from spacecraft transmitters with the power of a refrigerator light bulb. These engineering achievements challenged the metaphorical abilities of people trying to chronicle them, as in the frequent analogies to transcontinental golf putts or billiard shots to describe spacecraft navigation accuracy.[6]

JPL spacecraft returned scientific data and images that revealed astonishing complexity in other planets and their moons and dynamic phenomena, such as tectonics, volcanoes, and extreme weather systems, even in outer regions of the solar system previously thought cold and quiescent. These findings rewrote planetary astronomy textbooks, replacing Earth-centric theories with ones recognizing planetary diversity. In exposing this diversity JPL spacecraft affected more than science; they changed our view of our own planet and its place in the universe. If life exists on another planet, or an Earth-like planet around another star, JPL is humanity's best bet to detect it; and if it does it will profoundly alter our view of the cosmos and of ourselves.

JPL's actual and potential historical import encouraged participants and commentators to declare it the cockpit of a new Age of Discovery. JPL missions named Mariner, Voyager, and Magellan invoked an appeal that would continue through MER's journey "across sands of time and oceans of space," as one headline rhapsodized.[7] But this embrace of exploration did not much justify return visits for detailed science, and the dwindling list of unexplored sites in the solar system impelled a change in the justification for deep-space missions. In addition to exploration, deep-space missions were intended to serve science, and for space scientists, just getting to new planets and sending back pictures was not enough. A subtle shift to scientific goals was evident in the choice of names for later missions, such as Galileo and Cassini. Then, despite projects like Magellan and Pathfinder, more descriptive names began to appear, especially for Mars missions: Global Surveyor, Climate Orbiter, and Polar Lander. Romantic notions give way to practical realities in many long-term relationships.[8]

The debate over science and exploration returned to the constituency question (was it scientists or the public?) and went back to JPL's first missions—and even earlier, considering a similar interplay between scientific goals and exploration on eighteenth-century oceanic voyages or nineteenth-century geological surveys.[9] These earlier examples make clear that national governments rarely fund missions just for science. Although the space race pursued not so much imperial or colonial goals, but rather ones of national prestige and military relevance, science rode the coattails of other national interests. The difference between science and exploration showed up in hardware: for example, a three-axis stabilized platform for imaging or spinning spacecraft for particles-and-fields experiments. Galileo's dual-spin design, of 1970s vintage, represented a compromise between the two sides but also perhaps the high-water mark of the debate. The ever-higher resolution provided by spacecraft images, evident especially on Voyager, convinced scientists that pictures were not just for public relations but were an important part of the science too.[10]

A Fine Line

An irregular sine wave with a period of about five years traces JPL's fortunes over this period. It started with a low point circa 1977, with the impending post-Voyager bathtub and the fight to win Galileo; proceeded to the high of 1979 and the first Voyager encounters, followed by the planetary crisis of the early 1980s; recovery by 1984 and the growth of defense programs; the lows after Challenger in 1986 and highs when launches resumed in 1989; the post–cold war malaise of the early 1990s, Galileo's antenna problem, and the Mars Observer failure; the rebound owing to Galileo's encounter, Pathfinder, and Origins, and finally the funk following the Mars failures in 1999.

This curve may be coincidental, a space-age equivalent to the Kondratiev economic cycle, and the successes of 2004 might have broken the trend (though subsequent budget woes suggested the cycle could continue). But there may be an underlying cause for the lows that resulted from spacecraft failures: complacency. A successful mission or two could encourage JPL engineers to let down their guard and to forget about the one constant feature of deep-space missions: the exceedingly narrow margin between failure and success. Almost every successful planetary mission skated on very thin ice, from Voyager's post-launch emergencies to Magellan's lost heartbeat, Galileo's stuck antenna, and Mars Global Surveyor's broken wing. Failed missions highlighted the narrow margin, such as the units discrepancy on Mars Climate Orbiter or the faulty code that slipped through tests on Mars Polar Lander. Even defining failure or success proved problematic: NASA at first viewed Seasat as a failure but soon came around to see it as a scientific and technical success.

What made the difference between success and failure? Some JPL staff believed the lab's acronym stood for "Just Plain Luck."[11] Others attributed success to the quality of the people. Constant proclamations of superior competence fed perceptions of JPL's arrogance (and perhaps betrayed some insecurity in the lab's relation to Caltech). From the view of aerospace firms, JPL engineers could seem no smarter than their colleagues in industry, especially as companies matured and gained technical and managerial expertise; but the pipeline of Caltech graduates did help, and JPL perhaps boasted a richer mix of capabilities. A more important difference might have been JPL's mission: the chance to lead the exploration of outer space attracted good people and motivated them to work very hard.[12] Successful missions inspired an exceptional commitment from the project team, and concerns whether JPL could sustain such commitment faded as engineers geared up for the next neat mission.[13] The supreme self-confidence that some called arrogance could be helpful, by generating a belief that any problem, however intractable, would yield to rational analysis and hard work.[14]

JPL benefited also from a culture of peer review, an unfettered airing of opinions no matter how critical. Spacecraft design reviews, in particular, provided a trial by fire for people as well as for design concepts, forging stronger engineers and spacecraft. The association with Caltech perhaps contributed: JPL's origins in and continued ties with an academic environment steeped it in the tradition of critical peer review, more so than the civil service NASA centers. This culture of tolerating and encouraging dissenting views did not always overcome normal human failings, and JPL did not escape the accidents that plagued NASA, such as the Challenger and Columbia shuttle tragedies. In particular, in the 1990s NASA applied increasing pressure on JPL to toe the agency line, while the lab itself embraced new management initiatives promoting customer service and discouraging personal criticism. The resulting emphasis on presenting a positive image contributed to the Mars failures in 1999.

Diversification

Another long-term trend helped damp the amplitude of the success-failure curve. Planetary exploration was JPL's main mission in this period but not its only one, nor was it inevitable (after all, it was not the lab's original mission). In the 1970s the lab diversified into earth sciences and astronomy, fields within NASA's purview, and these programs reduced the impact of periodic crises in the planetary program. JPL had also diversified in direct response to earlier low points, first into energy in the 1970s, then into defense; in each case JPL staff considered the potential for a major second mission or even for a dominant one. Each of these programs grew quickly and then dwindled, and neither became a long-term mission. But energy and defense work did have long-term effects, as new skills and tools provided fruitful interactions. Energy work, for example, involved solid-state research on photovoltaics, which then fed the microelectronics program under defense sponsorship, which in turn became a prime source of planetary technologies.

These diverse lines contributed greatly to JPL's return on the national investment. In earth sciences, JPL spacecraft and instruments produced not only specific knowledge of such phenomena as the ozone hole and El Niño, but they also helped bring about the methodological embrace of remote sensing by geologists and oceanographers. In astronomy JPL built the two major orbital infrared observatories, IRAS and the Spitzer telescope, as well as the crucial camera that corrected the Hubble telescope's faulty optics, and thus greatly expanded our vision of the universe. Outside NASA's turf, JPL helped push the development of solar power, developed an array of micro-electronic sensors with defense support, and played a little-recognized role in the emergence of the electronic battlefield. JPL's contributions included technologies spun off from its planetary mission, such as synthetic aperture radar. Digital image processing in particular has found myriad applications ranging from medical radiology to fine-art photography.

Diversification also had important effects on JPL itself. As a risk-aversion strategy common to large organizations, it enabled JPL to ride out threats to its primary product line. But it also fragmented the lab: instead of a single large planetary project defining and driving the program, engineers and managers were scattered among a welter of missions and instruments. Some of these projects, such as earth science and astronomy instruments, relied on spacecraft systems engineering, but others—solar power or military command-and-control systems—appealed only to broad capabilities. Diversification may thus have diluted JPL's expertise and culture, which centered on the production of high-reliability spacecraft through the regime of systems engineering.[15]

Lab managers would consistently wonder whether diversification was hurting the lab. Had JPL become a jack of all trades and master of none? In 1988 Lew Allen asked: "Are we making a trade between diversity and focus? . . . The issue of focus was easy to satisfy when planetary programs were the main objective. On the other hand diversity helps us to survive. Historically, the best laboratories have been single-mission laboratories."[16] In 2001 JPL's visiting committee was still pondering the issue: "Is JPL trying to do too much? [Or] does it need to find a way to increase its core competencies to maintain a wider range of activities?"[17]

Questions of Identity

Diversification affected another constant issue in this history: the triangular relationship among JPL, Caltech, and NASA. Work for outside sponsors, an option unavailable to NASA's other civil service centers, increased the lab's independence and helped tilt the triangle toward Caltech and JPL in the 1970s and 1980s. It swung back toward NASA in the 1990s as JPL phased out non-NASA work. Other factors weighed on the balance: the personalities of the actors; JPL's programmatic and administrative performance; and, most notably, the post–cold war tightening of the regulatory environment. All of these combined in the 1990s to reduce JPL's autonomy, even as NASA touted the contractor model for its other centers. The common question—was it NASA's JPL or Caltech's JPL?—was increasingly answered for NASA, and the agency's sensitivity on the subject likely derived from JPL's exceptional status among the NASA centers. Similar university-run labs—for instance, the national labs under the Department of Energy—do not seem to have been so sensitive to this question of identity (although they certainly grappled with many other shared issues, especially accountability versus autonomy).[18]

The lab tried to maintain another sort of balance in its work, between the interests of scientists and those of engineers. As with other forms of modern science that entailed the construction of complex instruments, JPL's job building spacecraft for scientific missions mingled scientists and engineers.[19] Despite the popular conception of "rocket science" and a tendency by media to call JPL staff "scientists," engineers dominated.[20] That, at least, was the view of scientists, who first of all consistently bemoaned the poor status of science within JPL, where staff scientists had to spend too much time seeking funding and too little on their research. More broadly but as consistently, planetary scientists—even those expressing appreciation for JPL's engineering expertise—complained that engineering dictates trumped scientific goals on JPL missions. The purpose of these missions, after all, was science, and just delivering a mass of metal to a planet did no good if no interesting data came back. For their part, engineers seeking to ensure reliability could view scientists' demands—can we add extra electromagnetic shielding for our instrument? can we cut off radio contact by swinging behind a moon?—as incremental threats to spacecraft survival. Neat experiments meant nothing if the spacecraft did not get there in the first place.

Scientists could also constrain engineers in a different way, when engineers were willing to risk failure in order to try out new technologies. For instance, scientific commitment to big platforms, in the interest of obtaining comprehensive data sets, conflicted with the microspacecraft movement, the sort of blue-sky technology engineers viewed as fun. JPL and NASA recognized that new technology would pay dividends in the long run and hence gradually incorporated new technologies within flight projects, but NASA's short-term focus generally excluded advanced technology development from JPL's job description. The lab's own frame of reference centered on launching the current project successfully; the common attitude of "the better is the enemy of the good" did not encourage innovation.[21]

This identity question, of science versus engineering, had a third axis, that of management. The question posed by the orange report in 1976 echoed throughout this period: were JPL staff primarily scientists, engineers, or managers? JPL's accomplishments rested perhaps less on its ability to build hardware than on the regime of systems engineering, also known as systems management. The ambiguity of the term suggested the identity problem, and although there was no denying the importance of systems engineering, the proliferation of documentation and procedures it engendered led to fears that JPL was losing its technical skill and becoming a place of paper-shuffling job monitors.[22] The trend toward industry contracts instead of in-house engineering exaggerated the issue, as did the lab's standard career path for scientists and engineers, which led upward into management (although some shunned this track in order to keep their hands on research). Persistent questions about the source of JPL's capability—was it managerial or technical?—also affected relations with Caltech, since campus expertise was strictly technical.

Much of the literature in the history of science and technology focuses on scientists and engineers, to the neglect of managers.[23] Management deserves more attention. Not confined to JPL or the space program, it applies to big science more widely—that is, to research involving large, expensive instruments whose development requires coordination of large teams of scientists and engineers. Two examples suggest that JPL and the space program were more attuned to issues of management. The gravity-wave detector known as LIGO, a collaboration between Caltech and MIT, attempted in the 1980s to impose management discipline on squabbling academic physicists and brought in Frank Schutz from JPL as project manager; he quit a few years later and returned to JPL, frustrated by the physicists' inability to recognize that project management was not the same thing as research.[24] In high-energy physics, when the ill-fated Superconducting Super Collider sought a project manager in 1990, the search committee looked first not to high-energy physicists or to accelerator engineers, but instead to the civil and military space programs—and their top candidate was John Casani from JPL.[25]

JPL and NASA did not always share this appreciation for systems engineering. The Discovery program in the 1990s inverted the usual relation between scientists and managers. Instead of placing the project manager above the project scientist, Discovery missions had the scientist on top, thus ignoring a central lesson of the space program: that management was a separate discipline, one distinct from scientific expertise and acquired only through long experience. When some of these missions got into trouble during development, JPL managers blamed overindulgent scientists.[26] The failures at Mars in 1999 were similarly attributed to departures from the discipline of systems engineering.

The subject of management carries connotations of bureaucratic procedure and organization charts, which might explain the relative lack of scholarly attention. But management approaches ultimately reflected personal philosophies, from consensus-builders like Ed Stone to the leg breakers like John Casani, from the compassionate empowerment envisioned by reengineering to the autocratic rigor of systems engineering. Individuals make a difference. In particular, JPL directors stamped the lab with their personalities: the visionary, activist Murray; the measured gravitas of Lew Allen; the conservative revolutionary Stone, seeking cultural change through cautious consideration; the enthusiastic planning and marketing of Elachi. Each director's character determined his response to a crisis: budget cuts led Murray to look outward, to change the environment through public relations and political lobbying, whereas Stone looked inward and tried to change JPL. Allen, faced with Challenger, looked sideways, identifying advanced technology as a new primary mission for the lab.

Each director's approach affected the delicate balance among JPL, Caltech, and NASA. In particular, Murray was criticized by NASA for pushing back too much, yet Stone was criticized at JPL for not pushing back enough. Each man was perhaps justified: Murray antagonized NASA, but his activism helped save the planetary program; Stone sacrificed JPL's independence, but he stayed in NASA's high esteem and pulled JPL through a programmatic crisis. Each approach reflected not only the director's personality, but also the context—especially Stone's sense that the end of the cold war demanded fundamental changes, and also his need to deal with Dan Goldin. (Matching Murray with Goldin might have made for spontaneous combustion.) And Murray and Stone were united in their fixation on change, on JPL's need to adapt to new circumstances—although they differed in their approach, Murray sweeping into action, Stone advancing cautiously. Lew Allen, for his part, sailed a straighter course, one in between Murray's and Stone's approaches to NASA; his name carried enough weight in space policy circles to ensure JPL's independence, but as a former military man he knew when to accept orders from above—as in JPL's agreement to work on the space station, which Allen personally opposed.[27]

Strong leadership can benefit large laboratories in general, but the director was particularly important for JPL because of its centralized bureaucracy and the lack of programmatic direction from Caltech administrators or trustees.[28] Directors had to learn to work the throttle. Bruce Murray, for example, came accustomed to throwing out ideas as if he were in an academic seminar. "He tried that same stuff at JPL," said John Casani, "the next day there were fifty people working on it. He didn't mean for that to happen; he just wanted someone to tell him what a dumb idea it was."[29] Yet as a large organization JPL had institutional inertia; the daily work continued at lower levels through leadership changes, and group supervisors could claim that their level—the lowest level of management—was the most important, as scientists and engineers in small groups were the ultimate source of new ideas and the starting point on the path from lab bench to launch pad.[30]

The End of the Cold War

JPL, NASA, and planetary scientists looked on two levels for a post–cold war rationale. The Origins program represented an attempt to look beyond goals of national security to fundamental questions concerning all humankind: What were the origins of life and the cosmos? Are we alone in the universe? But underneath these transcendent goals lay more mundane motives, though no less comprehensive, namely, economic competitiveness. Appeals to the economic impact of space missions tried to tap the large majority of the American public, which had little interest in space but much interest in their job prospects. The new economic orientation appeared in JPL's redoubled emphasis on technology transfer; an increasing role for the aerospace industry through the partnering policy; and renewed appreciation for outreach, focused now especially on children, not current taxpayers, as a way to increase the future labor supply of scientists and engineers.

The commercialization of JPL extended to its practice, to the means as well as the ends of the space program. Total Quality Management and re-engineering applied techniques from for-profit manufacturing industry to advanced research and development, and faster-better-cheaper tried to instill commercial cost consciousness. Increasing government oversight meanwhile required JPL to comply with federal regulations developed primarily for industrial contractors, and thus forced JPL to adopt corporate business operations, including the appointment of a chief financial officer. Chief scientist Moustafa Chahine spoke of a cultural shift in the 1990s, from a university-type culture to an industrial environment.[31]

JPL had always nurtured an entrepreneurial spirit, apparent in references to "marketing" of proposals and jokes about "branding" with the Mariner Mark II series, seeking to capitalize on the Mariner name without really using its technological inheritance.[32] But appeals to "business models" multiplied in the 1990s, together with more concrete expressions of commercial enterprise in Caltech's increased licensing activity and the policy encouraging spin-off companies to cash in on JPL technologies. The use of an economic market system instead of centralized allocation of resources on Cassini exemplified the trend.

The commercial spirit threatened to upset the pattern of federal R&D funding, based on government contracts, that had predominated through the cold war. In 2002 NASA considered setting up its own venture capital firm to fund new technologies, on the model of the CIA's Incutel, established in 1999; instead of contracting for research, the venture-capital model hoped to tap fast-evolving elements of the private sector—"to try and ride some of these commercial waves that could be of benefit to NASA." Neither recognized legislative obstacles nor the end of the go-go business years of the 1990s dimmed NASA's hopes of catching the venture capital wave.[33]

But however much JPL staff embraced industrial approaches and talked of marketing or branding, the lab differed from industry in two crucial respects. First, it was owned and funded by the government. A government entity cannot operate like a business because it is not trying to turn a profit and must be politically accountable; whereas business managers can focus on tasks, government managers must focus on constraints, such as in allocation of revenues or definition of goals.[34] One of the reasons the CIA set up Incutel was to get around vexing federal contract and procurement regulations; and JPL's attempts at technology transfer were limited by NASA fears of private profiteering from taxpayer-supported research. Second, the raison d'être for government-owned labs, such as JPL, was to undertake high-risk, long-range R&D projects that industry could not or would not do. Despite the short-term focus of the federal government, JPL trained its eye on the cutting edge and beyond, not on the bottom line for shareholders. For these two reasons, attempts to apply industrial models to JPL were handicapped from the start, as were efforts to draw management lessons for industry from JPL.[35]

Civil Space Programs and the Military

The end of the cold war did not mean an end to its influence. Although competition with the Soviets no longer served as a justification for the space program, the cold war continued to make itself felt in the integration of military with civilian space programs. That is, there are two basic historical developments to consider: the renewed militarization of space starting in the late 1970s and the end of the cold war. The one determined the response to the other. In 1995 Ed Stone noted, "The end of the Cold War race has exposed more fundamental changes that had occurred several years earlier but until recently could be ignored"—namely, the "rapid growth of the non-NASA space program, so that for the last 10 years or so, NASA and the nation's space program are no longer synonymous." Some of this growth came from communications and weather satellites, but most of it came from the military.[36]

The military is the elephant in the living room of the U.S. space program; its presence is inescapable, however much public policy seems not to acknowledge it. JPL's remilitarization in the 1980s reflected that of the space program in general and left a significant legacy: in the Microdevices Lab, the microspacecraft program, and a cadre of managers who gained valuable experience on military projects and particular exposure to military management modes on such projects as SDI Pathfinder and MSTI. More broadly, the flood of military labs, technologies, people, and management techniques into civil space after the cold war—in particular, those that came out of the Strategic Defense Initiative—drove the shift to faster-better-cheaper. NASA for decades had sought a coherent, long-term program of cheap, frequent, focused missions, going back to the low-cost systems office of the 1970s and then the SSEC plan of the 1980s. Each time a variety of forces had combined to sink low-cost plans: scientists piling on too many mission goals, NASA managers indulging scientists to gain political support, launch vehicle capabilities (notably the shuttle program), and JPL's own engineering culture. Faster-better-cheaper differed in its post–cold war context of budget cuts and a NASA administrator committed to a new approach, but especially in its foundations in military space programs from the 1980s.

There is an analogy here to the 1960s, when NASA borrowed personnel and techniques from the air force to prosecute Apollo, and the 1990s, when NASA drew on military technologies, techniques, and models to implement faster-better-cheaper. The analogy extends from NASA to JPL itself, which started as a military lab; its development of systems engineering in the 1960s drew on previous experience for the army much like its programs thirty years later built on the 1980s remobilization. It became increasingly difficult in this period to distinguish the civil and military space programs. Institutionally, civilian labs like JPL undertook defense work and then military labs, such as APL and Livermore, began competing for NASA projects; industrial contractors like Lockheed-Martin built both military and NASA spacecraft. A bustling traffic in managers also ran between NASA and military programs in the 1980s and continued into the 1990s and beyond. To take just one example, in 1991 NASA picked SDI technology manager Michael Griffin to head its exploration office—and Griffin had worked at JPL before joining SDI. After stints in industry, leading the CIA's Incutel, and as director of APL's Space Department, Griffin ended up as head of NASA in 2005.[37]

Many technologies also straddled the boundary. SDI projects applied JPL expertise to military purposes while JPL engineers used SDI products and funding for civilian missions. Work on autonomous spacecraft served both deep-space and military missions: a microstep actuator for spacecraft scan platforms and cryogenic infrared sensors for astronomy and earth science jibed with experiments for ballistic missile defense; synthetic aperture radar, developed by the military and then adapted by JPL for Venus and oceanography, helped detect submarines and stealth airplanes. JPL contributed not just hardware but also software and systems engineering skills, as in its work on C^3I and the electronic battlefield.

The history of JPL might represent a broader, long-term trend for civil-military relations in the American space program. The trend follows the contours of the cold war: the initial integration or even identification of civil and military programs in the 1950s continued into the 1960s; a gradual divergence culminated in the mid-1970s; and renewed integration started in the late 1970s that continued beyond 1991, albeit with military programs now directed toward civilian ends. Historical literature tends to see the integration of planetary science and national security as harmful, but it could help, too, in overcoming a general lack of civilian support for advanced technology and in making connections to classified programs, albeit at the cost of subjecting science to military influence and vagaries in federal support.[38]

The militarization of space entailed not the wholesale capture of civil space programs by the military, but rather mutual interactions between the two. For instance, a NASA aide who had helped draft presidential directives for joint civil-military satellites in the Carter administration, amid remilitarization, hoped that defense connections would not only ensure budget support, but also provide a way to influence the military: "the 'civilizing' of our Defense establishments must begin from within."[39] JPL did not just respond to military requests but rather contributed to defense in some cases precisely because of its civilian orientation, as with synthetic aperture radar. In other cases, however, JPL's technological approach, grounded in the civil program, ran up against military tendencies—for instance, on SDI Pathfinder, where JPL pushed ultraviolet detection of missile exhaust, based on its experience with CCDs, against the military's ingrained preference for infrared sensors.

The genealogy of space technologies, like that of human populations, has grown increasingly entangled over time, precluding easy classification (in both senses of the term).[40] The relevance of space technology to national security, however, forced the federal government to make a hard distinction between secret and open technologies, no matter how blurry the boundary. How well did information cross the barrier of classification? At the top level, the NASA administrator was plugged into the black world, as was the JPL director either through advisory panels or personal experience. But what about at the operational level, for engineers designing specific spacecraft components? We have seen the worries of JPL managers about their ignorance of classified technologies, such as synthetic aperture radar and digital image processing, corroborated by comments from the military side. JPL's subsequent integration into military space programs increased its access; hence, for example, Seasat helped connect synthetic aperture radar engineers to military programs, and spacecraft engineers tapped military programs on instrument tracking and pointing in the 1980s.

A disconnect nevertheless persisted. In August 1993 a NASA panel, chaired by Allen and including members from the defense and reconnaissance communities, reviewed JPL's Pluto mission and a Goddard project. "A major purpose" of the panel was to ask if NASA missions "were adequately aware of emerging technology in other organizations, . . . including classified programs." It had no clear answer: JPL's Pluto team had drawn on military technologies, "but our reviewers were able to note technologies which the teams had not uncovered. . . . The classified programs are often difficult to penetrate although the relevant technologies can often be exchanged in an unclassified manner." The panel urged NASA to improve "mechanisms for exchange" with classified programs and specified in particular a "dialogue" with the National Reconnaissance Office (NRO).[41]

JPL followed this advice in the 1990s. Without the programmatic pressure to pursue big projects, and perhaps aided by declassification of certain programs under the NRO, JPL solidified its ties to the military even as it shrunk its defense effort. That at least was the judgment of Philip Eckman, who had returned from the CIA to JPL as liaison with military and intelligence agencies: "Our DoD relationship really began to grow in the '90s and then sort of flowered a little bit when . . . we developed formal relationships between JPL and the NRO and other parts of the DoD community."[42] At the programmatic level, JPL continued to work with the military in such areas as synthetic aperture radar, infrared cryogenic coolers, and C³I systems, while the top of JPL remained plugged into the black world through Stone's service on military and intelligence advisory committees.[43] In 2000 Stone and Barbara Wilson, head of JPL's microelectronics program (and later chief technologist for the air force), met with the director of the Ballistic Missile Defense Organization to discuss several products of the Microdevices Lab—the active pixel sensor, infrared sensors, a micro-machined gyroscope, and others—that would strengthen the partnership.[44] A few years earlier Eckman briefed the head of R&D for the NRO, Bob Pattishall, on thirteen JPL technologies. When asked which might interest him, Pattishall replied, "I want them all!"[45]

But there is no evidence that JPL received similar briefings in return from the NRO. If there was a pipeline between the black and open worlds, classification imposed a one-way valve. And however much the civil and military realms interacted, there remained basic distinctions between them. Murray and Allen referred to "cultural" differences between JPL and military, as did the Clementine review panel. Although JPL first matured under the army, by the late 1970s two decades under NASA had accustomed it to a civilian mission. Although the means of civilian and military programs overlapped, the ends fundamentally diverged: one pursued science and exploration; the other, spying and armed combat. Scholars of civil-military relations have noted that the cold war blurred but did not erase cultural distinctions between civilians and soldiers, and that the end of the cold war has exaggerated them.[46]

The encounter of two cultures can produce fruitful mutual interactions, such as appear in synthetic aperture radar, and change both cultures in a dynamic process. But one must also consider the relative power of the two cultures: in the 1980s the military space program was twice the size of NASA, not including the vast intelligence programs, and secrecy reinforced this outsized presence. The difference in cultures first limited JPL's penetration of military programs in the 1980s and then affected its reception of faster-better-cheaper. Barriers to integration were not all the result of cultural differences; some stemmed from JPL's "not-invented-here" philosophy of self-reliance, some from the usual bureaucratic fence-building of government agencies. And the military itself was of course not monolithic. In addition to the usual interservice rivalries, there were differences between the military services under the Department of Defense and the intelligence community of the CIA, NRO, and National Security Agency.[47] But the reception of faster-better-cheaper, in particular, suggested a cultural divide between civil and military space in levels of public scrutiny and attitudes toward risk. JPL and NASA operated not in the shadows of secrecy, but rather in the bright light, where failures were spotlighted.

Whither JPL?

Since its origins in the 1930s JPL has survived in part by adapting, by shifting from a small academic rocketry research project to an army rocket arsenal and then to a civilian space-exploration lab with increasingly diverse programs. It has remained in business through the end of the cold war because of the national services it provides—to science, exploration, defense, and industry—and also because of political support for a large Southern California enterprise. But the periodic crises in the past indicate that there is no guarantee that it will continue to survive or that it need not adapt again. JPL persists above all because it has produced results, whatever its mission. Whether lab staff keep building planetary spacecraft, find a new focus in astrophysics and cosmology, or perhaps change course altogether, they will no doubt continue to adhere to the common saying around JPL that "the lab is one failure away from closing, and one transistor away from failure."

The Ranger failures of the 1960s forged a new regime in the heat of public investigation. The Mars missions in 1999 showed that however different the context, the American public insisted on success, and JPL hence renewed its commitment to ensure accountability and reduce risk. The post–cold war environment has thus perpetuated the lab's balancing act between accountability and autonomy, between demands for success and the audacious enterprise of deep-space exploration.

Notes

Abbreviations Used in Notes

AW&ST = *Aviation Week and Space Technology*
CIT = California Institute of Technology
EC = JPL Executive Council
HSPS = *Historical Studies in the Physical and Biological Sciences*
Jet Propulsion Lab Archives, Pasadena, Calif.
    JPL 8 = Bruce Murray files, 1971–82
    JPL 92 = James Cutts files
    JPL 105 = Charles Kohlhase files
    JPL 110 = Arroyo Center collection
    JPL 119 = Jack James files
    JPL 142 = JPL Office of the Director files, 1959–82
    JPL 150 = JPL Executive Council files, 1960–82
    JPL 163 = John Casani files
    JPL 165 = JPL Executive Council files, 1987–98
    JPL 173 = Harris Schurmeier files
    JPL 198 = Lew Allen files
    JPL 216 = Bruce Murray files, 1975–82
    JPL 239 = Duane Dipprey files
    JPL 259 = Edward Stone files
    JPL-HC = JPL Historical Collection
JPL = Jet Propulsion Lab
JPL A/V = JPL Audiovisual Collection
Koppes = Clayton R. Koppes, *JPL and the American space program: A history of the Jet Propulsion Laboratory* (New Haven, 1982)
NASA History Office, NASA headquarters, Washington, D.C.
    NASA-Cassini = Cassini project file
    NASA-Clementine = Clementine project files
    NASA-CRAF = Comet Rendezvous and Asteroid Flyby project files
    NASA-Discovery = Discovery project files

NASA-IRAS = Infrared Astronomical Satellite files
NASA-JPL = JPL files
NASA-Magellan = Magellan project files
NASA-MO = Mars Observer project files
NASA-OSS = Office of Space Science files (unorganized)
NASA-Seasat = Seasat project files
NASA-SIRTF = Space Infrared Telescope Facility (Spitzer Telescope) project files
NASM = Space History Office, National Air and Space Museum, Washington, D.C.
POP = JPL Program Operating Plan
SSEEC = JPL Solar System Exploration Executive Committee

Preface

1. David H. DeVorkin, *Science with a vengeance: How the military created the U.S. space sciences after World War II* (New York, 1992); Joseph N. Tatarewicz, *Space technology and planetary astronomy* (Bloomington, 1990); Stephen G. Brush, *Fruitful encounters: The origins of the solar system and of the moon from Chamberlin to Apollo* (Cambridge, 1996); Ronald E. Doel, *Solar system astronomy in America: Communities, patronage, and interdisciplinary science, 1920–1960* (Cambridge, 1996); Doel, "Theories and origins in planetary physics," *Isis* 90 (1999): 563–68; Spencer R. Weart, *The discovery of global warming* (Cambridge, Mass., 2003); "Geophysics and the military," special issue, *HSPS* 30:2 (2000).

2. Daniel J. Kevles, "Big science and big politics in the United States: Reflections on the death of the SSC and the life of the Human Genome Project," *HSPS* 27:2 (1997): 269–97; Robert W. Smith, *The Space Telescope: A study of NASA, science, technology, and politics* (Cambridge, 1993).

3. E.g., Charles Thorpe and Steven Shapin, "Who was J. Robert Oppenheimer? Charisma and complex organization," *Social Studies of Science* 30:4 (2000): 545–90; Catherine Westfall, "A tale of two more laboratories: Readying for research at Fermilab and Jefferson Laboratory," *HSPS* 32:2 (2002): 369–407. As Thorpe and Shapin note, leadership itself is in practice a product of collective action.

4. On Voyager: Henry C. Dethloff and Ronald A. Schorn, *Voyager's grand tour* (Washington, D.C., 2003); Mark Washburn, *Distant encounters: The exploration of Jupiter and Saturn* (New York, 1983); Henry S. F. Cooper, Jr., *Imaging Saturn: The Voyager flights to Saturn* (New York, 1983); David Swift, *Voyager tales: Personal views of the grand tour* (Reston, Va., 1997). On Magellan: Henry S. F. Cooper, Jr., *The evening star: Venus observed* (Baltimore, 1994). On Mars Global Surveyor: Lawrence Bergreen, *Voyage to Mars: NASA's search for life beyond Earth* (New York, 2000). On Pathfinder: Donna Shirley, *Managing Martians* (New York, 1998); Andrew Mishkin, *Sojourner: An insider's view of the Mars Pathfinder mission* (New York, 2003). On the DSN: Douglas J. Mudgway, *Uplink-downlink: A history of the Deep Space Network, 1957–1997* (Washington, D.C., 2001).

5. William H. McNeill, "Mythistory, or, truth, myth, history, and historians," *American Historical Review* 91 (1986): 1–10, on 2.

6. Stephen B. Johnson, *The secret of Apollo: Systems management in American and European space programs* (Baltimore, 2002).

7. On the relation between civil and military space programs: Paul B. Stares, *The militarization of space: U.S. policy, 1945–1984* (Ithaca, 1985); Smith, *Space Telescope;* Eric J. Chaisson, *The Hubble wars* (New York, 1994); Dwayne A. Day, "Not so black and white . . . :

The military and the Hubble Space Telescope," *Space Times* 34 (Mar.–Apr. 1995): 20–21; Day, "Invitation to struggle: The history of civilian-military relations in space," in John Logsdon, ed., *Exploring the unknown*, vol. 2, *External relations* (Washington, D.C., 1995), 233–56; William E. Burrows, *Deep black: Space espionage and national security* (New York, 1986); John Cloud and Keith C. Clarke, "Through a shutter darkly: The tangled relationships between civilian, military, and intelligence remote sensing in the early U.S. space program," in Judith Reppy, ed., *Secrecy and knowledge production* (Cornell University Peace Studies Program, Occasional Paper no. 23, 2000), 36–56.

8. Samuel P. Huntington, *The soldier and the state: The theory and politics of civil-military relations* (Cambridge, Mass., 1957); Morris Janowitz, *The professional soldier: A social and political portrait* (New York, 1960); Peter D. Feaver, *Armed servants: Agency, oversight, and civil-military relations* (Cambridge, Mass., 2003); Philip Gummett and Judith Reppy, eds., *The relations between defence and civil technologies* (Dordrecht, 1988). Some of the civil-military literature does address the degree of interaction at operational levels as well as military political influence.

9. E.g., Derek Bok, *Universities in the marketplace: The commercialization of higher education* (Princeton, 2003).

Chapter 1. The Inheritance

1. Judith R. Goodstein, *Millikan's school: A history of the California Institute of Technology* (New York, 1991), 156–64; Koppes, 1–17.

2. Koppes, 18–20; on wartime contracts, see, e.g., Daniel J. Kevles, *The physicists: The history of a scientific community in modern America* (Cambridge, 1987), 298; Stuart W. Leslie, *The cold war and American science: The military-industrial-academic complex at MIT and Stanford* (New York, 1993), 6.

3. Koppes, 18–29; Leslie, *Cold war*, 14–43; David H. DeVorkin, *Science with a vengeance: How the military created the U.S. space sciences after World War II* (New York, 1992); Michael Aaron Dennis, "'Our first line of defense': Two university laboratories in the postwar American state," *Isis* 85 (1994): 427–55; Peter J. Westwick, *The national labs: Science in an American system, 1947–1974* (Cambridge, Mass., 2003).

4. Koppes, 30–31; Iris Chang, *Thread of the Silkworm* (New York, 1995). Tsien stayed at Caltech until 1955, when he returned to China and played a crucial role in developing China's ICBM capability.

5. Koppes, 38–61. The army deployed Corporal battalions in Europe starting in 1956.

6. Stephen B. Johnson, *The secret of Apollo: Systems management in American and European space programs* (Baltimore, 2002), 81–92.

7. Koppes, 47–51, 66–70, 238.

8. Koppes, 78–82, von Kármán quote on 22.

9. Walter A. McDougall, *The heavens and the earth: A political history of the space age* (New York, 1985), 141–56, on 154; Koppes, 82–91.

10. Koppes, 94–106.

11. Johnson, *Secret*, 99–102; Koppes, 117–18.

12. Johnson, *Secret*, on 102; "Systems engineering in space exploration," lectures presented by JPL staff at Stanford in 1963 (NASA-JPL, 4657). See also Glenn E. Bugos, "Manufacturing certainty: Testing and program management for the F-4 Phantom II," *Social Studies of Science* 23 (1993): 265–300.

13. R. Cargill Hall, *Lunar impact: A history of Project Ranger* (Washington, D.C., 1977), 35–36, 180; Koppes, 106–8, 132; Johnson, *Secret,* 102–3.

14. Koppes, 126–29, 165–72; Johnson, *Secret,* 107–11.

15. Douglas J. Mudgway, *Uplink-downlink: A history of the Deep Space Network, 1957–1997* (Washington, D.C., 2001), 2–79; Craig Waff, "The road to the Deep Space Network," *IEEE spectrum* (Apr. 1993): 50–57.

16. Norm Haynes interview, 11 Apr. 2003; Solomon Golomb, interview by Jose Alonso, 1 Sept. 1992 (JPL archives); Andrew Viterbi, interview by Alonso, 3 and 29 Oct. 1991 (JPL archives); Viterbi, interview by David Morton, 29 Oct. 1999 (Institute of Electrical and Electronics Engineers [IEEE] History Center, Rutgers University).

17. Koppes, 106–10, 134–60.

18. Koppes, 20, 31–32, 134–49.

19. Goodstein, *Millikan's school,* 161–62, 168–77.

20. Simon Ramo, *The business of science: Winning and losing in the high-tech age* (New York, 1988), 36–114; Allen J. Scott, *Technopolis: High-technology industry and regional development in Southern California* (Berkeley, 1993); Mike Davis, *City of quartz: Excavating the future in Los Angeles* (New York, 1990), 120–21; Ann Markusen et al., *Rise of the gunbelt: The military remapping of industrial America* (Oxford, 1991).

21. Alex Roland, *Model research: The National Advisory Committee for Aeronautics, 1915–1958,* vol. 1 (Washington D.C., 1985), 242–47, 302; Joan Lisa Bromberg, *NASA and the space industry* (Baltimore, 1999), 16–44; Koppes, 96–97, 115–16, 145.

22. Koppes, 172–80; Johnson, *Secret,* 104–6.

23. Koppes, 215. Women comprised about 1 percent of engineers in the United States through the 1950s: Alice S. Rossi, "Barriers to the career choice of engineering, medicine, or science among American women," in Jacquelyn A. Mattfeld and Carol G. Van Aken, eds., *Women and the scientific professions* (Cambridge, Mass., 1965), 51–127, on 58; Margaret W. Rossiter, *Women scientists in America: Before affirmative action, 1940–1972* (Baltimore, 1995).

24. Koppes, 46–47.

25. T. Keith Glennan to R. Cargill Hall, 22 Mar. 1976 (JPL 142, 23/380); James van Allen, in "Voyage to the morning star," *Time* (8 Mar. 1963), 76–80, on 79.

26. Koppes, 119.

27. Koppes, 250.

28. Stephen G. Brush, *A history of modern planetary physics,* vol. 3, *Fruitful encounters: The origin of the solar system and of the moon from Chamberlin to Apollo* (Cambridge, 1996), 131–38; Ronald E. Doel, "The earth sciences and geophysics," in John Krige and Dominique Pestre, eds., *Science in the twentieth century* (Amsterdam, 1997), 391–416, on 396, 406.

29. Robert S. Kraemer, *Beyond the moon: A golden age of planetary exploration, 1971–1978* (Washington D.C., 2000), 44–61; Bruce Murray, *Journey into space: The first three decades of space exploration* (New York, 1989), 41–65; Koppes, 220–21.

30. Koppes, 182–83; see also Ronald E. Doel, *Solar system astronomy in America: Communities, patronage, and interdisciplinary science, 1920–1960* (Cambridge, 1996), 134–50; Brush, *Fruitful encounters,* 218–33.

31. Koppes, 121–22, 132–33, 150–51, 164.

32. Howard E. McCurdy, *Space and the American imagination* (Washington D.C., 1997).

33. Koppes, 100.

34. "Voyage to the morning star," *Time* (8 Mar. 1963), 76–80; Fred Felberg, "Floating to Venus," JPL Story, 18 Apr. 2002, JPL Library.

35. Koppes; Doel, *Solar system;* Joseph N. Tatarewicz, *Space technology and planetary astronomy* (Bloomington, 1990).

36. McDougall, *Heavens,* 407; Kevles, *Physicists,* 393–424; Pickering quote in Rae Goodell, *The visible scientists* (Boston, 1977), 43.

37. Paul B. Stares, *The militarization of space: U.S. policy, 1945–1984* (Ithaca, 1985), appendix; McDougall, *Heavens,* appendix.

38. McDougall, *Heavens,* 423; T. A. Heppenheimer, *The space shuttle decision: NASA's search for a reusable space vehicle* (Washington, D.C., 1999); Joseph J. Trento, *Prescription for disaster* (New York, 1987), 93–121.

39. Joan Hoff, "The presidency, the Congress, and the deceleration of the U.S. space program in the 1970s," in Roger D. Launius and Howard E. McCurdy, eds, *Spaceflight and the myth of presidential leadership* (Urbana, 1997), 92–132.

40. Koppes, 137, 222, 226–30; Glenn E. Bugos, *Atmosphere of freedom: Sixty years at the NASA Ames Research Center,* NASA SP-4314 (Washington, 2000), 86–97.

41. "Institutional assessment," 25 Sept. 1975 (JPL 142, 46/757); Pickering to Elmer Groo, 21 Oct. 1975 (JPL 8, 1/35); JPL visiting committee, notes, 29–30 Jan. 1976 (JPL 142, 64/965); NASA, "Catalog of center roles," April 1976 and, revised, Dec. 1976 (JPL 142, 46/759 and 760).

42. Roger D. Launius, "Foreword," in Kraemer, *Beyond the moon,* xiv. The "golden age" characterization is Kraemer's.

43. Johnson, *Secret;* McDougall, *Heavens,* 436–37; David R. Jardini, "Out of the blue yonder: The RAND Corporation's diversification into social welfare research, 1946–1968" (PhD diss., Carnegie Mellon University, 1996).

44. Koppes, 232–36; on JPL's contributions to centralized surveillance and control, cf. Davis, *City of quartz,* 250–53.

45. Harold Brown remarks at Pickering retirement, 26 Mar. 1976 (JPL 8, 1/40).

Chapter 2. Planetary Exploration Triumphant

1. Koppes, 242.

2. Bruce Murray, *Journey into space: The first three decades of space exploration* (New York, 1989), 45.

3. Dick Lloyd, "Pickering recalls JPL glory," *Pasadena Star News,* 25 Mar. 1976. "Dreamers and visionaries" in Murray, state of the lab, 20 Apr. 1982 (JPL 8, 10/119).

4. Murray, *Journey,* 62, 49, 68–69; on Sagan's speculations, Keay Davidson, *Carl Sagan: A life* (New York, 1999), 185.

5. Murray, *Journey,* 54, 99.

6. Murray, "Technology, technologists, and the future," keynote speech to National Telecommunications Conference, 6 Dec. 1977 (JPL 8, 3/64); David F. Salisbury, "Prophet of tomorrow's redirected technology: Bruce Murray foresees return to small scale," *Christian Science Monitor,* 3 Nov. 1976.

7. D. R. Fowler to Murray, 2 Jan. 1976 (JPL 8, 1/32).

8. M. A. Minovitch, "A method for determining interplanetary free-fall reconnaissance trajectories," JPL Technical Memo 312–130, 23 Aug. 1961 (JPL HC5–623); Minovitch to

Charles Kohlhase, 30 Oct. 1989 and 20 Feb. 1990 (JPL 105, 1/4); Norriss S. Hetherington, "Interplanetary travel and gravitational thrust," unpub. manuscript, 18 Aug. 1972, and responses in JPL HC5–623.

9. Flandro in David Swift, *Voyager tales: Personal views of the grand tour* (Reston, Va., 1997), 62–65.

10. William E. Burrows, *Exploring space: Voyages in the solar system and beyond* (New York, 1991), 263; Henry C. Dethloff and Ronald A. Schorn, *Voyager's grand tour* (Washington, D.C., 2003), chaps. 2–3; James E. Long, "To the outer planets," *Astronautics & aeronautics* (June 1969), 32–47; Burrows, *This new ocean*, 477–79; Schurmeier in Swift, *Voyager tales*, 106; Robert S. Kraemer, *Beyond the moon: A golden age of planetary exploration, 1971–1978* (Washington, 2000), 163–73.

11. Kraemer, *Beyond*, 173–83; Dethloff and Schorn, *Grand tour*, chap. 3. Cost estimate given as $250 million in John Casani, "Flight projects cost history," Mar. 1992 (JPL 165, 1/8), and in David Morrison, *Voyages to Saturn*, NASA SP-451 (Washington, D.C., 1982), 32; given as $350 million in Dethloff and Schorn.

12. Dethloff and Schorn, *Grand tour*, 58; Andrew J. Butrica, "Voyager: The grand tour of big science," in Pamela E. Mack, ed., *From engineering to big science*, NASA SP-4219 (Washington, D.C., 1998), 251–76, on 253–54.

13. Roger Bourke, in Swift, *Voyager tales*, 77; Charles Kohlhase, "Navigation systems overview," 16 Mar. 1973 (JPL 105, 1/7).

14. Kohlhase in Swift, *Voyager tales*, 95; Kohlhase, author interview, 12 July 2002; Bourke in Swift, *Voyager tales*, 79–80; Stone, "Voyager—Journey of a lifetime," JPL Story, 18 July 2002 (on Saturn and fiscal year), JPL library.

15. Murray, *Journey*, 136; Don Rea interview, 2 May 2002.

16. Stone, JPL Story; Burrows, *This new ocean: The story of the first space age* (New York, 1998), 499.

17. Lane quoted in Burrows, *This new ocean*, 499.

18. Dethloff and Schorn, *Grand tour*, 72–74; Schurmeier in Swift, *Voyager tales*, 111; Kraemer, *Beyond*, 184.

19. Dethloff and Schorn, *Grand tour*, 78–82; Casani in Swift, *Voyager tales*, 116–17.

20. E.g., Burrows, *This new ocean*, 481.

21. Dethloff and Schorn, *Grand tour*, 99–100; Kraemer, *Beyond*, 182–83; Schurmeier in Swift, *Voyager tales*, 106–9.

22. Mariner Jupiter/Saturn 1977, Mission and Science Requirements Document, vol. 1, 1 Aug. 1976, JPL PD 618–51 rev. c (JPL 105, 1/14).

23. Casani to senior staff, 4 Mar. 1977, Casani to EC, 21 Jan. 1977, and R. L. Mills, proposed names for MJS77 (JPL 142, 60/994).

24. Casani to EC, 21 Jan. 1977; Burrows, *This new ocean*, 461–462.

25. Dethloff and Schorn, *Grand tour*, 39–40, 82, 88.

26. Raymond L. Heacock, "The Voyager spacecraft," *Proceedings of the Institute of Mechanical Engineers* 194 (1980): 211–24, on 218–19; Henry Cox in Swift, *Voyager tales*, 247; Dethloff and Schorn, *Grand tour*, 81; Morrison, *Voyages to Saturn*, 40.

27. Schurmeier and Thomas Gavin in Swift, *Voyager tales*, 107 and 250–51; Dethloff and Schorn, *Grand tour*, 71.

28. Koppes, 219; Burrows, *Exploring space*, 200.

29. Dethloff and Schorn, *Grand tour*, 84, 88–89.

30. See, e.g., the 33 boxes (11 cubic feet) in JPL 44.

31. Thomas Gavin in Swift, *Voyager tales*, on 229–30, 250–53, on 253.

32. Casani and Gavin in ibid., 119 and 253.

33. Heacock in ibid., 150; Murray, *Journey,* 145–46.

34. Heacock in Swift, *Voyager tales,* 150; Murray, *Journey,* 145–46.

35. Heacock in Swift, *Voyager tales,* 150; Murray, *Journey,* 147–48; Kohlhase interview, 12 July 2002.

36. David Morrison and Jane Samz, *Voyage to Jupiter,* NASA SP-439 (Washington, D.C., 1980), 52–56; Kohlhase in Swift, *Voyager tales,* 97–98.

37. Morrison and Samz, *Voyage to Jupiter,* 50–52; Murray, *Journey,* 152–55.

38. NASA, "Jet Propulsion Laboratory performance evaluation for the period October 1, 1977 to September 30, 1978," 7 June 1979 (JPL 142, 39/655); Heacock in Swift, *Voyager tales,* 150.

39. JPL performance evaluation (ibid.); Murray, state of the lab, 7 Apr. 1978 (JPL 150, 9/105); Murray, director's letter, 12 May 1978 (JPL 8, 4/69); R. J. Parks to senior staff, 8 June 1978 (JPL 150, 6/68); Murray, *Journey,* 152–53; Robert Parks and Peter Lyman in Swift, *Voyager tales,* 123–29 and 138–41.

40. Lyman and Richard Laeser in Swift, *Voyager tales,* 142–43 and 176–77; and Laeser, author interview, 12 Dec. 2001.

41. JPL performance evaluation; JPL mini-retreat summary, 13 Sept. 1977 (JPL 150, 20/238); Laeser in Swift, *Voyager tales,* 176.

42. Murray and Gavin in Swift, *Voyager tales,* 210 and 253; Morrison and Samz, *Voyage to Jupiter,* 50.

43. Jurrie van der Woude, Murray, and Stone in Swift, *Voyager tales,* 394, 210, and 57.

44. Scholarly compilations include *Journal of Geophysical Research* 86 (1981): 8123–41, and 88 (1983): 8625–9018; A. J. Dessler, ed., *Physics of the Jovian magnetosphere* (Cambridge, 1983); Michael Belton, Robert A. West, and Jürgen Rahe, eds., *Time variable phenomena in the Jovian system* (Washington, D.C., 1989); and Tom Gehrels and Mildred Shapley Mathews, *Saturn* (Tucson, 1984) (the last three include Pioneer results). Popular accounts: Morrison and Samz, *Voyage to Jupiter;* Morrison, *Voyages to Saturn;* Mark Washburn, *Distant encounters: The exploration of Jupiter and Saturn* (New York, 1983); Henry S. F. Cooper, Jr., *Imaging Saturn: The Voyager flights to Saturn* (New York, 1983).

45. Stone, interview by Dethloff and Schorn; Morrison and Samz, *Voyage to Jupiter,* 86; Washburn, *Distant encounters,* 115–17.

46. Stone in Swift, *Voyager tales,* 50; Morrison and Samz, *Voyage to Jupiter,* 87; Washburn, *Distant encounters,* 145–46.

47. Stone, interview by Dethloff and Schorn; Murray, *Journey,* 136.

48. Dethloff and Schorn, *Grand tour,* 160–61, 185–86; Morrison and Samz, *Voyage to Jupiter,* 79; Washburn, *Distant encounters,* 109–10, 208–11; Morrison, *Voyages to Saturn,* 146–47.

49. Dethloff and Schorn, *Grand tour,* 176–85; Morrison, *Voyages to Saturn,* 50–90; Cooper, *Imaging Saturn;* Washburn, *Distant encounters,* 189–91, 204–5; Murray, *Journey,* 156–57. On Jupiter's ring, cf. Stephen G. Brush, *Fruitful encounters: The origin of the solar system and of the moon from Chamberlin to Apollo* (Cambridge, 1996), 168–69.

50. Morrison and Samz, *Voyage to Jupiter,* 122–30; Morrison, *Voyages to Saturn,* 139–43; Washburn, *Distant encounters,* 147–49, 193–94; Cooper, *Imaging Saturn,* 142–44, 151–52.

51. Dethloff and Schorn, *Grand tour,* 147–50; cf. Ronald E. Doel, *Solar system astronomy in America: Communities, patronage, and interdisciplinary science, 1920–1960* (Cambridge, 1996).

52. *Science* 204 (1 June 1979): 945–1008; *Science* 212 (10 Apr. 1981): 159–243; *Science* 215 (29 Jan. 1982): 499–594; *Nature* 280 (30 Aug. 1979): 725–806; *Nature* 292 (20 Aug. 1981): 675–755; *Journal of Geophysical Research* 86 (1981): 8123–8841; *Journal of Geophysical Research* 88 (1983): 8625–9018.

53. Stone, interview by Dethloff and Schorn.

54. Thomas F. Gieryn, "The (cold) fusion of science, mass media, and politics," in Gieryn, *Cultural boundaries of science* (Chicago, 1999), 183–232; Bruce C. Lewinstein, "Cold fusion and hot history," *Osiris* 7 (1992): 135–63.

55. Frank Colella, interview with Don Bane, 11 May 1988, JPL archives; Horowitz quoted in Davidson, *Sagan*, on 280; on Mercury moon, Murray, *Journey*, 119, and Washburn, *Distant encounters*, 125; for Viking press accounts, see David Shaw, "Science news: Experts see distortions," *Los Angeles Times*, 13 Jan. 1977, and JPL news clips for late July 1976.

56. Robert C. Cowen, "Physics as a media event," *Christian Science Monitor*, 17 Oct. 1979; Andrew Pickering, *Constructing quarks: A sociological history of particle physics* (Chicago, 1984), 343–44.

57. Stone in Swift, *Voyager tales*, 40.

58. Frank Colella interview, 26 Feb. 2002.

59. Colella interview; see also Washburn, *Distant encounters*, 119; Cooper, *Imaging Saturn*, 59, 81; and Joel Davis, *Flyby: The interplanetary odyssey of Voyager 2* (New York, 1987), 55–57.

60. Stone in Swift, 39–41; Stone, author interview, 23 Oct. 2003.

61. Colella interview.

62. David E. Nye, *Image worlds: Corporate identities at General Electric, 1890–1930* (Cambridge, Mass., 1985), esp. 16–17; Marcel C. LaFollette, *Making science our own: Public images of science, 1910–1955* (Chicago, 1990), 53–61; Carol L. Rogers, "The practitioner in the middle," in Sharon M. Friedman, Sharon Dunwoody, and Carol L. Rogers, eds., *Scientists and journalists: Reporting science as news* (New York, 1986), 42–54; Sharon Dunwoody and Michael Ryan, "Public information persons as mediators between scientists and journalists," *Journalism Quarterly* 60 (1983): 647–56; Dorothy Nelkin, *Selling science: How the press covers science and technology* (New York, 1987), 132–53.

63. Colella interview.

64. James L. Baughman, *The republic of mass culture: Journalism, filmmaking, and broadcasting in America since 1941,* 2nd ed. (Baltimore, 1997), 92–98, 108–15, 158–170; Sharon M. Friedman, "The journalist's world," in Friedman, Dunwoody, and Rogers, eds., *Scientists and journalists*, 17–41, on 36–37.

65. Morrison, *Voyages to Saturn*, 115; Colella interview; Kohlhase interview, 12 July 2002.

66. R. B. Phillips (quote) to Terhune, 16 Mar. 1976 (JPL 142, 44/720); Colella interview.

67. John C. Burnham, *How superstition won and science lost: Popularizing science and health in the United States* (New Brunswick, N.J., 1987), 176; LaFollette, *Making science,* 46–47; Dunwoody, "The science writing inner club: A communication link between science and the lay public," in Friedman, Dunwoody, and Rogers, eds., *Scientists and journalists,* 155–69.

68. Burrows, *This new ocean,* 497–98.

69. "The science boom," *Newsweek* (17 Sept. 1979), 104–7; Richard Saltus, "Media gearing up to serve new wave of science fans," *Los Angeles Herald Examiner,* 15 Oct. 1979; Burnham, *How superstition won,* 171, 178–79.

70. K. M. Dawson to Murray, 30 June 1977 (JPL 142, 44/723); Earl C. Gottschalk, Jr., "With the devil's work done, film makers try cosmic capers," *Wall Street Journal,* 28

June 1977; Ben Bova, "Why Hollywood finds profits out of this world," *New York Times* editorial, 13 Nov. 1977.

71. On Star Trek fans and NASA, see Burrows, *This new ocean,* 522–23; Howard E. McCurdy, *Space and the American imagination* (Washington, 1997), 154; Constance Penley, *NASA/Trek: Popular science and sex in America* (New York, 1997), 15–20.

72. Mills, Proposed names for MJS77; Dethloff and Schorn, *Grand tour,* 4–5.

73. Dethloff and Schorn, *Grand tour,* 69, 102; Kohlhase interview, 12 July 2002.

74. Murray, *Journey,* 61–63; Ray Bradbury et al., *Mars and the mind of man* (New York, 1973).

75. Jerry Pournelle to James Fletcher, 21 July 1976 and 1 Sept. 1976 (JPL 142, 58/958).

76. David Gelman, "Seeking other worlds," *Newsweek* (15 Aug. 1977), 46–53; Davidson, *Sagan,* 318–40.

77. Glenn E. Bugos, *Atmosphere of freedom: Sixty years at the NASA Ames Research Center* (Washington D.C., 2000), 90–94; Davidson, *Sagan,* 163, 241–43.

78. Dethloff and Schorn, *Grand tour,* 89.

79. Carl Sagan et al., *Murmurs of Earth: The Voyager interstellar record* (New York, 1978), 9–12, 17, 40–43. See also Davidson, *Sagan,* 303–10.

80. Brian Duff to NASA deputy administrator, 25 Nov. 1980 (JPL 150, 6/68); Colella to Murray, 17 Dec. 1980 (JPL 8, 8/101).

81. Murray to JPL Advisory Council, 31 Aug. 1981 (JPL 8, 9/110).

82. Washburn, *Distant encounters,* 140.

83. All quoted in Morrison, *Voyages to Saturn,* 93.

84. Robert W. Smith, *The Space Telescope: A study of NASA, science, technology, and politics* (Cambridge, 1989), 259–313; Howard E. McCurdy, *Inside NASA: High technology and organizational change in the U.S. space program* (Baltimore, 1993).

85. Unidentified engineer quoted by William Shipley, in Swift, *Voyager tales,* 235.

86. Shipley in Swift, *Voyager tales,* 234–35.

87. Quoted in Murray, *Journey,* 101.

Chapter 3. Planetary Exploration in Extremis

1. Joint NASA Council/Center Directors meeting, 2–3 Dec. 1980 (JPL 150, 5/51); Hans Mark comments at NAS colloquium, 26–27 Oct. 1981 (JPL 150, 5/49).

2. J. R. Bruman memo on Salyut program, 27 Feb. 1978 (JPL 142, 52/851); D. G. Rea to Murray, 28 Apr. 1977 (JPL 142, 55/902); Murray to Noel Hinners, 8 July 1977 (JPL 142, 23/401); Gordon H. Pettengill to Thomas A. Mutch, 11 June 1980 (JPL 105, 1/17A).

3. William K. Hartmann to Murray, 30 July 1976 (JPL 142, 44/723); Arthur Unger, "Live from Mars—after this message," *Christian Science Monitor,* 23 July 1976; "The Viking miracle," *New York Times* editorial, 26 July 1976; Bella Stumbo, "Mars probe stirs the blood and brings a yawn," *Los Angeles Times,* 19 July 1976.

4. "No Mars life may curtail planet probes," *Pasadena Star News,* 5 July 1976; David Shaw, "Science news: Experts see distortions," *Los Angeles Times,* 13 Jan. 1977.

5. George C. Wilson, "House panel plans inquiry into Carter's space program," *Washington Post,* 18 Dec. 1977.

6. Jonathan Spivak, "Apathy is NASA's biggest foe," *Wall Street Journal,* 25 Feb. 1977; Gregg Kilday, "The space shot as a sham," *Los Angeles Times,* 13 Oct. 1976.

7. Bruce Murray, *Journey into space: The first three decades of space exploration* (New York, 1989), 197; Robert S. Kraemer, *Beyond the moon: A golden age of planetary exploration, 1971–1978* (Washington D.C., 2000), 183; shuttle launch statistics from Bette R. Janson and Eleanor H. Ritchie, *Astronautics and aeronautics, 1979–1984: A chronology,* NASA SP-4024 (Washington, D.C., 1990).

8. V. L. Melikan to Colella, 5 May 1978 (JPL 150, 8/94); *Aerospace Daily,* 25 Nov. 1981.

9. Burrows, *This new ocean,* 335–36, 437, David Helfand quote from 1989 on 336; Linda Neumann Ezell, *NASA historical data book,* vol. 3 (Washington D.C., 1988), 132.

10. Robert W. Smith, *The Space Telescope: A study of NASA, science, technology, and politics* (Cambridge, 1989); Eric J. Chaisson, *The Hubble wars* (New York, 1994), 27–29.

11. Pamela E. Mack, *Viewing the Earth: The social construction of the Landsat satellite system* (Cambridge, Mass., 1990).

12. NASA Space and Earth Science Advisory Committee, "The crisis in space and earth science," Nov. 1986 (JPL 198, 12/163).

13. "Outlook for Space: A synopsis," Jan. 1976 (JPL 142, 37/638).

14. Noel Hinners, interview by Robert Smith and Joseph Tatarewicz, 17 Oct. 1984, NASM; Memphis Norman, interview by Robert W. Smith, 6 and 12 Sept. 1984, NASM.

15. A. G. W. Cameron to James Fletcher, 23 Nov. 1976 (JPL 142, 31/544); Hinners, interview by Smith and Tatarewicz.

16. *NASA Historical Data Book,* vol. 3, 140, and NASA Space and Earth Science Advisory Committee, "Crisis in space and earth science."

17. Graph of JPL flight projects staffing, 9 June 1981 (JPL 150, 2/22); Robert Kraemer to Gerald Wasserburg, 27 July 1976 (JPL 142, 35/591); J. James draft memo on "Revitalization of the planetary exploration program," Dec. 1976 (JPL 142, 55/909).

18. Murray to John Naugle, 27 Aug. 1976 (JPL 142, 26/453).

19. Murray, "Planetary exploration and the U.S.: What's the future?" 15 Aug. 1976 (JPL 142, 37/627); Murray, *Journey,* 244–45; David F. Salisbury, "After Mars, next stop Titan?" *Christian Science Monitor,* 4 Aug. 1976.

20. Murray, *Journey,* 244.

21. Murray, remarks to JPL managers, 11 June 1976 (JPL 216, 2/24), and "Planetary exploration and the U.S.: What's the future?" 15 Aug. 1976 (JPL 142, 37/627).

22. Murray, remarks to JPL managers, 6 Aug. 1976 (JPL 216, 2/26); Frank Colella interview, 26 Feb. 2002.

23. Purple pigeon media response, July 1976 (JPL 8, 2/47); NASA Office of Space Science, five-year plan, c. 1976 (JPL 150, 17/210); Jesse Moore to Murray et al., 9 Aug. 1976 (JPL 142, 8/122).

24. Director's letter, 8 Dec. 1976 (JPL 8, 2/52), and Murray remarks to JPL managers, 14 Dec. 1976 (JPL 216, 2/28).

25. Murray, *Journey,* 189–92.

26. Murray, *Journey,* 193–94; Smith, *Space Telescope,* 184; *Washington Post* editorial, "On to Jupiter," 18 July 1977.

27. *Congressional Record* (19 July 1977), H7339–7355; Murray, *Journey,* 194.

28. W. Petit to G. Robillard, 1 June 1977 (JPL 142, 32/553).

29. Murray, state of the lab, 7 Apr. 1978 (JPL 150, 9/105).

30. George Alexander, "Space shuttle problems will alter Jupiter probe," *Los Angeles Times,* 6 Sept. 1979; "Stage constraints curb Galileo options," *AW&ST* (10 Sept. 1979).

31. Richard Saltus, "A hard look: Space exploration facing a gloomy decade in '80s," *San Francisco Examiner,* 27 Dec. 1979; Richard Kerr, "Planetary science on the brink again," *Science* (14 Dec. 1979): 1288–89.

32. Rea to Murray, 4 Jan. 1979 (JPL 8, 5/77).

33. K. Zebb to W. H. Bayley et al., 9 July 1976 (JPL 150, 17/208); Hinners to Murray, 26 June 1978 (JPL 150, 9/113); George Alexander, "'Solar polar' spectacular waits in wings," *Los Angeles Times,* 8 Jan. 1978.

34. SSEEC, 31 Mar. 1980 (JPL 150, 4/46); graph of JPL flight projects staffing, 9 June 1981 (JPL 150, 2/22).

35. Murray, handwritten notes on COMPLEX panel discussion, 20 Sept. 1976 (JPL 142, 8/124).

36. James and N. Haynes to A. J. Calio, 30 Nov. 1976, and James to Murray, with proposed draft of Murray to Hinners, 22 July 1977 (JPL 142, 27/463); Mutch, recommendations of Mars Science Working Group, 16 Mar. 1977 (JPL 142, 27/464); "1984 Mars mission, briefing to NASA cost review committee," 23 May 1977 (JPL 142, 27/466).

37. "Future exploration of Mars," briefing to C. C. Kraft, 2 May 1978, Louis Friedman to Murray and C. Terhune, 3 May 1978, and Friedman to James et al., 4 May 1978 (JPL 198, 9/132); Hinners ("or nothing") to Victor C. Clarke, 13 July 1978 (NASA-OSS); John Noble Wilford, "Space scientists, at seminar, urge new unmanned missions to Mars," *New York Times,* 18 Jan. 1979; Kraemer ("delusions"), *Beyond the moon,* 223.

38. On Galileo: Hinners to Murray, 27 June 1978 (JPL 150, 8/100).

39. "Venus Orbital Imaging Radar mission," July 1979 (JPL 8, 6/84); Mutch to Murray, 7 Aug. 1979 (NASA-Magellan, 5180).

40. SSEEC, 17 Aug. 1981 (JPL 150, 4/46).

41. James to Murray and Terhune, 24 Jan. 1977, and Friedman to Murray et al., 8 Feb. 1977 (JPL 142, 57/945).

42. John Logsdon, "Missing Halley's comet: The politics of big science," *Isis* 80 (1989): 254–80.

43. Murray, *Journey,* 246–47; Kraemer, *Beyond the moon,* 226; Logsdon, "Comet," 258.

44. Comet Halley Science Working Group, "Scientific rationale and strategies for a first comet mission," July 1977, NASA TM-78420 (JPL 142, 21/359); Terhune to senior staff, 22 June 1977, and ad hoc SEP/SAIL panel to Murray and Terhune, 20 July 77 (JPL 142, 22/370); Murray, *Journey,* 249–51; Logsdon, "Comet," 262.

45. C. R. Gates memo to file, "Very long range planning study," 8 Feb. 1979 (JPL 142, 58/949); "Space Horizons Study," 29 Mar. 1979 (JPL 8, 6/80).

46. Logsdon, "The survival crisis of the U.S. solar system exploration program," unpub. manuscript, June 1989. I thank Professor Logsdon for a copy of this essay.

47. *Congressional Record* (18 June 1980), H5165; Murray, "Special status report to JPL," 26 Feb. 1981 (JPL 150, 9/105); Andrew Stofan to Murray, 11 May 1981 (JPL 150, 4/43); *Aerospace Daily,* 16 Sept. 1981; SSEEC, 28 Sept. 1981 (JPL 150, 4/46).

48. Murray statement to House Subcommittee on Space Science and Technology, 21 Mar. 1981 (JPL 150, 4/35).

49. R. A. Frosch, statement to House Subcommittee on Appropriations, 28 Nov. 1979 (JPL 150, 8/100); SSEEC minutes, 3 and 10 Dec. 1979 and 3 Jan. 1980 (JPL 150, 4/46); Stofan to Murray, 30 Jan. 1981 (JPL 150, 4/42); Murray, *Journey,* 204–9.

50. Murray, *Journey,* 262–70; Logsdon, "Comet"; James Beggs to G. A. Keyworth, 16 Sept. 1981 (JPL 198, 10/145).

51. Murray statement to House Subcommittee on Space Science and Technology, 21 Mar. 1981 (JPL 150, 4/35); Mark to Murray, 23 May 1981 (JPL 8, 107).

52. POP 80–2, 30 June 1980 (JPL 150, 4/41).

53. Murray interview, 15 Jan. 03.

54. Murray to George F. Will, 11 Sept. 1981 (JPL 8, 9/111).

55. Beggs to Keyworth, 16 Sept. 1981, and Beggs to Keyworth, 17 Aug. 1981 (JPL 198, 10/145); Logsdon, "Comet," 278–79; Murray, *Journey*, 272–75.

56. Murray, midyear review, 1 Dec. 1981 (JPL 198, 1/2).

57. Murray to Beggs, 12 Oct. 1981 (JPL 150, 8/100).

58. Thomas O'Toole, "NASA weighs abandoning Voyager," *Washington Post,* 7 Oct. 1981, and George Alexander, "Planned NASA budget stirs rumors," *Los Angeles Times,* 9 Oct. 1981.

59. Logsdon, "Crisis," 13–14.

60. Beggs to Stockman, 29 Sept. 1981, and Beggs in *AW&ST* (24 June 1981), both quoted in Logsdon, "Crisis," 15.

61. Murray, director's letter, 12 Oct. 1981 and midyear review memo, 17 Nov. 1981 (JPL 216, 1/2).

62. Philip J. Hilts, "Science board to advise president proposed," *Washington Post,* 2 Dec. 1981; Alton K. Marsh, "Adviser urges shuttle emphasis," *AW&ST* (14 Dec. 1981): 16–18.

63. Quoted in Logsdon, "Crisis," 26.

64. Mark, "New enterprises in space," *Bulletin of the American Academy of Arts and Sciences* 28:4 (1975), quoted in Logsdon, "Crisis," on 19.

65. Mark to Thomas Young, 2 Mar. 1977 (JPL 142, 30/516).

66. Mark and Milton Silveira, "Notes on long-range planning," Aug. 1981 (JPL 198, 11/153).

67. M. Mitchell Waldrop, "Planetary science *in extremis,*" *Science* 214 (18 Dec. 1981); "Washington roundup," *AW&ST* (7 Dec. 1981): 17.

68. Logsdon, "Crisis."

69. K. Zebb to F. E. Goddard et al., 6 Aug. 1976 (JPL 150, 17/209); Friedman to Columbus team et al., 10 Dec. 1976, and Friedman and K. L. Atkins to J. N. James and C. R. Gates, 2 Aug. 1976 (JPL 142, 42/704); Friedman to V. Melikan, 2 Sept. 1976 (JPL 142, 9/148); Murray, *Journey*, 248–49.

70. Murray, *Journey*, 249n.

71. Joe Allen to Murray, 17 May 1977, with note added at top from Bill Porter's office (JPL 142, 32/560).

72. Petit to Robillard, 1 June 1977 (JPL 142, 32/553).

73. Mark to Murray, 26 Sept. 1975 (JPL 8, 1/34); Kerr, "On the brink."

74. Murray, *Journey*, appendix; Logsdon, "Crisis," 31.

75. Murray, talk at AIAA Global Technology 2000, 6 May 1980 (JPL 8, 7/94).

76. Daniel H. Herman (quote) to C. T. Russell, 14 May 1979, and Hinners to Clarke, 13 July 1978 (NASA-OSS); Herman in Comet Halley Science Working Group, meeting notes, 25–26 Jan. 1977 (JPL 142, 21/359).

77. Mary Scranton to Murray, 27 Oct. 1980 (JPL 198, 24/325).

78. Murray, *Journey*, 266.

79. Stanley R. Rawn, Jr., to George Bush, 13 Nov. 1980 (JPL 8, 8/100), and Rawn to James A. Baker III, 5 Feb. 1981 (JPL 216, 1/13); Murray, *Journey*, 267.

80. Murray to Edwin Meese III, 20 January 1981 (JPL 8, 8/102).

81. Baker to Rawn, 5 Mar. 1981, Meese to Murray, 11 Mar. 1981, in JPL Advisory Council, 9–10 Apr. 1981 (JPL 216, 1/13); Murray, *Journey,* 270.

82. See chronology in JPL Advisory Council, 9–10 Apr. 1981 (JPL 216, 1/13).

83. JPL Advisory Council, 9–10 Apr. 1981 (JPL 216, 1/13); Colella interview.

84. Murray oral history, CIT archives, 139; Murray interview, 15 Jan. 2003.

85. Sens. Strom Thurmond and Alan Cranston in *Congressional Record—Senate* (17 and 25 Nov. 1980).

86. Edmund G. (Pat) Brown, "Budget cuts could abort U.S. space research," *Los Angeles Times,* 23 Apr. 1981; George Will, "Columbia—The gem of the U.S. spirit," *Los Angeles Times,* 16 Apr. 1981; John Noble Wilford, "Space program faces hurdles despite cheers for Columbia," *New York Times,* 19 Apr. 1981; "Flying cathedrals," *Wall Street Journal,* 15 Apr. 1981.

87. "Our new, spaced-out governor," *Los Angeles Times* editorial, 5 Aug. 1977; Joseph Lelyveld, "Jerry Brown's space program," *New York Times Magazine* (17 July 1977).

88. *Aerospace Daily,* 8 Mar. 1982; Miles Beller, "Q&A" with Gingrich, *Los Angeles Herald Examiner,* 13 Apr. 1982.

89. Roger D. Launius and Howard E. McCurdy, "Epilogue: Beyond NASA exceptionalism," in Launius and McCurdy, eds., *Spaceflight and the myth of the presidential leadership* (Urbana, Ill., 1997), 221–50, on 234–40.

90. NBC News poll results, in Laurily Epstein to Louis Friedman, 30 Nov. 1981 (JPL 150, 11/146).

91. Goldberger to Walter Burke, 24 July 1981 (JPL 150, 5/51).

92. Goldberger to Ronald Reagan, 2 Oct. 1981, attached to Goldberger to William French Smith, 2 Oct. 1981, and Arnold Beckman to Meese, 5 Oct. 1981 (JPL 150, 12/163).

93. Murray to Beckman, 17 Nov. 1981, and Meese to Beckman, 17 Nov. 1981 (JPL 150, 3/24); Murray to Meese, 10 Dec. 1981 (JPL 150, 8/100); Scranton to Goldberger, 16 Dec. 1981, and Murray to Beckman, 17 Dec. 1981 (JPL 8, 9/115); Baker quoted in Logsdon, "Crisis," 37.

94. Murray to Keyworth, 15 Dec. 1981 (JPL 150, 12/168); *Aerospace Daily,* 21 Dec. 1981; Logsdon, "Crisis," 37–38; John Casani to Galileo review board, 6 Jan. 1982 (JPL 150, 8/100).

95. Murray, "Planetary exploration—evolution for a future," talk at AAS, Division of Planetary Science annual meeting, 14 Oct. 1980 (JPL 150, 11/141).

96. Murray oral history, CIT archives, 77, 141.

97. Murray, "Planetary exploration."

98. Murray, "Special status report to JPL," 26 Feb. 1981, and state of the lab, 2 Apr. 1981 (JPL 150, 9/105).

99. Murray, "Planetary exploration."

100. NASA, JPL performance evaluation for FY81, draft Dec. 1981 (JPL 150, 3/32); Casani interview, 9 Apr. 2004; Murray oral history, CIT archives, 140–41.

101. Quoted in Mark Washburn, *Distant encounters: The exploration of Jupiter and Saturn* (New York, 1983), 222.

102. Logsdon, "Crisis," 28–32.

103. NBC News poll results, 30 Nov. 1981.

Chapter 4. External Relations and the Internal Environment

1. Pickering remarks to JPL section managers, Feb. 1976 (JPL 142, 8/131); Murray inaugural speech, 2 Apr. 1976 (JPL 216, 2/23).

2. Koppes, 236–39; Report of the ad hoc study group on JPL/campus interactions [orange report], part 1, 2 Apr. 1976 (JPL 173, 3/35).

3. Orange report, part 2.

4. Orange report, part 1.

5. Ibid.

6. Ibid.

7. R. W. Davies, "Where to bite the orange?" c. Apr. 1976 (JPL 173, 3/37).

8. Davies, "Bite."

9. Murray remarks in faculty minutes, 9 June 1976, and Harold Brown to R. Vogt and Murray, 10 June 1976 (JPL 173, 3/38).

10. W. H. Padgham to Murray, 20 May 1976 (JPL 142, 7/104).

11. Ray Owen to Vogt, 14 Aug. 1978 (JPL 150, 1/12); M. L. Goldberger inaugural address, Nov. 1978 (JPL 8, 5/75); Murray in faculty minutes, 9 June 1976, and Brown to Vogt and Murray, 10 June 1976 (JPL 173, 3/38); faculty board minutes, 15 Nov. 1976 (JPL 8, 2/51).

12. Murray midyear report, 17 Oct. 1977 (JPL 216, 2/32); W. Victor to senior staff, 6 Mar. 1980 (JPL 150, 11/144).

13. Walt Victor to JPL senior staff, 5 Nov. 1979 (JPL 150, 2/14), and Victor to EC, 18 Mar. 1980 (JPL 150, 2/16).

14. Director's letter, 30 Sept. 1977 (JPL 8, 3/61), and Murray to senior staff, 24 Mar. 1978 (JPL 150, 8/103).

15. "Proposal to establish two upper-level scientist grades at JPL," 8 Aug. 1978 (JPL 8, 4/72).

16. Caltech/JPL cost comparison, Sept. 1977 (NASA-JPL, 4655).

17. Orange report, part 1.

18. D. R. Fowler, "Commentary on proposed resolution," 18 Feb. 1970 (JPL 142, 5/76).

19. Caltech/JPL comparison.

20. Peter J. Westwick, *The national labs: Science in an American system, 1947–1974* (Cambridge, Mass., 2003), 43–57; Stuart W. Leslie, *The cold war and American science: The military-industrial-academic complex at MIT and Stanford* (New York, 1993); Rebecca S. Lowen, *Creating the cold war university: The transformation of Stanford* (Berkeley, 1997), 177–86.

21. F. Felberg and K. Zebb, "Report on discussions at several universities and laboratories," 17 Dec. 1975 (JPL 142, 6/93).

22. Goldberger to Murray, 9 June 81, and Murray to Goldberger, 10 June 1981 (JPL 8, 9/108).

23. Murray oral history, CIT archives, 147.

24. Roger Geiger, *Research and relevant knowledge: American research universities since World War II* (Oxford, 1993), 243–46, 310–11.

25. Koppes, 146–49.

26. Donald Fowler to Allan Burke, 21 Feb. 1978 (NASA-JPL, 16151); Fowler to EC et al., 9 May 1978 (JPL 150, 1/11); Murray, state of the lab, 4 Apr. 1979 (JPL 150, 9/105).

27. NASA Management Instruction 1410.3B, 2 Dec. 1974; on lobbying, Joe Allen to Murray, 17 May 1977 (JPL 142, 32/560).

28. "Evaluation of Caltech's proposed increase in fee," including justification by Allan Burke, 24 Apr. 1975, "JPL fee," c. 1976, and John Naugle to Alan Lovelace, 23 Nov. 1977 (NASA-JPL, 16150); Fowler to E. F. Morriss, 12 May 1976 (JPL 142, 10/167).

29. NASA announcement, 1 Aug. 1979 (NASA-JPL, 4649); Fred Felberg to Murray, 2 Mar. 1982 (JPL 198, 1/4); Brent Bennett interview, 18 Apr. 2001.

30. Charles Pellerin, interview by Robert Smith, 1 Aug. 1983, NASM.

31. Briefing memo for Goldberger on MOU revision, 28 Mar. 1978 (JPL 198, 8/121); Koppes, 237.

32. Fowler, "Items for discussion with NASA," 25 July 1978 (JPL 198, 8/121); Naugle to Lovelace, 22 Nov. 1977, NASA-CIT MOU, 11 Dec. 1968, and "Guidelines for NASA work for non-NASA users under contract NAS7–100," 27 May 1975 (NASA-JPL, 16142); H. Schurmeier and G. Robillard to Fowler, 5 July 1978 (JPL 150, 20/243).

33. Ray Kline to Naugle, 26 July 1978 (NASA-JPL, 16142); Fowler, "Compilation of perceived problems or needs," 13 July 1978 (JPL 198, 8/121), and Schurmeier and Robillard to Fowler, 5 July 1978 (JPL 150, 20/243).

34. Fowler, "Questions concerning changes made by NASA," 15 Nov. 1978, Fowler to Murray, 29 Nov. 1978, and Murray to Naugle, 29 Nov. 1978 (JPL 198, 8/122); Ray Kline to Naugle, 25 Oct. 1978, and MOU revised by NASA, draft 8 Nov. 1978 (NASA-JPL, 16142); NASA-CIT MOU annotated for FY79, 21 Sept. 1979 (JPL 150, 5/50).

35. J. Garcia, 13 Jan. 1978, and J. Horvath, 17 Jan. 1978, memos on JPL contract renewal (NASA-JPL, 16151); John Pierce to Murray, 9 Jan. 1979 (JPL 8, 5/77); Murray to Lew Allen, 30 June 1982 (JPL 8, 10/122).

36. W. H. Bayley to EC, 3 Dec. 1976 (JPL 150, 25/234); draft performance evaluations for FY74 (JPL 150, 3/29), FY77 (JPL 150, 3/30); FY79 (JPL 150, 3/31), FY80 (JPL 142, 39/658), and FY81 (JPL 150, 3/32).

37. Fowler to EC et al., 9 May 1978 (JPL 150, 1/11).

38. Alex Roland, *Model research: The National Advisory Committee for Aeronautics, 1915–1958,* vol. 1, NASA-SP-4103 (Washington, D.C., 1985); Joan Lisa Bromberg, *NASA and the space industry* (Baltimore, 1999), 30–31.

39. Bromberg, *Space industry,* 18–25; Cummings quoted in Koppes, 96–97.

40. Brooks T. Morris to Pickering, 15 May 1967 (JPL 150, 1/3).

41. Albert Wheelon interview, 13 June 2002.

42. Aerospace firms employed more than 300,000 in Southern California by the 1970s; the missile and space industry alone, apart from aviation, employed about 150,000 in the United States, 60 percent of them white-collar. Allen J. Scott, *Technopolis: High-technology industry and regional development in Southern California* (Berkeley, 1993), 16, 121–22.

43. Fred Felberg to EC, 3 Feb. 1976 (JPL 150, 17/207).

44. Kirk Dawson, "Subsystem contracting mode," and Kane Casani, "Full system contracting," 6 July 1977 (JPL 150, 20/237).

45. J. N. James to all concerned, drafts 15 Apr. and 16 Sept. 1969 (JPL 142, 53.871); draft report of the System Contracting Concepts Committee, 7 May 1970 (JPL 142, 53/872); on the army arsenal model, see Bromberg, 16–17.

46. Donna Shirley e-mail to author, 6 Aug. 2001.

47. JPL mini-retreat summary, 6 July 1977 (JPL 150, 20/237).

48. Kraemer, *Beyond the moon,* 174–79.

49. Noel Hinners to Murray, 5 May 1977 (JPL 142, 20/326); W. Victor to Murray, 26 Apr. 1978 (JPL 150, 18/215).

50. J. James to Pickering and Terhune, 2 Oct. 1975 (JPL 142, 46/757).

51. "Make or buy considerations," distributed by Robillard to EC, 14 Dec. 1977, and Murray, "Laboratory policy: Make or buy," 7 Mar. 1978 (JPL 150, 18/214). "Smart buyers" appears, for example, in Don Rea (quoting Beggs memo) to EC, 2 Feb. 1982 (JPL 150, 22/257).

52. Ray Kline to Naugle, 26 July 1978, and revised MOU draft, 8 Nov. 1978 (NASA-JPL, 16142).

53. Memphis Norman interview with Robert W. Smith, 6 and 12 Sept. 1984, NASM.

54. Low cost meeting, AIA conference, May 1972 (JPL 142, 11/182); Aerospace Report, "Standardization and program practices analysis," 5 Dec. 1977 (JPL 142, 11/177); Low cost retreat minutes, July 1975 (JPL 142, 32/554); Naugle to Center directors et al., 15 June 1976 (JPL 142, 24/403).

55. Bill Becker to Frank Colella, 9 Dec. 1976 (JPL 150, 25/234); Felberg to Murray, 22 Aug. (quote) and 11 Sept. 1975 (JPL 8, 1/34).

56. "Burden pool application sequence," 23 July 1980 (NASA-JPL, 16150). JPL's "burden budget" for indirect costs covered administrative and support salaries as well as supplies and utilities, but its definition remained flexible. I thank Winston Gin and Gary Ureda for enlightenment on this subject.

57. Rocco Petrone to Center directors and HQ office heads, 3 Mar. 1975 (JPL 142, 32/554); see also Murray, oral history interview by Rachel Prud'homme (Oct. 1983–Feb. 1984), CIT archives, 94–95.

58. Low cost retreat minutes, July 1975 (JPL 142, 32/554).

59. Ibid.; Low Cost Systems Office, POP 76–1 guidelines (JPL 142, 41/696).

60. JPL performance evaluation for FY77, 23 Mar. 1978 (JPL 142, 39/653); Raymond L. Heacock, "The Voyager spacecraft," *Proceedings of the Institute of Mechanical Engineers* 194 (1980): 211–24, on 216.

61. NASA Advisory Council symposium notes, 10–16 June 1979 (JPL 142, 28/496); Rea memo for record, 15 June 1979 (JPL 142, 44/732); J. Beckman to Murray, 28 June 1979 (JPL 142, 31/546); SSEEC, 9 June, 18 June, and 6 July 1980 (JPL 150, 4/46); R. J. P. [Parks], "What [do] we do about planetary program decline problem," 26 Nov. 1980 (JPL 150, 21/249).

62. Morris to Parks, 2 Mar. 1976, and Robert S. Kraemer ["shortcuts"] to George Low et al., 27 Feb. 1976 (JPL 142, 26/461); Murray to EC, 5 May 1976 (JPL 8, 2/44); Donna Shirley, JPL Story, 2 Aug. 2001, JPL library.

63. Parks to Terhune, 17 June 1975 (JPL 142, 32/554); Shirley e-mail to author, 6 Aug. 2001.

64. Shirley, JPL Story.

65. Report of the Seasat Failure Review Board, 21 Dec. 1978 (JPL 142, 49/796).

66. Murray, state of the lab, 26 Mar. 1980, and midyear report, 2 Oct. 1980 (JPL 150, 9/105).

67. Felberg to Murray, 11 Sept. 1975 (JPL 8, 1/34).

68. Murray, "Planetary exploration—evolution for a future," talk at AAS Division of Planetary Science annual meeting, 14 Oct. 1980 (JPL 150, 11/141).

69. Hans Mark to Murray, 7 June 1982, and Murray to Mark, 2 June 1982 (JPL 150, 12/170). In his original quote Murray said, "once every N/2.35 years," although he clearly meant to multiply, not divide, by 2.35.

70. Stofan quoted in SSEEC, 8 June 1981 (JPL 150, 4/46); apparently based on Stofan to Murray, 13 May 1981 (JPL 150, 2/22).

71. JPL performance evaluation for FY81, 16 Feb. 1982 (JPL 150, 3/33).

72. Fowler to Murray, 11 July 1975 and 2 Jan. 1976 (JPL 8, 1/32).

73. Frank E. Goddard to Murray, 11 Aug. 1975 (JPL 8, 1/33); M. H. Cohen to Murray, 1 Mar. 1976 (JPL 8, 1/40); Fowler to Murray, 11 July 1975 and 2 Jan. 1976 (JPL 8, 1/32); David W. Morrisroe to Murray, 8 Jan. 1976 (JPL 8, 1/35); Terhune comments in EC retreat, 10 Dec. 1977 (JPL 8, 3/64).

74. Murray to James Fletcher, 14 July 1976, and director's letter, 30 July 1976 (JPL 8, 2/47); Murray to JPL management personnel, 6 Aug. 1976 (JPL 216, 2/26).

75. R. E. Sutherland to W. E. Strong, 11 Feb. 1977 (JPL 142, 39/661); Murray to all JPL engineers and scientists, 23 Feb. 1977 and 22 July 1977, and Strong to R. B. Gilmore, 5 July 1977 (JPL 142, 57/938). On termination policies, see Murray remarks to JPL management personnel, 6 Aug. 1976 (JPL 216, 2/26); Murray to Morrisroe, 24 May 1976 (JPL 8, 2/44); Murray, draft of director's letter 27 and 29 July 1976, and Steve Savage to Geoffrey Robillard, 4 Nov. 1976 (JPL 142, 44/736); Terhune memo on termination policy, 26 July 1976, and Robillard to Murray, 9 May 1977 (JPL 142, 57/927).

76. Murray remarks to JPL management personnel, 6 Aug. 1976 (JPL 216, 2/26), and Murray inaugural speech, 2 Apr. 1976 (JPL 216, 2/23).

77. Murray, state of the lab for 1 Apr. 1977 (JPL 216, 2/31), and 7 Apr. 1978, 4 Apr. 1979, and 26 Mar. 1980 (JPL 150, 9/105).

78. Norton Belknap to Murray, 18 Feb. 1977 (JPL 8, 3/54), and Stanley Rawn to Murray, 5 Nov. 1979 (JPL 8, 6/88).

79. Wheelon interview.

80. James to Murray, 29 Aug. 1975 (JPL 8, 1/33).

81. Karen R. Davidson, "Are things harder to get done at JPL than they used to be?" 26 Feb. 1981 (JPL 150, 21/251); Murray, state of the lab, 2 Apr. 1981 (JPL 150, 9/105).

82. Notes from section managers meetings, Dec. 1975 (JPL 142, 8/131).

83. "Personnel-related data study," 1977 (JPL 142, 40/667).

84. New Yorker (5 Dec. 1970), 166.

85. John Heie to Phil Click, 23 Jan. 1981; Gates to EC, 4 Mar. 81, and Davidson, "Are things harder?"

86. Murray, state of the lab, 2 Apr. 1981 (JPL 150, 9/105), and director's letters 14 July and 30 Nov. 1981 (JPL 150, 4/36).

87. J. A. Carr, JPL employee opinion survey, 19 Aug. 1980 (JPL 198, 4/49).

88. Headcount of engineers and scientists by age group (JPL 150, 22/257).

89. T. G. Meikle, Ethnic staffing by job categories, 28 Oct. 1976 (JPL 142, 16/265); Advisory Council on Minority Affairs minutes, 5 Oct. 1977 (JPL 142, 16/258).

90. Earl Lane, "Women lag in science pursuits," Los Angeles Times, 3 June 1977; Employment comparison in Advisory Council material, Feb. 1979 (JPL 8, 5/79).

91. Terhune to Lewis Sandler, 7 Mar. 1975 (JPL 142, 16/264); JPL charter 100-C5 (JPL 198, 51/1000); Murray to JPL managers, 14 Dec. 1976 (JPL 216, 2/28). Eighty women applied for the twenty or so available slots.

92. Notes on senior staff meeting, 17 Aug. 1976 (JPL 142, 49/805); Fowler to Murray, 11 July 1975 (JPL 8, 1/32); notes from section managers meetings, Dec. 1975 (JPL 142, 8/131), citing "a report that some engineers have remarked to the effect that the lab may be doing too much" relative to affirmative action.

93. Advisory Committee on Minority Affairs minutes, 6 Mar. 1975 (JPL 142, 16/258). NASA followed Carter's continued support of nonquota affirmative action programs after Bakke: Carter to executive agency heads, 20 July 1978, and Frosch to Murray, 8 Aug. 1978 (JPL 142, 16/265).

94. Murray, midyear review, 2 Oct. 1980 (JPL 198, 1/2).

95. Ibid.

96. JPL draft performance evaluation, draft 29 Nov. 1977 (JPL 150, 3/30).

97. Frank E. Goddard to Murray, 11 Aug. 1975 (JPL 8, 1/33).

98. John Pierce to Murray, 11 Oct. 1977 (JPL 8, 3/62).

99. Murray, "JPL financial status and prospects," 5 Aug. 1980 (JPL 150, 10/138); Heie, memo for record, 12 Nov. 1981 (JPL 150, 5/49).

100. Parks to Murray, 14 Oct. 1975 (JPL 8, 1/35).

101. Carr, JPL survey.

102. Felberg et al., "JPL Futures Study," July 1980 (JPL 142, 20/325); W. J. O'Neil to Murray, 8 Nov. 1979 (JPL 142, 27/477).

103. Bella Stumbo, "Mars probe stirs the blood and brings a yawn," *Los Angeles Times,* 19 July 1976.

104. JPL strategic plans for energy R&D, July 1976 (JPL 142, 15/147), and "Jet Propulsion Laboratory: An overview," 23 Apr. 1978 (JPL 150, 9/106).

105. Felberg to Murray, 10 June 1981 (JPL 230, 11/128); Robert Staehle interview, 12 Oct. 2001, Charles Kohlhase interview, 2 July 2002, and Norm Haynes interview, 13 Mar. 2003.

106. James Westphal, interview by Robert Smith, 27 Sept. 1991, NASM. Westphal attributed the saying to Goddard staff, but it applied equally to JPL.

107. Murray, "JPL financial status and prospects," 5 Aug. 1980 (JPL 150, 10/138).

108. James to Murray, 29 Aug. 1975 (JPL 8, 1/33).

109. James interview by John Bluth, 8 Dec. 1993, JPL archives.

110. R. J. Mackin to Murray, 26 Nov. 1979 (JPL 142, 19/312).

111. *Lab-oratory* and *JPL Universe* back issues, JPL archives.

Chapter 5. Diversification

1. Doren Roberts, CSPO data, 20 Nov. 1975 (JPL 142, 53/875); Dan Schneiderman, civil systems management review, 30 Sept. 1975 (JPL 142, 35/612), and Schneiderman to C. H. Terhune, 2 Dec. 1975 (JPL 142, 49/799).

2. Murray to Elmer S. Groo, 12 Sept. 1975, and F. Felberg to Murray, 22 Aug. 1975 (JPL 8, 1/34).

3. Daniel Yergin, *The prize: The epic quest for oil, money, and power* (New York, 1991), 663; reports quoted anonymously in Jack Anderson and Les Whitten, "Energy crisis may cause U.S. revolution," *Glendale News Press,* 6 July 1977.

4. Director's letter, 2 Apr. 1976 (JPL 8, 1/41).

5. D. R. Fowler, "Items for discussion with NASA," 25 July 1978 (JPL 198, 8/121); W. H. Bayley to Murray, 10 July 1975 (JPL 8, 1/33).

6. Murray, "Jet Propulsion Laboratory: An overview," 23 Apr. 1978 (JPL 150, 9/106); Murray in faculty board minutes, 17 May 1976 (JPL 142, 18/297); Murray to EC, 3 May 1976 (JPL 8, 2/44).

7. Mahlon Easterling and Joe Spiegel presentation at JPL mini-retreat, 12 Apr. 1977 (JPL 150, 20/236).

8. D. S. Halacy, Jr., *The coming age of solar energy* (New York, 1973), 75–96.

9. JPL mini-retreat, 12 Apr. 1977 (JPL 150, 20/236).

10. Orange report, part 1, 23; Harold Brown to J. J. Morgan et al., 9 July 1976 (JPL 142, 14/223); Murray, "Some thoughts about campus and JPL," 10 May 1976 (JPL 173, 3/38).

11. W. H. Corcoran to M. L. Goldberger, 15 May 1979 (JPL 142, 14/224).

12. Nuclear Waste Management Review Board briefing, 15 Feb. 1977 (JPL 142, 36/620).

13. "JPL's solar electric program," 13 Apr. 1978 (JPL 150, 8/95).

14. Allen Hammond and William D. Metz, "Solar energy research: Making solar after the nuclear model?" *Science* 197 (15 July 1977): 241.

15. E. F. Schumacher, *Small is beautiful: Economics as if people mattered* (New York, 1989), 190–201; Carroll Pursell, "The rise and fall of the appropriate technology movement in the United States, 1965–1985," *Technology and Culture* 34 (1993): 629–37.

16. Murray to Walt Victor, 24 Aug. 1976, Victor to Murray, 23 Aug. 1976, and M. Easterling to Schurmeier, 18 Aug. 1976 (JPL 142, 14/223); David F. Salisbury, "Prophet of tomorrow's redirected technology: Bruce Murray foresees return to small scale," *Christian Science Monitor*, 3 Nov. 1976; M. S. Reid to Murray, 27 Apr. 1979 (JPL 142, 1/14); Amory B. Lovins, *Soft energy paths: Toward a durable peace* (San Francisco, 1977), 11–12.

17. Joseph King and David Martin to Murray, 11 Jan. 1980 (JPL 142, 15/237); JPL strategic plans for energy R&D, draft July 1976 (JPL 142, 15/147); JPL press release (on California coal-use conference), 4 May 1978 (JPL 150, 1/11).

18. MacGregor Reid interview, 28 Mar. 2003.

19. Director's letter, 7 Mar. 1978 (JPL 8, 4/67); "The energy program future," 8 Dec. 1977 (JPL 150, 20/241).

20. Murray to Brown with draft of PAL concept, 21 July 1975, Brown to Murray, 30 July 1975, C. J. Pings to Brown, 22 Aug. 1975, and Bob Sharp to Murray, 11 Aug. 1975 (JPL 8, 1/32); Dan Schneiderman to Murray, 15 Oct. 1975 (JPL 8, 1/35); D. R. Fowler to Murray, 5 Aug. 1975 and 26 Nov. 1980 (JPL 8, 8/100); Murray interview, 15 Jan. 2003; EC retreat, 10–12 Dec. 1976 (JPL 150, 25/233); Schneiderman to Murray, 21 Mar. 1977 (JPL 142, 7/112).

21. Felberg, "JPL operation under multiple sponsor contracts," 1 Mar. 1976 (JPL 142, 63/481); Pickering to Brown, 4 Mar. 1976 (JPL 142, 27/481); Schneiderman, "Civil systems management review," 30 Sept. 1975 (JPL 142, 35/612); "Contractual and campus considerations of separate contracts and/or separate facilities and/or separate laboratories for the performance of energy work by JPL," 10 Dec. 1977 (JPL 150, 20/241).

22. EC summary, 10 Dec. 1977 (JPL 150, 25/241).

23. LSSA Project plan for FY77, 15 Oct. 1976 (JPL 142, 25/437); Elmer Christensen, "Flat-Plate Solar Array Project," Oct. 1985 (JPL 173, 6/84).

24. Jeffrey L. Smith, "Photovoltaics as a terrestrial energy source: Vol. III, an overview," Department of Energy report DOE/ET-20356-6, Oct. 1980; Smith, "Photovoltaics as a terrestrial energy source," 1 Apr. 1981 (JPL 150, 11/156); Schurmeier statement to House Committee on Science and Technology, 1 Mar. 1979 (JPL 8, 6/80).

25. Schurmeier statement to House Subcommittee on Energy Conservation and Power, 2 Dec. 1981 (JPL 150, 8/94).

26. Ranking of outstanding JPL commitments, 28 Mar. 1980 (JPL 150, 9/120).

27. Opinion survey results for JPL Advisory Council, 30 May 1980 (JPL 8, 7/94).

28. Bruce Murray, *Journey into space: The first three decades of space exploration* (New York, 1989), 143.

29. Murray, state of the lab, 4 Apr. 1979 (JPL 150, 9/105); JPL five-year plan, vol. 2, draft 30 May 1978 (JPL 150, 9/107); "JPL capabilities, facilities, and interests applicable to nuclear waste transport and disposal," 5 Mar. 1975 (JPL 142, 35/613).

30. John List to Murray, 1 Nov. 1978 (JPL 8, 5/75).

31. Norton Belknap to Murray, 18 Feb. 1977 (JPL 8, 3/54); Shirley Hufstedler to Murray, 30 Mar. 1977 (JPL 142, 1/6); Schurmeier to senior staff, 31 May 1978 (two memos) (JPL 8, 4/69), and 29 Sept. 1978 (JPL 8, 5/73).

32. Felberg et al., "JPL Futures Study," July 1980 (JPL 142, 20/325); Norm Haynes interview, 14 March 2003.

33. EC retreat notes, 10 Dec. 1977 (JPL 8, 3/64); Murray, state of the lab, 4 Apr. 1979 (JPL 150, 9/105).

34. JPL mini-retreat minutes, 12 Apr. 1977 (JPL 150, 20/236); Geoff Robillard to Murray, 3 Apr. 1980 (JPL 142, 46/756).

35. John Pierce to Murray, 1 Mar. 1977 (JPL 142, 6/85); Murray notes on Advisory Council meeting, 30 Oct. 1978 (JPL 8, 5/74); Robert Bacher to Murray, 2 Nov. 1978 (JPL 8, 5/75).

36. Bacher to Murray, 2 Nov. 1978; orange report, part 1, 14, 23.

37. Robillard to M. Alper, N. Nichols, and Schurmeier, 4 Oct. 1978 (JPL 8, 5/74).

38. JPL mini-retreat minutes, 12 Apr. 1977, and G. E. Nichols, "What should JPL's interface be with the private sector," 12 Apr. 1977 (JPL 150, 20/236); Murray, midyear review, 5 Oct. 1979 (JPL 150, 9/105); JPL Advisory Council notes, 27–28 Jan. 1977 (JPL 8, 2/53); Elmer Christensen, "Flat-Plate Solar Array Project," Oct. 1985 (JPL 173, 6/84); J. W. Doane statements at Advisory Council meeting, 13 Apr. 1978 (JPL 8, 4/71).

39. "The future of utilitarian, non-space, civilian activities at JPL," 10 Jan. 1980 (JPL 150, 10/129), and Robillard, "The energy program as a utilitarian mission for JPL," 30 May 1980 (JPL 142, 19/324).

40. "OMB slashes DOE FY83 budget by $3 billion," *Inside energy,* 4 Dec. 1981.

41. "The future of utilitarian, non-space, civilian activities at JPL," 10 Jan. 1980 (JPL 150, 10/129).

42. Al Hibbs (quote), "An investigation of how NASA's 'Outlook for Space' study might effect [sic] JPL," 31 Oct. 1975 (JPL 142, 37/637); NASA study group, "Outlook for space: A synopsis," Jan. 1976 (JPL 142, 37/638); Pickering to James Fletcher, 20 Feb. 1976 (JPL 142, 33/568).

43. JPL Science Office, briefing to Murray, 18 Nov. 1975 (JPL 150, 7/88).

44. Richard L. Haedrich and Kenneth O. Emery, "Growth of an oceanographic institution," in M. Sears and D. Merriman, eds., *Oceanography: The past* (New York, 1980), 67–82, on 73.

45. John Lucas to EC, 23 Apr. and 3 May 1976 (JPL 150, 17/207).

46. Don Rea interview, 2 May 2002, and Walt Brown interview, 14 Nov. 2002; Goddard Space Flight Center, "Seasat-A, Phase-A study presentation," 31 July 1973, and NASA press release, 15 Jan. 1975 (NASA-Seasat).

47. NASA, catalog of center roles, Dec. 1976 (JPL 8, 2/52); Murray, state of the lab, 4 Apr. 1979 (JPL 150, 9/105); JPL five-year plan, draft May 1978 (JPL 150, 9/107); Murray in faculty board minutes, 17 May 1976 (JPL 142, 18/297).

48. On Goddard squabbles: Murray to EC, 25 Aug. 1976 (JPL 150, 17/209); Jack James to Anthony Calio, 22 July 1978 (JPL 8, 4/71); Murray, state of the lab, 4 Apr. 1979; Harry Press to Schneiderman, 28 Mar. 1980 (JPL 142, 28/496). The Office of Applications separated from the Office of Space Science in 1972, was renamed the Office of Space and Terrestrial Applications in 1978, and rejoined Space Science in 1982.

49. Naugle to James Fletcher, 9 Dec. 1974, and Fletcher to H. G. Stever, 26 Aug. 1975 (NASA-Seasat); E. Loomis to Pickering et al., 20 Jan. 1975 (JPL 142, 64/789).

50. Walt Brown interview; Eileen Shea, *A history of NOAA* (Washington, 1987), avail-

able at http://www.lib.noaa.gov/edocs/. The Weather Bureau and Coast and Geodetic Survey were previously combined in the Environmental Science Services Administration.

51. NASA, "Project Seasat—A, Support Instrumentation Requirements Document," 12 Apr. 1976 (JPL 142, 48/791); Seasat—A mission operation report, June 1978.

52. Murray, state of the lab, 1 Apr. 1977 (JPL 216, 2/31).

53. JPL performance evaluation for FY1978, draft 16 May 1979 (JPL 142, 39/654); John Naugle to Calio, 14 Apr. 1977 (NASA-Seasat); *Aerospace Daily,* 19 Apr. 1977; Murray, state of the lab, 1 Apr. 1977 (JPL 216, 2/31).

54. JPL performance evaluation for FY78, draft 16 May 1979 (JPL 142, 39/654); Douglas Broome to Pat Rygh, 27 Sept. 1979 (JPL 142, 48/790).

55. Murray to Calio, 9 May 1979 (JPL 8, 6/82).

56. John Apel to Rygh, 14 Feb. 1979 (JPL 216, 1/20); Broome to Rygh, 27 Sept. 1979; JPL performance evaluation for FY79, 28 Mar. 1980 (JPL 142, 39/657).

57. *Science* 204:4400 (29 June 1979): 1405–24; *Journal of Geophysical Research: Oceans and Atmospheres* 87 (30 Apr. 1982); *Journal of Astronautical Sciences* 28:4 (1980).

58. "Notes by Loomis from the Seasat B presentation," 16 Feb. 1977 (JPL 142, 48/789).

59. "National Oceanic Satellite System," 25 May 1978 (JPL 150, 9/110); J. H. Gerpheide, "A plan to achieve an FY81 start for the National Oceanic Satellite System," 21 Feb. 1979 (JPL 142, 24/411).

60. David Williamson, Jr., to Murray, 26 Mar. 1980 (JPL 8, 7/92); *Aerospace Daily,* 28 Apr. and 11 June 1980 and 9 Mar. and 12 May 1981.

61. Murray, "JPL financial status and prospects," 4 Aug. 1981.

62. Murray to JPL Advisory Council, 20 Feb. 1980 (JPL 150, 11/150).

63. Don Rea interview, 2 May 2002, and Alexander Goetz interview, 25 Feb. 2003; Susan West, "A SERIES look at the Earth," *Science News* 115 (27 Jan. 1979), 58–61.

64. Ronald E. Doel, "The earth sciences and geophysics," in John Krige and Dominique Pestre, eds., *Science in the twentieth century* (Amsterdam, 1997), 391–416; Naomi Oreskes, *The rejection of continental drift: Theory and method in American earth science* (Oxford, 1999), 273–75.

65. Walt Brown interview, 14 Nov. 2002; T. D. Allan, "Seasat's short-lived mission," *Nature* 281 (11 Oct. 1979): 421–32.

66. Omar Shemdin to Murray, 8 July 1977 (JPL 142, 13/206).

67. Pitt G. Thome et al., "Assessment of Landsat and related R&D programs," Aug. 1982 (JPL 198, 13/179).

68. Eugene Linden, "Windows on a vast frontier," *Time* (12 Sept. 1988), 68; see also George Alexander, "High technology aids study of world's oceans," *Los Angeles Times,* 31 Mar. 1984.

69. Hibbs, "Investigation."

70. Pickering to Hinners, 16 Feb. 1976, Hinners to Murray, 12 Apr. 1976, and director's letter, 22 Apr. 1976 (JPL 142, 23/389); Conway W. Snyder, "History of the IRAS project," Oct. 1984 (NASA-IRAS, 6070).

71. Robert W. Smith, *The Space Telescope: A study of NASA, science, technology, and politics* (Cambridge, 1989), 240–53.

72. Smith, *Space Telescope,* 248–56; Murray to Calio, 28 Oct. 1976 (JPL 142, 52/860); Robillard to Murray, 24 Nov. 1976 (JPL 142, 12/195); Murray oral history, CIT archives, 105–7; James Westphal interview by Shirley K. Cohen, 23 July 1998, CIT archives; James Cutts interview, 21 March 2002; Krishna Koliwad interview, 28 Mar. 2003.

73. Murray to JPL Advisory Council, 8 Oct. 1979 (JPL 8, 7/90).

74. Murray oral history, CIT archives, 142–44; Norm Haynes interview, 11 Apr. 2003.

75. Douglas J. Mudgway, *Uplink-downlink: A history of the Deep Space Network, 1957–1997* (Washington, D.C., 2001), 133–35. X band covers about 8,000–9,000 MHz; S band about 2,000–3,000 MHz.

76. Andrew J. Butrica, *To see the unseen: A history of planetary radar astronomy* (Washington, D.C., 1996); Mudgway, *Uplink-downlink,* 502–79; Gordon Garmire to Murray, 3 Jan. 1980 (JPL 8, 7/90).

77. Steven J. Dick, *The biological universe: The twentieth-century extraterrestrial life debate and the limits of science* (Cambridge, 1996), 399–454; R. E. Edelson, draft final report of SETI Science Workshop, 13 Feb. 1976 (JPL 142, 47/776).

78. Calio to John Billingham, 17 Dec. 1975 (JPL 142, 47/772).

79. JPL director's letter, 1 Nov. 1976 (JPL 8, 2/51); Dick, *Biological universe,* 462–63.

80. Ames Research Center and JPL, "Search for Extraterrestrial Intelligence, project plan," Nov. 1976 (JPL 142, 48/782).

81. Roger D. Launius, "A Western mormon in Washington, D.C.: James C. Fletcher, NASA, and the final frontier," *Pacific Historical Review* 64 (May 1995): 217–41, on 233. On NASA program managers' resistance: R. E. Edelson to Murray and Terhune, 12 Jan. 1977, Hans Mark to Naugle, 3 Feb. 1977, Billingham to Murray, 5 Apr. 1977, Naugle to Mark, 25 Apr. 1977, and Hinners to Murray and to Mark, 15 June 1977 (JPL 142, 47/772).

82. Sen. William Proxmire press release, 16 Feb. 1978 (JPL 8, 4/66); NASA, "Response to queries" for SETI (JPL 142, 48/788).

83. Dick, *Biological universe,* 498; M. J. Klein to Murray et al., 15 Feb. 1982 (JPL 8, 10/117); Frank Drake and Dava Sobel, *Is anyone out there? The scientific search for extraterrestrial intelligence* (New York, 1992), 191–196.

84. W. A. Collier, "Flight science experiments at JPL," briefing to Murray, 13 Nov. 1975 (JPL 150, 7/87); Rea interview, 2 May 2002; Voyager science teams in David Morrison, *Voyages to Saturn* (Washington, D.C., 1982), appendix A.

85. Terhune to senior staff, 19 Mar. 1976 (JPL 142, 46/757).

86. Wes Huntress interview, 8 July 2003.

87. John E. Naugle, *First among equals: The selection of NASA space science experiments,* NASA SP-4215 (Washington, D.C., 1991), 63–65; Koppes, 121–22.

88. Herbert S. Bridge to Murray, 13 May 1977 (JPL 142, 28/487), and Norman Ness to Murray, 3 June 1977 (JPL 142, 30/518).

89. JPL five-year plan, draft May 1978 (JPL 150, 9/107).

90. Philip Abelson to Murray, 16 Jan. 1978 (JPL 8, 4/65).

91. Murray to EC, 29 Mar. 1977 (JPL 150, 20/235).

92. Roger Noll to Murray, 23 Nov. 1977, and Murray to Noll, 29 Nov. 1977 (JPL 8, 3/63); Noll to Murray, 1 Dec. 1977 (JPL 8, 3/64).

93. Murray to EC, 25 Aug. 1976 (JPL 8, 2/48).

94. JPL Advisory Council notes, 27–28 Jan. 1977 (JPL 8, 2/53), and Murray to EC, 29 Mar. 1977 (JPL 150, 20/235).

95. Hinners to colleague, 15 Dec. 1976, and Physical Sciences Committee report, 1 Apr. 1976 (JPL 142, 35/592).

96. Bruce Lundin to Murray, 1 Feb. 1977, with draft of study team report, Lundin to Rea, 28 June 1977, and Naugle to Lundin, 20 June 1977 (JPL 142, 30/528); Murray to

Rea, 11 Mar. 1977, and to Lundin, 21 Mar. 1977 (JPL 142, 30/527); Rea to Lundin, 1 Apr. 1977, Murray to Hinners, 21 Apr. 1977, and Hinners to Murray, 6 June 1977 (JPL 142, 35/591).

97. Tom Duxbury interview, 19 July 2001.

98. Walt Brown interview.

99. "Manyear distribution by programmatic goal," 16 Nov. 1979 (JPL 8, 7/90); Walt Victor to EC, 29 Oct. 1980 (JPL 150, 2/18).

100. Murray, "JPL financial status and prospects," 5 Aug. 1980 (JPL 150, 10/138); supporting material for EC retreat, 13 Nov. 1980 (JPL 150, 21/249).

101. "Items of key interest to section 312 personnel," 8 Nov. 1979 (JPL 142, 27/477); Murray, midyear report, 2 Oct. 1980 (JPL 150, 9/105).

102. Pierce, "Some thoughts about laboratories and JP[L]," 2 Sept. 1981 (JPL 150, 12/160), and Pierce, "JPL and technology," 27 Feb. 1980 (JPL 150, 10/130).

103. Felberg et al., "JPL Futures Study," July 1980 (JPL 142, 20/325).

104. B. T. Morris to Robillard, 18 Nov. 1975 (JPL 142, 27/480); Morris to Schurmeier, 9 Aug. 1979 (JPL 142, 44/728); Robillard to Morris, 13 Aug. 1979 (JPL 142, 46/756); Murray remarks to management personnel, 6 Aug. 1976 (JPL 216, 2/26); Felberg to Pickering, 14 Mar. 1972 (JPL 150, 25/226), and Felberg to EC, 5 Apr. 1974 (JPL 150, 25/229).

105. JPL mini-retreat, summary, 11 Oct. 1977 (JPL 150, 20/239); C. R. Gates to EC, 2 Dec. 1980 (JPL 150, 21/249).

106. JPL program prospects, Feb. 1982 (JPL 150, 22/255).

Chapter 6. Return to the Military

1. E.g., Thomas O'Toole, "The 'militarization' of the space agency," *Washington Post*, 8 May 1982; Paul B. Stares, *The militarization of space: U.S. policy, 1945–1984* (Ithaca, 1985).

2. *Aerospace Daily*, 2 June 1980; O'Toole, "Militarization"; Stares, *Militarization*, appendix 1. The budgets for military space programs do not include the classified budgets for reconnaissance satellites.

3. "DoD program development," 21 Nov. 1975, and briefing to Murray on Research and Advanced Development, [Nov.] 1975 (JPL 150, 7/88); author conversation with Winston Gin, 16 May 2001.

4. H. H. Haglund and P. K. Eckman to Pickering (quote), 16 Apr. 1975, and Eckman and Haglund memo, 7 Aug. 1975 (JPL 142, 54/891); "The Advanced Concepts Laboratory," 28 July 1975 (JPL 142, 2/25).

5. Eckman and Haglund memo, 7 Aug. 1975, Harold Brown to Pickering, 1 Aug. 1975, and to Pickering and F. E. Goddard (quote), 26 Sept. 1975 (JPL 142, 54/891).

6. Briefing to Murray on classified work, [Nov.] 1975 (JPL 150, 7/88).

7. Haglund and Eckman to Pickering, 16 Apr. 1975, and Brown to Pickering, 1 Aug. 1975 (JPL 142, 54/891).

8. Pickering to NASA assistant administrator for DOD & interagency affairs, 24 May 1973 (JPL 142, 60/986).

9. Eckman, interview by Russ Castonguay, 20 Nov. 2001 (JPL archives); James D. Burke interview, 5 Dec. 2003; Walt Brown interview, 14 Nov. 2002; Charles Kohlhase interview, 2 July 2002.

10. W. P. Spaulding to Murray, 12 Aug. 1976 (JPL 142, 64/986); Clifford Cummings to Murray (quote), 6 Oct. 1976 (JPL 142, 60/986); Cummings interview, 14 June 2001. On

protests, see, e.g., Dorothy Nelkin, *The university and military research: Moral politics at MIT* (Ithaca, 1972).

11. Cummings to Murray (quote), and Cummings interview.

12. Mary Lyle to Eckman, 8 Oct. 1976 (JPL 142, 60/986).

13. Cummings to Murray, 6 Oct. 1976; Gen. William W. Snavely, draft to Allen Burke, 15 July 1976, and draft MOU between NASA and Caltech-JPL (JPL 142, 64/986).

14. W. P. Spaulding, F. M. Riddle, and Eckman, minutes of Vista meeting, 5 Apr. 1976 (JPL 142, 64/986).

15. A. Loomis to W. Brown et al., 4 Apr. 1974 (JPL 150, 24/203).

16. W. E. Giberson to S. W. McCandless, 7 Nov. 1975 (JPL 142, 48/789); Charles W. Mathews to John Naugle, 13 Nov. 1975, F. L. Williams to Ross Williams, 24 Feb. 1977, and F. L. Williams to L. Jaffe, 15 Mar. 1977 (NASA-Seasat).

17. David Williamson, Jr., to John Naugle, 6 Aug. 1976 (NASA-Seasat); Giberson to R. J. Parks, 7 June 1976 (JPL 1442, 64/789).

18. Giberson to McCandless, 15 Mar. 1976 (JPL 142, 48/789); Murray to Harold Brown, 9 June 1976 (JPL 142, 64/789), and Murray to Brown, 18 Mar. 1977 (JPL 142, 48/790); Frederick Seitz to William Kellogg, 2 Dec. 1976, Kellogg to Seitz, 22 Nov. 1976 (NASA-Seasat); John Apel, draft (unsent) to James Fletcher, Nov. 1976 (JPL 142, 48/789).

19. *Aerospace Daily,* 29 Aug. and 12 Sept. 1977.

20. Walt Brown interview, 14 Nov. 2002.

21. Tony Spear interview, 12 Feb. 2004.

22. Dick Baumbach, "Did killer craft KO Seasat?" *TODAY,* 12 Oct. 1978. On Soviet ASATs and lasers, see Stares, *Militarization.*

23. Vernon A. Guidry, "Satellite's loss raises questions on U.S. subs," *Baltimore Sun,* 19 Sept. 1984. The spy case involving Peter Lee and China in 1997 involved synthetic aperture radar: William J. Broad, "U.S. loses hold on submarine-exposing radar technique," *New York Times,* 11 May 1999.

24. Murray to Maj. Gen. Jack Kulpa, 22 Jan. 1979, and Murray to David Mann, 22 Mar. 1979 (JPL 142, 53/887).

25. R. P. Mathison to Murray ("nervous"), 23 Apr. 1979, and Mathison to Murray, 25 June 1979 (JPL 142, 53/887); New Work Opportunity announcements, Jan.–May 1982 (JPL 150, 11/149); T. R. Scheck to senior staff, 19 Jan. 1982 (JPL 150, 23/172).

26. "Defense and national security implications of the U.S. deep space program," 6 Mar. 1981 (JPL 150, 18/220).

27. J. N. James, "Commentary on a major defense mission for JPL," 28 May 1980 (JPL 150, 11/148).

28. Murray, comments to faculty, 11 June 1980 (JPL 150, 5/50); JPL Proposal, Autonomous Spacecraft Project, 7 July 1980 (JPL 150, 23/148).

29. Murray, midyear report, 2 Oct. 1980 (JPL 150, 9/105).

30. Murray to Kulpa, 22 Jan. 1979.

31. Murray, state of the lab, 7 Apr. 1978 and 2 Apr. 1982 (quote) (JPL 150, 9/105); C. R. Gates, James, and G. Nichols to EC, 4 June 1981 (JPL 150, 22/252).

32. James to R. P. Sharp, 14 Aug. 1969 (JPL 119, 33/1968); orange report, part 1, 2 Apr. 1976 (JPL 173, 3/35).

33. Goldberger to voting faculty, draft May–early June 1980 (JPL 173, 3/39).

34. David D. Evans, "Classified work at JPL," 22 May 1980 (JPL 150, 10/133).

35. Pete Lyman interview, 1 Apr. 2004; U.S. General Accounting Office, "Security

clearances: Consideration of sexual orientation in the clearance process," GAO/NSIAD-95–21, 24 Mar. 1995 (available through www.gao.gov); Barbara Spector, "Security clearance delays hamper gays' careers," *The Scientist* 6:5 (2 Mar. 1992); *High Tech Gays v. Defense Industrial Security Clearance Office,* 895 F.2d 563 (9th Cir., 2 Feb. 1990); Gary Libman, "Scientists confront homophobia in their ranks," *Los Angeles Times,* 2 Feb. 1990. See also M. G. Lord, *Astro-turf: The private life of rocket science* (New York, 2005), 188–95.

36. Goldberger to faculty, 6 June 1980 (JPL 150, 10/133).

37. Faculty meeting minutes, 11 June 1980 (JPL 150, 5/50).

38. Murray to Goldberger, 8 July 1980 (JPL 150, 23/148).

39. Goldberger to faculty, 6 June 1980.

40. Murray to Goldberger, 8 July 1980. James's outfit was named the Advanced Technology Development Office, renamed the Defense Programs Office in 1981.

41. Murray and John D. Roberts to Goldberger, 20 June 1980 (JPL 150, 23/148); faculty meeting minutes, 15 Dec. 1980 (JPL 173, 3/39).

42. David Goodstein to Murray and Roberts, 6 Oct. 1980 (JPL 150, 11/148); faculty meeting minutes, 15 Dec. 1980 (JPL 173, 3/39).

43. Murray to Goldberger, 8 July 1980.

44. Hans Mark to Robert P. Sharp (quotes), 9 Apr. 1974, Mark to Sharp, 26 June 1975, and Sharp to Mark, 3 July 1975 (JPL 150, 12/170).

45. Mark to Murray, 14 Oct. 1981 (JPL 150, 12/170).

46. Murray to Mark, 10 July 1981 (JPL 198, 11/153); Mark to Murray, 16 August 1981, and Murray to Mark, 4 Nov. 1981 (JPL 150, 12/170).

47. Faculty board minutes, 12 Oct. 1981 (JPL 198, 1/2).

48. Murray, "Challenge facing JPL," 20 Oct. 1981 (JPL 150, 5/51).

49. David C. Elliott, addendum dated 21 Oct. 1981, on F. C. Anson to faculty, 16 Oct. 1981 (JPL 198, 1/2).

50. CIT board of trustees minutes, 23–25 Oct. 81 (JPL 198, 24/325).

51. Bruce Murray, midyear review, 1 Dec. 1981 (JPL 198, 1/2).

52. Murray comments to faculty meeting, 14 Dec. 1981 (JPL 150, 5/51).

53. Stares, *Militarization,* 201–5; Donald R. Baucom, *The origins of SDI, 1944–1983* (Lawrence, Kans., 1992), 97–129.

54. "Discussion topics" for meeting with Harold Brown, 4 Jan. 1982 (JPL 150, 3/25); *Aerospace Daily,* 7 Dec. 1981 and 24 June 1982.

55. J. N. James et al., "FY82 Defense Programs marketing plan," 28 Jan. 1982 (JPL 150, 22/255); New Work Opportunity announcements, Jan.–May 1982 (JPL 150, 11/149).

56. MOU between USAF Space Division and Caltech, 22 Oct. 1981 (JPL 173, 2/23); James to defense programs managers, 23 Nov. 1981 (JPL 150, 3/24); Murray to Lt. Gen. Richard C. Henry, 30 Nov. 1981 (JPL 150, 11/148); Murray, director's letter, 22 Feb. 1982 (JPL 150, 4/36); Talon Gold description in "FY82 defense programs marketing plan," 28 Jan. 1982 (JPL 150, 22/255).

57. James, report on Naval Post-Graduate School Symposium, 15 Oct. 1981 (JPL 150, 23/148); Tom Hamilton to Schurmeier, 13 Jan. 1982 (JPL 150, 23/149).

58. Murray, "Transition at JPL," 18 Mar. 1982, copy courtesy of Murray.

59. James to EC, 4 Feb. 1982 (JPL 150, 11/149).

60. Murray comments to faculty meeting, 14 Dec. 1981 (JPL 150, 5/51); "AF space obstacles to JPL's acquisition of DOD work," at EC retreat, 5 Feb. 1982 (JPL 150, 22/257); James to EC, 4 Feb. 1982.

61. James to EC, 4 Feb. 1982; Schurmeier, "Issues regarding JPL working for DoD,"

10 Feb. 1982 (JPL 150, 22/257); Hamilton to Schurmeier, notes on Fubini visit, 26 Jan. 1982 (JPL 198, 56/609).

62. Murray comments to faculty, 14 Dec. 1981 (JPL 150, 5/51).

63. Meeting of defense programs staff with Harold Brown, 4 Jan. 1982 (JPL 150, 3/25); J. Bryden (quote), report on Naval Post-Graduate School Symposium, 15 Oct. 1981 (JPL 150, 23/148).

64. Murray to James Beggs, draft c. Sept. 1981 (JPL 173, 4/51); James to defense programs managers, 23 Nov. 1981 (JPL 150, 3/24).

65. James to EC, notes on meeting with Mark, 11 June 1981 (JPL 150, 23/148); Hamilton to EC (quote), 28 Apr. 1982, notes on Gen. Alton B. Slay's visit to JPL (JPL 173, 5/62).

66. Hamilton, notes on Si Ramo's visit to JPL, 28 Jan. 1982 (JPL 173, 5/62); Cummings interview.

67. "Why C3I is the Pentagon's top priority," *Government Executive* (Jan. 1982), 14–20.

68. James, "An update on defense work at JPL," 2 June 1981 (JPL 150, 22/252); Terhune to senior staff (quote), 1 May 1980 (JPL 150, 4/35).

69. Utilitarian Programs Executive Committee, minutes, 2 Nov. 1981 (JPL 150, 5/48); MOU between U.S. Army and JPL, draft 16 Mar. 1982 (JPL 150, 11/149).

70. Defense Programs Office briefing to Mark, 15 Dec. 1982 (JPL 198, 5/72); Murray, state of the lab, 2 Apr. 1982 (JPL 150, 9/105).

71. J. A. Carr, JPL employee opinion survey, 19 Aug. 1980 (JPL 198, 4/49); Gates, "Aspirations of our staff," 3 Feb. 1982 (JPL 150, 22/257).

Chapter 7. Space Technology

1. Andrew J. Butrica, *To see the unseen: A history of planetary radar astronomy,* NASA SP-4218 (Washington, D.C., 1996), 162–67.

2. Charles Elachi, *Introduction to the physics and techniques of remote sensing* (New York, 1987), 193–221; Butrica, *See the unseen,* 167–68.

3. Elachi, *Introduction to the physics,* 193–221; Elachi, "Spaceborne imaging radar: Geologic and oceanographic applications," *Science* 209 (5 Sept. 80): 1073–82.

4. Walter E. Brown, Jr., "The rocket radar," unpub. manuscript, 9 Feb. 2002, and Brown interview, 14 Nov. 2002.

5. Butrica, *See the unseen,* 177–79.

6. Ibid., 167–68.

7. Brown e-mail to author, 27 Feb. 2003.

8. Brown interview; Bruce Murray, *Journey into space: The first three decades of space exploration* (New York, 1989), 127.

9. David Williamson to John Naugle, 11 May 1977 (NASA-Seasat).

10. Murray to Leonard Jaffe, 11 Jan. 1977, and Jaffe to Murray, 21 Jan. 1977 (JPL 8, 2/53); F. T. Barath to files, 8 Mar. 1977 (JPL 142, 53/888).

11. Brown interview; R. M. Goldstein to Murray, 29 Mar. 1979 (JPL 142, 53/887).

12. Douglas Broome to Pat Rygh, 27 Sept. 1979 (JPL 142, 48/790); Seasat mission operation report, 7 Dec. 1988 (NASA).

13. Elachi, "Spaceborne imaging radar."

14. "Crosscuts: A framework for advocating two programs," c. May 1977 (JPL 142, 12/185); J. N. James, "Crosscuts—a concept for additional emphasis," draft for Murray, 22 Apr. 1977, and A. R. Hibbs to Murray, 20 May 1977 (JPL 142, 30/531).

15. J. P. Ford, J. B. Cimino, and Elachi, "Space Shuttle Columbia views the world with imaging radar: The SIR-A experiment," JPL publication 82–95 (1 Jan. 1983).

16. John Noble Wilford, "Maya canals found by radar," *New York Times,* 3 June 1980; George Alexander, "Maya civilization looming larger," *Los Angeles Times,* 9 June 1980.

17. Elachi to C. Terhune, 30 Sept. 1982 (JPL 198, 3/41); J. F. McCauley et al., "Subsurface valleys and geoarcheology of the Eastern Sahara revealed by shuttle radar," *Science* 218 (3 Dec. 1982): 1004–20.

18. Elachi, JoBea Cimino, and M. Settle, "Overview of the Shuttle Imaging Radar-B preliminary scientific results," *Science* 232 (20 June 1986): 1511–16.

19. A. J. Spear to J. R. Hyde, 9 June 1978 (JPL 150, 9/111).

20. A. R. Hibbs, "An analysis of the effect on JPL of NASA's 'Outlook for Space' study," 5 Feb. 1976 (JPL 142, 37/639).

21. "Outlook for Space: A synopsis," Jan. 1976 (JPL 142, 37/638); James, "A search for the next technological themes that are right for JPL," 3 Aug. 1976 (JPL 8, 2/48); EC retreat, 10–12 Dec. 1976 (JPL 150, 25/233); Murray to senior staff, 28 Nov. 1977 (JPL 150, 9/112).

22. Hibbs, "Analysis."

23. For an introduction to the historiography of scientific images, see Alex Soojung-Kim Pang, "Visual representation and post-constructivist history of science," *HSPS* 28:1 (1997): 139–71. On Galileo, see Mary G. Winkler and Albert Van Helden, "Representing the heavens: Galileo and visual astronomy," *Isis* 83 (1992): 195–217; on bubble chambers, J. L. Heilbron, Robert W. Seidel, and Bruce R. Wheaton, *Lawrence and his laboratory: Nuclear science at Berkeley, 1931–1961* (Berkeley, 1981), 91–93, and Peter Galison, *Image and logic: A material culture of microphysics* (Chicago, 1997), 370–431.

24. William B. Green interview, 12 Feb. 2002.

25. T. Rindfleisch, "Getting more out of Ranger pictures by computer," *Astronautics and Aeronautics* (Jan. 1969): 70–74; Robert Nathan, interview by Cargill Hall, 22 Jan. 1975 (JPL archives).

26. Caltech/JPL Conference on Image-Processing Technology, *Proceedings,* 3–5 Nov. 1976, JPL report no. JPL SP-43–30.

27. E.g., Murray, *Journey,* 115–16.

28. Green interview; Kevin Hussey, Bob Mortensen, and Jeff Hall, "LA, the movie," 1987 (JPL A/V).

29. Kenneth R. Castleman, "A history of digital image processing at JPL," in Castleman, *Digital image processing* (Englewood Cliffs, N.J., 1979), 383–400; Azriel Rosenfeld, *Picture processing by computer* (New York, 1969); Maynard D. McFarlane, "Digital pictures fifty years ago," *Proceedings of the IEEE* 60:7 (1972): 768–70.

30. Esmond C. Lyons, Jr. [Comtal Corporation], "Digital image processing: An overview," *Computer* 10:8 (1977): 12–14; B. R. Hunt and D. H. Janney, "Digital image processing at Los Alamos Scientific Laboratory," *Computer* 7:5 (1974): 57–61; M. P. Ekstrom, "Digital image processing at Lawrence Livermore Laboratory, part 1—Diagnostic radiography applications," *Computer* 7:5 (1974): 72–80.

31. Special issues of *Proceedings of the IEEE* 60:7 (1972), and *Computer* 7:5 (1974) and 10:8 (1977); Castleman, *Digital image processing,* and William B. Green, *Digital image processing: A systems approach* (New York, 1983).

32. JPL performance evaluation for FY80, draft, 23 Dec. 1980 (JPL 142, 39/658).

33. Alexander Goetz interview, 25 Feb. 2003.

34. Green interview; on shared techniques, see Castleman, *Digital image processing,* 371–77.

35. Natalie Angier, "It was love at first byte," *Discover* (March 1981); David Salisbury, "Computer art takes off into space," *Christian Science Monitor*, 20 July 1979. Blinn stayed part time at JPL before moving to the Caltech campus, where he created the graphics for "The Mechanical Universe" video series; in 1995 he became a "graphics fellow" at Microsoft.

36. Green interview.

37. James A. Evans, "The reimbursable program," 28 Feb. 1995 (JPL 259, 50/553).

38. R. B. Gilmore to Murray, 29 Nov. 1976 (JPL 142, 23/384); Caltech/JPL Conference, *Proceedings.*

39. Nathan interview; Green to section 384 staff, 2 July 1979 (JPL 142, 2/34); Green to Murray, 24 Mar. 1977, J. King to Murray, 4 Apr. 1977, and Green, proposal for participation in Space Telescope, c. July 1977 (JPL 142, 52/860).

40. Nathan interview; Alan R. Gillispie (on Loch Ness photo) to Thomas Finley, 24 Mar. 1976 (JPL 142, 44/724); Julian Loewe, "JPL pair may test Shroud of Turin," *Pasadena Star-News*, 19 Aug. 1978; Barbara J. Culliton, "The mystery of the Shroud of Turin challenges twentieth-century science," *Science* 201 (21 July 1978): 235–39.

41. Green interview. On digital images in astronomy, see Michael Lynch and Samuel Y. Edgerton, Jr., "Aesthetics and digital image processing: Representational craft in contemporary astronomy," *Picturing power: Visual depiction and social relations* (New York, 1988), 184–220.

42. Nicholas Clapp, *The road to Ubar* (New York, 1998).

43. Clapp, *Road;* Elachi and Ronald Blom, "Transarabia expedition: Space technology and the discovery of the lost city of Ubar," talk to Caltech Management Association, 29 May 1992 (JPL A/V).

44. Brown interview.

45. F. E. C. Culick to Murray, 2 May 1977, and Walt Victor to Murray, 16 May 1977 (JPL 142, 6/92).

46. E.g., Robert Frosch to all center directors, 21 June 1977 (JPL 150, 1/10), naming technology utilization as a priority equal to flight programs.

47. Noel Hinners to C. Terhune, 2 Nov. 1982 (JPL 198, 21/292).

48. "Cooperative efforts with other NASA program offices," n.d. [c. 1977] (JPL 198, 9/132); Mark to Center directors and NASA staff, 13 Apr. 1982 (JPL 198, 11/153).

49. F. E. Goddard to Murray and Terhune, 16 July 1976 (JPL 142, 33/562).

50. Duane Dipprey interview, 15 Feb. 2002.

51. JPL performance evaluation for FY1979, 28 Mar. 1980 (JPL 142, 39/657).

52. Dipprey position paper, Mar. 1977, Terhune to R. R. Breshears, 9 May 1977, Dipprey to Terhune, 13 May 1977, and Breshears to Murray, 18 May 77 (JPL 142, 19/311).

53. Murray to David E. Mann, 22 Mar. 1979 (JPL 8, 6/80); "Image processing study," 9 May 1980 (JPL 142, 23/386).

54. E.g., J. N. James to Murray, 10 July 1979 (JPL 142, 24/412).

55. Orange report, part 1, 2 Apr. 1976 (JPL 173, 3/35).

56. Murray presentation to faculty board, 13 Nov. 1978 (JPL 8, 5/75).

57. Murray to Eugene Fubini, 15 Aug. 1977 (JPL 150, 1/10).

58. Handwritten notes [by Murray?] on meeting of JPL/Caltech and NASA representatives, c. Aug. 1978 (JPL 259, 36/356).

59. George A. Solomon to Murray, 10 Apr. 1978 (JPL 150, 1/11).

60. T. Hamilton, notes on A. D. Wheelon visit, 17 Feb. 1982, Hamilton to Schurmeier, 11 Jan. 1982, notes on Harold Brown visit, and Hamilton memo on Brown visit, 12 Jan. 1982 (JPL 173, 5/62).

61. Green interview.

62. Faculty board minutes, 7 Jan. 1980 (JPL 150, 5.50).

63. Koppes, 105; Stephen B. Johnson, *The secret of Apollo: Systems management in American and European space programs* (Baltimore, 2002), 97.

64. Anthony J. Calio to Alan Lovelace, 15 Mar. 1979 (NASA-Seasat); Murray interview, 15 Jan. 2003.

65. William E. Burrows, *Deep black: Space espionage and national security* (New York, 1986), 264–65.

66. Eric J. Chaisson, *The Hubble wars: Astrophysics meets astropolitics in the two-billion-dollar sruggle over the Hubble Space Telescope* (New York, 1994), 94–97; Charles Pellerin, interview by Robert Smith, 1 Aug. 1983, NASM.

67. Robert W. Smith, *The Space Telescope: A study of NASA, science, technology, and politics* (Cambridge, 1989), 147–48, 224, 383.

68. David D. Evans, "Classified work at JPL," 22 May 1980 (JPL 150, 10/133).

69. Henry C. Dethloff and Ronald A. Schorn, *Voyager's grand tour* (Washington, D.C., 2003), 136–37.

70. Green interview; James D. Burke interview, 5 Dec. 2003; Clifford Cummings interview, 14 June 2001; Eckman interview, by Russell Castonguay, 20 Nov. 2001, JPL archives.

71. Murray, *Journey,* 54; Murray interview, 31 Jan. 2003.

72. Merton E. Davies and Bruce Murray, *The view from space: Photographic exploration of the planets* (New York, 1971); Merton E. Davies and William R. Harris, *Rand's role in the evolution of balloon and satellite observation systems and related U.S. space technology* (Santa Monica, 1988).

73. Butrica, *See the unseen,* 167.

74. Wheelon interview.

75. Burrows, *Deep black,* 265.

76. Dwayne A. Day, "Not so black and white . . . : The military and the Hubble Space Telescope," *Space Times* 34 (Mar.–Apr. 1995): 20–21.

77. Murray, state of the lab, 2 Apr. 1982 (JPL 8, 10/119); Harold Brown's remarks on March 31, 1976 (JPL 8, 1/40).

78. Murray to Goldberger, 29 Mar. 1982 (JPL 8, 10/118); Murray oral history, CIT archives, 174.

Chapter 8. The Rise and Decline of Defense Programs

1. Lew Allen, interview by Heidi Aspaturian, 10 June and 31 July 1991 (CIT archives); Allen, author interview, 10 Dec. 2001.

2. Frank Colella interview, 26 Feb. 2002.

3. Albert D. Wheelon interview, 13 June 2002; Colella interview.

4. Allen, author interview; Murray quoted in Sara Terry, "Why put a general at helm of U.S. planetary space program?" *Christian Science Monitor,* 28 July 1982; "JPL takes on classified research," *Nature* (22 July 1982): 315; M. Mitchell Waldrop, "Air force general to head JPL," *Science* 217 (6 Aug. 1982): 517.

5. "Utilitarian program activities," 2 Nov. 1982 (JPL 198, 36/521).

6. Donald R. Baucom, *The origins of SDI, 1944–1983* (Lawrence, Kans., 1992); Frances FitzGerald, *Way out there in the blue: Reagan, Star Wars and the end of the cold war* (New York, 2000).

7. J. James to Allen, 11 Feb. 1984 (JPL 173, 3/39); memo on meeting at NASA of Allen, J. Beggs, B. Edelson, and H. Mark, 14 Feb. 1984, and Allen to M. Goldberger, R. Christy, and R. Vogt, 16 Feb. 1984 (JPL 198, 59/1005); William Goss, "Space Relay Experiment," 10 Oct. 1986 (JPL 198, 25/336). On Triad, see R. J. De Young et al., "A NASA high-power space based laser research and applications program," NASA SP-464 (1983); Baucom, *Origins*, 110–11, and Paul B. Stares, *The militarization of space: U.S. policy, 1945–1984* (Ithaca, 1985), 215.

8. There was another Pathfinder project at the same time, this one a collaboration between NASA and the European and Soviet missions to Halley's comet. Allen to Charles T. Force, 15 Mar. 1985 (JPL 198, 52/1010).

9. P. J. Rygh, "SDI activities at JPL," 26 Apr. 1985 (JPL 198, 6/82); Dave Evans, "Pathfinder," 10 Oct. 1986 (JPL 198, 25/336); James Cutts interview, 21 Mar. 2002; Arthur Lonne Lane phone interview, 31 Mar. 2005.

10. James to R. J. Parks, 8 July 1985 (JPL 119, 30//1821); James, "The Acquisition, Tracking, and Pointing (ATP) Space Experiments project," 22 July 1985 (JPL 119, 31/1852); James to Louis Marquet, 15 July 1985 (JPL 119, 28/1667); James to Marquet, 31 Oct. 1985 (JPL 119, 28/1674); Allen to James A. Abrahamson, 16 Nov. 1985 (JPL 198, 53/1015); D. F. Dipprey to Goldberger, 17 Jan. 1986, and to Marquet, 9 July 1986 (JPL 198, 5/73); Marquet to Dipprey, 30 June 1986 (JPL 198, 27/366); Evans to Allen, 23 Oct. 1986 (JPL 198, 25/336); on Delta, see Lane interview and J. W. Schomisch, ed., *Guide to the Strategic Defense Initiative* (Arlington, Va., 1990), 59–64.

11. James C. Fletcher, "The Strategic Defense Initiative," statement to U.S. House, 98:2 Congress, Committee on Armed Services, 1 Mar. 1984.

12. Beverly P. Mowery, "SDI: How much will fly?" *Signal* (July 1985): 47–51, on 48.

13. John L. Gardner, "Pilot Architecture Study," 30 Oct. 1984 (JPL 173, 1/12); James to Gardner, 28 Nov. 1984, and Richard A. Montgomery to H. Schurmeier, 7 Dec. 1984 (JPL 173, 1/13). Montgomery chaired the study's executive review panel at the same time he was directing JPL's Arroyo Center think tank.

14. Paul Weissman to Allen, 5 Apr. 1985 (JPL 173, 3/41).

15. Allan R. Klumpp et al. to editor, *Los Angeles Times,* 3 May 1982.

16. Weissman to Allen.

17. Terhune to senior staff, 5 Jan. 1979, with attached annotated copy of 1978 MOU (JPL 150, 22/257).

18. Mark Cohen to Allen, and to Goldberger and Vogt, 7 Aug. 1984; B. H. Rosker to Cohen, 17 July 1984 (JPL 173, 3/44); Allen (quote) to Cohen, 27 Aug. 1984 (JPL 198, 52/1008).

19. Advertisement, "Say no to 'Star Wars,'" *California Tech,* 1 Mar. 1985; Julian Loewe, "Local scientists blast 'Star Wars,'" *Pasadena Star-News,* 1 June 1985; Schurmeier to Vogt, 31 Aug. 1984, and Parks to Goldberger, 3 Oct. 1984 (JPL 173, 3/44); Goldberger to Cohen, 24 July 1984 (JPL 198, 23/312); Harold Brown to faculty, students, staff, 2 Oct. 1970 (JPL 198, 22/306).

20. Faculty board minutes, 14 May 1984 (JPL 198, 26/351).

21. Faculty meeting minutes, 6 June 1984 (JPL 173, 3/43).

22. Goldberger in faculty meeting minutes, 18 Feb. 1985 (JPL 173, 3/41); J. F. Benton, H. D. Politzer, and M. B. Kennedy, respectively, in faculty board minutes, 15 Oct. 1984 (JPL 173, 3/40).

23. James, "Defense Programs guidelines for the acquisition of new work," Sept. 1984 (JPL 198, 26/351).

24. Goldberger in faculty meeting minutes, 6 June 1984.

25. Goldberger to R. F. Christy, 18 Dec. 1981 (JPL 150, 3/24); faculty board minutes, 7 June 1982 (JPL 198, 26/350); Schurmeier to Allen, 23 Nov. 1982 (JPL 198, 27/363).

26. Faculty board minutes, 7 June 1982 (JPL 198, 26/350); Ken Whang, "JPL secret work questioned," *California Tech,* 1 June 1984.

27. Goldberger to Christy, 5 June 1984, and to John Seinfeld, 23 Oct. 1984 (JPL 198, 23/312); Goldberger to Allen and Vogt, 3 Oct. 1984, and faculty board minutes, 15 Oct. 1984 (JPL 173, 3/40).

28. Mary Scranton to Goldberger, 14 Feb. 1984 (JPL 198, 23/325); CIT board of trustees, 25 Oct. 1985 (JPL 198, 23/321).

29. Culick report in faculty board minutes, 16 Dec. 1985 (JPL 173, 3/46); on persistent concerns, see faculty meeting minutes, 18 Feb. 1985, and faculty board minutes, 18 Mar. 1985 (JPL 173, 3/41).

30. Goldberger in faculty meeting minutes, 6 June 1984 (JPL 173, 3/43).

31. Goldberger in faculty board minutes, 15 Oct. 1984 (JPL 173, 3/40).

32. Nick Nichols to Allen, 9 Nov. 1982 (JPL 198, 3/41).

33. "Professional disciplines of C.N.A. staff," 1982 (JPL 173, 2/23); David Jardini, "Out of the blue yonder: The RAND Corporation's diversification into social welfare research" (PhD diss., Carnegie Mellon University, 1996).

34. Faculty board minutes, 11 Oct. 1982 (JPL 173, 2/24); Brig. Gen. Victor Hugo, Jr., to James Ambrose, 11 May 1982, "Army external analysis center," 26 May 1982, and Tom Hamilton to Utilitarian Programs Executive Committee members, 9 June 1982 (JPL 110, 1/2). See also Philip M. Barnett, "The evolution of a federally funded research and development center: An analysis using four theoretical frameworks" (PhD diss., Claremont Graduate University, 2000), chap. 9.

35. Schurmeier to Allen, 23 Nov. 1982 (JPL 198, 27/363); "The Arroyo Center history and rationale," May 1984 (JPL 173, 2/28); Martin Goldsmith to Joann Langston, 4 Aug. 1982 (JPL 110, 1/2); brief for board of trustees, 20 Sept. 1982 (JPL 198, 36/533).

36. Faculty board minutes, 11 Oct. 1982 (JPL 173, 2/24).

37. Ibid.

38. "Army Analysis Program," presented to Caltech faculty board, 13 Dec. 1982 (JPL 173, 2/24); faculty board minutes, 13 Dec. 1982 (JPL 173, 2/25); "The Arroyo Center history and rationale," May 1984 (JPL 173, 2/28).

39. W. H. Pickering, "AAP Committee, chairman's final report," 15 Jan. 1983; Donald Cohen to Pickering, 26 Jan. 1983, Fred Culick to Pickering, 27 Jan. 1983, and Charles Plott to Pickering, 4 Feb. 1983 (JPL 173, 2/25); R. F. Bacher to Pickering, 25 Jan. 1983 (JPL 110, 1/3).

40. Culick to Pickering, 11 Oct. 1982 (JPL 110, 1/4).

41. Faculty board minutes, 28 Feb. 1983 (JPL 173, 2/24).

42. Schurmeier, "Management context for the Arroyo Center," draft 9 Jan. 1983, and "Concept of the Army Analysis Program at the Jet Propulsion Laboratory," 1 Apr. 1983 (JPL 173, 2/23); Schurmeier, "The Search Committee Charter," 11 Mar. 1983 (JPL 173, 2/26).

43. Arroyo Center, graph of staff (JPL 173, 2/28). By December, when staff approached 30, Goldberger noted that only 3 were new hires. Faculty board minutes, 12 Dec. 1983 (JPL 173, 2/24).

44. Systems Division charts, 1982 (JPL 198, 3/37). Section 311, in Systems Analysis, included ten PhDs in economics.

45. Hugo, quoted in Schurmeier to Goldsmith et al., 1 Oct. 1982 (JPL 110, 1/3); James, "Suggested discussion topics with Mr. James Ambrose," 8 June 1982 (JPL 110, 1/2); Goldsmith to Allen et al., 29 Oct. 1982 (JPL 198, 2/16); Barnett, "Evolution," 289–92.

46. Schurmeier, "Concept."

47. Schurmeier to Allen, 7 Mar. 1983 (JPL 173, 2/23); Goldsmith to Lt. Col. James Cravens, 4 May 1983, Langston to Goldsmith, 31 May 1983, and William B. Bridges to faculty board, 14 Nov. 1983 (JPL 110, 1/4). Other names considered were CASA (for Center for Army Studies and Analyses) and AASI (Army Advanced Studies Institute).

48. D. S. Cohen et al. to Vogt, 5 Dec. 1983 (JPL 110, 1/4).

49. Faculty board minutes, 12 Dec. 1983 (JPL 173, 2/24).

50. Handwritten notes by Schurmeier, 13 Jan. 1984 (JPL 173, 2/23).

51. Schurmeier, "Concept"; "Arroyo Center concept of operations," (quote) 19 Aug. 1983 (JPL 173, 2/28).

52. Roger Noll to Montgomery, 4 Jan. 1984 (JPL 173, 2/23).

53. Handwritten notes (by Schurmeier), "A/C facility location," 7 Jan. 1984 (JPL 173, 2/23).

54. Handwritten notes (by Schurmeier), "Comments to J.N.J[ames] by H. Gray and others just before Christmas," 1983 (JPL 173, 2/23).

55. "A/C facility location."

56. "AC 'questions,'" Dec. 1983–Jan. 1984, and handwritten notes by Schurmeier, 13 Jan. 1984 (JPL 173, 2/23); see answers to questions in Felberg et al. to Vogt, 17 Jan. 1984 (JPL 173, 2/30).

57. "Comments to J.N.J."

58. "Comments to J.N.J," and "Apparent positions," 7 Jan. 1984 (JPL 173, 2/23).

59. Goldberger in memo of meeting of Goldberger, Vogt, and Allen, 28 Dec. 1983 (JPL 198, 59/16); Goldberger to F. H. Felberg et al., c. early Jan. 1984 (JPL 173, 2/23).

60. Felberg, Parks, Schurmeier, and Montgomery to Vogt, 17 Jan. 1984 (JPL 173, 2/30); Montgomery to Goldberger, 17 Jan. 1984 (JPL 173, 2/23).

61. Montgomery to Allen, draft 12 Jan. 1984 (JPL 173, 2/23).

62. Vogt to voting faculty, 6 Jan. 1984 (JPL 173, 2/32); Lee Dembart, "Army think tank plan stirs Caltech," *Los Angeles Times,* 30 Jan. 1984; "Military think tank causes concern at Caltech," *Pasadena Star-News,* 29 Jan. 1984; Greg Critser, "Tough choices," *Altadena: The Weekly,* 19–26 Jan. 1984.

63. Goldberger and Vogt to the faculty, 23 Jan. 1984 (JPL 173, 2/31).

64. Caltech press release quoting resolution, 1 Feb. 1984 (JPL 110, 1/5). A resolution to divest "immediately" was defeated by a two-to-one vote. Faculty board minutes, 20 Feb. 1984 (JPL 198, 26/351).

65. Rochus Vogt interview, 24 Jan. 2001.

66. JPL Arroyo Center, "Summary report," 31 Jan. 1985 (JPL 110, 1/5).

67. James, "Comments on JPL staffing of army work," 26 May 1985 (JPL 198, 6/82); Terhune to Ambrose, 2 Aug. 1982 (JPL 198, 5/78); ASAS/ENSCE brochure (JPL 198, 25/336).

68. ASAS proposal authorization, 25 Oct. 1982 (JPL 198, 36/532).

69. Terhune to Ambrose, 2 Aug. 1982 (JPL 198, 5/78); H. W. Norris to Schurmeier, 18 Mar. 1985 (JPL 173, 10/59).

70. Norris to K. M. Dawson, 26 Feb. 1985 (JPL 119, 29/1720).

71. Allen to James et al., 16 May 1983 (JPL 119, 28/1651).

72. Notes for meeting of Allen with Ambrose, 2 May 1985 (JPL 198, 6/82); James

in Caltech trustees committee on JPL, minutes, 7 May 1985 (JPL 198, 24/332); James to Ambrose, 28 May 1985 (JPL 119, 28/1662); Cliff Cummings interview, 14 June 2001; Duane Dipprey interview, 15 Feb. 2002.

73. Notes on Caltech trustees committee on JPL, 27 July 1983 (JPL 198, 43/722).

74. James, "Comments on JPL staffing of army work," 26 May 1985 (JPL 198, 6/82).

75. Norris to Dawson (quote), 26 Feb. 85; Norris to Gates and Dawson, 22 Apr. 1985 (JPL 119, 29/1754); Allen to senior staff, 14 June 1983 (JPL 198, 51/1002), and Allen to senior staff, 15 Apr. 1985 (JPL 198, 53/1011); Philip Eckman, interview by Russ Castonguay, 20 Nov. 2001, JPL archives.

76. Allen to senior staff, 15 Apr. 1985 (JPL 198, 53/1011), and J. Scull, "ASAS/ENSCE," 10 Oct. 1986 (JPL 198, 25/336); JPL press release, 17 Feb. 1992 (NASA-JPL, 4674).

77. Dipprey interview.

78. Allen to senior staff, 14 June 1983 (JPL 198, 51/1002); Dipprey interview. On the military's early problems developing C³I, see Larry Waller, "The U.S. attacks the C³I problem," *Electronics* 56 (15 Dec. 1983): 98–107.

79. Norris to Schurmeier, 18 Mar. 1985 (JPL 173, 10/59).

80. JPL funding by source, FY85-FY90 (JPL 198, 9/126); Schurmeier to Allen, 12 Oct. 1984 (JPL 173, 10/40); Caltech trustees committee on JPL, minutes, 17 Aug. 1987 (JPL 198, 25/339).

81. Hans Mark to Norris, 23 Dec. 1982 (JPL 198, 11/154); Lt. Col. Ralph Freeman to Allen, 12 June 1986 (JPL 198, 27/368); "Synthetic aperture radar system support," task plan for DARPA, c. late 1988 (JPL 198, 56/1037); Walt Brown interview, 14 Nov. 2002.

82. Defense Programs Office, briefing to Mark, 15 Dec. 1982 (JPL 198, 5/72).

83. See Ivar Oswalt, "Current applications, trends, and organizations in U.S. military simulation and gaming," *Simulation and Gaming* 24:2 (1993): 153–89; Sharon Ghamari-Tabrizi, "Simulating the unthinkable: Gaming future war in the 1950s and 1960s," *Social Studies of Science* 30:2 (2000): 163–223.

84. Defense Information Systems Program, progress report, June 1982 (JPL 198, 5/72); Gen. Fred K. Mahaffey to Allen, 3 Feb. 1986, and Allen to Mahaffey, 10 Mar. 1986 (JPL 198, 54/1018); MOU between the U.S. Readiness Command and JPL concerning the Analysis and Training Systems Project, c. Oct. 1986 (JPL 198, 54/1022).

85. James to Technical Division managers, 11 Aug. 1982 (JPL 198, 5/72).

86. Schurmeier, "Utilitarian program, FY88 options," 6 Apr. 1983, and James, "Discussion of UPEC issues and concerns," 6 Apr. 1983 (JPL 173, 4/54); Felberg, notes on meeting re workforce planning, 8 July 1983 (JPL 173, 5/63); Gates, workforce implications for EC meeting, 15 May 1984 (JPL 173, 4/57).

87. Norris, material for EC retreat, 22 Mar. 1985 (JPL 173, 4/58); see also Dipprey, briefing for Caltech trustees committee on JPL, 13 Jan. 1987 (JPL 198, 25/337).

88. Norris to U.S. Army Communication Electronics Command, 8 Jan. 1985 (JPL 119, 28/1654); James to Marquet, 15 July 1985 (JPL 119, 28/1667); James to Allen and Parks, 22 Oct. 1985 (JPL 119, 32/1914); James to Allen, 1 Nov. 1985 (JPL 119, 32/1925); James to defense and civil programs managers, 2 Dec. 1985 (JPL 119, 32/1926).

89. JPL financial status and prospects, 7 July 1987 (JPL 198, 24/323).

90. Mal Yeater, "Options, prospects, plans," 12 Mar. 1992 (JPL 165, 1/8).

91. Faculty board minutes, 28 Feb. 1983 (JPL 173, 2/24).

92. Defense and Civil Programs, organization charts, 17 May 85 and 30 Sept. 1986 (JPL 119, 30/1768), and 2 Dec. 1985 (JPL 119, 32/1926).

93. James to Allen and Parks, 22 Oct. 1985 (JPL 119, 32/1914); Weissman (quote) to Allen, 5 Apr. 1985.

94. James to Allen and Parks, 22 Oct. 1985.

95. K. Zebb to Allen and Terhune, 7 Dec. 1982 (JPL 198, 2/11).

96. Goldsmith, "A proposal for separating the Jet Propulsion Laboratory from the campus of the California Institute of Technology," 13 Nov. 1984 (JPL 173, 3/45). This proposal called for JPL to report to the trustees instead of the Caltech president, thus bypassing faculty influence.

97. Jennifer Bingham Hill, "Defense contracts stir some student protests on college campuses," *Wall Street Journal,* 20 May 1983.

98. Caltech trustees committee on JPL, minutes, 25 Oct. 1986 (JPL 198, 25/336).

99. Allen interview, 10 Dec. 2001.

100. Handwritten queries, apparently Schurmeier to Culick, n.d. (JPL 173, 3/39).

101. James to Allen and Schurmeier, 7 Aug. 1985 (JPL 119, 31/1854).

Chapter 9. The Dividends of Defense Programs

1. Fred Felberg to Allen, 14 Dec. 1982 (JPL 198, 2/11); NASA Space Systems and Technology advisory committee, 2–3 Mar. 1982 (JPL 198, 19/257); K. C. Coon, "Technology program," 27 Sept. 1982 (JPL 198, 6/92); Allen to J. L. Kerrebrock, 10 May 1983 (JPL 198, 51/1002).

2. "Interview: Lew Allen," *Omni* (Jan. 1986): 78–90, on 88; Allen to David Packard, 19 Nov. 1982 (JPL 198, 51/1000).

3. Allen to Paul Weissman, draft 23 Apr. 1985 (JPL 173, 3/41).

4. Coon to Allen, 25 Apr. 1984 (JPL 198, 26/354).

5. Utilitarian Program activities, for Packard Panel review, 2 Nov. 1982 (JPL 198, 36/521); H. W. Norris to Schurmeier, 18 Mar. 1985 (JPL 173, 10/59); Allen, "Scientific spacecraft design," talk to AIAA conference, 9 Feb. 1988 (JPL 198, 44/755).

6. New work order 121, 2 Dec. 1985 (JPL 119, 33/1963); NASA Advisory Council minutes, 10–11 Feb. 1986 (JPL 198, 12/161).

7. On nuclear-electric: "Notes on TASP," 1 Nov. 1982 (JPL 198, 6/89); brief to CIT board of trustees on TASP, 20 Sept. 1982 (JPL 198, 6/88); Duane Dipprey interview, 15 Feb. 2002; Vincent Truscello, "SP-100," 10 Oct. 1986 (JPL 198, 25/336). On solar-electric: Lt. Michael R. Dickey, "Electric Insertion Transfer Experiment (ELITE)," Apr. 1989 (JPL 198, 5/74); Allen to Maj. Gen. Robert R. Rankine, Jr., and to Dale Myers, 24 Apr. 1989 (JPL 198, 57/1040); Dipprey to Robert Rosen and to Richard R. Weiss, 2 May 1989 (JPL 198, 47/702).

8. Handwritten notes on research seminar on VLSI, 17 Dec. 1981 (JPL 198, 40/587); Paul E. Ceruzzi, *A history of modern computing* (Cambridge, Mass., 1998), 217–24.

9. On DSN: P. T. Lyman to Terhune, 19 Feb. 1982 (JPL 198, 40/587).

10. Fred Felberg to Allen, 14 Dec. 1982 (JPL 198, 2/11); W. M. Whitney to VLSI management group, 16 June 1982 (JPL 198, 40/590).

11. Schurmeier to senior staff et al., 12 Sept. 1979 (JPL 142, 14/225).

12. Krishna Koliwad interview, 28 Mar. 2003.

13. Burton Edelson to Mary Scranton, 11 Aug. 1983, and Scranton to Allen, 3 Oct. 1983 (JPL 198, 24/325); Caltech trustees committee on JPL, 24 Sept. 1984 (JPL 198, 24/328); see also Allen to Edelson, 17 Apr. 1987 (JPL 198, 55/1526).

14. "Impact of delay in construction of the Microdevices Laboratory, JPL," 3 July 1985 (JPL 198, 3/35).

15. Allen to Edelson, 28 Sept. 1983 (JPL 198, 51/1003); E. O. Hinkley to Allen, 24 Apr. 1984 (JPL 198, 26/354); Allen interview, 10 Dec. 2001.

16. J. R. Pierce to Harold Brown, 19 Aug. 1976 (JPL 142, 6/97).

17. Allen to James Beggs, 15 July 1985 (JPL 198, 53/1012).

18. W. M. Whitney to VLSI management group, 16 June 1982 (JPL 198, 40/590); Carver Mead, interview by Shirley Cohen, 17 July 1996, CIT archives.

19. Allen to Edelson, 10 Dec. 1985 (JPL 198, 53/1016).

20. Allen retirement skit, 6 Dec. 1990 (JPL 235, 18/174).

21. Carl Kukkonen interview, 3 June 2003.

22. Dipprey interview; Allen interview; James Cutts interview, 21 Mar. 2002.

23. "Impact of delay in construction of the Microdevices Laboratory, JPL," 3 July 1985 (JPL 198, 3/35); Allen to Beggs, 15 July 1985; Allen to Edelson, 10 Dec. 1985.

24. Koliwad interview; Cutts interview.

25. Caltech trustees committee on JPL, 25 Oct. 1986 (JPL 198, 25/336).

26. Trustees meeting, 14 July 1986 (JPL 198, 24/335).

27. Caltech-NASA MOU on establishment of Center for Space Microelectronics Technology, 21 Jan. 1987 (JPL 198, 5/75); Goldberger to James Fletcher, 8 Jan. 1987 (JPL 198, 25/337).

28. CSMT, status report to board of governors, 17 Sept. 1987 (JPL 198, 5/75).

29. F. E. C. Culick to R. E. Vogt, 2 Feb. 1987 (JPL 198, 26/359).

30. Cutts interview; "Impact of delay in construction of the Microdevices Laboratory, JPL," 3 July 1985 (JPL 198, 3/35); Allen to Edelson.

31. Allen to Edelson; Cutts interview; Koliwad interview.

32. Kukkonen to Scranton, 16 Nov. 1989 (JPL 198, 25/347).

33. Descriptions of "Electron tunneling microsensors" and "Macro-scan-range tunneling microscope for device and material diagnostics," in Allen to Craig I. Fields, 31 Mar. 1988 (JPL 198, 56/1032); Koliwad interview; Cutts interview.

34. CSMT, Scientific Advisory Board, 12 Oct. 1988, and Dwight Duston to Allen, 20 May 1988 (JPL 198, 5/76). See also Albert Wheelon to Allen, 3 Jan. 1989 (JPL 198, 59/1049), judging the program "an outstanding achievement. One could ask for nothing finer."

35. Charles Seitz to Allen, 21 Feb. 1985, and Allen to Seitz, 27 Feb. 1985 (JPL 198, 52/1010); James C. Browne, "Parallel architectures for computer systems," *Physics Today* (May 1984): 28–35; Seitz and Juri Matisoo, "Engineering limits on computer performance," ibid., 38–45; Geoffrey C. Fox and Steve W. Otto, "Algorithms for concurrent processors," ibid., 50–59. On the hypercube's broader influence, see Alex Roland, *Strategic computing: DARPA and the quest for machine intelligence, 1983–1993* (Cambridge, Mass., 2002), on 151.

36. On Hypercube for SAR: Allen, Caltech Management Club talk, 29 Nov. 1984 (JPL 198, 43/735); on Fourier transforms: Fox and Otto, "Algorithms for concurrent processors," 57–59.

37. Allen to Wallace C. Henderson, 1 Oct. 1984 (JPL 198, 52/1009).

38. Allen to Paul Weissman, draft 23 Apr. 1985 (JPL 173, 3/41). See also Edelson to Allen, 22 July 1985 (JPL 198, 14/183: "NASA [has] not sponsored, to date, the Hypercube Research Project."

39. Background paper, attached to Allen to Lt. Gen. Don Kutyna, 9 Oct. 1989 (JPL 198, 57/1043).

40. Lt. Gen. Gordon Fornell to Allen, 9 Dec. 1988 (JPL 198, 5/76).

41. Kukkonen notes on meeting with Col. Mike Ryan, 14 Dec. 1988 (JPL 198, 5/76); Allen to Fornell, 22 Dec. 1988 (JPL 198, 56/1037).

42. Craig I. Fields to Allen, 1 Feb. 1988 (JPL 198, 5/75); Kukkonen interview.

43. Seitz to Allen, 21 Feb. 1985 (JPL 198, 52/1010); Vogt to Goldberger, 30 July 1984 (JPL 198, 23/312); MOU between Caltech and JPL and Ametek, Inc., Nov. 1985 (JPL 198, 53/1015); Allen to William F. Ballhaus, 8 July 1988 (JPL 198, 19/259); Allen to Lennard Fisk, 5 Dec. 1989 (JPL 198, 58/1044).

44. Peter Patton, "Supercomputing alternatives at NASA/JPL," 15 Aug. 1988, and Kukkonen and M. E. Alper, "JPL supercomputing initiative," draft 30 Aug. 1988 (JPL 198, 5/76); Allen to Dale L. Compton, 3 Mar. 1989 (JPL 198, 57/1040); Allen to Fisk, 20 Sept. 1990 (JPL 198, 58/1049); Allen to Fisk, to John Klineberg, and to Compton, 18 Dec. 1990 (JPL 198, 58/1050); B. Kamb to Robert W. Clayton, 30 Sept. 1988 (JPL 198, 26/359); Edward Stone to Lee B. Holcomb, 6 Nov. 1992 (JPL 259, 33/25); Stone comments at Cray T3D dedication, 13 Jan. 1994 (JPL 259, 44/474); Kukkonen interview.

45. Rob Staehle to Murray, 31 July 1979 (JPL 8, 6/84); Staehle, "Small planetary missions for the space shuttle," presented to American Astronautical Society annual meeting, 29 Oct. to 1 Nov. 1979, and J. D. Burke, "Micro-spacecraft," JPL publication 715–87, 15 Oct. 1981 (Ross Jones files), including Burke to A. R. Hibbs, 10 May 1979, with copies of doodles.

46. Burke, "Micro-spacecraft."

47. Robert L. Staehle interview, 12 Oct. 2001.

48. Ross Jones, microspacecraft timeline, 15 June 1996 (Ross Jones files); Jones interview, 2 May 2003; Jones, "Think small—in large numbers," Aerospace America (Oct. 1989): 14–17.

49. The solar panels and antenna determined the size of Burke's 66-cm solar microspacecraft: Burke, "Micro-spacecraft."

50. Jones, "Electromagnetically launched microspacecraft for space science missions," Journal of Spacecraft and Rockets 26:5 (1989): 38–342; Jones interview.

51. See the review article by A. Franks, "Nanotechnology," Journal of Physics E 20 (1987): 1442–51.

52. Bill Trimmer, "Micro Mechanical Systems," presentation to Microspacecraft for Space Science workshop, 6–7 July 1988 (Ross Jones files); Jones interview.

53. Donald C. Latham, "Space-based support of military operations," Armed Forces Journal (Nov. 1987): 38–46; Joan Lisa Bromberg, NASA and the space industry (Baltimore, 1999), 155–56; Burke, "Micro-spacecraft"; David W. Thompson, "The microspace revolution," 5 Sept. 1991 (copy courtesy of Orbital Sciences).

54. Freeman J. Dyson, Infinite in all directions (New York, 1988), 196–200; workshop panel members listed in Jones, microspacecraft timeline.

55. Microspacecraft for Space Science workshop, 6–7 July 1988, compiled presentations (Ross Jones files); "Microspacecraft conference," Spaceflight 30 (Nov. 1988): 426–27.

56. Allen, welcoming remarks, Micro Spacecraft workshop, draft 28 June 1988 (JPL 198, 5/76).

57. Jones and Christopher G. Salvo, "Microspacecraft technology for planetary missions," 42nd Congress of the International Astronautical Federation, 5–11 Oct. 1991, IAF-91–051 (Ross Jones files); Jones microspacecraft timeline.

58. Staehle, "The toughest part of the road to Pluto is the part from here to Washington," JPL Story, 15 Feb. 2001, JPL library; Staehle interview.

59. Rodney A. Brooks and Anita M. Flynn, "Rover on a chip," *Aerospace America* (Oct. 1989): 22–26; Staehle interview.

60. Jones interview; see also Cutts interview.

61. Cutts interview; Koliwad interview. On SDI and universities, see Council on Economic Priorities, *Star Wars: The economic fallout* (Cambridge, Mass., 1988), 88.

62. J. N. James to Pat Rygh, 12 June 1985 (JPL 119, 30/1795), and to Cliff Cummings, 10 June 1985 (JPL 119, 30/1793).

63. Allen in minutes of Caltech trustees committee on JPL, 31 Oct. 1987 (JPL 198, 25/340).

64. Allen to Wheelon, 17 Aug. 1988 (JPL 198, 41/599).

65. Allen to Dale Myers, 1 Dec. 1986 (JPL 198, 54/1023).

66. Allen to Wheelon, 17 Aug. 1988, and Wheelon, "Toward a new space policy," draft (JPL 198, 41/599).

67. Allen memo to Cole for Kukkonen, 12 Nov. 1984 (JPL 198, 52/1009); Gates, summary of EC retreat, 27 Apr. 1990 (JPL 198, 2/13); Allen to Fisk, 11 Sept. 1990 (JPL 198, 58/1049).

68. Jones interview; Staehle interview.

69. Tony Spear interview, 12 Feb. 2004.

70. Jones interview; Dipprey interview.

71. Allen to Fisk and to J. R. Thompson, 11 Sept. 1990 (JPL 198, 58/1049); Moustafa Chahine interview, 24 June 2003; author conversation with Philip Barnett, 10 Oct. 2001. The JPL visitors were Dipprey, Chahine, Norm Haynes, Barnett, and Frank Schutz.

72. Allen to Raymond Colladay, 23 June 1986, and Colladay to Allen, 30 July 1986 (JPL 198, 19/258); Daniel Fink for NASA Advisory Council to Fletcher, 14 Aug. 1986 (JPL 198, 11/148).

73. I. Bekey, "NASA long range plan to implement the recommendations of the National Commission on Space," 28 Feb. 1987 (JPL 198, 16/216); Allen to Colladay, 14 Apr. and 30 Apr. 1987, and Colladay to Allen, 24 Apr. 1987 (JPL 198, 19/259); Allen to Arnold D. Aldrich, 6 Dec. 1989, and to Geoffrey H. Vincent, 2 Nov. 1990 (JPL 198, 58/1045).

74. Gates, summary of EC retreat, 27 Apr. 1990 (JPL 198, 2/13).

Chapter 10. Space and Earth Science

1. James Westphal, interview by Robert Smith, 27 Sept. 1991, NASM; Westphal, interview by Shirley K. Cohen, 27 July 1998, CIT archives.

2. Westphal interview by Smith; Robert W. Smith, *The Space Telescope: A study of NASA, science, technology, and politics* (Cambridge, 1989), 330–31.

3. Smith, *Space Telescope,* 322–26.

4. Westphal interview by Cohen; Eric J. Chaisson, *The Hubble wars: Astrophysics meets astropolitics in the two-billion-dollar sruggle over the Hubble Space Telescope* (New York, 1994), 357–59; Ed Weiler interview, 24 Jan. 2004.

5. Allen to Burton Edelson with attached IRAS risk decision review, 21 Jan. 1983 (JPL 198, 51/1001); M. Mitchell Waldorp, "The Infrared Astronomy Satellite (I)," *Science* 220 (24 June 1983).

6. IRAS preshipment closeout review, 15 Dec. 1982 (JPL 198, 2/21).

7. G. Neugebauer et al., "Early results from the Infrared Astronomical Satellite,"

Science 224 (6 Apr. 1984): 14–21; Edelson, IRAS post-launch report, 28 Oct. 1985 (NASA-IRAS, 6070); "JPL highlights," IRAS report, 1984 (NASA-JPL, 4666); John Noble Wilford, "Astronomers' new data jolt vital part of Big Bang theory," *New York Times,* 3 Jan. 1991.

8. Thomas O'Toole, "Space telescope credited with more findings," *Washington Post,* 10 Nov. 1983; NASA, JPL performance review for FY1985 (quote) (JPL 198, 7/109).

9. Allen interview with Heidi Aspaturian, 31 Mar. 1994, CIT archives; Allen, author interview, 10 Dec. 2001; Goldberger to Vogt, 21 Mar. 1984 (JPL 198, 23/312).

10. *JPL Universe,* 19 Apr. 1985; William Green interview, 12 Feb. 2002.

11. Smith, *Space Telescope,* 337–52; Arthur J. Reetz, interview by Smith, 21 Sept. 1983, NASM; Weiler, interview by Smith, 20 Oct. 1983, NASM.

12. Benjamin M. Elson, "New Shuttle telescope in development," *AW&ST* (15 Sept. 1980): 41–47. The "s" in SIRTF initially stood for "shuttle."

13. EC minutes, 5 May 1988 (JPL 198, 25/342); L. Fisk to Allen et al., 5 Apr. 1989, Allen to Fisk, 23 May 1989, and JPL management plan for SIRTF, 26 May 1989 (JPL 198, 15/199); C. Pellerin to Allen et al., 5 Dec. 1989, and R. Truly to D. Compton (quote), 1 Dec. 1989 (JPL 198, 16/214); Fisk to Allen, 2 Jan. 1990 (JPL 198, 19/266); Norm Haynes interview, 11 Apr. 2003. On Caltech's interest, see G. Neugebauer to Allen, 23 Aug. 1988, and to T. Everhart and B. Kamb, 21 Mar. 1989 (JPL 198, 22/309).

14. Pellerin to Allen, Oct. 1987 (JPL 198, 15/213); see individual astrophysics projects for 1982 and 1988, in JPL 198, 15/213.

15. Ames and JPL, "A program plan for a Search for Extraterrestrial Intelligence," Mar. 1986 (JPL 198, 21/290); NASA, JPL performance evaluations for FY87 (JPL 198, 7/1115) and FY88 (JPL 198, 8/117); Steven J. Dick, *The biological universe: The twentieth-century extraterrestrial life debate and the limits of science* (Cambridge, 1996), 498–99.

16. "Interview: Lew Allen," *Omni* (Jan. 1986): 78–90, on 90.

17. Allen to Fisk, 10 July 1987 (JPL 198, 55/1028); Moustafa Chahine interview, 24 June 2003.

18. Allen talk to Caltech Associates, 14 Jan. 1985 (JPL 198, 43/736); Allen talk to AIAA aerospace engineering conference, 9 Feb. 1988 (JPL 198, 44/755); Allen to Gart Westerhout, 23 July 1986 (JPL 198, 54/1020); Allen interview, 10 Dec. 2001.

19. Ocean Topography Experiment (Topex), JPL study team prephase B report, Sept. 1982 (JPL 198, 6/98); Topex new start presentation, 1 Aug. 1985 (JPL 198, 3/28).

20. Don Rea to Bruce Murray, 2 June 1982, and to Shelby Tilford, 29 July 1982, and "JPL Oceans Program," July 1982 (JPL 198, 6/93); Chahine to C. H. Terhune, 16 Aug. 1982 (JPL 198, 6/97); J. King, Jr., to Terhune, 3 Aug. 1982 (JPL 198, 6/93); Allen to Edelson, 22 Oct. 1982, and Edelson to Allen, 9 Nov. 1982 (JPL 198, 13/180); Edelson to Allen, 21 Dec. 1982 (JPL 198, 13/180); Chahine interview.

21. Allen to Edelson, 29 July 1983 (JPL 198, 51/1003); NSCAT fact sheet, 14 Nov. 1985, and Edelson to Allen, 16 Dec. 1986 (JPL 198, 14/185); Fletcher to John Lehman, 12 Dec. 1986 (JPL 198, 11/148).

22. Chahine interview.

23. Faculty board minutes, 26 Nov. 1984 (JPL 198, 26/351); Allen to Edelson, 10 July 1985, and Edelson to Allen, 14 July 1985 (JPL 198, 14/183).

24. C. B. Farmer et al., "Stratospheric trace gases in the spring 1986 Antarctic atmosphere," *Nature* 329 (10 Sept. 1987): 126–30; John Maddox, "The great ozone controversy," ibid., 101; Michael D. Lemonick, "Culprits of the stratosphere," *Time* (21 Sept. 1987), 57; David E. Newton, *The ozone dilemma* (Santa Barbara, 1995).

25. James Beggs, speech to National Press Club, 5 Nov. 1982 (JPL 198, 10/146).

26. D. Schneiderman, "Short history of recent activities related to commercialization of civil remote sensing programs," 17 Nov. 1982, and Schneiderman to Rea, 22 Nov. 1982 (JPL 198, 6/89).

27. Fisk to Allen, 21 Oct. 1988 (JPL 198, 14/194); Caltech trustees committee on JPL, 29 Oct. 1988, 11 Jan. 1989, and 5 June 1990 (JPL 198, 25/323, 345, and 348); OSSA Strategic Plan, 1991 (NASA-OSS).

28. Allen, "Objectives of the Jet Propulsion Laboratory," 15 Nov. 1982, and Allen to Goldberger, 27 Oct. 1982 (JPL 198, 1/6).

29. Caltech trustees committee on JPL, 10 May 1988 (JPL 198, 25/342).

30. Caltech trustees committee on JPL, 11 Jan. 1989 (JPL 198, 25/345).

31. EC minutes, 5 May 1988 (JPL 198, 25/342).

32. Caltech trustees committee on JPL, 10 May 1988 (JPL 198, 25/342).

33. Albert Wheelon to Allen, 3 Jan. 1989 (JPL 198, 59/1049); Allen to Wheelon, 13 Feb. 1989 (JPL 198, 57/1039).

34. Chahine interview.

35. NASA Center Science Assessment Team, "Science at NASA field centers," May 1988, and D. James Baker to Allen, 30 June 1988 (JPL 198, 8125).

36. Rea and W. E. Giberson to H. M. Schurmeier, 3 May 1985, and Allen to Arden Albee, 11 June 1985 (JPL 198, 53/1012).

37. NASA flight project data book, 1992 (NASA-OSS).

Chapter 11. JPL under Allen

1. Murray, "Transition at JPL," 18 Mar. 1982 (Murray personal files).

2. Allen to John R. Pierce, 9 Mar. 1987 (JPL 198, 55/1025); Fred Felberg, interview by Michael Hooks, 6 Feb. 1990, JPL archives.

3. Allen to Caltech trustees committee on JPL, 25 Oct. 1986 (JPL 198, 25/336).

4. C. R. Gates to EC, 27 Apr. 1990 (JPL 198, 2/13).

5. Allen retirement skit, 6 Dec. 1990 (JPL 235, 18/174).

6. Moustafa Chahine interview, 24 June 2003; Charles Elachi interview.

7. Allen to senior staff, 9 May 1985 (JPL 198, 53/1011); Tom Duxbury interview, 19 July 2001.

8. *Lab-oratory* 5 (1976): 14–15 (JPL archives).

9. "Compendium of written comments, Open Landscaping Study," Nov. 1984 (JPL 198, 1/7).

10. Murray "Transition at JPL."

11. E.g., faculty meeting minutes, 26 Nov. 1984 (JPL 198, 26/351); John Benton to Allen, 15 Oct. 1984 (JPL 198, 22/306).

12. Faculty board minutes, 11 Oct. 1982 (JPL 173, 2/24); Murray, "Transition at JPL"; cf. Felberg, interview by Hooks.

13. Allen to M. Goldberger and to R. Vogt, 13 June 1983 (JPL 198, 51/1002); Bruce Murray interview, 31 Jan. 2003.

14. Allen interview, 10 Dec. 2001.

15. Allen presentation to Caltech faculty, 20 Nov. 1989 (JPL 198, 44/782); D. F. Dipprey, non-NASA support of campus-lab activities, 19 Sept. 1986, and T. Cole to Allen, 19 Sept. 1986 (JPL 198, 22/308).

16. D. R. Fowler and J. P. Click, "Institutional considerations," 2 Jan. 1980 (JPL 150, 21/245).

17. Terhune, "JPL financial status and prospects," 30 July 1982 (JPL 198, 59/315), and Allen, "JPL financial status and prospects," 7 July 1987 (JPL 198, 24/323).

18. Goldberger in faculty board minutes, 18 Jan. 1982 (JPL 198, 1/2); D. Morrisroe in faculty meeting minutes, 24 Nov. 1986 (JPL 198, 26/352).

19. Felberg, "The CEB facility project," 29 Jan. 1988 (JPL 230, 28/263).

20. IPAC presentation, Pasadena city board, 24 July 1984, and IPAC meeting, 22 Aug. 1984 (JPL 198, 27/365); "Caltech IRAS center deserves city's help," *Pasadena Star-News* editorial, 18 July 1984.

21. Allen, state of the lab, 24 Aug. 1984 (JPL 198, 43/733).

22. JPL institutional background and overview, 3 Oct. 1975 (JPL 142, 27/483).

23. "JPL is in Pasadena" (quote), *Pasadena Star News* editorial, 9 Mar. 1976; Harold Brown to Mortimer Mathews, 2 Dec. 1975, and Fowler to A. T. Burke, 2 Jan. 1976 (JPL 142, 24/420); "Pasadena to ask JPL land annexation," *Pasadena Star News*, 1 Jan. 1976; Jackie Knowles, "Pasadena fails in JPL annex" *Pasadena Star News*, 11 Mar. 1976; "The great battle for JPL," *La Canada Valley Sun* editorial, 18 Mar. 1976; Dick Lloyd, "JPL faces an identity crisis following incorporation vote," *Pasadena Star News*, 15 Nov. 1976; see additional clippings in NASA-JPL, 4649.

24. Beverly Place, "Foothill water wells checked for chemicals," *Montrose Ledger*, 19 Jan. 1980; Fred Felberg to speakers' bureau, with attached fact sheet, 25 Nov. 1986 (JPL 230, 26/246).

25. Felberg to speakers' bureau; W. E. Rains, memo to the record, with attached position paper, 20 Aug. 1986 (JPL 230, 26/241). The "good neighbor" phrase appears in both documents.

26. Management plan for remedial investigation/feasibility study, Jan. 1992 (JPL 239, 3/18); "Environmental cleanup review," JPL fact sheet, Apr. 1991 (JPL 239, 1/5); E. C. Stone to senior staff, 22 Oct. 1991 (JPL 239, 2/11); Marla Cone, "Jet Propulsion Lab added to Superfund list," *Los Angeles Times*, 15 Oct. 1992.

27. Tom Sauret interview, 25 Apr. 2001.

28. Robin Lloyd, "11 to join toxics suit against JPL," *Pasadena Star-News*, 18 June 1997; "Study clears NASA lab of alleged threat to public health," *San Diego Union-Tribune*, 23 Aug. 1998; Patti Paniccia, "The devil's advocate," *Los Angeles Times* magazine, 25 July 2004, p. 16.

29. Colin Macilwain, "Brookhaven contractor is sacked over tritium leak," *Nature* 387 (8 May 1997): 114; Andrew Lawler, "Meltdown on Long Island," *Science* 287 (25 Feb. 2000): 1382–88; Robert P. Crease, "Anxious history: The High Flux Beam Reactor and Brookhaven National Laboratory," *HSPS* 32:1 (2001): 41–56; Jack M. Holl, *Argonne National Laboratory, 1946–96* (Urbana, Ill., 1997), 485–88; Leland Johnson and Daniel Schaffer, *Oak Ridge National Laboratory: The first fifty years* (Knoxville, 1994), 225–29.

30. Spencer Weart, *Nuclear fear: A history of images* (Cambridge, 1988).

31. Felberg to speakers' bureau, 25 Nov. 1986 (JPL 230, 26/246); cf. Lawler, "Meltdown." Brookhaven scientists admitted their lack of public relations expertise.

32. Rains memo, 20 Aug. 1986.

33. Allen to Mary L. Scranton, 8 Apr. 1987 (JPL 198, 55/1026).

34. Ed Callan to Mary Lassiter, 31 Mar. 1989 (JPL 198, 42/700); Allen unsigned draft to Mikulski, and signed draft of 3 Apr. 1989, with Lorraine [Brakebill], memo to record, 24 Apr. 1989 (JPL 198, 57/1040).

35. Fowler to Everhart, 22 July 1988 (JPL 198, 26/358), and notes on contract NAS7–918-JPL, Caltech trustees committee on JPL, 29 Oct. 1988 (JPL 198, 25/343).

36. "Working paper on issues and strategies to be addressed in consideration of broader utilization of GOCO type of organization for NASA field centers," 17 Apr. 1986, and Ray Mayfield to R. Parks et al., 9 May 1986 (JPL 198, 18/244); advisory committee on the future of the U.S. space program (Augustine panel), summary and principal recommendations, advance copy, 10 Dec. 1990 (JPL 259, 18/228).

37. Report of the White House Science Council, Federal Laboratory Review Panel, May 1983.

38. Amendment to Caltech-NASA MOU, 11 Mar. 1985 (JPL 198, 15/206).

39. Allen to Hans Mark, 11 Nov. 1982 (JPL 198, 35/520); Wheelon to Allen, 3 Jan. 1989 (JPL 198, 59/1049).

40. Allen to Fisk, 20 Mar. 1990 (JPL 198, 58/1046); Chahine interview.

41. JPL office of patent council, briefing to Murray, 3 Oct. 1975 (JPL 142, 27/484); Terhune, notes on meeting with Fletcher, 4 Feb. 1976 (JPL 142, 29/507); D. Fowler to Allen, 1 Aug. 1985 (JPL 198, 26/356); Fowler to Morrisroe, 30 Dec. 1988 (JPL 198, 57/1038).

42. Fowler to John E. O'Brien, 20 Aug. 1985 (JPL 198, 26/356).

43. Michael Crow and Barry Bozeman, *Limited by design: R&D laboratories in the U.S. national innovation system* (New York, 1998), 64–67.

44. Robert J. Allnutt, "Space phase III: The commercial era dawns," speech to London aerospace conference, 2 Sept. 1982 (JPL 198, 16/222); Joan Lisa Bromberg, *NASA and the space industry* (Baltimore, 1999), 114–48.

45. CSMT board of directors, minutes, 14 Jan. 1988 (JPL 198, 56/1032); Edelson to Carl Kukkonen, 31 May 1988 (JPL 198, 5/75).

46. Edelson to Allen, 13 Oct. 1982 (JPL 198, 13/179), and Allen to Edelson, draft 9 Nov. 1982 (JPL 198, 13/180).

47. Fowler to Allen, 8 Jan. 1985 and 22 July 1985, and R. J. McEliece and E. C. Posner to Allen, 8 Jan. 1985 (JPL 198, 26/356); Panel on the Impact of National Security Controls on International Technology Transfer, *Balancing the national interest* (Washington, D.C., 1987); Allen, interview by Heidi Aspaturian, 4 Apr. 1994 (CIT archives).

48. Caltech trustees committee on JPL, 26 Oct. 1985 (JPL 198, 24/329); Allen to Edelson, 7 Nov. 1985 (JPL 198, 53/1015).

49. Wheelon to Allen, 3 Jan. 1989 (JPL 198, 59/1049); Wheelon interview, 13 June 2002; R. R. Green to K. M. Dawson, 9 Nov. 1990, and Allen to Wheelon, 15 Nov. 1990 (JPL 198, 58/1050).

Chapter 12. Recovery of Flight Projects

1. M. Mitchell Waldrop, "To the planets, cheaply," *Science* 213 (18 Sept. 1981): 1350; Solar System Exploration Committee, *Planetary exploration through year 2000: A core program* (Washington, D.C., 1983); John Noble Wilford, "No-frills plan to explore planets is urged," *New York Times,* 17 Apr. 1983; John Casani interview, 21 Nov. 2003. The "Observer" class was initially referred to as "Pioneer" class in the panel's deliberations.

2. Bruce Murray interview, 31 January 2003.

3. James R. Arnold to Allen, 26 Oct. 1982, Don Rea to Allen, 2 Nov. 1982, and Allen to Arnold, 21 Dec. 1982 (JPL 198, 51/1000).

4. Allen, "JPL—present and future," talk to Caltech Management Club, 16 Feb. 1983 (JPL 198, 42/714); notes on Caltech trustees committee on JPL, 27 July 1983 (JPL 198, 43/722).

5. SSEC, *Planetary exploration.*

6. Venus Radar Mapper, project initiation agreement, Sept.–Oct. 1982, and Warren W. James, "A new Venus initiative: Venus Radar Mapper," 9 Sept. 1982 (JPL 198, 3/25); Robert Buderi, *The invention that changed the world* (New York, 1996), 437–39; Andrew J. Butrica, *To see the unseen: A history of planetary radar astronomy* (Washington, D.C., 1996), 187–88.

7. Charles Polk, "Mars Observer Project History," Dec. 1990, JPL D-8095 (NASA-MO, 16614), 9–10.

8. Ulysses mission operation report, Oct. 1990, NASA History Office.

9. Edelson speech to Division of Planetary Sciences, 29 Oct. 1985 (JPL 198, 14/183); Lee Dye, "NASA primed for a year of spectaculars," *Los Angeles Times,* 2 Jan. 1986.

10. For JPL reaction, see, e.g., William E. Burrows, *Exploring space: Voyages in the solar system and beyond* (New York, 1991), 21–23.

11. "Challenger recovery assumptions," handout for EC, 13 Mar. 1986 (JPL 230, 24/231); Allen to Edelson, 18 Mar. 1986 (JPL 198, 54/1018).

12. NASA press release, 19 June 1986 (JPL 198, 24/334); W. E. Giberson to C. R. Gates, 21 Aug. 1987 (JPL 198, 16/216).

13. Lee Dye, "U.S. space failures force JPL into holding pattern," *Los Angeles Times,* 27 June 1986.

14. Allen to Brent Scowcroft, 31 Dec. 1987 (JPL 198, 38/569); Allen, "To boldly go—or what?" AIAA von Kármán lecture, 14 Jan. 1987 (JPL 198, 43/744).

15. "Report of the 90-day study on human exploration of the Moon and Mars," Nov. 1989 (JPL 198, 9/128); Burrows, *This new ocean: The story of the first space age* (New York, 1998), 566–69.

16. Caltech trustees committee on JPL, 13 Jan. 1987 (JPL 198, 25/337).

17. Augustine panel report, 10 Dec. 1990 (JPL 259, 18/228); Burrows, *This new ocean,* 568–569.

18. SSEEC, 7 and 14 Dec. 1981 (JPL 150, 5/47); Evan Thomas, "Roaming the high frontier," *Time* (26 Nov. 1984), 16–20; National Academy of Sciences, "Report of the committee on the space station," 1987 (JPL 198, 20/269).

19. Robert Staehle interview, 12 Oct. 2001.

20. W. Victor to Murray, 4 Aug. 1981 (JPL 150, 12/157); Don Rea to Terhune, 23 Aug. 1982, and D. Pivorotto, "Space station," 4 Oct. 1982 (JPL 198, 6/96).

21. Allen to Murray, 21 Nov. 1990 (JPL 198, 34/491).

22. Faculty meeting minutes, 24 Feb. 1986 (JPL 198, 26/352); Allen, interview with Heidi Aspaturian, 4 Apr. 1994, CIT archives.

23. R. P. Laeser, space station office presentation, 11 Jan. 1988 (JPL 198, 2/15); Laeser interview, 12 Dec. 2001; Norm Haynes interview, 13 Mar. 2003.

24. Burrows, *This new ocean,* 568–70.

25. Caltech trustees committee on JPL, minutes, 7 May 1985 (JPL 198, 24/332); Thomas Y. Canby, "Are the Soviets ahead in space?" *National Geographic* (Oct. 1986): 420–58.

26. Richard Barnes to Allen et al., 20 Mar. 1987 (JPL 198, 21/282); Jim Harford to Larry Adams, William Ballhaus, and Arthur Slotkin, 10 July 1987 (JPL 198, 28/385).

27. Eliot Marshall, "Mars mania and NASA," *Science* 240 (1 Apr. 1988); Arnold Beichman, "Ask the men who would be president about rescuing us from the 'Space Gap,'" *Los Angeles Times,* 19 Apr. 1988.

28. James Beggs speech to National Press Club, 5 Nov. 1982 (JPL 198, 10/146); NASA Advisory Council, "International space policy for the 1990s and beyond," 12 Oct. 1987

(JPL 198, 12/164); Burrows, *This new ocean*, 566–67; on Japan, see also Gates to Terhune, 8 July 1982 (JPL 198, 3/34), and Bradley K. Martin, "Now Japan plans to compete in space," *Wall Street Journal*, 10 Apr. 1984.

29. E.g., Peter J. Westwick, *The national labs: Science in an American system, 1947–1974* (Cambridge, Mass., 2003), 160–75.

30. Steven R. Weisman, "Reagan outlines steps to improve ties with Moscow," *New York Times*, 28 June 1984; Allen to Sen. Spark Matsunaga, 25 May 1984 (JPL 198, 52/1006); Senate Concurrent Resolution 16, *Congressional Record* 129 (10 Mar. 1983), 1; Allen to Burton Edelson, 11 June 1985 (JPL 198, 52/1012); Allen to Geoffrey Briggs and to Charles Pellerin, 13 Aug. 1985 (JPL 198, 53/1013); Allen to David Morrison, 2 Dec. 1985 (JPL 198, 53/1016).

31. US-USSR agreement on cooperation in outer space, 15 Apr. 1987 (JPL 198, 38/564); on DSN support, see Allen to James Beggs, 27 June 1985 (JPL 198, 1/5).

32. Memo on US-USSR space cooperation, Caltech trustees committee on JPL, 29 Oct. 1988 (JPL 198, 25/343); NASA memo, "Options for US/USSR space science cooperation," c. Dec. 1988, and handwritten notes (JPL 198, 38/569); Pete Smith to Allen and S. Fontana, 2 Oct. 1986, with draft of Fletcher to George Shultz and to John Poindexter (JPL 198, 16/222).

33. Tom Duxbury interview, 19 July 2001.

34. Bruce Murray interview, 23 Jan. 2003; Murray, *Journey into space: The first three decades of space exploration* (New York, 1989), 312–45; Burt Edelson and John Marks, "Go to Mars, but go together," *Los Angeles Times*, 18 Apr. 1988.

35. Charles Pellerin to Allen, 10 Mar. 1989, and Kenneth Kissell to John Lintott, 24 Jan. 1989 (JPL 198, 16/214).

36. David Morrison to SSEC members, 19 June 1986, Tobias Owen to Morrison, 9 June 1986, and Harold Masursky to Morrison, 16 June 1986 (JPL 198, 31/459).

37. Morrison to Fletcher, 5 June 1987 (JPL 198, 28/396).

38. Dan Hinks presentation to Caltech trustees, 14 July 1986 (JPL 198, 24/335); Morrison to Fletcher, 5 June 1987 (JPL 198, 28/396); Allen to Edelson, 13 Oct. 1986 (JPL 198, 54/1022); Space and Earth Science Advisory Committee, "The crisis in space and earth science," Nov. 1986 (JPL 198, 12/163).

39. Lennard Fisk, talk at symposium on space policy, 9 Dec. 1987 (JPL 198, 14/192).

40. Jay Berstralgh to DPS colleagues, Mar. 1987 (JPL 198, 27/375).

41. SESAC, "Crisis."

42. Jerry Wasserburg, remarks to Space Science Board symposium, 27 June 1988 (JPL 198, 22/309).

43. Murray interview, 31 Jan. 2003.

44. David Morrison to Lou Friedman ("conflict"), 27 Nov. 1987 (JPL 198, 31/459); Murray to Dale Myers ("resentment"), 16 Jan. 1987 (JPL 198, 36/528); Friedman to James Head ("soft"), 7 Nov. 1986 (JPL 198, 28/396).

45. E. J. Gaidos, "Project precedent," 31 July 1987 (JPL 198, 36/528).

46. Charles Polk, "Mars Observer project history," Dec. 1990, JPL D-8095 (NASA-MO, 16614), 14.

47. Lew Allen interview by Heidi Aspaturian, 4 Apr. 1994, CIT archives.

48. W. E. Giberson note on W. Purdy memo, 9 Mar. 1984, quoted in Polk, "Observer history," 15.

49. Polk, "Observer history," 23–38.

50. General Accounting Office, "Cost, schedule, and performance of NASA's Mars

Observer mission," May 1988; Mars Observer cost history, 6 Apr. 1992 (NASA-MO, 16614); Polk, "Observer history," 34.

51. Michael C. Malin to Allen, 8 Dec. 1988 (JPL 198, 2/23).

52. Polk, "Observer history," 45, 98.

53. Ibid., 50–81, William Purdy quote on 59.

54. On low bid: Jim Schefter, "Tragedy and triumph," *Popular Science* (Apr. 1994): 58–63, 94–95, on 62. On GE resistance: NASA performance evaluation of JPL for FY91, Mar. 1992 (JPL 259, 21//238). On "slow reveal": John Casani interview, 9 Apr. 2004.

55. NASA performance evaluation of JPL for FY88, Feb. 1989 (JPL 198, 8/117).

56. Polk, "Observer history," 90.

57. Allen to Edelson, 11 June 1985 (JPL 198, 53/1012).

58. Allen to Ralph Landau, 19 Nov. 1985 (JPL 198, 53/1015).

59. Allen to Edelson, 3 Sept. 1985 (JPL 198, 14/183); "CRAF/Cassini missions restored," *European Space Report* (17 Dec. 1990), 5.

60. NASA, draft performance review of JPL for FY88 (NASA-JPL, 16381).

61. Richard Truly to Albert Gore, Jr., 13 Nov. 1990 (NASA-CRAF, 5133).

Chapter 13. Voyager Redux, Galileo, and Magellan

1. Richard Laeser, in David Swift, *Voyager tales: Personal views of the Grand Tour* (Reston, Va., 1997), 177.

2. Richard Laeser, William I. McLaughlin, and Donna M. Wolff, "Engineering Voyager 2's encounter with Uranus," *Scientific American* (Nov. 1986): 36–45, on 38.

3. Laeser, McLaughlin, and Wolff, "Engineering," 38–39, 43; William E. Burrows, *Exploring space: Voyages in the solar system and beyond* (New York, 1990), 315–16; Joel Davis, *Flyby: The interplanetary odyssey of Voyager 2* (New York, 1987), 89–90.

4. Norm Haynes interview, 11 Apr. 2003.

5. Laeser, McLaughlin, and Wolff, "Engineering," 42; Douglas J. Mudgway, *Uplink-downlink: A history of the Deep Space Network, 1957–1997* (Washington, D.C., 2001), 193–201, 288–93; Davis, *Flyby,* 105–10, 112–13, 128–29.

6. Laeser, McLaughlin, and Wolff, "Engineering," 41; Raymond Heacock in Swift, *Voyager tales,* 153.

7. Laeser, McLaughlin, and Wolff, "Engineering," 42.

8. Ibid., 39; Burrows, *Exploring,* 317–18.

9. Henry C. Dethloff and Ronald A. Schorn, *Voyager's grand tour* (Washington, D.C., 2003), 209; Burrows, *Exploring,* 318–19.

10. Burrows, *Exploring,* 319; Dethloff and Schorn, *Grand tour,* 204.

11. John Noble Wilford, "Pictures of Triton, Neptune's icy moon, show signs of a never-seen icy volcanism," *New York Times,* 26 Aug. 1989; Dethloff and Schorn, *Grand tour,* 215–20; Burrows, *Exploring,* 399–417.

12. "Voyager 2's Neptune flyby leaves trail of stellar papers," *Science Watch* (Mar. 1991): 6.

13. Ingersoll in Burrows, *Exploring,* 414.

14. Edelson in Burrows, *Exploring,* 360; Laeser, McLaughlin, and Wolff, "Engineering," 40.

15. Frank Colella interview, 26 Feb. 2002; Bruce Murray interview, 15 Jan. 2003.

16. Burrows, *Exploring,* 21–23.

17. Laeser interview; Burrows, *Exploring,* 21–23.

18. Dorothy Nelkin, *Selling science: How the press covers science and technology* (New York, 1995), 159–60.

19. Sharon Begley and Mary Hager, "A fantastic voyage to Neptune," *Newsweek* cover story, 4 Sept. 1989; Leon Jaroff, "The last picture show," *Time*, 4 Sept. 1989; John Noble Wilford, "Voyager thrills scientists in farewell to solar system," *New York Times*, 26 Aug. 1989; Kathy Sawyer, "'Wow! What a way to leave the solar system,'" *Washington Post*, 26 Aug. 1989; "The wonders of Voyager," *Los Angeles Times* editorial, 29 Aug. 1989; "Voyager the intrepid," *AW&ST* editorial (with cover story), 28 Aug. 1989; and other material in JPL News Clips for August 1989 (JPL archives).

20. "The message from Neptune," *New York Times*, 24 Aug. 1989.

21. Michael Meltzer, *The Galileo mission to Jupiter* (Washington, D.C., forthcoming 2006), chap. 3; Burrows, *Exploring*, 332–35.

22. Meltzer, *Galileo*, chap. 2; John Casani interview, 21 Nov. 2003.

23. Casani interview; Meltzer, *Galileo*, chap. 2.

24. Casani interview; Meltzer, *Galileo*, chap. 2.

25. Murray, oral history interview by Rachel Prud'homme, Oct. 1983–Feb. 1984, CIT archives.

26. Casani interview; Robert S. Kraemer, *Beyond the moon: A golden age of planetary exploration, 1971–1978* (Washington, D.C., 2000), 228; David M. Harland, *Jupiter odyssey: The story of NASA's Galileo mission* (Chichester, U.K., 2000), 27–29.

27. Lew Allen, "Scientific spacecraft design," talk to AIAA, 9 Feb. 1988 (JPL 198, 44/755).

28. W. J. Downhower to Terhune, 4 May and 24 May 1978; J. Hyde, "Factors influencing 'quality' of cost reviews," 3 May 1978 (JPL 142, 11/177); A. Thomas Young to Downhower, 25 Aug. 1978 (NASA-Magellan, 5180).

29. Casani interview.

30. Norm Haynes interview, 13 Mar. 2003; Casani interview.

31. Murray interview, 15 Jan. 2003.

32. Casani interview.

33. Kraemer, *Beyond*, 54, 102, 230; Van Allen in Burrows, *Exploring space*, 338.

34. Burrows, *Exploring*, 340; Michael Benson, "What Galileo saw," *New Yorker* (8 Sept. 2003), 38–43; Casani afterword in Kristin Leutwyler, *The moons of Jupiter* (New York, 2003), 228.

35. Geoffrey Briggs to R. J. Parks, 27 Oct. 1986, and Parks to Briggs, 26 Mar. 1987 (JPL 198, 15/207); Meltzer, chap. 4; Burrows, *Exploring*, 341; Caltech trustees committee on JPL, 13 Jan. 1987 (JPL 198, 25/337); General Accounting Office, "NASA's deep space missions are experiencing long delays," May 1988 (NASA-Magellan, 5174).

36. Meltzer, *Galileo*, chap. 3.

37. Division 38 retreat, 18–20 May 1983 (JPL 92, 1/6).

38. Norm Haynes interview, 13 Mar. 2003; Casani interview.

39. Meltzer, *Galileo*, chap. 4; Caltech trustees committee on JPL, 10 May 1988 (JPL 198, 25/312).

40. Meltzer, *Galileo*, chap. 4; Burrows, *Exploring*, 342–49; Casani to F. Culick, 13 Jan. 1989, and Culick to Allen et al., 17 Jan. 1989 (JPL 198, 22/209).

41. Galileo prelaunch mission operation report, 1989, and Voyager prelaunch mission operation report, 4 Aug. 1977, NASA History Office.

42. Galileo prelaunch report; General Accounting Office, "NASA's deep space missions are experiencing long delays," May 1988 (NASA-Magellan, 5174).

43. Edelson to Beggs, 21 Dec. 1982, Edelson to Allen, 27 Dec. 1982, and Allen to Edelson, 2 Feb. 1983 (JPL 198, 3/25); JPL performance review for 1982, excerpt (NASA-JPL, 16381).

44. Magellan fact sheet, Apr. 1989 (JPL 198, 3/26).

45. General Accounting Office, "Cost, schedule, and performance of NASA's Magellan mission to Venus," May 1988 (NASA-Magellan, 5174).

46. On the SAR problems, see, e.g., Fisk to Allen, c. Jan. 1988 (JPL 198, 8/116).

47. Robert Buderi, *The invention that changed the world* (New York, 1996), 439.

48. Henry S. F. Cooper, Jr., *The evening star: Venus observed* (Baltimore, 1994), 38–42.

49. Magellan status reports, 1 p.m. 18 Aug, noon 19 Aug, and [no time] 19 Aug. 1990 (NASA-Magellan, 5174); handwritten notes on JPL press conference, 17 Aug. 1990 (NASA-JPL, 4674); Cooper, *Evening star*, 43–55.

50. David Okerson memos to NASA, 22 Aug. and 23 Aug. 1990 (NASA-Magellan, 5174); Jim Neuman quoted in Buderi, *Invention*, 443; Cooper, *Evening star*, 55–61.

51. Cooper, *Evening star*, 181–84, 209–21, 263–65; JPL press release, 15 Jan. 1992 (NASA-Magellan, 5174).

52. Cooper, *Evening star*, 129–33, 237–48; Buderi, *Invention*, 445–47; R. S. Saunders et al., "Magellan mission summary," *Journal of Geophysical Research* 97 (25 Aug. 1992): 13067–90 (special issues of the *Journal of Geophysical Research* on 25 Aug. and 25 Oct. 1992 reprinted as *Magellan at Venus*). On the ground slaps see Peter H. Schultz, "Atmospheric effects on ejecta emplacement and crater formation on Venus from Magellan," *Journal of Geophysical Research* 97 (25 Oct. 1992): 16183–248.

53. Cooper, *Evening star*, 275–83; Buderi, *Invention*, 447–48.

54. John Noble Wilford, "Ailing spacecraft to destroy itself on Venus," *New York Times*, 11 Oct. 1994; Cooper, *Evening star*, 265–74; Buderi, *Invention*, 450. On budget tolerance, see questions for Adm. Richard H. Truly from Senator Mikulski and Senator Wyche Fowler, c. Mar. 1992 (NASA-Magellan, 5174).

55. Larry Dumas interview, 14 Nov. 2003.

56. D. F. Dipprey, "Introducing JPL to the NASA TQM assessment team," 28 Apr. 1991 (JPL 239, 2/9).

Chapter 14. Faster, Better, Cheaper

1. Edward Stone interview, 23 Oct. 2003.

2. Moustafa Chahine interview, 24 June 2003; MacGregor Reid interview, 28 Mar. 2003.

3. Stone interview; Allen quoted in C. R. Gates to EC, summary of retreat 29 Mar.–1 Apr. 1990 (JPL 198, 2/13).

4. E.g., Stone, "Recent developments in the space program," talk to CIT executive forum, 8 June 1992 (JPL 259, 40/392); Stone interview.

5. Wesley T. Huntress, "Space science: Status and outlook," presentation to CIT trustees, 30 June 1993 (JPL 259, 32/326).

6. Charles Pellerin, "NASA strategic planning," 13 Apr. 1993 (JPL 259, 23/252).

7. FY93 budget outlook, June 1992 (JPL 259, 23/250).

8. NASA, "Aeronautics and space report of the president, fiscal year 1996 activities" (JPL 259, 20/232).

9. Caltech board of trustees and trustees subcommittee on JPL, minutes, 9 Mar. 1993 (JPL 259, 32/325).

10. Stone, notes on Caltech trustees committee on JPL, 10 Mar. 1992 (JPL 259, 32/323).

11. On the sense of crisis, see Douglas Isbell, "Budget alarms scientists," and Isbell and Andrew Lawler, "CRAF kill creates cost confusion," *Space News* (10–16 Feb. 1992), 1, 28.

12. NASA, "Payload flight assignments, NASA mixed fleet," Mar. 1988 (JPL 198, 17/233); Larry Dumas, JPL interview 1, 20 Sept. 2001.

13. William J. Broad, "NASA moves to end longtime reliance on big spacecraft," *New York Times,* 16 Sept. 1991; Norm Haynes interview, 11 Apr. 2003; Huntress interview with Rebecca Wright, 9 Jan. 2003, NASA History Office; Stephanie A. Roy, "The origin of the smaller, faster, cheaper approach in NASA's solar system exploration program," *Space Policy* 14 (1998): 153–71.

14. OSSA, presentation to NASA Strategic Planning Council, 25 Aug. 1987 (JPL 198, 16/216); OSSA Strategic Plan, 1991 (NASA-OSS); O'Toole, "New program development," Dec. 1991, and C. Elachi, "Desired program development attributes," 19 Dec. 1991 (JPL 165, 7/5).

15. Stone presentation to Caltech trustees committee on JPL, 10 Mar. 1992 (JPL 259, 32/323).

16. NASA, "Small planetary mission plan," report to Congress, Apr. 1992 (NASA history folder 16764).

17. Goldin remarks at AIAA annual meeting, 28 Apr. 1992 (JPL 259, 9/114); NASA press announcement, 22 May 1992 (JPL 259, 9/113). On Goldin's outsider image, see W. Henry Lambright, "Transforming government: Dan Goldin and the remaking of NASA," report for PricewaterhouseCoopers (Mar. 2001), 15.

18. Eliot Marshall, "Shakeup splits space science," *Science* 258 (23 Oct. 1992): 540; Lambright, "Transforming."

19. "A new NASA—the magic is back," memo on NASA senior management meeting, 1992 (JPL 259, 23/250).

20. Huntress NASA interview.

21. Howard E. McCurdy, *Faster better cheaper: Low-cost innovation in the U.S. space program* (Baltimore, 2001), 46; Roy, "Origin," 163.

22. Goldin, remarks to JPL workers, 28 May 1992, quoted in McCurdy, *Faster better cheaper,* 49; on battlestar galacticas, Huntress, author interview, 15 Dec. 2000. The quote appears as "battleship Galactica" in Eliot Marshall, "Space scientists get the jitters," *Science* 258 (20 Nov. 1992): 1296.

23. Roy, "Origin," 159, 167.

24. Harry Press, "Initiatives for future flight experiments and flight projects," 8 Mar. 1982 (JPL 198, 6/88).

25. Huntress, author interview, Huntress NASA interview, and author interview with Tony Spear, 12 Feb. 2004.

26. L. A. Fisk to Stone, 23 Jan. 1991 and 8 Nov. 1991 (JPL 259, 16/185); Broad, "NASA moves to end reliance."

27. Spear interview; Huntress, author interview, 8 July 2003; Haynes interview.

28. NASA, "Small planetary mission plan," Apr. 1992; Donna Shirley, *Managing Martians* (New York, 1998), 102–55; McCurdy, *Faster better cheaper,* 73.

29. Stone, state of the lab, 21 Apr. 1993 (JPL 259, 42/433).

30. Haynes interview.

31. Spear interview.

32. Fisk to Stone, 19 Mar. 1992, and Fisk to Stamatios Krimigis, 19 Mar. 1992 (JPL 259, 16/185); E. Kane Casani and Spear, "Low-cost spacecraft: The wave of the future," 27 Feb. 1992 (JPL A/V).

33. Discovery program handbook, Nov. 1992, and Discovery management workshop, final report, 13–15 Apr. 1993 (NASA-Discovery).

34. "Faster better cheaper: Science, mission design, and operations," panel discussion 22 Sept. 1994 (JPL A/V).

35. McCurdy, *Faster better cheaper,* 10.

36. Leising quote from "Faster better cheaper" panel discussion.

37. Goldin, "The future of NASA's science missions," talk at JPL, 25 Nov. 1992 (JPL A/V).

38. Huntress interview, 15 Dec. 2000.

39. "Small planetary mission plan," Apr. 1992.

40. Leising in "Faster better cheaper" panel discussion; Bruce Murray interview, 15 Jan. 2003.

41. EC retreat minutes, session 1, 1 Apr. 1993 (JPL 165, 7/15).

42. Discovery management option study team, 1992 (JPL 259, 89/1289).

43. JPL Discovery guidelines, 1992, Discovery management options, 23 July 1992, and Elachi to EC, 21 Sept. 1992 (JPL 259, 89/1289); Carl Pilcher memo on Discovery workshop, 8 Feb. 1993 (JPL 259, 89/1290).

44. Douglas Nash and Geoffrey Briggs to John Beckman, 16 July 1992 (JPL 259, 89/1289).

45. NASA press release 95–19, 28 Feb. 1995.

46. Roy, "Origin."

47. E.g., Lambright, "Transforming."

48. Roy, "Origin," 163–166; McCurdy, *Faster better cheaper,* 44–47; Lambright, "Transforming," 13–15.

49. On NRL: David H. DeVorkin, *Science with a vengeance: How the military created the U.S. space sciences after World War Two* (New York, 1992); Walter A. McDougall, *The heavens and the earth: A political history of the space age* (New York, 1985), 121–23, 154. On Livermore: Peter J. Westwick, *The national labs: Science in an American system, 1947–1974* (Cambridge, Mass., 2003), 204–10, 234–35.

50. Roderick A. Hyde, Muriel Y. Ishikawa, and Lowell L. Wood, "NASA assessment of the LLNL space exploration proposal and LLNL responses," LLNL report SS-90–9, 15 Jan. 1990; Roy, "Origin," 163–64.

51. Roy, "Origin," 162–63.

52. Huntress interview, July 2003.

53. Discovery management workshop, final report, 13–15 Apr. 1993 (NASA-Discovery).

54. Advisory committee on the future of the U.S. space program (Augustine panel), advance copy, 10 Dec. 1990 (JPL 259, 18/228); Michael Griffin interview, 21 Oct. 2004.

55. Huntress, "On the recommendations of the Augustine panel," 2 Jan. 1990 [*sic;* should be 1991] (JPL 259, 18/228).

56. Elachi, "JPL's future: Where do we go from here?" 12 Mar. 1992 (JPL 165, 7/8).

57. EC retreat notes, attachment 3, 14 Apr. 1992 (JPL 165, 7/6).

58. Stuart Nozette, "Concept on a napkin," in "Moonglow," *Final frontier* (Feb.–Mar. 1995), 35–37, on 37.

59. Garwin quoted in Vincent Kiernan and Andrew Lawler, "SDIO plans sensor tests near moon, asteroid in 1994," *Space News,* copy attached to Fred Vote and Roger Bedard,

"White paper: Potential JPL roles in SDIO's Clementine mission," 17 Feb. 1992 (JPL 259, 11/1283).

60. Committee on Planetary and Lunar Exploration, Space Studies Board, National Research Council, "Lessons learned from the Clementine mission" (Washington, D.C., 1997); Clementine mission summary (NASA-Clementine); Tom Duxbury interview, 19 July 2001; Trevor Sorensen interview, 24 Apr. 2001; Donald Horan, "The bat cave," in "Moonglow."

61. S. Nozette et al., "The Clementine bistatic radar experiment," *Science* 274 (29 Nov. 1996): 1495–98; Joseph C. Anselmo, "Evidence of ice raises interest in lunar missions," *AW&ST* (9 Dec. 1996): 27.

62. "Lessons learned."

63. Duxbury interview.

64. "Lessons learned," 17.

65. Ben Iannotta, "Clementine called model for NASA," *Space News* (25 Apr.–1 May 1994), 1; "Lessons learned," vii; Huntress in Liz Tucci, "Administrator blames bureaucracy for NASA waste," *Space News* (18–24 Apr. 1994), 10.

66. Sorensen interview.

67. Vote and Bedard, "White paper."

68. Col. Pedro Rustan interview, *Space News* (19–25 Sept. 1994), 22.

69. EC retreat minutes, Mar. 1991 (JPL 165, 7/4).

70. Miniature Seeker Technology Integration task plan, Oct. 1991 (JPL 259, 2/12).

71. E. Kane Casani, presentation on MSTI in Casani and Spear, "Low-cost spacecraft"; Stone to Caltech trustees committee on JPL, 31 Oct. 1992 (JPL 259, 31/311).

72. Stone, state of the lab, 19 Nov. 1991 (JPL 259, 39/381); see also Stone to all personnel, 20 Feb. 1992 (JPL 259, 2/16); Stone to Caltech trustees committee on JPL, 31 Oct. 1992 (JPL 259, 31/311).

73. Stone to Caltech trustees committee on JPL, 9 Mar. 1993 (JPL 259, 32/325).

74. Stone to all personnel, 16 Dec. 1992 (JPL 259, 3/26).

75. J. N. James to L. Allen and R. J. Parks, 22 Oct. 1985 (JPL 119, 32/1914); Lonne Lane phone interview, 31 Mar. 2005.

76. Caltech trustees committee on JPL, minutes, 10 May 1988 (JPL 198, 25/342).

77. Shirley, *Managing Martians,* 95; Spear interviews, 12 Feb. 2004 (quote) and 11 Mar. 2004 (on differences).

78. E.g., Goldin, "The future of NASA's science missions," talk at JPL, 25 Nov. 1992 (JPL A/V).

79. Carl Kukkonen interview, 3 June 2003.

80. Ross Jones and Chris Salvo, "FY-92 microspacecraft study program," 6 Mar. 1992, and Jones microspacecraft timeline (Ross Jones files); Ross Jones interview, 2 May 2003; Spear to Huntress, 24 Nov. 1993, and Spear (quote) to J. Casani, Elachi, J. Evans, J. King, and B. Shipley, 16 Nov. 1993 (Ross Jones files).

81. NASA, flight project data book, 1992 (NASA-OSS).

82. Robert Staehle, "Pluto mission development," 7 May 1992 (Staehle files); Staehle to Goldin, 28 May 1992, and Goldin to Staehle, 10 Aug. 1992 (JPL 259, 9/113); Staehle, "The toughest part of the road to Pluto is the part from here to Washington," 15 Feb. 2001, JPL Story; Staehle interview, 12 Oct. 2001.

83. Jones, microspacecraft timeline.

84. Eliot Marshall, "Space scientists get the jitters," *Science* 258 (20 Nov. 1992): 1296–97; Staehle to Goldin, 28 May 1992 (JPL 259, 9/113); Staehle interview.

85. Staehle interview; Jones interview.

86. Cassini briefing for Goldin, 29 Dec. 1992 (JPL 259, 9/115).

87. Stone interview.

88. Stone, state of the lab, 1 Apr. 1994 (JPL 259, 45/489).

89. Stone interview; Dumas, JPL interview 1, 20 Sept. 2001.

90. EC retreat minutes, 11–14 Mar. 1994 (JPL 165, 7/26).

91. Stone interview.

92. Dumas, author interview, 14 Nov. 2003.

93. Kirk Dawson, "Coping with a serious downturn in business," 14 Mar. 1992 (JPL 165, 1/9).

94. Huntress author interview, 8 July 2003; Tom Duxbury interview, 19 July 2001.

95. Wheelon interview, 13 June 2002.

96. Stuart Kerridge, Kendra Short, and Richard Wallace, "Planetary exploration 2012," briefing to EC, 29 Oct. 1992, and Elachi, "JPL 2000+, market and end products," 12 Nov. 1992 (JPL 165, 2/13).

97. Shirley, *Managing Martians,* 147–48.

98. Goldin address to JPL staff, 22 Sept. 1994 (JPL 259, 9/117).

99. Notes on Goldin visit, Sept. 1994 (JPL 259, 9/117); Caltech trustees committee on JPL, minutes, 2 Aug. 1994 (JPL 259, 33/329).

100. Chahine interview.

101. Chahine interview; Huntress author interview, 8 July 2003; Stone interview.

102. Stone, state of the lab, 1 Apr. 1994 (JPL 259, 45/489).

103. Dumas, JPL interview 1, 20 Sept. 2001.

104. Dumas, JPL interview 1; Stone, "Mars and the search for life elsewhere: Innovations in the third era of space exploration," von Kármán lecture at AIAA, 13 Jan. 1999.

105. "The objective of the Suess-Urey mission," Oct. 1995 (JPL 259, 96/1356).

106. McCurdy, *Faster better cheaper,* 120.

107. Ben Iannotta, "Congress, NASA dueling over reusable rocket management," *Space News* (23–29 Mar. 1994), 25.

108. "Clementine team comments on the NASA Discovery selections" (quote), Mar. 1995, and Stu Nozette to Col. Rich Davis, 29 Jan. 1995 (NASA-Clementine); "Clementine found still functioning; seen as argument for follow on," *Aerospace Daily,* 24 Feb. 1995.

109. John Noble Wilford, "With Observer silent, NASA now envisions 'Star Wars' explorers of Mars," *New York Times,* 27 Aug. 1993; Leon Jaroff, "Dreadfully sorry, Clementine," *Time* (27 Oct. 1997), 106.

110. "Lessons learned from the Clementine mission," 4.

Chapter 15. Reengineering JPL

1. William M. Tsutsui, *Manufacturing ideology: Scientific management in twentieth-century Japan* (Princeton, 1998), 190–235; Stephen P. Waring, *Taylorism transformed: Scientific management theory since 1945* (Chapel Hill, 1991).

2. Christopher Byron, "How Japan does it," *Time* (30 Mar. 1981), 54–60, on 60. See also William G. Ouchi, *Theory Z: How American business can meet the Japanese challenge* (Reading, Mass., 1981); Ezra F. Vogel, *Japan as number one: Lessons for America* (Cambridge, Mass., 1979).

3. On aerospace and quality circles: Waring, *Taylorism,* 166.

4. "A framework for action: Improving quality and productivity in government and industry," NASA report, Dec. 1984 (JPL 198, 12/158).

5. James Beggs to NASA associate administrator for management, 19 May 1982 (JPL 198, 10/145); "Suggestions for NASA/government improvements" (quote), 8 Jan. 1985 (JPL 198, 12/158).

6. Allen to S. J. Evans, 11 May 1987 (JPL 198, 55/1027); C. R. Gates, "JPL, the institution," Sept. 1990 (JPL 198, 9/127).

7. See, e.g., Fred Felberg handwritten post-it note, 9–10 Oct. 1985 (JPL 198, 12/159); Helen Benedict to Allen, 29 Sept. 1986 (JPL 198, 12/160), and handwritten note on Benedict to Allen, 12 Nov. 1982 (JPL 198, 18/246).

8. Allen to David Braunstein, 6 Dec. 1985 (JPL 198, 12/159).

9. Ed Stone interview, 14 Nov. 2003; this impression confirmed by Larry Dumas, JPL interview 3, 21 Sept. 2001.

10. Richard Laeser interview; 12 Dec. 2001; Norm Haynes interview, 11 Apr. 2003; EC retreat minutes, Mar. 1991 (JPL 165, 7/4); Stone, director's letter, 19 Apr. 1991 (JPL 163, 14/179).

11. Laeser interview.

12. J. Casani, "NASA's view of JPL," 19 Dec. 1991, and quote from D. McCleese, M. Sander, and T. Barber, "JPL↔NASA HQ, mutual perceptions," Dec. 1991 (JPL 165, 1/5); Huntress quoted in Casani, "Some inputs for off-site EC meeting," 24 July 1992 (JPL 165, 2/12).

13. Quote from Stone, "All-hands TQM talk," 7 Aug. 1992 (JPL 259, 40/397).

14. NASA administrator to all HQ employees, 5 June 1991, and Truly, personnel change announcement, 10 June 1991 (JPL 239, 2/7).

15. Daniel S. Goldin, "Total Quality Management—A culture change," 5 Dec. 1991 (JPL 198, 14/190); Goldin inaugural speech, 1 Apr. 1992, and Goldin, "The new NASA—faster, better, cheaper, without compromising safety," 18 May 1992 (JPL 259, 9/113).

16. Julia Malone, "Clinton trying out 'Total Quality Management,'" *Los Angeles Times*, 10 Mar. 1993; Al Gore, *Creating a government that works better & costs less: Report of the National Performance Review* (Washington, D.C., 1993), 66.

17. Moustafa Chahine interview, 24 June 2003; Wes Huntress interview, 8 July 2003.

18. Pete Lyman interview, 1 Apr. 2004.

19. D. F. Dipprey, quoted in Casani, draft notes on EC retreat, 17 Mar. 1992 (JPL 165, 1/6).

20. Stone quoted in ibid.

21. Stone interview, 14 Nov. 2003.

22. Casani to FPO managers, 8 Mar. 1993, and Laeser and Susan Stephenson to assistant lab directors, 11 Jan. 1994 (JPL 163, 14/189); Kirk Dawson, "JPL institutional overview," 7 Nov. 1994 (JPL 259, 20/229).

23. Casani, "Shadow activities," draft 7 July 1993 (JPL 163, 5/57); Laeser interview (quote).

24. E.g., Casani, "Systematic support systems and working groups: A holistic view," 29 Oct. 1993 (JPL 165, 2/17), and Office of Technical Divisions, "TDO 'care-abouts,'" 9 Sept. 1993 (JPL 165, 3/21).

25. Goldin inaugural speech, 1 Apr. 1992 (JPL 259, 9/113).

26. Casani, "Systematic support systems," and Casani to EC, 13 July 1993 (JPL 165, 2/17).

27. Willis Chapman to EC, 31 Mar. 1993 (JPL 165, 2/11).

28. Waring, *Taylorism*, 184.

29. Dumas JPL interview 1, 20 Sept. 2001.

30. Quoted in question to Dumas from JPL employee, Dumas JPL interview 1.

31. JPL employee surveys, May 1993 and June 1995 (JPL 259, 89/1293 and 1296).

32. Haynes interview.

33. Casani interview, 22 July 2004.

34. Laeser interview; for "manage by embarrassment": Winston Gin e-mail to author 9 May 2001. Cf. Lyman interview, 1 Apr. 2004.

35. Haynes and I. Cureton-Snead to R. O'Toole, 4 Aug. 1995 (JPL 163, 3/29).

36. Dumas JPL interview 3; Laeser interview.

37. "Laeser's hypotheses," c. Apr. 1993 (JPL 165, 2/11).

38. Michael Hammer and James Champy, *Reengineering the corporation: A manifesto for business revolution* (New York, 1993), and Hammer, *Beyond reengineering: How the process-centered organization is changing our work and our lives* (New York, 1996).

39. Laeser interview; Dumas JPL interview 3.

40. Dumas JPL interview 3.

41. Haynes and Cureton-Snead to O'Toole.

42. Laeser interview; Dumas JPL interview 1; Chahine, JPL Story; Stone interview.

43. "Issues from 10/26/95 management meeting" (JPL 165, 4/38).

44. Policy stated in Laeser, "Something's not right," 20 Feb. 1998 (JPL 163, 1/4).

45. Casani, "Rule making," n.d. [c. 1995] (JPL 163, 5/43); DMIE process redesign team, final report, 14 Feb. 1996 (JPL 163, 1/10).

46. Michael Hammer, "The road to the process organization," Nov. 1998 (JPL 163, 1/11).

47. Judith Gilliam, "Processes . . . the door to competitiveness" (JPL 163, 2/12).

48. Hammer, "Road."

49. Laeser to Winston Gin, c. 1997 (courtesy of Gin).

50. David Harvey, *The condition of postmodernity: An enquiry into the origins of cultural change* (Oxford, 1989); cf. Alvin Toffler, *Future shock* (New York, 1970), 112–35.

51. Laeser to Gin.

52. Kirk Dawson, "Best business practices," 13 Feb. 1998 (JPL 163, 1/4).

53. Stone, state of the lab, 1 Apr. 1994 (JPL 259, 45/489). An emphasis on development over operations also drove the restructuring.

54. Dumas JPL interview 3.

55. Stone interview, 14 Nov. 2003; Chahine interview.

56. Stone, "All hands TQM update," 7 Aug. 1992 (JPL 259, 40/397).

57. E.g., Stone to EC on "upward feedback facilitated discussion group," 4 Aug. 1999 (JPL 259, 7/94).

58. Dumas, author interview, 14 Nov. 2003.

59. Dumas JPL interview 2, 20 Sept. 2001; for Casani, see, e.g., "Reengineering the process for DMIE," 11 Sept. 1995 (JPL 165, 4/36), and Stone to senior staff, 20 Feb. 1998 (JPL 259, 6/76).

60. Laeser, "Something's not right," 20 Feb. 1998 (JPL 163, 1/4); Jody Brown ("purposeful") e-mail to Casani, 27 May 1997 (JPL 163, 1/8).

61. R. Stephenson in EC retreat, Mar. 1997 (JPL 165, 6/58).

62. Dumas JPL interview 3.

63. Casani, "JPL process map, draft 1," 14 Mar. 1995 (JPL 163, 2/12); "The JPL process map: A tangible view," 18 May 1995 (JPL 163, 2/13).

64. Laeser, "Something's not right."

65. On compensation, see the e-mail exchange between Casani and Laeser, 4–8 Aug. 1996 (JPL 163, 2/16).

66. Huntress interview, 15 Dec. 2000.

67. Dumas e-mail to author, 13 Mar. 2004; Waring, *Taylorism*, 128.

68. Tom Duxbury interview, 19 July 2001.

69. Tony Spear interview, 11 Mar. 2004. See also a similar expression in Duxbury interview.

70. Chahine interview, 24 June 2003.

71. Stone to all employees, 14 Feb. 1992 (JPL 239, 3/17).

72. Stone interview, 14 Nov. 2003; Laeser interview.

Chapter 16. The Tilting Triangle and Commercialization

1. Larry Dumas, author interview 14 Nov. 2003.

2. Dumas, chronology of JPL institutional events, 26 Sept. 2001 (courtesy of Dumas).

3. "JPL's institutional strategy," c. Jan. 1993, and EC meeting agenda, 1 Mar. 1993 (JPL 165, 2/11); Stone, state of the lab, 21 Apr. 1993 (JPL 259, 42/433); Kirk Dawson, "Workforce planning and allocation," 15 July 1993 (JPL 165, 2/17).

4. Zero Base self-assessment review, 27 Feb. 1995 (JPL 259, 50/552); Goldin talk on Zero Base review, 29 May 1995, and NASA news release, 19 May 1995 (JPL 259, 9/118); Stone to all employees, 20 Mar. 1995, and John Casani, handwritten notes on EC retreat, 7 Mar. 1996 (JPL 259, 4/41); graph of aerospace, and missiles and space, in Caltech trustees committee on JPL, 25 Mar. 1996 (JPL 259, 34/336); Stone, state of the lab, 21 Apr. 1993 (JPL 259, 42/433).

5. Stone presentation to Caltech trustees committee on JPL, 30 Oct. 1998 (JPL 259, 35/343); Stone to Edward Weiler, 7 Mar. 2000 (JPL 259, 7/101); Huntress to Stone, 6 Oct. 1998, and Huntress to Lon Rains, 27 Aug. 1998 (JPL 259, 16/188).

6. Sue Henry to D. W. Morrisroe, 19 Sept. 1994, Morrisroe to Stone, 21 Oct. 1994, and Thomas Sauret to Harry Yohalem, 21 Feb. 1996 (JPL 259, 16/188). Layoff figure derived from Stone presentation to Caltech trustees committee on JPL, 30 Oct. 1998 (JPL 259, 35/343).

7. Yohalem, "Managing workforce displacement and downsizing," 11 Mar. 1995 (JPL 165, 4/35); Dumas to John Heie and Jim King, 12 May 1994, with copy of Raymond R. Kepner and Richard E. Bromley, "How to minimize liability arising from reductions in force," Apr. 1992 (JPL 269, 2/25).

8. Stone presentation to Caltech trustees committee on JPL, 30 Oct. 1998 (JPL 259, 35/343).

9. "Messages from employees," 13 Mar. 1995 (JPL 165, 3/30); Dumas, "1995 employee survey, narrative synthesis," 26 July 1995 (JPL 259, 51/577); Richard Laeser interview, 12 Dec. 2001.

10. Henry to Morrisroe.

11. JPL, "Response to the NASA Federal Laboratory Task Force subcommittee questions," 31 Oct. 1994 (JPL 259, 20/231), and Dawson, "JPL institutional overview," 7 Nov. 1994 (JPL 259, 20/229); JPL employee survey, June 1995 (JPL 259, 89/1296).

12. JPL, "Response," and Dawson, "JPL institutional overview."

13. Carrie Patton, "Forget Venus; perhaps women are from Mars after all," *Working*

Woman (May 1999), 15; William J. Broad, "Three women wait anxiously for their spacecraft to reach Mars," *New York Times,* 18 Apr. 1999.

14. Women receiving bachelor's degrees in engineering increased from 10 percent in 1980 to over 15 percent in 1990, although concentrated in certain fields such as bioengineering and environmental engineering. Degrees in aeronautical/astronautical engineering to women increased from 8 percent in 1983 to 11 percent in 1993. Pamela E. Mack, "What difference has feminism made to engineering in the twentieth century?" in Angela N. H. Creager, Elizabeth Lunbeck, and Londa Schiebinger, eds., *Feminism in twentieth-century science, technology, and medicine* (Chicago, 2001), 149–68, on 158, 160.

15. See figures in JPL, "Response," and "NASA-wide metrics update to senior management," 13 Apr. 1993 (JPL 259, 23/252).

16. NASA equal opportunity and diversity management plan, 1 May 1994 (JPL 259, 24/256); Constance Penley, *NASA/Trek: Popular science and sex in America* (New York, 1997), 90–91, 94.

17. Goldin address at JPL, 22 Sept. 1994 (JPL 259, 9/117); Caltech trustees committee on JPL, minutes, 29 Oct. 1994 (JPL 259, 33/330).

18. Donna Shirley, *Managing Martians* (New York, 1998), 149, 224–25; see also Shirley retirement video, 25 Sept. 1998 (copy courtesy of Susan Foster). Cf. M. G. Lord, *Astroturf: The private life of rocket science* (New York, 2005).

19. Gavit quoted in Broad, "Three women." This view supports the recent, tentative conclusion that "the evidence for women bringing new ideas into engineering is mixed, at best," offered in Mack, "What difference," on 153.

20. Workforce age histograms in Dawson, "JPL institutional overview"; cf. headcount of engineers and scientists by age group for 1978 and 1981 (JPL 150, 22/257).

21. Yohalem, "Managing workforce displacement and downsizing," 11 Mar. 1995 (JPL 165, 4/35).

22. EC retreat minutes, 11–14 Mar. 1994 (JPL 165, 7/26); section 396 staff to Stone, 30 June 1994, James Erickson to Stone, 21 June 1994, Peter Doms to David Evans, 15 June 1994, Stone to all employees, 14 June 1994, and many other protests (JPL 259, 46/502); Stone remarks at town hall meeting, 6 July 1994 (JPL 259, 47/508); Karre Marino, "Stone discusses freeze on wages," *JPL Universe,* 15 July 1994.

23. Laeser interview.

24. JPL employee survey, vol. 1, May 1993 (JPL 259, 89/1293).

25. JPL employee survey, June 1995 (JPL 259, 89/1296).

26. Lewis A. Redding to Dumas, 8 Jan. 1997 (JPL 163, 2/17).

27. E.g., Kim A. McDonald, "U.S. auditors fault U. of California on management of 3 laboratories," *Chronicle of Higher Education* (7 Aug. 1991), A16.

28. Dick Oberman, consultant to House Subcommittee on Space, quoted in Caltech trustees committee on JPL, 2 Aug. 1994 (JPL 259, 33/329).

29. Dumas JPL interview 2, 20 Sept. 2001; Mark A. Stein, "Audit criticizes NASA's Caltech contract," *Los Angeles Times,* 31 July 1993; Kevin Keane, "Watchdog eyes NASA-Caltech contract talks," *Pasadena Star-News,* 30 July 1993.

30. Dumas JPL interview 2; Ed Stone interviews, 23 Oct. and 14 Nov. 2003. On correction of computer policy: Dumas to all personnel, 11 May 1994 (JPL 269, 2/25).

31. Brent Bennett interview, 18 Apr. 2001; Kurt Lindstrom interview, 24 Apr. 2001; Tom Sauret interview, 25 Apr. 2001.

32. Koppes, 147; Sauret interview, Bennett interview.

33. Bennett interview, Sauret interview.

34. Sauret interview. For fines, see JPL performance evaluation summary for FY94, 18 Aug. 1994 (JPL 259, 16/186).

35. Sauret interview.

36. Material for Caltech trustees committee on JPL, 29 Oct. 1994 (JPL 259, 33/330).

37. JPL, "Response to the NASA Federal Laboratory Task Force questions for JPL management," 21 Nov. 1994 (JPL 259, 20/231), and NASA Federal Laboratory Task Force, final report, Feb. 1995 (JPL 259, 22/244).

38. Dumas JPL interview 2.

39. Transcript of Goldin address at JPL, 22 Sept. 1994 (JPL 259, 9/117).

40. Huntress quoted in EC, summary and action items, 19 Nov. 1992 (JPL 165, 2/12).

41. Albert D. Wheelon interview, 13 June 2002; Dumas, author interview; Stone, "Challenges and issues," for Caltech trustees committee on JPL, 31 Oct. 1992 (JPL 259, 31/311); Caltech trustees committee on JPL, 29 Oct. 1994 and 26–27 June 1995 (JPL 259, 33/330 and 332); Stone to all personnel, 27 Jan. 1995 and 10 Aug. 1995 (JPL 259, 2/39 and 46); Stone to JPL employees, 1 Sept. 1999 (JPL 259, 7/95).

42. William B. Green to Robert J. Beale, 28 Sept. 1994 (JPL 259, 9/117).

43. "Pushback/pushforward," Mar. 1995 (JPL 165, 3/32); Casani, notes on EC retreat, 9 Mar. 1995, and Casani to Dawson with notes, 14 Mar. 1995 (JPL 165, 3/30).

44. Dumas JPL interview 2.

45. Goldin address to JPL employees, 22 Sept. 1994 (JPL 259, 9/117).

46. Stone interview, 14 Nov. 2003.

47. Lindstrom and Sauret interviews; Casani, handwritten notes on EC retreat, 13 Mar. 1997, and Larry Dumas to EC, 10 Apr. 1997 (JPL 165, 5/51).

48. Lindstrom interview; Dumas, author interview, 14 Nov. 2003; Dumas chronology.

49. Lindstrom interview.

50. Stone address to JPL employees, 21 Nov. 1994 (JPL 259, 49/536); faculty meeting minutes, 6 Dec. 1994 (JPL 259, 49/537); Stone, "JPL financial status and prospects," 14 July 1998 (JPL 259, 31/317). The 88 percent was applied to the performance-based portion of $12 million, resulting in $10.5 million; adding the guaranteed base fee of $6 million produced the total of $16.5 million.

51. Sauret interview.

52. Federal Laboratory Review report; "A proposed model for space science research at NASA centers," 11 May 1995 (JPL 259, 16/187); Andrew Lawler, "Goldin hopes to trim centers to stave off program cuts," *Science* 267 (24 Feb. 1995): 1087.

53. Glenn E. Bugos, *Atmosphere of freedom: Sixty years at NASA Ames Research Center* (Washington, D.C., 2000), 241.

54. Dumas interview 2, and Dumas, author interview.

55. Yohalem in EC retreat session 1, 23 Feb. 1998 (JPL 259, 58/690).

56. Memo for Caltech trustees committee on JPL, 19 June 1996 (JPL 259, 34/335).

57. Caltech IAC retreat agenda, 18–20 Sept. 1994 (JPL 259, 48/521); Wheelon interview.

58. Huntress quoted in Caltech trustees committee on JPL, minutes, 26–27 June 1995 (JPL 259, 33/332).

59. Material for Caltech-IAC retreat, Sept. 1995 (JPL 259, 51/583). Cf. Caltech trustees, budget presentation, 11 July 1995 (JPL 259, 31/315), which gives amount at 10 percent.

60. Stone presentation to Caltech trustees committee on JPL, 30 Oct. 1998 (JPL 259, 35/343).

61. David Baltimore in EC retreat session 1, 23 Feb. 1998 (JPL 259, 58/690).

62. JPL employee survey, May 1993, vol. 1 (JPL 259, 89/1293).

63. Wheelon interview.

64. EC retreat session 5, 23 Mar. 1998 (JPL 259/ 58/690).

65. Wheelon interview.

66. Moustafa Chahine interview, 24 June 2003.

67. Jim Evans, "JPL participation in the NASA space technology enterprise and the JPL reimbursable program," 7 Nov. 1994 (JPL 259, 20/230); Stone, FY96 presentation to the performance evaluation award evaluation board (JPL 259, 22/246).

68. Evans, "JPL participation"; W. H. Spuck, briefing for Goldin, 29 Dec. 1992 (JPL 259, 9/115).

69. Lawrence Gilbert, "The Caltech technology transfer program," 10 Mar. 1998 (JPL 259, 6/77).

70. Gilbert, "Technology transfer"; Carl Kukkonen interview, 3 June 2003.

71. "Photobit gains a third broad patent," *Machine vision online* (30 May 2000). Available at www.machinevisiononline.org.

72. Gilbert telephone interview, 15 Mar. 2005.

73. E.g., L. Van Warren to Stone et al., 30 Dec. 1992 (JPL 259, 9/115), and Stone, "Building the lab of the future," 24 Mar. 1994 (JPL 259, 45/487).

74. "Project implementation mode history," c. Apr. 1993 (JPL 165, 2/15); C. Elachi, "SESPD strategic plan alignment," 17 Mar. 1995 (JPL 165, 4/37); "Major contracts with unsatisfactory contractor's performance," c. Mar. 1988 (JPL 165, 1/1).

75. CSP Associates, "Make versus buy," 12 Aug. 1993 (JPL 165, 3/24).

76. Casani, "Suicide mission," 19 Feb. 1995, and "Impact of loss of in-house development," 27 Feb. 1995 (JPL 165, 3/31).

77. "Models for JPL downsizing," c. Mar. 1995 (JPL 165, 3/31); Elachi, "What is our strategy for guiding the focusing of our in-house skills," Mar. 1995 (JPL 165, 4/33).

78. J. J. Savino memo, 9 Mar. 1988, and "Associate contractor mode," 30 Mar. 1988 (JPL 165, 1/1).

79. "Combine strengths with partners," 22 June 1995, and Casani, notes on partnering to R. O'Toole, 4 Aug. 1995 (JPL 163, 4/31); CSP Associates, "Survey of industry attitudes towards partnering with JPL," 7 Nov. 1996 (JPL 163, 3/29).

80. M. Devirian, "Partnering subjects for discussion," Mar. 1997 (JPL 165, 5/52).

81. Lockheed Martin Astronautics, "Mars Surveyor program discussions," 14 Jan. 1997, and John McNamee to Casani et al., 20 Feb. 1997 (JPL 165, 5/52).

82. "Existing JPL 'partnerships,'" c. Apr. 1997 (JPL 163, 3/29).

83. Casani, notes on EC retreat, 13 Mar. 1997 (JPL 165, 5/51).

84. Casani, notes on EC retreat, 9 Mar. 1995, and Casani to Dawson, 14 Mar. 1995 (JPL 165, 3/30).

Chapter 17. A Break in the Storm

1. Michael Meltzer, *The Galileo mission to Jupiter* (Washington, D.C., forthcoming 2006), chap. 7; David M. Harland, *Jupiter odyssey: The story of NASA's Galileo mission* (Chichester, U.K., 2000), 56–57.

2. Meltzer, *Galileo,* chap. 7; John Casani interview, 9 Apr. 2004.

3. Michael Benson, "What Galileo saw," *New Yorker* (8 Sept. 2003), 38–43; Harland, *Jupiter,* 57, 70–71.

4. Jim Schefter, "Tragedy and triumph," *Popular Science* (Apr. 1994): 58–63, 94–95.

5. Lawrence Bergreen, *Voyage to Mars: NASA's search for life beyond Earth* (New York, 2000), 109.

6. See Murray inaugural speech, 2 Apr. 1976 (JPL 216, 2/23).

7. Mackie Lane, "Mars Observer photographed giant fish in space!" *Weekly World News* (26 Oct. 1993), 40–41.

8. Report of Mars Observer Mission Failure Investigation Board (NASA-MO, 16256); Final report of the JPL Mars Observer special review board, 2 Nov. 1993 (JPL 259, 90/1311); Mars Observer failure summary, Mar. 1994 (JPL 259, 33/328); Schefter, "Tragedy and triumph."

9. NASA and JPL review board reports; Cunningham quoted in Schefter, "Tragedy and triumph."

10. Timothy Coffey quoted in Kathy Sawyer, "NASA admits oversight on report," *Washington Post*, 11 Jan. 1994.

11. Report of NASA review board.

12. Larry Haskin to Allen, 16 July 1986, and Allen to Haskin, 30 July 1986 (JPL 198, 54/1020); Geoffrey Briggs to special assistant for strategic planning, 20 Mar. 1987 (JPL 198, 15/207).

13. Stone comments to Mars Observer team, 27 Aug. 1993 (JPL 259, 43/456).

14. Norm Haynes interview, 11 Apr. 2003; John Casani interview, 9 Apr. 2004; L. Fisk to Stone, 30 Jan. 1992 (JPL 259, 16/185); GAO draft report, "Causes and impacts of cutbacks to outer solar system exploration missions," Nov. 1993 (NASA-CRAF, 5133).

15. Fisk to Stone, 25 Feb. 1992 (JPL 259, 16/185).

16. "An approach for comparison of Voyager, Galileo, and Cassini," 11 Mar. 1992 (JPL 165, 1/7).

17. Stone quoted in Casani, handwritten notes on EC retreat, 12 Mar. 1992 (JPL 165, 1/6).

18. W. Downhower, "External environment—NASA," 26 Nov. 1991 (JPL 239, 2/13); Stone, "All hands budget talk," 18 Feb. 1994 (JPL 259, 45/481).

19. Kathy Sawyer, "Space budget battle: Humans 1, robots 0," *Washington Post,* 19 June 1991.

20. Stone, handwritten notes on Caltech trustees committee on JPL, 10 Mar. 1992 (JPL 259, 32/323); Cassini briefing to Goldin, 29 Dec. 1992 (JPL 259, 9/115).

21. Stone presentation to Caltech trustees committee on JPL, 31 Oct. 1992 (JPL 259, 31/311).

22. GAO report, "Causes and impacts"; Ralph Lorenz and Jacqueline Mitton, *Lifting Titan's veil: Exploring the giant moon of Saturn* (Cambridge, 2002), 179; Bruce Murray interview, 15 Jan. 2003.

23. Casani interview.

24. Report of JPL/planetary mission operations review board, 12 July 1991 (JPL 259, 16/190).

25. Dan Goldin, "The future of NASA's science missions," talk at JPL, 25 Nov. 1992 (JPL A/V). Cassini had $800 million for operations and the DSN, on top of $1.4 billion for the spacecraft and $450 million for the launch vehicle. Anne Eisele, "Cassini mission marks last of big spenders," *Space News* (6–12 Oct. 1997), 4.

26. Casani interview.

27. Haynes interview; Tony Spear interview, 11 Mar. 2004.

28. Tony Spear interview, 12 Feb. 2004.

29. On Spear as maverick: Wes Huntress interview, 8 July 2003. "Three-in-one" quote from Spear interview, 12 Feb. 2004.

30. Spear interview, 12 Feb. 2004.

31. Rob Manning, Brian Muirhead, and Richard Cook, "The true story behind the Mars Pathfinder success," 26 Sept. 2002, JPL Story, JPL library.

32. Spear interview, 12 Feb. 2004; Donna Shirley, *Managing Martians* (New York, 1998), 156–180; Andrew Mishkin, *Sojourner: An insider's view of the Mars Pathfinder mission* (New York, 2003), 97–106.

33. Spear interview, 12 Feb. 2004.

34. Huntress interview.

35. Kirk Dawson, "Organization possibilities," 19 Dec. 1991, and Dawson, "Features of Lockheed Skunk Works," Dec. 1991 (JPL 165, 1/5); Clarence L. Johnson, *Kelly: More than my share of it all* (Washington, D.C., 1985); Ben Rich and Leo Janos, *Skunk works* (New York, 1994).

36. Kirk Dawson to Judy Smith, 13 Apr. 1992, and Stone to Sherman N. Mullin, 17 Apr. 1992 (JPL 259, 2/18); Spear interview, 12 Feb. 2004.

37. Harland, *Jupiter odyssey,* 70–71; Benson, "What Galileo saw," 40–41.

38. Study team paper quoted in Benson, "What Galileo saw," 41; Harland, 70–72.

39. Benson, "What Galileo saw"; Huntress to Stone, 8 May 1992 (JPL 159, 16/191); Haynes interview.

40. Meltzer, *Galileo,* chap. 8; Harland, *Jupiter odyssey,* 94–96, and W. J. O'Neil, foreword to *Jupiter odyssey,* xxii.

41. W. J. O'Neil, presentation on Galileo to EC, 9 Mar. 1995 (JPL 165, 3/32).

42. Richard E. Young, "The Galileo probe mission to Jupiter: Science overview," *Journal of Geophysical Research* 103:E10 (25 Sept. 1998): 22,775–22,790; Meltzer, *Galileo,* chap. 8.

43. Gregory V. Hoppa et al., "Formation of cycloidal features on Europa," *Science* 285 (17 Sept. 1999): 1899–1902; Torrence V. Johnson, "A look at the Galilean satellites after the Galileo mission," *Physics Today* (Apr. 2004): 77–83; Benson, "What Voyager saw"; Harland, *Jupiter odyssey,* 230–32.

44. Galileo prelaunch mission operations report, NASA History Office; Usha Lee McFarling, "Stalwart Galileo is vaporized near Jupiter," *Los Angeles Times,* 22 Sept. 2003.

45. Usha Lee McFarling, "Fluke gives scientists double look at Jupiter," *Los Angeles Times,* 31 Dec. 2000.

46. O'Neil quoted in Benson, "What Galileo saw," 43.

47. William B. Green interview (quote), 12 Feb. 2002; Mars Pathfinder roundtable oral history, 5 Nov. 1998, NASA History Office; Mishkin, *Sojourner,* 306.

48. John Noble Wilford, "A new breed of scientists studying Mars takes control," *New York Times,* 14 July 1997.

49. Spear interview, 12 Feb. 2004.

50. On importance of Layman, see Shirley, *Managing Martians;* Mishkin, *Sojourner.*

51. Spear interview, 12 Feb. 2004.

52. Manning, Muirhead, and Cook, "True story."

53. Laurence Bergreen, *Voyage to Mars: NASA's search for life beyond Earth* (New York, 2000), 65–66, 86–87.

54. Shirley, *Martians,* 241–45; Mishkin, *Sojourner,* 261–64.

55. *Time* (14 July 1997) and *Newsweek* (14 July 1997).

56. Bernardo A. Huberman and Lada A. Adamic, "Internet: Growth dynamics of

the World-Wide Web," *Nature* 401 (9 Sept. 1999): 131; Steve Lawrence and C. Lee Giles, "Accessibility of information on the web," *Nature* 400 (8 July 1999): 107; Donna L. Hoffman, William D. Kalsbeek, and Thomas P. Novak, "Internet and Web use in the U.S.," *Communications of the Association for Computing Machinery* 39 (Dec. 1996): 36–46; Janet Abbate, *Inventing the Internet* (Cambridge, Mass., 1999), 214–17; Paul E. Ceruzzi, *A history of modern computing* (Cambridge, Mass., 1998), 302–3.

57. Mike Ebersole, in "Faster Better Cheaper: Science, mission design, and operations," panel discussion, 22 Sept. 1994 (JPL A/V).

58. Nona Yates, "Millions visit Mars on the Internet," *Los Angeles Times,* 14 July 1997; Amy Harmon, "Mars landing signals defining moment for Web use," *New York Times,* 14 July 1997.

59. "CRAF/Cassini missions restored," *European Space Report* (17 Dec. 1990), 5.

60. Renee Tawa, "Mission to Toyland," *Los Angeles Times,* 5 Oct. 1998.

61. President William J. Clinton, "Science in the national interest," 3 Aug. 1994 (Clinton1 .nara.gov/White_House/EOP/OSTP/Science/html/Sitni_Home.html); EC retreat minutes, Mar. 1991 (JPL 165, 7/4); Caltech trustees committee on JPL, minutes, 2 Aug. 1994 (JPL 259, 33/329); R. Rhoads Stephenson, "Technology transfer and educational outreach," presentation to EC, 30 Sept. 1994, and James A. Evans, "Outreach goal discussion," 18 Nov. 1994 (JPL 259, 49/535).

62. Peter Y. Hong, "Morale and image blast off at JPL," *Los Angeles Times,* 20 July 1997.

63. Brian Muirhead in Wilford, "New breed"; Daniel Goldin interview, 2 Apr. 2004.

64. Spear interview, 12 Feb. 2004, and Huntress interview, 8 July 2003.

65. Dumas JPL interview 1, 20 Sept. 2001.

66. Director's meeting with group supervisors, 22 Mar. 1995 (JPL 259, 50/557).

67. Spear interview, 12 Feb. 2004.

68. Ibid.

69. Mars Recovery Study Team, assessment, Sept. 1993 (JPL 259, 90/1310); Stone presentation to Caltech trustees committee on JPL, 9 Mar. 1994 (JPL 259, 33/328); Mars Global Surveyor, RFP issues, 20 Apr. 1994 (JPL 259, 91/1312).

70. Arden L. Albee, "Mars Global Surveyor: A success by any measure," *Engineering and science* 3/4 (2001): 31–41; Noel Hinners interview, 23 July 2003.

71. Albee, "MGS"; Bergreen, *Voyage,* 123–24. A magnetic field would offer no protection, though, against the ultraviolet radiation that floods through the thin Martian atmosphere.

72. Albee, "MGS"; Bergreen, *Voyage,* 304–6.

73. Albee, "MGS."

74. Dumas interview 3.

75. Casani interview; Randii R. Wessen and David Porter, "A management approach for allocating instrument development resources," *Space Policy* 13:3 (1997): 191–201.

76. Final environmental impact statement for the Cassini mission, June 1995 (NASA-Cassini); editorial, *AW&ST* (26 Sept. 1997): 66; Robert M. Nelson and D. L. Matson, "Cassini can unveil Saturn's secrets," *Los Angeles Times,* 3 Oct. 1997; Karl Grossman, "The risk of Cassini probe plutonium," *Christian Science Monitor,* 10 Oct. 1997; Reuters wire report, "Judge refuses to delay nuclear-powered launch," 12 Oct. 1997.

77. William Weber, "The 'new' JPL," 14 Mar. 1997 (JPL 165, 6/55).

78. Goldin quote from Tara Weingart, "Harpooning a comet—and other new space probes," *Newsweek* (15 Dec. 1997), 16; Deborah Zabarenko, "NASA's Stardust part of

bargain space mission era," Reuters news wire, 5 Feb. 1999; Casani, handwritten notes on EC retreat, 7 Mar. 1996 (JPL 165, 4/41).

79. Stone presentations to performance award evaluation board for 1995–1998 (JPL 259, 22/245–6 and 23/237–8).

80. Stone, FY98 presentation to the performance award evaluation board, 23 Oct. 1998 (JPL 259, 23/248). Flight instruments had 535 work-years, flight projects 472.

81. Stone presentation to Caltech trustees committee on JPL, 30 Mar.–1 Apr. 1998 (JPL 259, 34/341).

82. Michael Kobrick, "Planetary phrenology: The lumps and bumps of the Earth," *Engineering and Science* 1 (2002): 23–31.

83. Faculty meeting minutes, 6 Dec. 1994 (JPL 259, 49/537); SIRTF entries in NASA flight project data book for 1991, 1992, and 1995 (NASA-SIRTF). The plans for higher orbits first circulated after the Challenger accident: M. Werner, "Orbit comparison—scientific performance," and John Stauffer, "Operations related implications of differing orbits," 17 Oct. 1988, and SIRTF midterm review, 16 Nov. 1988 (NASA-SIRTF).

84. Stone in Caltech faculty board minutes, 12 May 1997 and 14 Dec. 1998 (JPL 259, 56/653 and 63/745); Stone, state of the lab, 19 Feb. 1998 (JPL 259, 58/682); Ed Weiler interview, 24 Jan. 2004; Goldin interview.

85. NASA/National Research Council, "The search for Origins: Findings of a space science workshop," 28–30 Oct. 1996, NASA press releases 96–159 and 96–160, 6 and 7 Aug. 1996, and President Clinton remarks, 7 Aug. 1996, all in John M. Logsdon, ed., *Exploring the unknown: Selected documents in the history of the U.S. civil space program,* vol. 5, *Exploring the cosmos* (Washington, D.C., 2001), 244–51, 488–93; Bergreen, *Voyage,* 38–57.

86. NASA/NRC, "Origins."

87. Stone, state of the lab, 19 Nov. 1991 (JPL 259, 39/381); Elachi, "Origins initiative," 23 Feb. 1998 (JPL 259, 58/683); Charles W. Petit, "Hunting new earths: Discovery of planetary system fuels search for others," *U.S. News and World Report* (26 Apr. 1999), 56–58. Interferometry also drew on the work at Caltech on the LIGO gravity-wave observatory. Ed Stone interview, 23 Oct. 2003.

88. On extrasolar planets, see Alan Boss, *Looking for earths: The race to find new solar systems* (New York, 1998).

89. Goldin interview; Eric J. Chaisson, "NASA's new science vision," *Science* 275 (7 Feb. 1997): 735.

90. "Martian chase" quote from Steven J. Dick, *The biological universe: The twentieth-century extraterrestrial life debate and the limits of science* (Cambridge, 1996), 469; Goldin quote from 1997 in Dick and James Strick, *The living universe: NASA and the origins of astrobiology* (New Brunswick, N.J., 2004), chap. 9; David Baltimore interview, 28 May 2004; "Exobiology program at the Jet Propulsion Laboratory," 1970 (copy courtesy of Steven Dick).

91. Gael Squibb notes on EC retreat, 11 Mar. 1999 (JPL 259, 64/758); James Graf quoted in Matthew Fordahl, "Deep Impact," AP newswire, 9 July 1999; NASA press releases on Deep Impact, 7 July 1999 and 4 June 2001; Andrew Murr and Jeff Giles, "The red planet takes a bow," *Newsweek* (6 Dec. 1999).

92. Elachi, "The post 'space summit' JPL program," 13 Mar. 1997 (JPL 165, 6/53); Stone, state of the lab outline, 19 Feb. 1998 (JPL 259, 58/682).

Chapter 18. Annus Miserabilis

1. Stone, state of the lab, 2 Mar. 1999 (JPL 259, 64/753).

2. Bruce Murray interview, 31 Jan. 2003; Norm Haynes interview, 11 Apr. 2003; Donna Shirley testimony, 30 Apr. 2000 (courtesy of Shirley); Human Exploration and Development of Space, strategic plan, 6 Apr. 1995 (JPL 259, 14/173), and NASA strategic plan, 1998 (JPL 259, 10/119).

3. Al Brejcha in EC retreat, concluding comments, Mar. 1997 (JPL 165, 6/58); Haynes interview; Noel Hinners interview, 23 July 2003.

4. Stone, "Loss of Mars Climate Orbiter," 7 Dec. 1999 (JPL 259, 68/806).

5. Haynes interview; Wes Huntress interview, 15 Dec. 2000; Larry Dumas JPL interview 1, 20 Sept. 2001.

6. Pete Lyman interview, 26 Mar. 2004.

7. Lyman interview.

8. Stone presentation to Caltech trustees committee on JPL, 30 Oct. 1999 (JPL 259, 35/344); Lyman interview; Hinners interview; Haynes interview; Dumas JPL interview 1.

9. D. F. Dipprey to A. V. Diaz, 5 Feb. 1992 (JPL 239, 3/17); Dumas to all employees, 9 Oct. 1992 (JPL 269, 1/4).

10. Stone video address to JPL employees/contractors, 1 Oct. 1999 (JPL 259, 67/793).

11. Dumas, author interview, 14 Nov. 2003.

12. Tony Spear interview, 11 Mar. 2004.

13. Stone in Mars press conference, 8 Nov. 1999 (JPL 259, 68/801).

14. Mars Pathfinder review board report, 7–8 Sept. 1994 (JPL 259, 91/1314); Howard E. McCurdy, *Faster better cheaper: Low-cost innovation in the U.S. space program* (Baltimore, 2001), 14–15; Lawrence Bergreen, *Voyage to Mars: NASA's search for life beyond Earth* (New York, 2000), 294–303.

15. Lyman interview; Haynes interview; McCurdy, *Faster better cheaper,* 15.

16. Mars Program Independent Assessment Team (hereafter Young panel), summary report, 14 Mar. 2000, 3.

17. JPL press release, 24 Mar. 2000.

18. Stone to Goldin, 14 Apr. 2000 (JPL 259, 8/102); Stone interview, 14 Nov. 2003; Hinners interview.

19. Stone presentation to Caltech trustees committee on JPL, 30 Oct. 1999 (JPL 259, 35/344).

20. Young panel, full report, 33–34.

21. Albert D. Wheelon interview, 13 June 2002.

22. Young panel, full report, 23.

23. Hinners interview.

24. Hinners interview; Haynes interview; Young summary report, 8.

25. Young report, 16–17, 27; Dumas JPL interview 1.

26. Lonne Lane, quoted in Shirley, *Managing Martians,* 159.

27. Lyman interview; Murray interview, 15 Jan. 2003; on arrogance see also Noel Hinners interview.

28. Haynes interview.

29. Stone to all employees, 9 July 1992, Office of Director, interoffice memoranda, and Stone, "All hands TQM update," 7 Aug. 1992 (JPL 259, 40/397).

30. Goldin address to JPL employees, 22 Sept. 1994 (JPL 259, 9/117); Moustafa Chahine interview, 24 June 2003.

31. Dumas, JPL interview 5, 24 Sept. 2001.

32. Dumas e-mail to author, 13 Mar. 2004; Casani interview, 22 July 2004.

33. Tom Duxbury interview, 19 July 2001.

34. Stone video address to JPL employees/contractors, 1 Oct. 1999 (JPL 259, 67/793).

35. Duxbury interview.

36. James Q. Wilson, *Bureaucracy: What government agencies do and why they do it* (New York, 1989), 319–20.

37. COMPLEX, "Lessons learned from the Clementine mission," National Academy of Sciences, 1997. The skunk works model, for example, relied on circumventing normal bureaucratic oversight.

38. James D. Burke interview, 5 Dec. 2003. On Corona, see William E. Burrows, *Deep black: Space espionage and national security* (New York, 1986), 107–11; Curtis Peebles, *The Corona project: America's first spy satellites* (Annapolis, Md., 1997); John Cloud, "Hidden in plain sight: The CORONA reconnaissance satellite programme and clandestine cold war science," *Annals of Science* 58 (2001): 203–9.

39. Goldin address at JPL, 22 Sept. 1994 (JPL 259, 9/117); Robert Lee Hotz, "Rocket with spy satellite explodes just after launch," *Los Angeles Times,* 3 Aug. 1993; Tim Weiner, "Lost Titan missile's secret cargo: Spy satellites worth $800 million," *New York Times,* 4 Aug. 1993; Hotz, "Sea satellites believed lost in blast," *Los Angeles Times,* 5 Aug. 1993; Mark A. Stein, "Mars Observer falls silent at critical point," *Los Angeles Times,* 23 Aug. 1993; Hotz, "Space probe asked to phone home; no reply," *Los Angeles Times,* 24 Aug. 1993; wire service report, "Contact with weather satellite lost," *Los Angeles Times,* 24 Aug. 1993; Hotz, "Mars probe still silent; hopes dim," *Los Angeles Times,* 25 Aug. 1993; Hotz, "Mars probe loss could change NASA's course," *Los Angeles Times*, 26 Aug. 1993; Hotz, "Transistor may be key to probe's failure," *Los Angeles Times*, 27 Aug. 1993; Hotz, "Mars devices failed in other spacecraft," *Los Angeles Times*, 28 Aug. 1993; Robert M. Nelson, "Rough weather for the space quest," *Los Angeles Times,* 27 Aug. 1993. On the reaction to the loss of another spy satellite with a Titan rocket failure in 1998: wire service report, "Spy satellite is destroyed as launch rocket explodes," *Los Angeles Times,* 13 Aug. 1998. This view confirmed in Eugene Tattini interview, 14 Oct. 2004.

40. David Baltimore to visiting committee for JPL, 3 Jan. 2001 (JPL 259, 25/346); Fred Culick interview, 17 Jan. 2001.

41. Huntress interview.

42. "NASA's critics in Congress sharpen up their knives," *Huntsville Times,* 2 Apr. 2000.

43. On Ranger: Koppes, 156–57.

44. Young panel, full report, 12.

45. Lyman interview.

46. Dumas, "JPL response to MPIAT lessons learned and recommendations," 10 Jan. 2001 (JPL 259, 35/348).

47. Haynes interview.

48. Duxbury interview.

49. Huntress interview, 8 July 2003.

50. Ed Weiler to Stone, 13 Jan. 1999 (JPL 259, 16/189); Stone to Weiler, 7 Mar. 2000 (JPL 259, 7/101); Haynes interview.

51. Usha Lee McFarling, "Missions to Pluto, Europa canceled," *Los Angeles Times,* 13 Apr. 2002.

52. Haynes interview.

53. Stone to lab employees, 18 May 2000 (JPL 259, 8/103). Stone stayed on an extra few months, until the end of April 2001, to give Caltech more time for the transition.

54. Dumas, JPL interview 3, 21 Sept. 2001.

Chapter 19. Epilogue, 2001–2004

1. David Baltimore interview, 28 May 2004.

2. I thank Winston Gin for this quote.

3. John Casani notes on EC retreat, 14 Mar. 1995 (JPL 165, 3/30).

4. Walt Brown interview, 14 Nov. 2002; Moustafa Chahine interview, 24 June 2003.

5. Ed Weiler interview, 24 Jan. 2004.

6. Charles Elachi interview, 25 May 2004.

7. Elachi all-hands talk, 2 May 2001, reprinted in *JPL Universe,* 4 May 2001; Richard Laeser interview, 12 Dec. 2001; Chahine interview.

8. Briefing book for JPL visiting committee, 9–11 Jan. 2001.

9. Baltimore interview; Ed Stone interview, 14 Nov. 2003.

10. Young report; Baltimore interview.

11. Elachi interview.

12. Elachi interview; Baltimore interview; Larry Dumas interview, 14 Nov. 2003.

13. Sam Venneri briefing to Goldin, 1 June 1998 (JPL 259, 11/140); Huntress to Stone, 27 Apr. 1998, with Goldin statement to Senate Appropriations Committee (JPL 259, 16/188); Stone presentation to Caltech trustees committee on JPL, 15 July 1998 (JPL 259, 34/342); Michael Sander briefing for JPL visiting committee, 10 Jan. 2001 (JPL 259, 35/347); Ed Weiler interview, 24 Jan. 2004.

14. Krishna Koliwad interview, 28 Mar. 2003.

15. Elachi interview, and Chahine interview.

16. Robert Staehle interview, 12 Oct. 2001; Elachi interview.

17. Chahine interview; Daniel J. Kevles, "Big chill in biotechnology," *Technology Review* (July 2003).

18. E.g., Michael Rogers, "Sounding the alarm for anthrax," *Caltech News* 37:2 (2003): 6–7; Chahine interview; Elachi interview, 15 June 2004.

19. Columbia Accident Investigation Board (CAIB), *Report,* vol. 1 (Aug. 2003), available at www.nasa.gov/columbia/caib; "Ground the space shuttle," editorial *Los Angeles Times,* 28 Dec. 2003; William Langewiesche, "Columbia's last flight," *Atlantic Monthly* (Nov. 2003), 58–87.

20. CAIB, *Report,* vol. 1, 191; Elachi interview, 15 June 2004; Ian Parker, "Absolute PowerPoint," *New Yorker* (28 May 2001), 76–87; Edward R. Tufte, *The cognitive style of PowerPoint* (Cheshire, Conn., 2003).

21. Bobby G. Williams, "The story of NEAR navigation: Extreme partnering for JPL," JPL Story, 27 Sept. 2001; Robert Roy Britt, "Comet fly-by success: Something to cheer about in dark times," *Space.Com,* 25 Sept. 2001. Available at www.space.com.

22. Usha Lee McFarling, "Odyssey probe detects vast ice deposits on red planet," *Los Angeles Times,* 29 May 2002.

23. Noel Hinners interview, 23 July 2003; Elachi interview, 15 June 2004.

24. A. Thomas Young to Goldin, 16 Nov. 2000 (JPL 259, 91/1317); Weiler interview.

25. Mars Exploration Rover landings, press kit, Jan. 2004.

26. Spear interview, 12 Feb. 2004.

27. Andrew Mishkin, *Sojourner: An insider's view of the Mars Pathfinder mission* (New York, 2003), 305–8; Weiler interview; Howard E. McCurdy, *Faster better cheaper: Low-cost innovation in the U.S. space program* (Baltimore, 2001), 9.

28. Weiler interview; Dumas, author interview, 14 Nov. 2003.

29. Spear interview, 11 Mar. 2004.

30. Charles Piller, "A fatal attraction in space," *Los Angeles Times,* 24 Dec. 2003.

31. Weiler interview.

32. Spear interview, 11 Mar. 2004.

33. O'Keefe comment at post-landing press conference at JPL, 3 Jan. 2004.

34. Jeanne Holm, "Metrics for Mars and NASA portals, 1/3–7/04"; MER press conference, 24 Jan. 2004.

35. On Spirit problems: JPL press releases, 21–24 Jan. 2004; Theisinger in MER press conference, 24 Jan. 2004.

36. JPL press release, 1 Feb. 2004.

37. Donna Shirley, *Managing Martians* (New York, 1998), 256; Mike Rogers, "Flights! Cameras! Mars!" *Caltech News* 37:4 (2003): 2, 12–13.

38. Piller, "Man on a mission heads rover team," *Los Angeles Times,* 5 Jan. 2004.

39. Elachi interview, 15 June 2004.

40. Douglas Smith, "Opportunity by the sea," *Engineering and Science* 67:1 (2004): 2; Guy Webster, "Rover finds rocks likely formed in salt water," *JPL Universe,* 26 Mar. 2004; John Updike, "Duet on Mars," *New Yorker* (1 Mar. 2004), 35.

41. Genesis and Stardust press kits; John Johnson, "Genesis crash blamed on installation error," *Los Angeles Times,* 15 Oct. 2004.

42. Thomas H. Maugh III, "A ringside seat reveals unexpected phenomena," *Los Angeles Times,* 2 July 2004; "'Flawless' flight takes Cassini to Saturn orbit" and Robert Mitchell interview, *JPL Universe,* 2 July 2004; John Johnson, "Titan images reveal dynamic surface and an apparent lake," *Los Angeles Times,* 29 Oct. 2004; Mark Alpert, "Strange new world," *Scientific American* 292:4 (2005): 22–24; C.C. Porco et al., "Cassini observes the active south pole of Enceladus," and J.R. Spencer et al., "Cassini encounters Enceladus: Background and the discovery of a south polar hot spot," *Science* 311 (10 Mar. 2006), 1393–1401 and 1401–5.

43. NASA, "Space science for the 21st century: The space science enterprise strategic plan," Aug. 1995, NASA-OSS.

44. Robert C. Cowen, "A new agenda for NASA beyond the pioneering stage," *Christian Science Monitor,* 28 Dec. 1983.

45. "Project Prometheus," overview handout, 8 Apr. 2003 (author copy); Spear interview, 11 Mar. 2004; Casani interview, 22 July 2004.

46. Weiler interview; Elachi interview, 15 June 2004.

47. Elachi interview, 15 June 2004; Michael Kobrick, "Planetary phrenology: The lumps and bumps of the Earth," *Engineering and Science* 1 (2002): 23–31; Gilles Peltzer and Paul Rosen, "Surface displacement of the 17 May 1993 Eureka Valley, California, earthquake observed by SAR interferometry," *Science* 268 (2 June 1995): 1333–36.

48. Smith, "The far, the cold, and the dusty," *Engineering and Science* 66:4 (2003): 9–19.

49. P. DeBernardis et al., "A flat universe from high-resolution maps of the cosmic

microwave background radiation," *Nature* 404 (27 Apr. 2000): 955–59, and Wayne Hu, "Ringing in the new cosmology," ibid., 939–40; see also Committee on the Physics of the Universe, National Research Council, *Connecting quarks with the cosmos: Eleven science questions for the new century* (Washington, D.C., 2003).

50. Elachi interview, 15 June 2004.

51. Ibid.

52. Voyager mission operations status report #2004–05–07.

Chapter 20. Conclusion

1. David Swift, *Voyager tales: Personal views of the Grand Tour* (Reston, Va., 1997), 395.

2. Bruce Mazlish, "Following the sun," *Wilson Quarterly* (autumn 1980): 90–93.

3. Bruce Murray, *Journey into space: The first three decades of space exploration* (New York, 1989). See also Timothy Ferris, "Ground NASA and start again," *New York Times*, 16 Mar. 1992.

4. Figure 2 in Office of Science and Technology Policy, "Funding trends in NASA's space science program," Sept. 1984 (JPL 173, 8/110).

5. Robert Staehle interview, 12 Oct. 2001.

6. E.g. Michael Meltzer, *The Galileo mission to Jupiter* (Washington, D.C., forthcoming 2006), chap. 1; Jerry Adler, "The riddles of Saturn," *Newsweek* (24 Nov. 1980).

7. Laurence Bergreen, "Across sands of time and oceans of space," *Los Angeles Times*, 5 Jan. 2004.

8. The hard-headed Soviets, by contrast, named spacecraft after their objectives, such as Venera, Mars, and Phobos.

9. E.g., Glyndwr Williams, "The *Endeavour* voyage: A coincidence of motives," in Margarette Lincoln, ed., *Science and exploration in the Pacific: European voyages to the southern oceans in the eighteenth century* (Suffolk, U.K., 1998), 3–18; John Gascoigne, *Science in the service of empire: Joseph Banks, the British state and the uses of science in the age of revolution* (Cambridge, 1998); Donald Worster, *A river running west: The life of John Wesley Powell* (Oxford, 2001), esp. 300–10 on artists.

10. Ed Stone interview, 14 Nov. 2003.

11. Winston Gin conversation, 9 Jan. 2004.

12. Noel Hinners interview, 23 July 2003; Albert D. Wheelon interview, 13 June 2002.

13. Charles Elachi interview, 15 June 2004.

14. Larry Dumas, JPL interview, 24 Sept. 2001.

15. Scholars have noted clear organizational goals as one feature of high-reliability organizations: Gene I. Rochlin, Todd R. LaPorte, and Karlene H. Roberts, "The self-designing high-reliability organization: Aircraft carrier flight operations at sea," *Naval War College Review* (autumn 1987): 76–90; LaPorte, "The United States air traffic control system: Increasing reliability in the midst of rapid growth," in R. Mayntz and T. Hughes, eds., *The development of large technical systems* (Boulder, 1988), 215–44. Cf. Charles Perrow, *Normal accidents: Living with high-risk technologies* (Princeton, 1999), and Scott D. Sagan, *The limits of safety: Organizations, accidents, and nuclear weapons* (Princeton, 1993).

16. EC minutes, 5 May 1988 (JPL 198, 25/.342); see also EC retreat minutes, Mar. 1991 (JPL 165, 7/4).

17. David Baltimore to visiting committee for JPL, 3 Jan. 2001 (JPL 259, 35/346).

18. Peter J. Westwick, *The national labs: Science in an American system, 1947–1974* (Cambridge, 2003).

19. E.g., J. L. Heilbron and Robert W. Seidel, *Lawrence and his laboratory* (Berkeley, 1989); Peter Galison, *Image and logic: A material culture of microphysics* (Chicago, 1997).

20. E.g., John Noble Wilford, "A new breed of scientists studying Mars takes control," *New York Times*, 14 July 1997. On the identification of technology with science, see also Michael L. Smith, "Selling the moon: The U.S. manned space program and the triumph of commodity scientism," in R. W. Fox and T. J. J. Lears, eds., *The culture of consumption: Critical essays in American history, 1880–1980* (New York, 1983), 177–236.

21. G. Ervin, in "New technology thrusts," 18–20 May 1983 (JPL 92, 1/6).

22. John Casani, handwritten notes on EC retreat, 12 Mar. 1992 (JPL 165, 1/6); James Westphal, interview by Robert Smith, 27 Sept. 1991, NASM.

23. Exceptions include Glenn Bugos, "Manufacturing certainty: Testing and program management for the F-4 Phantom II," *Social Studies of Science* 23 (1993): 265–300; Thomas P. Hughes, *Rescuing Prometheus: Four monumental projects that changed the modern world* (New York, 1998); Stephen B. Johnson, *The secret of Apollo: Systems management in American and European space programs* (Baltimore, 2002); Christophe Lécuyer, "High-tech corporatism: Management-employee relations in U.S. electronics firms, 1920s-1960s," *Enterprise & Society*, 4:3 (2003): 502–20.

24. H. M. Collins, "LIGO becomes big science," *HSPS* 33:2 (2003): 261–97, on 271.

25. Raphael Kasper to Lew Allen, 6 Apr. 1990 (JPL 198, 38/558). Casani was offered the job but declined it: Casani e-mail to author, 12 Aug. 2004.

26. Tony Spear interview, 12 Feb. 2004.

27. Murray interview, 15 Jan. 2002.

28. Fred Felberg to Murray, 23 June 1975 (JPL 8, 1/34); on lab leadership, see Charles Thorpe and Steven Shapin, "Who was J. Robert Oppenheimer? Charisma and complex organization," *Social Studies of Science* 30:4 (2000): 545–90; Catherine Westfall, "A tale of two more laboratories: Readying for research at Fermilab and Jefferson Laboratory," *HSPS* 32:2 (2002): 369–407.

29. John Casani retirement video, 27 Aug. 1999 (courtesy of Susan Foster).

30. Chahine interview, 24 June 2003; Walt Brown interview, 14 Nov. 2002.

31. Chahine interview.

32. On "branding": John Casani interview, 9 Apr. 2004.

33. NASA Advisory Council minutes, 11–12 June 2002 and 10–11 Sept. 2002 (quote). (www.hq.nasa.gov/office/codez/nac/mins, accessed 12 Aug. 2004); David Ignatius, "The CIA as venture capitalist," *Washington Post*, 29 Sept. 1999; Michael Griffin interview, 21 Oct. 2004.

34. James Q. Wilson, *Bureaucracy: What government agencies do and why they do it* (New York, 1989), 113–15.

35. E.g. Donna Shirley, *Managing Martians* (New York, 1998); Swift, *Voyager tales*, also sought managerial lessons.

36. Stone, town hall meeting, 3 May 1995 (JPL 259, 51/566).

37. Michael Griffin telephone interview, 21 Oct. 2004. The head of DARPA in the early 1980s, Robert S. Cooper, was previously director of Goddard, and one of his successors at DARPA, Raymond Colladay, came from NASA's technology office; the first director of SDI, Lt. Gen. James Abrahamson, had been head of space flight at NASA. And of course Dan Goldin came to lead NASA after managing an SDI program at TRW.

38. Koppes; Joseph N. Tatarewicz, *Space technology and planetary astronomy* (Bloomington, 1990); Ronald E. Doel, *Solar system astronomy in America: Communities, patronage, and interdisciplinary science, 1920–1960* (Cambridge, 1996).

39. David Williamson, Jr., to Murray, 26 Mar. 1980, responding to Pat Rygh, "The JPL NOSS experience," 13 Mar. 1980 (JPL 8, 7/92).

40. John Cloud and Keith Clarke have proposed a "shuttered box" model for how knowledge gets from secret to public realms. The questions remain: what particular knowledge gets out, and who controls the shutter? John Cloud and Keith C. Clarke, "Through a shutter darkly: The tangled relationships between civilian, military, and intelligence remote sensing in the early U.S. space program," in Judith Reppy, ed., *Secrecy and knowledge production* (Cornell University Peace Studies Program, Occasional Paper no. 23, 2000), 36–56.

41. Allen to Gregory M. Reck and Wesley Huntress, appendix C, 13 Aug. 1993 (JPL 259, 87/1268); Noel Hinners supported the view of a persistent disconnect; Hinners interview.

42. Philip K. Eckman, interview by Russ Castonguay, 20 Nov. 2001, JPL archives.

43. DCI Small Satellite Advisory Panel meeting at NRO, Apr. 1996, and "Independent panel review of small satellites," unclassified DCI report, 29 June 1996 (JPL 259, 53/609 and 54/626). Stone also sat on a Defense Science Board committee on satellite reconnaissance.

44. Meeting between Stone and Lt. Gen. Arnold Kadish, 29 June 2000 (JPl 259, 70/849).

45. Eckman interview.

46. Samuel P. Huntington, *The soldier and the state: The theory and politics of civil-military relations* (Cambridge, Mass., 1957); Morris Janowitz, *The professional soldier: A social and political portrait* (New York, 1960). Huntington and Janowitz continue to define the terms of scholarship on the subject: James Burk, "Theories of democratic civil-military relations," *Armed Forces & Society* 29:1 (2002): 7–29, and Peter D. Feaver, *Armed servants: Agency, oversight, and civil-military relations* (Cambridge, Mass., 2003), on 2. On the 1990s: Thomas E. Ricks, "The widening gap between the military and society," *Atlantic Monthly* (July 1997): 66–78.

47. Jim Burke interview, 5 Dec. 2003.

Index